China's Path to Modernization

A Historical Review from 1800 to the Present

Ranbir Vohra
Trinity College

Prentice Hall, Englewood Cliffs, New Jersey 07632

Library of Congress Cataloging-in-Publication Data

Vohra, Ranbir.
China's path to modernization : a historical review from 1800 to the present / Ranbir Vohra. — 2nd ed.
p. cm.

Includes bibliographical references and index.
ISBN 0-13-131525-0

1. China—History—19th century. 2. China—History—20th century.
I. Title.
DS755.V64 1992
951—dc20 91-23541
CIP

Acquisitions editor: Steve Dalphin
Editorial/production supervision
and interior design: Mary Anne Shahidi
Cover design: Rosemarie Paccione
Prepress buyer: Kelly Behr
Manufacturing buyer: Mary Ann Gloriande

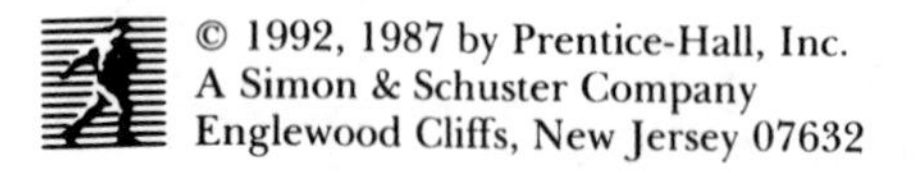

Printed in the United States of America
10 9 8 7 6 5 4 3 2

ISBN 0-13-131525-0

Prentice-Hall International (UK) Limited, *London*
Prentice-Hall of Australia Pty. Limited, *Sydney*
Prentice-Hall Canada Inc., *Toronto*
Prentice-Hall Hispanoamericana, S.A., *Mexico*
Prentice-Hall of India Private Limited, *New Delhi*
Prentice-Hall of Japan, Inc., *Tokyo*
Simon & Schuster Asia Pte. Ltd., *Singapore*
Editora Prentice-Hall do Brasil, Ltda., *Rio de Janeiro*

The book is dedicated
to
Carin and Meena

Contents

Preface

The field of modern Chinese studies has grown so rapidly in the last few decades that it has become almost impossible to find a single short book in the market that adequately compresses the scholarly information now available. However, I and many of my colleagues who teach survey courses on modern China have long felt the need for just such a text that could provide the nonspecialist college students and general readers an integrated overview of political, cultural, and economic developments in China since 1800. In this book I have attempted to present a readable account that avoids too many confusing Chinese names and terms, that is succinct, and that yet furnishes a comprehensive view of China's unique path to modernization.

Since it is becoming exceedingly clear that because of their diverse traditional cultures Third World countries are developing different paths to modernization than did the West, I have introduced a narrative line in the text that highlights the complex interaction between Chinese cultural tradition and the forces of change and modernity. As a background, the first chapter gives a brief summary of China's past history, focusing on the ideology and institutions that molded Chinese traditional political culture; it also has a section contrasting Confucian political ideals with the realities of the Manchu-gentry rule.

Later, the internal coherence of chapters provides the reader with a convenient foundation to grasp the sequence of fundamental changes in modern China. The survey offers fresh insights into critical transition periods in modern Chinese history, such as the collapse of the Manchu dynasty and the establishment of the first republic and the shift of power from the Nationalists to the Communists. The last chapter evaluates the dynamic and dramatic policy shifts and structural changes in post-Mao China.

In writing this book I have depended heavily on the works of China scholars, past and present, many more than named in the citations. I am deeply indebted to all of them. I am especially grateful to Professor John King Fairbank for his encouraging comments on the first few chapters, and I would like to express my profound gratitude to professors Fred Drake and David Arkush for their careful reading of the entire manuscript and their invaluable suggestions.

A NOTE ON THE SECOND EDITION

The first decade of Deng Xiao-ping's experimentation with modernization policies came to a tragic halt in 1989 when, backed by the Old Guard of the Communist party of China, he ruthlessly suppressed the pro-democracy student demonstrators at Tiananmen Square. This tragic event has raised some serious questions about the nature of post-Mao political developments and the future of China's modernization program. The revised edition of *China's Path to Modernization* could not have come at a more appropriate time.

The publisher's decision to bring out a second edition has not only made it possible for me to update the work by rewriting and enlarging the last chapter but also given me an opportunity to revise and correct the original text. In doing the latter I have depended heavily on suggestions provided by my colleagues in the field; I would, in particular, like to express my sincere thanks to Professor Don Starr (University of Durham) for his valuable comments.

The *Pinyin* System

The book uses the current *pinyin* system of romanization, but to make it easier for foreign readers, Chinese personal names have been hyphenated; thus Deng Xiaoping is shown as Deng Xiao-ping.

Following are selected elements from the *pinyin* alphabet, which are distinctly different from their English equivalents:

A: as in *(f)a(r)*
C: *ts* in *its*
CH: strongly aspirated *ch*
E: as in *her*
EI: as in *(h)eigh(t)*
I: (i) as in *ea(t)*
(ii) as in *(s)i(r)*
K: strongly aspirated *k*
O: as in *(l)oo(n)*
P: strongly aspirated *p*
Q: similar to *pinyin* CH
SH: as in *sh(ore)*
T: strongly aspirated *t*
U: as in German umlauted *ü*
X as in *sh(e)*
Y: as in *y(et)*; not to be pronounced when followed by an I
Z: pronounce as *tz*
ZH: as in *j(oe)*

The book follows *pinyin* romanization except for the following names, which are better known in their old form and for which the People's Republic continues to use the old form:

Sun Yat-sen
Chiang Kai-shek
Yangtze

CHAPTER 1

China on the Eve of European Aggression

PROLOGUE

The beginnings of revolutionary change and modernization in China have to be understood in the context of Western expansion in the nineteenth century, which created a West-centered world order. Regardless of how critically one views the nature of "imperialism" or the activities of Western men and Western governments during the period of Western dominance, the fact remains that the non-Western world was transformed by these activities.

During the Western century, as the period 1850–1950 may well be labeled, Western ideas, techniques, and institutions were either imposed on colonial peoples or accepted under pressure by the non-Western countries that still retained their "independence"; this acceptance was based on the recognition that the only hope for survival lay in Westernization.

Today, although the term *Westernization* has been discarded in favor of *modernization,* it remains an important component of modernization. As a supposedly universal phenomenon, modernization implies that all peoples sooner or later undergo similar processes of change to reach similar universal goals. The concept of modernization tends to bring a sense of dignity to non-Western people, who have been humiliated for so long and made to feel racially inferior. But one should not forget that the political ideologies (Western-style democracy, socialism, and communism) that have been accepted as the framework for modernization in Third World countries, are Western in origin. These ideologies and associated political practices and institutions (elections, legislative assemblies, etc.) are the product of European political thought and, to a lesser or greater extent, still remain foreign implants in many non-Western societies.

Therefore the story of change in non-Western societies concerns how and why the need arose to reappraise indigenous political cultures; what in Western ideas and institutions was found valuable for acceptance; and what process led to the rejection, modification, or retention of traditional elements to achieve the goals of modernization. Indeed, the quest for modernization may be a common challenge, but the fact that there is no single model of a "modern" society, that there is no single path to "modernization," that the advanced modern societies themselves now reject some elements that have been generally considered characteristics of modernization, and that the indigenous premodern cultures tend to react differently to the challenge makes the quest historically unique for each people.

True success in modernization, as may be the case of Japan, results only when what is borrowed is fully absorbed into the indigenous system and when modern science and technology become rooted in the native society. But sometimes what a country attempts to borrow is so alien to the native genius that it must be rejected. It is unfair, if not culturally parochial, to look on this as a failure of modernization. In China, for example, attempts to implant a liberal democratic system have, so far, met with little success. This should not lead one to condemn China; rather, it should inspire a greater effort to comprehend the complex interaction between the Chinese cultural tradition and the forces of Western impact. The resulting synthesis makes the Chinese polity what it is.

The collapse of the Chinese traditional order resulted from two major phenomena: internal decay and external aggression. Internal decay reflected a dynastic decline that was, to a considerable extent, traditional. External aggression, however, brought new forces into play that demanded nontraditional responses, which China found difficult to develop because it was in the throes of dynastic decline. Even if there had been no Western aggression, the Qing dynasty no doubt would have collapsed soon, perhaps even more quickly than it did, to be replaced by another traditional dynasty that would have brought new vigor to the administration. At one level the foreign impact aided in the death of the dynasty, but at another it undermined the entire traditional system. The result was that within 70 years of the First Opium War (or the first Anglo-Chinese War, 1839–1842), China saw the establishment of a modern republican form of government, and within 110 years, the present Communist government.

A youthful, vigorous, post-Industrial Revolution West may have been impatient to see quicker, or different, results. But societies are not blank sheets of paper on which new designs can be made at will. Indeed, it is only by keeping in mind the great Chinese tradition that we can comprehend both the time scale of change in China and the nature of its contemporary political developments, which have undeniable links with the past.

CHINA'S TRADITIONAL POLITICAL CULTURE

The Geographical Setting

Around 1800 the Chinese empire comprised two distinct parts: China "proper" and Chinese dependencies in the outlying regions in Inner Asia. China proper lies south of the Mongolian desert, is east of the Tibetan mountains, and is cut off from Southeast Asia by virtually impassable mountains, rivers, and forests. In the East it is bounded by the Pacific Ocean. Chinese dependencies, broadly speaking, covered Manchuria (shown in modern maps as the three northeastern provinces of China: Heilongjiang, Jilin, and Liaoning), Mongolia (today the People's Republic of Mongolia and Inner Mongolia), Central Asia (now the province of Xinjiang), Qinghai, and Tibet. These areas are contiguous to China proper and, in a manner of speaking, surround it.

China proper was densely populated by the Han people, the bulk of the Chinese population (somewhere around 95 percent), who gained their livelihood largely through settled agriculture; the dependencies were sparsely populated by nomadic or semi-agricultural tribes who lived mostly by hunting and raising cattle, sheep, and horses.

China proper was directly governed by Beijing through a tiered system of local government; the dependencies were "controlled" by various devices, such as appointing Han officials as "agents" of Beijing to advise local governments; giving official ranks to local rulers; helping friendly tribal leaders to gain power; and where necessary, encouraging wars between hostile tribes.

The non-Han "barbarians," particularly those from across the northern and northeastern borders, had posed a threat to China proper since the dawn of Chinese history. At the best of times, they could be expected to raid border settlements for booty; at the worst, when the tribes managed to unify, they even succeeded in conquering and ruling the whole of China. Conversely, when the Han governments were strong enough, they would strengthen their control over the outlying regions and keep the tribals "pacified." It was only in the eighteenth and nineteenth centuries that these areas were fully incorporated into the empire. Ironically this was achieved by the alien, "barbarian" Manchu dynasty, the Qing (1644–1912). From the end of the nineteenth century, voluntary or forced internal migration of Han Chinese to these territories began to change the demographic balance there; today the population of Manchuria is overwhelmingly Han, and the Han have also begun to outnumber the indigenous peoples in Xinjiang. Incidentally, the non-Han communities are now designated by the more respectable term *minority communities*.

The geopolitical interplay between the desert (or the steppe) and the arable land has left a lasting imprint on the Chinese psyche. It was this constant threat from the "northern barbarians" that had led to the building of the massive Great Wall in the third century B.C. The Wall, a tremendously impressive engineering feat, failed to provide the security the Chinese were seeking, with the result that Chinese attention has, historically, been focused landward. This, coupled with the fact that until the nineteenth century the ocean frontier had never posed a similar threat, is one important reason for China's not becoming a true sea power. It is noteworthy that after a century of imperialist aggression, primarily from the ocean side, China in recent decades once again came to perceive the greatest threat to its security to be on the landward side—from the Soviet Union in the north.

Although the northern barbarians periodically disturbed the peace and tranquility of the Chinese empire, they were never a menace to Chinese civilization. On the contrary, the invaders, with rare exception, were converted to Chinese culture. In due course they were assimilated into the Chinese population, thus proving to the Chinese that their culture was, indeed, superior. Of even greater significance, the inhospitable regions of outer China, by providing a geographical buffer between China and other advanced civilizations, furnished the Chinese an environment of relative isolation in which they could "sinicize" any foreign influences that crept into the country.

Such isolation was also possible because within the vast territory constituting China proper, China had all the necessary ingredients to make it economically self-sufficient. The fertile region of the Northern Plain watered by the Huang He (the Yellow River), of the central plains through which the Yangtze flows, of the West River basin in the south, and of the "Red Basin" (so called because of the color of the soil) in Sichuan, with their climatic variations, provided a rich diversity of agricultural products. Nature had also endowed the country with ample reserves of coal, iron, copper, tin, lead, and silver. China therefore never had to look beyond its borders for trade to supply any of its real needs.

The geographical setting in which Chinese civilization developed thus gave the Chinese a sense of self-sufficiency, exclusiveness, and cultural superiority, which they have not lost to this day.

The Historical Setting

China has over 3,000 years of historical continuity, and it is not the intention here to summarize the pre-1800 history, but only to highlight some of the historical developments that have contributed to the making of the great Chinese tradition.

Legend has it that after a series of semidivine beings had taught the Chinese rudiments of civilization (like agriculture, silk culture, and weaving), an ideal human ruler by the name of Yao came to control the Yellow River basin, the area that was to be the cradle of Chinese civilization. Yao was not only wise, compassionate, and benevolent but also decided to hand over the throne to a worthy official, Shun, with views similar to his own, rather than to his own unworthy son. During Shun's reign the Yellow River flooded, and he called on a man by the name of Yu to help control the flood waters that were devastating the land. Yu toiled for 13 years before he succeeded. During these many years he passed his own house three times, and he knew that his wife had given birth to a son, but he never once entered it.

This myth emphasizes certain values that later became a part of the Chinese social and political ideals: (1) The rulers' great concern is for the welfare of the people. (2) Yu is chosen for his talent, not because he is a high official. (3) The authority of the ruler is absolute, and Yu accepts the command without question. (4) Yu believes that the work given to him is of the highest importance and gives it precedence over his own personal needs and desires. (5) Unlike myths in other civilizations, the story of Yu has a very human content; it is all this-worldly. No gods or deities came to Yu's aid.

The story also indicates the preoccupation with water control that has characterized government activity in China since the dawn of history. The Yellow River, because of the high sedimentation rate that kept raising the river bed, had to be diked, and if the officials in charge of the dikes were negligent in their maintenance work, the dikes gave way and the ensuing floods destroyed thousands of square miles of farmland. The capricious river is appropriately called "China's Sorrow."

For his virtue and success Yu was made the ruler. He established the legendary Xia dynasty, which was ultimately overthrown by a hostile tribe, which in turn established the Shang dynasty (1766? B.C. to c. 1100 B.C.). The Shang is a historical dynasty, and the development of Chinese culture from this time on shows a remarkable continuity. In the Shang dynasty we have the beginnings of recorded history, written in a script that is clearly discernible as "Chinese."

In the twelth century B.C. China (and we can begin to use this term for this early heartland of the Chinese civilization) was invaded by a western tribe called the Zhou, who established a feudal state that lasted from c. 1100 B.C. to c. 250 B.C. From around 500 B.C. on, when the feudal order had begun to collapse, a great intellectual ferment took place, and many schools of philosophical thought flowered (e.g., Confucianism, Daoism, Legalism) that laid the foundations of Chinese traditional ideology.

The chief exponents of Confucianism, Confucius (c. 551–479 B.C.) himself and his follower Mencius (c. 372–289 B.C.), portrayed an idealized picture of the past when (supposedly) wise, moral rulers guided and led their people by the example of their own ethical conduct rather than by harsh laws; when the best in society, scholars of high character, advised the ruler and kept him from erring; when proper ritual and ceremonies held the people together, at various hierarchical levels, in close bonds of harmony; and when the government ensured the peasants their livelihood and provided education to all men. The Confucians were against war, not only because it was wasteful and brought human misery, but also because real authority came not from physical power but from virtue that radiated humanity and benevolence. By following these precepts the ruler could eradicate crime because crime was a product of poverty and ignorance.

There was no permanent "divine right" to rulership, and the ruler ruled only as long as he was virtuous and worked for the welfare of his people. The king did have a "mandate from Tian" (Heaven), but Tian was looked on as a moral force that guided the universe, and the responsibility of the ruler, the "Son of Heaven," was to bring humanity into harmony with Tian. This mandate could be withdrawn because "Heaven hears as the people hear, Heaven sees as the people see," and natural or man-made catastrophes leading to disorder and suffering were indications of Heaven's discontent. When bad events occurred, the mandate was taken to have expired; the Confucians approved of rebellion against a king who had thus proved himself lacking in virtue. No political philosophy until modern times has given the common man, in theory, such an important place in the state.

Confucianism stressed five human relationships (or bonds)—between father and son, husband and wife, elder brother and younger brother, prince and subject, and friend and friend—and maintained that if the rules governing these relationships were properly followed, society would achieve tranquility and harmony. Except for the last, these relationships were between a superior and an inferior, and although calling for obedience and loyalty from one side, presumed benign concern from the other. Three of these relationships are familial, but even the one between prince and subject can be considered an extension of the father-son relationship.

The Confucians looked on the family unit as the foundation of civilization. Not only was the individual totally subordinate to the family unit, but also all loyalty was focused on the family at the expense of every other social or political institution. The ideal family consisted of five, or at least four, generations who lived under one roof. In this state within the state, the grandfather or great-grandfather ruled the household with absolute authority. His word was final in all matters, and he managed the finances, arranged the marriages, hired tutors to educate the children, settled disputes between family members, and so forth. The complicated web of relationships within the extended family was clearly defined, and each person was expected to know exactly where he or she fit into the structure and to behave accordingly.

The cult of "ancestor worship" had existed long before Confucius, but he put great emphasis on it and also enlarged on the concept of "filial piety." If the family was to be the cornerstone of his society, the continuity of the family lineage was a must. Confucians did not stress life after death, so the word *worship* in ancestor worship needs to be understood in the Chinese context. Ancestor worship was a family affair and did not denote an organized religion in the Indian or the Middle Eastern sense. Since the number of generations of dead ancestors to be venerated was limited, the living were tied to the memory of those who had just preceded them. As Confucius said, "Filial piety is seen in the skillful carrying out of the wishes of our forefathers, and the skillful carrying forward of their undertakings."[1]

Filial piety came to influence not only the institution of marriage (marriages were arranged not for "love" but for the production of sons who would carry on the lineage and who were indispensable to ancestor worship) but also the development of Chinese humanism. If one could not love one's parents, how could one love those who were not even related by blood? An individual had to learn to serve and submit to one's parents with sincerity before becoming a parent and dispensing benevolence to one's own children and expecting them to be obedient. Cultivation of proper behavior for all members of the kinship group was essential to the proper regulation of a family. If all families were so regulated, the state would automatically be well regulated, and there would be universal tranquility and harmony.

Finally, since everything in Confucianism depended on correct behavior, and correct behavior, to be effective, had to reflect the inner man, the Confucians emphasized the need for self-discipline and self-examination and the continuous cultivation of the inner virtues of righteousness; propriety; wisdom; faithfulness; and most important, of *REN* (compassion, human-heartedness, goodness, and benevolence).

The one dark spot in the high ideology of Confucianism was that in the familial and social hierarchy of status it assigned a low position to women, who were inferior and subservient to men. A virtuous woman was supposed to uphold "three subordinations": be subordinate to her father before marriage, to her husband after marriage, and to her son after her husband died. Men could remarry and have concubines, whereas women were supposed to uphold the virtue of chastity when they lost their husbands. Although this has nothing to do with Confucianism as such, in the Song dynasty (960–1279) it became fashionable, among the upper classes, to bind women's feet when they were little girls so that the feet never grew to be more than a few inches long. This strange and painful fashion, which lasted into the twentieth century, gradually came to be accepted even by the peasantry. Thus the women of China came to be hobbled in more than one way.

Contrary to the Confucians, the Daoists discarded society and its burdens and rejected all rational, man-made concepts of ethics and morality. If people could understand the Dao, the way, of the cosmic order and seek harmony with it, they would realize the unity behind the diversity. This understanding could not come through reasoning or logic but through inner illumination. Like all schools of mysticism, Daoism is difficult to explain. Suffice it to say that it strengthened what probably was an ancient Chinese conception that the cosmic order was a united whole, that all things were relative, and that all contradictory phenomena supplied the correlates that went to prove the indivisibility of the whole. Daoism turned people's minds to nature and away from society because nature represented freedom from man-made restrictions and provided an opportunity for the expansion of the inner being.

Coexisting with Daoism was a belief that the cosmic order was influenced by the interplay of two forces, one positive and the other negative—Yang and Yin. The forces were contradictory yet complementary. They were represented by such opposite phenomena as the sun and the moon, day and night, summer and winter, heat and cold, male and female.

Daoism was antithetical to much of Confucianism and, if nothing else, helped to correct some of Confucianism's overemphasis on "man," which led to pomposity and rigidity of overly formalistic behavior. Daoist beliefs in a primitive society and minimum government died an early death, but philosophical Daoism left its abiding influence on the Chinese arts, particularly painting and poetry, in which the artist discarded Confucian rules and regulations and allowed the inner emotions to have freer play. With the passage of time Daoism also produced a popular religion, which attracted the common people with its rituals, magic, and a pantheon of divinities.

If Confucianism provided the framework for social behavior and the high ethical principles to guide good government, it was Legalism that actually eliminated the warring feudal states and unified China under a single imperial government. Unlike most Confucians, the Legalists were involved in the actual business of government. They were practical and forward-looking.

Instead of trying to revive the feudal order, they oversaw its burial. In contrast to the Confucians and Daoists, the Legalists looked on human nature as intrinsically evil and contended that laws (regulations) providing harsh punishments and bountiful rewards were essential for social peace and order. The Legalists advocated a strong autocratic government that would impartially administer the laws, conduct commerce, and own all resources of capital and labor. All power was to rest with the emperor, who was to exercise it with the help of administrators recruited for their talent and their loyalty to him. There was absolutely no need to depend on the moral example of the rulers or their advisors.

When the Qin, using Legalist practices, succeeded in putting China under its direct and absolute control in 211 B.C., the country underwent a major revolution. For a moment it appeared that with the abolition of hereditary nobles and their fiefs; the division of the country into districts under centrally appointed officers; the standardization of the writing system, money, weights, and measures; and the burning of books written by non-Legalist philosophers, not only feudalism but also Confucianism had been effaced. However, the ruthless Qin empire did not outlast its founder Shi Huang-di, the first emperor, by many years, and the feeling of revulsion against the tyranny and dictatorship that had characterized Qin rule led to the rise of pro-Confucian sentiment. In the Han dynasty that followed, the essential features of the ideology that guided imperial government for the next 2,000 years were formulated, but the structure of imperial government established by Shi Huang-di was accepted with little change.

Held up as an example of a wicked ruler for two millennia, Shi Huang-di was rehabilitated by the Chinese Communists and their great leader Mao Ze-dong, who otherwise found little in China's tradition worth saving. By using vast amounts of forced labor, Shi Huang-di built the Great Wall and an impressive network of roads; by forced transfer of population he extended the empire all the way down to present Vietnam and, of course, brought unity to China. The Maoists condone his ruthlessness (it is said that under every stone of the Great Wall lies buried a Chinese laborer) for his forward-looking policies and the greatness he brought to China.

The Making of Imperial Confucianism

During the Han dynasty (206 B.C.–A.D. 220) the classics proscribed by Qin Shi Huang-di were "rediscovered"—some were indeed found intact, some were rewritten from memory, but some were forged. The purity of pre-Qin Confucianism thought was lost, and the new Confucian scholars accepted many ideas as Confucian that actually had been propounded by philosophers antagonistic to Confucius. The final synthesis, which incorporated many Legalist elements such as the institution of an absolute monarch and his bureaucracy and the right of the state to establish legal codes, dispense harsh punishment, have an army, and indulge in commercial activities (e.g., monopolies in salt and iron production), is called Han Confucianism or Imperial Confucianism.

The Confucian element in this synthesis is the reassertion of the principle that in the ultimate analysis, good government depends not on laws and institutions but on ethics and moral leadership and that its primary duty is to look after the welfare of the people.

Realizing, no doubt, that high philosophical ideas may not in themselves be enough to check the absolute power of the Legalist emperor, Confucian thinkers tried to use the imperial system itself to achieve their ends. The bureaucracy, the key Legalist institution of the imperial order, was increasingly recruited through an examination system based on Confucian texts. Thus the best minds in the country came to be trained in Confucian classics, and the orthodox ideology was perpetuated.

Another institution that was established in the Han dynasty, and with various changes lasted to the end of the empire, was the Censorate. The censors, who were among the most learned of the Confucian scholars, were supposed to admonish the emperors for misgovernment and to impeach the officials who were corrupt or failed to perform their duties properly. As one can imagine, the first function was often difficult to fulfill, although there are many instances in Chinese history of censors who had the moral courage to reprimand the emperors even at the cost of their lives.

Accepting ideas from other schools of thought besides Legalism, Han Confucianism held that there was a basic unity in the universal order. All things were related to one another and influenced one another in the manner of Yin and Yang, which, though contradictory, were both essential to unity and harmony. In the following passage Dong Zhong-shu (c. 179–104 B.C.), one of the great synthesizers of Confucian thought, shows how Heaven, Earth, and Man were closely connected and how the ruler played a critical role in the universal scheme:

. . . Heaven, Earth and Man are the basis of all creatures. Heaven gives them birth, Earth nourishes them, and Man brings them to completion. Heaven provides them at birth with a sense of filial and brotherly love; Earth nourishes them with clothing and food; and Man completes them with rites and music [civilization]. The three act together as hands and feet join to complete the body and none can be dispensed with. . . .

. . . a worthy ruler . . . advances brotherly affection and encourages filial conduct. In this way he serves the basis of Heaven.

He personally grasps the plow handle and plows a furrow, plucks the mulberry himself and feeds the silkworms, breaks new ground to increase the grain supply, and opens the way for the sufficiency of clothing and food. In this way he serves the basis of Earth.

He sets up schools . . . in the towns and villages to teach filial piety and brotherly affection, reverence and humility. He enlightens the people with education and moves them with rites and music. Thus, he serves the basis of Man.[2]

The examination system based on Confucian texts later made Confucianism the official ideology of the bureaucracy, which meant the ideology of the educated class. It soon became the hallmark of high culture and gradually was accepted as national ideology by all Chinese.

One non-Chinese element that made a permanent mark on Chinese culture and even helped shape the metaphysics of Imperial Confucianism (hereafter referred to simply as Confucianism) was Buddhism. Entering China at the end of the Han dynasty, it spread over the entire country and reached its high point in the eighth century. Then, having lost its vigor, it continued to the present as a part of China's popular culture.

Buddhism came to China when the Han dynasty was collapsing; the country was torn by strife and was soon to enter a period of disunity that lasted three and a half centuries. In this time of political chaos and human misery, Buddhism, with its elaborate rituals, its explanation of suffering in this life, and its promise of a paradise after death, was attractive to the common person. It was also attractive to many intellectuals who had become disillusioned with the rigidity and superficiality of Confucianism as it had come to be practiced. Buddhism offered a highly sophisticated philosophy that dealt with the intellectual and spiritual life of the individual.

When Buddhism reached the height of its popularity, there were some 30,000 monasteries and thousands of pagodas and temples, which dotted the landscape in every part of the empire, and over 2 million monks and nuns who served the church. Every aspect of life was touched in one way or another by this alien religion. Apart from the realm of philosophy, Buddhism enriched the literature and the music of the country; added new styles to Chinese sculpture and painting; and contributed to Chinese science, especially astronomy, mathematics, and medicine.[3]

Buddhism, however, began to pose a dangerous challenge to the Confucian way of life, and an organized church with royal patronage began to exert an unacceptable political influence. Buddhism's advocacy of celibacy and withdrawal from society ran counter to the emphasis of Confucianism on filial piety, ancestor worship, and the need of all persons to be involved in productive social activities.

With the reunification of China in the Sui (581–618) and the Tang (618–907) dynasties and the institution of the examination system, there was a revival of Confucianism. At the popular level the Confucians found it comparatively easy to attack Buddhism for its antisocial attitudes, but at the intellectual and philosophical level they had to prove that the Buddhist doctrine of the Void was false. The doctrine of the Void posited that the phenomenal world was not real. There was nothing in Confucianism that could counter this postulate, so the Confucians added a new dimension to Han Confucianism, the concept of "The Great Ultimate." The Great Ultimate, they said, was not Void but an immaterial and immutable "Principle" inherent in all things. It operated through a "material force," which because of the interaction between Yin and Yang, condensed into the myriad phenomena of which we are cognizant (i.e., the world of reality). Reflecting the Buddhist idea that the *One* Buddha-mind was present in the *Many* (all sentient beings), the neo-Confucians declared that the Great Principle is found in all things and constitutes their essence. By proper cultivation of self, a person's mind could be made one with the "mind of the universe" and the Great Principle understood. When that happened an individual could comprehend the proper role of human ethics, the importance of social relations and filial piety, and the abiding need to help improve the environment in which one lived.

The link between the moral order of the universe and the social and political order on earth was revitalized. This doctrine became the basis of "Neo-Confucianism" and a part of the orthodox doctrine of the imperial state into the twentieth century, although a thinker in the Ming Dynasty (1368–1644), Wang Yang-ming (1472–1528), did add his school of thought to the mainstream. According to Wang, "knowledge" and "action" should be closely connected. Knowledge that did not result in action was useless; all people have "innate knowledge" of what is right, but they lose that knowledge when they allow selfishness to blind them. A person must, therefore, eliminate base selfish emotions to rediscover the virtues of benevolence, righteousness, loyalty, and so on.

Its traditional political culture made China synonymous with the greatest civilization on the face of the earth. Chinese culture provided the ultimate unity to the state, and that unity was strengthened by the belief that there could never be more than one Son of Heaven. In other words, there could never be more than one government over the state that coincided with the culture area. All peoples outside the culture area were barbarians.

There was only one orthodox ideology that all had to follow. No concept of a loyal opposition was permissible. This basically secular ideology (Confucianism) was all-embracing, relating humankind to the universe, the individual to the family, the family to society, private life to public life, and culture to politics.

The highest goal of humanity was to comprehend this ideology through education and self-discipline so as to better serve society, which could best be accomplished by participating in the government. Government was the hub of civilization. Commerce and trade were activities unworthy of the virtuous person.

The authority of the ruler as the ultimate protector of the ideology was all-pervasive, and the people were supposed to be beholden to him for everything. They could, therefore, have no "rights," only the obligation to serve him loyally and obediently. Individuals could fulfill themselves only through the group and the collective by recognizing their station within the hierarchical pattern of human relations. Outer action was a reflection of inner virtue. Conformity brought merit.

Obedience to authority was inculcated as a virtue.

MANCHU CHINA c. 1800: THE MYTH AND THE REALITY

China never came close to the Confucian utopian ideal, but the Confucian political, social, and economic framework did prove durable, and over the centuries, Chinese culture did possess enough vigor to outlast other civilizations. The distinctive political and cultural patterns that first became visible in the Han dynasty continued to develop creatively until about the fifteenth century, when the system can be said to have matured and further developments slowed down.

The following pages provide an overview of conditions that prevailed when China entered the nineteenth century and give a bleak picture of a state and society that appear to be on the verge of collapse; the sophisticated imperial system, which had once allowed for technical developments and economic growth, had lost its resilience and dynamism, and the gap between Confucian ideals and the sociopolitical reality had begun to widen beyond repair.

It has been suggested by some historians that in the late Ming-early Qing period, China saw a tremendous growth in silk and porcelain production, which led to the emergence of "workshops" and the "sprouts" of capitalism, and that had it not been for the destructive Western presence (appearing on the scene at the wrong time), China would have produced its own Industrial Revolution. Though the possibility of such a development cannot be wholly ruled out, the thesis becomes irrelevant in the face of actual historical progress, in which the West rapidly outpaced China. As a respected Communist historian, Bai Shouyi, has pointed out (and his pro-Chinese, anti-imperialist stand can hardly be doubted), "Though nascent capitalism made its appearance during the late Ming and early Qing period, it never had a chance to grow normally for several centuries." Among the reasons he gives are "inertia of a self-sufficient economy," limitations placed on capitalist development by "guilds and handicraftsmen," government oppression, diversion of investment capital to land, and the Ming-Qing "self-defeating" policy of imposing restrictions on foreign trade.[4]

The Political System: The Rulers

The Manchus. A small but significant problem that faces students of modern China is the use of the term *Chinese*. On the face of it, it is obviously correct to refer to the government at Beijing as the *Chinese government*, the emperor as the *Chinese emperor*, and the people of China as the *Chinese people*. The fact that the last dynasty was a Manchu dynasty introduces an element that sometimes makes the use of these terms misleading. The Qing dynasty (1644–1911) was established by *Man-ren* (men of the Manchu race), who were a tribal people from Manchuria, a territory that lies northeast of China proper. Although the rulers adapted themselves to the civilization of *Han-ren* (people of the Han, or "Chinese," race), they never came to be totally absorbed, and the distinction between *Han* and *Man* was never lost throughout the Qing dynasty. The term *Chinese* will generally be used in this and the following sections to cover both Han and Manchu aspects of Chinese polity; on occasion it will connote the majority community as juxtaposed to the Manchus.

The success of the Manchus in being accepted as the legitimate rulers of China was primarily due to the fact that having restored peace in the empire by the use of their superior military power, the Manchus went on to rule the country through existing imperial institutions and with the help of Han officials. The local Han landlord-scholar-gentry families (see p. 13) were allowed to function as heretofore, and their interests were not touched. In other words, the Manchus, who constituted only 2 percent of the population, moved in at the top of the existing political pyramid and became supervisors of a system that had been perfected over the centuries.

The Manchus tried to preserve their separate identity and continued predominance over the vastly larger Han population by trying to keep the *Man-ren* segregated from the Chinese (Han) and by maintaining a military establishment that was primarily Manchu and Mongol. The Chinese military units were deployed in areas of secondary importance and used largely as a police force. As time passed, Manchus at the lower levels, especially Manchu soldiers, broke the various bans imposed on them and began to wear Chinese dress, speak Chinese, and intermarry with the Chinese. But the sense of their being superior to the Chinese and the sense of antagonism between the two communities disappeared only with the collapse of the dynasty.

The most serious consequence of the Manchu domination of China was the increased concentration of power in the hands of the emperor. Theoretically, all Chinese emperors had been absolute despots, but the Manchu emperors circumscribed the power of the Han officials even more severely because of the inherent Manchu fear of the majority community. No Han officials were included in the department handling relations with dependencies; a Manchu was appointed, jointly with a Chinese, to head each ministry, and most governor-generals in the provincial administration were Manchus.

The Qian-long emperor (reigned 1736–1796) carried out a literary inquisition and suppressed thousands of works that were supposed to be seditious (many of them criticized the Manchus as barbarians) and punished the authors with death or banishment. Such actions of the Qing rulers increased the servility of the officials and the literati to the government and smothered those who could have provided more creative political solutions to the problems that arose in the nineteenth century.

The Qing continued the Ming approach to mercantilism. In internal trade this meant that the repressive system of tariffs, duties, and "squeeze" was perpetuated, and a national market was kept from developing. Some cities and areas did develop specialized products (e.g., porcelain at Jingdezhen; teas and silks in Jiangxi), but the government had no constructive policies that would have fostered manufacturing industries.

In external trade the Manchu policies were even more restrictive of growth than those of the insular Ming government. In the early decades of the Qing dynasty the Ming loyalists had continued to harass the new government from overseas bases. The Qing tried to cut off the connection between the Ming loyalists and the population inland by forcing the coastal inhabitants to withdraw several miles inland. The size of the merchant ships was reduced, and orders were issued forbidding overseas Chinese from returning to the mother country. Even when the government was securely in power, its suspicions of overseas Chinese and those involved in naval commerce never abated.

Cultural contacts with the West, tenuously maintained by the Jesuits, came to an end when Christianity was declared a heterodox cult in 1742. Around 1760 trade with the West was restricted to the one port of Canton, where it was carried on under strict official supervision.

In the century of isolation from the West that followed, China extended its authority over Tibet (1751) and Central Asia (1760s), which was later called Xinjiang ("New Frontier") and made a province of the empire in 1884. It also expanded its influence over Nepal and Burma through extensive military action. Thus the empire came to be a conglomerate of provinces, colonies, and protectorates. Manchuria, the homeland of the Manchus, was kept separate from China proper and given a special status; Mongolia was bound to the empire through ties of tribal loyalty to the Manchus; Xinjiang was administered by the military; and Tibet was a protectorate. By maintaining the fiction that these areas were dependencies and that their peoples were "minority" communities of China, and by suggesting that it was in this capacity that these people occasionally tried to become the rulers of China, the present government has avoided the issue of imperialist expansion. Otherwise one would have to recognize that China's occupation and absorption of the outlying regions was an act similar to that of the Western imperialists, who at this very time were beginning to carve out world empires.

Internally, however, the period was largely one of stability and prosperity, although signs of dynastic decline started to become visible by the late eighteenth century and multiplied in the nineteenth century.

The Emperor. The emperor played a key role in the Confucian sociopolitical system. The accepted myth was that the emperor was the Son of Heaven, the ruler of all humankind, the fountainhead of civilization, the ultimate defender of ideology, a most humane sovereign, whose only raison d'être was his concern for the welfare of the common man. And he was endowed with supreme power.

In actual fact few emperors had the physical stamina and the intellectual capacity to undertake the direct rulership of the country and to exercise this power. The first few emperors of the Qing dynasty, those who

The Jesuits

Jesuit missionaries first managed to reach Beijing in 1600, at the end of the Ming dynasty. They learned the Chinese language, studied the Chinese classics and Confucian philosophy, and changed their dress to that worn by the Chinese scholars, hoping that if they could find acceptance in the eyes of the Chinese upper classes they could propagate their religion among the Chinese intelligentsia. They achieved some success under the Ming, and even the early Manchu rulers were disposed to favor them. The situation changed after 1742 when the pope, siding with the Jesuits' opponents in the church, declared that the Chinese rites of ancestor worship and the worship of Confucius and of Tian (Heaven) were religious rites and not "civil" rites, and therefore Chinese converts were forbidden from participating in them. The Qing rulers could not accept this attack on what constituted the foundations of Chinese social and political ideology, and henceforth only those missionaries were allowed to stay who virtually denounced the papal decree. This extremely limited number of Jesuits was useful to the court because they served as calendar makers, interpreters, cartographers, painters, and so on. Christianity was declared to be a heterodox cult, and the Jesuits' work as missionaries basically came to an end. The last of the Jesuits in China died in 1805.

---

helped to establish it, were no doubt men of vigor, and they did actually "rule" the country. But with the passage of time weaker emperors emerged who were more content to "reign" through a bureaucracy that was becoming vastly inflated. At the same time, the military, which was under the direct command of the emperor and had not seen any real war for a century and a half, began to lose its fighting capacity.

There were other limitations, too, on the power of the later emperors. They were bound by Imperial House Laws (laid down by the emperor who founded the dynasty), by the edicts of their predecessors, and by custom and tradition. Raised by eunuchs and maid-servants, these emperors had hardly any contact with life outside their high palace walls. When in power they were caught up in palace intrigues; guided by eunuchs and sycophants, they hardly fit the Confucian myth. The need to uphold the myth, however, became greater as the reality slipped further and further from the ideal.

What, for example, could be more un-Confucian than a eunuch who could not continue his lineage, except a eunuch advising the emperor. Although the original reason for having eunuchs in the residential quarters of the imperial palace was to protect the emperor's wives and concubines from coming in contact with any male other than the emperor, the numbers and the duties of the eunuchs proliferated with time. The 3,000 eunuchs in the Forbidden City (the Imperial Palace compound) at the end of the Qing dynasty had among their tasks such items as transmitting imperial edicts, leading officials to audiences, receiving memorials, and receiving money and grain sent by treasuries outside the palace. The eunuchs thus came to control the communication links between the emperor and the outside world.

The Central Government. The emperor was assisted, at the highest level of government, by the Grand Council (*Junjichu*) and the Grand Secretariat (*Neige*). The Grand Council, comprising an equal number of Manchus and Chinese, met with the emperor every morning to discuss policy issues, usually raised by memorials sent by senior central and provincial officials, and to help draft imperial edicts that settled the issues and laid down policy. The Grand Secretariat oversaw the execution of policy through the activities of the six central ministries (sometimes referred to as "boards"), each headed by two presidents and four vice-presidents, half Chinese and half Manchu: Civil Affairs (appointment and dismissal of officials), Revenue, Rites (state ceremonials, tributary missions, and imperial examinations), War, Punishments, and Public Works (roads, dikes, canals, flood control, imperial buildings, etc.).

Other important organs of central government located in Beijing were a Censorate, which kept watch over the officials and reported incidents of impropriety and violations of moral and legal codes, and a Bureau of Dependency Affairs, handling relations with inner Asian dependencies.

Provincial Administration. China proper was divided into 18 provinces, which were further subdivided into circuits, prefectures, districts, and subprefectures.

Each province was under a governor, and most provinces were paired together under a governor-general, or viceroy. The governors were mostly Chinese; the governor-generals, mostly Manchu. In provinces that had a governor and governor-general, the two officials jointly reported important business to the emperor. Other important officials centrally appointed to the provincial capital were a financial commissioner, handling revenues; a judicial commissioner; and a provincial commander-in-chief, in charge of central military units in the province.

The basic local administrative unit was the district (*xian*), of which there were about 1,500 in the country. The district magistrate, appointed by Beijing, was a key imperial official because he came in direct contact with the local populace. He represented all government authority in his person, and his activities covered all fundamental branches of government. He collected the taxes, maintained peace and order, arrested the criminals, adjudicated the law, and looked after the public works and public welfare.

To avoid the possibility of establishing a local power base, no magistrate was appointed to his home province, and his tenure in any one district was usually no more than three years. He was helped in the difficult task of administering a district with a population of several hundred thousand by his personal staff (who moved from district to district with him), as well as a local staff of clerks, messengers, servants, and so forth and by the voluntary help of the local scholar-gentry.

The Examination System, the Gentry, and the Bureaucracy. The 40,000 officials who headed the civil service and the million or so degree holders who formed the scholar-gentry were all the product of the imperial examination system, which incidentally, was later copied by almost the whole world.

The examinations, which were held at various levels at regular intervals, led to three important degrees: *xiu-cai* ("flowering talent," may be taken to be the equivalent of the B.A. degree since it is the lowest of the three), *ju-ren* ("recommended person," M.A.), and *jin-shi* ("presented scholar," Ph.D.). The examinations, based on Confucian texts, were by no means easy to pass, but since they were the only avenue of upward mobility and since the rewards of passing them were so great, hundreds of thousands of the best minds in the country were continuously locked in rigorous preparation for this harrowing experience. Scholars who failed could take an examination repeatedly, and sometimes a grandfather would be enrolled for the same examination as his grandson.

Candidates would be placed in separate cubicles (that were not large enough for a person to stretch out in and sleep) and tested in several sessions of several days each. They were allowed to bring food, bedding, and writing materials but were thoroughly checked for any books or scraps of paper with writing on them that they might have secreted on their persons. When the examinations were over, "suffering from fatigue, and under heavy pressure, most candidates became a little strange in the head. . . . In the most severe cases men became sick or insane."[5]

Only those who passed the top two levels of the examinations were entitled to any official position, but the *xiu-cai,* too, played an extremely important role in the maintenance of the political system. They and the scholar-officials who had come to their home districts on leave or retirement formed the bulk of the literati class. They are known as *the gentry*, which should not be confused with the term as used in Britain. In China one attained gentry status and enjoyed certain well-defined social, economic, and legal privileges because of one's scholarly attainment. Gentry were the accepted leaders in their locality, and the magistrates treated them with respect. Not only were they their scholarly peers, but the magistrate also needed gentry goodwill to function effectively in an alien environment.

The privileges granted to the gentry put them in a category apart from the rest of the people. Socially, they were eligible to wear certain clothing that the common folk were denied and to have a flag post outside their residences with a pennant displaying the degree they had earned. Some of their taxes were reduced, and they were exempted from corvee labor. They were also exempted from judicial punishment short of penal servitude, and that punishment could be meted out only after they had been first deprived of their degree.

In return for these privileges the gentry were expected to perform certain unpaid functions. For example, they raised funds for the maintenance of public works (canals, dams, dikes, roads, bridges, etc.); they looked after the Confucian temples, set up schools, gave lectures on public morals, published local histories and gazetteers; they supported poor houses, widows' homes, and orphanages; and in times of flood or famine they organized relief work. In case there were local uprisings they were authorized to raise a militia for local defense. These functions paralleled the work of the government.

The million-plus members of the gentry constituted an important part of the ruling class of China. They were educated in the same Confucian texts and were imbued with the same ideology and world outlook; spread over the entire country, they had a deep-rooted, vested interest in the existing system and helped to strengthen the cultural unity of the country. The functions they performed made them an unofficial branch of the government. A dynasty could not last if they removed their support from it.

According to the Confucian myth, the officials and the gentry were the wise, sage leaders of society who helped sustain the moral order and who worked zealously for the welfare of the people. In reality, the gentry and the officials usually connived and competed with one another to squeeze as much as they could out of the peasantry in order to build up private fortunes. By the nineteenth century, as the central government became more inefficient and ineffective at the local level, the gentry increased their terribly un-Confucian activities, removing their land holdings from tax registers, grabbing land belonging to tenants in debt, gathering taxes from the peasants far in excess of government demand, and so forth.

Instead of being the "father-mother" officials the mandarins were supposed to be, they consciously separated themselves from the common people and ruled from a distance, not unlike the colonial British officials in India. Indeed, at one level, the Chinese political system can be compared to a colonial government, for the main thrust of the Manchu rulers was to preserve themselves by giving maximum free play to supportive traditional institutions, which indoctrinated the people to make them subservient. The Manchus spent more energy creating a network of checks and balances than fostering dynamic policies of growth and advancement. Thus the function of the Beijing government was negative rather than positive. In the face of European aggression, when the need arose to lead society, neither the emperor nor his officials were in a position to do so.

Over the centuries the examinations had become stereotyped, knowledge had become stultified, and there was little allowance for creative political thinking. Education was not for broadening mental horizons or liberating the spirit of enquiry but for memorizing texts that exulted in conservatism and a backward-looking Confucian ideology that effectively shut out the world beyond the borders of the Middle Kingdom. The few who survived the system and emerged with their intellectual vitality unimpaired were an exception to the rule.

The Manchu rulers, who themselves were "barbarians," should have been more aware of the danger that the "barbarians from the West" represented. But they had become so sinicized by 1800 that they too had acquired the Confucian blindfold. In fact, to gain legitimacy in the eyes of the Han population, the Manchus had to out-Confucian the Confucians.

Corruption. Behind the facade of Confucianism, which continued to be affirmed publicly in every possible manner, there was a vast web of nepotism and corruption, the like of which the world has rarely seen. Corruption had become a part of the system. For example, Chinese officials received rather meager salaries, not even enough to cover their legitimate expenses, and they were allowed to make up the balance through "customary dues," a polite term for graft. These officials were expected to maintain a style of life befitting their status; pay their staff from their own pocket; and provide for innumerable relatives who, because of the Confucian emphasis on kinship, could demand to be looked after. Besides all this, officials usually managed to amass a considerable fortune by the time they retired. To receive a post in which there were greater chances of making money or to avoid being sent to a hardship post, the officials had to bribe their superiors, who in turn had to bribe theirs. This resulted in a national system of graft and corruption that extended from the eunuchs and the princes in the Imperial Palace in Beijing down to the magistrate's clerk in the district. Ultimately, of course, it was the poor peasant at the bottom, whom they were all supposed to be serving so assiduously, who was wrung dry.

The most notorious example of corruption at this point in Qing history is no doubt He-shen (1750–1799), who because he was the favorite of the Qian-long emperor, rose from the position of a bodyguard to that of chief minister and who accumulated personal property worth the equivalent of $1.5 billion.

The Financial Base of the Empire. The imperial government kept a detailed record of the intake and outgo of national financial transactions, but these figures do not indicate the true nature of the economy because many of them were ritualistic. There was no "common purse" into which revenues were collected, nor indeed was there any system by which the government could know precisely what revenues were actually collected.

Central revenues were based on three sources: land-poll taxes (75 percent), commodity taxes (customs duties, 10 percent), and monopolies (the most important of which was salt, 15 percent). But since provincial and other local expenditures were deducted from the amounts forwarded to Beijing, the figures tell only half the story.

Consider, for example, the land-poll taxes. The figures for cash and grain reaching Beijing were, by and large, correct, but figures giving the total collections were more often than not totally false. One reason, as indicated earlier, was that the government did not make adequate provision for local administrative expenses or pay adequate salaries to the magistrates. Strangely enough, it recognized this problem, and even more strangely, it officially allowed an unofficial surcharge of 10 percent to be collected. But no magistrate was content with the 10 percent limit, and illegal exactions often were as high as 50 percent of the legal tax.

Another form of corruption resulted from the exchange rate. The tax was collected in terms of silver, and the official exchange rate was supposedly fixed at 1,000 copper cash for one tael of silver. Local officials, however, sometimes arbitrarily raised the rate to as high as 4,000 cash. Since the local gentry could actually pay in silver, they did not suffer from the system as did the poor peasants, who could hardly raise enough copper cash even to pay the fixed amount at the authorized rate of exchange.

The officials further abused their position by imposing various miscellaneous taxes.

Although the tax system was based on the amount of land under the plow and the number of adult males who worked it, the imperial government was not concerned with individual tax returns but allocated a quota to be collected by each province. If the contribution asked for was forthcoming, the central government had no further interest in local finances or in how much was actually being collected.

Similar corruption marked customs collection and the management of monopolies. The total amount of revenues reaching Beijing before 1850 was about 40 million taels, a fifth to a third of the official collections. When foreign aggression placed added financial demands on the central government, the antiquated revenue system could not meet the need. Additional levies on the land were impossible, for the peasants had been taxed to the limit. The development of new sources of wealth required a revolutionary change in the agrarian-based Confucian ideology, and China was not yet ready for such a change.

The Military System. All Chinese dynasties had come to power with the help of the military, and the ultimate source of imperial power was the army. Yet a myth had arisen that the Chinese were a pacifist people who had contempt for the military man and for military affairs. Whether this myth was a concession to Confucianism, which as an ideology looked askance at the military, or a product of the propaganda by the scholar-literati that they alone kept the empire going, is inconsequential. In fact, the Chinese are no more pacifist than any other people; their history is no less bloody than that of any other nation. Indeed, if one were to go by their operas, plays, and literature, they have a host of popular military heroes who have stirred the hearts of commoner and elite alike through the centuries. Perhaps the contempt for the military was also due to the fact that the Manchu dynasty not only kept the senior-most military posts in Manchu hands but also kept the Han out of the main fighting armies.

Although China had no military caste, the officers were considered members of the gentry, and many civil officials had military responsibilities. In the latter half of the nineteenth century some of the senior Confucian officials became prominent provincial military leaders.

The Manchu military was known as the "banner forces" (so called because each army had its own distinguishing banner), and after the occupation of China the Manchus used their own forces to garrison the capital and the key areas in China. The Chinese army, the "Army of the Green Standard," inherited by the Qing and about 600,000 in strength, was nearly twice the size of the Manchu forces. But it was decentralized and used primarily as a local police force. The banner garrisons occupied their own fortified residential quarters in a city, so even though the Manchus became sinicized, the Han could not quite forget that they were occupation troops.

Like the rest of the administration, the military gradually lost its efficiency and became corrupt. The banner forces were ill paid, ill trained, and ill supplied. From being proud Manchu soldiers who were not allowed to engage in trade or labor, many were now forced by adverse circumstances to work as artisans and peddlers. The forces of the Army of the Green Standard existed in full strength only on paper. The commanders, whose muster roles showed 100 to 500 percent more soldiers than existed in fact, appropriated military funds for private use, built up private fortunes, and lived a life of corruption and luxury.

The army had become so worthless that it often could not even enforce law and order. Indeed, at some locations the soldiers themselves were the cause of disorder, and their depredations were comparable to those of the local banditry. As a result, many localities began to form local corps for defense, under the leadership of the local gentry.

Law in Traditional China. Confucian ideology stressed the overriding obligation for all persons, from the emperor to the peasant, to preserve harmony and not disturb the natural order. It was reasoned that since this harmony could be achieved, in the nation and in the family, by following the ritualized rules of social conduct, by moral suasion, and by maintaining the proper attitude toward authority, there was no need for laws and punishments. However, even before the establishment of the Legalist imperial state, Confucians had recognized that only the educated superior person could be expected to have the moral understanding and self-discipline that would obviate the need for punishments. The common people, often referred to by the literati as "the foolish ones," might need to be disciplined by punishment. The Legalists, as their name implies, put great emphasis on laws (regulations) and prescribed harsh punishments for those who broke them.

Legal practice in imperial China reflected both these strains of thought. The so-called legal codes that had developed through the centuries were primarily administrative and penal and stressed both morality and harsh punishment. Civil law had a limited and stunted growth. Within the framework of Confucian society, the family, the clan, the group, and the collective were responsible for individual behavior. The individual therefore had no rights that needed to be protected. Any conflict between individuals was best mediated within the family or the group and settled by compromise and accommodation. Mutual surveillance and mutual responsibility were officially encouraged.

If, however, a crime was committed and the group failed to punish the culprit, it disturbed local harmony and endangered the state. The state then moved in with a heavy hand and severely punished the group to which the criminal belonged, unless, of course, the group on its own identified the criminal. Law, as dispensed in China, was less to distribute justice than to instill fear into the hearts of the evil-doers and to ensure that the people understood the terror of the law. Often an innocent person was punished, but that was secondary to the fact that the law had set an example.

Law was not transcendental. Keeping Confucian values in mind, the magistrate would punish a father lightly for killing his erring son but award the death penalty to a son who had merely injured his father. The preservation of the Confucian moral order was more important than any respect for an abstract legal doctrine. There was no development of an independent judiciary or a science of jurisprudence. The magistrate combined in his person the functions of the police (he was to ensure that the criminal was apprehended), the public prosecutor, the defense attorney, the coroner, the judge, and the jury.

Since crime meant disorder and a lack of harmony, it reflected on the magistrate's inner virtue. The greater the number of crimes in his district, the less virtuous he was seen to be; consequently the likelihood of not being promoted or receiving an increment was greater if crime was common in his district. Moreover, if a magistrate could not apprehend the criminal within a certain period, he might be suspended without pay or even demoted. It was therefore in the interest of the magistrate to cover up criminal activity in his district or connive to get the criminals to move into a neighboring district. As the Qing administration deteriorated, this practice meant that the government was progressively unaware of the actual conditions in the countryside. It also meant that bandits and other bad elements sought refuge on the borders of administrative areas (e.g., mountains separating provinces), where they were free from control.

Quoting cases in which the victims of injustice "had to fall back on the faith that supernatural power would help them . . . where human agencies had failed to do so," Sybille van der Sprenkel concludes that "legal institutions . . . may in fact have done as much to undermine the social order as to uphold it . . . [by] strengthening irrational tendencies which were at variance with the common-sense humanism of Confucianism."[6]

The Commoners: The Ruled

Peasants. In spite of the Confucian lip service to the peasants and their supposedly high position within the ranking structure of the Chinese classes—next below the all-important literati and above the artisans and merchants—the peasants, who constituted nearly 80 percent of the population, were in fact at the bottom of society. As a generalization it was true that the craftspeople and merchants, although in theory considered to be social inferiors, definitely enjoyed a more comfortable life than the majority of the peasants.

According to the Confucian myth, Chinese society was egalitarian, and the humblest male peasant could aspire to the highest pinnacle of social status by passing the imperial examinations, rising through the bureaucracy and perhaps even ending his career as a member of the Grand Council or as the head of one of the ministries. The fact that in some rare cases peasants actually had climbed this ladder of upward mobility had helped to perpetuate the myth. In reality China was a two-class society: the landlord-gentry-scholar-bureaucrats, forming the ruling elite, and the illiterate peasants (along with the numerically fewer artisans, merchants, and soldiers), the exploited masses.

Over the centuries elements of Confucian high culture had, indeed, trickled down to the peasantry and had come to provide basic family values and patterns of familial and social relationships. However, Confucianism never did wholly replace other elements that formed the living fabric of mass culture. Popular Buddhism and popular Daoism, with all their hells and heavens and myriads of gods and goddesses, continued to provide a much-needed spiritual solace to the peasants, whose precarious existence could be shattered by one bad harvest.

With an abundance of workers and limited technology, the agricultural economy worked fairly well until the nineteenth century. But for reasons not yet fully understood, a population explosion had occurred by this time. The population doubled in the 100 years preceding 1850, reaching the staggering figure of 400 plus million. This increase resulted in a definite decline in the peasant economic situation, manifested in decreasing acreage of small holdings, increasing tenancy, agricultural unemployment, indebtedness, and peasant rebellions.

Throughout history Chinese peasants had suffered periodically from devastating floods and famines, but agrarian distress from 1800 on resulted in death by the millions. During one famine alone, in 1877–1878, some 9 to 13 million persons perished in four northern provinces. The rapacity of the officials added to the cruelty of nature. By the mid-nineteenth century corruption in taxation practices often meant an increase of 300 to 1,000 percent in what the peasants had to pay. The imperial system of public granaries, where grain was stored for distribution during shortage, broke down and was abandoned. According to Barrington Moore, "the government and the upper classes performed no function that the peasants regarded as essential for their way of life."[7]

Unlike the ruling elite, the peasants generally did not live in extended family units. It was customary for them to live as a conjugal family, in their own home (however small) in the local village. The average family size was five. All members of the family who had the physical capacity to do so labored long hours intensively cultivating their land holding. Although not all peasants were poor, the number of those who owned comparatively small holdings, on which the family labored without outside help, and those who rented land as tenants formed the bulk of the peasantry. The practice of dividing the land equally between male offspring tended over time to reduce the size of the holdings even further. Dependable figures are not available, but it has been calculated that in the nineteenth century the average size of a farm in North China was three acres, and in South China, one and a half acres.

Two aspects of peasant life have come to leave their mark on Chinese society as a whole. One is that the peasants' preoccupation with maintaining the fertility of the soil led to their carefully collecting all refuse for use in the fields, particularly night soil. A perceptive foreigner who lived in China in the 1850s observed that the "preparation of manure from night soil . . . furnishes employment to multitudes who transport at all hours their noisome loads through narrow city streets. Tanks are dug by the wayside, pails are placed in the streets and retiring stalls opened among the dwellings, whose contents are carried away in boats and buckets. . . ."[8] This situation prevails in large areas of China even today.

The second aspect is that centuries of fighting famines and food shortages has led the Chinese to experiment with every possible source of nutrition. The beauty is that the ingredients, such as snakes, frogs, cats, and dogs, are transformed into the most appetizing dishes. The pity is that the peasants, who no doubt helped in the development of this culinary art, became so poor that they could rarely afford to eat any dishes made even of these ingredients.

The peasants lived in villages, but the imperial control system (the *bao-jia* system) organized the households in units of 10 (*pai*), 100 (*jia*), and 1,000 (*bao*) for collective responsibility, thus cutting across the limits of a single village. The natural village therefore could not acquire the independent identity it often did in other traditional societies. The *bao-jia*, as a police control system, collapsed by the middle of the nineteenth century, but by then banditry and internal wars had made village life chaotic.

Artisans and Merchants. The artisans and merchants were city dwellers, although the bulk of their clients lived in the rural areas. The artisans stood above the merchants in the Confucian social stratification, but they were numerically fewer and not as well off as the merchants. The artisans were organized into separate guilds for each of the main trades (shoemakers, weavers, carpenters, goldsmiths, etc.), which usually were located in separate neighborhoods. The masters and the apprentices established a familial relationship, living and working together until the apprentice had learned the trade and was ready to set up his own craft shop. The guild regulated the conditions of work, established quality control and prices, settled disputes, and collected taxes. It was also responsible to the government. In addition the guilds organized social entertainment and get-togethers for their members.

The merchant community ranged from itinerant peddlers, who carried their wares from village to village, and street vendors to large-scale traders, who were millionaires. Merchants who handled the interprovincial distribution of specialized products like salt, silk, and tea tended to be affluent, often many times richer than the wealthy bureaucrats, but their status in society did not match their prosperity. Even a petty official could make life difficult for them because they had no protection under the law. Confucianism considered their activities parasitic.

Although called a *class* in Confucian terminology, the merchants never came to form an independent class as they did in Japan or India. They established guilds, but unlike the guilds of Europe, Chinese guilds proved unable to promote effectively the special interests of the merchants or give them a voice in government affairs. Rather, Chinese guilds served more as control mechanisms for the government. In the cases of salt and foreign trade the guilds were established by the government itself. Trade and merchants thus remained subservient to government officials and dependent on official goodwill. Since the officials could, and did, squeeze the merchants, the merchants learned to work as allies of the government and kept high officials happy with "gifts" and "donations," thereby securing protection at the highest level and avoiding harassment at lower levels.

Despite the element of government control, guilds of course performed useful functions for Chinese merchants. For example, to protect merchants who were away from their home province, regional guilds were established in major trading centers in other provinces. As the conditions of law and order deteriorated, some of the richer guilds even began to organize their own militias. And by fixing prices and arbitrating disputes, the guilds tended to reduce competitive tensions between merchants.

To discard their lowly status and gain higher social honor, many wealthy merchants abandoned the mercantile world to join the gentry class. They became landlords and encouraged their children to take the imperial examinations. Thus the development of capitalism and the entrepreneurial spirit remained thwarted by unfavorable social circumstances.

Secret Societies and Peasant Rebellions. Confucian political theory accepted peasant rebellions as a legitimate response to dynastic decline. Indeed, such rebellions had usually helped to establish new dynasties throughout Chinese traditional history. Yet nothing was so abhorrent to Confucianism as "disorder" (*luan*). This ambivalence came to be resolved, in practice, by the acceptance of the leader of a successful rebellion as a man of great virtue who had received the heavenly mandate to rule China and by the condemnation of the leader of an unsuccessful rebellion as a "bandit" and a "traitor" who was sliced to death for having shown disloyalty to his prince. Peasant defiance of authority, however, was not limited to these relatively rare occasions of dynastic change. At any time when famines, floods, or the rapacity of landlords or officials made life impossible for the peasants and drove them beyond the limits of forbearance, uprisings occurred. When these uprisings became widespread and were led by secret societies, they were taken to be a sure indication of dynastic decline.

Usually associated with some Buddhist or Daoist religious cult, the secret societies had long histories, surviving through the centuries despite every type of effort by various dynasties to suppress them. Each secret society had developed elaborate rituals and secret signs that gave a sense of identity to their members. In times of peace and order they provided group security and advancement.

By 1800, as Qing power declined, peasant uprisings led by secret societies began to harass the government. The rising of the White Lotus Society in the region bounded by Hubei, Sichuan, and Shaanxi lasted nine years (1796–1804) and cost the government about 120 million silver taels to suppress (three times the annual state revenue). The Heavenly Reason Society staged an uprising in Henan, Shandong, and Zhili provinces in 1813 and even attempted to seize the Forbidden City. The slogan "Overthrow the Qing," which appeared at this time, served as a rallying cry for its opponents until the collapse of the dynasty. These early nineteenth-century uprisings were eventually quelled. But in the process it became abundantly clear that the Qing military had deteriorated because the government had to raise a militia force of several hundred thousands to achieve victory.

It can be concluded that by 1800 the Confucian imperial system had become too set in its ways. It was no longer possible for its operators to change it in any significant manner. Indeed, the ruling classes were themselves the prisoners of the system. The system still held the country together, but cracks had begun to mar the impressive facade of the ideal monolithic, centralized power structure, cracks created by the very real contradictions between the imperial Inner Court and the bureaucracy, the central government and the provinces, the bureaucracy and the gentry, the gentry and the people; in short, between the government as a whole and the people as a whole.

NOTES

1. See "Doctrine of the Mean," in *The Four Books*, trans. James Legge (Shanghai: The Chinese Book Co., n.d.), p. 377.

2. W. T. de Bary et al., eds., *Sources of Chinese Tradition* (New York: Columbia University Press, 1960), pp. 178–79. The quote is slightly amended.

3. See Chin-Keh-mu, *A Short History of Sino-Indian Friendship* (Beijing: Foreign Languages Press, 1958).

4. Bai Shouyi, *An Outline History of China* (Beijing: Foreign Languages Press, 1982), pp. 416–18.

5. Ichisada Miyazaki, *China's Examination Hell*, trans. Conrad Schirokauer (New Haven, CT: Yale University Press, 1981), p. 130.

6. Sybille van der Sprenkel, *Legal Institutions in Manchu China* (London: Athlone Press, 1962), p. 130.

7. Barrington Moore, Jr., *Social Origins of Dictatorship and Democracy* (Boston: Beacon Press, 1966), p. 205.

8. S. Wells Williams, *The Middle Kingdom*, vol. II (London: W. H. Allen, 1883), p. 8.

CHAPTER 2

The End of Isolation: 1800–1860

Despite the dynastic decline, when China entered the nineteenth century there was little reason for any Chinese to imagine that within a few decades their traditional polity would be shaken to its very roots and never recover from the shock. During 2,000 years of its imperial history, China had perfected one of the world's most durable political systems. And China had indeed developed a uniquely indigenous civilization that had not only deeply influenced the culture of the peripheral countries but also drawn them into a China-centered international order. The success of the system and its self-sufficiency had led to a sense of complacency, which was heightened by China's self-imposed isolation.

In the context of global history, China's isolationist policies came at a totally wrong time. When emperor Qian-long ordered all foreign trade to be restricted to the single port of Canton (Guangzhou), he was unaware that a new and potentially dangerous dynamism was emerging in the Occident that was bound to affect China and the Chinese world order. A revolution in science and technology led by Britain was transforming the Western nations into competitors in the global arena for markets, raw materials, and colonies. It was only a matter of time until the expansive, aggressive West, incapable of being contained within the Chinese international system of "tribute and trade," would shatter the isolationist walls raised by China. China's ignorance of the West was colossal, and although it is not suggested that better knowledge would have kept China from being defeated in war, it may have helped China to have been better prepared for the onslaught.

CHINA'S WORLD ORDER AND FOREIGN TRADE

The Chinese international structure was totally different from any that had evolved in other parts of the world. First, it was premised on the belief (not novel in itself because many other societies have tended to think of themselves in the same way) that China was the cultural center of the universe and that all non-Chinese were "uncivilized" barbarians. This belief was reflected in the Chinese name for their country, Zhongguo, which can be translated as "The Central Kingdom" or "The Middle Kingdom."

Second, since the Chinese ruler, "the Son of Heaven," was considered the ruler of all humankind, all other "barbarian" rulers were mere local chieftains owing allegiance to Beijing. There could be no Western-style diplomatic relations. Countries wanting to trade with China had to send "tribute" missions that legitimized Chinese suzerainty, and in return they could trade for a specified number of days at border points designated by Beijing. When received at the Imperial court the tributary envoy had to *ke-tou* (kowtow) before the emperor. The ritual of kowtow, which consisted of three kneelings, each involving three prostrations, was not specially devised for the foreigners and was an everyday ceremony in China. The non-Chinese Asians accepted it without difficulty, but the Europeans found it disconcerting and debasing.

Regulations did not allow any alien to enter or live within China without imperial permission or any Chinese to travel abroad. Except for officially designated institutions, even teaching the Chinese language to a foreigner was an act punishable under the law.

Since Asian states dealing with China continued to pay regular tribute to Beijing, there was little reason for the Chinese to doubt their predominance in their world order. Even the Europeans, who had first entered the Chinese waters as early as the sixteenth century, had submitted to trade within the highly restrictive Chinese system.

The tribute system of international relations was, however, not so uniform as ideology would have it. Mongolia, Xinjiang, and Tibet, although outside China proper, were considered within the pale, and Beijing had the right to post agents and armed forces there. Korea, the Ryukyu Islands, Annam (present-day Vietnam), Siam (Thailand), Burma, and Nepal were "tributary states," which sent regular tribute missions. The Europeans in Guangzhou, the "ocean barbarians," were considered to have come from too far to send regular tribute missions, but by recording their embassies as "tributary missions," the fiction was maintained that they, too, came from tributary states.

Russia fell into a different category altogether. Russian expansion into East Asia brought St. Petersburg into confrontation with China. The Manchus, themselves "barbarians" who had conquered China in 1644 and were not yet totally blinded by Confucian ideology, signed the Treaty of Nerchinsk (1689) and the Treaty of Kiakhta (1727) on the basis of equality. These treaties delimited borders, established trading points, allowed the Russians limited caravan trade with Beijing, and granted the Russians facilities to establish a church in Beijing and permission to send ecclesiastical missions that would include students of Chinese language. Much has been made of these treaties by historians wanting to show that China had a precedent for not pushing the idea of the universal rule of the Son of Heaven too far when the Anglo-Chinese crisis arose in the 1830s. The fact is that Beijing viewed the Russians as a Central Asian state, and there were precedents in Chinese history for dealing in a similar fashion with Central Asian rulers whose power China had reasons to fear.

Furthermore, with the passage of time the Sino-Russian arrangement lost the original sense of equality that may have marked the treaties. The Russians in Beijing were locally isolated, led an impoverished intellectual and physical existence, and performed no diplomatic function and hardly any ecclesiastic one. By the end of the eighteenth century Beijing had begun to use the language of superiority in its notes to the Russians.

Things were, however, about to change drastically for China. Not only was its world order about to collapse, but China would also soon find itself humiliated and degraded to the rank of a third-rate power in the new

West-centered world order. It all began in Guangzhou (Canton), the one southern port to which the trade of all European maritime powers was limited.

THE GUANGZHOU SYSTEM OF TRADE AND ITS COLLAPSE

The foreign trade system in Guangzhou reflected the Chinese government's attitude that trade was secondary to the maintenance of the Chinese world and internal order. The governor-general in charge of the two provinces of Guangdong and Guangxi, and the governor of Guangdong, both posted at Guangzhou, headed the local government and were responsible for local law and order. A Chinese commissioner for customs at Guangzhou (the Hoppo), directly appointed by Beijing but lower in rank than the other two officials, was in immediate charge of the guild of Chinese merchants, the Cohong, who had a monopoly of trade with the European merchants. The Cohong merchants were jointly responsible to the officials.

The 12 or 13 members of the Cohong, also known as the security merchants because they "secured," or guaranteed, every ship that came to Guangzhou, were responsible for selling the inbound cargo, procuring the Chinese goods sought by the foreign trader, and collecting all duties and other dues and transferring them to the office of the Hoppo. They were also responsible for looking after the needs of the captain and the crew of the foreign ship and were held liable if the foreigners broke any of the regulations governing their stay in Guangzhou.

The foreign traders could not communicate with the officials directly but had to send their "petitions" (a "letter" would have meant an assumption of equality) through the Cohong. In case of any infraction of the law, the foreigners were held jointly responsible. For example, in 1821 an American sailor on board the U.S. ship *Emily* accidentally killed a Chinese boatwoman. The Chinese demanded that the sailor be handed over for execution. The Americans, knowing that under the Chinese legal system the sailor would not get a fair trial, refused to surrender him, with the result that the Chinese threatened to stop all trade. Thereupon the Americans reluctantly complied, and the sailor was duly strangled publicly.

This and other similar incidents gave ample evidence that the Westerners, however dissatisfied with their circumstances, were willing to accept this type of humiliating treatment because they were loath to give up their highly profitable China trade. Indeed, the adverse conditions under which trade was carried on were clearly spelled out by an imperial edict. It stipulated that the Westerners could come to Guangzhou only for the duration of the trading season, not leave the limits of the factory grounds (residence and offices of the foreign "factors") outside the city of Guangzhou, never enter the city, never row on the river, never bring their families or any females with them, and never deal with any Chinese other than those officially permitted. The foreigners could not ride in a sedan chair (a mark of respectability in a privilege-conscious society) or even hire Chinese servants as a right (they did get them by connivance). When the summer trading months came to an end, the foreigners were expected to close their operations in Guangzhou and repair to the peninsula of Macao, where the Portuguese had been given an enclave for residence since the middle of the sixteenth century.

It should be recognized that by conforming to the conditions imposed on them and by accepting their inferior position, the Westerners strengthened the Chinese belief in the preeminence of the Middle Kingdom and in the tributary system of foreign relations. In a manner of speaking, the British East India Company, which dominated the trade at Guangzhou, was an ideal collaborator. Like the Cohong, it had a virtual monopoly of foreign trade, and again like the Cohong, it was a merchant organization. Its officers, although they may have been irritated by the system, did not consider it an unpardonable insult that they were not allowed to communicate directly with the Chinese officials. The head of the British East India Company (the taipan) could speak on behalf of the foreign merchants, be held responsible for their actions, and deal with his counterpart in the Cohong on equal terms.

But some irritants soon became a cause of more serious Sino-British trouble. Apart from the unsatisfactory personal conditions under which trade was carried on and the abhorrent Chinese legal practices, the conditions of trade itself left much to be desired. The foreigners were kept ignorant of the tariff schedules and were often charged many times the official rates. Not being able to complain or take their case to any higher agency, they were at the mercy of the Cohong. They were constantly subjected to demands for bribes and illicit commissions, called "customary dues," which had to be paid to customs officials, interpreters, river pilots, and so forth. If a Cohong merchant who had taken a loan or an advance to purchase next year's goods went bankrupt or reneged on the debt, no legal machinery could help the foreign merchant recover the money.

If the Chinese had not been so self-absorbed and so intent on keeping their country as closed off as possible, they might have at least realized that the Guangzhou system of trade was collapsing and that if it did collapse, the tribute system would go down with it. The relationship between tribute and trade was established by China as an instrument for controlling the barbarian. For the Chinese tribute was far more important than the trade element in the equation; for the Westerner, in contrast, the compelling motive for being in China was trade. If this tribute business got in the way, it would have to be eliminated as a totally unacceptable hindrance.

By the time the eighteenth century came to a close, British trade with China had expanded tremendously. The exports of tea alone rose from c. 400,000 pounds in 1725 to c. 26 million pounds in 1808. The number of Westerners who gathered for trade at Guangzhou began to make the fiction that the ocean barbarians came from too far to be asked for regular tribute missions sound hollow.

This trade was one-sided in the beginning because the Chinese agrarian-based economy was relatively self-sufficient, and there was almost no demand for European goods in China. The British therefore had to pay in silver for the teas, silks, porcelain, lacquerware, and nankeen (a cotton fabric made in Nanking). Gradually the deficits were redressed by the development of what is known as the "country trade" between India and Guangzhou. The country traders were mostly private English merchants who brought raw cotton, cotton piece goods, and opium from India. As the demand for these goods, particularly opium (from c. 150,000 pounds in 1767 to c. 6 million pounds in 1838), increased in China, the trade balance reversed in favor of Britain. But the private merchants circumvented the control of the East India Company and, by establishing illicit contacts with Chinese smugglers, that of the Cohong, too. They grew, enlarged their arena of commercial activities, and became a force undermining the Guangzhou system, which, they felt, kept the Chinese market from being opened further. These merchants received help from an unexpected source—the Americans. America entered the China trade in 1784 but soon became the second most important trading partner of China. The Chinese tried to get the Americans to organize themselves into a group and appoint one person who would be responsible for the others, but they failed in the endeavor because the Americans were ardent believers in individualism and free trade.

In England, too, the British "free traders" and industrial manufacturers, who upheld the new philosophy of capitalism and laissez-faire, pressured the British government to end the age of mercantilism by abolishing the East India Company's monopoly. To these merchants free trade was a birthright that could be denied neither by Britain nor by China. With the company out of the way and the Guangzhou system demolished, the rising class of British industrialists would surely find a ready market for their woolens and cotton textiles with China's population of 300 million.

The East India Company's monopoly finally ended in 1834. This was an event of great local importance because the taipan, representing a mercantile company, was now replaced by an officer commissioned by the British government "not only as a protector of [British] subjects and an overseer of their commercial activities but as a political and diplomatic representative" of the Crown.[1] Surely a representative of His Britannic Majesty could not be expected to deal with the Chinese officials through the Cohong merchants. The stage was set therefore for the confrontation that contributed to the first Anglo-Chinese War of 1839–1842 (also known as the Opium War), which "opened" China and forced it onto the tortuous path of modernization it has since followed.

BRITAIN'S ATTEMPT TO OPEN CHINA DIPLOMATICALLY

Even before the East India Company's monopoly had ended, the pressures on the British government to help expand overseas markets resulted in three official missions to Beijing to negotiate a more acceptable framework for trade and establish some form of treaty relations. The first embassy set out in 1787 but never reached Beijing because the envoy, Colonel Charles Cathcart, died on the way. The second and third embassies, 1793 and 1816, headed by Lord Macartney and Lord Amherst, succeeded in reaching Beijing but totally failed to achieve any of their goals.

Macartney's instructions clearly reflected the concerns of the free traders and the industrialists of Manchester, Liverpool, and Birmingham. He was to ask for three new ports to be opened, one of them as far north as Tianjin (i.e., open China to foreign trade); a reduction in the duties; a published tariff (a commercial treaty); one or more island depots "near to the tea and silk-producing and woolen-consuming areas, where the English traders might reside and where English jurisdiction might be exercised" (cessions of territory); the accreditation of a British minister to the court at Beijing (Western-style diplomatic relations); and the freedom to propagate Christianity. He was also given samples of British woolens to distribute in China to help create a taste for British products.[2]

But Macartney, with all his resplendent embroidered velvet dress; his mantle of the Order of the Bath; his entourage of some 95 persons in uniforms of scarlet, green, and gold; and his 600 packages of presents failed to impress Emperor Qian-long. The only concession he received was permission to pay homage to the Son of Heaven on bended knee instead of kowtowing. The embassy was recorded as a "tribute-bearing mission" and the gifts as "tribute." The emperor had allowed him to kneel instead of kowtow because the barbarian was too ignorant to learn proper behavior (although in the official record it was said that Macartney had kowtowed). Ignorance was also proved by the inclusion, among the presents, of an elegant, well-sprung carriage, which though more comfortable than the ones the emperor used, had the coachman's seat elevated above that of the emperor![3] Even worse, the embassy had used the services of 12-year-old George Staunton (his father was an aide of Lord Macartney) to copy diplomatic papers in Chinese (a language he had picked up on the voyage out) because the person who made the original translation was afraid he would be recognized by his calligraphy and consequently be punished for helping the barbarians. One can imagine what impression this made on the Chinese officials, who laid such great store on the art of writing.

Emperor Qian-long must have been a bit nonplussed by Lord Macartney's requests, but in his several exhaustive mandates (replies) to George III, Qian-long made the Chinese position absolutely clear. The first edict opened with this statement:

> You, O king, live beyond the confines of many seas, nevertheless, impelled by your humble desire to partake of the benefits of our civilisation,

you have dispatched a mission respectfully bearing your memorial. . . . To show your devotion, you have also sent offerings of your country's produce.

and concluded with this admonition:

I confer upon you, O King, valuable presents. . . . Do you reverently receive them and take note of my tender goodwill toward you! A special mandate![4]

First and foremost from the British point of view was the desirability of increasing trade and opening more ports. Qian-long dismissed that request with this remark:

Our dynasty's majestic virtue has penetrated unto every country under Heaven, and Kings of all nations have offered their costly tribute by land and sea. As your Ambassador can see for himself, we possess all things. I set no value on objects strange or ingenious, and have no use for your country's manufactures. . . .

[As for opening more ports] I decree that your request is refused and that the trade shall be limited to [Guangzhou].

It appears that the proposal that Qian-long found most difficult to comprehend was the British "entreaty to send one of [her] nationals to be accredited to [the] Celestial Court." His explanation for why this request was wholly unacceptable shows how wide the gap was between the Chinese and British views of international relations and trade.

First, wrote the emperor, no foreigners were allowed to reside at the capital. There were a handful of Jesuit missionaries at the court, but they offered no precedent because these Europeans were in the service of China. As such they were "compelled to adopt Chinese dress," their movements were restricted, they could not correspond with anyone in their own country, and they were "never permitted to return home."

It is interesting to note that Qian-long makes it a point to mention that the Russians had once been allowed to trade in Beijing but were "compelled to withdraw" after Kiakhta was opened for trade; he does not refer to the presence of the Russian "embassy" in Beijing. Indeed, Lord Macartney inquired about it but was told by the Chinese government that the Russians owed their presence in Beijing "to a peculiar history in which England, as yet, had no part."[5]

A second reason given by Qian-long against establishing embassies in Beijing was that foreign tributary envoys were "provided for" by the Chinese government. How was Britain going to look after its envoy in Beijing? Indeed, according to the Chinese system, from the day a tribute mission entered Chinese territory to the day it departed, the Office for Tributary States was responsible for all aspects of transportation, housing, and food connected with the mission. Consider, for example, Lord Macartney's mission itself. Certain high officials and hundreds of lower-ranking mandarins received Macartney and accompanied him throughout his stay. He was wined and dined by them, and his entourage was given "120 sheep, 120 hogs, 100 fowls, 100 ducks, 20 bullocks, 14 boxes of Tartar bread, 400 melons, 22 boxes of dried peaches . . . vegetables, candies, red rice, tea, wine . . ." on the day they landed on Chinese soil as the first of an ongoing series of "gifts." The mission was provided with junks, sailors, and coolies to transport it upriver and 3,000 porters, carters, coolies, and guards, along with horses, wagons, carts, carriages, and sedan chairs to help it on the road journey.[6] How was Britain expected to make such arrangements in China, a country so tightly organized that a foreigner could not even hire a single Chinese without official permission?

Third, asked Qian-long, how was the British representative expected to exercise control over British trade from Beijing, which was so far (1,200 miles) from Guangzhou!

To bring home the absurdity of the request, the emperor further pointed out that the problems would be magnified many times over because he would have to allow envoys from all other European nations to reside in Beijing, too. "How can our dynasty alter its whole procedure and system of etiquette . . . in order to meet your individual views?"

As far as the other demands were concerned, the emperor rejected them one by one, giving a variety of reasons, all reinforcing the obvious conclusion that the foreigners must work within the Guangzhou system. He was incensed with the proposal that he cede territory for British residence. "Consider, moreover, that England is not the only barbarian land that wishes to establish relations with our civilisation and trade with our Empire: supposing that other nations were all to imitate your evil example and beseech me to present them each and all with a site for trading purposes, how could I possibly comply? This also is a flagrant infringement of the usage of my Empire and cannot possibly be entertained." As for the dissemination of Christianity, Qian-long found the request "utterly unreasonable."[7]

Qian-long sent such a detailed reply because he wanted to clarify, once and for all, the ordinances that applied to foreigners and foreign trade. "It may be, O king, that the above proposals have been wantonly made by your ambassador on his own responsibility, or per adventure you yourself are ignorant of our dynastic regulations and had no intention of transgressing them when you expressed all these wild ideas and hopes."[8]

The British mission ended in failure, but Lord Macartney's perceptive analysis of China is worth recording: "The Empire of China is an old, crazy first rate Man of War. . . . She may, perhaps, not sink outright; she may drift some time as a wreck, and will then be dashed to pieces on the shore; but she can never be rebuilt on the old bottom. . . ."[9]

Macartney's failure and Emperor Qian-long's rebuke did not keep the British from trying the diplomatic path once more in 1816, when they were much better prepared for sending a mission. Unlike in 1793, when the British had to hunt all over the continent for an interpreter, Lord Amherst had the help of George Staunton (who from the small beginnings mentioned became a proficient Chinese linguist, took on work with the East India Company, and by 1816 had become the president of the Select Committee) and of Reverend Robert Morrison (a Presbyterian missionary who was working for the company as a Chinese translator), both well recognized as China experts.

The only change on the Chinese side, however, was that the reigning emperor, the Jia-qing emperor, was not inclined to be as lax over the question of the kowtow as his father had been. The Chinese officials in charge of the mission could not get Lord Amherst to agree to perform the kowtow, and they dared not inform the emperor of their failure. When Lord Amherst, who had been traveling all night and did not have his official dress with him, refused to be rushed into an audience, the Chinese officials heaved a sigh of relief. The emperor was informed that the ambassador was sick with diarrhea. When ordered to send the deputies of Lord Amherst, the emperor was told that they, too, were sick. The emperor was so incensed that he expelled the embassy. Later, on learning the real truth, he remarked, "The Middle Kingdom is the common sovereign of all nations under Heaven. How can We suffer such an insult due to [British] pride and arrogance?"[10]

In his edict to the king of England Emperor Jia-qing recalled that at first, "not being accustomed to our good manners," Lord Macartney, too, had not followed "our etiquette which required him to kowtow," but on instruction from high Chinese officials, "your ambassador performed the etiquette both of kneeling and kowtowing according to Our ceremonials." The virtuous Son of Heaven was not above telling a blatant lie to defend Confucian ideology! Since, however, Lord Amherst had "failed to carry out his mission in proper form and to accord us proof of your genuine loyalty," the memorial sent by London could not be accepted and was being returned with the ambassador.

Emperor Jia-qing then gave a list of the presents he was "bestowing" on the king of England and added that no more attempts need be made to send missions to Beijing:

> . . . your ambassadors are ignorant of our Chinese etiquette. Though we have repeatedly instructed

China—Mid-nineteenth Century

them, they pay no heed. . . . There is no need for you to send an embassy on this long and tiring journey. If you will remain sincerely loyal to us, then your ambassadors need not come to Our Court. We regard this as your inclination toward our civilization. We hope you will always observe this edict. Thus We have decreed.[11]

On their return journey Lord Amherst and his party were treated very shabbily. "There were now no soldiers to clear the way, no guides with lanterns to light up the road; and the animosity of the mandarins was amply displayed next morning when a beggar, standing up as Lord Amherst passed by, was instantly ordered to sit down again."[12]

The Chinese, who obviously considered this embassy of little consequence and probably felt that they had put an end to future missions and the irritation they caused, did not realize that in England more and more people were coming to the conclusion that since all civil attempts to establish fair relations with China only resulted in insults to Britain, China would have to be dealt with in a more forceful fashion. The Opium War took place within a decade and a half of the Amherst embassy.

WAR AS AN EXTENSION OF DIPLOMACY

The first serious instance of friction between China and Britain occurred in 1834 when Lord Napier arrived to replace the taipan of the now-defunct East India Company. His title, chief superintendent of trade at Canton, and his duties, to protect the interests of English merchants and English trade, were similar to that of his predecessor. But, unlike him, Napier had received his appointment from the British crown and not from a commercial company. His instructions were to respect the laws and prejudices of China and to behave in a reasonable and circumspect manner, to be conciliatory, and not to use menacing language. However, he was to announce his arrival to the viceroy of Guangdong "by letter," and he could call on the help of the Royal Navy in an "extreme case" of emergency. The situation was by no means clear-cut. In the absence of proper diplomatic relations Lord Napier could not be considered a full-fledged diplomatic representative of Britain in a proper consular post (indeed, no advance information had been sent to Beijing or Guangzhou regarding his appointment), but neither could he be considered a merchant representative.

Whatever the intent of his instructions, Lord Napier looked upon himself as an envoy of Britain, a protector of British dignity and honor, who would deal only with the high officials of China directly and not through the Cohong, who would not be soft on the Chinese, and who would help expand British trade by getting more ports opened to commerce. When Napier left Macao for Guangzhou and sent his letter to the viceroy, he broke several important regulations. He did not apply for permission to go to Guangzhou, he had no customs permit to reside in the Guangzhou factory, he sent his communication to the viceroy not as a humble "petition" from an inferior to a superior but as a "letter" to an equal, the letter was in Chinese and not in English, and he tried to get the letter delivered directly and not through the Cohong merchants.

From the Chinese point of view this was highly unacceptable behavior, and the most charitable interpretation was that the barbarian was totally ignorant of the civilized laws of China. Napier's letter was not accepted by the mandarin at the city gate. It was noted, with horror, that it had "the form and style of equality." The viceroy promptly sent a communication to the Cohong, meant to be conveyed to Napier, which said in part,

> The object of the said barbarian headman [here Lord Napier's name is transliterated by characters that may be translated as "Laboriously Vile"] in coming to Canton is for commercial business. The Celestial Empire appoints officials—civilian to rule the people, military to intimidate the wicked; but the petty affairs of commerce are to be directed by the merchants themselves. The officials are not concerned with such matters. In the trade of the said barbarians, if there are any changes to be made in regulations, in all cases the Hong merchants are to consult together, and make a joint statement to the superintendent of customs and to my office, and they will then be informed officially whether the proposals are to be allowed or disallowed. . . .
>
> The great ministers of the Celestial Empire are not permitted to have private intercourse by letters with outside barbarians. . . .
>
> To sum up the whole matter: the nation has its laws; it is so everywhere. Even England has its laws; how much more the Celestial Empire! How flaming bright are its great laws and ordinances! More terrible than the awful thunderbolt! . . .[13]

A Chinese official, however high, could not sanction a change in the Guangzhou system without prior approval of the emperor. And in any case, there was no reason for the Chinese even to think of changing a system that had worked so well for so long. The only bothersome element was Napier because he did not fit into the system.

After various further acts of mutual irritation, when Napier realized that the viceroy might order the cessation of trade, Napier did the most foolish thing possible: He circulated a proclamation, written in Chinese, attacking the "obstinacy" of the viceroy for not receiving his letter and the "perversity" of the Chinese government, which by suspending trade, would bring immense suffering to the hard-working Chinese, who depended on trade with Britain. Napier incorrectly presumed that the common Chinese hated their government and that they shared a common interest with the British. Indeed, Napier had interfered in the internal affairs of China. The viceroy, in keeping with Chinese traditional practice, issued a special edict prohibiting all further commercial transactions between the Chinese and the British as long as Napier stayed on in Guangzhou.

Lord Napier, true to character, responded by ordering two frigates of the Royal Navy to sail upriver to Guangzhou. The time had come for a show of force. Chinese forts protecting the river fired on the frigates, and though not much damage was inflicted, Napier warned the viceroy that it was a "very serious offence to fire upon or otherwise insult the British flag," that the viceroy had "opened the preliminaries of war," and that his (Britannic) Majesty would not let such folly go unpunished. "Therefore tremble, Viceroy Loo, intensely tremble."[14] The tables had been turned. The British had begun using the language reserved by the Chinese for the barbarians.

The British government, although it failed to provide Lord Napier with well-defined instructions, had never wanted him to act in this manner and had in no way encouraged him in his rash behavior. Most of the British merchants, too, were unhappy at the developments because, instead of serving their interests, Napier had undermined them. Ill and frustrated, Napier finally gave in to Chinese pressure and retired to Macao, where he died a few days later.

The entire crisis had lasted only a little over two months, and since the superintendents of trade who succeeded Napier made no attempt to open direct intercourse with the viceroy, the next few years were a quiescent period. However, the "Napier fizzle" left an impression behind that shaped future Western policy in China: The only way to negotiate with China was under the threat of military force. As Lord Napier wrote to Lord Grey, "I feel satisfied your Lordship will see the urgent necessity of negotiating with such a government, having in your hands at the same time the means of compulsion; to negotiate with them otherwise would be an idle waste of time."[15]

On the Chinese side during the crisis, Beijing had admonished the viceroy for having failed in his duties and had punished him by depriving him of his rank (restored when Napier left Guangzhou); the viceroy, in turn, had punished the Cohong merchants for having failed in their duty to control the barbarian. When the crisis ended, the Chinese had succeeded in reaffirming the Chinese system of trade and tribute and in reconfirming China's superiority over the trade-hungry barbarians. Another irritation had been satisfactorily dealt with from the Chinese point of view.

The second act of open conflict was the result of Chinese action to suppress the opium traffic.

THE FIRST OPIUM WAR: 1839–1842

The quiescent policy followed by the superintendents of trade came to an end with the appointment of Captain Charles Elliot to this post in December 1836. With far more subtlety than Napier had shown, Captain Elliot tried, once again, to force the viceroy to accept direct communication from him. At the same time he requested London to send naval units from India to the China coast so that the Chinese might be pressured to legalize the opium trade and release it "from its actual condition of stagnation."[16] The forces requested arrived in Chinese waters in mid-1838. However, by this time it had become amply clear that the Chinese government was determined to suppress rather than legalize the opium trade.

In 1839, after making a thorough investigation of the opium problem in Guangzhou, Commissioner Lin concluded that action had to be taken against the foreign merchants involved in the trade. Lin's position was in no way antagonistic to the interests of foreign merchants carrying on legitimate trade. Un-

The Opium Problem

Though opium had been used occasionally by the Chinese as a medicinal drug for centuries, its importation was extremely limited until the eighteenth century, when the opium-smoking habit began to spread throughout the country. By the early decades of the nineteenth century, opium became the major item of British imports into China, more than balancing the tea, silk, and porcelain exports from China. Starting with fewer than 1,000 chests (approximately 135 pounds to a chest) at the end of the eighteenth century, the amount of opium unloaded in China stood at 5,000 chests in 1821, 22,000 chests in 1831, and 35,000 chests in 1837.

Although the British were the biggest suppliers of opium, almost all the other merchants from the United States and Europe were also involved in the nefarious traffic. Since China had prohibited the import, sale, or consumption of opium, trade in the drug was totally illegal, so opium had to be smuggled into China. The British did not create the opium habit in China, but surely Britain cannot avoid being condemned for ruthlessly and callously exploiting this demand, helping it to grow by ensuring increased supplies of opium from its base in India. Technically, the East India Company in Guangzhou was not involved in the drug trade, but the Company in India monopolized both its manufacture in India and its sale to private "country traders," who smuggled it into China. The British government in India earned about 10 percent of its total revenues from taxes on opium.

The question of the opium trade had been debated heatedly in the British press and in Parliament, and though condemned by many as immoral, a parliamentary committee had declared, in 1832, that it was "inadvisable to abandon so important a [source of] revenue." There is no question that the British government was deeply involved in this disgraceful trade.

But regardless of the differing public positions on the opium question, on one point British public opinion was reaching a consensus. Even those who were strongly against the trade felt at one with the hawks, that the Chinese had to be taught some kind of a lesson for their overbearing and insulting behavior in foreign relations. Not surprisingly, the most vocal of the warmongers were the opium traders, like William Jardine and James Matheson, whose profits were often as high as $1,000 per chest, and who returned with their millions to England to enter Parliament or receive a knighthood and settle down as highly respected citizens.

The Chinese government's first edict prohibiting transactions in opium had been issued in 1729, the second in 1780, and the third in 1796. From that year to 1839 over 40 edicts were issued by two emperors and their viceroys, which reconfirmed the prohibition and increased the punishments to be meted out to opium addicts, sellers of opium, merchants smuggling opium, and officials conniving in the trade. The number and frequency of these edicts only proved that though the government was fully aware of the gravity of the situation, it was ineffective in stamping out the traffic in "foreign mud." Too many corrupt officials were colluding with the foreign merchants. Opium was being off-loaded up the coast as far as Tianjin.

The rapid growth of the opium-smoking habit in China is difficult to explain, but its deleterious effects can be readily analyzed. First, it corroded the morals and the health of the millions who were addicted to it: Addicts ranged from princes in the Forbidden City and officials in the bureaucracy to soldiers, merchants, artisans, coolies, and city riffraff. The degeneration of the army, where the habit was extremely widespread, was of particular concern to the government. The use of the narcotic also led to greater demands for bribes and increased corruption among the bureaucracy, and of course, it led to an increase of all types of crimes at the lower levels of society.

Second, the opium traffic had serious economic repercussions. A large percentage of the addicts belonged to the poorer sections of society, and since they had limited purchasing power, the regular market in consumer goods became depressed. Much more important, as the balance of trade shifted to favor the British, there began an outflow of silver. According to one estimate, one-fifth of all silver in circulation in China left the country between 1821 and 1840. Thus the value of silver appreciated in terms of the Chinese copper currency with devastating effects on the poor Chinese peasant masses, who had to pay taxes in silver. For example, the exchange rate in the province of Shandong rose from 1,450 to 1,650 copper cash for 1 silver tael in 1800 to 2,700 in 1830. Not all provinces were affected as badly as Shandong, but the situation had become critical nationwide.

In the 1830s concerned high officials began to write memorials to the emperor suggesting various means for the suppression of the opium traffic. Some suggested that if the trade was legalized, smuggling would stop and foreign trade would once again be restricted to the one port of Guangzhou; the government could increase its revenues by imposing a duty on opium and also control the distribution of the drug within the country. Others proposed that the immoral traffic in the drug had to be totally eradicated within the country by harsher punishments of those involved. This would halt the degeneration of society, stem the outflow of silver, and make it unattractive for foreigners to bring opium to China.

The emperor finally sided with the prohibitionists and appointed Lin Ze-xu as imperial commissioner at Guangzhou to carry out the new policies. Lin had said in his memorial that if the traffic in opium was not eradicated, "a few decades from now we shall not only be without soldiers to resist the enemy, but also in want of silver to provide an army."[17] Lin arrived in Guangzhou in 1839 to find that the viceroy in Guangzhou had already taken several vigorous measures to stamp out the sale and use of opium in the city and the surrounding areas. Although the viceroy's demand that the leading foreign opium dealers should leave China had been contemptuously ignored, the opium trade already had begun to languish.

---

fortunately for Lin, however, so many merchants were involved in both the legitimate and the contraband trade that he had to confront virtually the entire foreign community. He ordered the traders to hand over their stocks of opium for destruction and to sign a bond guaranteeing that they would never again smuggle opium in their ships. His stand was moral and legal.

Lin presumed that the British government was not a party to this illegal trade, as is apparent in his letter to the "ruler of England," in which he appealed to him (Lin did not know that Queen Victoria was the reigning monarch) to "check your wicked and sift your vicious people before they come to China":

. . . The wealth of China is used to profit the barbarians [through legitimate trade]. . . . By what right do they in return use the poisonous drug to injure the Chinese people? . . . Since [opium] is not permitted to do harm to your own country, then even less should you let it be passed on to the harm of other countries—how much less to China? Of all that China exports to foreign countries, there is not a single thing that is not beneficial to people. . . . Take tea and rhubarb, for example; the foreign countries cannot get along a single day without them. . . .

. . . Indeed you, O King, can eradicate the

opium plant in (India), hoe over the fields entirely, and sow in its stead the five grains. . . .

. . . Suppose a man of another country comes to England to trade, he still has to obey the English laws; how much more should he obey the laws of the Celestial Dynasty?[18]

Believing that Elliot might not forward the letter to the English ruler, Commissioner Lin sent it with the captain of an ordinary ship sailing to England. The letter never reached her Britannic Majesty. So much for the Chinese style of international relations and for Lin's understanding of Britain. The naivete displayed in Lin's letter also underlay his belief that the Royal Navy would not intervene on behalf of the barbarian lawbreakers.

Lin was correct, but only to a point. To force the merchants to hand over their opium stocks, Lin suspended trade, blockaded the foreign factories, ordered all Chinese (cooks, servants, compradors, etc.) to withdraw, and confined the entire merchant community to this open prison for 47 days. Lin had used the time-honored techniques of controlling the barbarians. When the opium was surrendered, Lin had succeeded in his goal and the traditional techniques had been reconfirmed.

However, when Elliot, "in the name and on behalf of her Britannic majesty's government," collected the 20,283 chests of opium (guaranteeing indemnity for all stocks handed over to him) and surrendered them to Lin, the matter had been raised to the level of an international issue. Lin did not realize that there was a crucial difference, from the Western point of view, between his confiscating contraband from individual merchants and his seizing it from the representative of the government, who had acted under duress to protect "British life, liberty, and property." The Chinese had unwittingly insulted British dignity and rendered themselves liable to the British government.

Even after the destruction of the opium, trade was still denied to British merchants. Under advice from Elliot, they had refused to sign the bond guaranteeing that there would be no more smuggling of opium. The ostensible reason for this stand was the fear that even if one sailor secretly smuggled in some opium, the entire crew would be punished under Chinese law. Elliot, who had skillfully prepared the ground for intervention by the British government, withdrew to Macao along with the British merchant community. Meanwhile, smuggling in opium had resumed with heightened vigor, and the British merchants managed to carry on their legitimate trade by using American ships. The Americans had signed the necessary bond.

At this stage the main issue became complicated when a party of drunken British sailors killed a Chinese citizen in a brawl in Kowloon. Elliot held a trial but could not identify the person responsible. He punished some of the sailors and compensated the family of the victim. Lin, however, in keeping with Chinese legal practice, demanded that an Englishman be handed over for punishment, which in this case meant death. When the Portuguese authorities in Macao declined to shield the British from Chinese pressure, the British withdrew in their ships to the waters around Hong Kong and made the island their headquarters. War broke out in November 1839.

From the Chinese point of view the Celestial Empire was chastening foreign barbarians who had failed to follow Chinese regulations and laws. Lin's action was influenced by several popular misconceptions: The Europeans could not survive without rhubarb and tea (their food habits made them constipated and blocked their bladders—they needed rhubarb and tea to relieve themselves); the profit motive was so strong among the foreigners that they could be controlled by the threat that trade would be denied to them (this had worked in the past); the power of the British warships was overrated and they were unwieldy in shallow waters; British soldiers were buttoned up so tight that once knocked over they could not get up again. Information about the West in official literature was no less confused: Portugal was near Malacca and was the same as France, England was the same as Holland, and so forth. Nobody, obviously, had bothered to look at the globe presented to the emperor by Lord Macartney.

Theoretically, from the British point of view, unless China accepted the independence and equality of other nations and realized that it was obligated to open the country to commercial intercourse, the relations between China and the West could never be satisfactory. In fact, it would be a truer estimation of the situation to say that the British wanted to force China to become a subservient and pliant state that would willingly accept European supremacy. Opium was only a part of the problem. Of much greater importance was the issue of British manufactures; the industrial capitalists in England were consumed by the desire to open (what they considered to be) the vast Chinese market for their goods.

War began in earnest in mid-1840, after the arrival of a British expeditionary force with instructions to help Captain Elliot deliver a letter from Lord Palmerston, British foreign minister, to a responsible Chinese official for onward transmission to the emperor. The naval force went up the coast, reducing coastal defenses on the way; it occupied Dinghai and finally reached Tianjin before the emperor decided to send officials to receive the communication from Palmerston and deal with Elliot. Negotiations were opened outside Guangzhou between Elliot and the Manchu grandee, Qi-shan, in January 1841. By the resulting Chuenpi (Chuan-bi) Convention, China was to cede Hong Kong to Britain, pay an indemnity, accept the principle of diplomatic equality, and reopen Guangzhou for trade. But neither Beijing nor London was pleased with the settlement: One side felt that too much had been conceded; the other, that too little had been gained. Qi-shan was dismissed and Elliot was recalled.

The British decided that they had to prove their military capability once again before the Chinese would surrender to their demands. So the British destroyed the Chinese southern fleet; Guangzhou was held to ransom; Xiamen, Dinghai, Ningbo, and Shanghai were occupied. When the squadron occupied Chenjiang, at the junction of the Grand Canal and the Yangtze River and began to sail upriver to Nanjing, the British threatened to cut off Beijing from the rich and fertile provinces of South China, which were its main source of food and revenue. By now the emperor, who at the beginning of the war had been getting many false reports of military successes, was convinced that the British could not be subdued by force. He agreed to negotiate without preconditions. Negotiations were opened in Nanjing and resulted in the first unequal treaty with the West, the Treaty of Nanjing (August 1842).

The view of Communist Chinese historians today is that the war was lost because the "reactionary, feudal" Manchu government could not afford to harness the militant spirit of the masses, who were, supposedly, ready and willing to fight the enemy. The data provided to prove this thesis are superficial and weak. The facts appear to be that the Manchu forces lacked national coordination; that the officers showed poor command of strategy and tactics; and that the soldiers were poorly trained, poorly equipped, and often highly demoralized. In some places the Manchu forces, outnumbered and outgunned, fought and died bravely; but by and large they were a cowardly lot. Except for one or two incidents, the general populace watched the battles with cynical indifference. Those who had to flee the battle areas and lost their property, as a result of the war, looked on it as a blight; others looked on it as an opportunity to loot the abandoned shops and the houses of the wealthy. It must be added that the victorious British forces did not distinguish themselves by their discipline and humanity. Looting, burning, and indiscriminate killing made the war more brutal than it need have been.

Under the Treaty of Nanjing and the supplementary treaties signed in 1843, Britain gained the following rights and privileges, many of which were first officially sought by Lord Macartney:

1. The cession of the island of Hong Kong to England.
2. An indemnity of 21 million Mexican silver dollars as compensation for the confiscated opium, war expenses, and debts owed by the Cohong merchants to British merchants. This sum did not include the $6 million received as ransom for Guangzhou.
3. The opening of the ports of Guangzhou, Xiamen, Fuzhou, Ningbo, and Shanghai for residence and trade.
4. The abolition of the Cohong and the establishment of a fixed tariff, which was 5 percent ad valorem on most important items. China could not alter the tariff without British consent.
5. The appointment of consuls at the treaty ports who could communicate directly with Chinese officials of equal rank.
6. Consular jurisdiction over British subjects involved in disputes with Chinese citizens, which meant that the British citizen would be tried, by the consul, under British law, and the Chinese would be judged according to the laws of China. The principle of extraterritoriality was extended to both civil and criminal cases. This provision violated China's judicial powers and gave the lowliest British citizen a privileged status higher than that of the highest Chinese official.
6. The "most favored nation" status, which meant that Britain would, automatically, receive any privilege that China might later extend to any other nation.

Other Western powers naturally took advantage of the British victory and also entered into treaty relations with China. The Chinese had, on their own, decided to give the other powers the same privileges accorded to the British, so that these powers would feel beholden to China rather than to Britain. The treaties with other Western powers, therefore, covered the same ground as those with Britain. They also had a few extra elements, which under the "most favored nation" clause, were immediately shared by everyone.

The American Treaty of Wanghia (Wangxia), 1844, made the right of extraterritoriality ("extrality" for short) more explicit, put American commercial vessels in Chinese waters under the jurisdiction of the American consuls, and allowed the Americans to build their own churches in the treaty ports. The French Treaty of Whampoa (Huangbu), 1844, granted the French the right to build cemeteries and Roman Catholic churches in the treaty ports and made it obligatory for the Chinese government to punish trespassers in these places. The French also pressed the Chinese government to rescind the ban on Roman Catholicism, which Beijing did in early 1846.

The treaties were subject to revision in 12 years, which meant in 1854, as far as the British were concerned. Two issues, not touched on in the first set of treaties, would then be taken up: legalizing the opium trade and opening Beijing to foreign embassies.

Although neither the Chinese nor the foreign powers realized this immediately, these treaties (and those obtained subsequently in the same aggressive fashion) had a serious impact on the future Chinese polity. The treaties, originally intended to force China to recognize that foreign powers were "equal" to China, impaired its sovereignty and made it less than equal. The historian H. B. Morse has rightly categorized the period 1834–1860 as one of "conflict," 1861–1893 as one of "submission," and 1894–1911 as one of "subjection." The government of China gradually became a tool in the hands of the foreign powers, useful for the exploitation of China.

Of course, all this did not happen overnight. The encroachment of the foreign powers increased from decade to decade because of the unsatisfied Western appetite for trade or competition among Western states for control of foreign markets. Also missionaries had to be backed in their demand that the Chinese stop interfering with their "right" to work freely in the interior.

To the Chinese the 1840 war had been irksome, but it had not conclusively proved that their civilization was not, indeed, superior or that their emperor was not a universal ruler. The Westerners were still not allowed into the country as a whole and were isolated in the five treaty ports. No diplomatic representation had been allowed in the capital. The biggest danger to the empire was not perceived, at this time, to come from external aggression but from internal rebellion and domestic crisis.

INTERNAL DECAY

The critical Confucian values that held state and society together had begun to erode by the opening decades of the nineteenth century. A population explosion; natural disasters; declining rural economy; massive corruption in the bureaucracy; and ineffectual, incompetent leadership in Beijing presaged the end of the dynasty. If there had been no Western intrusion, it is possible that the Qing dynasty soon would have passed from the scene, giving place to a new, more vigorous dynasty that would have revived Confucian values, reintroduced efficiency into the government, and given a further lease on life to Chinese tradition.

But the Western presence made it impossible for either the internal antidynastic developments or the imperial attempts at crisis handling to follow purely traditional formulas or have a purely traditional content. This interplay between internal and external causes for the disintegration of the dynasty is extremely complex and does not lend itself to a simple analysis.

The Opium War had not only revealed the military weakness of the Manchu dynasty (thus encouraging would-be rebels) but also increased the financial hardship of the peasantry. First, the war had made it possible for opium smuggling to be carried on more brazenly, without further fears of punitive action. Consequently, the import of opium increased to 70,000 chests a year in the 1850s, and after legalization in 1858, imports of the drug touched the high point of 81,000 chests in 1884. The resulting outflow of silver steadily raised its value in terms of copper cash and exacerbated the problems of taxpaying peasants.

Second, the war caused increasing fiscal problems for the state. It and subsequent conflicts ultimately led to bankruptcy. At the end of the Opium War Beijing had to pay 23 million silver dollars (Mexican) as indemnity; at the end of the 1860 war (the Second Opium War), Beijing was forced to pay 16 million silver taels (1 tael was 70 U.S. cents in local value). The imperial financial reserves disappeared in 1860. After that China was continually in debt until the establishment of the People's Republic in 1949. Beijing imposed several additional levies, hoping to relieve the exchequer, but these further impoverished the already suffering peasantry.

Third, the Western presence had brought zealous, dedicated Christian missionaries to China's shores. Even before they were allowed into the interior, they had begun to undermine the traditional order.

Fourth, although this affected only small areas adjacent to the treaty ports, the import of foreign cloth and yarn caused a certain amount of decline in the native handicraft textile industry.

Last, the war contributed to social disorder. The opening of Shanghai as a new center for trade brought the foreign merchants closer to the tea and silk production areas, which meant that thousands of coolies and boatmen, who earlier had been employed in transporting these commodities to Guangzhou, were thrown out of work. Coastal pirates, cleared from the high seas by the British navy, invaded the river systems of Guangdong and Guangxi to harass and pillage. The ranks of the lawless were further swelled by the soldiers discharged from local militias after the conclusion of the war.

It was under these internal and external circumstances that large-scale peasant rebellions arose to threaten the Qing dynasty. The greatest and best organized of these antidynastic insurrections was, without doubt, the Taiping Rebellion (1850–1864).

This uprising, which covered the whole of South China, was accompanied or followed by several others: the Nian Rebellion in Anhui and Shandong (1853–1868); the Southwest Muslim Rebellion in Yunnan (1855–1873); and the Northwest Muslim Rebellion in Gansu, Shaanxi, and Chinese Turkestan (1862–1877).

The Taiping Insurrection

There were over a hundred armed uprisings in China between 1840 and 1850. Most of them were led by the dozens of traditional secret societies that had surfaced in these troubled times; many of the more significant ones called for the overthrow of the Manchus and the return of a native regime.

The Taiping insurrection (called a "rebellion" by traditional Chinese historians, a "revolution" by many others) was significantly different from the other uprisings, for it was influenced by Christianity. It was not Roman Catholicism (which had existed in China in restricted form since the sixteenth century) that tinctured the ideology of the Taiping movement but Protestant fundamentalism, which had seeped in from Guangzhou even before the Opium War.

Hong Xiu-quan (1814–1864), the founder and leader of the Taiping movement, was born to a respected, though by no means affluent, Hakka farmer in a village near Guangzhou. The family made sacrifices to get Xiu-quan, the brightest of the children, through school. Hong went to Guangzhou in 1836 and 1837 to take the civil-service examinations but failed on both occasions. After the second attempt he fell seriously ill. In his deliriums he saw himself in the palace of an aged heavenly king, who gave him a sword to go forth and kill the devils pestering his countrymen. In the palace he also met a younger man, whom he addressed as "Elder Brother."

On recovering from his illness Hong became a teacher in a village school. Six years later, in 1843, he chanced on a book given to him during his first visit to Guangzhou by a Chinese Protestant, Liang A-fa (an assistant of the British missionary Robert Morrison), who had used the occasion of the examinations to hand out Christian propaganda literature to the students. The book, *Good Words for Exhorting the Age,* consisted of translations of sections from the Bible and some sermons. Hong's earlier visions suddenly made sense. Hong had met God, his father, and Jesus Christ, his elder brother, and he had been given a heavenly mandate to destroy the Manchu scourge. Incidentally, 1843 was the last year that Hong attempted the official examinations.

For the next several years Hong and his close associates propagated their form of Christianity, established a Society for the Worship of God, made converts among the local elements declassé, and prepared the nucleus of an armed unit that was to challenge not only the Manchu authority but also traditional Confucian beliefs.

Hong's creed included a mixture of Judaic monotheism and iconoclasm; Protestant egalitarianism and equality between the sexes; an ancient Confucian ideal of equal distribution of land; and an ancient Chinese vision of the "Great Harmony," which called for communal ownership of all property. In 1847 Hong returned to Guangzhou to receive instruction from the American missionary Issachar J. Roberts, but Roberts found it difficult to baptize this Chinese Christ. Hong left after two months to carry on his ministry in his own way.

Hong's rebellion began in 1850; by 1853 the Taiping army, now over a million strong, had advanced from its base in Guangxi, overrun Hunan and Hubei, defeated Manchu armies in Anhui and the lower reaches of the Yangtze River, and established the capital of Taiping Tianguo (The Heavenly Kingdom of the Great Peace) at Nanjing. Taiping influence extended over six of the richest provinces of China. Hong installed himself as the Heavenly King.

China now had two dynasties, two kingdoms, vying for total control of the country. The Taiping government, however, lacked the stable underpinnings of the traditional Confucian state that served the Qing, and

Taiping leadership lacked unity and the organizational capacity that might have tilted the final outcome in its favor. The Taiping uprising attained the high point of its success and power by 1856; thereafter the movement lost its vigor and the upstart dynasty was liquidated in 1864.

Although comparatively short-lived, this vast upheaval left its mark on the country. The Chinese state that emerged from this bloodletting (around 30 million persons lost their lives in the civil war) was in many significant ways different from what it had been in 1850, 14 years earlier.

The Revolutionary Aspect of the Taiping Movement

The ideology and goals of the Taiping leaders had many elements that can be called revolutionary, but to evaluate their true worth one must analyze the source of each and, furthermore, view them in the context of Taiping practice.

In the political arena the Taiping attack on the Manchus as foreign, barbarian rulers who were exploiting the Han Chinese is considered by some to represent the beginning of modern nationalism, and therefore, as revolutionary. This is not necessarily true. The Taiping anti-Manchuism was in consonance with the aims of most of the Chinese secret societies, whose goals were represented by such slogans as "Overthrow the Qing, Restore the Ming." Although Hong rejected the idea of a Ming restoration, he nevertheless did establish his capital in Nanjing, which had been the Ming capital, and revive the Ming style of court dress. He also built a lavish imperial palace (well stocked with concubines) and set up the traditional Six Ministries, although his bureaucracy was recruited through examinations that tested students on the basis of Christian texts rather than Confucian classics. But since the Taiping never came to establish a firm central hold over the lands they had occupied, their ideas of a revolutionary civil and military local government never were translated into practice.

The details of the civil and military local government and the new society it was to oversee were spelled out in the "Land System of the Celestial Dynasty," promulgated in 1853. The system was premised on the belief that "the empire is like a large family of the Heavenly Father, Supreme Lord, and Almighty God; no one is selfish, and everything is turned over to the Supreme Lord, so that he will have goods at his disposal,"[19] which in actuality meant that the state was to have total control over all land, goods, and life.

The Taiping state, theocratic in theory, had a strong military character, reflecting the obvious insecurity of the state and the paramount need to keep the army well supplied. From the Heavenly King down to the local level, all administrators had civil and military functions. The organization of the military into armies, divisions, brigades, companies, and platoons, with a strict segregation of the sexes (women were enrolled in combat units), was projected into civil institutions.

According to the new land system, all land was to be distributed equally among the people, regardless of the sex of the recipient, except that those under 16 received only half a share; the size of a lot depended on its productive capacity. Every 25 families were to form a basic unit with its own church and treasury. Each family was to provide one soldier for a local platoon; the platoon leader was to be the local army officer who administered the unit. Successively bigger administrative units, paralleling the military structure, finally resulted in a unit of 13,156 families under the control of the "army" commander. Rural families were to work on the land but not own it. After their basic needs had been met, their surplus production was to go into the communal treasury. Thus political, economic, civil, and military functions were to be unified under army officers, who were to ensure that land, food, clothing, and money were shared equally by all. The heavenly land system was, however, never implemented on any wide scale.

The thrust of the Taiping movement was

not only egalitarian and "socialistic"; it also had strong puritanical and feminist elements. The banning of adultery, slavery, prostitution, opium smoking, and gambling were Taiping goals that China would achieve only a century later under communism, although they were pushed vigorously for some time by Hong's followers. The most revolutionary act of the Taipings was, no doubt, the emancipation of women. Women, whose lowly status in society was written into the Confucian doctrine, now fought alongside men as their equals and became officers in the army and administration. Footbinding, concubinage, and arranged marriages were abolished.

Although the program and the policies of the Taiping appear to have elements that can be associated with modern revolutions, it must not be forgotten that they were also rooted in China's popular culture. Taiping egalitarianism can be traced to *Zhou-li* (Rites of Zhou), a work produced in the pre-Christian era, which presents a vivid picture of a socialistic society. Similarly, equal land distribution can be traced to Mencius and the various experiments of imperial dynasties through the Tang era. Paramilitary social organization also had historical precedent, as had female armies. Hong as reincarnation of the Christian God had parallels in the so-called appearance of Maitreya Buddhas as leaders of rebellious secret societies.

If there was any real attempt to learn from the West and transform China into a modern state, it came with the appointment of Hong Ren-gan (1822–1864) as prime minister in 1859. Until 1850 Ren-gan's career had duplicated that of his cousin, Hong Xiu-quan: He had failed the imperial examinations, taken up a teaching career, and converted to Christianity. Ren-gan was deeply influenced by Xiu-quan but for various reasons did not join the Taiping campaign. Instead, he spent nearly six years in Hong Kong and Shanghai gaining Western knowledge from his Christian mentors and employers in the London Missionary Society and the American Baptist Church. When he finally did get to Nanjing in 1859, he was promptly given the high office of prime minister.

Hong Ren-gan elaborated his political program in a work entitled *New Guide to Government.* He advocated Western-style institutions for centralizing power and ending factional politics, which had been plaguing Nanjing; cleaning up the bureaucracy to eliminate corruption; a rational accounting system; a reform of the penal code; and the development of public opinion through the establishment of newspapers. He emphasized the need for modern transportation and communications (railways, highways, steamer service, postal service); new-style schools and hospitals; and modern banking, insurance, and technology.

In foreign relations Hong Ren-gan favored opening China to trade and cultural relations with foreign nations on a basis of true equality: China would discard its superior attitude and stop calling the foreigners "barbarians," and the foreigners would not interfere in China's internal affairs.

Neither Hong Xiu-quan's land system nor Hong Ren-gan's new political and economic system had any real impact on the Taiping kingdom. Even before 1860 (when it faced not only the better-organized Qing forces but also the active intervention of the British and French on behalf of Beijing), it had lost its revolutionary ardor and become a faction-ridden military state in which the leaders fought one another for personal power and wealth. The peasants in this "utopian" state often found themselves exploited more ruthlessly than they had been by their Qing overlords.

Chinese Communist historians, although praising the "revolutionary" qualities of the Taiping ("its marvelous contribution to the forward march of history will last for ever"[20]), relate the failure of the movement to the class background of the leaders. With what appears to be a bizarre sense of historical logic, they declare that the Taiping "was after all a peasant revolutionary movement . . . [and] could not benefit from the leadership of the Chinese working class and its Party."[21] Incidentally, Karl Marx called the Taiping a "greater scourge to the population than the older rulers" and saw its vocation as "destruction, in grotesque horrifying form, without any seeds for a renaissance."[22]

The Taiping government consistently had tried hard to gain the recognition and support of the foreign powers, their "Christian brothers," but the Westerners, who had rather callously exploited the civil war to make a war of their own on Beijing and gain a revision of the treaties in 1860, now decided that the time had come to give up their attitude of neutrality and help the Qing.

THE FIFTEEN CRITICAL YEARS: 1842–1857

The jubilation with which the foreigners in China had greeted the first set of treaties did not last long. It was soon felt that the "opening" of the five treaty ports was, in actual fact, no more than the "confining" of foreign trade and foreign traders to these port cities. Furthermore, it became apparent that of the five ports only Guangzhou and Shanghai had potential for growth. Even in these cities, particularly in Guangzhou, antagonistic officials and harassing bureaucratic practices continued to mock the spirit of the treaties.

To fulfill their great commercial expectations, which had not been realized by the opening of the five ports, the British merchants began to clamor for free access to other ports and to the presumed fabulous market that existed in the vast interior. Indeed, except for opium, China's import of British manufactures had declined in the decade following the Nanjing Treaty. The voices of these merchants were joined by those of Protestant missionaries who wanted the rights gained by the Catholic missionaries under the Sino-French treaty plus the right to move freely in the hinterland.

In the beginning the British government was not overly anxious to become militarily involved in China once again. It did not consider the pressures exerted by the merchants and the missionaries to be fully justified. However, the Chinese reluctance or incapacity to follow Western norms of international relations and allow for more open contact between Western diplomats and high Chinese officials, as spelled out in the treaties, led to an increasing number of diplomatic incidents and a spate of letters from the Crown's representatives in China, recommending that London take some kind of "strong" action against Beijing.

The basic trouble was that China had no institution that could handle "foreign relations," as the West understood the term. Until 1841 the Cohong merchants were the only contact point between the "ocean barbarians" and China. After signing the treaties, the foreign consuls in the treaty ports could deal directly with the local circuit intendant, and *dao-tai* (who, apart from being the intermediary in diplomatic intercourse, was also the superintendent of customs), and through the *dao-tai,* with the governor and governor-general (the viceroy, in Western terminology of the day) in charge of the province in which the treaty port was located. An imperial commissioner, posted at Guangzhou and especially appointed to handle foreign affairs, was the highest official in this hierarchy, and it was he who received the credentials of foreign heads of missions.

Therefore all serious correspondence and negotiations had to be carried on with the imperial commissioner in Guangzhou, over a thousand miles from Beijing. In Beijing no special office was established to handle Western foreign relations. Westerners expected some change after the Treaty of Nanjing, but none came because the idea of treating the barbarians as equals was still too abhorrent. The emperor, helped by the Grand Council (made up of five officials), personally dealt with any issues brought to his notice through memorials from the imperial commissioner or other concerned officials. Since Western diplomats had no right to communicate directly with the emperor, their cases were presented through such memorials. Of course, the memorialist could always distort the truth to suit his purpose.

With the passage of time it became apparent that Beijing had little intention of abiding by the diplomatic aspects of the treaties that it had conceded at gunpoint. For example, no attempt was made by the Chinese government to announce the contents of the treaties to the populace at large or even to the people in the port cities, where they were bound to come in contact with the foreigners. The original and ratified copies of the treaties were kept in Guangzhou and not even forwarded to Beijing. Yet, by and large, this lack of preparation for a new order did not affect the four new ports, where the population had not come in contact with the foreigners earlier and had no bitter feelings against them. But it did result in a worsening of relations at Guangzhou.

The British maintained that the treaties had given them the right to enter the walls of Guangzhou (a debatable issue because the Chinese version of the Treaty of Nanjing could not be so interpreted), but the imperial commissioners managed to keep postponing the date of entry on the grounds that it would take time to calm the unruly citizens of Guangzhou, who were violently hostile to the foreigners. It was, indeed, true that the people of Guangzhou showed a strong antiforeign disposition, but it was equally true that they were incited by the officials and the local gentry. In 1847, when the British sent gunboats upriver and destroyed the city's defenses in retaliation for the manhandling of two British sailors who had gone into the city, the imperial commissioner finally agreed to open Guangzhou in 1849. But when the time came to carry out the agreement, the imperial commissioner, Xu Guang-jin, and the governor, Ye Ming-chen, "incited the people of Canton [Guangzhou] to gather several ten thousands of militiamen to threaten Bonham (the British Superintendent of Trade and the Governor of Hong Kong) when the latter was having a conference with Xu."[23] Under the circumstances, Sir George Bonham reluctantly decided to postpone the issue to a still later date; this so pleased the emperor that both Xu and Ye were awarded higher titles. The emperor's edict is instructive: "The Central Empire [China] cannot oppose the people in order to yield to men from a distance."[24] The will of the people had suddenly become a convenient, although questionable, weapon in China's diplomatic armory. A few years later, when Guangzhou was occupied by the British in 1857, the Cantonese showed no sign of unruliness and foreigners could walk about unmolested, "without the slightest sign of resistance or animosity."[25]

Although the imperial commissioners in Guangzhou were proving their capability in handling the Western barbarians by prevarication and equivocation, the Taiping uprising soon created a political situation that demanded careful assessment by the foreign powers. Was it likely that the Taipings would be the next government? Would it not be better to back the Taipings who were, after all, Christians and who might open the entire country to foreign trade and missionary activities? In any case, since the Taipings controlled the tea- and silk-producing areas, they should be made aware of Western interests and told to abide by the treaties.

In 1853, when Bonham led the first foreign mission to Nanjing, he found that the second Son of God was also the "Lord of the whole world," who demanded that the inferior foreigners kowtow before him. Although Bonham did not gain an interview with Hong, he did manage to make an agreement with the Taipings for the British to trade freely in Taiping territory. Bonham's recommendation to London was that Britain should maintain a neutral stand in the Chinese civil war but be prepared to defend its citizens in case they came under attack from the Taipings. Following Bonham, the French minister, deBourboulon, and the American minister, Robert McLane, also visited Nanjing and came to conclusions more or less similar to those of Bonham.

The foreign merchants were not too unhappy with the situation because, despite the war, trade was not affected. The missionaries, however, were disillusioned with the Taipings: The Protestants because of the scandalous claims of Hong; the Catholics because the Taipings did not recognize them as legitimate Christians.

By 1856 several developments had prepared the ground for the next major war and the final destruction of the Chinese self-imposed wall of isolation. First, Ye Ming-chen, who had been promoted to imperial commissioner at Guangzhou in 1852, had by his haughty and intransigent attitude annoyed all the foreign diplomats. He was an expert in delaying tactics and in making it impossible for Western diplomats to secure interviews with him. Consider, for example, the case of Humphrey Marshall, the American minister, who on arrival in China followed the prescribed procedure by going to Guangzhou to present his credentials to Commissioner Ye. He was told that Ye was busy with the local rebels and not available. Marshall then proceeded to Shanghai, hoping to present his credentials to the viceroy of Jiangsu through the good offices of the local *dao-tai.* The *dao-tai,* not empowered to act in this fashion, refused to help Marshall. Marshall then took the last recourse; he threatened to sail to Tianjin and seek redress from the court at Beijing. This threat brought prompt results, and he was asked to return to Guangzhou, where Ye would see him. Indeed, Ye did. But Marshall had hardly presented his credentials when he was replaced by Robert McLane. It comes as no surprise that McLane underwent exactly the same treatment as his predecessor.

Obviously, Ye was not acting in this recalcitrant fashion without the emperor's approval. Witness the pride with which he reported to the emperor in 1855: "First McLane came to Canton [Guangzhou] in the middle of the month; in the latter part, Bowring (Sir John Bowring who had replaced Bonham), with several warships, also came to Canton, and sent a man to give notice and to fix a date for an interview, insisting that it be in the *yamen* to accord with propriety. Your official answered that he was really so desirous of a meeting that, no matter what the place, he should consent, but as the *yamen* was inside the city it was virtually impossible to agree. They stayed in Canton some three weeks but never came back to repeat the request."[26] The emperor, no doubt, was thrilled by this report.

Second, while Ye was trying to revive the traditional system of managing the barbarians, Beijing appears to have forgotten the treaty-revision clause. In 1854, the year the British treaties were due to come up for revision, Britain decided to act in concert with France and America. It was agreed among the powers that China should be asked to open the entire country to foreign trade, or at least allow free navigation in the Yangtze River; abolish internal duties; legalize the opium trade; agree to the establishment of embassies in Beijing or, failing this, the right of consuls to correspond with responsible officials of the Chinese government.

British, American, and French consuls approached Ye with these proposals, but he replied that his government felt that revisions were unnecessary. Bowring and McLane then did what was becoming the common diplomatic practice—they went to Shanghai and, gaining no response from Chinese officials in Shanghai, on to Tianjin to push for recognition of their claims. In Tianjin they were joined by the French representative. Not being accompanied by a military force, they were subjected to the usual delaying tactics and finally returned to Guangzhou, having accomplished nothing substantial. Although efforts at treaty revision in 1854 came to nought (partly because, from 1854 to 1856, Britain and France were preoccupied with the Crimean War), the attempt resulted in a greater awareness in Western capitals that only force would bring results.

Third, by 1856 it was becoming clear that the Taiping kingdom was itself experiencing internal difficulties and was perhaps disintegrating. The Western powers had little choice but to deal with the Qing government, compelling it to give in to their demands, while ensuring at the same time that it did not collapse.

THE SECOND OPIUM WAR: 1857–1860

The real cause of the Second Opium War was the continuing conflict between the Chinese and European views of international relations. The Chinese were aware of European expansion in Asia, particularly of the British occupation of India, but China was entrapped by its all-encompassing sociopolitical tradition. It was impossible to give up China's sense of superiority and world outlook to accept the "superiority" and "universality" of Western civilization or the validity of Western-style "international law." China had yet to learn the lesson that in the modern world "superiority" is allied to military power.

It is fascinating to note that both sides considered the other barbaric and inscrutable. The emperor was repeatedly informed that "what goes on in the (barbarian) mind is inscrutable."[27] (The Westerners were still referred to as barbarians in all official correspondence. The practice was stopped only after the 1860 war, on the insistence of the European powers.) On the British side, Lord Elgin, who headed the expedition to chastise China, viewed the people of the Middle Kingdom as "these incomprehensible Chinese."[28]

Two incidents involving France and Britain served as the immediate cause of war. The first was the arrest and execution by the local Chinese authorities of a French Catholic missionary in February 1856. Auguste Chapdelaine had been traveling in the interior of Guangxi in contravention of the treaty regulations stipulating that foreigners could not go beyond the treaty ports. The French were incensed by the execution; they called it a "judicial murder," in violation of France's extraterritorial rights.

The second cause was the notorious Lorcha (a ship with a European hull and Chinese rig) *Arrow* incident. The *Arrow* was owned by a Chinese and had a Chinese crew, but it was captained by a British subject. It was registered in Hong Kong and flew the British flag. On October 8, 1856, while lying at anchor in Guangzhou, it was boarded by Chinese officials, who arrested 12 of the crew of 14 on charges of an earlier act of piracy. The British consul at Guangzhou, Harry Parkes, protested to Commissioner Ye because the crew was entitled to British protection; hauling down the British flag was an insulting act. In fact, the boat's registry had expired in September, and it is questionable whether she was flying the British flag while she lay to, but these legalisms had little impact on the issue, which now became politically explosive. Parkes was a hard-liner who would have used any pretense to create an "incident." Hong Kong backed Parkes, demanding an apology and further assurances. After a series of charges and countercharges, Ye first returned some of the prisoners and finally all of them. But since they were not accompanied by a Chinese officer of rank or an apology, Parkes refused to accept their release.

The British then went a step further. Their naval force bombarded the river forts, breached the city wall, lobbed shells into Ye's residence, and stood ready to seize the city, but had no authorization from London to do so. When they withdrew, the Chinese burned down the foreign factories. Ye did not know it, but war had begun. Ye, in his ignorance of the larger world outside China and with his strange sense of logic, actually felt that he had won the battle. He sent a glowing report to the emperor, giving details of how the barbarians had lost their warships, how their troops had been massacred by the brave Chinese soldiers, and how their admiral Seymour had met his well-deserved and dishonorable end. The emperor was pleased to record that "Yeh Ming-ch'en [Ye Ming-chen] understands barbarian affairs thoroughly and can certainly find means to control them."[29] An empire that relied on such a tissue of misunderstandings could not last very long.

In 1857 a British expeditionary force under Lord Elgin and a French force under Baron Gros reached China to revise the treaties; in the process they taught the Chinese a lesson that they would not forget as easily as they had forgotten the first war. Action began in Guangzhou in December after Ye refused to submit to the demands of the two plenipotentiaries. Guangzhou was seized in January 1858. It remained under foreign occupation and was ruled by an Anglo-French commission acting through Chinese officials until the end of the war in 1860. Imperial Commissioner Ye was taken prisoner and exiled to Calcutta, where he died in 1859. Ironically, it was Seymour (already "killed" in Ye's despatches) who arranged Ye's sea passage to India.

Whereas the first Opium War two decades earlier had been fought by the British alone, in this war not only were the British and the French allied against China but even the Americans and the Russians collaborated with Elgin and Gros. The four powers, by prearrangement, sent similar notes to the grand secretary ("The Senior Secretary of State at Beijing," as Elgin addressed him) in Beijing asking for the appointment of a responsible high-level official to negotiate with them in Shanghai. The British and French letters were, of course, more bellicose. When the grand secretary sent word that he could not, in all propriety, correspond with the foreigners and that they should go back to Guangzhou (the envoys were now in Shanghai) and deal with the imperial commissioner there (the Guangdong governor working under the Anglo-French commission was entitled to communicate with the emperor), the Anglo-French forces sailed north to the mouth of the Beihe in Zhili Bay. The American and the Russian representatives accompanied Elgin and Gros as "neutrals," deeply interested in the outcome of the operation and ready to act as intermediaries between the belligerent nations.

Forced to respond, Beijing appointed the viceroy of the metropolitan province to meet with the plenipotentiaries, but Elgin considered him to be lacking the power and authority to negotiate a treaty. Beijing prevaricated. On May 20 the Anglo-French naval forces opened fire on the four Dagu forts that guarded the mouth of the river. Within a few hours the British and French flags were flying from the forts, and the expeditionary force pushed on to Tianjin, fewer than 100 miles from Beijing.

Dismayed by the turn of events and further shocked to learn that the British had brought with them highly confidential imperial edicts and memorials dealing with "barbarian affairs," taken from Commissioner Ye's office when Guangzhou was occupied, Beijing felt humiliated but had no recourse but to yield to the Western powers. The Anglo-Chinese Treaty, signed on June 26, 1858, provided the general sense for the treaties with the other three powers, which followed in quick succession.

The British treaty made it absolutely clear that Britain not only had the right to post a resident minister at Beijing but also that this gentleman, representing a nation equal to China, would not perform ceremonies like the kowtow. Of course, the Chinese also had the right to appoint their representative to the Court of St. James, but all diplomatic practice would follow the precedents laid down in Europe.

Apart from the opening of ten new treaty ports and the right of British ships to sail up the Yangtze, the treaty also gained the right for British subjects to travel to all parts of the interior under a passport issued by their consul and countersigned by a Chinese official. China was also forced not only to grant toleration to Christianity but also to protect officially the missionaries and their converts.

The definition of extraterritoriality was further clarified: Disputes between foreigners were to be handled by the foreign consuls concerned; a Chinese guilty of a crime against a foreigner was to be tried by the laws of China; a foreigner guilty of a crime in China was to be tried by the consul of his country according to the laws of his native land; cases between a Chinese and a foreigner were to be tried by a mixed court formed of a Chinese magistrate and a foreign consul.

Since foreigners (missionaries not excluded) enjoyed the right of extrality, the right to travel in the interior meant that they became a privileged class that could not be controlled by the Chinese legal system.

The indemnity of 4 million taels of silver sought by Britain to cover the cost of the war in Guangzhou and the expedition north was seen by the Chinese as the least of the demands. From the Chinese point of view, the residence of an envoy in Beijing was the worst blow.

From Tianjin the foreign plenipotentiaries retired to Shanghai to carry on further negotiations regarding tariff readjustments, it having been agreed that they would return north in 1859 to ratify the treaties at Beijing. The treaties had been hurriedly accepted by China because Beijing was threatened by foreign forces; now that the threat had disappeared, the emperor and his advisers began to discuss ways of altering the treaties to eliminate the residence clause. There was even a suggestion made, in all seriousness, that Beijing would forgo all customs duties if the Westerners agreed to drop the demand to establish embassies in Beijing.

While in Shanghai, Elgin, whom the Chinese rightly considered the main culprit responsible for the new treaty system, was approached by the imperial commissioners with the request that the right of permanent residence of an ambassador to Beijing be changed to an "occasional" visit (under Chinese advice, the American and the Russian representatives had actually recommended to Elgin that he not insist on the residency clause; the French did not favor the idea but went along with Elgin). The reason given was "in her present crisis of domestic troubles," the presence of foreign envoys in Beijing "would cause a loss of respect for their Government in the minds of her subjects."[30] Not wanting to undermine the authority of the emperor and in the interest of better relations, Elgin yielded; it was agreed that though the right would remain as a clause in the treaty, the British would not insist on immediate compliance.

Having thus satisfactorily settled the treaty problem and having also seen to the revision of the tariff and the legalization of the opium trade, Elgin sailed home. Everyone, including the Chinese, realized that since the opium trade could not be suppressed, it was better to legalize it because it would then at least yield considerable revenues for the impoverished Beijing government. Elgin had come to China with an open mind and in the beginning had felt that the responsibility for the poor relationship between China and the West lay more with the rapacious, arrogantly aggressive foreigners than with the Chinese. But by the time he left for England, he had become convinced that hawks like Parkes were right. The "stupid" Chinese yielded nothing except under fear, and Elgin had to play the role of "an uncontrollably fierce barbarian," even though this went against his grain.

Beijing's preparations to receive the foreign envoys for ratification of the treaties were in keeping with its revived spirit of confidence. The Dagu forts were rearmed and the mouth of the river blocked with sunken barges and chains. This act was supposed to force the envoys to leave their ships behind and travel to Beijing by the land route north of Dagu. Instructions were issued that the envoys could not bring more than ten attendants each and that no one must bear arms. The envoys would not be allowed to ride in sedan chairs; they must leave Beijing as soon as the treaties had been ratified.

In June 1859 Frederick Bruce (Lord Elgin's brother), deBourbolon, and John E. Ward—representing Britain, France, and America—sailed to Dagu, where they were instructed to proceed north to Beitang, from where they would be conveyed to Beijing by road. Ward accepted the instructions, but the Anglo-French envoys did not. Showing a certain lack of caution, presumably because all earlier military action in China had been comparatively easy, the British admiral approached the barrier to clear a passage upstream. Suddenly the Dagu guns opened heavy, and surprisingly accurate, fire; the allies suffered a heavy enough loss in men and boats that they were forced to repair to Shanghai. Since the British were the real leaders of the campaign and the prime challengers of the Chinese empire, this battle can be considered a humiliating defeat for the British.

Meanwhile, because of the Dagu success or perhaps just because of their ingrained sense of "propriety," the Chinese treated Ward in a rather shabby fashion. After a three-week delay in Beitang, Ward and his party were taken to Beijing in closed, unsprung carts of the type used to convey Korean tributary missions. There Ward learned that the Russian delegation had already arrived overland and had exchanged ratification, but he was not allowed to meet or communicate with the Russians. Held virtually as a prisoner, Ward was harangued about the need to perform the kowtow, or some ceremony that came near enough to it, when he was received in audience by the emperor. However, when the day of the audience arrived, it became clear that no deviation from the orthodox kowtow was possible. Ward was ordered to return to Beitang, and the ratifications were exchanged there instead of at Beijing.

The news of the Dagu debacle was received with anger and dismay in England and France. The press and public were outraged. There was a cry for the governments to avenge the honor of their countries and "the blood of our murdered soldiers." Finally, acting in concert in 1860, the British and the French governments dispatched the old Elgin and Gros team, backed by a suitable force.

Action began on August 1. The Dagu forts were taken without much difficulty, and the expeditionary force moved on to Tianjin and then on to a position 12 miles outside Beijing, defeating the imperial army in several engagements on the way. All negotiations en route were of no avail because the Chinese officials did not have the power to sign a convention. In mid-September, when it appeared that the Chinese were at least ready to negotiate in earnest, attitudes in Beijing suddenly hardened. The Chinese found Elgin's demands that he be allowed to enter Beijing with an armed escort and seek an audience with the emperor particularly unacceptable. The Anglo-French spokespersons, heading an advance party of 37 persons to confer under a flag of truce with the Chinese officials, were made prisoners. Although the concept of a flag of truce may not have been fully appreciated by the Chinese, there was no call for suddenly taking as hostages the spokespersons with whom they had been negotiating all along, nor for the brutality with which the prisoners were handled. Twenty of the prisoners were dead by the time the others were released.

Incensed by these developments, the allied forces now took the offensive and easily defeated the Chinese armies under the hardline Mongol general Seng-ge-lin-chin, thus clearing the way for the occupation of Beijing. The emperor, and all other high officials who could do so, fled from Beijing. It was left to Prince Gong, the emperor's half-brother, who had been given the authority to deal with the enemy, to accept the terms of the humiliating surrender. Before that happened, however, Lord Elgin decided that the emperor needed to be taught a personal lesson, and so he ordered his troops to burn the Summer Palace, which stood just outside Beijing. The palace grounds extended over several hundred acres of land and were dotted with innumerable residences, temples, pagodas, landscaped gardens, fountains, artificial lakes, and hills. Before the palace was set to the torch, it was methodically looted by the British and the French forces.

The Beijing Convention confirmed the treaties of Tianjin, doubled the indemnities asked for in 1858, added Tianjin to the list of treaty ports, restored Catholic property confiscated since the banning of that religion, allowed priests to buy land and build churches in the interior (the clause was surreptitiously introduced by the French, but the right was naturally extended to the Protestants under the "most favored nation" principle), and ceded the Kowloon peninsula (opposite Hong Kong) to Britain in perpetuity.

Russian-Chinese Relations

China's special relations with Russia continued to operate until the opening of the nineteenth century, when Russia began to focus greater attention on eastern Siberia. The Treaty of Nanjing and the advantages gained by the Western European naval powers in China increased Russian concern for protecting and developing its interests in the Russian Far East.

Russia was an Asian land power, so its concern was different from that of the Western European nations. More than trade and missionary activity, Russia wanted to consolidate its hold over this remote part of its empire and ensure that Russian strategic interests there could not be undermined by European enemies. The attack on Petropavlovsk in Kamchatka by an Anglo-French fleet in 1854, during the Crimean War, proved that Russian fears were not baseless.

In violation of the earlier Russo-Chinese treaties, the Russians began to explore the region of the Amur basin and look for suitable ports on the Pacific. After sending three expeditions down the entire length of the Amur River, by 1858 the Russians had effectively isolated the territory stretching from the northern bank of the river to the border delimited by the Treaty of Nerchinsk. The island of Sakhalin had already been annexed in 1853.

In 1858 Russia sent Count Putiatin to China to ensure that Russia was not denied any of the rights that Britain and France would gain in their revision of the 1840 treaties. In June, Putiatin was one of the envoys who signed the Tianjin treaties. But, although gaining all the other rights, he could not get the Chinese to open the Amur question. Putiatin was not aware that Count Muraviev, the governor-general of Eastern Siberia, had already confronted the Chinese frontier forces; Muraviev had in May 1858 signed a treaty at Aigun by which Russia had acquired all lands north of the Amur and the right to control jointly the territory lying between the Amur and the Ussuri rivers and the Pacific (the Maritime Province).

At the ratification of the Tianjin Treaty between Russia and China at Beijing in 1859, it became clear that the Chinese had repudiated the Aigun Treaty, particularly as far as the trans-Ussuri territory was concerned. However, in 1860 the Russian envoy, Major General Ignatiev, exploited the war situation by showing friendliness to both sides—giving information to Elgin and Gros and assuring Prince Gong that he would use his influence to get the allied armies out of Beijing. Prince Gong, not necessarily deceived by Ignatiev, felt it expedient to sign a convention, which not only confirmed the Aigun and Tianjin treaties but also ceded the Maritime Province to Russia.

Although defeated by the Anglo-French forces, Prince Gong still felt that the real threat to China came not from the maritime powers but from Russia. As he wrote to the emperor, "in my opinion all the barbarians have the nature of brute beasts. The British are the most unruly, but the Russians are the most cunning. The rebels [the Taipings] menace our heart, the Russians our trunk, while the British are merely a threat to our limbs."[31] Exactly a hundred years later, in 1960, a serious split, with international consequences, developed between the two Communist giants, the U.S.S.R. and the People's Republic of China; among the reasons for the break were the territorial expansion of Tsarist Russia and the suspicion of Russia, which China has harbored since the 1860s.

The result of the treaty system was that China was forced not only to discard its traditional world view and accept the Western international order but also to open the country to Western trade, Western religions, and Western ideas. The Western nations had proved beyond any doubt that they had the "right" to conduct diplomatic relations along lines they were used to; the "right" to trade freely anywhere they chose; the "right" to protect their citizens, and the property of their citizens, with weapons of war and their national legal systems; and the "right" to propagate their civilization and their religion without let or hindrance. That they achieved this advantage by acts of high-handed imperialism, savagery, and vandalism was bound to leave lasting anger and hatred in the Chinese, a feeling that has tinged Chinese developments to this day.

The only "right" the Chinese government gained from the treaties was the right to protect foreign interests at the cost of their own. This is not to say that the Chinese government had no faults or was not responsible for its own downfall and degradation. The Chinese had wasted the 15 years between 1842 and 1857, learning nothing and forgetting nothing, hoping that somehow the new evil from across the ocean would disappear on its own, leaving no trace behind.

Communist historians trace all modern China's troubles to "imperialism" and see the Qing as "shamelessly" acceding "to all the rapacious demands of these foreign pirates, in order to secure in exchange their cooperation in the suppression of the people's revolution" (the Taipings, Nian, etc.).[32] One need hardly pause to examine this simplistic distortion of history.

Some Western historians feel that the word *imperialism,* used as a blanket term to condemn all Western activity (*economic imperialism, cultural imperialism, political imperialism*) as aggressive and exploitative, is meaningless because it overlooks the fact that China's traditional economic structure and the balance of internal supply and demand limited the economic exploitation of China, that imperialism had a positive impact in propelling China toward modernization, and that in the development of Western-Chinese relations many philanthropic souls dedicated themselves to the welfare of China.

Such historians miss a basic point: Indeed, the forces of historical development have to be viewed with objectivity, but there is no reason not to exercise a value judgment where the people or governments involved with the historical process are concerned. Chenghis Khan's conquests brought Europe and Asia closer together and helped advance historical changes (e.g., the introduction of gunpowder and paper into Europe), but this does not mean that Chenghis cannot be condemned for the ruthlessness with which he destroyed peoples and cities that got in his way.

However, regardless of how one may view these developments, 1860 marks the beginning of the new order for China.

NOTES

1. C. Costin, *Great Britain and China, 1833–1860* (London: Oxford University Press, 1937), p. 21.
2. Earl H. Pritchard, *The Crucial Years of Anglo-Chinese Relations, 1750–1800* (Pullman: Washington State College, 1936), p. 307.
3. See Christopher Hibbert, *The Dragon Awakes: China and the West, 1793–1911* (New York: Harper & Row, 1970), p. 52.
4. Harley F. MacNair, *Modern Chinese History: Selected Readings* (Shanghai: Commercial Press, 1923), pp. 2–4.
5. See Eric Widmer, *The Russian Ecclesiastical Mission in Peking During the Eighteenth Century* (Cambridge, MA: Harvard University Press, 1976), p. 180.
6. Hibbert, *Dragon Awakes,* pp. 9–19.
7. MacNair, *Modern Chinese History,* p. 8.
8. Ibid.
9. Quoted in John King Fairbank et al., *East Asia: The Modern Transformation* (Boston: Houghton Mifflin, 1965), p. 77.
10. Lo-shu Fu, *A Documentary Chronicle of Sino-Western Relations 1644–1820* (Tucson: University of Arizona Press, 1966), p. 406.
11. Ibid., p. 405.
12. Hibbert, *Dragon Awakes,* p. 66.
13. H. B. Morse, *The International Relations of the Chinese Empire,* vol. I, 1834–1860 (London: Longmans Green, 1910), pp. 126–27.
14. Quoted in Hibbert, *Dragon Awakes,* pp. 99–100.
15. Morse, *International Relations,* p. 142.
16. Ibid., p. 102.
17. See Hsin-pao Chang, *Commissioner Lin and the Opium War* (Cambridge, MA: Harvard University Press, 1964), p. 96.
18. Ssu-yu Teng and John K. Fairbank, *China's Response to the West: A Documentary Survey, 1839–1923* (Cambridge, MA: Harvard University Press, 1965), pp. 24–27.
19. See Li Chien-nung, *The Political History of China, 1840–1928* (Palo Alto, CA: Stanford University Press, 1956), pp. 63–64.

20. *The Taiping Revolution* (Beijing: Foreign Languages Press, 1976), p. 173.

21. Ibid., pp. 172–73.

22. Karl Marx, "Chinese Affairs," *Die Press* (Vienna), July 7, 1862, quoted in Shlomo Avineri, *Karl Marx on Colonialism and Modernization* (New York: Anchor Books), p. 442.

23. Li Chien-nung, *Political History*, p. 82.

24. Quoted in Emily Hahn, *China Only Yesterday* (London: Weidenfeld & Nicolson, 1963), p. 41.

25. See Hibbert, *Dragon Awakes*, p. 229.

26. Earl Swisher, *China's Management of the American Barbarians* (New Haven, CT: Yale University Press, 1953), p. 303.

27. For example, see ibid. (pp. 242 and 326).

28. Quoted in Hibbert, *Dragon Awakes*, p. 226.

29. Swisher, *China's Management*, p. 327.

30. MacNair, *Modern Chinese History*, p. 291.

31. Wu Hsiang-hsiang, *O-ti ch'in-lueh Chung-kuo shih* (Taipei: 1954), p. 48; quoted in Henry McAleavy, *The Modern History of China* (New York: Praeger, 1967), p. 100.

32. Jian Bozan et al., *A Concise History of China* (Beijing: Foreign Languages Press, 1981), p. 94.

CHAPTER 3

Decline of the Old Order, Beginning of the New: 1860–1895

During the 34 years that followed the signing of the Beijing treaties, internal rebellion was put down, some new ("modern") political and economic institutions were added to the traditional system, the armed forces were "modernized," a few Western-style defense and commercial industries were established, railways and telegraphs were introduced, and diplomatic posts were opened abroad. The dynasty, which seemed on the verge of collapse in the 1850s, now appeared to be fully restored to power. China gave the impression of progressing satisfactorily, albeit slowly.

However, in 1894–1895 the actual incompetence and weakness of the Chinese government system that lay behind the facade of growth and development was exposed when this Asian giant was abjectly defeated by Japan, the island nation that had been "opened" by the United States in 1854. This defeat virtually spelled the end of the Chinese traditional order and put China on the path of revolutionary change, which ultimately led to the establishment of a Communist government in 1949.

China's defeat in the 1894–1895 war was a symptom of the Qing failure to renovate successfully its moribund traditional political-economic system. This failure was the result of many forces, national and international, but if there was one preponderant reason for China's plight, it was the poor leadership of the incompetent, conservative, unimaginative Manchus, who sought to preserve their position even at the cost of further decentralization of power. What China needed was a strong center that could pull the country together and mobilize all possible resources to confront its internal and external problems. Indeed, had this been done, even the dynasty might have been saved.

CENTRAL LEADERSHIP

Occupants of the Dragon Throne

The most important figure at the court during these 34 years was Yehonala (1835–1908), whose career began in 1851 as a low-ranking Manchu concubine in the imperial palace. Her status was raised when she became the mother in 1856 of the only son and heir of Emperor Xian-feng (born 1831; reigned 1851–1861). She was well versed in the Chinese language and began to take a keen interest in the affairs of state; the emperor even allowed her to classify his memorials.

Xian-feng was extremely antiforeign and was particularly incensed at the idea of granting an audience to foreign envoys, who refused to kowtow before him. The success of his imperial forces at Dagu in 1859 gave him the false impression that the foreigners could be militarily contained. However, the debacle in 1860 destroyed his sense of self-respect, and he gave up all interest in national affairs when he fled to Rehe. He could not see himself returning to Beijing to be humiliated by Westerners, who not only had burned down his favorite summer palace but whose envoys now had also gained the right to stand upright in his presence. So he lingered on in Rehe, indulging in excesses ("debauchery," as a more frank appraisal would have described it). As a result of these excesses, he died in the fall of 1861.

Just before his death, eight of his rabidly antiforeign advisers were appointed as joint regents of his four-year-old son. Yehonala, although given the rank of empress dowager, was deprived of all power.

In a brilliantly organized coup, the details of which read like an exciting thriller, Yehonala connived with Prince Gong to arrest the eight regents and eliminate them from the political scene; one was executed and two were allowed to hang themselves, and the others were suitably punished in other ways. The empress consort (the legitimate wife of the Xien-feng emperor) and the empress dowager were appointed coregents. Prince Gong, their adviser, was given the rank of prince Counselor.

The empress consort was happy to allow Prince Gong to work unhampered, but the empress dowager (also known by her title as Ci-xi or by the popular expression "the Old Buddha") was more ambitious. In 1865, when she had consolidated her power, Ci-xi deprived Prince Gong of the special rank of prince counselor, although he was allowed to retain his other offices.

This regency lasted until 1873, when the Tong-zhi emperor (born 1856; reigned 1861–1875) came of age. The court now once again faced the audience question, which had been shelved since 1860. Despite two wars and the humiliating occupation of Beijing, the decision to allow foreign envoys to bow three times when received in audience was made with painful reluctance. The diehard conservatives, however, still managed to win a psychological victory and save face for the emperor. The audiences were held in a pavilion used for receiving tribute missions from minor vassal states, like the Ryukyu Islands (great loss of face for the foreigners); the envoys were kept waiting for a long time (greater loss of face) before they were conducted before the Imperial Presence; they entered through a side gate, normally used by lesser officials (terrible loss of face)!

The young emperor, given to excesses like his father, had hardly begun to understand the business of governing his empire when he fell sick and died (January 1875). He was 19 and left no heir, although his consort was pregnant.

Ci-xi, breaking all dynastic laws, hurriedly had her sister's three-year-old son appointed heir. (Under the dynastic laws an heir could not belong to the same generation as the last ruler.) As adoptive mother of her nephew, Ci-xi again became regent, and except for a brief time, she managed to keep the Guang-xu emperor from exercising his royal prerogative. Guang-xu (born 1872; reigned 1875–1908) died one day before the Old

Buddha; it was rumored that she had him poisoned because she feared he might malign her after her death.

In 1875, to avoid the possibility of the Tong-zhi emperor's consort giving birth to a son and thereby complicating Ci-xi's plans, the dowager empress forced the pregnant princess to commit suicide. From 1875 Ci-xi's position was so well consolidated and her powers so enhanced that she gradually reduced the authority of Prince Gong and finally dismissed him in 1884. This act proved shortsighted because Prince Gong had emerged after 1860 as one of the ablest Qing officials. Not only was he skillful in handling foreign relations but also he was capable of understanding the needs of the times, something quite beyond Ci-xi's limited intellectual capacity.

From 1875 until her death in 1908 Ci-xi retained her key position in the state, seldom losing her capacity to influence national policies. She maintained this position by playing one senior official against another, adroitly undermining the influence of those who were against her, and operating through palace eunuchs. However beneficial to her, such techniques of control made China even less centralized than it had been before 1860.

RISE TO POWER OF HAN OFFICIALS

The major anti-Qing rebellions were suppressed, ultimately, less by the imperial armies than by Han provincial militias raised by Han provincial officials. The most important of these officials were Zeng Guo-fan (1811–1872) and his subordinates Li Hong-zhang (1823–1901) and Zuo Zong-tang (1812–1885).

Zeng was a fairly senior official when he returned home to Hunan in 1852 to observe the customary mourning period for his dead mother. While at home he received orders from the emperor to organize a militia to expel the Taipings, who had invaded Hunan and the adjacent provinces. Zeng's militia, later known as the Hunan Braves or the Hunan Army, was well trained, well paid, and well indoctrinated in Confucian ethics. Zeng was handicapped by poor finances, however, for he depended on voluntary contributions from the local officials and local gentry. Only after Zeng gained an official post, placing him in control of the provincial finances, could he enlarge his army, build gunboats, and train naval forces.

Zeng won several significant victories, but Beijing was hesitant to give him a free hand to campaign beyond Hunan's borders. Many Manchu grandees feared that a Han would gain too much military power. The one voice in his favor, surprisingly enough, was that of the 25-year-old Yehonala, who managed to sway the emperor's opinion.

In August 1860, a month before Xianfeng fled the capital, orders were issued promoting Zeng to the rank of governor-general of Jiangsu and Jiangxi. After the emperor's death, Zeng in addition was given supreme military control over the provinces of Jiangsu, Anhui, Jiangxi, and Zhejiang. These rich provinces formed the heartland of the Taiping kingdom. Zeng coopted Zuo Zong-tang and Li Hong-zhang and set up three military bases: in Jiangsu, under Li as governor; in Zhejiang, under Zuo as governor; and in Anhui, under his own control. Like Zeng, Zuo and Li raised militias (Li's became famous as the Anhui Army) in their own provinces. They received financial and other help not only from the provincial literati but also from the Chinese merchants in the treaty ports, as well as from the British and the French.

In 1860, to defend Shanghai from the rebels, Chinese merchants and local officials had backed the formation of a unit of foreign mercenaries, which was led by an American adventurer, Frederick Townsend Ward. Ward's successes against the Taipings led his backers to encourage him to expand his "army" by recruiting several thousand Chinese. Ward proved that the Chinese, given proper training and modern weapons, were as good soldiers as any. In 1862 Ward's imperial masters honored his force by giving it the name Ever Victorious Army. After the ratification of the 1860 treaties, the British and French had every reason to support the dynasty against the rebels. So in 1862, when Ward was killed in action and his adjutant found unfit to take command, the British loaned one of their regular officers, Major Charles Gordon, to head the Ever Victorious Army and work under Li Hong-zhang. Units similar to the Ever Victorious Army were also formed by the French to help Zuo in Zhejiang.

Although the Taipings were not totally bereft of capable generals, the sustaining power of ideology had already drained out of the system. It was too late for the faction-ridden Heavenly Kingdom to consolidate its hold over the widespread but poorly organized territories. The imperial forces, spearheaded by the armies of Zeng, Li, and Zuo and assisted by foreign units, brought the Taiping war to a successful, although bloody, conclusion in June 1864; Hong committed suicide just before the fall of Nanjing. Gordon was showered with gifts and honors by Beijing before he went back to his post in the British army. Many years later General Gordon was to become a national hero in England, when he fell at the seige of Khartoum.

The pacification of China, although helped by the purchase of Western arms and the assistance of Western military units, was primarily carried out by the Chinese themselves. After the Taiping collapse, Beijing ordered Zeng to turn his forces against the Nian rebels. The Nians, who were skilled in the use of guerrilla tactics, had operated with considerable success in the Anhui, Henan, Jiangsu, and Shandong area since 1853. The imperial armies had carried on a long campaign against them but to no avail. Zeng and later Li, using Confucian techniques to gain support of the local peasantry, consolidated their hold over the countryside surrounding the Nian. The Nian were thus forced to withdraw into an ever more constricted area and were finally eliminated in 1868.

Qing authority had also been challenged by the Muslim minority communities in Southwest and Northwest China. Indeed, in the Southwest a Muslim state had been established in 1865, but since it was not supported by the local non-Muslim Chinese population, it did not pose as severe a threat as the Taipings and the Nians. After a protracted war and much wanton slaughter (nearly half the local population was annihilated), the rebellion was suppressed in 1873.

The Northwest Muslim Rebellion (1862–1873) was a more serious affair. Since the Shaanxi-Gansu panhandle (where the rebellion occurred) linked China proper to its Central Asian dependencies, a rebellion in this region could cut off communications between Beijing and Central Asia. In 1868, after the subjugation of the Taiping and the Nian rebels, Zuo Zong-tang was ordered to the Northwest to complete the task of internal pacification. It took him five years, but in the end he managed to bring the area firmly under central control and rehabilitate its economy.

The value of this operation became apparent within a few years when China saved Chinese Turkestan (modern-day Xinjiang) from falling into foreign hands. The Northwest Muslim Rebellion had inspired a Muslim uprising in Chinese Turkestan, leading to the establishment in 1865, of an independent kingdom in Kashgar under Yakub Beg, an adventurer from Khokand, a state that lay on the Chinese western border. In the absence of effective Chinese authority in this region, and fearing the extension of British influence in the area, Russia moved into Kuldja and Ili in 1871.

By this date the Russians had already advanced into Tashkent, Samarkand, Bokhara, and Khokand. After moving into the Ili valley, they felt strong enough to contain Yakub Beg and so gave him recognition in 1872. The British followed suit in 1873 (the year Zuo completed the pacification of the Northwest). The situation, naturally, worried the Chinese.

In 1875 Zuo, now a grand secretary and governor-general, was put in charge of military affairs in Chinese Turkestan. Zuo planned the campaign, which was to take him through many hundred miles of an arid desert, with the same meticulousness he had shown in Gansu. This was an expensive undertaking, and Zuo's request for funds was opposed by those (Li Hong-zhang among them) who regarded the ocean frontier as more important and who suggested that building a navy took precedence over the recovery of wasteland. However, Zuo and other like-minded traditionalists won their point that China could not allow any encroachment on Chinese territory.

The success of the Central Asian campaign was a tribute to Zuo's military genius. By early 1878 all lost territory, except that under Russian occupation, had been recovered. (Yakub Beg had committed suicide in 1877.) This was China's last traditional-style military victory, but it was impressive enough to influence the final outcome of the treaty negotiations between Russia and China. By the Treaty of St. Petersburg (1881) most of Ili valley reverted to China. In 1884 Chinese Turkestan was absorbed into China proper. It was made a centrally administered province and given the name of Xinjiang ("New Frontier").

"Restoration"

The period following the suppression of the Taipings has been looked on as one in which a conservative "restoration" of the Confucian empire took place. In many ways Zeng was its symbol. He was an ideal Confucian official: honest, frugal, hard-working, and dedicated. With the return of peace he turned his attention to reviving and strengthening the traditional order. He rehabilitated the agrarian economy (the basis of the Confucian state) by encouraging the movement of the people back to lands abandoned during the war; remitting or lowering taxes; and undertaking the repair of public works (canals, dykes, etc.), which had been damaged by neglect and civil turmoil. He revived the imperial examination system in the liberated areas to ensure the continued supply of Confucian literati to staff the bureaucracy and shore up the traditional order.

The "restoration," however, introduced certain important nontraditional elements into the Chinese scene. The Han civil officials, indeed, did begin their military careers with the aim of restoring national power to the Qing and the traditional order to the country, but without intending to do so, their activities resulted in undermining both.

On the broadest level the "restoration" had failed to bring back an order based on true Confucian moral and political principles. In the liberated provinces the peasant masses gained far less than the corrupt landowning gentry class and the exploitative government officials.

At a more crucial level, by highlighting the bankruptcy of the imperial armed forces and thereby the weakness of the Qing dynasty, the "restoration" led to the increased transfer of political and (something wholly new) military power to Han provincial officials. The significance of this development may not have been fully appreciated at the time, either by the court or by the provincial leaders themselves.

The armies that Zeng, Li, and Zuo had raised and directed were private armies, not under the Board of War; they owed loyalty to their creators rather than to the state. These armies, each numbering several tens of thousands (at its high point the Hunan Army was around 100,000 strong) and recruited from the commanders' home provinces, were officered by the relatives and close friends of the commanders. Except for a minimal central subsidy, the commanders had to arrange their own sources of funds to pay the forces. After the rebellions were put down, the militia armies were demobilized or reduced in size and an attempt was made to absorb what remained into the central system; but personal ties and personal loyalties between the militia units and their Han generals could not be replaced with a higher loyalty to the Manchu rulers.

The combination of political status (the commanders all became governors-general) and military power made these Han provincial officials key figures at the national level. This was particularly true of Li Hong-zhang, who as governor-general of Zhili province from 1870 to 1895 (concurrently grand secretary and commissioner of the northern ports) became the virtual foreign minister of China and the main arbiter of its modernization program. When Li moved to Zhili, he took his armies with him.

Officials like Li created a private source of power based on their regional armies, their control over regional officials, and their manipulation of regional economies. When at last an attempt was made to create a modern army under central control, units of Li's forces were used as the nucleus. One of his proteges, Yuan Shi-kai, was appointed commander. After 1908, when Yuan was dismissed from office, officers of the Beiyang Army (as the new model army was called) refused to cooperate with the new commander, and Yuan finally had to be recalled to service in a last-ditch effort to save the dynasty. Later, in the 1910s and 1920s the generals of the Beiyang Army continued to exploit private loyalties in the armed forces and established regional power bases, splitting the country into autonomous "warlord" zones.

Thus the "restoration," by failing to restore central authority over the militia armies, led to the reduction of central control over the provinces. The increase in the number and power of Han officials fostered fear and jealousy in the hearts of the conservative Manchus entrenched around the throne. The possibility of the center effectively promoting national policies, pulling the Han and the Manchus together, became even more remote.

The use of modern arms and the exposure to Western-style military training and tactics stimulated the restorationists to move, albeit hesitatingly, in the direction of establishing modern defense and other industries. This move, in turn, led to the introduction of Western science and technology and, ultimately, to the questioning of Confucian concepts.

TOWARD A NEW ORDER

The Contribution of the West

In the immediate context Western action in China can be seen as having a positive or a negative impact. However, in the long run both kinds of activities contributed to change because, one way or the other, they undermined tradition and helped to introduce new ideas, values, and institutions.

As China became enmeshed in the West-centered global historical process, officials who had had to deal with Westerners realized that the Chinese needed to acquire the weaponry of the West to ward off the West; some even concluded that the Chinese ignorance of the West would have to yield to a greater understanding of the sources of Western wealth and power.

The Chinese need to study Western methods and the opportunity to do so both increased with the passage of time. Before 1839 there were few contacts between Chinese officials and Westerners. Between 1840 and 1860, however, contact was officially authorized between the Western consuls and the imperial commissioner at Guangzhou (representing the government of China) and with certain provincial officials in the treaty ports. The number of Chinese officials who handled foreign affairs was still extremely small, but after 1860, when embassies were established in Beijing and a Chinese "foreign office" opened, the contacts became more widespread.

Contacts between foreign merchants and their Chinese counterparts, restricted to the Cohong merchants for eight decades before 1839, also increased. A new class of Chinese merchants emerged, the compradors, who acted as liaison between the foreign traders and the native producers or buyers. The compradors became indispensable because on the one hand they had a working knowledge of the foreigner's language and understood the foreign system of commerce, and on the other they knew the Chinese market and could deal effectively with Chinese traders in the interior.

Missionary Activities: The Positive Side. Of the two groups of missionaries active in China, the Roman Catholics and the Protestants, it was primarily the latter who went beyond evangelism to become involved with good works and social changes. In fact, considering the growth in the number of missionaries, the number of converts was rather discouraging. In 1860 there were about 100 Protestant missionaries active on the China coast; in 1870, 350; in 1890, 1,350; and in 1898, 2,458. The number of converts in 1898 was, however, only about 80,000.

From the 1870s, when some Protestant missionaries secularized their work, their activities, particularly in the major treaty ports, led to the establishment of schools (many of which later became renowned universities), libraries, museums, magazines, and newspapers. Here was a ready source of Western knowledge for the Chinese. Enrollment in mission schools stood at about 17,000 by 1890, but most of the students were from nonliterati backgrounds and hoped to gain employment with the foreigners on completing their studies.

As Irwin Hyatt has pointed out, "Education and medicine were made into institutions during the 1880s . . . by missionary specialists. By 1890 these practitioners had established professional societies and publications and had to a significant degree assumed professional attitudes."[1] Organizations such as the Society for the Diffusion of Useful Knowledge in China and the Society for the Diffusion of Christian and General Knowledge promoted the translation of Western works and introduced, among other subjects, European science and technology.

Viewed in the context of China as a whole, the positive achievement of these well-meaning foreign endeavors was extremely limited: geographically, to a few coastal cities, and socially, to a few enlightened Chinese. The vast hinterland, by and large, remained impervious to new ideas and techniques. Indeed, missionary and other foreign activity in the remoter areas created strong antiforeign sentiment. The government of China was torn between adjustment to "modern" pressures emanating from the treaty ports and the traditional system, with which it continued to govern the Chinese land mass and the bulk of the Chinese people. Nevertheless, this limited contribution of the West would in time be the catalyst for reform and change in China.

Foreign Settlements. The treaty system had created another unique situation in some of the treaty ports. Grants of lands given as "concessions" for foreign residence became autonomous and developed municipal governments under the Western consuls. The foreign settlements in Shanghai (later identified as the Anglo-American International Settlement and the French Concession) turned into foreign-governed enclaves with jurisdiction over the thousands of Chinese who had sought shelter in them.

By 1895 the International Settlement boasted paved roads, street lights, running water, schools (including the famous St. John's College), law courts, modern hospitals, postal service, telegraph connections to the rest of the world, English- and Chinese-language newspapers, publishing houses, and of course a cricket club and a race course. A similar development took place in Hong Kong, which as a British Crown colony had the legitimate right to exercise foreign-style government over the territory and the large number of Chinese who lived there.

These self-governing enclaves provided a local showcase of European municipal and community life and could be viewed as models for reform-minded Chinese. Chinese dissidents sought refuge in the International Settlement, the French Concession, or Hong Kong, where they could express their views in relative freedom.

Between 1860 and 1895 the negative side of the imperialist impact was far greater than its positive contribution to China's modernization. Almost all Westerners who went to China in the nineteenth century regarded Western civilization as being far superior to that of China and showed open contempt for the Chinese. The sign "Chinese and dogs not allowed" outside a Shanghai park symbolized an extreme example of this attitude. It is therefore not surprising that even the Chinese revolutionaries who took sanctuary in Shanghai to escape persecution by Beijing attacked their own government for not being powerful enough to get rid of the imperialists, who had established virtual colonies in China.

Missionary Activities: The Negative Side. Widespread contact between the Chinese people and Westerners developed only after the missionaries were allowed into the hinterland. The Western traders had no desire to change China, other than to lift restrictions on commerce; the diplomats could impress senior officials of the empire with the need to make institutional changes that would help ease international relations or modernize China; but it was the missionaries who took upon themselves the task of providing an alternative to Chinese social tradition.

Having entered the local scene, protected by extrality, the missionaries propagated a religion that attacked Confucian values and mores: People owed absolute obedience to God and not to an emperor; ancestor worship was a pagan rite; all human beings were equal in the eyes of God, and justice should not discriminate between people on the basis of hierarchical status; Confucian ideas of graded love must give way to the Christian ideal of universal love; men and women were equal; marriages should be a product of mutual love and not parental arrangement; and footbinding was an act against nature.

The missionaries took on the role of teachers and protectors of the socially underprivileged. Apart from erecting houses of worship, they established orphanages and homes for widows, schools, and medical clinics; at times of floods and famines they acted as relief agencies, setting up soup kitchens. Because of their special and unassailable position, they could even pressure the local officials to favor members of their flock.

Thus the missionaries came to challenge the traditional order and assail the local gentry, who were supposed to propagate Confucianism, establish Confucian schools, and look after local welfare. Consequently the gentry, concerned for their vested interests, became implacable enemies of the missionaries; indeed, it is not difficult to imagine why missionary attacks on Chinese tradition would make even the common folk resentful of the missionary presence.

Within a few years of the opening of China to missionary activity, antimissionary riots began to mar China's relations with the European powers. The treaties gave missionaries the freedom to preach, whereas the Chinese government had the responsibility of protecting their persons and property. In case of trouble the powers were committed to intercede on behalf of the missionary and demand compensation for any damage done to the missionary's person or property. In any conflict between a missionary and the local gentry or local government, the powers forced Beijing to side with the missionary against its own local upholders of Confucian society and state. Indeed, the central government often had to punish or transfer offending officials and to order the gentry to raise money to pay compensation or an indemnity. From being a protector of Confucianism, the treaties turned the emperor into a protector of a foreign heterodox cult. The European powers thus were led by the missionaries to interfere in China's internal affairs and further weaken its government.

Antimissionary incidents and riots started in the 1860s and continued into the twentieth century. Between 1867 and 1869 there was trouble in Dayong, Liuzhou, Gengshan, Yantai, Yangzhou, Fuzhou, and Wuchang. In many cases a broader antiforeignism was closely mixed with purely anti-Christian sentiments; in all cases the powers used the treaties to gain redress; in some cases they intervened directly with gunboats to put down local unrest.

A far more serious incident, known as the Tianjin massacre, took place in 1870 and brought to a close the so-called period of cooperation between China and the West. The details of the incident provide a good example of the friction that missionary activity was causing in Sino-foreign relations. By 1870 anti-Christian tracts were circulating widely in the provinces. They charged that the missionaries forced their converts to show dishonor to their ancestors and undergo baptism with an unguent made from the corpses of priests; that they tore out the eyes and hearts of the dying to make drugs; and that they encouraged sodomy and sex between parents and children and between brothers and sisters.

In Tianjin the French were doubly detested because, without legal title, they not only had erected a Roman Catholic cathedral but also had done so on the site of an imperial temple. Rumor had it that the French Sisters of Mercy, who had established an orphanage, were buying up children and killing them for their eyes and hearts. Indeed, the sisters did give some gratuity to those who brought orphans to their institutions (which probably encouraged some kidnapping), and since most of these orphans were in poor health, they often died soon after they were taken in. Just at this time an epidemic raised the death rate even higher. The rites of baptism and last unction (pouring holy oil in the eyes) and the seemingly secret burial of the children in the Christian cemetery appeared to confirm the rumors. On June 21 a mob gathered to take direct action against the sisters.

Before the ranking Chinese official of the area could pacify the angry mob, the impetuous local French consul, M. Fontanier, armed with two pistols, took direct action by firing at the crowd and the local magistrate.

There was no controlling the crowd now. The Chinese slaughtered the consul and his assistant and went on a rampage. Before the evening was out they had burned down the French consulate, the cathedral, the orphanage, and four English and American chapels; raped and butchered ten sisters; and killed two priests and seven other "French" men and women, three of whom were actually Russians.

There was a cry for war in France and for vengeance in other European capitals. Foreign gunboats were moved to Tianjin, and seven foreign powers sent a collective note of protest to Beijing. The French demanded the lives of several senior officers posted at Tianjin. Zeng and then Li were brought in by Beijing to negotiate a settlement, which became comparatively easier because France had just suffered a defeat in the Franco-Prussian War and was powerless to exert its authority abroad. Apart from paying indemnities, Beijing had to send an "apology mission" (carrying a letter of apology from the emperor) to Paris, indemnify the French for the loss of lives and property, banish the prefect and magistrate of Tianjin to a penal colony on the Amur, and punish 51 other Chinese with decapitation and exile.

After the Tianjin massacre, antimissionary incidents increased as purely anti-Christian sentiment got mixed with antiforeign and anti-Manchu hatred. Since the foreign powers could neither control the missionaries nor dissociate themselves from them, imperialist policies became more and more involved with missionary causes. According to Edmund Wehrle, in 1891 riots in the Yangtze valley made the missionary problem "the foremost concern of British policy in China . . . [and] almost simultaneous calls for [gunboats, came from] virtually every treaty port on the Yangtze."[2] After the "Kut'ien [Gutian] Massacre" in 1895 the British ambassador managed to get high Chinese officials punished for the first time and urged London that in the future the Chinese government be forced to punish the literati and officials when an antimissionary outbreak took place. According to Wehrle, "By forcing the regime to humble itself publicly [the British ambassador] may have played into the hands of those who sought to overthrow the dynasty."[3] In 1897 the German seizure of Jiaozhou was associated with missionary trouble, and this in turn led to a scramble for concessions and the partitioning of China into spheres of influence by the imperialist powers. In 1900 the missionaries were a catalyst in the Boxer uprising, which resulted in the occupation of Beijing by the imperialist powers and the virtual end of the Chinese traditional imperial system.

The Finalization of the Unequal Treaties. In accordance with the clause in the Tianjin treaties providing for a revision every ten years, negotiations began in 1869. Sir Rutherford Alcock, the British envoy in Beijing, served as the main Western negotiator. He consulted the foreign chambers of commerce in China and the envoys of other powers. The merchants were adamant that China be forced to remove "unjust restrictions" on trade, open the interior further to facilitate merchant travel and residence, and throw open "the producing and consuming districts to foreign capital and energy." Alcock was of the opinion that it would be counterproductive to push China to move any faster. China should be left alone to work out things for itself. The British government agreed that a full revision of the treaties could wait for a few years, at least until 1873 when the emperor attained his majority. London reached this view partly because of the exhortations of China's ambassador-extraordinary, the American diplomat Mr. Anson Burlingame, who was in England in 1868 and who explained that unfriendly pressure on China could jeopardize its independence.

Alcock's negotiations did lead to a convention, the Alcock Convention, which even contained some clauses favorable to China. London, however, failed to ratify the convention because of pressure from the merchants, who felt that it conceded too much to the Chinese. The matter of treaty revision remained in suspension until the Margary incident in 1875.

The British, who had already occupied a part of Burma, speculated on the possibility of reaching Yunnan from India through northern Burma. An exploratory mission was mounted, and A. R. Margary, a British consular officer posted to Beijing and a member of the expedition, was killed by tribes in the remote, lawless borderland. It was not clear whether the Burmese king, who was strongly opposed to opening any trade routes, the almost independent local tribespeople, or the Chinese were responsible for the outrage. To the petulant British minister in Beijing, Sir Thomas Wade, known for his rages and outbursts, this was a God-sent opportunity to settle all outstanding matters between the two countries and give final shape to the treaties. It mattered little to him that Margary's five Chinese associates had also been killed in the same ambush or that the other foreign ministers were not favorably inclined to broadening the negotiations to include issues other than redress for Margary's death.

To put pressure on the Chinese government, Wade even threatened to break relations with China. Negotiations opened between him and Li Hong-zhang in Yantai (known as Chefoo to the Westerners) in 1876 resulted in the Chefoo Convention, "the final capstone of the treaty system," according to John King Fairbank. The agreement was in three parts. Section I, which dealt with the Yunnan case, opened frontier trade between Burma and Yunnan, allowed British officials to be stationed at Dali, fixed the amount of indemnity to 200,000 taels of silver, and declared that a Chinese mission would be sent to England carrying an imperial letter of apology.

Section II, which dealt with the problem of official intercourse, announced that the Chinese Foreign Office would prepare a code of etiquette after consulting foreign diplomats, and it also elaborated on the conduct of judicial proceedings in mixed courts.

The last part of the convention dealt with trade. *Likin* (an inland transit duty) was abolished from the concession areas; four more cities were opened as treaty ports; six more places on the Yangtze were opened, not as treaty ports, but as ports of call for steamers; duty and *Likin* on opium were combined, and some other transit dues were rationalized. A separate article ensured proper protection for a contemplated British "mission of exploration" that would go from Beijing to India through Tibet.

The convention did not contribute to any

significant increase in trade, but it did mark the beginning of Li Hong-zhang's rise to prominence as the de facto foreign minister of China, and it did result in the establishment of the first Chinese legation abroad. Guo Song-dao, who headed the mission of apology in 1877, set up the Chinese embassy and served as China's ambassador to the Court of St. James.

Dismantling the Chinese World Order. In the 1870s the world was entering the period of "New Imperialism." By 1870 Italy and Germany had emerged as vigorous nation-states, and the post-Civil War United States had entered a period of rapid industrialization. These countries now joined the reinvigorated Third Republic of France (established in 1870) and England in competing for foreign markets for trade and capital investment. In the next 50 years Europe reached the high point of its expansion over the globe. The compulsion for political and territorial domination to protect their financial interests led the Western powers to partition Africa and Asia among themselves and to establish colonies, protectorates, and spheres of influence.

What were the pressures behind this aggressiveness? Debate on the meaning of the term *imperialism* began in the late nineteenth century and has not yet drawn to a close. Was it due to surplus capital in the industrial countries that needed to be invested in colonies and spheres of influence ("economic colonies," as J. A. Hobson put it)? Or was imperialism simply the monopoly state of capitalism and historically inevitable, as Vladimir Lenin analyzed it? Should one agree with Joseph Schumpeter that imperialism was not an economic instrument after all but a blind tribal impulse driving the state to "unlimited forcible expansion"? Or with A. J. P. Taylor that it was a byproduct of the conflict of European state interests? Many in the nineteenth and early twentieth centuries believed that the white race had the duty, the burden to spread higher, white civilization throughout the world: to convert the heathens to Christianity to save their souls and give them Western knowledge and techniques to save their bodies.

Whatever the nature of imperialism—indeed, it may be a varying mix of all the elements mentioned—it had a profound impact on the subject areas, where the fundamentals of native culture and civilization came under an attack that could not be warded off. In China, until 1895, the economic gains made by the Western nations were, relatively speaking, so disappointing that imperialism cannot be explained on that basis alone. The vision of an inexhaustible market for Western industrial products never really died, but every step that opened China to further trade proved futile. The total annual value of the foreign trade of China in 1896 was a little over 50 million pounds sterling, of which Britain's exports to China amounted to only 7 million pounds.[4]

Chinese exports of tea and silk also began to decline after reaching their high point in the 1880s. Teas from India, Ceylon, and Japan began to capture the British and American markets, and better-quality silks from Japan and Europe started replacing the Chinese silks. Opium consumption continued to rise in China, but the imports peaked by 1880 (c. 87,000 chests) when the Chinese indigenous production, many times the quantity imported, began to saturate the market.

The competition between imperialist powers in China spilled over into the states on its periphery, resulting in weakening China in another unexpected way. The concept of the Central (Middle) Kingdom was good only as long as China was surrounded by the ring of tributary states: Burma, Siam (now Thailand), Annam (now Vietnam), Ryukyu Islands, Korea, Mongolia, Chinese Turkestan, and Tibet (the last three were much more closely tied to Beijing and fell into the different category of "dependencies"). By 1895 many of these states were removed from China's orbit, thus destroying the world order to which China was "central."

At this stage a new imperialist power arrived on the Chinese scene: Japan. The Japanese, after their country was "opened" by the United States in 1854, went through a political revolution (the Meiji Restoration, 1868) and began to Westernize rapidly. Unlike China, Japan was sensitive about its vulnerability to Western expansion and was particularly fearful of Russia. It saw its line of strategic defense as lying on the continent and so began to take increasing interest in the peripheral areas. Japanese imperialism aped its Western counterpart but lacked the ingredients that made Western imperialism a world phenomenon. However, its impact on China was to be even more devastating than that of the West.

Japan's treaty of peace and friendship with China, signed in 1871 without any threat of force, marked the beginning of China's modern relationship with an Asian power. The treaty did not include the "most favored nation" clause and therefore denied Japan the privileges accorded to Western states.

The first indication of future discord between the two Asian neighbors came shortly thereafter, when Japan absorbed the Ryukyu Islands into its newly unified empire. The Ryukyus had paid tribute to China but had also been considered vassals of the feudal lord of Satsuma, a powerful domain in southern Japan. When the Meiji government abolished feudalism, the Ryukyus were automatically considered to belong to Japan. In 1873 the Japanese sought, but did not immediately gain, redress from China for the killing of some Ryukyuan shipwrecked sailors by Taiwanese aborigines. Japan followed up its diplomatic action by a military expedition to Taiwan to chastise the Taiwanese. In 1874 China negotiated a settlement and paid an indemnity to Japan, thus unwittingly recognizing Japan's sovereignty over the Ryukyu Islands. In 1878 Japan stopped the king of the Ryukyus from sending tribute to China, and in 1879 the islands were incorporated into Okinawa Prefecture. The Chinese protested, to no avail.

The importance of the Ryukyuan incident is that it was the first act in the dismemberment of the Chinese tributary order and a signal indication of how successfully Japan had learned the Western concept of nation-state boundaries and the value of Western-style international treaty relations.

Li is reported to have tried to reduce the significance of this development by saying "this dot on the map [the Ryukyus] is closer to Japan than to us." He could, however, not have said the same of Burma and Annam, which were shortly to be taken over by the British and the French.

The French had first entered Indochina in the mid-eighteenth century. The area then comprised Cambodia, Laos, and Annam (roughly present-day Vietnam), and the emperor of Annam was the primary power. It was, however, only in the mid-nineteenth century that France began to use military power to gain political ascendancy in this region. By 1863 France had established a protectorate over Cambodia and forced Annam to cede the three eastern provinces of Cochin-China.

A treaty signed in 1874 (the same year that the Ryukyus were lost) gave France control over the foreign relations of Annam and navigation rights in the Red River, confirmed their possession of Cochin-China, and provided extraterritoriality for French citizens and protection for missionaries. Thus Vietnam also became a protectorate, although technically it retained its independence. The emperor of Annam appealed to China for help. The Chinese refused to recognize the treaties on the ground that Annam was a tributary state, "whose ruler," Paris was informed by China in a letter sent in 1880, "down to the present day has received his investiture from the Emperor of China."[5] But China could do little to enforce its position. The French replied that the Treaty of 1874 recognized the independence of Vietnam.

In 1880 France stationed troops in Hanoi and Haiphong, whereas Hue (the capital of Annam) sent a tribute mission to China in an attempt to strengthen its ties with Beijing. In 1882 the French occupied Hanoi.

Beijing was divided between those who championed war and those, like Li, who advocated a more cautious approach. The basic issue was whether Vietnam was an independent country or under Chinese sovereignty. The young, hot-blooded conservative officials, who had formed a "party of purists" (*qing liu dang*) and who had been encouraged by Zuo's success in Xinjiang, attacked Li for his capitulationism. The first agreement worked out between Li and the French minister Bouree collapsed in 1883, and the purists gained ground. Yunnan and Guangxi armies were ordered to advance into Tongking.

The French response was to occupy Hue and sign another treaty (the Treaty of Hue, 1883), which without any ambiguity, reduced Vietnam to the position of an outright protectorate. Beijing announced, in November 1883, that any attack on the Chinese forces would signal the beginning of a war. In March 1884, French troops inflicted a humiliating defeat on the Chinese armies, but the action brought neither a declaration of war from Beijing nor a move for peace.

The empress dowager, however, took this opportunity to strengthen her hold over the government by dismissing Prince Gong, the head of the Zongli Yamen (the Chinese Foreign Office), ostensibly because he was in favor of a negotiated settlement. But in reality she had carried a personal grudge against him for a long time. This action of Ci-xi gave the appearance that the officials favoring war had gained ascendance. In fact, there was still no firm policy on war or peace.

At this stage Captain Fournier of the French navy appeared on the scene and offered to help negotiate a conciliatory settlement of the controversy. In May 1884 the Li-Fournier Convention was signed. It provided that China was to withdraw "immediately" its troops from Tongking, respect the treaties between France and Vietnam, and open the southern border to French trade (via Tongking). In return, France would respect China's southern border and not use any expressions in its forthcoming treaty with Vietnam "calculated to affect prejudicially the prestige of the Celestial Empire." Li, afraid of the court's reaction, failed to inform Beijing of the date on which the Chinese troops were supposed to withdraw. The result was that in June there was a skirmish between French and Chinese forces (who had not withdrawn because they had received no orders to do so) at Bac-le in which the French were defeated.

The French now added a demand for indemnity to the Li-Fournier agreement, but Beijing was adamant that China was not responsible for the Bac-le incident and rejected all French ultimatums. A state of undeclared war resulted. In August 1884 the French navy destroyed the Fuzhou shipyard (established in 1866 with French aid and technical help) along with 9 of the 11 steam warships built at the yard.

While China was recovering from this shock, news came that the Japanese had backed a coup in Korea to overthrow the pro-Chinese ruler. The coup was thwarted by the Chinese garrison, but relations between China and Japan came to a breaking point. The Japanese garrison, which had had to retreat from Seoul, was now back in greater strength, and there was strong prowar sentiment in Japan.

With the help of negotiations in Paris by Robert Hart's agent (Hart was the inspector general of the Chinese Maritime Customs Service, 1868–1907) in London, Paris and Beijing finally agreed to end hostilities. The protocol, signed in April 1885, was essentially a confirmation of the Li-Fournier agreement. The French reverses at Langson, a strategic town just south of the Chinese border, which had been recovered by the Chinese in March, saved Chinese face somewhat.

In 1887 the French unified their administrative control over Vietnam and Cambodia and established the Union Indo-Chinois; in 1893 they acquired Laos, which had long been in dispute between Annam and Siam.

The Annam affair showed that two and a half decades after the second set of treaties, China was still caught between its traditional tributary system and the new Western-style international relations. Although China was no longer in a position to protect its dependencies, the concept of tributary states was difficult to discard. Lacking a unified leadership, Beijing could make only ad hoc policy decisions, which vacillated between half-hearted resistance to the West and humiliating appeasement. As one senior Chinese official put it, "In the morning an order [is] issued; in the evening it is changed. Unavoidably outsiders will laugh. But there is nothing that can be done about it."[6] Beijing's troubles were not to end with Annam.

The British, already in possession of eastern India, had begun their penetration and occupation of Burma in the 1820s. By the time of the Margary affair (1875) the British had fought two wars and absorbed Arakan, the Tenasserim coast, and Pegu. Fear of the French moving from Annam into Burma precipitated the third war in 1885, and the British annexed Burma.

Since Burma was also a dependency of China, the British felt it proper to clear the matter with Beijing. It appears that a few years after the Cheefoo Convention, Thomas Wade had told Li Hong-zhang that "we British like Burma very much: it is a place worth having." Li's reply was, "If you should decide to go to war with Burma let us know beforehand, so that it will not cause any trouble between us."[7] Now that Burma had been conquered, the British made the act more palatable by agreeing (1886) that the Burmese would continue to send their tribute missions. A Burmese mission was sent in 1895, but after China's defeat by Japan in the 1894–1895 war, even this face-saving act was no longer necessary.

Siam (modern-day Thailand) was lost to the Chinese much earlier than Vietnam and Burma, but its last days as a tributary state may be mentioned here to complete the picture of developments in Southeast Asia. Siam, like Annam, was required to send a tributary mission every three years, and it followed the practice unfailingly until 1853. Indeed, in 1852 the new king of Siam sent an envoy to Beijing to request investiture.

However, when danger of foreign aggression came to Siam with the expansion of the British into Burma and the French into Annam, instead of looking to Beijing for help, the wise and reform-minded King Rama IV (reigned 1851–1868) willingly concluded treaties with Britain (1855), France, and America (1856). While opening the country to foreign trade and missionary activity, he began a program of modernization that saved the country from China's fate. By balancing British and French interests this small kingdom assured its independence. It sent no more tribute missions to China after 1855.

Like Vietnam, Korea was a tributary state with a predominantly Confucian sociopolitical culture and had close geographical and historical links with China. Indeed, if one considers the frequency of the tribute missions, it was even closer than Vietnam because it sent a mission every year.

Of the tributary states discussed so far, Korea came nearest to the Chinese ideal because, except for a limited contact with Japan, it followed an aggressive policy of total seclusion (thereby earning the name Hermit Kingdom) and let Beijing handle all its foreign relations. But as with other tributary states, China was no longer strong enough to prevent foreign powers from interfering in Korea. This left Korea caught between the dying Chinese international order and the one that the imperialist powers were in the process of forging.

At the outset Korea was successful in keeping the foreign powers out. The French fleet, sent in 1866 to seek redress for the murder of some French priests, failed to "open" Korea. The Americans, encouraged by their success in opening Japan, sent an expedition in 1871 and met the same fate. The Koreans asked Beijing to explain their exclusion policies to the Americans and to urge them not to try to deal directly with Seoul. As a result, China announced to the powers that "although Korea is a country subordinate to China, nevertheless, it is wholly self-determining in government, religion, prohibitions and laws."[8] The statement sounded rather ambiguous to the legal-minded Western diplomats.

Japan, itself just recently opened, now took upon itself the task of opening Korea. It is startling to note how modern Japan had become in just a few years, how quickly it had become conscious of its strategic interests on the continent, and how keenly it was following the tactics established by the West in dealing with Asian nations. Within a year of having gained suzerainty over the Ryukyus through the Taiwan Settlement of 1874, Japan sent a surveying party to the mouth of the Han River, which led upriver to the Korean capital. The Japanese had to withdraw after their vessel was fired on, and their request for a treaty was refused on the grounds that Korea was a vassal of China. Japan now turned to Beijing and asked for credentials to be granted that would facilitate another mission to Seoul. Since it would have been totally against the spirit of the tributary relations for China to open Korean doors to a hostile barbarian country, Beijing refused. Tokyo was given the same answer as the other powers, that Korea was self-governing. Japan chose to interpret this term to mean that Korea was an independent state.

Li Hong-zhang, realizing the gravity of the situation and fearing a Japanese attack on Korea, advised the Zongli Yamen to send secret instructions to Seoul to receive the Japanese mission with "proper courtesy." As a result, Korea and Japan signed a treaty (1876) that confirmed the right of the two countries to exchange envoys, forced Korea to open certain ports for trade, and granted extrality to the Japanese.

Despite this treaty Korea continued to maintain its special relations with China and to resist opening the country to other powers.

In 1880 Li Hong-zhang was given full authority to handle Korean affairs. Li's endeavor was twofold: to protect Korea's independence and to preserve China's dominance in that country. To preserve Korean territorial integrity and counter Japan's ambitions in Korea, Li encouraged Korea to establish diplomatic relations with as many powers as possible. At the same time he insisted that the treaties include a clause recognizing China's suzerainty over Korea. As an adjunct measure Li began to strengthen China's northern naval force. Between 1882 and 1886 Korea signed treaties with the United States, Britain, Germany, Italy, Russia, and France. Although the powers refused to include a clause in the treaties recognizing Korea's dependence on China, in letters accompanying the treaties Korea made a formal declaration of its vassal status.

Li also managed to increase the Chinese presence in Seoul. Chinese commercial agents were appointed to advise the Korean ruler, a Chinese became the inspector general of Korean Customs, and Chinese troops under Yuan Shi-kai (later an important figure in Chinese history) were dispatched to restore order after an abortive coup by a pro-Japanese clique in 1882. Since the Japanese legation had been attacked during the coup, the Japanese, apart from exacting an apology and an indemnity, also sent troops to Korea and stationed them there to protect their nationals.

The situation was rather anomalous. China was intervening in Korea's internal affairs as a suzerain, and the Japanese were acting as if Korea were independent. In 1884 another coup took place, and the pro-Japanese Korean "progressives" seized the king and appealed to the Japanese for help. Yuan Shi-kai, taking action on behalf of the ruler, defeated the Japanese and restored the king to the throne.

This was a great victory for China in a year that otherwise had brought endless bad news: The French had destroyed the Chinese ships and arsenal at the Fuzhou shipyard and were about to take over Vietnam. After the Korean incident, the Japanese exacted another indemnity from Korea but, at the same time, sent an envoy to China to discuss the Korean question with Li Hong-zhang. The resulting Convention of Tianjin (1885) was looked on as a victory by both sides. China and Japan agreed to withdraw troops from Seoul, but both nations reserved the right to send troops to Korea in case of future trouble, after notifying the other side. For Japan this was a victory because the convention put

China and Japan on an equal footing. For Li it was a victory because he felt that China's traditional interest in Korea had been tacitly recognized and that China could always ship its troops from Port Arthur to reach Seoul much faster than any Japanese army.

Between 1885 and 1894 Li, working through Yuan Shi-kai, who had been appointed China's resident in Korea, made China the paramount power in Korea. He also got Beijing to increase funding to build a navy, and he developed naval bases in Weihaiwei, Shandong, and Lushunkou (Port Arthur) on the Liaodong peninsula. It appeared that Li had learned a great deal from China's earlier foreign policy failures and that Korea would not become another Annam or Burma.

But there was a serious flaw in Li's Korean policies. He confused legitimate national strategic interests (a modern concept) with a traditional Confucian stand. In 1894, because of domestic rebellion, the Korean ruler requested and received Chinese military help. Li informed Japan of this action but implied that China had the right to send troops to help a vassal ruler. The Japanese refused to recognize Korea as a dependency of China and replied that they, too, would dispatch troops, as had been agreed on in the Tianjin Convention.

It turned out that in fact no outside troops were needed to quell the rebellion, but that was no longer relevant to further developments. The Japanese, not getting a categorical declaration from Seoul that Korea was not a vassal of China, seized the palace and installed a pro-Japanese ruler who "requested" Japan to help in the expulsion of the Chinese. The Sino-Japanese War had begun.

The Western powers, although maintaining neutrality, were generally in favor of China and not too worried about the outcome because China's modernization efforts appeared to be far more impressive than those of Japan. China had had 34 years to prepare (1860–1894), whereas Japan, a much smaller power, had begun these efforts only around 1870. The Chinese forces that crossed the Yalu into Korea were much larger than the Japanese troops; the Chinese naval force off the mouth of the Yalu (13 ships against the Japanese 12) had superior gun power and included two ironclads of over 7,000 tons, whereas the largest Japanese ship was 4,000 tons. But the effectiveness of young Japan's military machine startled the world.

On land the Japanese routed the Chinese forces, pushed into Manchuria, and captured Port Arthur. On water the Chinese humiliation was even greater. In a four-hour battle the Japanese trounced the Chinese, sinking four of their vessels without losing any of their own. The rest of the Chinese fleet sought refuge in Weihaiwei, where it finally surrendered to the Japanese troops who had entered the port from the landward side.

The Sino-Japanese War and the Treaty of Shimonoseki (1895) that concluded it marked the beginning of a new era in East Asia. Japan emerged as a key imperialist power and, henceforth, a permanent factor in the regional and world power play. Although it would take Japan 10 years to draw Korea fully into its sphere of influence and 15 to make it an outright colony, the "liberation" of Korea in 1895 was a positive step forward in the fulfillment of Japanese ambitions. The treaty forced the Qing government to cede Liaodong Peninsula, the Pescadores, and Taiwan to Japan; pay an indemnity of 200 million taels (nearly 270 million ounces of silver); grant the Japanese "most favored nation" treatment (since the original Sino-Japanese treaty was between equal powers, this change made it an "unequal" treaty and put Japan in the category of the Western powers); and open seven new treaty ports. Incidentally, Russia, finding Japan's occupation of Liaodong strategically unacceptable, used diplomatic pressure in cooperation with Germany and France to force Japan to return Liaodong to China, for an additional monetary compensation, of course. This event marks the beginning of the Russian-Japanese conflict in Northeast Asia.

Last, and most important, in a supplementary commercial treaty signed in 1896, Japanese nationals were permitted to set up and run industries in the treaty ports of China. Under the "most favored nation" clause, all other powers automatically gained the same privilege, and this new development added a crucial dimension to imperialist exploitation of China. Since the foreign capitalists could use cheap Chinese labor and did not have to pay local Chinese taxes, they gained a competitive edge over the native Chinese industrialists. In the long run, this development thwarted the growth of national Chinese capitalist enterprises.

For China the war was a most shattering experience. A crippling defeat at the hands of the "dwarf" Asian barbarians, who had historically been looked down on as vastly inferior to the inhabitants of the Middle Kingdom, was psychologically unnerving. China was finally divested of its principal tributary states, and the traditional Confucian view of international relations was irrevocably put to rest. The country could now turn its full attention to the building of a modern nation-state. Thirty-five years of modernization programs (see the next section) carried out halfheartedly in the context of the traditional political-social context had proved a total failure. Any respect that the foreign powers may have had for the Qing government was now replaced with a scramble to extract as many privileges as possible out of a dying dynasty. Within China, too, the corrupt and inefficient dynasty lost its legitimacy in the eyes of many Chinese, some of whom, for the first time, began to think in terms of a modern revolution.

Later, when distinction between the Chinese traditional empire and modern empires got blurred, many patriotic Chinese strongly resented the loss of the tributary states. Looking back at the nineteenth-century developments, Mao Ze-dong, the greatest of the twentieth-century Chinese revolutionary leaders, wrote in 1939,

> Japan appropriated Korea, Taiwan, the Ryukyu Islands, the Pescadores and Port Arthur; England took Burma, Bhutan, Nepal, and Hongkong; France seized Annam; even a miserable little country like Portugal took Macao from us. At the same time that they took away part of her territory, the imperialists obliged China to pay enormous indemnities.[9]

Internal Changes

China had wasted the 15 years between 1842 and 1857 in following delaying tactics that were intended to conciliate and pacify the barbarians temporarily but that aimed at a return of the status quo ante. The war of 1860 proved the bankruptcy of this traditional concept for the management of barbarians and forced Beijing to adjust, however reluctantly, to the new political environment. The Sino-Japanese War of 1894 demonstrated that the changes introduced by the Chinese between 1860 and 1894 had not been effective in truly strengthening China. Apparently China had found it impossible to achieve a viable accommodation between its traditional political style and the new elements of Westernization.

However, there was a vast difference between the China of 1895 and the China of 1860 proved the bankruptcy of this traditional concept for the management of barbarians and forced Beijing to adjust, however reluctantly, to the new political environment. The Sino-Japanese War of 1894 demonstrated that the changes introduced by the Chinese between 1860 and 1894 had not been effective in truly strengthening China. Apparently China had found it impossible to achieve a viable accommodation between its traditional political style and the new elements of Westernization.

As noted earlier, one cause of friction between the Westerners and the Chinese was the lack of a proper institution in Beijing that could handle Western-style foreign relations. After the occupation of Beijing, when the British made it absolutely clear that they would no longer deal diplomatically with a provincial-level official, even if he carried the title of imperial commissioner, China added a new institution, the Zongli Yamen (Office of the General Administration of the Affairs of the Different Nations, or simply the Chinese Foreign Office), to the existing political edifice.

The Zongli Yamen. Established in 1861, the Zongli Yamen was staffed primarily by powerful members of the Grand Council. It was supposed to be a temporary agency, whose powers to deal with foreign diplomats would revert to the Grand Council as soon as the foreign crisis was over. Although a new institution, the Zongli Yamen was handicapped in its function because it had to fit into the old system of government communication and decision making. For example, memorials from senior provincial officials, even if they concerned foreign affairs, were still to be sent to the emperor. The Grand Council was then to make copies of these memorials and forward them to the Zongli Yamen. This lack of centralization of power did not affect the Zongli Yamen as long as the attitude of the government to the foreigners was conciliatory and as long as the power holders in the Grand Council were also the directors of Zongli Yamen.

Despite the original intention, the Zongli Yamen was never dispensed with, but with the passage of years its powers were severely diminished. Of its three original leaders, one died in 1862, Prince Gong came under attack from Empress Ci-xi, and the Grand Councilor Wen-xiang lacked the courage to stand up to the growing influence of the antiforeign clique. In the meantime, after the suppression of the Taiping rebellion, new regional power holders like Zeng Guo-fan and Li Hong-zhang gained tremendous political influence. After his appointment as governor-general of Zhili province in 1870, Li gradually took over many of the functions of the Zongli Yamen, and finally his personal office became the center for the conduct of foreign affairs. It was only in 1901, when China made a concerted effort to reorganize the government on Western lines, that a Ministry of Foreign Affairs was established.

The posting of resident ministers to Beijing by foreign powers physically confirmed the introduction of the new diplomatic order, but China still had some way to go before it could fully accept Western-style foreign relations. Apart from the audience question, China had yet to reach that stage of maturity when it could learn to use the new system to its own advantage by posting its own ambassadors abroad. But despite all its limitations, the Zongli Yamen did become a catalyst for change.

To carry out its duties (among them the supervision of the proper collection of maritime customs), the Yamen needed dependable translators and linguists. It immediately established two new subordinate institutions: the Inspectorate General of Customs and the College of Foreign Languages (Tong-wen Guan).

The Inspectorate General of Customs. When rebels occupied the Chinese city of Shanghai in 1853, the Chinese customs official fled. With no one around to collect maritime customs, the port of Shanghai became a tariff-free paradise for ten months. However, the British who handled the bulk of the China trade, were worried that demands for retrospective payments were sure to be made once Chinese authority returned to Shanghai. After giving some thought to this matter, the British consul, with the approval of the American and the French consuls and the Chinese authorities, established a foreign-managed customs service in 1854. This Foreign Inspectorate of Customs at Shanghai, headed by Horatio Nelson Lay and staffed at the top by foreigners, functioned as a "Chinese" customs office. Lay had given up his British consular service to become a Chinese employee.

This strange hybrid institution was later to play a significant role in China's modernization programs, but the impression cannot be avoided that it was basically a foreign device thrust on the Chinese, who had no substitute solution of their own for the unique situation created in Shanghai by the civil war. The foreigners in the service, though employees of Beijing, had extraterritorial standing and had fixed their own salaries at scales far higher than those received by the Chinese. The irony of the situation could not have been lost on anyone with the slightest sensitivity when Lay, who was fluent in Chinese, was "borrowed" by Lord Elgin in 1858 to accompany the British expedition as an interpreter. During the negotiations, Lay, the "loyal Chinese official," harangued the emperor's envoy and embarrassed him with information the British had gained from the Chinese archives captured in Guangzhou.

Even more ironic was the fact that when, under the Tianjin treaties and associated protocols, the Chinese agreed to the expansion of the foreign inspectorate of customs to all ports, Beijing promoted Lay to become the first Inspector General of Customs. He was confirmed in this post by the Zongli Yamen in 1861. The Chinese reasoning was that although Lay, "the most crafty of barbarians," had made a "great display of violence" in Tianjin to ingratiate "himself with the barbarian chief" (Lord Elgin), he was actually "grateful" to China for his "generous pay" and "looks out for smuggling for us, so in recent years barbarian customs have been three or four times as much as when the ports were opened."[10] An honest barbarian was preferable to the corrupt Chinese mandarins. The expanding customs revenues were absolutely indispensable to maintain an increasingly bankrupt government.

When Lay went on home leave in 1861, Robert Hart, who like Lay had left the British consular service in 1859 to become the assistant commissioner of customs at Guangzhou, was appointed acting inspector general. During his leave in England, Lay had been instructed to purchase a flotilla of ships for the Chinese navy. Because of the totally unacceptable manner in which he handled this affair, Lay was dismissed on his return to China in 1863. The 28-year-old Hart now replaced Lay and for the next 45 years administered the Customs Service as inspector general.

During his long tenure Hart established a model Western-style organization, but despite his personal loyalty to China, the service in many ways remained a foreign implant. Although Hart insisted that the Inspectorate of Customs was "a Chinese and not a Foreign Service" and that the foreigners "who take the pay and who are the servants of the Chinese Government" should not behave as superiors of the Chinese,[11] the foreigners remained elitists. By 1895 there were 700 Western and 3,500 Chinese employees in the Customs Service. However, few Chinese could ever hope to rise to the higher posts. Hart ran the organization as a one-man show. All the employees were responsible to him, and he alone was responsible to the Zongli Yamen. Hart, of course, cannot be blamed for this state of affairs. If the Qing government had had a positive national policy and greater confidence in its own officials, Hart could have been replaced by a Chinese as soon as one had been trained for the purpose.

After his office was shifted to Beijing in 1865, Hart became an even more trusted advisor of his superiors in the Zongli Yamen and played an important role in pushing for China's modernization. Like the great regional leader Li Hong-zhang, Hart got involved in China's diplomatic and reform efforts. He helped establish the Tong-wen Guan, helped to end the Sino-French war in 1885, pushed for the development of a Chinese navy in the 1880s, advocated the modernization of the traditional examination system (mathematics was added to the *ju-ren* degree examination in 1888), established the national postal service (1896), and helped popularize scientific and technical subjects through publications and exhibits.

That Hart was an effective intermediary between China and the West was recognized by the British government, which conferred knighthood on him in 1882 and three years later offered him the British ambassadorship to China (which he declined).

By 1895 Hart had begun to lose patience with the Manchu dynasty. Looking back in 1893 on the work he had done, or tried to do, in China, he said, "The country changes very slowly for the better, and most of what we do is merely to keep the tyre on the wheel." In 1895 his conclusion was, "I fear, as far as the dynasty is concerned, it is hopeless; in ten years time revolution will do the trick."[12] The revolution came in 16 years.

To sum up, the customs Service, apart from supporting the dynasty with dependable revenues (supplying 25 percent of the total central revenues in the 1890s and 34 percent in the early 1900s), became an important modern part of the Chinese government. It introduced the principle of central fiscal control (totally absent in traditional Chinese fiscal structure), which helped foster the concept of political unity. It also helped in promoting other modernization programs.

The Tong-Wen Guan and China's Foreign Service. Like the Customs Service, the Tong-wen Guan, the College of Foreign Languages, or Interpreters College as it was sometimes known, was also an institution in which the Westerners and the Chinese collaborated. When Prince Gong accepted the advice of foreigners, such as Hart, and established this college in 1862, he was doing no more than what was absolutely necessary to run the Zongli Yamen. Increasing contacts between the Zongli Yamen and the foreign governments meant that Beijing could no longer rely on the untrained Guangzhou "linguists" (whose English was often appalling) or on foreigners like Lay. The Tianjin treaties had stipulated that all British and French communications with Beijing would be in both English and French and that the texts in these languages would be held as authoritative. So Chinese translators were needed, but training language experts meant depending on foreign instructors. To silence critics of this policy, precedence was found in the early Qing employment of Jesuits for calendar making. And it was obviously easier to explain away the hiring of foreigners in the Customs Service, where they were not in a position to undermine the Confucian educational system.

The Tong-wen Guan hired foreign instructors to teach English, French, Russian, and German. In the beginning, since no self-respecting Confucian scholar would be caught dead studying a foreign language, the Manchu bannermen (often middle-aged), who were *ordered* to enroll at the college, proved to be indifferent students. In time the prestige of the institution improved as it became much more of a liberal arts college. Other subjects, such as science, astronomy, mathematics, and international law, were added to the curriculum, and the period of study was lengthened to eight years.

The growth and development of the Tong-wen Guan owed a special debt to W. A. P. Martin, an American missionary educator, who having served as an English instructor for some years, was appointed its president in 1869. He held the post until 1894. By 1873 the college had its own printing press, which made it easier for professors and students to publish the books they had translated or compiled. Among the books produced by the staff that can be considered helpful in introducing Western and international law to China were translations of Wheaton's *Elements of International Law, Code Napoleon,* Woolsey's *International Law,* and Bluntschli's *International Law.*

That Western international law could be used by the Chinese against the West itself was proved early when the Zongli Yamen used information gained from Wheaton's book (translated by Martin in 1863) to force the Prussians in 1864 to release the Danish "enemy" ships they had seized in Chinese "neutral" waters.

Other centers similar to the Tong-wen Guan were set up in Shanghai (1863), Guangzhou (1864), and Fuzhou (1866). By 1895 these institutions were supplying all of the interpreters for the Zongli Yamen and the legations abroad. And yet the impact of these schools on the Chinese educational system or on the attitude of the majority of the literati was virtually nil. The reasons for this are not hard to find. The traditional examination system, which attracted thousands of ambitious, bright men from all over the empire, had not changed its emphasis on Confucianism. It continued to produce a conservative, backward-looking intelligentsia, who would have agreed with Grand Secretary

Wo-ren's memorial of 1867, which stated in part that subjects such as astronomy and mathematics, introduced into the curriculum of the translation schools by barbarian teachers, were of little use in strengthening the nation. "From ancient down to modern times, your slave has never heard of anyone who could use mathematics to raise the nation from a state of decline."[13] His recommendation was that these studies be "abolished instantly," before the barbarians had an opportunity to undermine the loyalty of the Chinese multitudes to the dynasty.

Diplomatic Missions Abroad. Robert Hart, who had done so much to support the development of the Tong-wen Guan, was also eager that China establish its own diplomatic missions abroad. Chinese envoys in Western capitals could help defend China's national interests and, because of their firsthand experience of conditions in the West, help encourage China's modernization.

In 1866, when Hart was going on a six-month leave to Europe, he proposed to the Zongli Yamen that a Chinese official accompany him, in an informal capacity, primarily to see what the outside world looked like. Beijing agreed, and a delegation consisting of a 64-year-old, middle-ranking Manchu official, Pin-chun, and four students got an opportunity to visit London, Copenhagen, Stockholm, St. Petersburg, Berlin, and Paris. According to Morse, Pin-chun, though feted and well received in the various capitals,

> was disgusted with the discomforts of travel in countries whose customs he abhorred with all the dislike of a fossil and a Manchu. His tour was cut short and he was allowed to . . . . leave the scenes of mental disturbance created by steam and electricity, and of moral disturbance caused by the indecorum and bad manners everywhere manifest in his eyes. He produced no favorable impression of Chinese civilization, and he could have nothing favorable to report of the West; and his mission must be pronounced a failure.[14]

This failure did not dishearten Hart, who continued to advise the Zongli Yamen that China must discard her psychology of seclusion and send ambassadors to the capitals of the treaty powers, "to cultivate and conserve friendly relations by explaining to the Treaty Powers the many difficulties that China cannot fail to experience in attempting to change existing conditions; to bespeak forbearance and prevent [them from resorting] to hostile pressure to wring from China concessions for which the government did not as yet feel itself ready."[15]

The Zongli Yamen appreciated the value of Hart's advice (incidentally, he was not the only foreigner who was giving such advice). Fearing that hostile pressures might, indeed, be exerted on China when the treaties came up for revision in 1868, the Zongli Yamen consulted the leading statesmen concerning how far China should go in the modernization programs advocated by the powers. There were differences of opinion on matters such as greater freedom to the missionaries or the opening of railroads and mines, but it was generally agreed (the two most important officials, Zeng Guo-fan and Li Hong-zhang favored the proposal) that sending diplomatic missions abroad might be worth the effort.

In November 1867 the Zongli Yamen appointed the U.S. minister, Anson Burlingame, who was about to retire from his post in Beijing, to be China's ambassador-extraordinary to all the world capitals. A high rank was conferred on Burlingame, and he was made a Chinese civil servant. Using barbarians to serve China seemed to have become the mode. Obviously, to placate the jealousies of the other powers, an Englishman from the British embassy was commissioned as first secretary and a Frenchman from the Customs Service as the second secretary. A Manchu and a Han official, of the second civil rank, were appointed coenvoys, and they had an entourage of 30 secretaries and aides.

The mission left China in May 1868 and for all practical purposes ended in February 1870, when Burlingame died of pneumonia in St. Petersburg. In its 28 months abroad the mission visited Washington, London, Paris, Stockholm, Copenhagen, The Hague, Berlin, St. Petersburg, Brussels, and Rome, the last two under the headship of the Manchu Zhi-gang.

While in the United States Burlingame took it on himself to portray a "progressive" China, opening its arms wide to receive "the shining banners of Western civilization," welcoming the missionaries to "plant the shining cross on every hill and in every valley," and engaging engineers to open mines and build railways.[16] Burlingame's exaggerations shocked both the foreigners in China and the Chinese government, but he impressed his fellow citizens favorably. Forever afterward many Americans have been guilty of deceiving themselves with favorable, though false, images of China. Burlingame was certainly responsible for inspiring large numbers of missionaries to rush off to plant their shining crosses in China.

In Washington, Burlingame (without consulting Beijing) negotiated eight supplementary articles that revised the American Tianjin Treaty. These articles guaranteed China's territorial integrity; Chinese control over its internal trade; its right to construct railroads whenever it chose to do so; and the rights of Chinese in America and Americans in China to enjoy the freedoms of religion, residence, and travel. The articles also confirmed "the inalienable right of man to change his home and allegiance," which strengthened the position of American missionaries in China and made it easier to import cheap Chinese labor to America. That the clause was one-sided became evident when the Americans, feeling threatened by the numbers of Chinese entering California, passed laws discriminating against the Chinese, culminating in making them ineligible for American citizenship (1871).

The Chinese government ratified the Burlingame treaty because, despite Burlingame's portrayal of a China dying to Westernize (a picture most abhorrent to the Chinese leaders), he had presented China's case with passion, and the new clauses did strengthen Beijing's hand in dealing with the problems arising out of the revision of treaties. The Alcock Convention failed to be ratified partly because of Burlingame's mission.

In England the mission's success was limited. It got the British government to declare that as a matter of policy "unfriendly pressure would not be applied inconsistent with the independence and safety of China," as long as Britain could deal directly with Beijing and not the local authorities and as long as China abided by its treaty obligations. Paris agreed with the British stand. Burlingame's success in the other European capitals was even less spectacular. The mission achieved no long-term results.

Between 1870 and 1877, when China finally decided to establish diplomatic missions abroad, three further incidents took place to undermine the Chinese traditional world view. In 1873, the audience question was finally more or less settled when the Tong-zhi emperor, having come of age, had to receive the foreign ambassadors in audience, European style. Instead of kowtowing, the ministers, representing Britain, America, France, Russia, Holland, and Japan, bowed five times to the Son of Heaven. The question whether the emperor would continue to grant special or annual audiences remained unanswered because he died in 1875. The subtle suggestion of superiority, indicated in the manner in which the audience was held, was repeated in 1890 when the Guang-xu emperor came of age and the next set of audiences was granted. Only after the outbreak of the war with Japan in 1894 was the audience question finally put to rest. Foreign envoys were now received in a proper hall in the palace under a fully acceptable protocol.

The other two incidents were connected with the Tianjin massacre (1870) and the Margary affair (1875). On both these occasions diplomatic missions, if they can be dubbed such, were sent with letters of apology to Paris and London. The Chinese official, Guo Song-dao (1818–1891), who led the mission to London stayed on to become the first permanent Chinese diplomatic envoy to Britain and France (1877). China's entry into the world of diplomatic relations did not have an auspicious beginning. However, in 1878 a legation was opened in Washington, and by 1880 missions had been established in most European states and Japan.

The embassies were established hesitatingly and under strong foreign pressure. Many Chinese were reluctant to be appointed abroad, and even those who did accept the posts were often attacked upon their return for their changed attitude toward the world. For example, during his two years in London, Guo was converted to the idea that institutional reforms were a prerequisite to progress and that only with internal change would China be able to resist external aggression. His rational approach to European development and his non-Confucian recommendations for China's progress made him a target of attack by the conservatives in Beijing. When the Zongli Yamen decided to publish Guo's official diary, in which he had sketched the history of Western civilization, the critics managed to persuade the emperor to order the destruction of the printing blocks.

Between 1880 and 1896 China lost its tributary states; after its defeat in the Sino-Japanese War, China was at last relieved of its burden of superiority. Only then was it finally ready to enter the so-called family of nations. The irony is that to reach this stage it had to give up its own empire and recognize the legitimacy of the empires being established by Western nations; it had to give up its own sense of superiority and recognize the superiority of the West.

Western Knowledge, Self-Strengthening, and Reform Ideas

In the two decades that followed the First Anglo-Chinese War, little was done by the Beijing government to prepare for the next round of Western aggression. The reason was that officials (like Commissioner Lin Zexu) who had come in direct contact with Westerners for the first time in their lives could not dare to inform Beijing truthfully that the foreigners possessed some knowledge (e.g., science and technology) that was not available to the Chinese. To have done so would have made the barbarian Westerners superior to the Chinese, albeit in a limited sphere. Such an opinion would have been counter to the conscious policy of rejecting outside knowledge, and the holder of it would have become a traitor to Confucian China. The result was that although personally recognizing Western superiority in weapons and military techniques (in the face of defeat, it was impossible not to do so), the officials continued to belittle the "ocean barbarians" in their memorials to the emperor.

Even when it became an open secret that the Western military was superior to that of China, an attempt was made to separate guns and ships from the Western civilization and polity that had produced these instruments of aggression. This dichotomy marked the developments in China for the entire period until 1895.

However, some of the more thoughtful Chinese officials, even as early as 1839, felt that it was necessary to inquire into the sources of Western wealth and power. They were men of intellectual courage because they knew that they could be condemned for associating with the hated foreigners (from whom they got their information) and for subverting Confucianism with their new-fangled ideas.

During the two decades 1840–1860 that otherwise appear so barren, three Chinese officials prepared the ground for a better understanding of the world beyond China. Commissioner Lin was shocked into a new awareness when he saw how the Western steamers "came and went as they pleased," heedless of tide and wind, and how effective their fire power was. He realized that the "barbarians are superior in three ways: firstly, warships; secondly, firearms; and thirdly, methods of military training and discipline of soldiers."[17]

In an intelligent response to the new situation developing on the South China coast, Lin promptly after his arrival in Guangzhou began to gather information on the West through translations of materials selected from Western books and periodicials. The selections included excerpts from Murray's *Cyclopedia* and Vattel's *Law of Nations*. His observations and inquires led Lin to the conclusion that China should endeavor to become a modern maritime power by hiring British and American technicians to help build warships and train a naval force. Unlike the Japanese leaders of 1868, who made the search of "knowledge throughout the world" their national policy, Lin could not even give his advice openly. He could only convey his feelings in confidence to his closest friends. One of them, the official Wei Yuan, also received Lin's collected translations in 1841.

Wei Yuan (1794–1856), although a junior official working in the Grand Secretariat, was intensely interested in national affairs. China's defeat in 1842 led him to turn his attention to the problem of relations with Western powers. With the help of Lin's papers and other sources, Wei completed, within months of the signing of the Treaty of Nanjing, a political geography of foreign nations. The work appeared in 1844, under the title *Hai-guo tu-zhi* (*An illustrated Gazetteer of the Countries Overseas*). The book was revised and enlarged in 1847 and expanded again in 1852. The publication became popular in China and Japan and is said to have helped inspire Japan's modernization efforts.

Wei's compilation was rather uneven, a patchwork of translations not without errors, but it marked the beginning of a serious effort to seek knowledge of the world beyond China. Wei's work was acceptable because he put it in the context of China's traditional approach to barbarian management: "Use the barbarian to control the barbarian." However, he also implied that the superior technology of the Western barbarians should be learned to ward them off.

A far more scientifically accurate and scholarly work, which dealt with the nations of the world, their history, and their political and economic systems, was that of Xu Ji-yu (1795–1873). In the beginning, like Lin and other officials, Xu had little knowledge of the Westerners and, for example, readily believed that "their knees do not easily bend." But his postings in Fujian, Guangdong, and Guangxi from 1840 to 1851 (he was governor of Fujian, 1847–1851) brought him in contact with Westerners, and he developed a far more sophisticated attitude toward the West. Xu began researching his subject in 1843, taking the help of such foreigners as the American missionary David Abeel, and finished writing it in 1848. *Ying-huan zhi-lüeh* (*A Short Account of the Maritime Circuit*) was published in 1850.

Because of its objectivity, Xu's book challenged the premises of China's traditional view of the world and the absolute superiority of Chinese civilization. In a manner of speaking, Xu scored the emergence of a new international order and prompted China to secure its proper place in it by reforming its institutions and borrowing Western techniques. He was perhaps the first to employ the ancient Confucian term *self-strengthening* to indicate China's needed response to Western imperialism.

Like Lin and Wei, Xu was no traitor to Confucianism, but unlike them, he went far beyond guns and ships in his search for the sources of Western power. Because of his objectivity and his attempt at a sympathetic understanding of the West and because of his close relationship with the foreigners who supplied him information, Xu was reprimanded, demoted, and dismissed from service. Only after the 1860 debacle was Xu not only reinstated but also given posts in the Zongli Yamen and the Tong-wen Guan. His book, now printed by the government itself, became a standard work, read by every reformer into the twentieth century.

Although in the 1840s and 1850s, activities of officials like Lin, Wei, and Xu were marginal to the intellectual world of the Chinese literati, their importance lies in the fact that in the 1860s, when the need for knowledge of the West became apparent, the pioneering groundwork had already been laid. In this context the contribution made by the secular writings of Western missionaries (even though their Chinese language lacked elegance and style) was also significant. For example, three books in Chinese, Elijah Bridgman's *Brief History of the United States* and Karl Gutzlaff's *Illustrated Universal Geography* and *Universal History,* were available to Xu and the others.[18]

After the 1860 debacle the newly emerging provincial leaders began to absorb Western technology and science under the slogan Self-Strengthening. The expression *self-strengthening* (*zi-qiang*), used by Xu Ji-yu, was made popular by the official Feng Gui-fen, who at one time or another worked with or had come in contact with Lin Ze-xu, Zeng Guo-fan, and Li Hong-zhang. Feng posed the question "Why are [the Western countries] small and yet strong? Why are we large and yet weak?"[19] And his answer was that China must master Western science and technology to gain the prosperity and strength of the Western nations.

In the aftermath of the 1860 war and with the establishment of the Zongli Yamen and the Tong-wen Guan, leaders like Prince Gong, Zeng Guo-fan, and Li Hong-Zhang had little difficulty in accepting the need to acquire Western arms. Indeed, the provincial leaders had already bought Western arms to suppress the rebellions. But now their goal was self-sufficiency, so they began to buy Western machinery to manufacture arms. With foreign technical help, arsenals and shipyards were established in quick succession: the Jiangnan arsenal at Shanghai under Zeng's sponsorship (1865), Fuzhou shipyard under Zuo Zong-tang (1866), and Nanjing arsenal under Li Hong-zhang (1867).

Zeng acquired the machinery for the Jiangnan arsenal from America, using a Chinese Yale graduate, Yung Wing, as his agent. The arsenal soon became one of the biggest industrial units of its type in the whole world, constructing steamships, cannons, guns, and ammunition. By 1872, the year Zeng passed away, the Jiangnan arsenal had produced five steam-powered gun boats (the last of 400 horsepower) and other sundry arms. The arsenal also had a translation bureau and a technical school attached to it. The head foreigner employed in the translation bureau was an Englishman, John Fryer, who by 1896 had helped produce over a hundred translations of books on mathematics, military affairs, navigation, engineering, chemistry, physics, medicine, law, and political economy.

The Fuzhou shipyard, set up with the help of two Frenchmen, also had an arsenal and a technical school. By 1874, 15 ships had been built at the naval yard, most of them of 150 horsepower.

More than most other officials, Li Hongzhang realized that China needed to progress much faster, not only in the manufacture of arms but also in communications and modern economic enterprises. From 1870 to 1895, as governor-general of Zhili province posted to Tianjin, Li was the preeminent statesman in the empire (particularly after the death of Zeng in 1872). His efforts, or patronage, led to many significant self-strengthening developments in various fields.

To prepare the Chinese to officer modern naval and army units, naval and military academies were established by 1885 and trainees sent to England, France, and Germany to study military tactics, shipbuilding, and navigation. Between 1872 and 1881, under the care of Yung Wing, 120 young boys were sent to schools in the United States to acquire Western knowledge.

In the realm of transportation and communications the China Merchants' Steam Navigation Company (CMSNC), established in 1872, ran commercial ships between the northern and southern ports and to Japan, the Phillippines, and Singapore; telegraph and railways were inaugurated in 1881. Coal mines to supply the fuel for the ships and railways were opened in Kaiping in 1877.

Heavy industry was introduced with iron mines and iron works (1889–1890) and light industry with cotton mills, textile factories, paper mills, and match companies (all between 1885 and 1895).

Although the list of enterprises looks impressive (many Westerners were impressed enough to believe that China would win the 1894 war), the achievements were disappointing. The arsenals could not keep up with the improvements in arms in the West, and as the cost of building ships became excessively heavy, it was found advisable to buy, from abroad, more advanced ships of greater tonnage and better guns. The Fuzhou shipyard (built with French help) and ten Chinese naval vessels were destroyed by the French in the war of 1884–1885, and the shipyard never fully recovered from the blow. Fryer's translations were read by very few, and as he himself said, they never came "into general notice." The educational mission to the United States was withdrawn five years before its completion because the Chinese boys had become too Americanized and had lost their own culture. The CMSNC did well enough to buy out the competing American firm of Russell and Co. in 1877 and increase its fleet to 31 ships, but thereafter it stagnated because of corrupt practices and lost its edge over the British coastal lines. Similarly, the Kaiping Mining Company, which did well until 1892, fell into debt and was taken over by a British company in 1900. After 1896, foreign industries began to be established in treaty ports on the basis of the privileges granted to the Japanese at the conclusion of the Sino-Japanese War.

Reasons for Failure. As Jonathan Spence has put it, "The 'self-strengthening' movement never really took off; indeed, it was more a succession of experiments than a movement. The various projects undertaken . . . remained isolated phenomena."[20] The authority and resources of the central government had become severely limited. Besides, Beijing had neither the understanding nor the vision that could have compelled it to play the unifying role necessary to coordinate a national program of modernization. A representative example of this situation can be seen in the development of the Imperial Navy after the Fuzhou shipyard was destroyed by the French. A Naval Yamen (Board of Admiralty) was created in 1885, presumably to centralize the four regional fleets. The centralization did not take place. Li Hong-zhang, who was more interested in building up the northern navy (the Beiyang fleet), which was under his command, ensured his dominant position in the Naval Yamen by diverting 36 million taels of the naval funds to the empress dowager for the building of a new summer palace. When the war with Japan came, Li's navy was short of ammunition for the heavy guns (some of the torpedoes were filled with scrap iron instead of gunpowder because of corrupt officials); the admiral could not communicate with the British master-gunner; the southern navy would not spare ships for the war; and after the Japanese had captured all the ships at Weihaiwei, the captain of a ship from the Guangdong fleet, caught in the war, pleaded that he be allowed to leave with his ship because his squadron had not taken part in the war.[21]

The regional officials, who promoted modernization efforts, were required to receive central permission for their projects, but in practice the efforts remained personal, leading to personal aggrandizement. The rivalries between regional power holders and the system of overlapping bureaucratic authority made it impossible for the center to coordinate even defense activities.

Most of the funds for industrial enterprises had to be raised locally by the regional officials. The result was joint official-merchant undertakings, the officials supervising the operation and the merchants providing the bulk of the capital. The system came to be known as *guan-du shang-ban* (Official Supervision and Merchant Management). The grafting of traditional bureaucratic practices onto modern industrial and commercial ventures was bound to lead to failure; officials, themselves Confucian generalists, could not foster functional specialization (there was excessive dependence on foreign experts; incidentally, the Communists would find themselves in the same predicament in the 1980s and the 1990s); nepotism brought inefficient operators into the system; and official exactions and other corrupt practices siphoned off profits and kept them from being plowed back into the enterprise. According to Albert Feuerwerker, "the *guan-du shang-ban* industries remained marginal undertakings within their own environment. Their establishment and operation did not represent a fundamental break with traditional agrarian economy and the conservative economic outlook that reflected it . . . [the lesson to be drawn is that] one institutional breakthrough is worth a dozen textile mills or shipping companies established within the framework of the traditional society and its system of values."[22]

Some scholars have found the cause for China's failure at industrialization in the unhealthy relationship between the government (as represented by the regional officials) and the merchants, which constrained the development of free enterprise. But this in itself is not necessarily true. Some of the most rapidly developing economies in the world today are in countries where the government's relations with the industrial sector are close (e.g., Japan, Taiwan, and Singapore). Indeed, the Chinese failure may be seen as resulting from the absence of a strong central government that could lead and guide economic growth.

Changing Intellectual Environment. Despite the failures already mentioned, China by 1895 had established the beginnings of an industrial base (mostly in the treaty ports along the coast). As a consequence, new technical and working classes emerged. What is perhaps even more important, the trend hesitatingly set by Lin Ze-xu, Wei Yuan, and Xu Ji-yu now spread to Confucian scholars who had not even gained official status. In other words, political developments and loss of central authority had made it possible for some literati to become involved with foreign matters.

Although their number was small, scholars like Kang You-wei and Liang Qi-chao rose to national prominence after 1895. Their education and lives before 1895 show how the intellectual environment was already changing under the old regime.

Kang You-wei (1858–1927), who came from a family of scholars in a village near Guangzhou, received formal Confucian education in his youth. However, he failed to pass the *ju-ren* examination in 1876. Shortly thereafter, for personal reasons, he temporarily turned away from classical education to study Daoism and Buddhism. His new scholarship inspired him to such a degree that he considered becoming a "sage" and working for the salvation of the world. In his preparation to reach sagehood, he read books on history and geography and gained an interest in the West. He visited Hong Kong and Shanghai, read translations by the missionary press and the Jiangnan arsenal, and became a student of Western civilization.

In 1888, following the Chinese failure in the Sino-French War (1884–1885), which disturbed him very much, Kang wrote a memorial to the emperor urging reforms in the administration; the memorial from such a humble source naturally never reached the emperor. In 1891 Kang founded a school in Guangzhou, where apart from the classical subjects, he taught Western learning and other modern subjects such as mathematics and military drill. It was during this time that Kang began to study the Han *gu-wen* (old text) classics (the basis of orthodox Confucian education) critically and to assail their authenticity. He developed theories to prove that Confucius and Confucian classics, when culled of forgeries, encouraged political reform. His book dealing with forgeries raised a storm of protest and was banned in 1894. Kang, wanting to legitimize reform within the framework of Confucian ideology, refused to give up his efforts and produced another controversial book, *Confucius as a Reformer,* in 1897.

In 1893 Kang passed the *ju-ren* examination and in 1895 gained the final degree of *jin-shi.* On hearing of China's acceptance of the humiliating terms ending the Sino-Japanese War, Kang got 1,200 imperial examination candidates to sign a petition urging the government to reject the treaty and carry on the war. Kang followed up the Candidates Memorial, which had had no effect on the government, with two other memorials recommending a systematic program of administrative, economic, military, and educational reform. In mid-1895 Kang, along with his student Liang Qi-chao, established the Society for the Study of National Strengthening (*Qiang-xue hui*) and a newspaper associated with it. Because of the opposition and hostility that his activities had created, the *Qiang-xue hui* was proscribed in 1896 and Kang was forced to leave Beijing and withdraw to Guangzhou. Although Kang's early efforts to change China failed, he gained a national reputation that helped him later to become the leader of the reform movement in China.

Liang Qi-chao (1873–1929), also from Guangdong province, was instructed in Confucian classics from the age of 4 or 5 and became a *ju-ren* at the age of 16. In 1890 on his way back from Beijing, where he had gone to take the *jin-shi* examination (which he failed), he passed through Shanghai and bought a copy of Xu's geography and other translations. Later in the same year Liang met Kang You-wei and became his student. On Liang's urging Kang set up his school in Guangzhou. Here, where Liang heard Kang's lectures, in which he took "Western affairs for comparison and illustration,"[23] Liang gained an opportunity to air his own views as an instructor beginning in 1893.

In 1895 Liang helped Kang draft the Candidates Memorial and served the reform movement as secretary to the Society for the Study of National Strengthening. Later Liang became one of the most active spokespersons for progress and radical reform in China.

While discussing the failures of the self-strengthening movement, students of Chinese history often fail to see that in the realm of ideas, Chinese scholars had already begun to probe Western political, economic, and social institutions and the civilization that lay behind them and to seek ways of using this information to renovate China. Such progressive, reform-minded scholars were few and their understanding of the West was limited, but their influence, in the long run, would far outweigh their numerical strength.

NOTES

1. See Irwin Hyatt, "Protestant Missions in China, 1877–1890," *Papers on China* (East Asia Center, Harvard University), no. 17 (1963), 67–100.

2. Edmund S. Wehrle, *Britain, China, and the Anti-Missionary Riots, 1891–1900* (Minneapolis: University of Minnesota Press, 1966), pp. 29–30.

3. Ibid., p. 91.

4. British Public Record Office, F.O. 881/7118.

5. Marquis Zeng to the French Foreign Office, quoted in Henry McAleavy, *Black Flags in Vietnam* (New York: Macmillan, 1968), p. 184.

6. Quoted in Lloyd E. Eastman, *Throne and Mandarins* (Cambridge, MA: Harvard University Press, 1967), p. 211.

7. See McAleavy, *Black Flags*, p. 164.

8. T. C. Lin, "Li Hung-chang: His Korean Policies, 1870–1885." *The Chinese Social and Political Science Review*, 19 (1935), p. 214.

9. Stuart R. Schram, *The Political Thought of Mao Tse-tung* (New York: Praeger, 1963), p. 375.

10. Earl Swisher, *China's Management of the American Barbarians* (New Haven, CT: Yale University Press, 1953), p. 522.

11. Harley F. MacNair, *Modern Chinese History: Selected Readings* (Shanghai: Commercial Press, 1923), pp. 384–85.

12. J. K. Fairbank et al., eds., *The I.G. in Peking*, vol. 1 (Cambridge, MA: Harvard University Press, 1975), pp. 18–19.

13. S. Y. Teng and John K. Fairbank, *China's Response to the West: A Documentary Survey, 1839–1923* (Cambridge, MA: Harvard University Press, 1965), pp. 52–53.

14. H. B. Morse, *The International Relations of the Chinese Empire*, vol. II (London: Longmans Green, 1910), p. 186.

15. Ibid., pp. 190–91.

16. Ibid., p. 195.

17. See Gideon Chen, *The Pioneer Promoters of Modern Industrial Techniques in China*, Part I (New York: Paragon, 1968), p. 5.

18. For an excellent treatment of Xu Ji-yu, see Fred W. Drake, *China Charts the World: Hsu Chi-yu and His Geography of 1848* (Cambridge, MA: Harvard University Press, 1975).

19. Teng and Fairbank, *China's Response to the West*, pp. 52–53.

20. Jonathan Spence, *To Change China* (Boston: Little, Brown, 1969), p. 154.

21. See John L. Rawlinson, "China's Failure to Coordinate Her Modern Fleets in the Late Nineteenth Century," in Albert Feuerwerker et al., eds., *Approaches to Modern Chinese History* (Berkeley: California University Press, 1967), p. 130.

22. Albert Feuerwerker, *China's Early Industrialization* (Cambridge, MA: Harvard University Press, 1958), p. 242.

23. Quoted in Chi-yun Chen, "Liang Ch'i-ch'ao's Missionary Education," *Harvard Papers on China*, no. 15 (1962), 80.

CHAPTER 4

China Turns to Revolution: 1895–1911

The last 16 years of the Manchu dynasty, 1895–1911, witnessed hectic political activity. China's humiliating defeat by Japan precipitated a series of aggressive actions by the imperialist powers that reduced China to a semicolony and parceled up its territory as separate spheres of influence. This development in turn led to national movements for reform and revolution, culminating in the 1911 revolution and the establishment of the first Chinese Republic.

THE IMPERIALIST RAPE OF CHINA: 1895–1898

Despite their victories in China the Western powers had treated it with a certain amount of respect, but China's defeat at the hands of a small Asian nation changed their attitude drastically. Fearful that the Manchu dynasty was on the verge of collapse, the powers vied with one another to exact as many concessions as possible from the Beijing government. To a certain degree their behavior in China reflected their views of how the Treaty of Shimonoseki had altered the balance of power in East Asia.

Russia, itself interested in the warm-water harbor of Port Arthur on the Liaodong Peninsula, could not tolerate the idea of its acquisition by Japan. With the help of Germany and France, Russia forced Japan to renounce possession of Liaodong for an additional indemnity of 30 million taels. Although some Chinese viewed this as a friendly Russian action, Russia was only maneuvering to keep Japan out of what the Russians considered their area of strategic interest.

Until the Sino-Japanese War, China had borrowed little from abroad, but now her reserves were totally depleted. To finance the war China had to borrow 4.635 million pounds sterling from the British Hong Kong and Shanghai Bank. After the war it faced an indemnity of 230 million taels (about 23 million pounds). With an annual revenue of 89 million taels, China was in no position to pay the indemnity without borrowing heavily from abroad. Countries wanting to dominate Beijing and also to profit financially from the transaction rushed to lend money to the bankrupt government. In 1895 the Russians, who had just proved their "disinterested" friendship for China, were anxious to keep China from becoming indebted to Britain. They loaned Beijing 400 million francs (15.8 million pounds) through a Franco-Russian syndicate, due in 36 years and secured against customs revenues. In 1896 an Anglo-German consortium of banks loaned 16 million pounds, also for 36 years. It, too, was secured against customs revenues. Two years later an Anglo-German syndicate of bankers advanced another 16 million pounds for 45 years. This loan was secured against customs revenues and internal transit taxes. China's dependable revenues were now under foreign control; China was not to escape this foreign financial grip until the establishment of the Communist government in 1949.

In 1896, during his visit to Russia to represent China at the coronation of Czar Nicholas II, Li Hong-zhang signed a secret defense treaty with Russia, providing for joint Sino-Russian resistance to any Japanese aggression. (There is every reason to believe that he was heavily bribed by the Russians.) In return, China allowed the Russian trans-Siberian railway to cut across Manchuria to reach Vladivostok. Theoretically, the China segment of the railroad, later known as the Chinese Eastern Railway, was under the joint control of the two countries operating through a Sino-Russian bank; in fact, since the Chinese did not contribute their share of the capital, the railroad was operated by the Russians and gave the Russians an opportunity to extend their political and economic influence into Manchuria. The treaty gave them "absolute and exclusive right of administration" over the lands granted to the railroad, and they could move troops and munitions without interference. When the details of the treaty leaked out, the Japanese were naturally infuriated and stepped up their military preparations. The Chinese Eastern Railway was completed in 1904. The Russo-Japanese War followed in 1905.

France and Germany, the other two members of the Triple Alliance that had caused Japan to evacuate Liaodong, expected to be as well rewarded as Russia. In 1895 France secured extensive territorial and commercial concessions in Yunnan, Guangxi, and Guangdong, provinces bordering French-controlled Vietnam. The French gained mining rights in these provinces and, in 1896, a concession to construct a railroad from the border of Vietnam into Guangxi. China also agreed to the nonalienation of Hainan to any other power.

In 1896, as part of the treaty settlement, Japan had gained "most favored nation" status and the right to establish industries in treaty ports (all other powers automatically gained the same right). The immediate result was that within a year the British had established two cotton mills and a flour mill in Shanghai, the Americans a cotton mill, the Japanese a textile and a flour mill, and the Germans a cotton mill.

In February 1897 the British countered the French move in the south by gaining concessions in Yunnan and the right to extend Burmese railways into that province (which later proved to be futile).

However, the big "scramble for concessions" began after the Germans, using the pretext of the murder of two German missionaries (who had been killed along with many Chinese by bandits and not by anti-foreign or anti-Christian mobs) in Shandong, occupied Jiaozhou Bay and the city of Qingdao in November 1897. Here was an example of the blatant use of military force to gain imperialistic ends. When China appealed to the other powers to intervene, Russia and France backed Germany and England remained neutral. European international law, which China had been asked to study so assiduously, was relevant only to those who were not militarily weak. In March 1898 China signed a convention that gave Germany a 99-year lease on Jiaozhou Bay and exclusive rights to build railroads and to open mines in Shandong. Thus Germany had gained lease territory and a sphere of exclusive influence where it could invest capital in building railroads and opening mines. Other powers followed suit.

Within three days of the German convention Russia secured a 25-year lease of Port Arthur and Dalian (on the Liaodong Peninsula, which only three years earlier they had "saved" from Japanese occupation) and the right to build a railroad to connect Dalian with Harbin. France promptly demanded and received a 99-year lease of Guangzhou Bay, the right to build a railway from Tonkin to Kunming, and the nonalienation of territories bordering Vietnam. The British, not to be outdone, compelled Beijing to open inland waters to foreign steamers and to declare that the Yangtze valley would not be alienated to any other power. The British also gained a 99-year lease of land adjacent to Kowloon (New Territories), a lease on the port of Weihaiwei for as long as the Russians held Port Arthur, and concessions to build 2,800 miles of railroads. Japan got Beijing to declare that Fujian, the province opposite Japan-held Taiwan, would not be alienated to any other power and thus made it Japan's sphere of influence.

By the end of 1898 it appeared that China was about to be dismembered. Even though this did not happen, it was clear that China's sovereignty had been seriously impaired. A helpless, impotent Manchu government had allowed the foreigners to slice the country into spheres of influence. The foreign missionaries, who had entered the interior of China propagating a foreign religion and spreading foreign ideas, were now joined by their compatriots, who were going to invest capital to exploit China's natural wealth, administer and control China's railroads, and sail their commercial vessels in all the major waterways of China. They were protected, of course, by extraterritoriality and consular gunboats.

The only country that did not participate in the looting of China was the United States; it was busy in 1898 conquering the Philippines. Only one country, Italy, was refused a concession when it joined the scramble and, in 1899, asked for port facilities in Zhejiang.

REFORMERS AND REACTIONARIES: 1895–1898

Shocked by their defeat to Japan and the imperialist activities that followed in its wake, many Chinese, including some who had attacked Kang You-wei for his radical ideas, now agreed that only major political and institutional changes could save China. From 1895 there was significant open public discussion of national issues. Kang's Candidates Memorial of 1895 had shown how the literati, otherwise steeped in Confucian ideas, could respond to a national crisis and think in terms of change.

Societies promoting the study of ways and means to strengthen the nation, *qiang-xue hui,* were established by reform-minded scholars in various provinces. For the first time privately published periodicals appeared within China (a dozen or so Chinese-language newspapers and periodicals already existed in the treaty ports, run by Chinese businesspersons or missionaries) and began to circulate new ideas. Interestingly provincial governors-general often financed these activities. By 1901 there were about 120 newspapers and periodicals.

Even the young Guang-xu emperor had become interested in learning more about world affairs. When he reached the age of majority in 1889, theoretically the empress dowager handed over the reins of power to him. In fact she still wielded enormous influence because the emperor was her son through adoption, had to refer to her as his Imperial Father, and could not go against her wishes. She had forced him to marry her niece. Moreover, Ci-xi commanded the loyalty of a large number of bureaucrats who owed their position to her patronage. So the imperial court came to be split between those who wanted to strengthen the hands of the emperor and those who still relied on the Old Buddha.

After 1895 Guang-xu's tutor, Weng Tong-he, concurrently appointed grand councilor (1894), member of the Zongli Yamen (1895), and associate grand secretary (1897), realized the necessity for reforms and began to introduce the emperor to books on world history and other Western subjects. Thus the emperor's faction came to be associated with reform and Ci-xi's with conservatism.

The most ardent and active reformers were Kang You-wei, Liang Qi-chao, and Tan Si-tong. They were helped, of course, by the writings and ideas of many others, like Yan Fu, Wang Tao, and the missionary Timothy Richard. Kang's first efforts in establishing study societies in Beijing and Shanghai and a periodical in Beijing came to naught when the empress dowager ordered the emperor to proscribe his society and the magazine in 1896. In the same year she also terminated Weng's tutorship of the emperor.

But because of his high office, Weng still had access to the emperor, and because of the heightened imperialist activity, the "hunger for [new] knowledge" (as Liang Qi-chao later put it) could not be suppressed by the conservatives. By 1897 study circles and clubs, on *qiang-xue hui* lines, were established in Zhili, Hubei, Hunan, Guangxi, Shaanxi, and Shanghai. Among the 25 periodicals that began publication between 1896 and 1898, Kang's periodical *Shiwu Bao* (*Contemporary Affairs*) in Shanghai, Yan Fu's *Guowen Bao* (*National News*) in Tianjin, and *Xiangxue Xin Bao* (*New Hunan Study Journal;* later the *Hunan Study Journal*) played leading roles. The articles in these journals introduced ideas on modernization and reform, going so far as to suggest a constitutional monarchy for China.

Of the provincial governors-general and governors, most were conservative, and even those like Li Hong-zhang and Zhang Zhi-dong, who advocated self-strengthening, trimmed their sails according to the changing winds in the capital; if the empress dowager's party was in the ascendancy, they withdrew their support from the reformers and their activities. Only the Governor of Hunan took an active personal interest in reform and encouraged study circles, schools, and magazines that propagated reform ideas. The School of Contemporary Affairs was established in Changsha in 1897, and Liang Qi-chao and Tan Si-tong were invited to teach there. In 1898 the Southern Study Society (*Nanxue hui*) was established in Changsha with branches in every county. The society brought new ideas to the people through a wide-ranging lecture series. Thus Hunan became a center for reform and revolution, maintaining that position through the first half of the twentieth century.

The reformers were mostly junior officials or higher-ranking gentry. By 1897 Kang You-wei, Liang Qi-chao, and Tan Si-tong had emerged as their national leaders. To a lesser or greater extent they were all influenced by Yan Fu. The background of Kang and Liang was introduced in the last chapter; however, more needs to be said about Tan Si-tong and Yan Fu.

Tan Si-tong (1865–1898) was born into a Hunanese gentry family (his father was governor of Hubei from 1890 to 1898), but because of his unhappy family circumstances, he followed an unorthodox path to education and a bureaucratic career. He read widely and traveled extensively for ten years, visiting historical places and tombs of China's past heroes in many provinces. By 1894 Tan had begun to study Western knowledge. In 1895 he was inspired by Kang's memorial and Kang's reform ideas, and he met Liang. In 1897 he went with Liang to Hunan, at the invitation of the progressive provincial governor, to help run the School of Contemporary Affairs. Later the same year he became editor of the *New Hunan Study Journal* and chairperson of the Southern Study Society.

Tan was a poet and an essayist of considerable merit. However, his most important work, as far as the reform movement is concerned, was a book entitled *A Study of Benevolence* (*Ren-xue*), in which he denounced Confucian values and expressed the need for Chinese to "break out of all entangling nets" (bureaucratism, formalistic Confucian teachings, authoritarian government, and Confucian family and social relations) so that knowledge could be sought throughout the world. He was the most forthright advocate of Westernization. He spoke of the "beauty and perfection of Western legal systems and political institutions."[1]

Yan Fu (1853–1921) came from a respectable scholar-gentry family in Fujian. His father's death in 1866 left the family in dire straits and brought to a sudden end Yan Fu's classical education and preparation for a bureaucratic career. In 1867 Yan Fu, then 14 years old, was admitted as a student in the newly opened naval school attached to the Fuzhou shipyard. After his graduation he was sent to study at Greenwich Naval College, England, from 1877 to 1879. On his return he taught at various naval academies and later became the president of Beijing University.

Yan Fu was one of the few Chinese who had mastered a foreign language (English in his case) and is best known for his translations of Western works. In the hectic days of the reform movement, Yan Fu was posted at the naval academy of Tianjin. He wrote a number of articles of current interest on subjects such as "Radical Changes in the World" and "How to Make China Strong." In his periodical *National News* he not only covered domestic and foreign news but also published translations of articles from the foreign press. But his biggest contribution to the reform movement was his translation of Thomas Huxley's *Evolution and Ethics,* which was serialized in the *National News* and later published in book form in 1898.

This was the first translation of a serious Western theoretical work into Chinese by a Chinese. Yan's translation became very popular, and the book went through a number of printings. Huxley's application of Darwin's evolutionary theories to human societies led to the concept of social Darwinism: that societies existed in mutual competition, that they engaged in a struggle for survival in which only the strongest survived and the weak were eliminated, and that in the process the strongest and the most self-assertive tended to trample on the weak. These ideas caught the imagination of the Chinese reformers because they helped explain the dismemberment of China and also provided support to the reformers' thesis that the survival of China as a nation depended entirely on its capacity to adapt itself to changing circumstances and to make itself fit and strong.

Yan Fu said that developments similar to those that China had witnessed from 1860 to 1895, ranging from the creation of the Foreign Office (Zongli Yamen) to the construction of steamships and railways, had served as the foundation on which European states had built their strength and power. But these developments had failed to produce the desired effect in China because the Chinese were backward-looking and lacked the concept of progress. The Westerners struggled "in the present in order to supersede the past" and consider "*that daily progress should be endless*" (emphasis added).[2]

Although Yan Fu exerted a profound influence on the reformers, particularly on Liang Qi-chao, he was not directly associated with their activities; as far as action is concerned, he remained outside the mainstream of the reform movement. When the movement failed, he carried on his work of introducing the West to China by producing Chinese translations of John Stuart Mill's *On Liberty and Logic,* Herbert Spencer's *Study of Sociology,* and Adam Smith's *The Wealth of Nations.*

The Year of Great Reforms: 1898

In 1897, when the Germans forcibly occupied Jiaozhou Bay and the powers began to "scramble for concessions," it appeared that Kang You-wei's predictions had proved correct. He had warned in one of his 1895 memorials that the Sino-Japanese War had "opened the door to the partition of China by the powers. . . . The danger facing our country has never been so great as it is today."[3]

Before 1897 ended Kang sent his fifth memorial to the emperor, in which he used harsh language to warn that if reforms were not made, China would disappear as a nation and the emperor and his ministers might not even be able "to live the life of commoners."[4] Kang recommended three plans, the best being that the Guang-xu emperor follow the example of Peter the Great of Russia and the Meiji emperor of Japan to initiate reforms, preferably using the Japanese model. The memorial was not forwarded to the emperor, but Kang was asked to defend his case before a panel of high officials that included Weng Tong-he (January 24, 1898). His basic defense was to raise the question: When the ancestors' homeland was lost, who would remain to follow the ancestors' way?

The next day Weng Tong-he reported the discussion to the emperor and recommended that he grant an audience to Kang. But conservative officials again managed to sabotage the meeting, and Kang was asked instead to send his proposals and his books on Japan and Russia for the emperor's perusal. Kang did so and presented the emperor with a wide range of recommendations that touched on almost every aspect of political life in China.

In April Kang established the Protect the Country Society (*Bao-guo-hui*), whose constitution aimed at drawing together like-minded people to protect China's sovereignty, territorial integrity, and racial independence through selective political and economic reforms. The society was to have head offices in Beijing and Shanghai and branches in the provinces and the counties. The first signs of patriotism and nationalism were becoming evident in the younger members of the scholar-gentry-bureaucratic class, among whom it also became fashionable to talk of reform. But pro-Ci-xi conservative officials, particularly some high-ranking Manchus, still had the power to attack the reformers and suggest that they wanted to save China at the expense of the Qing dynasty and that, in any case, the reformers were men of little consequence who arrogantly talked of such big issues as saving China. Because of these pressures, the Protect the Country Society soon ceased its activities.

Meanwhile, despite these developments, the 27-year-old emperor's imagination was fired by Kang's writings, which he reread several times, and he decided to become another Meiji emperor. On June 11 the emperor issued an addict expressing his resolution that Chian embark on a reform program:

> . . . Those who claim to be Conservative patriots consider that all the old customs should be upheld and the new ideas repudiated without compromise. Such querulous opinions are worthless. Consider the needs of the times and the weakness of our Empire! If we continue to drift with an army untrained, our revenues disorganized, our scholars ignorant, and our artisans without technical training, how can we possibly hope to hold our own among the nations. . . . The virtuous rulers of remote antiquity did not cling obstinately to existing needs, but were ready to accept change, even as one wears grass-cloth garments in summer and furs in winter.
>
> We now issue this special Decree so that all our subjects, from the Imperial family downwards, may hereafter exert themselves in the cause of reform. . . .[5]

Kang was finally summoned to an audience on June 16, 1898. The meeting was exceptionally long, and Kang is reported to have urged the sympathetic emperor to break through the barrier of conservatism surrounding him by appointing vigorous lower officials to carry out the program and by not throwing open the contents of the program for discussion among the senior officials, "who may refuse to put it into effect."

Before long the emperor also met with Liang and Tan Si-tong. Kang, Liang, and Tan were given posts in Beijing. Although the posts were not senior positions, the incumbents were granted permission to memorialize the emperor directly. On the basis of proposals and memorials submitted by Kang and his colleagues, the emperor issued decree after decree ordering the remaking of China. In 103 days 110 imperial edicts were issued, leading to the term *Hundred Days of Reform.*

The new order envisaged a changed examination system that would deal with practical subjects, subjects of contemporary interest, and economics; a new hierarchical school system that would include Western disciplines along with Chinese subjects; conversion of shrines and temples into schools; sending students abroad for study; encouragement of inventions; encouragement of a free press and freedom of the citizens to address the emperor; encouragement of agriculture, industry, and commerce by the establishment of specialized bureaus, specialized schools, trade journals, and chambers of commerce; government sponsorship of railroads and mining; inauguration of a nationwide postal service; rationalization and simplification of the bureaucracy and abolition of sinecure posts; centralization of the fiscal system; modernization and enlargement of the land and naval forces and standardization of the defense industry; and abolition of state allowances for Manchu bannermen.

These reforms covered almost every aspect of China's political, economic, military, educational, and cultural life; if carried out they would have radically changed China. Kang also urged that a constitutional monarchy be established and a national assembly convened, but the emperor did not issue a decree on that subject.

In early September the emperor dismissed certain high officials for obstructing the implementation of reforms. For the same reason he ordered Li Hong-zhang not to attend the Zongli Yamen. This act made the diehard conservatives and Manchu grandees in sinecure posts even more fearful of the emperor and his reforms. They had already been pressuring the empress dowager to intercede on their behalf when, on September 14, the edict stipulating that bannermen earn their own living was issued; the Manchu emperor had obviously turned against his own people. Ci-xi, however, recommended patience to the agitated Manchu grandees.

The emperor, aware of the danger he was in, accepted Kang's advice that he seek the active support of Yuan Shi-kai, the head of the New Army (with perhaps the best troops available in the country), which was in the Metropolitan province (Zhili province). The easiest way to neutralize Ci-xi was to have Yuan eliminate Ronglu, her close confidant and trusted lieutenant. Ci-xi had arranged to have Ronglu posted as governor-general of Zhili and commander of the Northern Armies, which included Yuan's force. The emperor summoned Yuan to an audience on September 16 and promoted him to the honorary rank of vice-president of one of the six boards and placed him in charge of army training. On the eighteenth Tan Si-tong called on Yuan, informed him of the threat to Emperor Guang-xi, and asked him to join the plot against Ci-xi to save His Majesty. Yuan is reported to have said that "killing Ronglu would be as easy as killing a dog."

But Yuan betrayed the plot to Ronglu, who warned the empress dowager. Ci-xi acted swiftly. In a countercoup she seized the emperor on September 21, 1898, and put him under house arrest. An edict was issued in the emperor's name in which he said that Her Majesty had graciously answered his prayer and "condescended . . . to administer the government." The emperor, who spent the rest of his days in close confinement, never forgave Yuan Shi-kai for having betrayed him, and it is said that his last words to his brothers before he died were that they should take revenge on the traitor. Thus ended the great promise of a China revolutionized by imperial fiat.

Warned by the emperor, Kang You-wei and Liang Qi-chao escaped, Kang to Hong Kong and Liang to Japan, but Tan Si-tong refused to flee the country and, along with five others, was executed. For four days, until the twenty-fifth, Tan calmly waited for his arrest, telling his friends who recommended escape that without shedding blood there was no hope for a new China. The Six Martyrs of the reform movement of 1898 were executed on the twenty-eighth; many other supporters of the reform movement were imprisoned or dismissed from office.

The reasons for the failure of the reform movement are many. It must not be presumed that the emperor acted against Ci-xi's wishes from the beginning. On the contrary, he had consulted her and received her approval for the first reform decree, which set broad guidelines for the new policy. Indeed, the idea that reforms of some kind were necessary was accepted by many conservatives. Even Ronglu sent memorials suggesting reforms. Only when the edicts began to specify details of the reforms did the conservatives start having second thoughts. Even the moderates turned against the emperor when they realized that the reforms would undermine their privileges and vested interests.

Since most of the high-ranking officials were far more conservative than the low-ranking youthful reformers, the emperor had to dismiss or reprimand the politically important and depend on the politically weak junior officials. The reformers had no effective factional base and could not save the emperor when the need arose. The empress dowager had never lost her power to interfere in political affairs; she strengthened it further by having Weng Tong-he dismissed within five days of the first reform edict. The decree dismissing Weng was no doubt written by Ci-xi, and the emperor was powerless to overrule it. This weakened Guang-xu's position because he trusted Weng and depended on him to be the link between himself and the reformers (the reformers were too low on the bureaucratic scale to meet the emperor freely). She further consolidated her position by securing Ronglu's appointment as governor-general of Zhili (June 14, 1898); this action put him in direct control of the armies near Beijing. She also appointed a henchman to head the Beijing garrison.

Orders to abolish redundant offices and to dismiss sinecure officials meant an immediate loss of jobs for many high officials, most of them Manchus. Similarly, the decree that Manchu bannermen could no longer depend on government pensions created the impression that the reforms were at the cost of the Manchus. Indeed, the reformers were Han Chinese and belonged to the southern faction (South China had few Manchus; most lived in Beijing or in the North), whereas Manchu conservatives belonged to the pro-Ci-xi northern faction. Kang was bitterly attacked for establishing the Protect the Country Society because the task of protecting the country, according to the Manchus, fell on imperial nobles (mostly Manchu) and court ministers (many of them Manchu), not on lowly officials. A censor accused Kang of "protecting the 400,000,000 [Han] Chinese at the expense of the illustrious Qing [Manchu] Dynasty."[6]

Apart from angering the Manchus, the senior Han officials, and the bannermen, the reforms threatened the interests of thousands of literati who had studied the Confucian classics for years to take the imperial examinations; some of them had already passed the first or second levels. Abolishing the traditional examination system thus hit a class of people whose support was necessary to maintain the dynasty. Many of these scholars may have sympathized with Kang, but when they saw they would have to retrain themselves to take the new types of examinations, their essential conservatism emerged. The pleas of the nuns and monks, whose temples or monasteries were to be converted into new-style schools, also reached the ears of the religious-minded Ci-xi.

The young, inexperienced emperor and his equally young, inexperienced, and idealistic advisors did not realize until it was too late that the supposedly all-powerful emperor of China in fact was severely limited in his exercise of power. The emperor's power was circumscribed by traditional ideology and traditional bureaucratic practices. When Guang-xu stepped out of the limits set by tradition, he found himself truly powerless. The extraordinary influence wielded by the empress dowager only added to his troubles. Guang-xu visited the summer palace every week or so to pay his respects to Her Majesty and consult her before issuing important decrees. When visiting her, he could not announce his arrival himself but had to kneel at the inner gate until the chief eunuch admitted him. He was sometimes kept waiting in this position for half an hour before the infamous Li Lian-ying, who hated Guang-xu, informed Ci-xi of his arrival—this, despite the fact that the emperor had paid the customary bribe to the eunuch!

Some 20 years later, looking back at the events of 1898, Liang Qi-chao wrote that Kang, Liang, and Tan hoped to found a new school of learning that would be "neither Chinese nor Western but in fact both Chinese and Western. . . . This possibility was already precluded by that time, since not only was the indigenous traditional thinking too inveterate and deep-rooted, but the new foreign thought had too shallow and meager a source, which dried up easily once tapped and, quite expectedly, died of exhaustion."[7]

CI-XI IN CONTROL — PHASE I: 1898–1901

Ci-xi, issuing new decrees in the name of the emperor, reversed the reform policies, while blaming officials for creating confusion among the masses by not carrying out the reform orders in a "proper way." The reformers were ordered to be executed because they had taken advantage of the situation and conspired to overthrow the dynasty. "We are further informed that, greatly daring, these traitors have organized a secret Society, the objects of which are to overthrow the Manchu dynasty for the benefit of the Chinese [Han] . . . the writings of K'ang Yuwei [Kang You-wei] were . . . depraved and immoral. . . . [He] intended to flout and destroy the doctrines of the Sages. . . . Our dynasty rules in accordance with the teachings of Confucius."[8]

The fact that they were upholders of the traditional ways made the empress dowager and the conservatives antiforeign. They became even more so because the reformers were helped by foreigners and had the backing of the foreign powers. It is no doubt true that missionaries like Timothy Richard had influenced Kang and Liang in the drafting of the reform proposals. Richard and other missionaries had been invited to dine with members of the Beijing *qiang-xue* society, and says Richard, "we in turn invited them back. At each dinner speeches were delivered bearing on reform in China, and discussions followed in which the members took the keenest interest. They invited me to remain in Peking a few months so as to give them advice as to how they should proceed."[9] It is equally true that there were proposals made publicly in the missionary press that China should appoint foreigners as advisers to the throne; that Richard had suggested to Governor-General Zhang Zhi-dong that China should allow a foreign power to handle its foreign affairs and oversee a program of reform; that in 1898, Kang had suggested to the emperor that he should make Richard an adviser with ministerial rank (Richard was summoned for an audience by the emperor, but this was on the day the emperor lost power); and that Kang and Liang had sought British and Japanese aid in fleeing China.

The empress dowager was further angered when the British minister and others, believing the popular rumor that the emperor was about to be executed, warned the Chinese government that European states would view with grave displeasure the sudden death of the emperor. By seeking foreign sympathy and support, the reformers thus had proven themselves to be traitors. The popular sentiment that they were traitors strengthened the hands of Ci-xi, as did her reversal of the decree to abolish old-style examinations, which had shaken the loyalty of the literati.

The work of modernization, however, was not halted with the return of Ci-xi to power. It was allowed to continue in the old, diffused manner under the auspices of the provincial leaders. The most notable of these was now Zhang Zhi-dong (1837–1909). Zhang, a native of Zhili, came from a family that had produced officials for many generations. He had won the *jin-shi* degree in 1863 and by 1880 had brought himself to the empress dowager's favorable attention by his strong antiforeign stand during the Ili crisis. As governor of Shanxi (1882–1884), governor-general of Guangdong and Guangxi (1884–1889), and governor-general of Hubei and Hunan (1889–1907, with a short break as governor-general at Nanjing),

Zhang proved himself to be an honest, dedicated bureaucrat and effective proponent of "self-strengthening." He was successful in improving tax-collection practices; he bought warships for the southern fleet, established military schools, and opened the first modern mint in Canton; he pushed for the building of railways, started the Han-Ye-Ping iron and steel works, and established a modern military unit drilled by German instructors in Hunan.

Initially sympathetic to the reformers in 1898, he soon revealed his personal difference of view when, in the middle of the Hundred Days of Reform, he published an essay entitled "Exhortation to Study." Zhang emphasized that Chinese learning must provide the fundamental principles, and Western learning should be used only for its practical utility (popularized in the slogan *zhong-xue wei ti, xi-xue wei yong*). Unquestioningly loyal to the Manchu dynasty, Zhang believed that the dynasty and China could be saved by a revival of Confucianism, not by the introduction of anti-Confucian, foreign political practices. Proper schooling and inculcating proper Confucian virtues and the necessary "self-strengthening" subjects, such as diplomacy, industry, and commerce, therefore were absolutely necessary. Zhang felt that reformers who spoke of "people's rights" incited disorder; unity and strength could come to China not through this foreign notion but through the Confucian virtues of "loyalty and righteousness." When the reform movement collapsed, Zhang telegraphed Ci-xi, urging that the reformers be severely punished.

Zhang was the embodiment of a conservative Han reformer. He believed in the Confucian ideals, owed absolute loyalty to the empress, belonged to the northern faction, had been in the war party during the 1880s, and yet encouraged a modicum of Westernization.

The Boxer Uprising

Antiforeignism in the court was paralleled by growing antiforeignism among the peasant masses. From 1894 to 1899, three things were happening simultaneously: The Qing government, burdened by war indemnities and loans, was becoming more exploitative; foreigners, having divided the country into spheres of influence, were developing railroads and expanding their economic activities in the interior; and the missionaries, who had penetrated the countryside, were busy undermining the local social order. In one way or another, all these developments affected the peasantry.

For example, the government increased taxes to pay for the cost of the war, foreign goods displaced some local handicraft industries, and railroads threw landless labor out of employment as traditional transporters of goods. These developments created unrest in the countryside, and anger was turned against the missionaries, the local symbols of foreign aggression. In 1896–1897 there were antimissionary riots in six provinces in central China—Hubei, Hunan, Sichuan, Jiangxi, Jiangsu, and Shandong.

The province that had suffered most was Shandong. Between 1895 and 1898 there was not one year that large areas in Shandong had not been hit by natural disasters. At the same time, because of the Sino-Japanese War and the developments that followed, taxes were increased, and Shandong was forced to raise a domestic loan. After the war, Japan occupied Weihaiwei for three years, refusing to leave until the indemnity had been paid. Hardly had Japan vacated the port when the Germans took control of Jiaozhou Bay and Britain occupied Weihaiwei. Anti-Christian feelings ran high in Shandong (Shandong had to pay 104,000 taels in damages to missionaries between 1897 and 1899 for the destruction of missionary property by rioters), although the murder of two German missionaries, which led to the German military action, was not the work of any antimissionary group.

In 1898 the Germans acquired railroad-building and mining rights in Shandong and built the Jiaozhou-Jinan Railway, throwing many coolies out of work. Because of the railways and coastal shipping, commerce along the Grand Canal began to decline, and many lost their livelihood. In the same year the Yellow River flooded, inundating large areas of Shandong, while drought hit the rest of the province. Literally millions suffered.

Among the various secret societies in Shandong was one called *Yi-he-quan* (Society of Righteous and Harmonious Fists), a distant offshoot of the White Lotus Society, which had existed for centuries. Members of *Yi-he-quan* practiced Chinese boxing," hence acquiring the foreign name *Boxers*. In 1898, as a result of the disturbed conditions, the society became openly active among the peasants, water and land transport workers, and handicraftsworkers. At first their targets were both the Qing government and the foreigners, but by mid-1899, encouraged by some local conservative, antiforeign officials, the Boxers changed their slogan to "Protect the Qing, destroy the Foreigners." The society then changed its name to *Yi-he-tuan* (Righteous and Harmonious Militia), which gave it a semiofficial standing because militias were government supported. Divided into squads and brigades, the Boxers were a fairly disciplined group, although they lacked centralized leadership.

The empress dowager was caught in a dilemma. On taking over the government she had declared that China would resist all further foreign encroachment. Indeed, in March 1899, when the Italians sent a fleet to Zhejiang and demanded that Sanmen Bay be leased to them, she ordered the local forces to resist. Italy eventually withdrew its demand, giving Beijing the impression that the new, tough line was paying off. In November an edict was issued: "Never shall the word 'peace' fall from the mouths of our high officials nor should they harbor it for a moment in their breasts."[10] The Boxers' antiforeign activities had brought protests and pressure from the foreign powers; but if Beijing were to follow the dictates of the powers, would it not prove itself to be a tool of the foreigners and would it not be suppressing Chinese people supporting the dynasty?

Foreign pressure and the advice from the moderates, who did not believe that the Boxers had magical powers that made them invulnerable to bullets, forced Ci-xi to replace Yu-xian, the governor of Shandong, with Yuan Shi-kai in December 1899. By spring 1900, with his New Army and other forces raised locally, Yuan checked the Boxer movement and brought law and order back to Shandong. The Boxers, however, shifted their main force to Zhili.

The Boxer bands grew and spread through the Metropolitan province, destroying churches, killing Chinese Christians, and burning railway stations. The court was divided on how to handle the situation, with the empress dowager favoring the appeasement of the Boxers. A halfhearted attempt to suppress the Boxers failed, and they defeated the imperial troops sent against them. By late April the Boxers had captured several towns and had begun infiltrating Beijing. In May the Beijing city guards were no longer checking the identity of the insurgents entering the city, which was shortly dominated by the Boxers. Among the posters that appeared on the streets one said, "Most bitterly do we hate the treaties which harm the country and bring calamities on the people. High officials betray the country. Lower ranks follow suit. The people find no redress for their grievances."[11]

In early June, when the killings and pillage had reached intolerable levels, it also became clear that the court had decided to side openly with the Boxers. The foreign legations in Beijing felt threatened, and on June 10, the powers decided to take the matter into their own hands. Two thousand troops representing Britain, Germany, Russia, France, America, Japan, Italy, and Austria, under Britain's Admiral Seymour, started out from Tianjin to protect the Beijing legations. On June 13, the Boxers took over Beijing and besieged the legations, pillaging and burning other foreign establishments and massacring Chinese Christians.

About the same time the Boxers also entered Tianjin and spread terror there by killing Christian converts, burning churches, destroying electricity poles, wrecking the office of the intendant of customs, and attacking foreign concessions. Seymour's relief column, attacked by Boxers and imperial troops and finding that the railway line to Beijing had been cut, had to fall back to Tianjin, where it remained holed up until July 14.

On June 17 foreign warships attacked and occupied the Dagu forts and opened the passage to Tianjin and Beijing for more troops. In Beijing it was rumored that the allies had decided to demand that the empress dowager restore power to the proforeign Guangxu emperor. This naturally enraged the empress, who on June 21 issued an edict declaring war on the powers and commanding the provincial leaders to mobilize for action. On the previous day the German minister, Baron von Ketteler, had been killed in Beijing, and the Boxers had begun their attack on the legations.

For all practical purposes the "war" lasted until August 14, when the international relief force of 20,000 men broke into Beijing and rescued the foreign community and Chinese Christians (nearly 7,500), who had been besieged in the legation quarters and the Beitang Roman Catholic cathedral. The force had relieved the siege of Tianjin on July 14 but had been delayed in its advance until August 4 because of rivalries between the powers. The war was fought mainly in Zhili and on the Chinese side involved both the Boxers and the imperial troops. In some of the other northern provinces, particularly Shanxi and Dongbei, the war meant a license for killing a few hundred foreigners, mostly missionaries. The rabidly antiforeign Yuxian, who had been shifted from Shandong to Shanxi, took the declaration of war seriously and personally supervised the execution of 46 foreigners.

In the rest of China (Anhui, Jiangxi, Hubei, Hunan, Jiangsu, Guangdong, Shandong, Zhejiang, Fujian, Sichuan, Henan, and Shanxi) the governors and governors-general, some of whom had memorialized the throne to suppress the Boxers, ignored the declaration of war and came to an agreement with foreign consuls in the treaty ports for a "mutual guarantee for the protection of south and east China." In other words, the Chinese officials collaborated with the foreign powers to maintain law and order in their areas. There could be no better evidence of the weakness of the central government and the rise of regionalism in China. Governor-General Zhang Zhi-dong even took it upon himself to telegraph the Chinese envoy in London and instruct him to reassure the British government that foreign life and property would be protected in south and east China. Both sides were happy to maintain the fiction that the Boxer movement was a rebellion against the dynasty.

Even in the north the war was fought halfheartedly because the court did not have a determined and fixed policy. At the end of June the Zongli Yamen sent instructions to Chinese envoys abroad to explain to foreign governments that the "mobs" in Zhili had temporarily gotten out of hand but that the legations would be protected. Powerful figures like Ronglu kept the Boxers from making an all-out attack on the legations; otherwise it would have been hard for the besieged foreigners, despite their bravery and courage, to have held out so long. For 13 days, beginning with July 14, there was a sort of truce and the court sent cartloads of vegetables, fruit, rice, and flour to the besieged. This no doubt had something to do with the fall of Tianjin, although the legations had no information of that development.

On August 15, before the main body of the relief force had entered Beijing, the empress dowager and the emperor (suitably dressed as peasants), along with Manchu princes and other high officials, fled Beijing. The imperial party, ostensibly on a "tour of the West," headed to Xian. The aging Li Hong-zhang, currently governor-general of the distant southern provinces of Guangdong and Guangxi, was recalled to deal with the situation. Li's pro-Western stand in the south and his earlier diplomatic record were supposed to make him an acceptable spokesperson for China. Li tried hard to keep the allies from being too vindictive, and particularly from humiliating the empress dowager.

As wars go, this was a particularly dirty

one. If the Boxers can be condemned for their wanton killings, rape, and looting ("women and children hacked to pieces, men trussed like fowls, with noses and ears cut off and eyes gouged out"[12]), the allied armies cannot be exonerated for their willful plunder of the innocent. In the words of Savage-Landor, "If looting is looked upon as a crime, the soldiers of all nations, none excepted, disgraced themselves alike. The Russians, the British, the American, the Japanese, the French, all looted alike. They one and all were looters of the very first water."[13] Not only did the allied armies systematically loot the city, but even the diplomatic staff, not excluding Lady MacDonald, the wife of the British minister, went out foraging. Hundreds of Chinese women committed suicide because they were afraid of being raped by the troops.

After the occupation of Beijing the allied forces, numbering around 50,000 by the end of the year, went on punitive expeditions in areas surrounding the capital. The Russians in the meantime had already occupied Manchuria. This disturbed the Japanese, who had been asked to forego their interest in Manchuria five years earlier. Incidentally, the Japanese, who had contributed the biggest unit in the relief force, had taken the brunt of the fighting and impressed the world by their strict discipline and competence.

The Russians were pleased to accept their friend Li Hong-zhang's credentials as China's plenipotentiary and hoped that he would help them gain special status in Manchuria. Afraid of just this result, Britain and Japan insisted on getting Liu Kun-yi and Zhang Zhi-dong added to the delegation. The draft protocol, prepared by the allies for the post-Boxer settlement, was accepted by the empress dowager on December 27, 1900, but because of squabbling among the powers over details (e.g., the amount of the indemnity and how it was to be collected), the final protocol was not signed until September 7, 1901.

The main terms of the Boxer protocol were:

1. China had to pay an indemnity of 450 million taels of silver (about $333 million) over 39 years (the payments were secured against the maritime customs, inland customs, and salt revenues and, with interest, would amount to 982 million taels).
2. China had to raze the Dagu forts and other military installations between Dagu and Beijing and allow foreign troops to be stationed at 12 strategic points and at the legation quarters.
3. China was to execute 10 high officials and punish 100 others for their antiforeign activities, suspend for five years imperial examinations in 45 towns where foreigners had been killed or maltreated (to penalize the antiforeign gentry), dismiss any governor or governor-general who allowed an antiforeign disturbance in his area, execute and publicly announce the names of all officials who joined an antiforeign society during the next two years, and erect expiatory monuments in foreign cemeteries that had been desecrated.
4. China was to send diplomatic missions to Japan and Germany to apologize for the murder of the Japanese and German diplomats and was not to import any arms and ammunition for two years.

The allies had found it convenient to accept the fiction that the Boxer movement was a rebellion against the dynasty. Therefore the Boxer protocol was directed against those who had sided with or abetted the Boxers; the empress dowager was absolved, but not her antiforeign high ministers and the antimissionary literati. In fact, the staggering indemnity punished the country as a whole. Annual remittances on foreign debts amounted to about 40 percent of the annual revenue of the central government. In the words of Alexander Eckstein, "The fact remains . . . that from 1896 until the Second World War China's payments abroad on loans and indemnities constituted a sizable and constant financial drain which inevitably impaired her capacity for domestic capital formation, both governmental and private."[14] Furthermore, the unilateral posting of foreign troops reduced the sovereignty of the Chinese state, the punishment of officials and the suspension of examinations demoralized the gentry-bureaucrats, and the edicts threatening punishment to high officials for antiforeign disturbances reduced China to a state of vassalage.

If the history of past Sino-foreign relations had not embittered the Chinese already, the Boxer protocol ensured that a strong antiforeign streak would mark the next five decades until the foreigners were literally thrown out of China.

Some Communist Chinese historians view the Boxer uprising as a spontaneous revolutionary anti-imperialist people's movement. According to them, although the movement failed because of the "immaturity of the peasants" and the lack of progressive leadership, "it gave the invaders a taste of the people's heavy fist and shattered their fond dream of partitioning China."[15]

It can hardly be doubted that the movement was anti-Christian and antiforeign. Therefore, it was popular, attracting followers in the hundreds of thousands. To that extent it can be called anti-imperialist, as long as it is kept in mind that the Boxers had no understanding of the Marxist term *imperialism* and were only attacking the local manifestation of imperialist activity that hurt them socially or economically. But to call the movement "nationalistic" is farfetched. The tradition-minded Boxers had no concept of "nation" or "state." Similarly, although in the beginning the Boxers were anti-Manchu, too, this did not make them "antifeudal," as some Chinese Communist historians insist.

As it evolved, the simple antidynastic, antiforeign, peasant-based secret society uprising became complicated when gentry and bureaucrat elements began to support the movement and use it to their advantage. These conservative, antiforeign upper classes found satisfaction in seeing the Boxers destroy churches and kill foreigners. This tolerance allowed the uprising to get out of control (As one official put it, "The disturbances are so widespread that neither extermination nor pacification is an easy matter"[16]) and forced the court to declare its hand. In taking the fateful decision to back the Boxers, Ci-xi had countered the arguments of the anti-Boxer officials with the time-honored Confucian axiom that the ruler must rely on the loyalty of the people to maintain the state. But her rhetoric sounded hollow because there was no real union of the court and the people. Within the court, officials like Ronglu were against the Boxers; outside the court most provinces refused to go along with Ci-xi.

America's "Open Door" Notes

The Boxer story would not be complete without mentioning the American Open Door notes, the first set of which was issued by Secretary of State John Hay in September 1899. The September notes, sent to the governments of Britain, Germany, and Russia (followed by similar notes to Japan, Italy, and France in November) implied America's nonacceptance of any monopoly rights that might become associated with foreign spheres of influence in China. The notes requested the powers not to interfere with "any treaty port or any vested interest" or with the treaty tariffs or the right of the Chinese government to collect duties or to charge higher harbor or railroad dues from other nations, "within any so-called 'sphere of interest' or leased territory."

The impression given was that the United States was against the partitioning of China and thus was "saving" China from that horrible fate. Actually the first set of notes ensured not the integrity of the Chinese state but America's right to an equal opportunity to trade anywhere in China or, to put it more crudely, an equal opportunity to exploit China. The notes could hardly be anti-imperialist, coming as they did in the wake of American annexation of the Hawaiian Islands, Pago Pago, and the Philippines.

The Open Door policy in fact originally had been suggested to the Americans by the British in 1898, when they felt their interests in China threatened by the German and Russian scramble for leaseholds and concessions. By the time the notes were issued, the British had already acquired their own leaseholds and concessions and were therefore no longer interested in the "open door." The powers were halfhearted in their response to the notes, but Hay announced that he had received "satisfactory assurances," thus creating the fiction that American had saved China.

In July 1900, at the height of the Boxer trouble, Hay sent another note to the powers in which he asserted that the United States sought a solution "which may bring about permanent safety and peace in China, [and] preserve Chinese territorial and administrative entity." He went on to say that the solution would also "protect all rights guaranteed to friendly Powers by treaty and international law, and safeguard for the world the principle of equal and impartial trade with all parts of the Chinese Empire." Except for Britain, none of the powers replied to this circular, which sought a "collective guarantee" for China.

The high-sounding American moral stand on China had no practical repercussions other than to bolster the Americans' image of themselves. The United States was not strong enough to impose its policy on the other powers, although the notes did imply that America had now acquired world stature.

If China was not partitioned it was neither because of the Boxers nor because of the Americans but because of the jealousies among the powers, none of whom felt strong enough to fight a war to turn a part of China into an outright colony.

CI-XI IN CONTROL—PHASE II: 1902–1908

The empress dowager's vain attempt to stem the tide of change, resulting in the tragic developments of 1900, only heightened the consciousness among the gentry and the officials, even the conservative ones, that China absolutely had to reform its institutions to save itself from the onslaught of imperialism.

Indeed, the reform movement of 1898, which had met a temporary setback with the return of the conservatives to power, had pushed China to a stage from which there was no withdrawing. The conservatives had brought only greater disrepute to the institution of the emperor and the ruling Manchu dynasty. The feeling became sharper that the Manchus were out to protect their limited personal interest at the expense of the country as a whole. And as Confucian solutions became less relevant and change, based on the Western and Japanese experience, more acceptable, a sense of modern nationalism began to emerge in China.

The feeling gained ground that the nation was more important than any particular ruler and led many to the conclusion that to save China they did not have to save the Qing dynasty. The extreme logic of this kind of thinking was represented by the early revolutionaries, who believed that if saving China demanded the sacrifice of the dynasty, then that was the course to follow.

In the larger context Western learning had gained respectability, and new ideas were no longer as threatening as before. Newspapers, magazines, and publishing houses had brought national issues to the public forum. The number involved was still small, but there was a qualitative change in the intellectual environment. The traditional contempt for the merchant class was being replaced by considerable respect for commercial activity, and many members of the gentry had begun to invest in industry and commerce. Similarly, a military career was no longer looked down on by respectable gentry. The demand was growing for the "people's" (meaning the gentry class's) right to participate in making national decisions.

Indeed, Ci-xi herself, finally forced to accept the logic of the situation, became an enthusiastic leader of institutional change. From her return to Beijing in January 1902 to her death in November 1908, the empress dowager decreed many far-reaching reforms that gave a major impetus to the modernization of China. Even though her intention was to save the dynasty, many of Ci-xi's reforms had the contrary effect and contributed to the revolutionary overthrow of the Qing.

Although the powers had accepted the continuity of the central government under the empress dowager and there was no longer talk of partitioning China, the reforms were carried out in an international environment that continued to threaten the territorial integrity of the Chinese state. During the Boxer trouble, 175,000 Russian troops had entered Manchuria, ostensibly to protect the Chinese Eastern Railway, which Russia was currently in the process of building. However, even after the Boxer protocol had been signed, Russia continued its occupation of Manchurian cities, hoping to get Beijing to grant it special rights in that province. To counter the Russian move, the other powers pressured China not to sign a separate treaty with Russia, and the British concluded an alliance with Japan (January 1902) that pledged the two parties to support the "independence and territorial integrity" of China and Korea, while recognizing the special interests of Britain and Japan in China and those of Japan in Korea. This was the first alliance between a European and an Asian state, and it elevated Japan's status to that of a great power.

Russia made an agreement with China (April 1902) to evacuate its troops in stages, but instead of doing that Russia made new demands on China (April 1903) that would have turned Manchuria into a protectorate. The Japanese decided to acknowledge Russian rights in Manchuria in return for Russian acceptance of Japan's special position in Korea. Not gaining an answer, the Japanese went to war and soundly defeated Russia on land (in North Korea and Manchuria) and on sea, 1904–1905. By the Treaty of Portsmouth (September 1905) Japan acquired the Russian leasehold in Liaodong, the southern half of the Chinese Eastern Railway, and a recognition of Japan's paramount interest in Korea. In a separate treaty with China, signed in December 1905, the Japanese secured these rights from Beijing. The Qing government, aware of the new danger in the north, reorganized Manchuria into three centrally administered provinces and opened the Manchu homeland to Han migration (1907).

Within China proper the imperialist powers were focusing their attention on developing railways, which would provide access to their mineral rights and open the interior to foreign goods. Since the capital required was large, its inflow only increased the Chinese servitude to the foreigners.

The imperial reform program covered five fields: military, education, administration, state constitution, and law. In all cases the approach was radical and serious; in the cases of the military, education, and constitutional program, substantial progress changed the nature of China's future society and polity.

Military Reforms

The self-strengthening movement had led to the borrowing of Western technological innovations, but the post-Boxer reforms called for institutional reorganization of the armed forces. A percentage of the traditional Banner forces was demobilized, and old-style military examinations were replaced by a nationwide system of military academies. Modern specialized military units were created, officered by a class of specialists who received their training in the academies and often in military colleges abroad, particularly in Japan.

The key figure in the military reforms was Yuan Shi-kai, who had assumed the posts of governor-general of Zhili province and commissioner of the northern ports on the death of Li Hong-zhang in late 1901. In 1903 the Manchurian situation and the possibility of a Russo-Japanese war spurred the military reform program, and Yuan was appointed assistant commissioner of the Army Reorganization Council. Although the new officer corps, having received modern education and being imbued with a patriotic spirit, became a new elite vying for power with the nonmilitary scholar class, the goal of establishing a *centralized*, national standing army of 450,000 men was never reached. The new armies remained fragmented because of regional-provincial interests.

Because of his official position and the funds that he could divert to his use, Yuan's own new army, the Beiyang Army, comprising six divisions (around 70,000 men), soon became a model for the country. The traditional sense of loyalty, which bound the officers to their generals, later created problems for China. For example, the commanders in the Beiyang Army established the Beiyang Clique, owing loyalty to Yuan. Yuan exploited this loyalty to become president of the Chinese Republic in 1911, and he maintained that position by appointing ten of his Beiyang generals as military governors. After he died, the Beiyang generals not only took over power in their areas, establishing warlord satrapies, but also contributed five presidents to the phoney republican government in Beijing.

One graduate from Yuan's Baoding military school, however, turned out to be a revolutionary who destroyed the warlords' power and established the Nationalist Republic in 1927. He was Chiang Kai-shek (Jiang Jie-shi) who was trained in Baoding in 1907–1908 and in Japan from 1908 to 1911.

The principal achievement of the army reform was social. As military careers became respectable, they attracted men from the scholar-gentry class who looked on the new military as a means of recovering national honor and dignity. The new modern army thus became a symbol of patriotism and nationalism.

Educational Reforms

The educational reforms were the most revolutionary in their effect on China. As early as September 1901 the court decreed that a countrywide hierarchy of schools (primary and middle schools, topped by universities) be established to teach modern as well as classical subjects, that students be sent abroad for education, and that current affairs and other Western subjects be incorporated into the imperial examinations. However, shortages of teachers and educational equipment, limited finances, the ambiguous relationship between the old and the new subjects in the imperial examinations, inertia, and inexperience made the provinces hesitant to adopt the new program.

The abolition of the traditional examinations in 1905 changed the situation radically. Since the government still aimed at using the schools to train officials, the channel of upward mobility shifted from traditional education to modern schooling. Provincial authorities and the gentry enthusiastically founded various grades of schools in the county, district, and provincial-capital levels. Girls' schools, normal schools, and vocational schools were also started. Since teachers of modern subjects were still in short supply, more students were sent abroad for training. Japan became the favored country for the Chinese educationists because the Japanese language used the Chinese script and therefore was easier to learn. Besides, the proximity of Japan to China made it relatively cheaper to send students there.

The victory of Japan over Russia in 1904–1905 (which made the Japanese heroes in Asian eyes) was a further confirmation of the fact that the Japanese path to modernization was relevant to China and added to the impetus for change. The number of students in Japan increased rapidly from about 1,300 in 1904 to about 13,000 in 1906. At the same time Japanese professors were hired to teach in China.

Students also went to America and Europe, but their numbers remained small. After 1908 the United States returned a part of the Boxer indemnity to China, the funds being used to establish a college in Beijing and to support students coming to the United States. By 1911 there were about 800 Chinese students in the United States and half that number in Europe.

By 1910 China had established over 57,000 modern schools, with an enrollment of over 1.6 million students. One can add to these figures the 60,000 students in missionary schools. However, the pioneering work done by the missionary schools in introducing Western ideas was now taken over by the

Chinese themselves; the revolutionary potential of Western education was no longer the preserve of the Westerners.

By dissociating Confucianism from the educational system the reforms had opened new intellectual vistas for the vast majority of the gentry youths, who could now turn to Western studies with enthusiasm, without feeling alienated from the rest of society. Once this happened it was no longer necessary (as it had been only a few years earlier for Kang You-wei) to justify change on the basis of reinterpreted Confucian ideology. Confucianism began to lose its relevance, and it was only a question of time before Confucian philosophy would come under open attack.

Unlike the traditional classical education, which could be imparted informally in one's own home in a village, the new education demanded formal schoolhouses with laboratories and other physical facilities and teachers who had specialized in various disciplines. Schools, therefore, particularly middle schools and colleges, had to be located in urban centers and students had to live in dormitories. The modern students found intellectual stimulation in being in residential institutions; they could make intimate friends with like-minded students and debate issues with them, go to the library and read books on Western subjects that ranged from political philosophy to art and literature, keep abreast of current affairs by reading local newspapers, and express their opinions in the new journals. Thus a new kind of patriotic, nationalistic, yet cosmopolitan, urban, intellectual class began to replace the traditional scholar-gentry.

Fortuitously, just as the environment within China became more receptive to radical ideas, Chinese students in Japan became a rich source of revolutionary thought. Troubled by Japanese arrogance and contempt for China but desirous of learning from Japan, these students became bitter toward the Qing dynasty, which had thwarted change and allowed the Chinese image to fall so low. While in Japan they also came under the influence of reformers and revolutionaries who had found refuge in that country. Both Liang Qi-chao and Kang You-wei had fled to Japan, which had also provided a haven to the revolutionary leader Sun Yat-sen.

Liang, recognized as the most powerful writer of the age, immersed himself in Western knowledge and, through the various journals he edited in Japan (particularly the *Xin-min cong-bao, New People's Review,* established in 1902), introduced the students to a wide variety of subjects. He wrote lucidly and forcefully on constitutional monarchy, popular sovereignty, republicanism, nationalism, human rights, and so on. His articles on Western philosophers and historical figures treated Luther, Bacon, Descartes, Hobbes, Spinoza, Montewquieu, Voltaire, Rousseau, Tolstoy, Kant, Cromwell, Napoleon, Bismarck, and Mazzini. There is, perhaps, no modern Chinese leader who has not been deeply influenced by Liang Qi-chao. Mao Zedong, who in due course would become the greatest Communist leader of modern China, was 16 in 1910 when he first read some of Liang's articles, and he recorded later that he "read and re-read these until I knew them by heart. I worshipped . . . Liang Chi'i-ch'ao."[17] Mao modeled his writing style on Liang's.

In 1905 Sun Yat-sen, taking advantage of the large numbers of students in Japan and other revolutionary leaders who had had to flee China because of their conspiratorial activities, established an open revolutionary organization, the *Tongmenghui* (the United Association, which because of its goals, can be better termed the Revolutionary Alliance), Sun was elected president of the Revolutionary Alliance. In the same year the Revolutionary Alliance established its official organ, the *Min-bao* (*People's Journal*), which gave Sun an opportunity to explain his ideology of *san-min-zhu-yi,* the Three People's Principles. The first principle, nationalism, was basically an anti-Manchu stand, aimed at the overthrow of the Manchus and returning political power to the Han people in a republican form of government; the second, democracy, implied modern egalitarianism guaranteed by a constitution; the third, people's live-

Sun Yat-sen (1866–1925)

Sun, born in a village near Macao, was China's first professional modern revolutionary. He left home at the age of 13 to join his elder brother in Honolulu, where he enrolled in a three-year boarding school run by the Church of England. He was given instruction in English, Christianity, science, and history. He returned home in 1882, only to be expelled by the village for his iconoclastic act of trying to smash an idol in the village temple. From 1883 he lived mostly in Hong Kong, where he received further education and gained a medical degree in 1892. In Honk Kong, Sun also converted to Christianity.

Sun's interest in China's future was quickened by China's defeats at the hands of the foreign nations, and he began to entertain ideas of rebellion against the Qing dynasty. However, he first tried the path of the reformers and in 1894 wrote to Li Hong-zhang making certain proposals. Li ignored his letter and did not grant him an interview. Later that year, Sun, with financial help from overseas Chinese, organized his first secret society, the Revive China Society, which aimed at overthrowing the Manchu government and establishing a republic.

In 1895 Sun plotted an uprising in Guangzhou, but the plot was discovered and several of the conspirators were arrested and executed. Sun sought refuge in Japan because the Hong Kong authorities, under pressure from Beijing, ordered him to leave the colony. From then on, until the end of his life, Sun remained committed to revolution. In China, he came to be universally recognized as a symbol of nationalism and patriotism. After his death he was canonized as *Guo-fu,* the father of the nation.

lihood, emphasized the necessity to eliminate social inequities by establishing state socialism to control industries and communications and by creating a tax system that would not allow the owners of real estate to profit from future rises in land values. Although the last principle has often been translated as socialism, Sun seemed more concerned with urban problems than with rural ones. However, his ideology was broad enough to be attractive to large numbers of Chinese who represented a wide spectrum of political opinion.

Between 1905 and 1910 the revolutionaries organized several uprisings in China, working through students who returned to China to teach or join the military. Although the uprisings failed, the radicalization process was heightened. Something was attractive about the idea that the single act of revolution would put China on a par with the foreign nations that had been humiliating it. Even Liang Qi-chao, who attacked the revolutionaries and propagated gradualist reform and constitutional monarchy, contributed to this radicalization with his articles on the corruption and inefficiency of the Manchu regime (Kang and Liang were loyal to the emperor, not to the empress dowager), his propagation of nationalism, and his call for a spirit of destruction to cast off the enslavement to the past. As Timothy Richard noted in 1906, "the sons of the Chinese nobility and ruling classes are being educated in Japan by the thousands and return home fired by her example and emulous to repeat it."[18]

Anti-Manchu feeling was also growing on the mainland, where intellectuals used the protection offered by the treaty ports to establish revolutionary societies and journals. For example, in 1902 two well-respected scholars, Cai Yuan-pei and Zhang Bing-lin (who in 1900 had publicly cut off his queue, a symbol of subservience to the Manchus), established the Patriotic Academy in Shanghai International Settlement and under the guise of education carried on anti-Manchu activities. Protected in the foreign settlement, the Shanghai paper, *Su-bao* (*Jiangsu*

Journal), published the radical speeches made at the Patriotic Academy and provided financial aid. Zhang used the columns of *Su-bao* to refute the arguments of the reformists who advocated a constitutional monarchy, referring to the Guang-xu emperor by name and calling him a "little clown."

In 1903 an 18-year-old Japan-returned student, Zou Rong, published a pamphlet entitled *Ge-ming zhun* (*The Revolutionary Army*), with a forward by Zhang Bing-lin. *The Revolutionary Army* was the most outrageous and outspoken attack on the Manchus. *Su-bao* gave it favorable reviews. Zou wrote that the only solution to China's problems lay in the violent overthrow of the "barbarous Beijing government" and the establishment of a republic modeled on the United States:

> The autocracy of the last few thousand years must be swept away, the slavery of thousands of years abolished. The 5,000,000 barbarian Manchus . . . must be destroyed, and the great shame they have inflicted in their 260 years of cruel and harsh treatment expunged, that the Chinese mainland may be purified. . . .
>
> [The Manchus] have lived off the food of our fellow countrymen, lived off our land, and benefited from the great generosity of our compatriots to such an extent that they could not repay us with the minutest particle of gratitude, even if they drank our urine and licked our ordure.[19]

Apart from suggesting that the Manchus, including the emperor, should be killed in revenge, Zou made a remarkably clear analysis of China's current problems. His booklet reflected his admiration of America and his passionate faith in constitutional government.

At the request of the Manchu government the authorities of the International Settlement sent out orders to arrest the various persons connected with the Patriotic Academy and *Su-bao*. Many fled from Shanghai, but Zhang and Zou stayed on to court arrest. The newspaper and the academy were closed down; Zou was given a two years' sentence and Zhang, three. Zou died in prison in 1905 and gained the martyrdom he had sought. Zou's booklet became a bestseller and went through several printings.

These years of hectic anti-Manchu thinking and activity also produced the first modern woman revolutionary martyr, Qiu Jin (1879?–1907). At age 24 already married and a mother of two children, Qiu Jin was so moved by the post-Boxer developments that she decided to give up her family and dedicate her life to the revolutionary cause. She went to Japan in 1904, joined the Revolutionary Alliance, and on her return to China in 1906 became a schoolteacher in Zhejiang as a cover for her secret activities. However, her plot for an armed uprising (1907) became known and she was arrested and executed. Known as Woman Warrior of Jianhu Lake, Qiu Jin's death inspired many young intellectuals to follow her path.

Constitutional Reforms

The victory of Japan over Russia in the 1904–1905 war served to convince many vacillating Chinese that a constitutional monarchy was the only path to national strength. Had not the well-respected scholar-industrialist Zhang Jian written, even before the Russo-Japanese War had ended, that "the outcome of this war depends on which nation has gained a constitutional government"?[20] The new education and the new press had created a sense of nationalism among the educated and the commercial classes, which resulted in the rise of direct popular responses to political developments. For example, anti-Russian demonstrations in 1903 to protest Russian occupation of Manchuria were followed by the far more widespread anti-American boycott in 1905–1906 to protest U.S. laws prohibiting the immigration of Chinese labor into America. The effectiveness of the boycott can be seen in the fall of Standard Oil Company sales in Guangzhou by 80 percent between July and November 1905.

The empress dowager could no longer resist the growing demand of her loyal ministers and the public that constitutional reforms be instituted. In 1905 she reluctantly agreed to send five high officials on a mission abroad to investigate various constitutional governments and in 1906 finally proclaimed her commitment to the principle of constitutionalism. There were public celebrations in many cities marking the issuance of this decree. Self-government societies were established and experiments begun in local self-government.

For a whole year there was no further news on the subject. In anticipation of the constitution, the court turned to the reorganization of the executive and administrative organs of the government. The traditional 6 boards were converted into 11 Western-style ministries (some of which, like the Ministry of Foreign Affairs, had come into operation immediately after the Boxer trouble). Theoretically, the racial qualifications for appointment of ministers and vice-ministers were eliminated (the boards had two ministers and two vice-ministers each, one a Manchu, the other a Han), and the ministries were headed by a single person. However, in practice these high posts were still evenly divided between the Manchus and the Han. The Ministry of War was entirely staffed by Manchus. An attempt was also made to separate the three powers of government (the executive, the legislative, and the judicial), but the country had a long way to go in establishing a parliament, assemblies, and a legal code before these schemes could become operable.

Late in 1907 the court announced that China would have a National Assembly, with half its members elected, and fully elected deliberative assemblies at the provincial and local levels. But there was still no indication when all this was to come about. The urban elite clamored for an early decision.

When the draft constitution was approved in August 1908, it turned out to be a copy of the Japanese constitution, with a few amendments that gave even more power to the throne. The most glaring of these was that members of parliament were forbidden to petition the emperor. All power was vested in the emperor; the executive, the legislature, and the judiciary were only advisory bodies. Moreover, full constitutional government was to be introduced gradually over a period of nine years. In 1908 preparations were to be made for convening the provincial assemblies in 1909; in 1910 a National Assembly, with half the members nominated and the other half representing the provincial assemblies, was to be convened to oversee the preparations for the next five years (taking a census, introducing local self-government, codifying laws, establishing local courts, collecting revenue data, etc.) and generally to ready the country for the promulgation of the constitution and the parliament in 1916.

On November 15, 1908 the empress dowager died, preceded by a day by the Guang-xu emperor. Three-year-old Pu-yi, son of Prince Chun (half-brother of Guang-xu), succeeded to the throne (reign title Xuan-tong), with his father acting as regent.

THE END OF THE MANCHU DYNASTY: 1909–1911

It is said that the dying emperor had advised Prince Chun that when Pu-yi ascended to the throne, Yuan Shi-kai should be beheaded because he was a traitor responsible for the emperor's downfall. Apparently Prince Chun did not feel confident enough to act on this advice, but early in 1909 he ordered Yuan to retire from office and return to his native place to treat an imaginary ailment in his foot.

With the death of Zhang Zhi-dong, the last of the great provincial leaders, in October 1909, China was left without any mature leadership. Even Robert Hart, the grand old man of the Customs Service and long-time adviser of China, retired in 1908 and left for England. Prince Chun now became the de facto ruler of China, but he lacked the vision and the qualities of a great leader and was wholly incapable of handling the explosive political situation. The Manchu ruling clan, loath to part with power, was becoming more and more antagonistic to Han ambitions; the Han gentry and merchants were demanding greater participation in politics; the revolutionaries had spread their activities throughout the country (between 1906 and 1908, there were seven uprisings against the Manchus in Guangdong, Guangxi, Yunnan, and Hunan); bomb-throwing anarchists were becoming popular heroes; and anti-Manchu sentiment had affected even the Han, who had no interest in revolution.

Prince Chun followed the original schedule for the constitutional program: The provincial assemblies were organized in October 1909, and in January 1910 the regulations for local government and the drafting of the law codes were announced. Since the vote was restricted to teachers at certain levels, graduates from middle schools, degree holders, officials above a certain rank, and owners of property valued at $5,000, the elected assembly members were all members of the established elite: the officials, the gentry, and the affluent merchants. As expected, the gentry predominated. The elections gave an opportunity to these constitutionalists to heighten their activities and their demands. Representatives of the provinces met in late 1909 and established the Federation of Provincial Assemblies (FPA), which began to lobby at the national level for a change in the timetable, petitioning the court to summon parliament immediately.

By the time the FPA made its third petition, the National Assembly had been convened (October 1910), according to schedule. The petition received the backing of the National Assembly and virtually all of the governors and governors-general. The court had to give in to this pressure, and on November 4 it was announced that the parliament would be convened in 1913 instead of 1916.

Having made the announcement, the court tried to reimpose control over the constitutionalists by decreeing that it was illegal to petition the court. Some provincial leaders who attempted to do so were arrested and exiled. But the National Assembly could not be dissolved, and members of that body continued to question the role and the authority of the grand councilors; they requested that a cabinet responsible to the National Assembly be appointed to replace them. The imperial reply was curt:

> Whether the grand councilors are responsible or irresponsible and whether a responsible cabinet should be organized or not, are problems to be decided by the court and should not be interfered with by the chief members of the assembly. Therefore the request is to be dismissed without any further discussion.[21]

The conflict between the members of the National Assembly and the court (for that matter, between the provincial assembly members and the government) arose out of differing perceptions of the nature of constitutional government. In the eyes of the court the National Assembly and the provincial assemblies were *advisory* bodies, not *legislative* organs. Although technically that was true, the elected representatives, having realized that they had considerable power based on national sentiment and public opinion, clamored for the right to participate in government. They wanted a genuine parliament and a cabinet that was responsible to it.

In May 1911, when the National Assembly was not in session, Prince Chun abolished the old cabinet and the Grand Council, replacing them with a new cabinet. The constitution of the cabinet dispelled any doubts regarding Prince Chun's lack of vision, his incapacity to lead the country as a whole, or his strong anti-Han bias. Of the 13 cabinet members, 8 were Manchus, 1 was a Mongol bannerman, and only 4 were Han. Imperial clansmen, close relatives of Prince Chun, were given the prime ministership and the ministries of foreign affairs, finance, agriculture, industry, commerce, and the navy. Other Manchus looked after civil affairs, defense, justice, and territories. Of the four Han, one was vice-premier, one was vice-minister of foreign affairs, and the other two were to look after education and communications. The new cabinet was still individually and collectively responsible to the emperor. How was this cabinet supposed to lead the country to constitutional government?

As if this was not enough to shatter the

new elite's faith in the Qing dynasty, the court took two further actions in May that made it appear as a pawn for the foreign powers and an enemy of the people: the nationalization of all private trunk railway lines and the Hu-guang railway loan agreement with Britain, France, Germany, and America.

The monopoly rights obtained by the imperialist powers to build railways in China, either by giving loans or making direct investments, had become visible symbols of imperialist aggression. The growth of nationalism led the patriotic Chinese to demand that these rights be recovered to ensure China's sovereignty. The gentry and the merchants in the provinces set up private railway companies and raised funds to redeem the foreign lines. This movement made the railways a provincial, rather than a national, issue. But the local funds raised were far too meager to fulfill the aspirations of the people involved.

When the court decided to centralize and nationalize the railways and to compensate local private railway shareholders, the act should have been hailed as a victory for nationalism. Instead, the provincial leaders were outraged. Sentiments of parochial provincialism and nationalism became intermixed. Railway protection societies sprang up in Sichuan, Guangdong, Hunan, Hubei, and other provinces to oppose the central plan and fight the nationalization of railways.

The fact that seven days after issuing the decree nationalizing railways the government had contracted a huge loan from the four-power consortium to build the Hankou to Guangzhou and Hankou to Sichuan trunk lines (Hu-guang railways) made the court suspect in public eyes. The Manchus were buying out the Chinese and gratuitously selling national interests to foreign powers. There were mass meetings, hunger strikes, student protests, the closing of shops by merchants, strong-worded articles in the press, and a flood of petitions to the court to rescind the loans and punish the ministers concerned. Public opinion was inflamed even further when the rumor began to circulate that the foreign powers were planning to dismember China.

The gap between the reformer-constitutionalists and the revolutionaries began to close. For example, in Sichuan the movement to stop paying taxes to Beijing (on the grounds that they would be used to service foreign loans) and the anti-imperialist slogan "Sichuan for the Sichuanese," raised by the gentry and the merchants, acquired a strong antidynastic content. On September 7, when the governor-general of Sichuan arrested some leaders of the local railway company, there was mob rioting. The police opened fire, leading to the "Chengdu massacre." It appeared that the Manchus had joined the imperialists and turned their guns against patriotic Chinese.

As the provincial leaders became estranged from the government, their views began to synchronize with those of the revolutionaries: The Manchus had no intention of sharing power with the Han Chinese; the Manchus must go. During this entire period Sun Yat-sen's Revolutionary Alliance had also been active, although it suffered from many handicaps. Since the alliance had to operate from headquarters outside China and act in secrecy within China, it could not develop a strong organizational setup. The situation became worse in 1907 when the Japanese, pressured by the Qing government, expelled Sun from Japan and he moved to Hanoi in French Indochina.

During the next two years, Sun staged six fruitless uprisings in the provinces bordering Indochina before being asked by the French to leave Hanoi.

The headquarters then shifted to Hong Kong, and the Revolutionary Alliance now concentrated its activities in the Qing New Army, infiltrating its officer corps and spreading propaganda among the soldiers. On April 27, 1911, Huang Xing, a close associate of Sun, led an attack on the governor-general's office in Guangzhou. Despite the planning, things went wrong: Arms did not arrive in time; there was a lack of communication between the revolutionaries and the prorevolutionary city guards; and in any case, the government had received information about the attack and was forewarned. Some revolutionaries killed one another by mistake, and Huang Xing lost three fingers in the foray. However, the uprising did produce "72 martyrs," who became a source of inspiration to others, and their common grave serves as a historic landmark in Guangzhou.

As far as the alliance was concerned, the Guangzhou fiasco was a bitter setback. Huang Xing went into hiding in Hong Kong while Sun was traveling in America. In October an uprising similar to the one in Guangzhou was planned in Wuchang (one of the three cities that form Wuhan, the others being Hankou and Hanyang), Hubei province. The revolt was planned for October 16, but because of an inadvertent explosion of revolutionary ammunition on October 9 (which made the authorities aware of the plot), the uprising was staged on October 10. The revolutionaries had infiltrated units of the New Army, won over some of the officers, and recruited 3,000 soldiers to their cause. The Eighth Engineering Battalion of the New Army was the first to revolt. Four other battalions, out of a total of 22, joined the uprising and attacked the governor-general's office. The Manchu governor-general, the military commander, and the loyalist troops fled the scene.

The revolutionaries had succeeded in taking over Wuchang when they discovered that they had no leader. All the major leaders of the Revolutionary Alliance were nowhere near the scene of action, and even the minor ones were not easily reachable or available. Looking for someone well known, the important members of the local revolutionary organizations chose to invite brigade-commander Li Yuan-hong to become the military governor of "independent" Hubei province. Not only was Li not a member of the Revolutionary Alliance, but also he was anti-Republican. The story goes that the revolutionaries pulled him out from under the bed where he was hiding and, holding a gun to his head, asked him whether he would like to be the George Washington of China or die on the spot. Having forced Li to be "elected" to the post of military governor, the revolutionaries then "elected" Tan Hua-long, chair of the provincial assembly, to head the civil government.

This was not an auspicious start for the revolution. The revolutionaries had handed over power to an antirevolutionary and to a constitutionalist. But the revolutionaries were right on one count: Li and Tan did lend dignity to the uprising, which may otherwise have been no more than another incident of no import. Although the activities of the Revolutionary Alliance were poorly organized and poorly coordinated and suffered from a perennial shortage of funds, its ideology and goals, however loosely defined, provided an alternative to the Qing government. The reformers and the constitutionalists found it easier to accommodate themselves to a constitutional republic than to the Manchu autocracy. The manifesto, which was to be proclaimed by the revolutionary military governors of "liberated" provinces, was drafted by the Revolutionary Alliance and spelled out the basic ideology of the Three People's Principles.

By the end of November, all provinces south of the Great Wall except Zhili, Henan, Gansu, and Shandong had established military governments and declared their independence of the Qing government. In several provinces the central authority melted away without a fight; in some there was token resistance; and in the few where there was fighting, the imperial troops lost heart when their generals were killed. After the October 10 uprising in Wuchang (celebrated today in Taiwan as the Double Ten festival—tenth day of the tenth month), the court realized that it could not do without Yuan Shi-kai because of his military talents and also because his commanders in the elite New Army units, which he had built up, refused to take orders from the Manchu general. Prince Chun, who hated Yuan, was forced to recall him by appointing him governor-general of Hubei and Hunan and giving him overall military command. Yuan, however, had not forgotten the insulting manner in which he had been dismissed, so he delayed accepting the imperial order on the excuse that his foot had not yet healed. In any case, Yuan was not a loyalist and a diehard conservative, ready to sacrifice himself for the Manchu dynasty. Indeed, despite the fact that he had "betrayed" the emperor, Yuan, a protege of Li Hong-zhang and a one-time self-strengthener, had done much to introduce progressive reforms in the post-Boxer period. He now proved himself to be an astute politician by not responding to the court overtures until Beijing could meet his demands: opening parliament in 1912, amnesty for all revolutionaries, legal recognition of the Revolutionary Alliance, full authority to himself to reorganize the armed forces, and adequate military funds. Thus he made himself out to be a friend both of the court and the revolutionaries and emerged as the only possible arbitrator between the two.

As the situation worsened the Manchus panicked. Accepting Yuan's demands, the court appointed him imperial envoy with full powers over the army and navy; the cabinet was dissolved, and Yuan was appointed prime minister with the authority to organize his own cabinet (November 2). When the National Assembly elected Yuan as the new prime minister on November 8, he had already assumed command of the military. At this juncture, only Zhili, Shandong, Henan, and three Manchurian provinces were still loyal to the court.

Yuan's troops reoccupied Hankou and proved to the fledgling revolutionary governments that he still had the military power to undo their work. But Yuan did not proceed with the suppression of the revolutionaries because he had already made contact with them and offered to negotiate a settlement. By early November there was talk among the revolutionaries that Yuan should be offered the presidency of the republic; by mid-November, Sun, who was abroad, approved the proposal by telegraph. Yuan kept the pressure on the revolutionaries by occupying Hanyang on November 27 and threatening Wuchang, which was looked on as a sort of headquarters of the provisional revolutionary government. On December 2 the representatives of the revolutionary provinces formally resolved that Yuan be elected president if he shifted his allegiance from the Manchus to the republic. The same day, Nanjing fell into the hands of the revolutionaries and was soon declared the future capital of the republic.

Peace negotiations between the north (representing Yuan more than the Qing government) and the south (the revolutionaries) began in earnest on December 17 in Shanghai. The foreign powers, although "neutral," heavily favored the strongman Yuan Shi-kai, who could bring peace to the country. The compromise solution worked out by the negotiators was that Yuan would be made president if he could persuade the Manchu emperor to abdicate.

On December 25 Sun returned to China and was elected president by representatives of 17 revolutionary provinces (December 29). Sun agreed to concede the post to Yuan if Yuan joined the republican cause. On January 1, 1912, Sun took the presidential oath and declared the founding of the Republic of China. Li Yuan-hong was made vice-president, a cabinet was appointed, and the provisional government of the Republic of China came into existence. On January 22 Sun informed Yuan that as soon as the emperor abdicated and Yuan publicly declared support for the republic, Sun would resign in favor of Yuan. Having been convinced by Yuan that the future safety of the Manchus lay in their voluntary acceptance of the republic, the emperor abdicated on February 12 (the abdication edict vested sovereignty in the people and gave Yuan Shi-kai full powers to organize a provisional republican government); on the fourteenth Sun resigned; on the fifteenth Yuan was elected president unanimously by the representatives of the 17 provinces.

It was with surprising ease that the 2,000-year-old Confucian imperial structure was abolished, but the manner in which the transfer of power took place did not augur well for the future of either the revolutionaries or of the constitutionalists.

NOTES

[1]Ssu-yu Teng and John K. Fairbank, *China's Response to the West: A Documentary Survey, 1839–1923* (Cambridge, MA: Harvard University Press, 1965), p. 159.

[2]Ibid., p. 151.

[3]Hu Sheng, *Imperialism and Chinese Politics* (Beijing: Foreign Languages Press, 1955), p. 121.

[4]Ibid., p. 122.

[5]J. O. Bland and E. Backhouse, *China Under the Empress Dowager* (London: William Heinemann, 1910), p. 186.

[6]*The Reform Movement of 1898* (Beijing: Foreign Languages Press, 1976), p. 79.

[7]Immanuel C. Y. Hsu, trans., *Intellectual Trends in the Ch'ing Period, by Liang Ch'i-ch'ao* (Cambridge, MA: Harvard University Press, 1959), p. 113.

[8]Bland and Backhouse, *China Under the Empress Dowager,* p. 226.

[9]Timothy Richard, *Forty-five Years in China* (New York: F. A. Stokes, 1916), p. 255.

[10]Chester Tan, *The Boxer Catastrophe* (New York: Columbia University Press, 1955), p. 32.

[11]*The Yi Ho Tuan Movement of 1900* (Beijing: Foreign Languages Press, 1976), pp. 31–32.

[12]Peter Fleming, *The Siege at Peking* (New York: Harper, Collins, 1959), p. 95.

[13]Quoted in *The Yi Ho Tuan Movement,* p. 93.

[14]Alexander Eckstein, *China's Modern Development* (Ann Arbor: University of Michigan Press, 1976), p. 118.

[15]*The Yi Ho Tuan Movement,* p. 124.

[16]Hu, *Imperialism,* p. 139.

[17]See Edgar Snow, *Red Star Over China* (New York: Grove Press, 1961), p. 133.

[18]T. Richard, "China and the West," *Living Age,* March 10, 1906.

[19]See Chün-tu Hsüeh and Geraldine R. Schiff, "The Life and Writings of Tsou Jung," in Chün-tu Hsüeh, ed., *Revolutionary Leaders of Modern China* (London: Oxford University Press, 1971), pp. 164, 186.

[20]See Li Chien-nung, *The Political History of China, 1840–1928* (Palo Alto, CA: Stanford University Press, 1956), p. 199.

[21]Ibid., p. 234.

CHAPTER 5

The Republic That Never Was: 1912–1927

THE FAILURE OF THE REVOLUTION

The way the revolutionaries and the constitutionalists had joined hands in the final act of the revolution, the way the revolution was carried out, and the way Yuan Shi-kai ascended to the presidency meant several things, none of which boded well for the future of constitutionalism in China.

At the national level Sun Yat-sen's ideas of the revolutionary process and the stage-by-stage organization of the government had to be discarded. Sun had envisioned a three-stage introduction of democracy. The first stage was to be a military unification of China, with the military exercising authority at all levels, from the center to the districts. After three years of this purely military government, the next stage (lasting six years) was expected to oversee the introduction of provisional constitutional government under military tutelage. At the end of nine years a full-fledged constitutional government was to be established, and the military government was to cease functioning. This plan could have been followed only if Sun Yat-sen and the Revolutionary Alliance had led the military insurrection and been in total command of the situation.

The revolution, as it had taken place, was, however, the combined product of reformist and revolutionary forces. The reforms produced social disequilibrium by creating new values and rising expectations among the politicized intellectuals and the new merchant class, which in turn put pressure on an inept leadership to concede even greater reforms, which were not forthcoming. This fostered a "revolutionary" ambience. The Revolutionary Alliance, exploiting the new values and the new nationalism, provided an alternative to the traditional monarchical system (a democratic republic), and by staging rebellions, added to social dysfunction. Both forces found common ground in constitutionalism, and growing anti-Manchu sentiment weakened the stand of those who favored a constitutional monarchy.

At the provincial level the provincial assemblies and local self-government had brought local leadership to the fore and bred provincialism; slogans such as "Guangdong for the Guangdongese" and "Sichuan for the Sichuanese" became popular. These tendencies were strengthened when the provinces declared themselves independent of the national government. But the heightened autonomy of the provinces made it difficult to reimpose central authority, revolutionary or otherwise, or to work out a national consensus.

Yuan Shi-kai and the Constitution

Sun and the revolutionaries had offered the presidency to Yuan because they were aware of their military weakness. They also were afraid that an extended operation might invite foreign intervention and lead to the dreaded partitioning of China. But the revolutionaries also wanted to ensure that Yuan would serve the republic; so before yielding power to Yuan, they enacted a provisional constitution, which enshrined a bill of rights and provided for a cabinet form of government. The cabinet was to be approved by the senate (made up of representatives of all provinces, Mongolia, and Tibet) and be responsible to the parliament. The constitution was drawn up in haste because the revolutionaries had not envisioned the possibility of having to hand over power to a person like Yuan, who had dubious political credentials. When the issue of the constitution was debated, it was obvious that there was no unanimity among the revolutionary leaders. Indeed, as late as December 1911, Sun himself was in favor of a presidential form of government, which would have placed all executive power in his hands as provisional president. However, once it was apparent that Yuan Shi-kai, and not Sun, would be the president, the framers of the provisional constitution hastily shifted to a "responsible cabinet" system.

The president, under the provisional constitution, was in charge of political affairs; served as commander-in-chief of the army and navy; and had the authority to appoint ministers and diplomatic envoys, declare war, negotiate peace, and sign treaties. But he could take none of these actions without the approval of the senate. The provisional constitution was designed to make the prime minister the de facto custodian of political power, but the division of power between the president and the prime minister was not clear-cut.

The provisional constitution was to remain in force until the parliament, to be convened within ten months, drew up the formal constitution.

The first issue that arose between the revolutionaries and Yuan was the location of the capital. The Nanjing assembly, knowing that the strength of the revolutionaries lay in the south, voted for Nanjing to be the capital, but Yuan managed to manipulate the situation and get Beijing declared the capital of the republic. This act was backed by many Chinese as well as the foreign powers, who had their embassies in Beijing.

The second issue was that of sharing power with the cabinet. On assuming the presidency, Yuan appointed Tang Shao-yi (1860–1938) prime minister. Tang, who had been sent by the China Educational Mission to study in the United States in the 1870s and later risen to high official rank, was the chief negotiator between Yuan and the revolutionaries. He was eminently acceptable to both sides; he was a friend of Yuan and had won the confidence of Sun. He even joined the Revolutionary Alliance to allay any doubts about his loyalty to the republican cause.

However, once made prime minister, Tang tried to live up to the spirit of the constitution and refused to rubber-stamp Yuan's appointments and policies. The clashes between the two continued until Yuan proved by his arbitrary actions that he did not consider the premier to wield superior power. In June 1912 Tang resigned in frustration. He had been prime minister for less than three months. Historians have blamed Yuan for undermining the constitution, but the constitution itself was to blame for most of the confusion. Yuan had no control over the cabinet, and neither did the prime minister. The prime minister did not represent a majority party, and he had no control over the budget or the local governments. The legislature could impeach ministers, but the prime minister could not dissolve the legislature. Yuan could operate only by working around the system, which had no roots in Chinese social consciousness or polity.

Since the Revolutionary Alliance members of the cabinet resigned along with Tang, Yuan was given an opportunity to appoint more pliable premiers and cabinet members. The legislative assembly, torn between factions and lacking a unified sense of constitutional powers, grudgingly approved the appointments.

The hope of the revolutionaries now lay in the parliamentary elections that were held in the winter of 1912–1913. The Revolutionary Alliance and four other political groups were reorganized as a political party, the Guomindang (the Nationalist party), which emerged as the majority party in the new parliament. The organizer of the Nationalist party and its de facto leader was Song Jiao-ren (1882–1913), who had carried on a vigorous election campaign in which he bitterly denounced Yuan's government and its policies. Song presumed that he would head the new, single-party cabinet and bring the constitution closer to the British model. Yuan, fearing a serious confrontation with Song and the parliament, solved the problem by having Song assassinated (March 20, 1913). Song's death marked the end of the democratic experiment.

Meanwhile, Yuan had expanded his control over the provinces through the appointment of loyal military governors. Incidentally, the idea that the provinces should be headed by military rather than civil governors came from the revolutionaries. They wrote this clause into the provisional constitution, no doubt as a concession to Sun's three-staged approach to democracy (the first stage being military unification).

However, Yuan could not exercise autocratic power without adequate finances. Having inherited the empty Qing coffers and the debts and indemnities of the Manchu government, he lacked funds. He knew that he could not obtain them from the provinces, which had become more autonomous and were diverting most of the provincial monies to local use. Besides, the needs of the state were far greater than could be fulfilled by revenues from the provinces, even if these had been forthcoming. In April Yuan concluded a $125 million "Reorganization Loan" from the five-power banking consortium (Britain, France, Germany, Russia, and Japan) without gaining the approval of the parliament. The loan was secured against China's salt taxes, which were henceforth to be administered under foreign supervision.

The strongman Yuan, preserver of China's revolution and the Chinese Republic, had willingly allowed the foreigners to have greater control over China's finances. The news of this autocratic act was met with consternation by many constitutionalists and revolutionaries. The Guomindang opposition was further stirred by the findings of the committee inquiring into Song's death that the government had a hand in the assassination (published on the same day that Yuan signed the loan). On May 5 the parliament, led by the Guomindang, voted a resolution declaring the loan agreement illegal.

But Yuan, strengthened by the loan, no longer had any reason to tolerate Guomindang opposition. He severed relations with the Guomindang, dismissed three Nationalist military governors who had opposed the loans, and moved his troops south in anticipation of possible trouble. In July seven provinces (Jiangxi, Anhui, Jiangsu, Guangdong, Sichuan, Fujian, and Hunan), following the precedent of 1911, declared their independence of Beijing and began the "second revolution." Badly organized, badly planned, and lacking popular backing, this revolution collapsed within two months. Sun and other revolutionary leaders fled to Japan or sought sanctuary in the treaty ports. By September Yuan was militarily in control of the whole country.

Sun had failed to recreate the revolutionary spirit of 1911, proving that in 1911 it was the anti-Manchu sentiment and not the ideology of revolution that had united the students, gentry, merchants, and the military. In 1913 most social elements that had revolted against the Manchus no longer felt psychologically compelled to take up arms again. They saw in Yuan a strongman who could unify and lead the country. More important, they were convinced that no one else could take his place. They lacked a deep commitment to the constitutional process, which they hardly understood, and they had little faith in the so-called political parties, which were open to bribes and whose factional bickering had destroyed their prestige.

After the second revolution Yuan did not need the parliament, except to legalize his position. He was technically still the provisional president, and only the duly elected parliament could formally elect the president of the republic for a tenure of five years. Parliament was supposed to enact a constitution before electing the president. But bribed or browbeaten by Yuan and pressured by the senior generals, members of parliament reversed the procedure and elected Yuan on October 6. Foreign powers that had withheld recognition of the government now extended recognition to Yuan in time for his formal inauguration as the first president of the Republic of China on October 10, 1913, the second anniversary of the revolution.

During the next year Yuan moved step by step to dismantle the constitutional structure. In early November he ordered the dissolution of the Guomindang and the arrest of its members still in Beijing on the grounds of security because the party had been involved in the summer rebellion. In January 1914 Yuan dissolved the parliament (which in any case now lacked a quorum), the provincial assemblies, and the local governments. Numerous newspapers were suppressed and "subversive" political associations banned. Yuan had taken China back to where the empress dowager had left it.

Working through the Political Council, a puppet body that Yuan had brought into existence in late 1913, the president created a constitutional council, which drafted a new constitution. The Constitutional Compact, as Yuan's constitution was called, was promulgated on May 1, 1914, and gave Yuan all the dictatorial powers the Manchus had sought for the emperor in 1910. The cabinet was replaced by a secretary of state, appointed by and responsible to the president; the legislature, whenever it came into being, was to have only advisory powers. The difference between 1910 and 1914 was that a weak Manchu court, which was giving in to public pressure for the advancement of the constitutional cause, had been replaced by a strong dictator, who could (and did) reverse the constitutional process. Yuan used bribery, espionage, and political assassination to run his government.

In December 1914 Yuan, by an amendment to the Constitutional Compact, had his term extended indefinitely and obtained the right to appoint his successor. He then did something even more shocking, something totally unexpected from a republican president: He carried out the imposing ceremony of offering sacrifice to Tian at the Temple of Heaven, a ceremony that could be carried out only by an emperor. Yuan also revived the sacrificial rites to Confucius that had been suspended since 1911 and got the Political Council to endorse their restoration officially. To a discerning eye it would have been obvious that Yuan not only was out to destroy republicanism but also had monarchical ambitions.

Yuan and Imperialism

The aim of the revolution had been to establish a strong national government that could counter imperialist encroachment, but without a secure financial base no Chinese government, Manchu or Republican, could be forceful. One of the last acts of the Manchu government had been to allow the foreign commissioners of the Maritime Customs Service to collect customs revenues directly and forward them, not to Beijing, but to the International Commission of Bankers at Shanghai for distribution among th creditor nations (November 1911). As noted earlier, Yuan could not have survived without the reorganization loan. But to secure it he had to weaken China's sovereignty even further by allowing foreign control over the restructured Salt Revenue Administration.

Moreover, to gain the loan Yuan had to recognize Britain's interest in Tibet and Russia's in Outer Mongolia. Afraid that the economic independence and political autonomy of Outer Mongolia would be destroyed by the influx of Han Chinese, as had happened in Inner Mongolia, the Living Buddha at Urga (a Tibetan by birth), backed by Moscow, declared Outer Mongolia independent on December 28, 1911. The Russians, not wanting to arouse Japanese fears or draw the attention of other powers to this area, worked out a formula with Yuan whereby Outer Mongolia was recognized as "autonomous" under China's "suzerainty." Outer Mongolia in fact became a Russian protectorate.

The British government in India, afraid of the expansion of Russian influence in Tibet, began to view Tibet as an area of legitimate British interest and a possible buffer state between British India and Russian Central Asia. In 1904 the British sent an armed expedition to Lhasa, the "forbidden city," and signed an Anglo-Tibetan convention that might have made Tibet a British protectorate had their anxiety regarding Russia not been allayed soon thereafter. The Chinese reasserted their authority over Tibet briefly in 1910 but lost it again in 1912. In 1913 the Dalai Lama, the spiritual and secular head of Tibet, declared independence and made a treaty with the Living Buddha at Urga. Britain recognized Tibet's independence in 1914, and although China refused to do so, Yuan had no power to stop Britain from developing direct relations with Lhasa.

Until 1914 mutual jealousies among the imperialists had kept any single power from trying to turn China into a protectorate or from carving out a colony in China proper. However, as the European nations became involved with World War I, Japan gained a free hand to expand its influence in China. The Anglo-Japanese alliance of 1902 did not legally bind Japan to any action against Germany, and the war in no way adversely affected Japan's territorial or other interests in the Pacific or China. However, paying no heed to the Chinese proclamation of neutrality, Japan proceeded to attack the Germans in Qingdao. The Chinese tried to limit the area of Japanese action by declaring a "war zone," but Japan contemptuously disregarded the attempt. After the fall of Qingdao (November 1914), Japan took over the German leased territory in Shandong as well as all other rights and interests the Germans had secured in that province.

When hostilities between the Japanese and the Germans had ceased with the collapse of German resistance, Yuan informed the Japanese (January 7, 1915) that China's neutrality would once again extend over Shandong, except for the leased territory. The Japanese protested that this was an unfriendly act and on January 18 presented Yuan with their own demands, the nefarious Twenty-One Demands. The demands were divided into five groups: Group I transferred German rights in Shandong to Japan and made it exclusively a Japanese sphere of interest. Group II confirmed Japan's paramount position in eastern Inner Mongolia and South Manchuria; extended leases for a period of 99 years; gave the Japanese subjects rights to lease or own land for trade, manufacturing, or farming; and ensured that no third power would be granted any privileges without Japanese consent. Group III gave Japan the right to become the joint operator of the Han-ye-ping Iron and Steel Works in Hubei and denied China the right to open mines in the neighborhood of those owned by the Han-ye-ping Company without Japanese permission. Group IV demanded a promise from China not to cede or lease any harbor, bay, or island along the coast of China to any third power.

Group V contained the most vicious demands of all. If accepted, these would have made China a protectorate of Japan. The Chinese central government was to employ Japanese advisors in political, financial, and military affairs; "numerous Japanese" were to be employed to administer jointly the police departments of major cities; Japanese were to administer jointly Chinese arsenals and provide the bulk of China's military needs; Japan was to be consulted first for China's foreign capital needs; and Japanese missionaries were to have the right to propagate Buddhism in China.

These demands were presented directly to Yuan, and he was admonished to keep them secret. However, the astute politician allowed certain details to be leaked to the national and foreign press, thus creating a strong anti-Japanese sentiment within China and a suspicion of Japanese intentions in Britain and the United States. After four months of parlays in which China tried its best to wear down the Japanese negotiators, Japan presented an ultimatum (May 7, a day which came to be marked annually as National Humiliation Day) saying that if matters were not settled by a certain date, force might be used. Yuan then accepted most of the demands, with the proviso that group V should be further negotiated. In face of the widespread hostility that the demands had created, Japan agreed to the compromise. The Sino-Japanese treaties were signed on May 25, 1915.

The unity that the nation had shown in anti-Japanese demonstrations, boycotts, and riots gave Yuan the impression that the country was wholly behind him. He was soon to learn the shocking truth that this was not so.

Yuan Restores the Monarchy

The Constitutional Compact already had given Yuan all the power that he could ever have hoped for, but he still chose to dismantle the republican system altogether and to establish a constitutional monarchy. Chinese historians and most foreign scholars have long denounced Yuan as a three-time traitor who betrayed the Guang-xu emperor in 1898, the Manchu dynasty in 1911, and the republic in 1916. Without denying Yuan's talent for intrigue and deception, it can be argued that Yuan was a product of unique circumstances, not a maker of them. After all, the monarchists and the revolutionaries came seeking him to head the government, not the other way around.

Yuan, more than anyone else, realized the bankruptcy of the republican movement, which had resulted in strengthening provincialism rather than in helping to reintegrate the Chinese political system. Yuan's control over the country was superficially maintained through the loyalty of his generals, but even this loyalty was not absolute, as events were soon to prove.

The debate over China's future constitution was far from over. The Manchus had abdicated, but those who had struggled for a constitutional monarchy were still influential and were not yet convinced that a republican form of government would work. To aid in formulating his policies, Yuan engaged Chinese and foreign consultants to advise him on constitutional and government matters. Buttressed by the advice of these specialists, particularly that of the American political scientist Frank J. Goodnow (professor of Columbia University and later president of Johns Hopkins University), Yuan came to the conclusion that national integration could only be ensured through a monarchical system. Goodnow wrote,

> It is of course not susceptible of doubt that a monarchy is better suited than a republic to China. China's history and traditions, her social and economic conditions, her relations with foreign powers all make it probable that the country would develop that constitutional government, which it must develop if it is to preserve its independence as a state, more easily as a monarchy than as a republic.[1]

Goodnow had qualified his statement with the condition that the restoration of monarchy must meet public approval. Yuan set about to gain it by having six well-known personalities, including Yan Fu (who later said that he had been coerced into joining), organize a "society for planning peace" to study whether monarchism or republicanism was more suited to China and start a nationwide campaign to poll public opinion.

The government was soon flooded with petitions asking for a monarchical system. Representatives of the provinces, whose members had been handpicked by provincial governors to form the so-called National People's Assembly, were polled. They made a unanimous declaration (November 20):

> Reverently representing the public opinion of the nation, we request that the president, Yuan Shih-k'ai, be made emperor of the Chinese empire. He will have the highest and the most complete authority and sovereignty over the nation. The throne will be handed down in his royal family from generation to generation through ten thousand generations.[2]

On December 11 the Political Council petitioned Yuan to ascend the Dragon Throne. It is possible that Yuan was not fully aware of how his loyal henchmen had arranged the puppet show, but he was pleased to begin preparations to become the new monarch, creating five ranks of nobility, choosing the reign title of Hong-xian (Grand Constitutional Era, to begin on January 1, 1916), and minting coins bearing his image.

These developments did not disturb the mass of common people, the peasantry, few of whom had any idea what was happening in Beijing. But Yuan and his close advisors had underestimated the resentment and opposition that had been growing in the gagged, silent majority of the educated urban classes. Sun, who in exile had established a new revolutionary party, was of course vociferously against the monarchical move; Liang Qi-chao, head of the Progressive party, which had initially supported the president, bitterly attacked Yuan; Japan and the other foreign powers registered their objections; most ironically, even Yuan's own generals, who had accepted his dissolution of the parliament and the elimination of political parties, turned against him.

The military governor of Yunnan, Cai E, incited by his one-time mentor, Liang Qichao, revolted against Beijing, denounced Yuan, and declared Yunnan's independence on December 25. Guizhou followed suit in January 1916, and Guangxi in March. Realizing that he could not militarily suppress the rebellion and facing a national outpouring of criticism, Yuan restored republican government on March 22.

But Cai E and Liang demanded that Yuan resign his post and leave China. Since imperial restoration threatened provincial autonomy in a way that suppressing parliament and Guomindang had not, they found backing in provinces that seceded from the center in April and May: Guangdong, Zhejiang, Shaanxi, Sichuan, and Hunan. Yuan's top Beiyang generals, Duan Qi-rui and Feng Guo-zhang, now played a key role in undermining Yuan's position by joining the banned Guomindang parliamentarians and other leaders of the opposition and demanding Yuan's retirement.

One wonders what would have happened next if Yuan had not died on June 6, 1916.

WARLORD POLITICS AND THE MAKING OF A NEW CHINA: 1916–1927

The revolutionaries had been optimistic that after the abolition of the Confucian monarchy, a rapid national integration would take place under a democratic, constitutional republican government. This optimism was totally baseless because China was wholly unprepared for representative democracy. The ideal of democracy is not easy to achieve and requires a foundation that few countries outside Western Europe and North America have been able to develop. China, with its authority-dependency orientation, its lack of an ideal of rule by law or the concept of individual rights, and its lack of a tradition of loyal opposition, had few of the ingredients that would have been conducive to the transplant of liberal democratic institutions.

Yuan, the "elected" monarch, tried to rebuild the Chinese polity by combining the traditional ingrained attitudes of the masses toward monarchy with the modern notion of a "social contract" as reflected in the constitutional movement. But lacking both the traditional sanction for authority that came with the mandate of heaven and the modern sanction that came with the people's will, he had to rely on military force.

The events of 1915–1916 led to three parallel developments. First, provincial military power holders, by proving the impotence of Beijing, further undermined the efforts to centralize power and strengthened the forces of regionalism. For almost the whole of the next decade, although the fiction of a central government was maintained (primarily because the foreign powers continued to deal with the militarist in control of Beijing as if he represented the government of China), provincial militarists (the warlords) made alliances and counteralliances to expand their territorial domains and take over Beijing. Second, the Japanese emerged as the key imperialist nation, with ambitions to subdue China to its will. Third, Yuan's monarchical movement, the Japanese Twenty-one Demands, and the rise of warlords heightened the sense of urgency among the nationalistic and patriotic intelligentsia in finding a new solution to China's ills.

Warlord Politics

Yuan Shi-kai was succeeded by Li Yuan-hong, who had been vice-president under Yuan. Li revived the 1912 constitution, recalled the members of the old National Assembly, and reconstituted the cabinet with Duan Qi-rui (1865–1936) as prime minister. If it was Li's desire to return the country to the situation that had existed in 1913, on the eve of the dissolution of the National Assembly, he succeeded beyond any doubt.

However, like Yuan, Li was soon at odds with his prime minister, and the members of the National Assembly, representing the old Guomindang and the Progressive parties, were sharply divided over every possible issue. Working under the old constitution, which weighted the prime minister over the president, Duan tried to make himself the center of executive authority, although he depended more on his comrades-in-arms, the Beiyang military governors, who dominated most of the provinces, than on the National Assembly.

The issue that brought matters to a head was the war against Germany. It was rumored, correctly, that Duan was pushing the country into war, under Japanese pressure, because he had received secret loans from the Japanese. Li, backed by the parliament, dismissed Duan in May 1917, but Duan got the Beiyang militarists to rally to his side. Eight provinces, including the Metropolitan province of Zhili, declared their independence and condemned the president and the National Assembly for Duan's dismissal. In desperation Li accepted the offer of Zhang Xun, the "pigtailed" general (because he and his troops had retained their queues as a sign of loyalty to the Manchus), to intercede. Zhang was a Beiyang general and military governor of Anhui but had not proclaimed his independence.

Zhang, however, had some plans of his own. After he got Li to suspend the meddlesome National Assembly (June 12, 1917), he moved into Beijing at the head of his troops to effect the restoration of the Manchu dynasty (July 1). The imperial edict proclaiming the return of the emperor was drafted by the one-time hero of the reformists, Kang You-wei. But the country that had just denied Yuan the throne was in no mood to accept the return of the Manchus. The Beiyang generals retracted their declarations of independence and prepared to attack Beijing. Duan headed the antirestoration army.

Li, who had taken refuge in the Japanese legation, reappointed Duan as prime minister. On July 14 Duan entered Beijing as the savior of the republic. There was very little fighting, Zhang Xun retired from politics, and the young emperor disappeared from view without any further fuss. Duan consolidated his position by forcing Li Yuan-hong to retire in favor of the vice-president, the Beiyang General Feng Guo-zhang. On August 14 China declared war on Germany, and Duan negotiated another loan from Japan.

Like Yuan, Duan wanted to free himself from the parliament, which was vociferously attacking his arbitrary actions, and like Yuan, he abrogated the provisional constitution, revised the Organic Law of the parliament, reduced the electorate still further, and created a new National Assembly packed by his followers. Once again the southwestern provinces expressed opposition, and Guangdong, Guangxi, and Yunnan declared their independence. Sun Yat-sen, now back in Shanghai, started the Constitution Protection Movement. Joined by the minister of navy (who had resigned in protest and taken the navy with him), he sailed south to establish a rival military government in Guangzhou (August 1917), Sun took on the military rank of generalissimo. The Guomindang-dominated parliament also moved to Guangzhou.

From 1917 to 1927 two governments were vying for national recognition—one in the south at Guangzhou, the other in the north at Beijing. Neither of them had jurisdiction over extensive territories, nor did they control national organizations or exercise national authority. And both were challenged by other, rival governments, which periodically replaced them. There were many scores of major and minor warlords, whose activities would be fundamental to understanding the history of the autonomous or semiautonomous provinces. They, however, remained marginal to the politics of Beijing and Guangzhou and so have to be ignored in a broad overview of the warlord decade.

The warlords came from diverse backgrounds. Some were illiterate, some highly educated, some traditional, some Westernized, some rose from the ranks, some had seen service as high officials in the Imperial Army, some came from impoverished families (a few had been bandits), and some were from well-established and affluent families.

Some warlords were interested in developing and modernizing their areas, but most had little consideration for public welfare and exploited the countryside to the maximum for finances and recruits for their ever-growing armies. A warlord would issue paper money, which often lost even the limited value it had to begin with when another warlord took over the territory. The parasitic armies increased from 500,000 in 1914 to 900,000 in 1920 to 1.5 million in 1925.

As far as national finances are concerned, the provinces stopped contributing to the central exchequer after 1919. Beijing depended on the surplus funds released to the central government from the salt and maritime customs revenues, after the foreign debts had been serviced. In 1919 these receipts amount to $7 million, and the expenditures to $10 million. The deficit was made up by borrowing from native banks. As expenditures increased, militarists like Duan Qi-rui took secret and open loans from foreign powers, pledging whatever remained unpledged. In 1922 China defaulted on its foreign loans for the first time, and in 1923 it was calculated that government expenditure was 17 times its income. Chaotic politics and national bankruptcy went hand in hand.

Warlord politics during the decade 1917–1927 is so tangled and confusing that it is impossible to delineate it in a brief overview. As a broad generalization it can be said that in the north, the Beiyang commanders split into two warring cliques, both contending to gain power over the government in Beijing and thereby tap the foreign loan market: the Anfu clique under Duan Qi-rui and the Zhili clique under Feng Guo-zhang. When they felt threatened or saw an opportunity to improve their situation, other warlords not belonging to these cliques joined one side or the other or took independent action.

In October 1918 the Anfu-controlled parliament managed to remove Feng as president and replace him with one of Duan's lieutenants. The Zhili group, capitalizing on Duan's connections with the Japanese, began to condemn him for "selling out China" in return for loans. In 1919, when the Versailles Conference decided that Japan could retain the German claims in Shandong, the infuriated Chinese educated elite demonstrated against Japan; demanded that China not sign the peace treaty; and sought the expulsion of the members of the Anfu government, who had collaborated with the Japanese. The May Fourth Incident, named after the student demonstrations on that date, led to a nationalistic upsurge, and Duan was forced to dismiss some high-ranking officials. (The incident is discussed in greater detail later in the chapter.)

While Duan was trying to restabilize his position, Wu Pei-fu (a warlord with a base in Sichuan and western Henan), who felt threatened by Duan's moves, joined some other militarists and attacked Duan. Wu also managed to get the bandit-turned-warlord Zhang Zuo-lin (based in Manchuria; head of the Fengtian clique) to join the fray. In June 1920 the Anfu forces melted away before the advancing armies, Duan went into retirement, and the enlarged Zhili clique (now headed by Wu), supported by Zhang Zuo-lin, took over power. Although Zhang would not accept Wu's leadership, this unstable coalition lasted through 1921. But the break between Zhang and Wu came into the open in 1922. Wu managed to receive added help from the independent warlord Feng Yu-xiang (based in Shaanxi; often referred to as the Christian general because he had converted to Christianity), and Zhang was forced to withdraw beyond the Great Wall to his territorial base in Manchuria.

Wu Pei-fu recalled the supposedly innocuous Li Yuang-hong to take over the presidency. The Zhili clique, posing as protector of the republic, convened the "legitimate" parliament (August 1922), which had been dissolved in 1917 by Zhang Xun, and hoped that the presence of Li and the recall of the parliament would help in winning back the south. There was a flurry of meetings, and talk spread of adopting a federal system of government, which would give autonomy to the provinces but have only one national government. These discussions were academic, however, for before anything could be worked out, Cao Kun, a Zhili warlord, took over the leadership of the Zhili faction, ousted President Li, and got himself elected president by heavily bribing the members of parliament (1923). Wu Pei-fu, still the head of the Zhili forces, retired to his home base.

In 1924 Zhang Zuo-lin tried to reenter Beijing politics by joining a local war against Wu Pei-fu. In autumn 1924, after Zhili had declared war against Zhang, Wu marched his troops northeast to invade Manchuria through the Shanhaiguan pass, where the Great Wall meets the ocean. Parallel to this move, Wu ordered Feng Yu-xiang to move to the western passes so that Zhang could not make an encircling movement and attack Wu from behind. Instead of following Wu's orders, Feng double-crossed him. Feng turned back from the Great Wall, seized Beijing, imprisoned Cao Kun, and ordered the arrest of the members of parliament.

The affairs of China were further complicated by the support the major warlords received from foreign powers. Zhang was aided by the Japanese, who wanted to build up their position in Manchuria; Wu was supported by the British, who had interests in the Yangtze valley; Feng was given some aid by the Soviet Union, which was also now backing Sun Yat-sen in the south.

The situation in the south was no different from that in the north. As mentioned earlier, in 1917 Generalissimo Sun Yat-sen tried to establish himself at the head of a republican government in Guangzhou. But without an army of his own, Sun's authority depended on the goodwill of the Guangdong and Guangxi warlords. In 1918 the unsympathetic Guangxi clique came to dominate Guangzhou, abolished the "generalissimoship," and forced Sun to retire to Shanghai. Sun used his time to ponder the nature of politics and write a book expounding his political ideas. In October 1920 Chen Jiong-ming, the Guangdong warlord, a member of the Guomindang and a follower of Sun, expelled the Guangxi militarists and invited Sun to return as head of the new military government. In May 1921 Sun, having got himself elected president by the southern rump parliament, declared his intention to launch a northern expedition to unify China. But Chen had no desire to involve his armies in a war with the powerful northern warlords. Besides, he favored the much-touted federal system that would give him an opportunity to entrench himself in Guangdong. So

Chen, while assuring the Zhili clique that he had no intention to start any military action, turned against Sun, forcing him to retire once again to Shanghai (August 1922).

In 1923 Sun, having accepted the Soviet offer of arms and financial aid, at last managed to consolidate his hold over the military government at Guangzhou. Rather naively, Sun still hoped that China's affairs could be settled constitutionally, and therefore he entered into talks with the enemies of Cao Kun because Cao had "usurped" the presidency. When the anti-Cao generals took power, Sun decided to go to Beijing to discuss the formation of a national government on lines satisfactory to his vision of a unified China (December 31, 1924). He died in Beijing in March 1925 without having achieved any results. Backed by Zhang Zuo-lin, the old fox Duan Qi-rui had been installed Chief Executive (the office of presidency was dropped) without regard to any constitution.

In 1926, in the face of the growing threat from Sun's reconstituted and newly armed Nationalist party (Guomindang), which under its new military leader, Chiang Kai-shek (Jiang Jie-shi), had launched its northern expedition to unify China militarily, Zhang reunited with the forces of Wu Pei-fu. Feng was ousted from Beijing, and there was no further use for Duan, who once again retired from active politics. However, Zhang and Wu failed to agree on the formation of a civil government, and for a year no president was appointed. In 1927 Zhang assumed control as military dictator but in the following year was compelled to retreat to Manchuria when the Nationalist forces swept north and brought China proper under their domination. By the end of 1928 the Nationalist government had occupied Beijing, established its capital at Nanjing, and gained the recognition of foreign powers.

In the end the south won over the north, but it was a totally new combination of forces that succeeded in the military unification of China. In 1923–1924 Sun Yat-sen, helped by the Soviet Union, reorganized the Nationalist party along lines of the Russian Communist party, added a Bolshevik-style party army to the organization, and agreed to cooperate with the newly established Communist party of China (which was also, naturally, being helped by the Soviet Union). After Sun's death, it was this new Guomindang that fulfilled Sun's goal and brought about the Nationalist revolution.

Since developments from this stage on were intricately connected with the weakening of traditional social attitudes, the rise of Chinese nationalism, the leftward shift of Guomindang politics, and the role of the Soviet Union in the Chinese revolution, it is necessary to shift attention to the larger social and intellectual scene.

NEW CULTURE, NATIONALISM, AND NEW POLITICAL IDEALS

Surprising as it may seem, political turmoil connected with the warlords did not produce a corresponding chaos in the modern economic sector of China or in its urban social life. Warlordism unquestionably had a negative impact on rural China, and it made little contribution to the progress of the modern industrial sector of the economy, but it could not thwart the trend toward the growth of urbanization, particularly the growth of treaty ports. Trade and industries continued to expand, schools and colleges continued to grow in numbers, and magazines and newspapers proliferated.

Trade and Industry

China's foreign trade rose 350 percent in the first three decades of this century. But what is even more important, the nature of the trade changed significantly. The import of opium, which had first turned the balance of trade against China, was phased out by 1917. (This, of course, did not mean that the Chinese had also stopped producing opium within the country.) China now increasingly imported commodities like raw cotton, machinery, kerosene, paper, telephone and telegraph supplies, and scientific instruments, which reflected the trend toward industrialization and modernization.

Similarly, changes in the export trade showed that China was in the intermediary stage between a traditional economy and a modern one. The traditional items of Chinese export, produced by traditional methods, had lost out to countries that had begun to produce these items by using modern techniques and paying careful regard to standards and standardization. The export of tea, which had represented nearly 50 percent of the export trade in 1880, declined to about 5 percent in the 1920s. Silk also suffered a decline, although relatively less than that of tea. In the 1920s China was exporting goods such as soya beans, bean cake, vegetable oils, pig bristles, hides, and skins—products of cheap labor.

Modern industry also made considerable advances. By 1914 China was extracting nearly 13 million tons of coal and .5 million tons of iron ore, and it had modern mills producing iron, textiles, cotton yarn, cigarettes, electric power, and cement. Despite warlord disruptions, the average annual rate of industrial growth from 1912 to 1929 was 13.8 percent. Although the foreign capitalists had led the way in industrial development, native capitalists gradually increased their role. World War I gave the Chinese capitalists an excellent opportunity to expand their enterprises; the Western powers, diverted by the war in Europe, had not only loosened their grip in China but also needed to import processed goods, which their own factories were no longer in a position to produce. Between 1914 and 1918 Chinese mills increased from 75 to over 110, the most noteworthy expansion taking place in the textile industry. By 1933, 67 percent of the industrial gross output value was produced in Chinese factories, which employed 73 percent of the labor force.

In the context of China as a whole, however, the industrial sector of the economy was minuscule. For example, handicraft production accounted for 95 percent of the cloth consumed in 1919. However, the few centers (such as Shanghai, Wuhan, Tianjin, Qingdao, Guangzhou, and Mukden) in which industries were established became the nuclei of future industrial growth and the training ground for the new class of industrial workers. By 1920 China had about a million industrial workers.

By 1919 Western-style permanent labor organizations came into existence. The establishment of the Communist party of China in 1921 and the reorganization of the Nationalist party on Communist Russian lines politicized labor unions and encouraged their expansion. Strikes for economic gains and political strikes became common. One newspaper calculated that in the last quarter of 1922 there were 41 strikes. Approximately 71 percent of these were for increases in wages, 12 percent opposed the supervisors, 12 percent were sympathetic, and 5 percent were for the right to organize unions.

However, in the absence of effective labor regulations, strikes could not make a significant change in the overall labor conditions, which remained poor for a long time. Low wages, unhygienic living and working quarters, long work hours—even for women and children—and contract labor provided by unethical and criminal organizations were the rule rather than the exception.

Intellectual Life

The failure of the 1911 revolution, the two attempts to revive the monarchy, and the drift of China into warlordism led many revolutionary intellectuals to turn their backs on politics in disgust and frustration. It was clear that paper drafts of constitutions were unlikely to change the nature of politics. Only a revolutionized society could do that.

The need to forge a new society had been recognized by Liang Qi-chao even before the Qing dynasty had fallen, and a debate on what ingredients should go into the making of "new culture" had been carried on by the Chinese students studying in Japan. After 1911 most revolutionaries became involved with the affairs of the state, and there was a short pause in the debate, which was reignited in 1915, the year of the Twenty-one Demands and Yuan's monarchical movement. It is no coincidence that in 1915 Chen Du-xiu (1879–1942) founded the magazine *New Youth,* which began an all-out attack on Chinese tradition and soon became the most influential magazine in China.

The May Fourth Era, as the period 1915–1923 came to be known, brought to a logical conclusion the intellectual trends that had begun, three-quarters of a century earlier, with Lin Ze-xu's and Xu Ji-yu's recommendations for change that would strengthen China. As the imperialist threat to China's sovereignty and integrity increased and the Qing dynasty failed to meet the challenge, Chinese intellectuals' perceptions of the national problems changed. By the end of the nineteenth century the realization had dawned that it was not the traditional Confucian culture and its adjunct, the traditional political system, that needed saving but the entity called "the Chinese state." The Western concept of a nation-state was new, but once Western learning brought it home, nationalism made its first appearance and intellectuals began to seek the sources of national power, even if it implied a rejection of tradition.

Liang Qi-chao and Kang You-wei, still closely tied to tradition, had tried to change the nature of Confucianism to make Western learning acceptable. The post-1900 generation of Chinese intellectuals, products of the new school system and foreign education, far more nationalistic and anti-imperialist than Kang and Liang and far less bound to tradition, felt that only Westernization and the discarding of tradition could save China. By 1921 there were 10 university-level institutions of higher learning, 41 provincial collegiate schools, 189 provincial normal schools, and thousands of junior and elementary schools, all geared to Western learning in one form or another. By 1930 there were about 130,000 schools, ranging from the primary to the university level, with an enrollment of approximately 4.25 million students. The two most prestigious universities were Beijing National University and Qing Hua University, both in Beijing.

The question this generation faced was not how to introduce Western ideologies but what Western ideology would be most suitable. Most thinkers were in favor of a parliamentary democracy. A few had dabbled with bomb-throwing anarchism before 1911, and anarchism continued to attract youthful minds, but in the larger context, this ideology had few followers. Since China was not an advanced industrial country and, therefore, lacked the presumed prerequisite for a Marxian revolution, Marxism had attracted little interest. A strain of socialism, however, was visible in both Liang Qi-chao's writings and the ideology professed by Sun Yat-sen. It was neither well defined nor did it form the main plank of their thinking, but Sun and Liang, although they were not "'good' socialists . . . did much to make socialism 'good' for China. They pioneered in giving it respectability, and the vital connection with the themes of 'nationalism' and 'democracy' which it needed."[3]

Parliamentary democracy, however, remained the main goal of most intellectuals. The failure of the republic did not turn them against representative government, but instead it led them to probe the deeper causes of that failure. Chen Du-xiu's analysis, expressed in his forceful articles in the *New Youth* magazine, was that Confucian social culture lay at the heart of China's troubles and that the absence of a tradition of democracy and science had made it difficult to make the republic work. Confucian culture was predisposed to despotism, demanding servility and abjuring individual independence. It was narrowly elitist, exploiting the many to serve the few. Inherently conservative and isolationist, it put hurdles in the path of progress, cosmopolitanism, and the scientific outlook. This "old and rotten" culture, as Chen put it, had to be destroyed in toto, so that youth could be liberated from the bondage of the tyrannical Confucian family system and the energies of the nation released for creative growth and development.

In 1917 Chen Du-xiu, now recognized as the champion of China's new culture movement, was invited to serve as dean of the College of Letters in Beijing University. Here he and his magazine became the centers of the intellectual ferment that made Beijing University the vanguard educational institution in China. In 1917 and 1918 Hu Shi (1891–1962; Hu Shi received his doctorate from Columbia University, United States and was later appointed professor of philosophy at Beijing University) published articles in the *New Youth* magazine advocating the use of the vernacular (*bai-hua*) to replace the classical written language (*wen-yan*) because *wen-yan* was the language of Confucian high culture, was difficult to master, and had resulted in scholarly elitism. *Wen-yan,* however elegant and sophisticated, was a dead language. It could not be spoken and served only as a medium of written expression. By adopting *bai-hua,* the written and spoken languages could be made to conform and the problem of education and mass literacy be simplified; *bai-hua* would thus help in bringing modern ideas to larger numbers. Hu Shi also proposed that *bai-hua* be used to create a new popular literature based on Western forms (short stories, plays, novels, and poetry)—a literature that would deal with the life of the common people and expose the evils of traditional ways. Hu Shi advised the writers to discard clichés and classical allusions and to stop imitating classical writing and artificiality. All writing, he said, should have meaning and substance.

The debate on the literary revolution was carried on in *wen-yan!* It was only from 1918 that *New Youth* was published entirely in *bai-hua,* and it was also in that year that the magazine carried Lu Xun's first short story written in *bai-hua,* "The Diary of a Madman." The story attacked Confucian morality for being hypocritical and for using lofty sentiments and ideas to camouflage a "man-eat-man" society, which it in fact fostered. The story was an immediate success.

The literary revolution, like the movement for new culture, was a conscious attempt by intellectuals to serve a national cause. The need for literature to bear a heavy social responsibility is represented dramatically in the life of Lu Xun (1881–1936), China's greatest modern writer. Lu Xun went to Japan in 1902 to study medicine. "I dreamed a beautiful dream," he writes, "that on my return to China I would cure patients . . . who had been wrongly treated. If a war broke out I would serve as an army doctor. At the same time I would strengthen my countrymen's faith in reform." He worked hard in medical school, until one day, during the Russo-Japanese War in 1905, the teacher showed lantern slides in which a Chinese, allegedly working as a spy for the Russians, was executed by the Japanese. Lu Xun felt humiliated by the manner in which the Japanese students cheered the incident, but what shocked him even more was that the film showed a crowd of Chinese standing around apathetically watching the beheading. "Because of this film I felt that medical science was not so important after all. The people of a weak and backward country, however strong and healthy they may be can only serve to be made examples of. . . . It is not necessarily deplorable no matter how many of them die of illness. The most important thing, therefore, was to change their spirit, and since at this time I felt that literature was the best means to this end, I determined to promote a literary movement."[4]

This group of intellectual leaders, bold and iconoclastic, found it easy to win over youthful minds in debunking Confucianism, but they could not readily fill the void being created in cultural values. Democracy and science, held up as substitutes for the national heritage, remained rhetorical expressions, not easy to realize.

THE MAY FOURTH INCIDENT: 1919

China had entered the war against Germany in 1917, but it could not take over German interests in Shandong because Japanese actions there had already precluded that possibility. China, however, hoped that the Allies, particularly the United States, would help in getting the Japanese to vacate Shandong. These hopes were shattered when it was revealed at the Versailles peace negotiations that England, France, and Italy had signed secret treaties agreeing to Japan's claims to Shandong. Even America had recognized that Japan had special interests in China. The news stunned China.

Students in Beijing, who had planned to demonstrate on May 7 (National Humiliation Day) in 1919, advanced the date to May 4 to combine their protest against Japan with that against the injustice of the Versailles decision. Three thousand students marched through Beijing, shouting slogans and carrying banners, some with inscriptions written in blood, that denounced the Twenty-one Demands, international justice, and Duan Qi-rui's warlord government. Under pressure from the Japanese, the government tried to suppress the students by arresting them, but Beijing rulers had underestimated public sentiment. The arrest of over 1,000 students filled the jails to capacity but failed to halt the demonstrations. For the first time large numbers of women students joined their male colleagues in demonstrations and courted arrest. Teachers, journalists, lawyers, doctors, other professionals, merchants, shopkeepers, and even workers all over the country responded with sympathetic strikes, boycotts, and demonstrations. The government finally gave in to the pressure. The pro-Japanese ministers were dismissed, and the Chinese delegation refused to sign the Versailles Treaty.

The importance of the nationwide disturbances and protests that lasted for two months lies not in the impact they had on the treaty powers (which was nil) or on warlord politics (which continued unchanged despite Duan's resignation) but in being the first sign of mass nationalism in urban China. The seven-day general strike in Shanghai in June was remarkable because it showed how students, merchants, industrialists, workers, and shopkeepers could create ad hoc organizations and collaborate in shutting down the biggest industrial city in the country.

The famous writer Ba Jin recalls in his autobiographical novel *Jia* (*The Family*) how the May Fourth happenings affected his hometown in remote Sichuan:

> . . . in 1919 the May Fourth Movement began. Fiery, bitter newspaper articles awakened in Chueh-hsin memories of his youth. Like his two younger brothers he avidly read the Peking dispatches carried in the local press, and news of the big strike in Shanghai on June 3, which followed. When the local paper reprinted articles from the *New Youth* and *Weekly Review* magazines, he hurried to the only bookstore in town that was selling these journals and bought the latest issue of the first, and two or three issues of the second. Their words were like sparks setting off a conflagration in the brothers' hearts. Aroused by the fresh approach and the ardent phrases, the brothers found themselves in complete agreement with the writer's sentiments.[5]

This intellectual and nationalistic ferment led to a rapid expansion of the press in China and with it the spread of "new culture." Hundreds of new periodicals, written in the vernacular, introduced every kind of Western idea to readers hungry for new ideas. The popular use of the term *new* in the titles of many of these magazines reflects the passionate desire of the educated classes to revitalize China: *The New Man, New China, The New Life, The New Student.*

The May Fourth Incident shifted the intellectual movement from culture to politics. In late 1919 *New Youth* published a manifesto that articulated the need for a new political philosophy:

> Although we do not believe in the omnipotence of politics, we recognize that politics is an important aspect of public life. And we believe that in a genuine democracy, political rights must be distributed to all people. Even though there may be limitations, the criteria for distribution will be whether people work or not, rather than whether they own property or not. This kind of politics is really inevitable in the process of introducing the new era and a useful instrument in the development of the new society.[6]

However, as intellectuals turned to politics questions of political ideology began to split the intelligentsia, which had so far been united in its attacks on Confucian conservatism. Politicians like Sun Yat-sen, quick to recognize the emergence of the urban classes, particularly the students, as a valuable patriotic force, began to woo them to their side. It cannot be doubted that the May Fourth Movement led to the establishment of the National Students Union (1919) or that it paved the way for the founding of the Chinese Communist party (1921), the General Labor Union (1922), and the reorganization of the Guomindang (1924).

THE SOVIET UNION AND CHINA

To those Chinese who had believed that the postwar peace would bring morality to international relations along the lines enunciated in President Wilson's Fourteen Points (among which were evacuation of occupied territory and the right of national self-determination), the Versailles Treaty was not only disappointing but brought anger and revulsion against the immorality of the West. In the words of Li Da-zhao (1889–1927), professor of history and head of the library at Beijing University and a contributor to *New Youth,* "When the war ended, we had dreams about the victory of humanism and peace. . . . When we look . . . at the Paris Peace Conference . . . where have the freedom and rights of the small and weak peoples not been sacrificed to a few robber states?"[7] Even Liang Qi-chao, for so long an ardent advocate of Westernization, revised his admiration of the West and declared that a blind worship of science had made the West spiritually bankrupt. He recommended that China, while accepting science and technology, should not give up its traditional moral idealism.

At this critical juncture the Russian Revolution provided an alternative solution to China's problems. The October Revolution that established the Communist government in Russia was a happening that in time would have a most far-reaching impact on the politics of the modern world. But in 1917 the fledgling state was internally unstable and externally hemmed in by antagonistic capitalist states. However, from its very inception the Soviet Union became a symbol of hope for many revolutionary groups in colonial countries, and it took on itself the role of leading world revolutionary movements. The Soviet Union worked through the Communist International, or Comintern, which became an organ for the exercise of Soviet foreign policy by means other than conventional state-to-state relations.

The Establishment of the Chinese Communist Party

The success of the Communist revolution in Russia proved that Marxism could be efficacious in an industrially backward country. Moreover, Marxism offered a satisfactory explanation for China's ills. China was backward not because of its culture but because foreign imperialists and feudal warlords were collaborating to keep it poor and weak. Culture would change with the change in the ruling class. China did not have to reject its past but put it in the context of universal historical change. Lenin's thesis—that imperialism was the highest stage of capitalism and that anti-imperialistic nationalist revolt in colonial and semicolonial countries could hasten the downfall of capitalism in advanced industrial countries and further world revolution—was attractive to political activists in China. According to Lenin, this anti-imperialist revolution in the colonial and semicolonial countries need not be based on the industrial proletariat and could have a national-bourgeois character. With the collapse of imperialism and thereby of capitalism, the colonial and semicolonial countries could move on to the socialist stage, bypassing the capitalist stage.

Russian experience had shown that instead of depending on the spontaneous uprising of the working classes, the revolution could be led by a politically active intelligentsia, who would head a Communist party, the vanguard of the revolution. By embracing Marxism, the Chinese would find themselves a part of the historical progression that placed them ahead of the capitalist West. Yet all these ideas took some time to develop because not many Chinese intellectuals were immediately touched by the events in Russia. Among the first to respond enthusiastically to the Bolshevik Revolution was Li Da-zhao, who published an article in *New Youth* in October 1918 entitled "The Victory of Bolshevism." He hailed the Russian Revolution and said, "Henceforth all national boundaries, all differences of classes, all barriers to freedom will be swept away. . . . [Bolshevism] expresses the common sentiments of twentieth century mankind."[8] Li had accepted the messianic claims of the Marxist revolution without knowing much about Marxism. However, he soon established a circle of students to study and discuss the ideology. A young intellectual from Hunan, Mao Ze-dong (1893–1976), was part of this group. In May 1919 Li edited an issue of *New Youth* entirely devoted to Marxism.

In July, against the background of the Chinese demonstrations attacking the West, Moscow elaborated on the Soviet Union's repudiation, first made in 1918, of imperialist rights gained in China by czarist Russia. The Soviet Union announced that it would voluntarily and unilaterally withdraw from the territories acquired by the czars; renounce the Boxer indemnities; and return, without compensation, the Chinese Eastern Railway and other concessions. Although ultimately the Soviet Union did not give up many of the privileges gained under the unequal treaties, this announcement naturally had a powerful pro-Soviet impact on the radical Chinese intellectuals. In 1920, with the secret help of the Comintern agent Gregory Voitinsky, Communist cells were established in Beijing, Shanghai, Hunan (under Mao Ze-dong), and Hubei. Chen Du-xiu, who after his arrest by the authorities as one of the leaders of the May Fourth Movement had left Beijing for Shanghai, also met with Voitinsky and was totally won over to communism. In 1921 the Communist Party of China (CPC) was formally established by 12 or 13 delegates (there is debate about the exact figure), representing less than a 100 members, who met secretly in Shanghai. Chen was elected secretary general of the party.

Since from these small beginnings the party ultimately was to bring about a Communist revolution, the question is worth asking, How could intellectuals like Chen Du-xiu who appeared so deeply committed to democracy turn so quickly to an authoritarian ideology? The answer lies in the fact that these intellectuals were committed to saving China and not to any particular political ideology. Their approach was basically pragmatic. When the Russian experience made Marxism a possible practical guide to Chinese revolution, they turned to it and found it more appealing than the liberal democratic model. In an age when science was made so much of, the Communist creed was "scientific." It provided a rational explanation of world history, put China in the context of universal progression, and gave the frustrated Chinese an optimistic view of their future.

It was also far easier for the Chinese intellectuals, with a tradition of a totalistic Confucian ideology, to replace Confucianism with the new totalistic ideology of communism. Like Confucianism, communism presented a single universal truth, a doctrine that emphasized the group over the individual while sanctioning a leadership role to the intellectuals. That Confucian "harmony" was replaced with Communist "struggle" did not jar the subconscious of the intellectuals, who were consciously involved in an attempt to make a wholesale change in traditional values.

The Soviet Union and Sun Yat-sen

As we have seen, Sun Yat-sen's political fortune was at a low point in 1922, when he was expelled from Guangzhou by the warlord Chen Jiong-ming. So far, Sun, who had maintained a sporadic correspondence with Moscow and met some of the Russian agents in China, had basically kept aloof from the

Soviets, perhaps because of his fear of British intervention in Guangzhou or because he was confident of achieving success on his own. Besides, even the Soviet Union had made no definite overture to which Sun could give serious consideration. In 1922–1923 Moscow's reading of the Chinese situation changed critically. The Russian agent in China, Adolf Joffe, after meeting Beijing militarists and other public leaders, came to the conclusion that Sun personified the Chinese revolution and that a united front between the Guomindang and the CPC could lead to the reunification of China and the ousting of the imperialists.

When approached by Joffe in 1922, Sun, who by this time had lost faith in his warlord friends and had despaired of getting any recognition or aid from the West, was highly receptive to the Soviet offer of aid. The negotiations between the two resulted in the Sun-Joffe declaration of January 1923. Sun got Joffe to agree that conditions in China were not suitable for communism or the Soviet system but that China needed unification and independence on the basis of his Three Principles. In return for Soviet aid, Sun agreed to collaborate with the CPC and accepted the postponement of the issues connected with the Chinese Eastern Railway and the withdrawal of Soviet troops from Outer Mongolia. Shortly thereafter, Moscow supplied the Guomindang with monetary and military aid, military experts, and a political advisor in the person of Michael Borodin.

Many in Sun's party doubted the wisdom of the Guomindang-CPC alliance, but Sun managed to allay most of their fears by publicly announcing that in case the Communists went counter to Guomindang policies, they would be expelled, and that in case the Soviets tried to subvert the Guomindang, he would oppose Russia. Sun explained that in following the propaganda and organization techniques of the Soviet Union, the Guomindang would become a mass party, something it had never been before.

In the meantime, Chen Jiong-ming was forced out of Guangzhou, and the new power holders invited the generalissimo to return to Guangzhou. In March 1923 Sun established a military government in Guangzhou, which laid the foundations of the future government of China. A few months later, Sun sent his military aide, Chiang Kai-shek, to the Soviet Union to study the Bolshevik army and party systems. Although Sun had insisted that Moscow recognize that the Soviet system was unsuitable for China, he in fact borrowed heavily from it because it strengthened his own ideas of revolutionary strategy. During the three stages of his revolution (military conquest, political tutelage, and finally constitutional government), Sun emphasized the need for his party to wield a monopoly of power for the initial two stages, and he demanded personal allegiance and obedience from the members of the party. The Leninist party and army organizations reinforced his views of how power should be organized.

The Three People's Principles, which had first been enunciated before the collapse of the Qing dynasty, were redefined. The principle of nationalism, which had earlier meant anti-Manchuism, was now interpreted to mean the unification of races within China, elimination of inequalities among the nations of the world, and a struggle against foreign imperialism. The last part, added after Sun failed to get control over Guangzhou customs revenues in late 1923, appealed to the emerging national consciousness.

Sun gave an original twist to the principle of democracy by making a distinction between "sovereign power" and "ability." The people, although lacking ability, retained sovereign power and could use it through the institutions of suffrage, recall, initiative, and referendum, but the high-powered government was to be run by men of ability, a group of experts. Sun wanted to ensure that China would have strong political leadership. The government was to be organized on the basis of a five-power constitution that added a censorate and an examination branch, taken from Chinese tradition, to the modern branches of executive, legislature, and judiciary. Sun extended the meaning of "the people's livelihood" by adding "control of capital" to the "equalization of land rights." Although categorically rejecting Marxism, Sun envisaged a kind of state socialism, but he still showed limited understanding of the problems of the peasants. At the same time he made statements that were vague enough to give the impression that he was for communism. Thus, he says at one place, "Not only should we not say that communism conflicts with the *Min-sheng* [people's livelihood] Principle, but we should even claim communism as a good friend. . . . Our Principle of Livelihood is a form of communism. . . . [Its] great aim . . . is communism."[9]

The Guomindang was reorganized with the help of the Soviet advisor, Michael Borodin, and its final pyramidal structure, as approved by the First Party Congress of the Guomindang in January 1924, was much like that of any Communist party: four tiers of authority constituting the central, the provincial, the county, and the district party organizations. The National Party Congress (NPC) theoretically possessed the highest authority and was supposed to meet every other year. Actually it met only five times in 20 years. In the absence of the NPC, its authority was exercised by the Central Executive Committee, in fact by the few who made up the Standing Committee of the Central Executive Committee. Parallel to the Central Executive Committee was the Central Supervisory Committee, which was concerned with matters of discipline and finance. The party worked on the principle of democratic centralism, which meant that once the decisions had been reached (presumably democratically), the lower levels had to accept them unquestioningly. The most important person in the party of course was Sun, who was constitutionally made president for life and given the power to approve or disapprove resolutions of the party congress.

The first congress also approved the collaboration between the Guomindang and the CPC. The CPC members could join the Guomindang in their *individual* capacity and had to accept Guomindang discipline. The orthodox Moscow view was that the revolution would be carried to culmination in two stages—the bourgeois-national stage and the socialist stage. The first stage had to be led by a bourgeois-nationalist party representing *all four classes* of society (bourgeois, petty bourgeois, workers, and peasants). The Communists joining the Guomindang would form a "bloc within," which would gradually expand its activities and hold over the inner machinery of the party and government. Called the First United Front, the alliance lasted from 1924 to 1927.

The CPC under Chen Du-xiu was reluctant to accept this arrangement, which made the CPC subservient to a bourgeois party and took away CPC independence. However, Chen, who would have preferred a "bloc without" approach, which would have given a sense of equality between the parties, was forced by the Comintern to agree to the policies framed in Moscow. As Borodin advised them, the Communists would have to be the "coolies" of the revolution until the right time came for them to take power. Perhaps Moscow was right, because in 1924 the CPC was hardly a party with any strength. The alliance promptly gave it a framework within which it could expand. Among the 24 members of the newly elected Central Executive Committee of the Guomindang were 4 Communists, including Li-Da-zhao; among the 17 alternate members were 3 Communists, including Mao Ze-dong and Qu Qiu-bai. Naturally, all these Communists were required to take out Guomindang membership.

In May 1924 the Guomindang military academy, headed by Chiang Kai-shek, opened in Whampoa (Huangpu), near Guangzhou. Sun at last had not only an army of his own but also, following the Leninist principle, an army subordinate to the party. In the Soviet style the academy had a political wing to provide political indoctrination (based on the Three People's Principles) to the military officers. Among those holding seniormost posts in the political department was the young Communist party member Zhou En-lai (1898–1976), who often had to act as the director of the department. But Communist influence was limited and indeed could not counter the growing mystique of Chiang Kai-shek. One of the few Communists who graduated from the academy was Lin Biao, who later rose to the top of the power pyramid in Communist China. The new army got an opportunity to show its capability in fall 1924, when it crushed a British-inspired uprising by the Guangzhou Merchant Volunteers and in the process expanded the area under Nationalist control.

The years 1924 to 1926 were good for the CPC. The party expanded its mass organization operations, and its membership increased rapidly, helped by a new wave of anti-imperialist nationalism that followed the May Thirtieth and June Twenty-third incidents in 1925. In May the workers of a Japanese-owned Shanghai cotton mill went on strike to protest the dismissal of some of their colleagues. The factory guards opened fire, killing one and wounding several workers. This act resulted in widespread resentment, and on May 30, 10,000 persons gathered in the International Settlement to demonstrate against the Japanese imperialists. A clash developed between the demonstrators and the British police; the police opened fire on the crowd, killing and wounding several persons in the process. The result was that 200,000 workers downed tools, 50,000 students quit their schools and colleges, and many merchants closed their business establishments on June 1. On June 11 the Shanghai Federation of Workers, Merchants, and Students held a mass meeting and passed a resolution making 17 demands, among which were withdrawal of foreign forces from China; abrogation of extraterritoriality; freedom of speech, publication, and assembly; and the right to strike and organize trade unions.

Nothing came of the demands, and for political reasons, the organizers called off the strikes at the end of June, but events in Shanghai reflected the new mood of the country. The May Thirtieth incident inflamed national sentiment and angered the Chinese, who demonstrated in most of the major cities, formed anti-imperialist associations, and demanded the end of unequal treaties. The strikes, protests, and boycotts that swept the country exceeded anything the nation had witnessed earlier.

The response in the industrially and commercially advanced Hong Kong-Guangzhou area was particularly bitter. In mid-June a sympathy strike involving many tens of thousands of workers was organized in Hong Kong and led to the imposition of martial law in the colony. On June 23 100,000 persons, including workers, students, military cadets from Whampoa academy, and other citizens of Guangzhou, demonstrated outside the foreign concession area in that city. Just as in Shanghai, this demonstration led to foreign troops opening fire and killing 52 demonstrators and wounding over 100 others. A strike involving 200,000 workers followed in Hong Kong, which tied up the port for 16 months. The strike was led by the Communists.

In this feverish anticapitalist, anti-imperialist milieu, the CPC found ample opportunity to exert its influence and acquire a leadership role in the labor movement. The growth of the CPC was phenomenal. From 57 members in 1921, it rose slowly to a strength of 980 in January 1925; then within a year and a half, it expanded to over 30,000 members. By mid-1927 the membership soared to 58,000, with another 30,000 in the Communist Youth League. These figures amply prove that although working under the Guomindang banner and within the Guomindang framework, the CPC had managed to maintain its independent identity. Its success was partly due to the fact that the Guomindang mass movement programs were directed by Communists, which implied that the CPC was assuming the confrontational role of a party within a party.

The Guomindang, already a large party in 1923, also expanded its membership during these years; but after the death of Sun Yatsen in March 1925, the Nationalist leadership split up, and troubles also began between the Nationalists and the Communists. During his lifetime Sun had kept the various factions in the Nationalist party working together; after him no leader of stature could command the allegiance of all party members.

The three most important leaders of the Guomindang, who had all been close associates of Sun and who aspired to his position, were Hu Han-min (1879–1936), Wang Jing-wei (1883–1944), and Liao Zhong-kai (1878–1925). Wang and Liao belonged to the left wing of the party (Liao being far more pro-Communist than Wang), and Hu can be said to have headed the right wing. At the death of Sun Yat-sen a collective leadership, which included Hu, Wang, and Liao, declared the establishment of the national government of China on July 1, 1925. However, the collective approach collapsed when Liao was assassinated in August 1925. Although the murder still remains a mystery, Hu was implicated in the plot and forced to leave Guangzhou on a mission to Moscow. Some of the rightist dissidents in the party met in November in the Buddhist temple in the western hills outside Beijing, where Sun's remains had been temporarily interred, and called for the expulsion of the Communists from the Guomindang, retirement of Borodin from his office as advisor to the party, and the suspension of Wang Jing-wei's party membership for six months.

However, in the absence of Hu, the party came to be dominated by Wang Jing-wei and the Communists, reflected in the composition of the various leading committees at the Second National Conference of the Guomindang in February 1926. More than 33 percent of the delegates to the congress were Communists, who also represented 20 percent of the membership in the Central Executive Committee. The congress took action against the Western Hills faction by expelling some of those involved and reprimanding the others. Under Borodin's advice Chiang Kai-shek, who had so far remained aloof from the civilian leadership of the party, was brought in as a member of the Central Executive Committee and the Standing Committee. There was every reason to believe that Chiang, the passionately loyal follower of Sun Yat-sen, the man who had suppressed several right-wing military threats to the regime and had made many anti-imperialist speeches, was a trustworthy leftist.

The new balance of power was shortly destroyed by the notorious *Zhong-shan* incident. On March 18, 1926 the *Zhong-shan,* a Nationalist gunboat under the command of a Communist, moved to the vicinity of Whampoa Military Academy. It is not known even today who ordered the transfer of the gunboat (the Communists say that it was Chiang himself who did it); Chiang looked on this act as a Communist plot to kidnap him, and he staged a countercoup. He declared martial law in Guangzhou; disarmed the Communist-directed workers' militias of the Guangzhou-Hong Kong Strike Committee; detained many Communists, including those attached to the Military Academy; and put the Soviet advisors under house arrest. Since Chiang had taken this action without authorization from Wang Jing-wei, who was his superior and head of state, Wang showed his resentment by withdrawing from active politics and leaving in May for France for a "vacation."

With the leaders of the left and right wings out of the way, Chiang was now unquestionably in control of Guomindang affairs. All these events occurred when Borodin was away in the north negotiating with the warlord Feng Yu-xiang, who had moved to the Soviet side in 1926. When he returned to Guangzhou in April, Borodin found the situation not entirely to his liking, but he could not afford to have his masters in Moscow believe that he had failed in maintaining control of the Chinese revolution. In the power struggle that had developed in Russia after Lenin's death in 1924, Stalin had to prove that his policies in China were correct. In any case, Chiang needed Soviet aid as much as the Soviets needed the Guomindang.

Borodin was satisfied with Chiang's reconfirmation of his loyalty to the Three Great Policies of Sun Yat-sen (alliance with the Soviet Union, collaboration with the CPC, and development of mass movements), with Chiang's denunciation of the Guomindang right wing, and with the actions meant to heal the breach between him and the CPC. There was no real evidence to prove that Chiang was not indeed basically a leftist. Did

Chiang Kai-shek (1887–1975): Early Years

Chiang Kai-shek was born in the coastal province of Zhejiang in a merchant family of modest means. His father died when Chiang was nine years old and his mother had to make many sacrifices to bring up six children.

Troubled by China's plight in the post-Boxer period and inspired by Japan's victory over Russia in the 1904–1905 war, Chiang decided on a military career. He entered Baoding Military School (which later became famous as Baoding Military Academy) in 1907 and was sent to Japan for advanced military training from 1908 to 1910. Upon completing his studies, Chiang served for a brief time in the regular Japanese army.

Chiang, who already had strong anti-Manchu feelings, became a more ardent revolutionary after meeting Sun Yat-sen and other members of the *Tong-meng-hui* in Japan. When news of the Wuchang uprising reached Japan, Chiang hurried back to help the republican cause. He was involved in some military action but never rose to any position of prominence.

After Yuan's usurpation of power and the failure of the 1911 revolution, Chiang once again left for Japan, returning briefly to take part in the abortive second revolution. Soon thereafter, in 1914, Chiang joined Sun's new Revolutionary Party and became a sworn follower of Sun, who had also sought refuge in Japan. In 1915 Chiang came back to China to participate in the movement against Yuan's attempt to become monarch. It is during these years that Chiang developed a close friendship with the brothers Chen Guo-fu and Chen Li-fu, who were later to play an important role in Chiang's government.

Many details of Chiang's activities from 1915 to 1921 are missing, but it is known that during this period he occasionally helped Sun in fund raising and as a military advisor and that he was somehow involved with the business community and the stock exchange in Shanghai. He does not appear to have taken any part in the May Fourth Movement.

From 1922, when Sun appointed him chief of staff, Chiang rose to become one of the most important lieutenants of Sun; in 1923, after Sun's alliance with the Soviet Union, Chiang was sent to Russia to study the Soviet military system. On his return he headed the Whampoa (Huangpu) Military Academy, which provided the Guomindang with its own army and finally gave Sun an opportunity to carry out his revolutionary goals for China.

---

not the Western press in Shanghai and Hong Kong call him the "red general"? On his part, Borodin blamed the CPC for some of the troubles and agreed to limit Communist influence in the Nationalist party. The Comintern also tended to belittle the importance of the *Zhong-shan* incident, claiming that it was an invention of the imperialists. Some in the CPC suggested that the Communist party withdraw from the alliance and follow an independent policy, but Borodin and the Comintern would not accept that course of action, knowing that the CPC, despite its impressive successes in the mass movement, could be easily crushed out of existence.

Another major concession that Borodin had to make to reestablish the Guangzhou-Moscow alliance was to agree to Chiang's timetable for the northern expedition. Military operations to unify China began in May 1926 with Chiang as commander-in-chief. The expeditionary force, numbering about 100,000 men, was divided into two main flanks. The left flank, driving directly north, gained rapid success and reached Wuhan by the end of the year; the right flank, under Chiang, occupied Jiangxi and Fujian. The heavily left-wing government council, left behind in Guangzhou (which included two CPC members and Borodin), wanted to shift the government from Guangzhou to Wuhan. Chiang, along with the Central Executive Committee members who favored him, declared for Nanchang, which was Chiang's new base. The transfer of the government to Wuhan (January 1, 1927) made it obvious that Borodin and the party left were going to resist Chiang. Incidentally, when the revolutionaries occupied the British settlement in Hankou, the British government decided to relinquish its concessions in Hankou and Jiujiang. This was the first success of the revolutionaries against imperialism.

The points of conflict between the Wuhan and the Nanchang camps became further complicated by the entry into the picture of warlords, who decided to join the Nationalists, by Chiang Kai-shek's political volte face, and by the contradictory policies emanating from Moscow. The commanders of the left flank, advised by Borodin, wanted to continue their northward march to link with Feng Yu-xiang, whose base was Inner Mongolia and who was now considered a pro-Soviet revolutionary. Chiang wanted to move eastward to occupy Nanjing and Shanghai. In the meantime the Nationalist armies had nearly trebled by the incorporation of troops belonging to warlords who had switched to the Nationalist side. These militarists, although opportunistic, could hardly be expected to support radical policies. The Communists, whose mass organizations in the countryside had provided invaluable help to the expedition, were caught in a dilemma. They had aroused the peasantry with their revolutionary antilandlord and land-to-the-tiller slogans, but their alliance with the Guomindang meant that they could not deliver on their promises.

While Wuhan was becoming increasingly anti-Chiang and Chiang was growing weary of the leftists, Chiang's forces continued to be successful in the eastern sector. Hangzhou was occupied on February 19, 1927. The Communist-organized armed workers in Shanghai, despite the brutal manner in which the local warlord tried to suppress them, arose and liberated the Chinese city of Shanghai on March 21 and thus enabled the expeditionary force to occupy Shanghai with ease on March 23. Nanjing was captured on March 24. However, because some foreigners had been attacked by troops from one of the revolutionary units (the British consul was wounded, and among the killed was an American missionary), the British and Americans retaliated by ordering their gunboats, anchored on the Yangtze, to bombard the city, and foreign forces in the International Settlement were reinforced. Chiang went to Shanghai and tried to assure the foreigners that the Nationalists, although determined to rid the country of imperialism, were not out to harm them individually or to change the international treaty system by mob violence.

It is not known at what stage Chiang was assured of the financial support from the Shanghai mercantile interests that was to enable him to break from Wuhan, but it must have been in fall 1926 and early 1927, when his old friends from Shanghai visited him in Nanchang. In any case, it is known that the anti-Chiang campaign in Wuhan was assuming alarming proportions and that Wuhan was denying Chiang the finances and supplies he needed. The return of Wang Jingwei to Wuhan in April strengthened the left-wing leadership, and Borodin managed to increase the role of the CPC within the Guomindang. The growing power of the CPC and its Soviet backers alarmed many in the country, and diverse forces began to gel in favor of Chiang Kai-shek. These forces included the conservatives inside and outside the Guomindang party, the Chinese mercantile community, the pro-British and pro-Japanese warlords, and of course the imperialist powers.

On April 6, 1927, the Beijing warlord authorities raided the Soviet embassy and confiscated documents proving that the Soviet diplomats were actively supporting subversion by Chinese Communists. Beijing broke off diplomatic relations with Moscow and arrested and executed many Communists with Soviet connections, one of whom was Li Dazhao. On April 12, Chiang ordered the disarming of the Workers' General Union in

Shanghai. The action resulted in a reign of terror and a brutal massacre of the labor leaders and members of the Communist party. On April 15 the pro-Chiang Guomindang authorities in Guangzhou suppressed the Communist-directed mass organizations in Guangzhou, killing over 2,000 Communists in the process. On April 18 Chiang, supported by most of the members of the Guomindang Central Executive Committee, set up his own national government in Nanjing. In the middle of April the Wuhan government had dismissed Chiang from his post of commander-in-chief of the Nationalist army and from membership in the Guomindang.

Even more than in the cities, Communist activity in the countryside was causing the conservatives to fear the CPC alliance. During the first year of the northern expedition, as the expeditionary forces moved through the crowded southern provinces, the Communist-inspired peasant associations exploded in numbers. For example, consider the single province of Hunan. It is calculated that whereas only about 200,000 peasants were organized in associations on the eve of the northern expedition, their number in mid-1927 was over 4.5 million.[10] The radicalized peasants often refused to pay rents and at places even seized the land. Mao Ze-dong, in his enthusiastic report entitled the "Peasant Movement in Hunan," delivered in March 1927, said,

> "All power to the peasant association" has become a reality. . . . The local tyrants, evil gentry and lawless landlords have been deprived of all rights to speak, and none of them dares even mutter dissent. . . . [Although "terrible" and "excessive" this] rural revolution is a revolution by which the peasantry overthrows the power of the feudal landlord class.[11]

Many of the officers in the Guomindang armies and members of the Guomindang, who came from the landlord-gentry class, obviously felt threatened by this aspect of the revolution. The peasants did not even spare the parents of CPC members. The father of Li Li-san, one of the most prominent Communist leaders, was killed by the peasants in his Hunan village home, even though he had in his possession a letter written by his son guaranteeing that the old man was in favor of peasant associations.

Having "lost" Chiang Kai-shek, Moscow tried to concentrate the left-wing forces in Wuhan, eliminate the bourgeoisie from the alliance, and deprive Chiang of his powers. The CPC dilemma was that the party was directed by Moscow to heighten agrarian revolution without jeopardizing its collaboration with the Guomindang. These were mutually incompatible goals. The issues were further clouded because of the debate between Borodin and the newly arrived (April 2, 1927) Comintern agent M. N. Roy. Borodin wanted to continue the northern expedition to link up with Feng Yu-xiang. To ensure the loyalty of the army officers, he wanted to put restraints on the peasant movement; Roy wanted the left to consolidate the revolutionary base by carrying out the agrarian revolution before further military expansion. At the end of April, the fifth congress of the CPC approved both the continuation of the northern expedition and the radical land program!

Moscow had overlooked the fact that most of the troops under Wuhan belonged to warlords who had opportunistically joined the Guomindang. By appointing them to Guomindang military posts and allowing them to retain control of their armies (although these armies were now units of the Guomindang force), the Wuhan government had not only diluted the ideological purity of the Nationalist military but also weakened its own power and authority. Thus, for example, on May 21, 1927, the Guomindang commander-in-chief for Hunan, the former warlord Tang Sheng-zhi, realizing that the Wuhan government decrees (advising mass organizations to restrain peasant excesses) carried no weight, took direct action against peasant associations and labor unions. Many hundreds of peasants and Communist organizers were executed for sabotaging the rear lines of the northern expedition. Under these circumstances, how could the CPC carry on its revolutionary activities in the countryside? And what role could the Guomindang "left" play?

On June 1, 1927, Stalin sent a cable to Roy giving new guidelines for the Chinese revolution:

> Without an agrarian revolution victory is impossible. . . . We are decidedly in favor of the land actually being seized by masses from below. . . . A large number of new peasants and working class leaders from the ranks must be drawn into the Central Committee of the Kuomintang [Guomindang]. . . . It is necessary to liquidate the dependence on unreliable generals. Mobilize about 20,000 Communists and about 50,000 revolutionary workers and peasants . . . and organize your own reliable army before it is too late. . . . If the Kuomintangists do not learn to be revolutionary Jacobins, they will be lost both to the people and to the revolution.[12]

According to Zhang Guo-tao, a founding member of the CPC, "When this telegram was read at the meeting of the Politbureau of the Central Committee of the CPC, everyone had the reaction of not knowing whether to cry or to laugh. They unanimously felt that it was impossible to implement the order."[13] It appears that Stalin presumed that Soviet aid, along with the Comintern agents and Soviet advisors, was indispensable to the Chinese revolution. Stalin did not realize that without the "unreliable generals," Wuhan was militarily vulnerable. In any case, the Guomindang left wing may have been left of center but was by no means Marxist-Leninist in its thinking. Roy, for some inexplicable reason, showed the telegram to Wang Jing-wei, hoping perhaps to win over the radical Wang to Stalin's cause. Wang was shocked. He felt that Moscow wanted to turn the Guomindang into a tool of the CPC and bring communism to China. This policy went against the goals laid down by Sun Yat-sen, who had clearly stated that the Communist, or the Soviet, system was not applicable to China. There was no way the United Front could now be saved.

At the same time Borodin also failed in his mission to gain the support of Feng Yu-xiang and the northern provinces. Both Wuhan and Nanjing were wooing Feng. On June 6 the Shanxi warlord Yan Xi-shan, a neighbor of Feng, joined Chiang Kai-shek and was appointed commander-in-chief of the National Revolutionary Army in the north. On June 21, Feng sent a secret telegram to the Wuhan government, expressing dissatisfaction with the Communist presence in the Guomindang and suggesting that Borodin be sent back to Russia and that the party leaders in Wuhan agree to join the government in Nanjing.

On June 20 the CPC had abjectly conceded everything that the Guomindang could have asked of it, even the leadership and control of the mass organizations and the armed pickets, but to no avail. The suppression of peasant and labor movements continued. On July 13 the Central Committee of the CPC issued a declaration condemning the Wuhan authorities for serving "the reactionary army officers who rose from the ranks of local bullies and evil gentry . . . [and for opposing] the interests of the great majority of the Chinese people."[14] This declaration finally confirmed, if any confirmation was needed, that the CPC was untrustworthy and acting seditiously. On July 23 the government finally expelled all Communists who were working in the Nationalist party, government, and army and ordered the CPC to cease all activity for the duration of the national revolution. On July 24 Wang Jing-wei sent a telegram to Feng Yu-xiang stating that the CPC and Borodin had been dealt with and that the party was ready to move to Nanjing.

The decade of Soviet intervention in Chinese politics ended ignominiously, but it left an indelible mark on the future of the Chinese revolution. Borodin and other Soviet advisors left hurriedly for Russia. Some new Comintern agents arrived to carry on the liaison work with the CPC, which became an underground party harassed and persecuted by the "legitimate" national government at Nanjing.

To strengthen the unity of the party and

enable the senior members of the Guomindang, his superiors, to come to Nanjing without losing face, Chiang Kai-shek resigned his posts and retired from active politics in August 1927. He used the vacation, for that is what it really was, to marry Sun Yat-sen's sister-in-law, Soong Mei-ling. The marriage strengthened Chiang's political connections. T. V. Soong, Mei-ling's brother, was minister of finance in the national government, and her brother-in-law (sister's husband), H. H. Kung, was a banker and a businessperson who joined the government as minister of industry in 1928.

In early 1928 Chiang Kai-shek, back in his post as the head of the Nationalist military force, resumed the northern expedition to complete the reunification of China.

THE FOREIGN POWERS AND CHINA: 1920–1927

In the decade following World War I the Western powers missed their greatest opportunity to influence the modernization of China. Even America, with its heritage of revolution and its moral view of world politics, could not see Sun Yat-sen's potential and reach out to him. Sun had literally begged for help from various Western powers, including America and England. It appears that well-established capitalist democracies, intent on dealing with legitimate governments, have a limited capacity to give positive help to nationalistic revolutionary movements but a limitless capacity to exploit, undermine, and destabilize weak nations struggling for modernization.

After World War I, Japan emerged as a major Pacific power and a potential threat to British and American interests. To stop the naval race among Japan, Britain, and the United States and to restrict the expansion of Japanese influence in Asia, the Washington Conference was held from November 1921 to February 1922. Among the participants were Britain, France, Holland, Belgium, Portugal (representing European interests in East Asia and the Pacific), the United States, Japan, and China. Russia was not invited. The conference produced a series of treaties. One of them, the Four Powers Pact, spelled the end of the Anglo-Japanese alliance, replacing it with a pledge by major Western powers of nonintervention in East Asia. Another limited the strength of the capital navies of Britain, the United States, and Japan to a 5:5:3 ratio. Thus Japan, with no navy in the Atlantic, was ensured a superiority in the western Pacific, as against any one of the other two powers taken singly. The Nine-Power Treaty formally declared the support of the powers to the principle of the Open Door, that is, the territorial integrity and administrative independence of China, but this in no way meant an immediate end to the foreign rights and special privileges already squeezed out of China. China, lacking even an effective central government, had no leverage to change the existing unequal treaty system; the foreign powers, although conscious that the time was not far off when they would have to liquidate extraterritoriality and other rights, were not eager to hurry the process.

NOTES

1. Quoted in Hu Sheng, *Imperialism and Chinese Politics* (Beijing: Foreign Languages Press, 1955), p. 208.

2. See Li Chien-nung, *The Political History of China, 1840–1928* (Palo Alto, CA: Stanford University Press, 1967), pp. 316–17.

3. R. A. Scalapino and Harold Schiffrin, "Early Socialist Currents in the Chinese Revolutionary Movement," *The Journal of Asian Studies*, 18, no. 3 (May 1959), 342.

4. *Selected Works of Lu Hsun*, vol. I (Beijing: Foreign Languages Press, 1956), pp. 2–3.

5. Pa Chin (Ba Jin), *The Family*, trans. Sidney Shapiro (Beijing: Foreign Languages Press, 1964), p. 36.

6. See Jonathan D. Spence, *The Gate of Hevenly Peace* (New York: Penguin Books, 1982), pp. 159–60.

7. Quoted in Maurice Meisner, *Li Ta-chao and the Origins of Chinese Marxism* (Cambridge, MA: Harvard University Press, 1967), p. 96.

8. Quoted in Benjamin I. Schwartz, *Chinese Communism and the Rise of Mao* (Cambridge, MA: Harvard University Press, 1951), p. 14.

9. Sun Yat-sen, *San Min Chu I: The Three Principles of the People,* trans. Frank W. Price (Shanghai: Institute of Pacific Relations, 1927), pp. 428–34.

10The figures vary in different accounts. This is the highest figure I have come across. See Chang Kuo-t'ao, *The Rise of the Chinese Communist Party, 1921–1927* (Lawrence: University Press of Kansas, 1971), p. 603.

11. *Selected Works of Mao Tse-Tung,* vol. I (Beijing: Peking Foreign Languages Press, 1967), pp. 25–28.

12. Robert C. North and Xenia J. Eudin, *M. N. Roy's Mission to China* (Berkeley: University of California Press, 1963), pp. 106–7.

13. Chang Kuo-t'ao, *Rise of the Chinese Communist Party,* p. 637.

14. Ibid., p. 651.

CHAPTER 6

The Nationalist Government: 1928–1937

THE FAILURE OF NATIONAL REINTEGRATION

The unification of China was officially announced when the Guomindang forces occupied Beijing in June 1928. The formal structure of the Nationalist government, under Chiang Kai-shek as president, was inaugurated in Nanjing on October 10, the anniversary of the 1911 revolution. Beijing (Northern Capital) was renamed Beiping (Northern Peace). Technically, the first stage of Sun Yat-sen's three stages to constitutional government (military unification, followed by six years of political tutelage, leading to constitutional democracy) had been completed.

The Guomindang, having established a single-party dictatorship, theoretically could now begin the process of instructing and guiding the people toward democracy. It is debatable whether a conservative party leaning toward authoritarianism could have achieved this goal even under ideal circumstances. But the circumstances were far from ideal. Behind the facade of unification the country still remained divided, and periodic rebellions forced Nanjing to continue to concentrate its efforts on internal pacification at the expense of constructive national endeavors. This circumstance and the Japanese policies aimed at dominating China strengthened the militarist faction of the Guomindang. Military expenditures and foreign debt payments absorbed over 80 percent of the revenues in 1928–1929, and between 1929 and 1937 the figure never fell much below 66 percent. Most important, factional and clique troubles within the Guomindang kept the party from functioning as a monolithic body providing cohesive and uniform policies that could have helped national reintegration.

Party Troubles and Civil War

The Guomindang success was hailed by the war-weary Chinese, particularly by the urban intelligentsia, who hoped that the revolution would at last bring strength and prosperity to the nation and restore its dignity in the eyes of the world. National elation, however, did not last long. Within a year or two it became clear that the Guomindang had lost its revolutionary drive and that its leaders were squabbling for public office to gain personal status and build up private fortunes.

By its very nature the national government during the period of political tutelage (which because of political reasons was never concluded during Guomindang's rule over mainland China, 1927–1949, and is just being brought to an end in Taiwan) was not popularly elected. In the absence of any democratic controls, the power of the executive could only be checked by the party because the other branches of government, lacking a system of mutual checks and balances, were weak and could not make the president and the Political Council responsible to them. But the party also could not perform this supervisory function because there was no separation between the party and the government. Indeed, the Political Council was a subcommittee of the Central Executive Committee of the party. Furthermore, the party lacked a tight organization, as well as a clear-cut ideology and discipline. It was also badly split between the left and the right wings under Wang Jing-wei and Hu Han-min, respectively. While appearing to act as a mediator between Wang and Hu, Chiang was able to strengthen his own position and even managed to separate his military command from the offices of the national government.

Chiang had no great respect for the party. As early as 1928 he declared that party members had become degenerate and were "struggling for power and profit" instead of making sacrifices for the revolution.[1] He was right in his estimation, but it obviously did not occur to him that he was partly responsible for this state of affairs. The indiscriminate expansion of the party and the absorption of the warlords and old-style bureaucrats into its organization had diluted the idealism that may have existed before 1927. After the break with the CPC in 1927, the party's purge of its Communist and pro-Communist, left-oriented liberals, although in no way helping to bring unity to those who remained behind, did mean that the party had lost its dedicated activists. It now became dangerous for party members to display any signs of revolutionary activism associated with mass movements.

Chiang, whose devotion to the cause of Chinese nationalism cannot be questioned, sincerely believed that he alone was a true follower of Sun Yat-sen and that he was Sun's worthy heir. He therefore had to ensure that he was in an unassailable position to carry on his work as the unifier of the nation and as its modernizer. Since Chiang's self-perception was challenged by Wang Jing-wei and Hu Han-min, who also believed that they were rightful inheritors of the revolutionary legacy, Chiang employed various methods to maintain his position. Western scholars have condemned these methods because they were counter to the expectations of liberal thinkers who wanted Chiang to introduce democracy into China. But however deplorable Chiang's actions may appear, they fitted into the pattern of political behavior of the day.

The party, the army, and the government were riven by numerous small and large factions, but Chiang managed to get his own cliques into positions of power while balancing and playing off antagonistic groups. He developed a tight police and security network and gained control over financial, military, and party affairs.[2]

The C.C. Clique became the most important faction within the party to back Chiang. Led by the brothers Chen Guo-fu and Chen Li-fu, close friends of Chiang Kai-shek, the C.C.Clique represented the hard-core anti-Communist elements in the party. By the 1930s over 25 percent of the Central Executive Committee members belonged to the C.C. Clique; it controlled the intelligence network and dominated the party organization department; it had branches in the government at national and local levels; its members had penetrated the military, trade unions, education, cultural, youth, and other popular organizations; and it influenced the communication media by establishing newspapers, journals, and publishing houses. The C.C. Clique also got into banking operations. It had its own recruiting and training organization, and it drew its membership from intellectuals, bureaucrats, military officers, and leading business entrepreneurs.

Whampoa military graduates (many of whom rose to become high military officers) who swore loyalty to Chiang Kai-shek contributed to the establishment of the Whampoa Clique and the Blue Shirt Society. The Whampoa Clique constituted over 50 percent of the military men in the Central Executive Committee; according to Ch'ien Tuan-sheng, it controlled the party organization in the army and represented the power of what may be termed Chiang's personal army.[3]

Chiang publicly extolled Sun Yat-sen's Three Principles of the People ideology, but he was actively concerned only with that part of Sun's philosophy that demanded the establishment of a strong, single-party state under a strong leader. Chiang interpreted this concept to mean that individual freedom and state authority were equated. As he put it, "The command of the state should be regarded as the free and voluntary will of the individual."[4] Instead of giving the country human rights and a rule of law, Chiang called for absolute loyalty to the state by an ethically enlightened citizenry. The ethics were to come from a revival of traditional Confucian virtues of loyalty, filial piety, benevolence, love, sincerity, righteousness, harmony, and peace. This doctrine formed the basis of Chiang's New Life Movement, inaugurated in 1934 and intended to renovate the moral life of Chinese society.

The Blue Shirt Society was a well-organized political machine whose activities have been compared by some scholars with the Fascist movements in Europe and with Mussolini's Black Shirts and Hitler's Brown Shirts. Like their European counterparts the Blue Shirts glorified their leader, exalted the state, accepted the need for totalitarian controls, rejected democracy, and used terrorism and violence to liquidate opponents of the party and the leader. The Blue Shirts invoked the restoration of certain traditional Confucian cultural values, which Chiang also supported in his New Life Movement.

However, the manner in which the Blue Shirts tried to propagate these noble values proved terribly counterproductive. Their clandestine activities brought terror and fear to the hearts of many innocent citizens of China, undermining the morale of those in government and the military who may have displayed an independent attitude. The Blue Shirts made China a more authoritarian state than it need have been. The costly activities of the Blue Shirts were financed by Chiang Kai-shek himself.

Another clique worthy of mention was the Political Study Clique, an extra-party faction whose members were interested in "increasing their hold on the provincial administration and also on the larger financial and business concerns of the country, whether private or government."[5] The Political Study Clique also supported Chiang Kai-shek and looked on him as their patron.

These and other cliques came into conflict, and mutual rivalries developed that only helped to strengthen Chiang's position. However, factional politics meant that the party could not work out a cohesive policy of reform and, more important, that Chiang lacked absolute authority even while appearing to be in total control.

Chiang's Internal and External Troubles: 1929–1936

From the very day Chiang Kai-shek assumed power he faced major trouble from four sources, three from within the country and one from without. Within, Wang Jingwei and Hu Han-min challenged him for national leadership; the erstwhile warlords resisted Chiang's attempts at centralization of authority; and the CPC, after being ousted from the united front, began to build up its armed forces and establish an independent government in the countryside. All these rivals, at one time or another, posed a military threat; between 1928 and 1936 Chiang had to suppress no less than 23 revolts. Externally, the Japanese expanded their aggressive activities, absorbed Manchuria into their empire in 1932, and began to encroach on China's northern provinces, which led to full-scale war in 1937.

Chiang realized that the unity of China was illusory and that internal pacification was necessary before Nanjing could declare war on Japan. Although he was to be condemned for this attitude, as a military thinker he was right in his assessment.

Trouble from Warlords and Party Leaders: 1929–1930. Although it may be technically incorrect to use the term *warlords* to designate the locally powerful military commanders who had opportunistically joined the Guomindang and were now in command of Guomindang armies (which were often no other than their own troops from the pre-Guomindang days), the term is valid because these figures retained warlord attitudes and tried desperately to retain their autonomy within the Nationalist government. They resented Chiang's efforts at demobilizing the inflated army, since warlord forces would have been the first to be disbanded, and his efforts to increase provincial contributions to the central revenue. The major warlord areas were Gansu-Henan-Shaanxi under Feng Yu-xiang, Shanxi-Hebei under Yan Xi-shan, and Guangxi-Hunan-Hubei under Li Zong-ren and Bai Chong-xi. Feng also laid claim to Shandong, which was actually under Japanese control from 1915. The provinces of Yunnan, Guizhou, Sichuan, Chahar, Ningxia, Xigang, Qinghai, and Xinjiang had yet to be fully incorporated into unified China and continued to be ruled by several minor warlords. Zhang Xue-liang, a case unto himself, had taken over power in Manchuria on the death of his bandit-turned-warlord father, Zhang Zuo-lin, who had been assassinated by the Japanese in 1928. This left Chiang Kai-shek in control of the rich lower Yangtze valley provinces of Zhejiang, Anhui, Jiangsu, and Jiangsi and with influence in Guangdong.

The first challenge to Chiang's authority came from the Guangxi generals Li Zong-ren and Bai Chong-xi. These generals split from the Nanjing government in early 1929 over the question of territorial control and began military operations to expand their area of influence. Chiang had to take punitive action to quell this rebellion.

Later in the same year it was the turn of the "Christian General," Feng Yu-xiang, to rise against the Nationalist government. Some idea of the confused nature of affairs becomes apparent when it is borne in mind that Feng was a member of the State Council, vice-president of the executive Yuan (deputy prime minister), and minister of war when he turned against Chiang. To Feng the maintenance of his hold over his private army was far more important than all these offices. The trouble began with Chiang's attempt to demobilize some of the troops in the swollen armies of the warlords. The situation became acute when Japan, which finally recognized the Nationalist government in March 1929, several months after the other major powers had done so, agreed to withdraw its forces from Shangdong. In April Chiang took control of Shandong, thus denying Feng the right to extend his authority over an area that Feng believed fell legitimately into his zone of control.

Feng accused Chiang of designs that favored his own troops over those of Feng and of policies that were intended to starve Feng's army by withholding funds. Feng declared his independence of Nanjing and in turn was dismissed from all his posts. Chiang bought off some of Feng's generals, who defected to the national government with 100,000 of Feng's best troops and also opened Henan to central control. When war came in October 1929, Feng was defeated.

These developments troubled Yan Xi-shan because every move that strengthened the hand of Chiang Kai-shek spelled the end of warlord power, his own included. In early 1930 Yan joined forces with Feng; gained the backing of Li Zong-ren and Bai Chong-xi; and far more important, won the support of Wang Jing-wei and other factions in the Guomindang that opposed Chiang and wanted to reorganize the party. The "reorganizationist" members of the Guomindang met in Beiping and established an opposition government with Wang, Feng, and Li Zong-ren in the leading posts and Yan as chair of the State Council. This formidable coalition posed the most serious threat Chiang had faced so far. Fifty-seven generals and dozens of politicians, headed by Wang Jing-wei, sent a spate of telegrams to Chiang denouncing his government for bribery, corruption, and dictatorship and demanding that Chiang resign from the presidency and retire from politics.

Chiang defeated the Guangxi generals before the coalition was fully established, but the heavy fighting in Henan and Shandong was indecisive. At this critical moment the balance of power was held by Zhang Xueliang, and both sides approached him for support. On September 19 Zhang, won over by various promises, declared his loyalty to Nanjing and moved his troops south to Beiping. The coalition and the short-lived Beiping regime collapsed and another crisis was over, although not without some further bitter fighting. The war had cost 240,000 casualties, with thousands of peasants uprooted and the province of Henan laid waste.

Trouble from the Communists: 1930–1931. By the end of 1930 the frontline leaders of the CPC operating in the countryside, particularly Mao Ze-dong and Zhu De, had built up an army of several tens of thousands (the Red Army). Taking advantage of the difficulties faced by Chiang Kai-shek, they had established a territorial base, an autonomous soviet, in southern Jiangxi. The word *soviet,* borrowed from the Soviet Union and used in transliteration by the CPC, meant a government run by the local masses. There were similar soviets in other parts of the country, but the one under Mao, with its capital at Ruijin, was the biggest and the most important.

However, the underground headquarters of the CPC was still in Shanghai, and the official policy of the CPC still aimed at leading a city-based proletarian revolution. In mid-1930 the frontline leaders were ordered to capture the cities of Changsha and Nanchang and thus help promote the true revolutionary cause. Although the Red Armies failed to take Nanchang and held Changsha for ten days only, it was becoming apparent that CPC armies had begun to pose a real threat to the central government. After defeating the Feng-Yan coalition, Chiang Kai-shek turned to the problem of suppressing the Communists. The first Communist-suppression campaign (sometimes also referred to as the Communist-encirclement or Communist-annihilation campaign) was launched in December 1930. It was a total failure. What the Communist troops had failed to achieve in the cities, Mao managed to achieve in the countryside. Using guerrilla tactics Mao mauled the Nationalist armies, capturing a general, killing 9,000, and destroying large quantities of supplies.

Chiang Kai-shek was not accustomed to military failure, so he followed up the first campaign with another in April 1931. The Nationalist troops, numbering over 100,000, were under a well-known general, but their fate was no different from that of their comrades in the earlier expedition. It has been suggested that Chiang did not use his best troops and that the armies of the second Communist-suppression campaign were made of units belonging to warlord armies (like the troops of Feng Yu-xiang, who had defected to Nanjing in 1930), which Chiang was happy to see destroyed—therefore, the failure. Regardless of how true this assessment is, and indeed it may be very true, the fact remains that Mao Ze-dong's guerrilla-style warfare was something new. The Nationalists had yet to learn how to deal with an elusive enemy who became visible only when least expected.

In July 1931 Chiang opened the third campaign against the Communists, this time putting himself in direct command. The Nationalist forces were successful in the beginning, driving the Red Armies before them and forcing them to retreat in the direction favorable to the Nationalists. In August, however, heavy rains set in, which favored the guerrillas, and Mao was once again able to extricate his troops and inflict heavy damage on the enemy. But the campaign was by no means over when Chiang had to turn his attention to crises elsewhere. Trouble came from Manchuria in the north and Guangdong in the south.

Japan's Invasion of Manchuria: 1931. On the night of September 18, 1931, while Chiang Kai-shek was bogged down in Guangxi and a considerable part of Zhang Xue-liang's forces were south of the Great Wall in Beiping, Japanese troops set off a bomb on the SMR railway track just outside Mukden (Shenyang). Then, on the pretext of protecting the railway from an attack by the Chinese, they seized Mukden. Within the next few weeks they took possession of several other key centers.

Chiang Kai-shek's reaction to this development was to halt the campaign against the Communists and promptly return to Nanjing to face the Manchurian crisis. As can be imagined, the Chinese were shocked by the Japanese action. There were massive anti-Japanese demonstrations in the cities and boycotts of Japanese goods. Most segments of the urban population publicly demanded that Nanjing turn its guns against the invaders. But Chiang, who calculated that it would be better to entrust China's case to the League of Nations than to start a war, instructed Zhang Xue-liang (whose forces still in Manchuria outnumbered those of the Japanese and could have put up a resistance) not to fight.

By the end of the year the Japanese had cleared Manchuria of Zhang's troops. In March 1932, scorning the findings of the League of Nations and the weight of world opinion, Japan established the puppet state of Manchukuo under the regency of Pu-yi, the last Qing emperor, who had abdicated the Dragon Throne in 1912. The Japanese action had far-reaching repercussions: It changed the power balance in East Asia; it helped drive Japan onto the path of militarism; it made the West suspicious of Japanese long-range goals; and it can be seen to mark the first stage leading toward World War II.

Another Rival "National" Government—Guangzhou: 1931. The trouble in south China was connected with Chiang's differences with Hu Han-min. As a response to the demands made by the leaders of the 1930 abortive rebellion (Wang Jing-wei, Feng Yuxiang, and Yan Xi-shan) that China should have a constitution, Chiang decided to convoke a national assembly and adopt a provisional constitution. Hu Han-min was adamantly opposed to this move because he believed that, as Sun Yat-sen had planned, a period of political tutelage was absolutely necessary before a constitution could be inaugurated. Rather unwisely, Chiang put Hu Han-min under house arrest (February 1931), which only precipitated another major party crisis. Some members of the Central Supervisory Committee of the Guomindang impeached Chiang for his illegal action. Southern warlords supported the impeachment, and in collaboration with anti-Chiang politicians, Wang Jing-wei included, they set up a parallel "national" government in Guangzhou (May).

In September, when the Nationalist troops were locked in combat with the Communists, troops from Guangdong and Guangxi marched into Hunan. But the September 18 Mukden incident, when the Japanese unleashed their forces in Manchuria, saved the nation from becoming embroiled in another civil war, and the southerners agreed to a peace conference in October. There the southerners demanded that Chiang resign his position as chair of the State Council; that the post of commander-in-chief of the land, naval, and air forces be abolished; and that no military man should be president of any of the five Yuan. Obviously their intention was to eliminate Chiang from the political arena.

These were dark days for Chiang. Condemned within the party by both Wang Jing-wei and Hu Han-min, the greatest of the

Background of the Manchurian Crisis

Officers of the Japanese troops posted in Manchuria (the Kwantung Army) to protect Japanese interests there assassinated the Manchurian warlord, Zhang Zuo-lin, in June 1928, just days before the Nationalist northern expedition had triumphantly entered Beijing. Their hope was that Zhang Zuo-lin's son, Zhang Xue-liang ("the Young Marshall"), known as a weak-charactered playboy addicted to drugs, would be more friendly to Japan and keep Manchuria out of the Nationalist jurisdiction. Despite Japanese pressure on Zhang Xue-liang to preserve Manchurian autonomy, in December 1928 Zhang finally pledged his loyalty to Nanjing and raised the Nationalist flag in Mukden, the capital of Manchuria. In return Nanjing confirmed Zhang's authority in the province and rewarded him with the post of commander-in-chief of the Northeastern Border Defense Army.

This act of Zhang led to a confrontation between Nanjing and the Soviet Union. The break between the Nationalists and the Soviets in 1927 had ended direct contact between them, but the Soviet position in Manchuria had remained unimpaired because Zhang Zuo-lin had never accepted the authority of the Nationalist government in Wuhan. Besides, the Soviet Union technically still maintained diplomatic relations with China, which it had established with the pre-1928 warlord government in Beijing. Now, however, it was the unrecognized Nationalist government that had extended its authority over the northeastern provinces. The Nationalists, who resented Soviet domination of the Chinese Eastern Railway (CER was supposed to be run jointly by the Russians and the Chinese) and looked with suspicion on Soviet activities that were aimed at promoting communism in the region, took action to reassert control over the CER (July 1929).

The Soviet Union broke off diplomatic relations and attacked China with aircraft and tanks. The Chinese suffered heavy casualties, and the undeclared war ended with Nanjing signing the Khabarovsk Protocol (December 1929), which restored the status quo ante. Nanjing also agreed to hold negotiations to settle other outstanding issues and to resume diplomatic relations. Bilateral meetings were begun in 1930 but ended inconclusively when the Japanese invaded Manchuria in September 1931.

Zhang and Nanjing had underestimated Japan's involvement in Manchuria. From the Japanese point of view, both the Soviet victory and the rising tide of anti-Japanese sentiment were a threat to Japan's strategic and economic interests. While procrastinating over Japanese requests to implement the agreement they had worked out with Zhang Zuo-lin in 1928 to build certain railway lines, Nanjing built a separate railway system to compete with the Japanese-run Southern Manchurian Railway (SMR) and also began a campaign for the recovery of the SMR.

The world economic depression of 1929–1930 had a particularly harsh impact on Japan, which was so heavily dependent on foreign markets for the surplus it needed to buy raw materials, especially iron, that the homeland lacked. The militarists and the ultranationalists in Japan felt that resource-rich Manchuria could provide Japan with coal and iron and also be a market for Japanese goods, if only it could be firmly brought into the Japanese sphere of influence.

Guomindang leaders, he was also attacked publicly, particularly by nationwide student organizations, for having betrayed China. Saying that "the affairs of the country have come to such a critical pass that unless we can step up the process of national unity and solidarity, we will not be able to meet successfully either the problem of foreign aggression or the aspirations of the Chinese people,"[6] Chiang resigned from his various posts on

December 15. Chiang's retirement, which reminds one of a similar action he had taken in 1927, saved face for those who had opposed him and gave the two sides an opportunity to achieve a measure of national reconciliation. But as in 1927, it was not long before the Guomindang was forced to persuade Chiang to resume office.

The Reorganized Nationalist Government

While the Central Executive Committee of the Guomindang was trying to rework the constitution to reduce the powers of the president and ensure that the executive Yuan would control the armed forces, the Japanese forces began an offensive against Jinzhou (December 24), the last major Nationalist stronghold in Manchuria. Zhang was asked to make a stand, but his demoralized troops withdrew. The opening days of the new year, 1932, saw the Japanese complete their conquest of Manchuria. The inexperienced leaders of the reorganized Nationalist government (in which neither Hu Han-min nor Wang Jing-wei was in a position of authority) panicked and begged Chiang to return to Nanjing. Chiang delayed his acceptance of the invitation until he had the top party politicians, military figures, civic leaders, and even students beseech him to return and until he felt sure that he would not be denied real power.

After his release from house arrest, Hu Han-min had shifted his residence to the British colony of Hong Kong in late 1931. Although he continued to give moral support to the leaders of Guangdong and Guangxi (who maintained a state of virtual autonomy) and persisted in attacking Chiang Kai-shek, Hu Han-min withdrew from active national politics. He died in 1936.

Wang Jing-wei, who had opposed Chiang Kai-shek ever since 1927, headed the Association for Reorganization of the Guomindang, which aimed primarily at reducing the growing power of Chiang. He had twice tried to establish a rival national government but failed. The Japanese aggression in Manchuria impressed the feuding Guomindang factions with the need to put aside their differences and caused Wang to make peace with Nanjing. Encouraged by the party leaders, Wang met with Chiang in the middle of January 1932, and by the end of the month both of them were holding important government offices. However, whereas Wang was appointed president of the executive Yuan (the equivalent of prime minister), a post he held from 1932 to 1935, Chiang was only made a member of the Military Affairs Commission. Theoretically, this appointment not only reduced the civil powers that Chiang had exercised before his resignation but also severely limited his current military authority because the other members of the commission were his erstwhile enemies Feng Yu-xiang and Yan Xi-shan and his erstwhile subordinate Zhang Xue-liang.

But Chiang knew that all this maneuvering could not take away from his real power. A few weeks after Chiang took office, the government was forced to appoint him chair of the Military Affairs Commission and chief of the general staff. These appointments were supposed to give him a freer hand in the exercise of his military authority, but Chiang soon stopped consulting the other commission members altogether and started using the commission's powers arbitrarily. His authority and role were further enhanced because of the continued military aggression by the Japanese and the internal war that Nanjing had to wage against the Communists. It must be remembered that Wang Jing-wei was no more enamored of the Communists than was Chiang.

Chiang also made effective use of the various party, civil, and military factions that dominated politics and were sworn to support him. Over and above all these developments, Chiang's relatives H. H. Kung and T. V. Soong held important posts in the cabinet and could thwart Wang Jing-wei's plans. Indeed, by the end of 1932 Wang felt so frustrated that he departed for Europe for six months, leaving the government in the hands of T. V. Soong. It should be noted that during the years 1932–1935 Chiang did not occupy the position of absolute power that he had before his resignation; despite his frustrations, Wang Jing-wei was the head of the civil government. If most foreigners continued to look on Chiang as the number-one person in China, as no doubt many of the Chinese did, too, it was only because in those troubled years the commander of the armed forces was always in the news and in the public eye.

More Trouble with Japan—The Shanghai Incident: 1932. The strong anti-Japanese feelings, which were further inflamed by the collapse of Jinzhou, created an explosive situation in Shanghai, where several thousand Japanese resided in the International Settlement or the adjoining Chinese district of Chapei. On January 18 a group of Japanese was attacked by some Chinese, and one person subsequently died of his injuries. The Chinese police arrived too late to arrest the culprits. Over the next few days some of the local Japanese residents retaliated by attacking Chinese property; other Japanese held a mass protest meeting and passed resolutions calling on the Japanese government to send a military force to suppress the anti-Japanese activities.

The Japanese consul-general then presented to the mayor of Shanghai a series of demands, the most important of which were a formal apology, arrest of those responsible for the death of the Japanese, suppression of the anti-Japanese movement, and immediate dissolution of all anti-Japanese organizations. The mayor protested that he could not comply with the last three demands. However, when the commander of the Japanese naval forces lying off Shanghai threatened to take direct action if a satisfactory reply was not forthcoming, and faced with an ultimatum (deadline 6 P.M., January 27), the mayor accepted the demands. To prove his sincerity, the mayor went so far as to order the Shanghai Anti-Japanese National Salvation Association to close down.

On the night of January 28, with no consideration of the manner in which the mayor had humbled himself, the arrogant and self-confident commander of the Japanese navy marched his marines into Chapei to remove all "hostile defenses." But he had not reckoned that the locally stationed troops of the Nineteenth Route Army would offer a stiff resistance. Infuriated, the Japanese commander ordered an aerial bombardment of Chapei and sent for reinforcements from Japan.

Despite the terrible civilian losses and material destruction, the Japanese reign of terror could not immediately subdue the fighting spirit of the Chinese troops. War continued through February. By the end of this period about 50,000 Japanese troops and a flotilla of cruisers and destroyers had been rushed to Shanghai. Three cruisers and four destroyers were sent upstream and anchored off Nanjing; one of them even fired a few rounds into the capital city. The Nationalist government moved to Luoyang. The Chinese forces, however, could no longer defend their positions after the Japanese landed troops in the open country near Wusong and outflanked Chapei. After 33 days of a bloody but heroic defense, the Chinese troops were forced to withdraw and a truce was declared (March).

The Nineteenth Route Army had become a national symbol of courage and patriotism, and the names of their commanders became household words. Shortly after the signing of the truce Chiang moved the Nineteenth Route Army from Shanghai to Fujian (May 1932), ostensibly to fight the Communists entrenched there. It has been suggested that since this army belonged to the Guangdong faction of the Guomindang and therefore did not owe loyalty to Chiang Kai-shek, its popularity posed a threat to Chiang's power and he hoped that it would be destroyed by the Communist forces. This would perhaps explain why the Nineteenth Route Army later revolted against Nanjing.

The truce agreement with Japan was, to say the least, extremely unpopular. Many felt that the Nationalist government should have made an all-out effort against the enemy. But Chiang saw the situation differently. Shanghai was only a pinprick. Real Japanese aggression was in the north. There, taking advantage of the fact that Nanjing's attention was temporarily diverted to Shanghai, the Japanese were completing their subjugation of Manchuria. Chiang foresaw that Japanese aggression would not stop with Manchuria, but he felt that Nanjing, weakened by internal discord, was not in a position to confront the sophisticated, modern armies of Japan. China had to deal with its domestic problems first, to attain true internal unity and pacification before it could declare war on Japan.

The Communist and Japanese Fronts: 1932–1933. The third Communist-suppression campaign had been halted because of the Manchurian crisis. The Communists used this period of respite to enlarge and reorganize their armies and to set up a rival central government of their own. Within a month and a half of the Mukden incident, the CPC held the First All-China Soviet Congress (November 1931) at Ruijin and promulgated the constitution of the Chinese Soviet Republic (CSR). Mao Ze-dong was elected chair (president) of the CSR and Zhu De, chair of the Military Commission. Apart from Mao's Central Soviet District (the Jiangxi Soviet), the CSR exercised jurisdiction over seven other, smaller soviets, isolated pockets under Communist control, located in seven central and southern provinces of China. According to Mao's estimate, the CSR had a population of 9 million. In April 1932, just after truce was declared in Shanghai and just before the ceasefire agreement was formally signed, the CSR declared war on Japan. Since there was no point of contact between the soviet districts and Japan, this was a political move intended to gain popular support and put Nanjing in a bad light. Chiang was not impressed.

He launched the fourth Communist-suppression campaign in June 1932, with the Nationalist troops simultaneously attacking the more important of the soviet zones. Chiang transferred his personal headquarters to Hankou and moved against the Hubei-Henan-Anhui Soviet District, the second biggest soviet, with a population of 2 million and an army numbering over 100,000 men. Chiang was successful in driving the Communists out of this strategic area, which lay in the heart of the rich Yangtze valley and straddled the north-south railway link; however, he failed to annihilate the Red Armies, many of which just melted away from the front only to reappear elsewhere later. Thus, for example, Zhang Guotao entered Sichuan with his Fourth Front Army and established a soviet there.

In December, after completing his part of the campaign, Chiang Kai-shek returned to Nanjing and prepared to turn his attention to Jiangxi, where the campaign was not progressing well. Once again Japanese aggressive actions intruded on the internal scene. Ever since the establishment of Manchukuo, Nanjing had been aware of Japan's intention to absorb the northern province of Jehol (Rehe). In the eyes of the Japanese, that Jehol had been under the control of Zhang Zuo-lin and Zhang Xue-liang, the warlords of Manchuria, was reason enough for it to continue to remain under the jurisdiction of Mukden. Besides, Jehol was strategically located as a buffer between Manchukuo and both China proper and the Soviet Union.

On the night of January 23 the Japanese army created an incident at Shanhaiguan (the pass where the Great Wall meets the Yellow Sea) and forcibly occupied it after bombarding it from the ground, the air, and the sea. Nanjing ordered Zhang Xue-liang to move his troops north to protect Jehol. This was looked on as a provocation, and the Japanese foreign minister declared that

> . . . the Great Wall is the dividing line between China on the one hand and Manchuria and Mongolia on the other. . . . Regular troops of Chang Hsueh-liang's [Zhang Xue-liang] army have crossed national boundaries into Jehol province. . . . The so-called Jehol question is purely a matter of domestic concern for Manchukuo.[7]

On February 25, 1933, the day after the assembly of the League of Nations adopted a resolution that its members would not recognize Manchukuo, the Japanese Kwantung Army invaded Jehol and within days took it over. In the next two months the Japanese occupied the passes in the Great Wall and threatened Beiping itself. The Nationalist troops made a better showing in Hebei than they had in Jehol, but in the long run Nanjing had to acquiesce to Japanese demands and sign a truce agreement (Tanggu, May 31, 1933). The humiliating agreement allowed for the creation of a demilitarized, neutral zone between the Great Wall and Beiping, an autonomous buffer zone in China proper where Nanjing could not exercise its sovereignty to post Chinese troops but where the Japanese, by virtue of the Boxer protocol, could maintain garrisons.

Chiang Kai-shek looked on these developments as a national humiliation, but he still maintained that Nanjing's enemy of the moment was the CPC and its soviets:

> Our country is confronted with a crisis which is both internal and external. Internally, the ruthless Communists have been killing and burning day after day. Externally the Japanese imperialists have been committing incessant aggression against our country. The Japanese imperialists attack us and even plan for our extinction. Owing to the existence of the Communist bandits, we cannot offer unified, effective resistance to the aggressor. . . . Internal disorder is the surest way to invite foreign aggression.[8]

But the fourth campaign against Jiangxi ended as disastrously as the previous three. By March the Nationalist armies were in disarray; three divisions had been destroyed, and over 20,000 soldiers had been taken prisoner. But if they had failed to dislodge the Communists, the Communists also had failed to force the Guomindang withdrawal from Jiangxi.

The Last Anti-Communist Campaign: 1933–1934. Correctly believing that the Japanese had achieved their immediate goals and were unlikely to create any more trouble for some time, Chiang Kai-shek turned his full attention to the anti-Communist campaign. He moved his headquarters to Nanchang and made careful preparations to ensure success. His strategies were both modern and traditional. The modern elements included sophisticated weapons (scouting planes and bombers) and a group of German generals (including Von Seeckt, who later commanded Hitler's army of occupation in Belgium) who were helping to train the troops in techniques of modern warfare. Chiang borrowed traditional elements from the tactics employed by Zeng Guo-fan to suppress the Taiping rebels: Increase the sense of loyalty and discipline among the troops and raise their morale by combating corruption; establish strict control over the countryside surrounding the enemy by raising self-defense units in the villages and introducing a system of mutual responsibility on the "bao-jia" basis. The aim was to deny the enemy support or help from the surrounding countryside and force it to withdraw into an ever-shrinking pocket. Chiang called this plan "70 percent political, 30 percent military."

Chiang discarded conventional modern tactics of pitched battles and attack. His army of nearly 800,000 moved slowly, building roads and countless blockhouses interconnected with machine-gun and artillery fire. It imposed an economic blockade on the enemy and forced it to counterattack.

While the Nationalist troops were converging on the Jiangxi soviet and all appeared to go well with the campaign, an incident took place that proved, if proof was still necessary, that Nanjing commanded precious little unity within its own ranks. In November the Nineteenth Route Army, posted in Fujian and supposedly playing an important part in the current anti-Communist campaign, revolted and proclaimed the establishment of the People's Revolutionary Government. Some of the generals of the Nineteenth Route Army, the anti-Japanese heroes from Shanghai who had long harbored ill will against Chiang, were persuaded by certain anti-Chiang liberal and left-wing Guomindang politicians that they would get popular support and the backing of various warlords if they called for a national united front to fight the Japanese. They were also assured help by the Communists.

But when the showdown came the rebels got no help from any source. It would have been tactically advantageous to the Communists if they had come to the support of the Nineteenth Route Army and broken the stranglehold of the encirclement campaign. However, there was a factional struggle within the CPC leadership, and Mao managed to thwart those who wanted to help the army. On the other hand, the army's alliance with the Communists had alienated the conservative warlords and other Guomindang leaders. Chiang moved swiftly against the rebels. Within two months the crisis was over and the leaders of the rebellion forced to flee to Hong Kong.

Chiang could now turn once again to his main task of liquidating the Communists. By May 1934, it was becoming clear to the CPC leadership that the Communist territory was fast shrinking, that the dwindling and impoverished peasant population was no longer in a position to offer adequate support, that there was a growing shortage of military and other supplies with no chance of replacement, and that the Red Army was uniformly unsuccessful in holding back the enemy. In July the Communists tried to sneak out two columns of about 8,000 men each to divert the Nationalists, but the tactic only resulted in the bulk of this force being annihilated. With no alternative left but flight, the Communists decided to abandon the Jiangxi soviet. Thus, on October 14, 1934, began the long march of the main forces of the Red Army and some support units, numbering about 100,000 persons. Twelve months and 12,500 kilometers later, about 10,000 reached the safety of northern Shaanxi. Before the fifth campaign the Red Army had grown to a strength of 300,000; at the end, it was less than 30,000. However, the CPC under the leadership of Mao Ze-dong entrenched itself in Shaanxi and began its recovery, which ultimately led to its victory over the Nationalists.

In January 1933 the CPC headquarters had at last been shifted from Shanghai to Ruijin. The Central Committee of the CPC could now take cognizance of the unorthodox policies followed by Mao Ze-dong. Mao was removed from several of the important posts he occupied and his guerrilla warfare and other policies discarded. Later, after Mao had gained control of the CPC, Communist historians contended that if he had still been in command the Communists would not have suffered this debacle. It appears that regardless of who was in command the Communists could not successfully have countered the carefully organized campaign of Chiang Kai-shek. However, total victory eluded Chiang Kai-shek because the Communists had after all slipped through his net.

Sino-Japanese Relations: 1934–1936

From the Mukden incident (1931) through the Shanghai incident (1932), the occupation of Manchuria (1932), the annexation of Jehol (1933), the declaration of east Hebei as a demilitarized zone (1933), and the establishment of the independent kingdom of Manchukuo under Emperor Kang De (from regent, Pu Yi was made emperor) in January 1934, the cumulative effect of the Japanese actions was to keep Chinese passions inflamed.

No major incidents took place in 1934, although the Japanese enunciation of their official policy toward China (the Amau Declaration, April 1934) was most disturbing because it asserted that Japan would not permit any foreign power to limit Japan's special rights and interests in China. The statement was received with alarm not only in China but also in all the Western capitals, and Japan had to confirm that it would continue to observe the Nine-Power Treaty (1922) and the principle of the Open Door.

Moscow, conscious of the danger posed to the Soviet Union by the Axis powers in the West and Japan in the East, in March 1935 sold the Chinese Eastern Railway to Manchukuo (which meant to the Japanese) in an effort to consolidate its eastern front. This sale naturally also aided Japan's consolidation of power in Manchuria and eliminated Chinese national interests in the railway.

In May, on the pretext that two Chinese editors of pro-Japanese newspapers had been assassinated in Tianjin, allegedly by anti-Japanese elements, the Japanese army demonstrated before the offices of the Hebei provincial government; also, Japan pressured Nanjing to agree to the withdrawal of Nationalist troops from Hebei and the abolition of all Guomindang secret service organizations in Beiping, Tianjin, and the province of Hebei (Ho-Umezu Agreement, June 1935).

Elsewhere, using a similarly flimsy pretext, the Japanese pressured Nanjing to dissolve the Guomindang organs in Chahar, vacate their troops from central north Chahar, and suppress all anti-Japanese organizations.

If Nanjing hoped that these concessions would placate the Japanese and help to bring about a rapprochement between China and Japan, it was mistaken. By September the Japanese military, which was acting with hardly any restraints from Tokyo, began to hint at the need to remove the five northern provinces of Hebei, Shandong, Shanxi, Chahar, and Suiyuan from Nationalist jurisdiction and make them "autonomous." It was made to appear that the local Chinese themselves were demanding autonomy. As an example of how this could be implemented, the Japanese established the East Hebei Anti-Communist Autonomous Government, a puppet regime staffed by Chinese collaborators (November).

From January 1932 to November 1935, China's foreign policy was conducted by Wang Jing-wei in his capacity as prime minister and foreign minister. Although Chiang Kai-shek's influence in the formulation of foreign policy was not nominal, he remained in the background. Inside China mounting public sentiment against Japan was coupled with a sense of frustration and anger against the Nationalist government, which continued to appease Japan and repress anti-Japanese organizations. On November 1, Wang Jing-wei, who was suspected of personally being pro-Japanese, was shot and wounded by an irate citizen. Wang resigned his official posts and left for Europe to seek medical care, whereupon Chiang Kai-shek was elected to replace him as president of the executive Yuan (prime minister).

Chiang, once again the civil and military leader of the Nationalist government, was forced to face the brunt of all the criticism: from patriotic nationalistic Chinese, who demanded resistance to Japan; from politically active students, who re-created the spirit of the May Fourth Movement (known as the December Ninth Movement after a demonstration on that date in Beiping); from liberals, who wanted reforms that would make the Guomindang more democratic; and from the Communists, who exploited the situation by advocating a united front to fight the Japanese.

The Japanese-sponsored autonomy movement was vigorously opposed by students and professors in Beiping. In November they passed a resolution urging the central government to "use the strength of the entire nation to maintain the territorial and administrative integrity of China."[9] The resolution was signed by the chancellors of Beijing National, Qinghua (Tsinghua), and Yanjing (Yenching) universities; professor Hu Shi; and several other cultural and educational leaders. The Japanese, behaving as if they were already masters of Beiping, forcibly detained the chancellor of Beijing National University for questioning. This was the background to the December Ninth Movement, and it led to a massive resurgence of student demonstrations in almost every city of China. Associations for national salvation, backed by Communists and liberal thinkers, were formed across the country.

Hoping to take the initiative out of Japanese hands (December 1935), Chiang tried to solve the autonomy issue by reorganizing the government of the Hebei-Chahar region and to make it semiautonomous and ostensibly "neutral." Of the 17 members of the Hebei-Chahar Political Council, 7 were well known as pro-Japanese. The chair of the council, however, was General Song Zhe-yuan, in command of the Twenty-ninth Army, whose troops were the first to take part in the Sino-Japanese War when it started on July 7, 1937. With General Song in a position to counter pro-Japanese influence, Chiang's strategy did work, and the Japanese were temporarily forced to postpone their plans for North China.

Nanjing, however, could not stop the Japanese from using their dominant position in the area to smuggle Japanese goods into northern China, which meant a considerable loss to the Chinese Customs. Even worse, the Japanese also tacitly encouraged the growth of narcotic traffic (heroin and cocaine) in the demilitarized and autonomous zones.

The respite for Nanjing was short-lived. In the latter half of 1936 anti-Japanese incidents were on the rise again (a few Japanese were attacked and some were assassinated in various parts of the country), leading the Japanese to present a set of seven demands to the Nationalist government (September 26, 1936). The most important of these were autonomy for Hebei, Chahar, Shandong, Shanxi, and Suiyuan; a joint Sino-Japanese front against communism; employment of Japanese advisers by Nanjing; and suppression of all anti-Japanese movements. Nanjing countered with a set of its own demands, which called for an annulment of the Shanghai and Tanggu agreements, dissolution of the East Hebei government, and suppression of smuggling. While negotiations dragged on, an incident took place in Chinese politics that changed the course of history.

The Xian Incident: December 1936

Japanese pressure on northern China and the Nanjing regime had created national sentiment that opposed the continuation of the civil war between the Nationalists and the Communists. Even the Guangdong-Guangxi warlords stirred up an abortive rebellion in 1936, ostensibly to force Nanjing to resist Japan. The CPC, now established in Shaanxi, also exploited this sentiment and called for an anti-Japanese, national united front.

The Communists had long recognized the propaganda value of an anti-Japanese stand. As early as 1932 they had declared war on Japan, and when they escaped from Jiangxi in 1934 they announced that they were "marching north to fight the Japanese invaders";[10] in August 1935, the CPC issued an "Open Letter to All Fellow Countrymen on Resisting Japan and Saving the Nation"; in December 1935 Mao Ze-dong delivered a report entitled "On Tactics against Japanese Imperialism," which recommended that the party should be prepared to unite with "the students, the petty bourgeoisie and the national bourgeoisie throughout the country"[11] to form a revolutionary united front.

The CPC propaganda appealed particularly to the Manchurian troops, the Northeastern Army of Zhang Xue-liang, who had been shifted to the northwest after their withdrawal from Manchuria to suppress the Communists in the Shaanxi-Gansu area. In January 1936, Mao Ze-dong, Zhou En-lai, and Zhu De issued a "Letter to All Officers and Men of the Northeastern Army," which appealed to Zhang and his troops to cease fire and join hands with the Communists to drive the Japanese out of China. If this were done, the troops naturally could go back home to Manchuria.

By midyear secret contacts were established between the Communists and Zhang Xue-liang (Zhou En-lai personally met with Zhang in April), and they agreed on "mutual non-aggression, mutual help, [and] exchange of representatives."[12] It appears that Zhang was won over to the united front cause and that he willingly accepted Communist representatives to help promote anti-Japanese propaganda in his army. The Communists had similarly infiltrated the Seventeenth Route Army of General Yang Hu-cheng, who was the other important commander of the Communist-suppression forces.

The Nationalist military action against the Communists thus came to a virtual halt. Chiang was not entirely ignorant of Zhang's and Yang's interest in the united front, but he was busy from June to October suppressing the Guangdong-Guangxi warlords. In October Chiang visited Xian to impress on Zhang and Yang the need to vigorously carry out the annihilation campaign. He reprimanded them for their halfhearted approach and, of course, rejected their suggestions regarding a united front. Chiang then moved to Luoyang and began personally to map out plans for the campaign. He redeployed 30 of his crack divisions and ordered the air force to the front.

On December 4 Chiang returned to Xian to announce that the campaign would be launched on December 12. Having failed to convince Chiang of their point of view, Zhang and Yang faced the prospect of either fighting the Communists—which they themselves were not inclined to do, and their officers and men may have refused to do—or facing a humiliating transfer. So they placed Chiang Kai-shek under house arrest (the term *kidnap,* used popularly for the incident, is not appropriate) on the night of December 11–12.

The next two weeks were a period of high drama: Zhang did not know what to do with his "prisoner," who showed great personal courage and demanded that he be either released or shot; the Communists were caught by surprise—some of them (it appears that Mao may have been one of these) wanted Chiang to be executed; Moscow, fearing that the death of Chiang would result in civil war and serve Japan's imperialistic designs, called for the release of Chiang and forced the CPC to follow suit; for reasons similar to those of the Soviets, the British and the Americans also wanted to see Chiang released; some pro-Japanese and anti-Chiang Chinese called for punitive action against the rebels, including aerial bombardment of Xian, without regard to the fact that Chiang was in Xian and might thus be killed.

Zhang Xue-liang was caught in a dilemma. He had wanted to remonstrate with Chiang but was not a disloyal officer who wanted to get rid of his commander-in-chief. He invited a Communist delegation, headed by Zhou En-lai, to Xian and also welcomed a group from Nanjing that included Soong Mei-ling (Chiang's wife), T. V. Soong, and William Henry Donald (Chiang's friend and advisor). The secret and open negotiations among the three parties, Zhang/Yang, the Communists, and Chiang's people from Nanjing, were carried on until December 24, when agreement was reached on six points. The most important of them called for ending the anti-Communist war and establishing a united front to fight the Japanese. According to recent revelations by Beijing, Zhou En-lai finally met Chiang Kai-shek on December 24, and Chiang accepted the six-point proposal. In Chiang's published account, he denied any such pledge. But from later developments one can surmise that Chiang, although he signed no documents, did agree to form some kind of a united front with the Communists.

Against the wishes of many in Xian who would have liked to lay down conditions for Chiang's release, Zhang Xue-liang saved Chiang's face by spiriting him out of Xian on December 25. Zhang accompanied Chiang to Nanjing, where Zhang was put under house arrest as Chiang's prisoner; he is still under house arrest in Taiwan.

Ironically, the Xian incident created a strong nationwide adverse reaction to Chiang's detention, and the generalissimo regained much of the stature he had acquired during the northern expedition. When the news of his release was broadcast, there was spontaneous rejoicing, and expressions of relief and thanksgiving were voiced everywhere. His authority was strengthened further when it came to be known that the civil war was over and that Chiang was going to lead the nation against Japan.

Since the actual conditions under which the united front was to function were yet to be fully defined, the first months of 1937 were spent by the two sides exchanging proposals and counterproposals. Before the final agreement could be announced, the war with Japan had begun on July 7, 1937. Under the terms of their collaboration, the CPC discontinued its policy of armed uprising to overthrow the Nationalist government, renamed its Shaanxi soviet Special Region of the Republic of China, allowed its army to become a part of the National Revolutionary Army under the jurisdiction of Chiang Kai-shek's Military Commission (its name was changed from Red Army to the Eighth Route Army), discontinued its policy of confiscating land from the landlords, and accepted a democratic system based on universal suffrage. In practice these changes meant little because they neither brought a greater Nationalist presence to the Communist area nor took away from the civil and military power and authority the Communists actually exercised.

The Nanjing decade (1928–1937) ended without Chinese society being truly reintegrated and without a central government that truly exercised jurisdiction over the whole country. The Guomindang had failed to produce an ideology or an organization that could bind the nation together. Many provincial governors, who were often the local warlords from pre-Nanjing days, not only retained a sense of independence and autonomy but also periodically chose to form alliances and rebel against Nanjing; the Guomindang was grievously factionalized, and leaders of Wang Jing-wei's stature tried to establish parallel "national" governments; the military component of the Nationalist government was virtually outside the control of the civil government; the armies of the Nationalist government owed loyalty to their commanders rather than to the state; political participation was limited; and programs of social reform had marginal significance.

Why did the Guomindang fail? Many reasons may be cited, but the primary one was built into Sun Yat-sen's program of a three-stage approach to constitutional government. By 1937 the Guomindang had yet to complete the first stage: the military unification of China. Theoretically that stage was achieved in 1928, but the northern expedition had perpetuated warlordism rather than destroyed it. Most scholars have blamed Chiang Kai-shek for Nanjing's failures. It is true that Chiang emerged as the key figure in China and soon after the start of the Sino-Japanese War became a virtual dictator, but can he be held responsible for the weaknesses of the party and the government? These weaknesses reflected the shortcomings of traditional Chinese political culture that still held China in thrall: the authority-dependency syndrome; the ingrained habit of looking for a single powerful figure to lead politics rather than an acceptance of politics through a complex network of institutions; politics through factional loyalties, nepotism, corruption, and intrigue; and lack of distinction between public office and private life, between public property and private property. China had not found it easy to introduce modern institutions that could impose accountability on the party or the government. This development has not taken place even today in Communist China, over 50 years later. If Chiang is to be blamed, it should be for insisting that the northern expedition start in 1926. Had he waited a few years or even a year, the Guomindang might have been in a position militarily to defeat the warlords and not be forced to make alliances with them.

Regardless of these considerations, on the eve of the Sino-Japanese War (1937–1945) China was more unified than it had been for a long time; Nanjing controlled 25 percent of the land area and 66 percent of the population of China.[13] Could Chiang have done better than he did? Yes, perhaps, if he had not been so obsessed with finding a military solution to all his problems.

THE MODERNIZATION OF CHINA: 1928–1937

By the 1930s China presented that unique combination of modern and traditional elements that many Westerners seem to find so attractive and that still exists in contemporary China. Basically, this was a mix of Westernized life-style, a product of modern cities, and the traditional life-style followed by the majority of the population in the countryside. The major cities of China had become cosmopolitan: A visitor could live comfortably in a modern hotel with modern conveniences like flush toilets and bathtubs, travel in imported limousines, use conveniently located post and telegraph offices for sending messages back home, meet Westernized Chinese who dressed in Western clothing and spoke English (the most popular foreign language), and do business with modern-style firms and banks.

This thin veneer of modernization gave the wrong impression to many who came to believe that China had made tremendous progress under the Nationalists. In the larger context of the country as a whole, the achievements of the Nanjing regime were significant but limited.

The weaknesses of the central government lay in four spheres. The first was lack of coordination among the five Yuan, the five branches of government; and within the executive Yuan, the most powerful Yuan, the military was virtually independent. Second, since authority was in the hands of the military chief, Chiang Kai-shek, national priorities were viewed as analogous to military goals, and 60 to 80 percent of the scarce resources were allocated to the maintenance of the military and the servicing of foreign debts, both nonproductive expenditures. Third, because a majority of government officials owed their jobs to various warlords and influential politicians, the central bureaucracy lacked cohesion and efficiency, which was made worse because senior officials had multiple overlapping appointments; central authority did not extend over al the provinces. Fourth, the government's administrative control ended at the district level, even in the provinces over which Nanjing had direct jurisdiction.

In an attempt to provide cohesion to the government and the people and revitalize the nation, Chiang Kai-shek inaugurated the New Life Movement in 1934. According to Chiang the revolution demanded discipline, which the Chinese people sadly lacked because of selfishness and the absence of social consciousness. However, the nation could be transformed if the Confucian virtues of *li, yi, lian,* and *chi* (propriety, justice, honesty, and self-respect) could be revived and popularized. To achieve this end, 95 rules of proper conduct were enunciated and propagated among the people. Obviously Chiang was trying to inculcate new habits that conformed to ideas of modern hygiene (e.g., not to spit in public) and new attitudes that conformed to modern ideas of loyalty and self-sacrifice for a national cause by turning to traditional morality.

The heart of the movement lay in Chiang's desire to mobilize the nation on military lines. As he himself put it, "Stated simply [the New Life Movement] is to thoroughly militarize the lives of the citizens of the entire nation so that they can cultivate courage and swiftness, the endurance of suffering and a tolerance for hard work, and especially the habit and ability of unified action, so that they will at any time sacrifice for the nation."[14] Within a year it was clear that the New Life Movement had failed because its neotraditional ideology was out of joint with the needs of the times and because it attempted to revolutionize society from above and came to be identified with authoritarian and repressive leaders who reflected none of the New Life virtues in their own lives.

As for economic growth and development, China continued to expand, albeit slowly, its light and staple industries and communication systems, the foundations for which had been laid in the early decades of the twentieth century, most of them centered in the coastal and riverine cities connected with the foreign presence. The Nationalist government helped this process by introducing a modern financial system: an annual budget; streamlined revenue collection and centralized industrial taxation; establishment of the Central Bank of China; restoration of tariff autonomy to China (a major change in the unequal treaty relationship); abolition of the likin tax, which had become an impediment in the growth of internal trade; and the abolition of the variable unit, the tael, to be replaced by the silver dollar (*yuan*) as the standard national legal tender. The government also founded the China Development Finance Corporation, whose goal was to promote industry and commerce by developing the domestic money market and encouraging foreign investment. Another achievement during the Nanjing decade was the completion of the Guangzhou-Hankou railroad trunk line and several branch lines (about 3,000 miles); also about 15,000 miles of highways were constructed. Much of the credit for these accomplishments goes to T. V. Soong, the financial genius of the Guomindang.

But even in this successful modern sector, Guomindang policies were basically regressive and did not encourage capital growth, savings, and investment. On the larger national level the Guomindang, representing the landlord-bourgeois class and lacking authority at the local level, could neither gather any of the land taxes (it had agreed in 1928 that the provinces could retain them for their use) nor carry out any of the much-needed land reforms. By the same token it could not even implement the Land Laws, which had been so enthusiastically enacted in 1930. The Land Laws would have reduced the land rent to 37.5 percent of the harvest and thus ameliorated the plight of the exploited tenant farmers, who formed the bulk of the peasantry and lived in abject poverty. As for the provincial authorities, most of them were more interested in squeezing as much as they could out of the land than in reconstruction projects.

Some considerable advance was made in the educational field, although actual achievements fell far short of the idealistic plans announced by the government. Under these plans, the government was given the authority to establish direct, centralized control over all levels of the national educational system, from the primary schools at the bottom to the universities at the top (including privately run schools), so that it could achieve, in stages, universal primary education and the eradication of adult illiteracy by the year 1949 and could modernize education at the secondary and tertiary levels. At the primary and secondary levels, common textbooks, approved by the central government, were to be used throughout the country; the curricula, which allowed for no electives, were devised to improve the students' physical bodies, inculcate traditional ethics and nationalistic values, and train them in subjects that would provide skills to build the country.

In actual practice, the plans came to naught because of the loose hold of the central government over the provinces and the lack of funds for education. Indeed, the financial mechanism that put the burden of funding primary schools on the counties and of secondary schools on the provinces (the center only funded the universities) meant that primary education made few gains; although there was a fourfold growth in secondary education during the Nanjing decade, it is higher education that benefited most from the new policies.

The lack of balance evidenced between the economic development of the coastal regions and the hinterland was also reflected in the educational sphere; the modern coastal and riverine cities had the best educational facilities (all the best-known universities were there), whereas some provinces in the interior had no institutions of higher learning at all. In many fields, the Western model had been so closely followed that the educational system was divorced from China's needs and circumstances; also, a great majority of the students devoted themselves to theoretical studies. The government did try to encourage higher education in the interior, and it also tried to make higher education more oriented toward science and technology. The total number of college and university students rose from 37,570 in 1930 to 41,610 in 1936, of which the number in natural sciences, agriculture, engineering, and medicine increased from 9,380 to 18,460, and the number in humanities, social sciences, education, and commerce dropped from 28,190 to 23,150 (all figures have been rounded off to the nearest 10). In any case .09 percent of the population could hardly be expected to introduce any significant social changes. They were elites who perpetuated elitism.

THE NANJING DECADE: A SUMMARY

Some historians of the Nanjing decade have praised the efforts of the Nationalist government, saying that although success was limited, the achievements indicated a trend that would have brought unification and reconstruction to China had the Japanese war not intervened. Others have condemned it because they believe that even if there had been no war with Japan, the Guomindang could not have brought about the socioeconomic revolution that China needed and many patriotic Chinese had been hoping for since 1911 because Guomindang ideology and organization failed to create the necessary infrastructure.

The truth, as is often the case, lies somewhere between these two extreme points of view. A decade is not a long enough period for any regime to have radically reorganized a state and society the size of China with all its multifarious problems. However, China was in the process of change, a process that had begun long before the Guomindang came into power. What we must attempt to do is to assess the impact the Guomindang had on this process. Many successes of the Nanjing regime in the modernization of China were built on the developments that had already begun before it came into power (e.g., in the realms of education, industry, commerce, banking, communications, and transportation). Similarly, many failures of the regime were the result of traditional factors that still were very much alive (such as the authority-obedience syndrome, paternalism in politics, factional loyalties, and bureaucratism) or of the hybrids that had emerged during the last half-century (such as the role of a modernized military in central and regional politics).

What role did the Nanjing regime play, in this historical context, in the process of change? First, the Guomindang, after having accepted aid from the Soviet Union, became Bolshevized and turned against Western, democratic political models. The party could now compromise with tradition and confirm that the state was more important than the individual, that democratic rights protecting the individual (or for that matter, the goals of democracy) were to be given lower priority than the goal of unifying and strengthening the state. It advocated the paternalistic, authoritarian rule of a single party, putting the party (like the traditional emperors) above the state. In this the Guomindang had the backing of many intellectuals who had become disillusioned with democratic experiments and who had shifted their demand from individual justice to justice for society. The frustration these intellectuals felt with the Guomindang, however, was not that the Guomindang had become dictatorial but that the dictatorship was ineffective in working for the benefit and welfare of society. By contrast, the benevolent authoritarianism of the CPC came to be looked on as a viable alternative. The milieu of the 1930s rejected the liberal democratic model and effectively killed the weak individual-oriented democratic movement that had emerged in the May Fourth era.

Second, although the Guomindang turned against the left and acquired a rightist coloration, the revolutionary socioeconomic goals it had initially advocated (e.g., the Principle of the People's Livelihood) continued to have a strong appeal. The regime's repressive policies only made the intelligentsia more acutely aware of the bankruptcy of the party, which still tried to hide its incapacities behind empty progressive mottoes and slogans. It is in this context that the attractiveness of the CPC has to be seen; however limited its political power, the CPC held forth a nobler vision of the future.

That politics in the 1920s and 1930s had become more left wing was also reflected in the growing field of modern Chinese literature, whose contribution to the making of the new milieu cannot be overestimated. The anti-Western, anti-imperialist reaction, which had begun with the May Fourth incident and the subsequent radicalization of the intellectuals, had a strong influence in shaping the literary world in the 1930s. Western imitation was not given up, but the writers turned increasingly to an investigation of the nature and function of literature. Reaching the conclusion that literature had a serious social purpose (in many ways similar to the view held by traditional Confucian scholars) and was therefore a didactic instrument, the writers, including those who had earlier clamored for "art for art's sake," accepted the path of social realism. The League of Left-Wing Writers was established in 1930, and most of China's outstanding writers became its members. Even those who kept aloof from the league accepted the idea that literature bore a heavy social responsibility. The harsh treatment meted out to liberal thinkers and writers by the Nanjing government only reinforced this trend.

These writers, by attacking the decadence of traditional society and demanding a social revolution, became harsh critics of the Guomindang and supporters, consciously or unconsciously, of the CPC. The nature of contemporary politics led even Lu Xun, who was not by instinct a Communist, to side with the CPC. Another popular writer, the novelist Mao Dun, used Marxist analysis in his novels to depict the exploitative nature of foreign and indigenous capitalists. Ba Jin, with leanings toward anarchism, became the idol of the younger generation because he described the sufferings and tribulations of youths trying to break away from the hold of the traditional family system. Lao She, who never joined any political or literary group, portrayed the lives of the common people, contrasting the intrinsic goodness of their nature and character with the rapaciousness of the society that exploited and destroyed them. Ding Ling, the most well-known woman writer of modern China, who first gained fame in 1928 (at the age of 26) with her stories depicting daring and independent heroines, turned to producing proletarian literature by 1931 and joined the CPC in 1933.

Third, the Guomindang, while exploiting nationalism, was unable to satisfy the nationalistic, antiforeign, patriotic urge for national unity. On the contrary, it helped to widen the gulf, albeit unconsciously, between the ruling classes and the ruled, between the Westernized high officials (70 to 80 percent of whom had been educated abroad) and the lower echelons of the bureaucracy, between the educated elite and the masses, and between the modern industrial and commercial sectors and the traditional agricultural sector (i.e., between the city and the countryside). At the same time it failed to institutionalize avenues of group or sectional representation, thus leading to alienation, frustration, and socially destructive behavior such as nepotism, bribery, riots, strikes, demonstrations, and coups. This negative situation helped strengthen the revolutionary forces that promised to reintegrate the fractionalized society and politics of the day.

Last, and most important, the Guomindang failed to produce a constitution that could guarantee civilian control of the government and a proper balance of power within its main branches. A Provisional Constitution of the Republic of China for the Period of Tutelage was promulgated by Nanjing in June 1931, an Organic Law of the National Government was passed by the Central Executive Committee of the Guomindang in December 1931, and a Draft Constitution of the Republic of China was promulgated by the Nationalist government in May 1936. These constitutional documents reflected shifting views on how to keep the military out of the executive and decrease or increase the powers of the presidency but had little impact on the actual function of power and authority in the government. There was little in Chinese political tradition to sanctify these paper constitutions. For this same reason the Communist constitutions, later, would provide no better protection to the people than those of the Nationalists.

MAO ZE-DONG AND THE CPC: 1927–1935

The history of the CPC from 1927 to 1935 is crucial to understanding modern China because it was during this time that Mao Ze-dong rose to power and began to enunciate his ideas on the organization of the party and the army and on revolutionary strategy. This body of ideas and theories, modified with the passage of time, came to be known as Maoism outside China and as The Thought of Mao Ze-dong inside China.

The period 1927–1935 can be divided into two phases: 1927–1932, when the CPC headquarters remained underground in Shanghai and soviets were established in the countryside, and 1933–1935, when the headquarters were shifted to Ruijin and took over direct control of the soviets.

From 1928 to 1932, operating in the countryside in a relatively independent fashion, Mao rose to prominence as a civil and military leader. He proved that he had the genius and the capacity to lead the revolution by organizing the peasantry. But not everyone in the party leadership agreed with Mao's ideas and policies. This became apparent from 1933 to 1935, when Mao came under attack and was removed from several of his key posts. But the collapse of the Jiangxi soviet helped Mao to return to power, and he assumed leadership of the party in 1935, during the Long March. He held this position until his death in 1976.

Mao's success in the late 1930s and in the 1940s made him a legendary figure in his own time and led to his virtual deification. However, because he made serious leadership mistakes that caused much harm to the party and the country after the establishment of the People's Republic in 1949, since his death many of his policies have been denounced and discarded, and his contribution to the revolution is now being reevaluated.

A debate continues on how far Mao departed from orthodox Communist doctrine and added creatively to Marxism-Leninism. Even before the demythification of Mao began, many scholars had contended that Mao was in no way original and that most, if not all, elements of his ideas were available to him from one source or another. It is not possible here to relate the details of the Mao debate; it will suffice to note the techniques and ideas Mao used to achieve his success and the reasons for his failures. It should also be noted that even Mao's harshest critics recognize his outstanding contribution to the Chinese revolution.

CPC Leadership: 1927–1932

From 1927 to 1932 the CPC leaders continued to formulate their policies on the presumption that the socialist revolution must necessarily have a proletariat base; therefore the party's future lay in the cities. In this it was closely directed by Moscow through the Comintern. What was new in the picture was the establishment of the Red Army, which was based in the countryside. Supposedly, this force would provide auxiliary help to the proletarian uprising. The party leader, not always the secretary general of the CPC, himself living a precarious underground existence in Shanghai, would evaluate the national situation. At some stage he would declare that the tide of revolution was rising and the time had come to occupy those cities where the proletariat was thought to be ripe for action. Orders would then be sent from Shanghai to the Red Army in the countryside to attack the targeted cities.

These operations invariably ended in disastrous failure. The Comintern would blame the failure on the current leader of the party and promptly replace him. Thus in 1927 Chen Du-xiu was replaced by Qu Qiubai; Qu, in turn, was deposed in 1928 in favor of Li Li-san; Li, who ordered attacks on Wuhan, Nanchang, and Changsha in mid-1930, was ousted by the end of the year. In 1931 the 28 Bolsheviks, a group of young Chinese students of Pavel Mif (director of the Sun Yat-sen University in Moscow and the chief Comintern expert on China), who were headed by Wang Ming, were given the leadership of the party. This group was also referred to as the Internationalists. By this time the Communist-backed, city-based labor movement had totally collapsed. No intelligent worker would risk joining a "red" union when it was virtually assured that its members would be massacred by the Guomindang. Finally, at the end of 1932 the par-

Mao Ze-dong's Background: 1893–1927

Born into a comparatively well-to-do peasant family ("rich peasant" in Communist terminology) in Hunan in 1893, Mao was the eldest of four children. He seems to have favored his warm-hearted mother, a devout Buddhist, and hated his harsh, autocratic father, against whose authority he rebelled when he was only 15 or 16 years old. Psychohistorians trace many of his later actions to this love-hate relationship.

Mao insisted on becoming educated, against his father's wishes, and succeeded in going to a higher primary school in 1909. Although his schoolmates generally did not accept him because he was six years older than most of them and far less affluent, Mao found modern education at the school exciting. He was particularly thrilled by the ideas on reform and revolution of such writers as Kang You-wei and Liang Qi-chao. In 1911 he went to study at the provincial capital, Changsha, and in the fall of that year became briefly involved with the 1911 revolution when he joined a revolutionary volunteer corps.

In Changsha Mao spent endless hours poring over magazines and books at the provincial library. He was a voracious reader and was soon familiar with the translated works of Thomas Huxley, J. S. Mill, Charles Darwin, and Adam Smith. In 1913 Mao entered the Fourth (later called the First) Teachers' Training School in Changsha. He graduated from this school in 1918. These were the heady days of the May Fourth Movement, and Mao, like so many others, was fired by the spirit of the times. He had developed strong revolutionary instincts, but his ideas were still largely unstructured.

In 1918, at age 24, Mao went to Beijing University, where he worked as a library assistant under Li Da-zhao. Here he met Chen Du-xiu and other intellectuals who were soon to establish the CPC. Mao was deeply impressed by the views of the brilliant Li Dazhao, who inspired his students with a vision of a new, self-reliant China and was one of the first Chinese to hail the success of the Russian Revolution. Mao's thinking also turned left, but he was more of an anarchist than a Communist. Only in 1920 did he first begin to read Marxist writings. On his return to Changsha that year, he founded the Russian Affairs Study Group. The following year he served as one of the delegates to the first congress of the CPC and became secretary of the party's Hunan branch.

From 1921 to 1923 Mao engaged in the more orthodox activities of the CPC such as the organization of labor unions and labor strikes. After the First United Front was established in 1923, Mao worked in the Guomindang organization in various posts, ending with the directorship of the Peasant Movement Training Institute in 1926. In 1927 he returned to his home province of Hunan to survey the condition of the peasant movement there. This led to his famous "Report of an Investigation into the Peasant Movement in Hunan."

Mao Ze-dong's 1927 report indicated his growing faith in the possibility that the peasants could serve as the main force of the revolution, "a mighty storm, like a hurricane, a force so swift and violent that no power, however great, will be able to hold it back. They will smash all the trammels that bind them and rush forward along the road to liberation. They will sweep all the imperialists, warlords, corrupt officials, local tyrants and evil gentry into their graves."[15] It was the debacle of 1927, when the First United Front came to its bitter end, that gave Mao Ze-dong an opportunity to establish a base in rural China and put into practice the ideas he had formulated during his early years with the CPC.

ty Central Committee shifted to Ruijin, at last accepting the notion long held by Mao that the revolution could be won from the countryside.

Mao Ze-dong and the Party: 1928–1934

After the disaster of 1927, when party membership had fallen from 60,000 to about 10,000, Moscow directed the CPC to carry out an agrarian revolution, arm the peasants and workers for "spontaneous" revolutionary struggle, establish city-based soviets (local government of "soldiers, workers, and peasants"), and develop guerrilla warfare. Of course, nobody was certain how all this was to be done. Where were the new party members to come from—from the proletariat only, or could the peasants be included? Where were the soldiers for the army to come from? Should there be a standing army, which ran counter to the idea of a spontaneous uprising, or should there be only local recruits who would temporarily join in a local insurrection? If all efforts were direct in gaining city bases, what role were the guerrillas to play? Who was to train them and coordinate their hit-and-run campaigns?

The Comintern and CPC leaders provided a shifting theoretical basis for action, but only those actually involved with activities in the countryside had to face the difficulties created by the contradictory, vague, or ill-defined guidelines. By early 1928 Mao Ze-dong, Zhu De, Peng De-huai, and others, having failed in their attacks on the cities and in inciting peasant uprisings (Mao had led the abortive Autumn Harvest Uprising in Hunan), had taken refuge in the Jinggang Mountains on the Hunan-Jiangxi border, traditionally a haven for bandits, and established a revolutionary base there. The idea of organizing a city-based soviet was given up. The Mao-Zhu forces, about 10,000 strong but with only 2,000 rifles in good repair, became the nucleus of the First Division of the Chinese Workers' and Peasants' Revolutionary Army; Zhu was the commander and Mao the political commisar. In Jinggangshan (Jinggang Mountains) Mao first began to experiment with his style of party organization, guerrilla warfare, and the mobilization of the peasantry. Here he enunciated his famous tactical guidelines for guerrilla forces: "The enemy advances, we retreat; the enemy camps, we harass; the enemy tires, we attack; the enemy retreats, we pursue."

In 1929, forced to retreat from Jinggangshan, Mao moved to Ruijin in southeast Jiangxi. Under Mao's guidance, this area eventually became the biggest Communist base, the Central Soviet. As chair of the Front Committee, Mao commanded civil and military power, and he increasingly used his own judgment to strengthen the Red Army, expand the territory under his control, and fight off the Guomindang anti-Communist campaigns. These goals sometimes meant bypassing or rejecting instructions from the Central Committee and, consequently, friction between Mao and the party leaders. As early as 1929, Mao was criticized by the party headquarters for allowing peasant mentality to undermine the revolution and the party and for forgetting that the ultimate aim of the small soviets was to help the struggle in the cities and not sink into peasant guerrillaism. This was a touchy subject with Mao because he was convinced that only the peasant masses could help the revolutionary movement. So Mao, in his reply to the Central Committee, although politely agreeing with the committee's criticism, added,

> . . . in our opinion it would also be wrong for any of our Party members to fear the growth of peasant strength lest it should outstrip the worker's strength and harm the revolution. For in the revolution in semi-colonial China, the peasant struggle must always fail if it does not have the leadership of the workers [meaning the leadership of the CPC, which of course in Mao's mind meant the leadership of Mao himself], but the revolution is never harmed if the peasant struggle outstrips the forces of the workers.[16]

By 1932 Mao was convinced more than ever before that in the absence of any control over urban areas and the proletariat, it was from the peasantry, particularly its poorer segments, that the party could draw its members and recruit its armies. However, to gain the confidence of this section of the people, who formed a large percentage of the population and who were either tenant farmers or landless laborers, the party had to patiently and assiduously cultivate them. This could be done by distributing land to them, protecting them from the exploitative control of the rich landlords (executing the landlords and confiscating their land was the practice generally followed; this act gave confidence to the poor peasants and served as a lesson for the rich peasants who were allowed to retain their lands), educating and politicizing them, and always ensuring that the military treated them fairly and with respect. The masses were the water and the party the fish; without water the fish could not survive. These truths were self-evident, although it was never to be forgotten that the *elements déclassés* recruited into the army needed a thorough indoctrination to become dependably "Red." For that matter indoctrination and political education could convert anyone to the proper proletarian attitude. Mao had even recruited some of the local bandits into his army in Jinggangshan.

Since the warlord and Guomindang armies had alienated the peasantry with their brutal behavior, Mao attempted to convert his soldiers into local heroes who could be loved by the villagers. He insisted that they meticulously follow certain rules: not take "a single needle or piece of thread from the masses," turn in everything captured, speak politely, pay fairly for all they bought, pay for things they damaged, not hit or swear at people, not damage any crops, not take liberties with women, and not ill treat captives.[17] Like most of Mao's "creative thought," this approach to military discipline and political training was a pragmatic response to a practical necessity. Mao wanted his army to be much more than a fighting force; it was to be a political instrument that spread propaganda among the masses, gave adult literacy classes, helped the peasants in farm work, and trained them as local militia; it was to be "a most powerful instrument of all in the coming revolution." Mao was the only CPC leader who wrote so extensively on war and military strategy.

From 1928 to 1930–1931, when the CPC was sill trying to create a nationwide uprising, Mao had quietly come to the conclusion that the party did not need an urban base and that it could work out its destiny by holding one Red area in the countryside, slowly expanding it to engulf the entire country. The growth of the Jiangxi soviet testifies to the correctness of his view. By dividing the soviet into military districts and subdistricts and by getting all citizens between the ages of 18 and 40 to join the "young vanguard" and the "Red guard" militia battalions or the women's associations, Mao had mobilized the entire population to provide intelligence, transportation, and supplies to the highly mobile units of the regular army. Nearly 80 percent of the army was locally recruited; 70 percent of it came from peasant background. When Mao wrote to the Central Committee in January 1930 that "the tactics we have derived from the struggle of the past three years are indeed different from any other tactics, ancient or modern, Chinese or foreign,"[18] his pride is understandable and his exaggeration forgivable. By the end of 1931 Mao had not only been able to neutralize three encirclement campaigns by using guerrilla tactics but also severely mauled the Nationalist forces. Massive desertions of the Nanjing troops to the Communist side had augmented Mao's armies and equipment.

Until 1931 the dozen or so soviets, scattered in several provinces, remained autonomous units and were not organizationally integrated. In November 1931 the All China Soviet Congress, held at Ruijin, established the Chinese Soviet Republic and appointed a central government with Mao Ze-dong as president.

This change affected Mao's power base. Although raised in status, Mao lost direct command over the armies, and the organizational base on which power had so far rested was changed. Mao had fused the party, state, and military systems into one and established an independent kingdom within the Communist movement. The constitution of the Chinese Soviet Republic separated the state and military structures, and Mao was given command of the civil apparatus. As far as the military was concerned, Mao was made political commissar of the entire Red Army in January 1931; this act removed him from direct contact with his First Front Army. He was also excluded from the Military Commission, which had supreme command over the Red Army and which was overwhelmingly comprised of the internationalists.

This government was still a part of the local party structure, for the CPC underground headquarters was still in Shanghai, where party members continued being caught by the British or the Chinese police and executed. Ultimately the situation became so difficult that the leadership was driven to move to Ruijin in the winter of 1932–1933. The Internationalists now increased their criticism of Mao's deviations from the official line, accusing him of guerrillaism, factionalism, peasant mentality, and party monopolization.

Seen from the Communist side the significance of the fourth Communist-suppression campaign of 1932 (discussed earlier) lies in the fact that it resulted in an open clash between the Internationalists and Mao over military tactics. Chiang had personally led his troops against the soviets in the central provinces of Hubei, Hunan, and Anhui and successfully defeated the Communist forces there. The Internationalists, backed by Zhou En-lai, favored a "forward and offensive line," which advocated the use of the Red Army as a regular army (vs. a guerrilla force), which would move "beyond the passes" (i.e., make a preemptive strike outside its area of strategic control to relieve the pressure on the besieged soviets). Mao dissented. Basing his opinion on his earlier experience, Mao felt that the chances of success would be greater if the enemy were "lured in deep" into the mountainous base area and destroyed by organized guerrilla tactics. Mao's recommendation was rejected. The Japanese activities in the north, which diverted Chiang's attention from Jiangxi, may have had something to do with the final outcome of the war, but the Internationalists felt smug because their plan appeared successful although the Hubei-Henan-Anhui and the Hunan-West Hubei soviets had been liquidated. Mao withdrew from active participation in deliberations, and his post of political commissar was formally assigned to Zhou En-lai in mid-1933.

In 1933 the Internationalists also started other political and economic campaigns in the Central Soviet that were intended to further diminish the power of Mao Ze-dong. The bigger danger facing them, however, was not Mao but Chiang Kai-shek. Although Chiang had lost the fourth Communist-suppression campaign, all the signs indicated that he was going to return and that the next assault would be far more serious, perhaps impossible, to deal with. In fact, many local peasants had begun to flee the area, and the CPC, mobilizing for the Nationalist fifth encirclement campaign, found it difficult to reach its quota of new recruits to expand the strength of the Red Army to 1 million. Under these circumstances it would have been politically wise for the CPC to support the People's Revolutionary Government established in Fujian by the Nineteenth Route Army, which had revolted against the Nanjing government in 1933. But for various reasons this was not done.

In a meeting of the Central Committee in January 1934, Mao and his proteges, one of whom was Deng Xiao-ping, came under further attack, and Mao was dropped from the Political Bureau (Politburo), the highest organ of the party leadership. A few days after this meeting, the Second All-China Soviet Congress was held. When the Central Executive Committee of the Soviet government was announced, all of Mao's lieutenants were missing. With an alien Central Executive Committee Mao became a figurehead. He was also removed from his post of chair of the Council of People's Commissars.

After having suppressed the rebellion of the Nineteenth Route Army, Chiang began his fifth campaign against the Jiangxi soviet. The strategy and tactics employed in this campaign were totally new. Neither the Internationalists' "forward and offensive line" nor Mao's "luring the enemy in deep" could have succeeded in coping with the new situation. Both tactics were tried after the Nationalists advanced into the Soviet territory, but they were ineffective. The Communists therefore decided, after radio consultation with Moscow, to retreat toward the northwest. In keeping with the Communists practice, someone had to be blamed for this debacle—obviously it could not be Mao Ze-dong, who was out of power. In the "Resolution on Certain Questions in the History of Our Party since the Founding of the People's Republic," adopted on June 27, 1981, the current view upholds Mao's a posteriori judgment: ". . . because of Wang Ming's 'Left' adventurist leadership, the struggle against the Kuomintang's [Guomindang's] fifth 'encirclement and suppression' campaign ended in failure. The First Front Army was forced to embark on the 25,000-li Long March and made its way to northern Shaanxi. . . . The Red Army of 300,000 men was reduced to about 30,000 and the Communist Party of 300,000 members to about 40,000."[19]

The Long March: 1934–1935

The Long March, which began on October 16, 1934, and took over a year to complete, was a desperate attempt at survival. A total of about 100,000 persons, including combat troops, cadres, and transport corps, carrying as much equipment as they could, fled westward. Women and children and 20,000 of the wounded had to be left behind, protected by an inadequate guerrilla force.

There were no definite plans about where the Communists were heading except that, at first, the goal was to join with the other Red forces still operating in Hunan. But the Nationalists had foreseen the possibility of this linkup; the Communists, who had moved west, through Guangdong into Guangxi, found the enemy waiting for them on the banks of the Xiang River. The battle that followed devastated the Red forces. The CPC, forced to give up its objective of joining with the Red Army in Hunan, decided to move to northern Sichuan, where the Oyuwan Soviet, under Zhang Guo-tao and his Fourth Red Army, was still intact. Pursued and harassed by the Nationalists, the Communists lost one-half to three-quarters of their force by the end of the year. They had also discarded all the heavy equipment they had brought with them.

At this stage Mao reentered the leadership circle with a suggestion that the Communists take the back route to Sichuan through Guizhou, where the Nationalists were weak. The First Army occupied the town of Zunyi, in northern Guizhou, on January 5, 1935. On the following day the leaders convened an enlarged conference of the Politburo (enlarged by including pro-Mao Communist members who were not already in the Politburo). The Internationalists came under heavy criticism for their theories and policies, and they were blamed for all the failures and setbacks suffered by the party; Mao gained majority support for his mobile warfare and guerrilla military tactics, for which he had been disgraced. Zhou En-lai joined Mao in attacking the Internationalists, although Zhou earlier had been working with them against Mao. Mao's resumption of control over military affairs (as chair of the Military Commission and leader of the First Front Army), at a time when military affairs dominated all other party affairs, gave him the leading position in the party. Since there was no possibility of communicating with Moscow, Mao gained this status without Moscow's sanction. Mao's position was finally legitimized in 1943 when he became the chairman of the party.

After the Zunyi conference, the Long Marchers zigzagged their way through Guizhou and Yunnan to western Sichuan, crossing fast-flowing rivers and scaling steep mountains. Only about 10,000 of the original 100,000 reached the little town of Mougong in June 1935. Here this bedraggled group was joined by the 70,000 men of Zhang Guo-tao's much better equipped Fourth Front Army (the armies were now called Front Armies). Zhang, a graduate of Beijing University and a close associate of Chen Du-xiu and Li Da-zhao, and who had been to Moscow and met Stalin, refused to recognize the legitimacy of the decisions taken at the Zunyi conference, which had not been approved by a party congress or by the Comintern. He believed that he was the rightful leader of the party, so he challenged Mao's newly acquired status. Zhang disagreed with Mao that the Communists should march north to Shaanxi. Instead he proposed alternative destinations. An attempt was made to placate Zhang by making him political commissar for the Red Army, which was divided into two columns: the right column under Mao and the left column under general headquarters, led by Zhu De, the commander-in-chief, and Zhang Guo-tao, the chief political commissar. By this time the Red forces had reached the town of Maoergai.

This was Mao's first struggle for power. He solved the problem by surreptitiously slipping away with his units of the First Front Army and the central organs of the party while the rest of the troops were engaged in various military actions. According to Zhang Guo-tao,

> The extraordinary move of Mao Tse-tung and others caused quite a stir among us. . . . Some of us pointed out frankly that Mao Tse-tung was playing the trick of the cicada shedding its shell. Taking advantage of the occasion when the northern route was cleared by the Fourth Front Army after heavy losses, he went away quietly, without sparing a thought for the majority of his comrades and the other army units.[20]

In a huff, Zhang set up his own Central Committee and, instead of following in Mao's track, decided to go his own way, southwest to Xigang. After many further hardships, Mao reached northern Shaanxi in October 1935. In the summer of 1935 Zhang was forced to revise his plans and move to Gansu. There some of his troops joined Mao, but Zhang with 20,000 troops marched westward to Xinjiang, in the hope, perhaps, of making contact with the Soviets. He was routed on the way by the Muslim general Ma Pu-feng and had to retreat to Shaanxi, a broken man, no longer in a position to challenge Mao.

For Mao and his men the journey from Maoergai to Shaanxi, through the Qinghai swampy grasslands, had been difficult and nightmarish. Short of food and medical supplies, exhausted and cold, the Communists had to walk through the swamps, where one false step meant death. They had to drink stagnant water and eat wild plants and often had to sleep standing. When they emerged from the grasslands they were surrounded by hostile tribes, which fled the villages on seeing the Han soldiers, taking everything with them and hiding their food stock. "Some men boiled cowhides [left behind by the tribals] for twenty-four hours and then ate; or they boiled big leather boots and drank the broth."[21] Starvation, disease, cold, and accidents killed off large numbers. According to Dick Wilson's calculation, of the original 100,000 only 5,000 had survived the Long March.[22]

Politically speaking, this force and the poverty-stricken soviet it had reached in northern Shaanxi represented no threat to the Nationalists, but the Long Marchers had a symbolic value that far transcended their numbers or their physical condition. They had become a legend: an indestructible force led by an indestructible leader, who could never be defeated in their quest for a just society.

Speaking in December 1935, shortly after his arrival in northern Shaanxi, Mao displayed a remarkable sense of self-confidence and optimism:

> [The significance of] the Long March [is that it] is the first of its kind in the annals of history, that it is a manifesto, a propaganda force, a seeding machine. . . . The Long March is a manifesto. It has proclaimed to the world that the Red Army is an army of heroes, while the imperialists and their running dogs, Chiang Kai-shek and his like, are impotent. . . . The Long March is also a propaganda force. It has announced to some 200 mil-

lion people in eleven provinces that the road of the Red Army is their only road to liberation. . . . The Long March is also a seeding machine. In the eleven provinces it has sown many seeds which will sprout, leaf, blossom, and bear fruit, and will yield a harvest in the future.[23]

NOTES

[1]Quoted in Lloyd E. Eastman, *The Abortive Revolution: China Under the Nationalist Rule, 1927–1937* (Cambridge, MA: Harvard University Press, 1974), p. 5.

[2]For an overview of the Guomindang cliques, see Hung Mao-tien, *Government and Politics in Kuomintang China* (Palo Alto, CA: Stanford University Press, 1972).

[3]Ch'ien Tuan-sheng, *The Government and Politics of China* (Cambridge, MA: Harvard University Press, 1950), p. 131.

[4]Quoted in Chester C. Tan, *Chinese Political Thought in the Twentieth Century* (Garden City, NY: Doubleday, 1971), p. 164.

[5]Ch'ien Tuan-sheng, *The Government and Politics of China*, p. 130.

[6]Quoted in Keiji Furuya, *Chiang Kai-shek: His Life and Times* (New York: St. John's University, 1981), p. 344.

[7]Ibid., p. 392.

[8]Ibid., pp. 377–88.

[9]Ibid., p. 487.

[10]Luo Ruiqing et al., *Zhou Enlai and the Xi'an Incident* (Beijing: Foreign Languages Press, 1983), p. 11.

[11]*Selected Works of Mao Zedong*, vol. 1 (Beijing: Foreign Languages Press, 1977), p. 161.

[12]Luo Ruiqing, *Zhou Enlai*, p. 30.

[13]Eastman, *Abortive Revolution*, p. 272.

[14]Ibid., p. 68.

[15]*Selected Works of Mao Tse-tung*, vol. I (Beijing: Foreign Languages Press, 1967), pp. 23–24 [hereafter cited as *SWM*].

[16]Ibid., p. 123.

[17]Ibid., vol. IV (1961), p. 155.

[18]Ibid., vol. I, p. 124.

[19]*Resolution on CPC History (1941–1981)* (Beijing: Foreign Languages Press, 1981), p. 6.

[20]Chang Kuo-t'ao, *The Rise of the Chinese Communist Party, 1928–1938* (Lawrence: University Press of Kansas, 1972), p. 422.

[21]Dick Wilson, *The Long March, 1935* (New York: Penguin Books, 1982), p. 216.

[22]Ibid., p. 227.

[23]*SWM*, vol. I, p. 160.

CHAPTER 7

The Rise of Chinese Communists to Power: 1937–1949

In addition to regaining full tariff autonomy in 1929, the Nationalist government recovered control of some foreign settlements and leased territories. The occupation of the British concessions in Hankou and Jiujiang by Nationalist troops during the northern expedition in 1927 had led to negotiations resulting in their surrender by the British. This was followed by the retrocession of British concessions in Zhenchang and Xiamen (Amoy) and of the leased territory of Weihaiwei. Since these were the least important of the areas under British jurisdiction, these acts did little more than confirm that all concessions and leased territories legally belonged to China and that China, at some stage, could be expected to reexert its sovereignty over them. The superior position of the foreigners had not been substantially disturbed; nothing had been done to upset their legal privileges and rights, which included extraterritoriality, the right to patrol Chinese waters and to maintain garrisons on Chinese soil.

The Chinese looked on their country as a semicolony, and so did the Japanese. But whereas China included Japan among the colonial powers, considering it to be the worst imperialist, the Japanese viewed China as being enslaved to the West and saw themselves as liberators of China. Japan's long-term goal was to establish a "New Order in East Asia" (enunciated in 1938), which would save China from the internal and external "Red menace" as well as from "improper white influences" that were inimical to China's territorial integrity. Through a series of strangely convoluted arguments Japan tried to prove that it was a friend of China and that its actions in China were all for China's good. Matsuoka Yosuke, who was later to become foreign minister of Japan, expressed this idea in a colorful fashion in 1937:

One thing is clear even to a donkey running along an Asian highway: constant and hearty cooperation between the peoples of Japan and China

. . . alone can work out the destiny of Asia. . . . China and Japan are two brothers who have inherited a great mansion called Eastern Asia. Adversity sent them both down to the depths of poverty. The ne'er-do-well elder brother [China] turned a dope fiend and a rogue but the younger [Japan], lean but rugged, and ambitious, ever dreamed of bringing back past glories to the old house . . . and worked hard to support the house. The elder . . . sold him out to their common enemy. The younger in a towering rage beat up the elder—trying to beat into him some sense of shame and awaken some pride in the noble traditions of the great house. After many scraps the younger finally made up his mind to stage a showdown fight.[1]

The showdown fight came in 1937 and ended only with the Japanese defeat at the hands of the United States in 1945. The Japanese had presumed that they would gain a quick military victory, which would lead to the fall of the Nationalist government and enable Tokyo to establish a friendly puppet government in China, as it had done in Manchuria. Japan did not have the human resources to occupy China physically. Its calculations went wrong when the Nationalists decided not to surrender but to withdraw into the interior to carry on the war from Chongqing, the wartime capital. Chiang Kai-shek had traded space for time; he had abandoned China's modern cities and the industrial/commercial sector for the agricultural hinterland.

Consequently, although the Japanese did gain quick military victories, they could only consolidate their hold over the northern provinces of Hebei, Chahar, Suiyuan, Shanxi, and Shandong; occupy the lower and middle reaches of the Yangtze valley, which contained the important industrial cities of Shanghai and Wuhan as well as the Nationalist capital at Nanjing; and occupy some coastal cities and the Guangzhou area in south China. Vast areas of China remained outside Japanese control, and both Nationalists and Communists contested Japanese attempts to control districts peripheral to their areas of direct occupation.

THE SINO-JAPANESE WAR: 1937–1945

The details of the Second United Front between the Nationalists and the Communists were yet to be fully worked out when the Lugouqiao (also popularly known as the Marco Polo Bridge because the Venetian had mentioned it in his memoirs) Incident took place on July 7, 1937. On the night of what came to be known as the Double Seventh, the local Japanese forces on maneuvers near the Chinese garrison town of Wanping, a few miles from Beiping, reported one of their soldiers missing. The Japanese commander demanded that he be allowed to search the town but was denied permission. Although the missing soldier turned up shortly afterward, a skirmish occurred between the Japanese and the Chinese troops, with neither side gaining any major advantage.

On the surface this was a trivial incident, and the local Chinese officials tried to pacify the Japanese to avoid further trouble. But locally arranged terms did not bring peace. Tokyo had decided to use the incident to further its designs on northern China, and within a few weeks Japanese troops in the area increased from 7,000 to 160,000 men. Chiang Kai-shek, too, concluded that the time for determined resistance had arrived and decided to check any further encroachment on Chinese territory; he ordered four divisions north of the Yellow River, while suggesting to the Japanese that the matter should not be settled at the local level but diplomatically between the two national governments.

Chiang, however, had not worked out any proper plan for the defense of the northern provinces. Indeed, his chief representative in the area, General Song Zhe-yuan, chairperson of the Hebei-Chahar Political Affairs Council and commander of the Twenty-ninth Army, made a detailed agreement with the Japanese commanders on July 19 without informing Nanjing. But incidents continued, culminating in a Japanese ultimatum to Song to withdraw his troops from the Marco Polo Bridge sector by July 27. Song rejected the ultimatum but chose at the same time to withdraw his troops from Beiping. When the Japanese started large-scale operations on the morning of July 28, World War II had begun.

The Japanese did not declare war on China and continued to refer to this massive military operation as the China Incident or the China Affair. Nor did the Chinese, for that matter, make a declaration of war until December 9, 1941, two days after the Japanese attack on Pearl Harbor and the entry of the United States into the war against Japan. It is a reflection on the nature of modern international law that until December 1941 neither the League of Nations nor any third power used the term *war* for what was going on in China.

The first and the most aggressive phase of the war lasted for a year and a half, until the end of 1938, when the Japanese had achieved all their major military goals.

In north China the Japanese advanced west into Inner Mongolia to Baotou on the edge of the Gobi Desert; southwest to Taiyuan, the capital of Shanxi; south to Kaifeng in Henan; and southeast to Jinan, the capital of Shandong. By the end of 1937, other than the part of Inner Mongolia that lay beyond the Great Wall, all the area enclosed by the Great Wall in the north, the Yellow River in the west and south, and the ocean in the east was in the hands of the Japanese. The Japa-

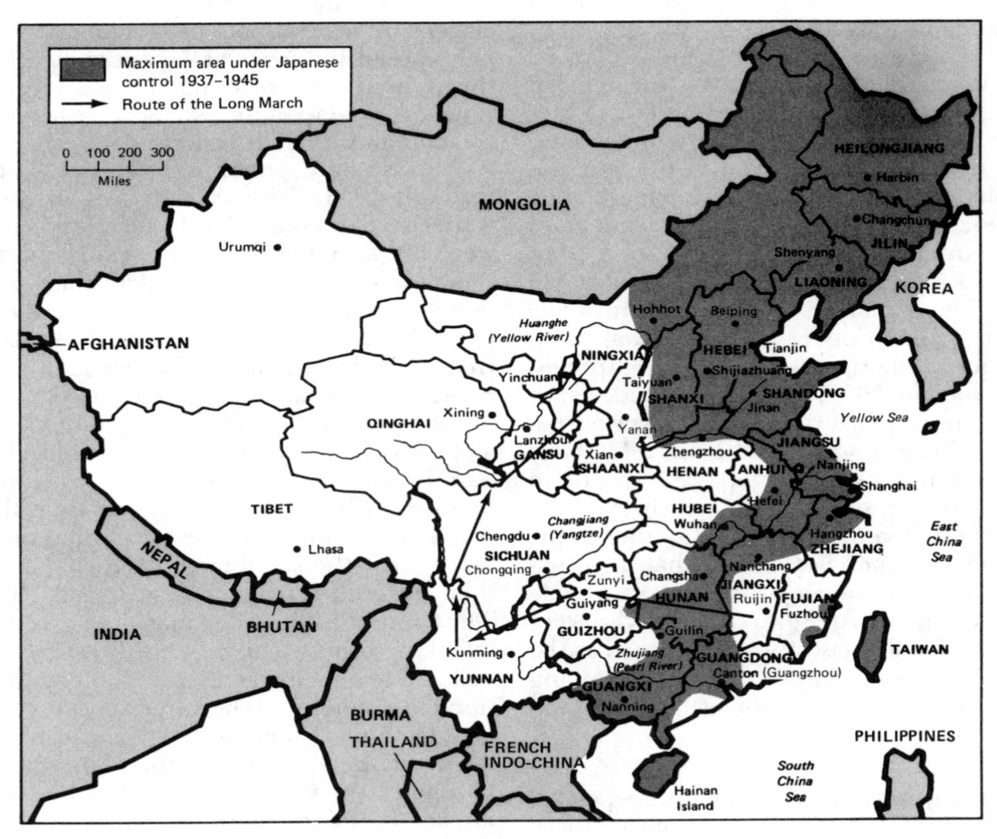

China During World War II

nese line of occupation on the west was the traditional border between the provinces of Shanxi and Shaanxi. Since Shaanxi was the headquarters of the Communists, this became the line of confrontation between them and the enemy. By August the Second United Front had finally been regularized, and the main body of the Red Army was named the Eighth Route Army of the Nationalist forces. At places the Nationalist and the Communist troops had offered strong resistance and fought with great courage, but they were no match for the better-equipped and better-trained Japanese.

In December 1937 the Japanese set up a provisional government at Beiping under a Chinese collaborator to administer the provinces south of the Great Wall. They also established an autonomous government of Mongolia in Kalgan.

Developments in central China followed the pattern set in the north: An "incident" in Shanghai in August led to the landing of Japanese troops and large-scale military confrontation between 300,000 of the best Nationalist troops and 200,000 Japanese. The Chinese troops fought with determination and courage, sustaining terrible losses, but by early November they were forced to retreat. The Nationalist government formally declared the transfer of the capital from Nanjing to Chongqing, 1,500 miles upriver, in November 1937, although it made Hankou its headquarters for a brief period before withdrawing to Chongqing. The way was now open for the Japanese troops to move upriver to Nanjing, which they occupied on December 13. The looting, rape, murder, and merciless killing that the Japanese troops indulged in there were widely reported by the foreign residents who were citizens of still "neutral" nations, such as the following description of the fall of Nanjing by an American professor at Nanjing University:

> On Tuesday the 14th the Japanese were pouring into the city—tanks, artillery, infantry, trucks. The reign of terror commenced, and it was to increase in severity and horror with each of the succeeding ten days. . . . Over a hundred women that we knew were taken away by soldiers . . . but there must have been many times that number who were raped in their homes. . . . Several big fires raging . . . started by the soldiers. . . . Some houses are entered from five to ten times in one day and the poor people looted and robbed and the women raped. Several were killed in cold blood, for no apparent reason whatever.[2]

It is estimated that over 200,000 persons were massacred in Nanjing, and one-third of the buildings in the city burned down. A certain amount of savagery and brutality accompanies all military action, but the behavior of the Japanese troops was shocking because of the general image that the Japanese, as a people, were highly disciplined and decorous. The diplomats, journalists, and other citizens of neutral nations residing in Nanjing spread the news of Japanese atrocities throughout the world and helped create a wave of anti-Japanese feeling in reaction to the bestiality of their actions.

The second phase of the war lasted through 1938. Instead of driving on westward to Hankou, where the Nationalists were preparing to make the next stand, the Japanese decided to consolidate their position by linking their forces in north and central China and encircling the Nationalist troops in the Shandong-Henan area. The operation was far from a total success. The Japanese northern armies, coming south along the Tianjin-Pukou railway, seized Jinan in December 1937, but they found themselves overextended by the time they reached the southern border of Shandong. Here, near the small town of Taierzhaung, they suffered a heavy defeat (April 1938). The Chinese armies then managed to retreat by taking drastic action: They breached the Yellow River dykes near Kaifeng and flooded millions of hectares of the countryside. This victory, although it caused the death of millions of peasants, boosted the morale of the Chinese troops but had little impact on the course of the war.

The Japanese then turned their campaign westward and moved up the Yangtze to

Wuhan. By the end of October the great industrial and commercial center was in their hands, and the Nationalists retreated further west toward Chongqing.

In the same month the Japanese opened a southern front in Guangdong and occupied the important port city of Guangzhou, thus blocking the last ocean route for Nationalist supplies from abroad. Access through Indochina via the rail route from Haiphong to Kunming was cut with the fall of France in 1940; that via the Burma Road, from Lashio to Kunming, was lost when Japan occupied Burma in 1942.

Despite their success, the Japanese had failed in their primary aim, which was to destroy the Nationalist government and replace it with a pliable, friendly regime that would willingly collaborate with Tokyo. They had achieved control over the northern and central plains and the coastal cities, but a much larger part of China remained in the hands of the Nationalists and the Communists. According to a U.S. War Department report (July 1945), the total area of occupied China proper in 1943 (i.e., China below the Great Wall) was nearly 345,000 square miles, with a population of 183 million. But of this area the Japanese actually controlled only about 82,000 square miles, with a population of 70 million (the total population of China at this time was about 450 million); the Nationalists controlled 41,000 square miles (population 16 million) of this supposedly Japanese territory; the Communists controlled 155,000 square miles of it (population 54 million); and the remaining 67,000 square miles was "no man's land" (population 43 million), contested by the Nanjing puppet regime, the Nationalists, and the Communist guerrillas.

Popular resistance continued to grow, although anti-Japanese sentiment became widespread only during the later stages of the war when the Japanese in utter desperation unleashed the barbarous policy of "burn all, kill all, and loot all."

From 1939 to 1944 there was a general lull in the operations. The Japanese capacity for further expansion in China was acutely impaired when the United States entered the war in December 1941. Chiang Kai-shek continued a halfhearted war, correctly anticipating that sooner or later Japan would be defeated by the Allies. Having lost the biggest arsenals in Nanjing, Hankou, and Taiyuan, Chiang was left with a huge army that sorely lacked sophisticated weaponry.

Harassed by the U.S. air force and fearing that the U.S. navy might cut the sea connection with their Southeast Asian territories, the Japanese started a series of campaigns in 1944 in south and central China to destroy American air bases and to take over the remaining southern railroads to establish an overland link with Indochina. But this was the last gasp of a nation that was on the verge of total collapse.

THE WAR AND THE FOREIGN POWERS

When the Sino-Japanese War began in 1937, the major foreign powers were sympathetic to China but did little to help the country. The British maintained strict neutrality to protect their interests in China which lay in Japanese-held territories. In any case the attention of Britain and France was soon absorbed by the aggressive policies of Hitler's Germany. Germany's occupation of Austria in 1938 and of Czechoslovakia and Poland in 1939 led to the outbreak of World War II in that year. The United States, which had yet to recover fully from the devastating economic crisis of the early 1930s, also followed a policy of nonintervention and limited its actions to the issuing of high-sounding moral statements about the need for nations to observe international agreements faithfully and avoid interfering in the internal affairs of other countries. At the same time the United States continued to supply Japan with petroleum, iron, steel, and other goods that could be considered war materials, even though its Neutrality Act (proclaimed in September 1937) barred the transportation of arms, ammunitions, or implements of war in vessels owned by the U.S. government or flying the American flag. This action could only hurt the Chinese.

By September 1937 the Japanese had proclaimed a blockade of the entire China coast, except for Qingdao and Hong Kong. Although the blockade was illegal (there was still no declaration of war), it resulted in the European powers' canceling many of their military supply agreements with China. No one wanted to annoy the Japanese, even though British and American ships on the Yangtze had come under Japanese air attack.

A similar spirit of appeasement dominated the meeting of the signatories of the Nine-Power Treaty (signed in 1922 to protect the territorial integrity of China), who met in Brussels in November 1937. Japan did not attend. While recognizing that the war in the Far East was of concern to the whole world, the powers felt it sufficient to urge upon Japan and China that they resort to peaceful processes. There was not even a discussion of Japan's violation of the terms of the Nine-Power Treaty.

Only the Soviet Union came to China's aid. The Soviet Union, faced by potential trouble from the Axis powers on both its western and eastern fronts, and in an attempt to safeguard its eastern frontier by weakening Japan, concluded a nonaggression pact with the Nationalists in August 1937. This pact included the clause that if China were attacked by a third power, the Soviet Union would give no aid to the aggressor. Between 1937 and 1939, when the war in Europe made things difficult for the Soviet Union, Soviet aid to the Nationalists amounted to about $300 million, which more than equaled all the credits China received from the Western powers from 1937 to 1941. Soviet supplies, most of which came overland, included aircraft, arms and ammunition, military vehicles, and gasoline. Soviet volunteer airmen also helped the young Chinese air force in the defense of China. But Soviet aid dwindled after 1939 and ended when Moscow, in direct violation of its treaty with China, signed a neutrality agreement with Japan in April 1941. Soviet national interest had prevailed over its solemn international pacts with China.

Germany, which had been helping Chiang Kai-shek modernize his military and whose advisors were still working for Chiang, had signed an anti-Comintern pact with Japan in 1936. It is probable that Germany encouraged Japan to bring the China war to a negotiated conclusion, fearing that unless Japan could get out of the China quagmire, it would lose its value as an ally against the Soviet Union.

In October 1937 German diplomats in Japan and China entered the picture as mediators, but the terms of settlement submitted by Japan were totally unacceptable to Chiang Kai-shek, who rejected them in no uncertain terms (November). However, negotiations continued, and although the Japanese demands became stiffer after the fall of Shanghai and Nanjing, some in the Nationalist party felt that capitulation would be better than utter defeat. Chiang, however, stood firm. On New Year's Day 1938 he gave up all his political posts (temporarily) to devote himself entirely to the war. By the end of the month the two countries withdrew their ambassadors; Japan declared that it would no longer deal with the Nationalists but would help in the establishment of an independent Chinese regime. Wang Jing-wei was one of those who would have liked to come to terms with Japan.

In mid-1938, having failed to win over Chiang Kai-shek, Japan inaugurated the Reformed Government of the Chinese Republic at Nanjing but could find no Chinese personality of any stature to head it. The Japanese approached some well-known figures such as Wu Pei-fu, the veteran warlord who was living in retirement in Beiping. But these people turned down the invitation, fearing that they would be looked on as traitors by their compatriots.

So it must have been most gratifying to the Japanese to learn that Wang Jing-wei, a leader who had been so close to Sun Yat-sen, had surreptitiously fled in frustration from Chongqing to Hanoi on December 21, 1938.

In mid-year, in a special session of the National Congress, Chiang Kai-shek had been elected *zong-cai* (the title is often translated as Director-General, but since the office gave virtually absolute power to Chiang, a better translation is The Leader). Wang Jing-wei, although given the title of deputy-*zong-cai,* was left without power. It was thus no coincidence that the prime minister of Japan made a statement on December 22, announcing that Tokyo was ready to collaborate with a new Chinese regime to establish its "New Order in East Asia." Wang, who had maintained secret contacts with the Japanese and was known to have pro-Japan sentiments, promptly issued a telegram to Chiang recommending that the generalissimo make peace with Japan. Chiang, of course, rejected the overture.

By mid-1939 Wang had made his way to Shanghai, where he spent the rest of the year secretly negotiating with the Japanese on a plan for a respectable and autonomous Chinese regime to work closely with Japan. However, this "new order" that Japan devised made China a dependency. In early 1940 the plan was leaked to the press in Hong Kong and Chongqing. Wang came under strong public condemnation in Free China, but he nevertheless proceeded to establish a "National Government of China" in Nanjing that he patterned after the government in Chongqing, using the Nationalist flag and swearing allegiance to the Three Principles of the People. As head of the "legal" government of China, Wang invited the Nationalist party and government officials in Chongqing to join him. Although some members of the Guomindang Central Executive Committee and a few of the generals went over to Nanjing, the gesture was largely futile.

As a result of Japan's declining fortunes from 1940 until his death in late 1944, Wang succeeded in raising the prestige of Nanjing and gained for his China the nominal status of an ally of Japan (October 1943). Whatever else he may have failed to do, Wang helped to ameliorate the condition of the Chinese under his administration and was fairly successful in keeping them from being molested and attacked by the Japanese troops. Consequently, when Japan fell there was little public violence directed against those who had run Wang's government.

For Chiang's government in Chongqing, Wang's defection and creation of a puppet government had been merely one of a number of blows. In a manner of speaking, 1942 was the darkest war year for Chongqing—the Japanese not only having effectively blockaded the Chongqing government by seizing all of China's ports but also having cut off the rail connection to Vietnam and the road link to Burma. Access to the Soviet Union was still open, but the Soviets had already signed a neutrality pact with Japan and acknowledged the independent status of Manchukuo (April 1941).

The American entry into the war, however, began to alter the situation for China, and Chongqing at last declared war against the Axis powers. The Allies established a China-Burma-India theater of war and appointed Chiang Kai-shek as the supreme commander of the China theater (January 1942). In the summer of 1941 a group of American volunteer pilots, the famed Flying Tigers under General Claire Chennault, had already begun to fly supplies over the "hump" (the Himalayan Mountains) from India. Later the group was formally activated as the U.S. Fourteenth Air Force. Supplies by air, however, were not an adequate substitute for road or rail transportation, and many of the heavier weapons could not be gotten to Chongqing. During the first three years the total tonnage airlifted to China was about 650,000 tons, but most of it was intended for Chennault and his air force; nearly 60 percent of the cargo was gasoline and oil. Not until the opening of the Burma Road in 1945 did the situation really improve for Chongqing.

From 1942 to 1946 the United States gave the Nationalists nearly $2 billion in credits and lend-lease aid. But more than the aid, which in view of China's size was not really that considerable, China was at last accepted as one of the Big Four, a power equal theoretically to the other three allies. This great power status was bestowed on China by President Roosevelt, over British and Soviet objections, in the hope that a strong, unified China would exert an effective influence in establishing peace and stability in postwar East Asia. Britain and America revised their treaties with China, ending the unequal treaty system; they also pledged that Manchuria, Formosa (Taiwan), and the Pescadores would revert to China after Japan was defeated. In 1945, when the United Nations came into being, China was alloted a permanent seat on the Security Council.

The Americans had been greatly impressed with the image of the plucky, poorly armed Chinese putting up a heroic resistance against the Japanese juggernaut. However, as Chinese-American military collaboration increased and America prepared an extensive program to train and equip Chinese air and ground forces, frictions began to arise. The Americans became critical of Chiang's incapacity, or lack of desire, to reform the inefficient army organization and eradicate deeply rooted abuses in the government system. Impatience and contempt began to replace their original sympathy, and apprehensions grew that Chiang, who had 400,000 of his best troops deployed in blockading the Communists rather than in fighting the Japanese, was not directing his main efforts against Japan but preparing for another war with the CPC.

However, as Barbara Tuchman points out, the corruption and the contempt were mutually shared:

> . . . The average American [soldier] in China, without his usual beer and PX supplies for which [air transportation] space could not be spared, disgusted by the surrounding squalor and filth which afflicted him with diarrhea, worms and every variety of intestinal disease, alienated by the callous cruelties of Chinese life, and with little understanding of the long deprivation and hunger for goods that led Chinese theft and graft to flourish . . . came to regard all Chinese as corrupt inefficient, unreliable, triple-damned, steal-you-blind, hopeless, sloppy sons-of-bitches. . . . The average Chinese found the Americans stupid, profligate, coarse, contemptuous, often brutal and easily corruptible. . . .
>
> Lend-lease provided limitless opportunity for mutual antipathies. No item, from medicine to half-ton trucks, was not for sale on the black markets of Kunming. . . . Americans were not slow to share the graft. Smuggling of gold, sulfa drugs, foreign currency, cigarets [sic], gems . . . was carried on by American Air Force, Army, Red Cross and civilian personnel for an estimated take of over $4,000,000 by the end of 1944.[3]

In 1945 there were 70,000 American servicemen in China, half of them posted at Kunming. The American attitude toward women was particularly reprehensible; an official inquiry had to be instituted to investigate the Bordello affair, which involved smuggling girls from India and Guilin into Kunming.

Even more important was the friction between Americans and Chinese at the highest level. During the first two years of the alliance, Generalissimo Chiang Kai-shek put pressure on Washington for increased supplies by periodically hinting of a separate peace with Japan. General Stilwell, a blunt, outspoken man who served as chief of staff to Chiang, found it difficult to work with the generalissimo because Chiang was a master in delaying tactics—postponing decisions, watering down proposals, and avoiding issues that did not appeal to him. In 1944, to counter the Japanese offensive in China, President Roosevelt asked Chiang to give Stilwell unquestioned authority to command all Chinese and American forces in China. Chiang, who feared that this would lessen his military and financial power, countered by demanding Stilwell's recall. Chiang reasoned that since Stilwell had brought the message to him, he had been made in effect Stilwell's subordinate, a situation no nationalist Chinese would tolerate. Chiang threatened to break with the Allies and fight the war without foreign aid. So Chiang got his way, and General Albert Wedemeyer replaced Stilwell.

In any case, the U.S. decision to attack Japan from the ocean (island-hopping strategy) rather than from the Chinese mainland reduced China's importance in the war. The United States also compromised on the notion that China could become a great power and help in establishing postwar stability. Instead, Roosevelt and Churchill turned to the Soviet Union to play this role. At the Yalta conference in February 1945, in return for Stalin's agreement to enter the anti-Japanese war after the defeat of Germany, they accepted his demand for the Soviet Union to be allowed to regain the rights in China that it had lost to Japan in 1904. Despite China's theoretical status as a great power, this agreement, kept secret from Chongqing, decided the future disposition of Chinese territory without consulting China. The Soviet demands included the restoration of the Russian lease of Port Arthur as a naval base; the internationalization of the port of Dalian, with recognition that the Soviets held a preeminent interest in the port; Sino-Soviet joint operation of the South Manchurian and the Chinese Eastern Railways; and the preservation of the status quo of Outer Mongolia, which meant the recognition of the independence of the People's Republic of Outer Mongolia.

Because of the adverse reports from disgruntled Americans in China and the resulting negative image of China, many have tended to ignore China's contribution to the Allied victory over Japan. It would be unfair to China to forget that the Nationalist army lost nearly 3 million officers and men (206 of them generals) in the war and that the Chinese forces kept 1.28 million Japanese troops tied down in China—troops that could have been effectively used against the United States in the Pacific.

NATIONALIST CHINA: 1937–1945

If the relatively favorable prewar conditions had not helped the Nationalist party to introduce reforms and truly reintegrate society, the wartime situation could only make matters worse. The Japanese invasion had, more or less, isolated the Nationalist government from the rest of the world; it was cut off from the coastal cities and the lower Yangtze economic zone, the industrial and commercial areas from where it had drawn its income and financial support.

In 1937 the Nationalists had moved some factories into the interior and later tried to establish a few industries in west China. These efforts were not inconsiderable, but industrial production was still far below Free China's needs. The scarcity of raw materials and finished products became a fact of life. Inflation and prices spiraled, making life difficult for the average wage earner; the wholesale price index increased from 100 in 1937 to 2,617,781 in 1947,[4] and interest rates on loans went up proportionately.

One reason for this development was that the Nationalist government, deprived of its earlier revenues, now became primarily dependent on the land tax, which on the average amounted to about 15 percent of its total expenditures. The government financed its deficit by issuing new notes, which in turn contributed to the inflationary forces. The note issue increased from 1.7 billion Nationalist dollars in 1937 to 163,332.8 billion in 1948.[5]

Inflation bred massive corruption, and corruption bred demoralization.

One segment of the population that became increasingly alienated from the government was the intellectuals. At the beginning of the war China's intellectual elite had accepted Chiang as the leader of the country and given him wholehearted support for standing up to the Japanese. Entire universities, with all the students and professors, moved into the southwest, carting their libraries with them. They used whatever means of transport they could get and often traversed long distances on foot. When the war resulted in a stalemate and government policies toward the Communists began to change, the intellectuals became disillusioned. Shrinking wages and smaller allowances meant deprivation but may not necessarily have driven the intellectuals to revolt. It was the government's attempts to intimidate intellectuals and suppress all critical and liberal opinion (condemned as leftism) and its use of repressive measures (such as arrest, physical torture, and sometimes execution) that turned their bitterness against the Guomindang into support for the Communists. John King Fairbank records a conversation he had in 1943 with the left-wing novelist Mao Dun in Chongqing that sheds some light on the plight of the writers:

[Mao Dun said] everyone is publishing more and more translations because they are easier to get past the censors . . . (and) one is likely to make enough to eat, whereas if you write an article or short story in the effort to feed yourself and the wrong idea slips in, there goes your rice [livelihood]. He says the censorship and secret police are now annoying every writer he knows or has heard of.[6]

The press was gagged, and large signs announcing "It is forbidden to discuss national affairs" were posted in every teahouse. Secret police frequented restaurants, clubs, schools, and colleges to listen to conversations and catch the unwary.

Adding to this depressing intellectual environment, in 1943 Chiang Kai-shek published *China's Destiny,* in which he gave his analysis of China's ills and prescriptions for treating them. Chiang distorted history and used bits and pieces of undigested information regarding the West to "prove" that China's political, social, and economic problems all stemmed from the pernicious effect of the unequal treaty system. He castigated Westernized Chinese intellectuals and advocated the revival of traditional Confucian social and political values, particularly the need for the people to follow authority loyally and unquestioningly. Chiang had failed to understand both the depth of the popular resentment against his government and the intellectual climate of the day, as may be seen from the following excerpts from *China's Destiny:*

We [can] rightly claim that the unequal treaties were the main cause for our failure to build a nation. For the past hundred years, the oppression of the unequal treaties caused political disunity, economic paralysis, and social chaos in China. The people developed a sense of inferiority; their ethical standards degenerated; and they were unable to feel a sense of shame.[7]

After the conclusion of the unequal treaties, China's academic and intellectual circles lost their self-confidence and blindly echoed foreign theories. . . . They came across Rousseau's doctrine of "the natural rights of man" and then maintained that China's Revolution and the European Revolution of the 18th and 19th centuries were part of the same fight for "freedom." . . . [The Europeans] subject to ruthless absolutism . . . [had no solution but] to fight for "freedom."

. . . the government of China under successive dynasties . . . generally adopted a magnanimous attitude towards the people. . . . According to Sun Yat-sen, "The Chinese people had long had great 'freedom' and it was not necessary for them to fight for it." Therefore, he said that the objective of the Chinese Revolution was opposite to that of the European Revolution. . . . "To resist foreign oppression, we must curtail 'individual freedom' and form a solid organization."[8]

Today the unequal treaties have been abolished. . . . Our citizens must awake and repent, mutually encouraging each other to regard the observance of the law [i.e., following the fiat of the government] as a virtue and the shouldering of responsibility as an honor. . . . To seek "freedom" we must understand its intrinsic nature; to uphold government by law we must form the habit of obedience to law.[9]

As difficulties increased, Chiang Kai-shek became more dictatorial and more aloof. He surrounded himself with sycophants and yes men—mediocrities because he put a premium on loyalty rather than ability. High officials found it difficult to get an audience. Often after waiting for weeks, they would have to get the leader's ear through his charming American-educated wife, Soong Mei-ling. The confidantes of his court were members of three families, two of them connected with his wife: her brother, T. V. Soong, and her brother-in-law, H. H. Kung (married to Soong Ai-ling); the third family was that of the Chen brothers, Chen Guo-fu and Chen Li-fu (the organizers of the C.C. Clique). Between them they controlled the party, the government, the military, and all the national finances. They, or those close to them, amassed huge fortunes while millions of Chinese starved.

Chiang, the leader, held 82 civil and military positions. He believed that he knew what was best for the country and that he was competent to direct personally all matters of policy. He often interfered in the work of his subordinates and did not hesitate to bypass responsible officials to give direct and contradictory orders to those below them. (It will be seen later that Mao Ze-dong had a similar view of his competence and leadership role.) Chiang took an inordinate interest in trivial matters, such as personally screening students applying to go to the United States for studies, while weighty national issues requiring urgent consideration lay pending. This practice led to confusion and a drastic decline in the effectiveness and morale of the government and military personnel.

As a military leader, Chiang should at least have kept his army in shape, but even here he lost contact with the fighting man and tended to accept the glowing reports submitted to him by his corrupt but loyal generals. Indeed, on paper the Nationalist forces looked formidable, but Chiang's armies were in poor fighting condition. As General Stilwell, whose objective and expert judgment can be trusted, summed up the situation in 1944, his findings were:

1. That the average strength per division instead of 10,000 is not more than 5,000.
2. That the troops are unpaid, unfed, shot with sickness and malnutrition.
3. The equipment is old, inadequate, and unserviceable.
4. That training is unexistent [sic].
5. That the officers are jobholders.
6. That there is no artillery, transport, medical services [etc., etc.].[10]

According to General Wedemeyer, Stilwell's successor in 1944, half of Chiang's troops were suffering from starvation.

When Japan surrendered suddenly after the Americans dropped the deadly atom bombs over Hiroshima and Nagasaki in August 1945, China entered a new phase. There was a moment of great jubilation, and Chiang Kai-shek's prestige soared again. But nagging questions bothered thoughtful Chinese, and only time could provide the answers. Was the Nationalist government, now back in Nanjing, ready for the task of social and economic reconstruction? Would the National Constituent Assembly, promised within a year of the cessation of the war, end the paternalistic authoritarianism of the regime and introduce democracy to the country? Would Nanjing be able to pacify the Communist opposition and reexert control over north China? As it turned out, the Guomindang failed in all these spheres. By the end of 1949 it was driven out of the mainland and forced to retreat to Taiwan. Why this happened may be understood in light of the growth of Communist party power during the war.

THE CPC AND THE SINO-JAPANESE WAR

Mao and the Second United Front: 1936–1945

As noted earlier, the Japanese troop movements in North China in the 1930s had created a national sentiment demanding that the Nationalists cease their internal war and turn their attention to defending the country from Japanese aggression. In mid-1935 the Comintern, reflecting Moscow's fears of the Axis powers, had called for the Communist parties all over the world to establish united fronts (UFs) with domestic regimes. The CPC leaders, who had long advocated that the Chinese must unite to face the Japanese challenge, issued a declaration of war against Japan on August 1, 1935, while they were still on their exhausting Long March. However, it was not the intention of the CPC leaders to collaborate with the Guomindang; the envisaged united front was to include "all people, all parties, all armed forces, and all classes" opposed both to Japanese imperialism and to Chiang Kai-shek. It was Comintern pressure that forced the CPC to change its policy and accept the idea of a united front with Chiang.

By the end of 1936, as a result of the Communist propaganda among Zhang Xueliang's troops and the house arrest of Chiang Kai-shek, the Second United Front was established. There was, however, a significant difference between the Second United Front and the first. The First United Front (1922–1927) had been a "united front from below," in which the Communists had worked as "a bloc within" the Guomindang to help the bourgeois-democratic stage of the revolution. The Second United Front, although accepting the leadership of the Nationalist government, was a "united front from above" because, despite the superficial changes in the structure and policies of the Communist soviet, it was an alliance of two parties, if not two independently armed governments. This structure can be seen from Zhou Enlai's analysis of the Second United Front, which he made ten years later in 1945, when the united front for all practical purposes had already collapsed:

> [In 1937, the Guomindang had four demands] . . . that we abolish the Red Army, abolish the political power of the Soviets, discontinue Red propaganda and stop class struggle. The word "abolish" was open to different interpretations. Once the Red Army was redesignated, you could say there was no longer a Red Army, but it would still exist; once the name of the Soviet areas was changed, you could also say there were no more Soviets, but they would still exist. "Discontinue Red propaganda and stop class struggle" meant that we were not to carry on political activities in the area under Kuomintang [Guomindang] rule [but could continue to do so in the Communist-held areas]. So there was peace, but beneath the calm waters there was a reef. And it is still there today [1945], they are bent on physically abolishing our armed forces and political power."[11]

In the Second United Front the Communists managed to retain their territorial base, their political autonomy, and their armed forces.

The Second United Front was based on mutual suspicion and distrust between the two sides, but there were members of the CPC who would have liked to offer more genuine cooperation to Chiang than Mao intended to give. Between 1937 and 1942 Mao managed to get rid of this opposition. Only after 1943, when Mao became the chairman of the CPC, can he be said to have come into full power. The fact that he could retain his dominant position between 1936 and 1942 was due to his control of the armed forces. Like Chiang, Mao had realized that power stemmed from the barrel of a gun, but unlike Chiang, Mao also wanted to be a genuine leader of a strong party. For this reason Mao never took on a military rank, although he controlled the military and even personally directed some battles the Communists had fought.

Two of the CPC leaders who contended for Mao's position, or at least strongly opposed Mao's interpretation of Comintern policies, were Zhang Guo-tao and Wang Ming. Zhang had lost much of his credibility because of the failure of his attempts to chalk out an independent course of action during the Long March. Mao had further helped in Zhang's fall by not sending any relief when Zhang was under attack by General Ma in Gansu in mid-November 1936. After his defeat, when Zhang returned to the CPC headquarters (Mao's headquarters) in Baoan in Shaanxi, he had no army left and posed little threat to Mao. Mao's supporters attacked Zhang for the crimes of "right opportunism, bankruptcy of leadership with regard to the Fourth Front Army, and opposition to the Party and the Central Committee [banditism]."[12] In 1938 Zhang defected to Chiang Kai-shek; in 1949, when the People's Republic was established, he moved to Hong Kong and later to Canada, where he wrote his memoirs.

Wang Ming, a graduate of Sun Yat-sen University in Moscow and leader of the 28 Bolsheviks, had become general secretary of the CPC in 1931. He was then only 24 years old. From 1932 to 1937, Wang was Chinese representative to the Comintern and a member of the Comintern's Executive Committee; he acquired the reputation of being a theorist and gained the respect of Stalin. It was to be expected that when he returned to China in 1937, he would consider himself an official interpreter of Comintern policies. He favored close cooperation with the Guomindang, even recommending the integration of the Red forces with those of the Nationalists so that all armies could be under a single, unified high command. Mao, of course, did not want to lose his capacity for independent action.

The united front appeared to work fairly well in 1938, but troubles between the two parties began in 1939 when local Nationalist and Communist guerrilla forces operating behind enemy lines began to clash over jurisdictional rights. By the end of the year Wang Jing-wei defected to the Japanese and the CPC was not sure that the Nationalist government would not come to terms with the Japanese. That Chiang had periodically threatened the Americans that he might make a separate peace with Japan only added to Mao's suspicions. On the other side, the Nationalists had no reason not to doubt the CPC guarantees when, in the same year, 1939, Mao openly supported the Soviet-Nazi nonaggression pact and argued that Chamberlain was as much to blame for the war as Hitler.

In the winter of 1939–1940, because of the lack of a unified military command, the Nationalist Ninety-seventh Army was attacked by the Communist Eighth Route Army for entering "Communist territory". In 1940 the Nationalists started a blockade of the Communist base area and ordered the Communist New Fourth Army to move north of the Yangtze River. On the pretext that the New Fourth Army had not followed the instructions, the Nationalist forces attacked it and almost wiped it out. The New Fourth Army was abolished by Chongqing, but it was re-formed by the Communists and continued to operate south of the Yangtze. This was the first major clash between the Guomindang and the CPC, and it was an indication of how the future relations were going to unfold.

With these developments, Wang Ming's importance had waned. From 1938 on he came under increasing attack from Mao's supporters. But apart from outmaneuvering his rivals, Mao had also proved that his policies could succeed in expanding the power of the CPC. The Guomindang strategy of positional warfare (which Chiang also wanted the Communists to follow) had led to defeat and retreat, whereas Mao's guerrilla units managed to establish anti-Japanese guerrilla zones behind enemy lines or in provincial areas where neither the Nationalists nor the Nanjing puppet regime had strong control. The only positional battle fought by the Communists was the Hundred Regiments Campaign in 1940, under the command of Peng De-huai, who had not consulted Mao. The campaign ended in defeat and heavy losses.

As the Communists managed to enlarge their control over the guerrilla zones, the zones were gradually converted to "liberated areas," with local party committees and a government structure paralleling the headquarters in Yanan. By the end of the Sino-Japanese War, liberated areas existed in much of north and central China: the Shanxi-Chahar-Hebei base with a population of 25 million and covering 108 *xian* (districts); the Shanxi-Hebei-Henan base, population 7 million in 59 *xian;* the Hebei-Shandong-Henan base, 18 *xian;* the Shanxi-Suiyuan base, population 3 million spread over 330,000 square kilometers; the Shandong base, population under control by 1943, 15 million; and the bases established by the New Fourth Army in Hubei-Henan-Anhui, Jiangsu, and Zhejiang. There were also some smaller bases in the south, in Guangdong, in the Guangzhou delta region, and on Hainan Island.

The CPC territorial expansion helped the growth of the Communist army and the party. This growth took place primarily between 1937 and 1939, when the Japanese had left the countryside of north and central China virtually uncontrolled and from 1944 to 1945, when the Japanese had to withdraw many of their troops. By 1940 the main Red armies, the Eighth Route and the New

Fourth, had grown to 400,000 and 100,000, respectively. However, from 1940 to 1943 the Japanese fort and blockade strategy, similar to the one used by Chiang in his fifth Communist-suppression campaign, plus a policy of "burn all, loot all, kill all," was temporarily successful in containing further Communist expansion; indeed, the numbers of Communist troops fell some. But when the Japanese, because of the demands of the Pacific war, had to reduce their local forces, the Communists heightened their activity, and within two years their regular armies numbered about 1 million, in control of areas with a total population of 100 million. Of course, all this expansion was done in defiance of the Chongqing government (the territorial expansion was at the expense of Guomindang areas far more than Japanese-occupied areas) and the Comintern line, which continued to stress cooperation with the Guomindang.

The membership of the party rose from 40,000 in 1937 to several hundred thousand in 1942, to 1.2 million in 1945.

Mao's Doctrines and the Rectification Campaign

The establishment of the scattered "liberated areas," some of them with little contact with the Communist capital at Yanan; the rapid expansion of the party and the army; and the continued presence of leaders like Wang Ming posed several problems for Mao Ze-dong. It was necessary for all party members and troops to be so thoroughly indoctrinated that even when located far from Yanan, in some remote base area and in a situation in which they had to act independently without being able to consult with headquarters, they would act in keeping with party policies. Many of the newly recruited party members were illiterate or semiliterate peasants. The local cadres often made serious political mistakes, such as killing off rich peasants and landlords and dislocating production.

It was also necessary for the indoctrination to be based on a single body of thought, not open to contradictory interpretation. As long as Wang Ming and his supporters remained unchecked, there was always the danger of the emergence of two lines. For example, it was intolerable to Mao that Peng De-huai had followed the Wang Ming line when he fought his Hundred Regiments campaign.

So, early in 1942 Mao launched a massive campaign for the Rectification of the Party's Style of Work (*zheng feng*). The campaign aimed at cleansing the party of incorrect ideas and purging it of undesirable elements because, as Mao said,

> [For the complete overthrow of the enemy] we must keep our ranks in good order, we must march in step, our troops must be picked troops and our weapons good weapons. Without these conditions the enemy cannot be overthrown. . . . (The problem facing our Party) is quite serious . . . [T]here is still something wrong with our style of study, with our style in the Party's internal and external relations.[13]

The rectification of "the style of study" meant establishment of Mao's "thought," which had sinified Marxism-Leninism as the sole orthodox ideology. As early as 1938 Mao had insisted that "Marxism must take on a national form before it can be applied." Now he was going to see to it that this was done, for it would not only bring uniformity to party thinking but consolidate his hold over the party.

Mao particularly denounced "foreign formalism," attacking doctrinaires who quoted Marx and Lenin but did not comprehend the reality of the Chinese situation (Wang Ming being one such theorist). The campaign can thus be seen as an indirect attack on the Soviet influence in the CPC and Mao's attempts to exert his independence of all foreign interference and provide the CPC with an independent philosophic basis. Although the Comintern had not interfered with the CPC since 1935, Mao welcomed its dissolution in 1943.

By 1942 Mao had written extensively on party and military affairs and even had dealt with theoretical issues—two and one-half volumes of the first three volumes of Mao's works consist of his writings between 1936 and 1945. Although Mao was at his best when dealing with concrete issues and his essays on philosophical subjects displayed a certain lack of depth, Mao's writing provided ample material for study during the rectification campaign of 1942.

The goal of the rectification campaign was to weed out three wrong tendencies that had emerged in the work style of party members: subjectivism, sectarianism, and formalism. Subjectivism, which led to dogmatism, came from overemphasis on book learning ("many intellectuals . . . fancy themselves very learned and assume airs of erudition without realizing that such airs are bad and harmful . . . workers and peasants know more than they do"[14]) and could be rectified by involvement with practical work. Sectarianism was an assertion of independence and an incapacity to wholeheartedly subordinate oneself to the majority decision as represented in central orders. Formalism was reflected in stereotyped writing, replete with meaningless but high-sounding quotations from theories worked out in the Soviet Union that had little relevance to Chinese reality. Such writing intimidated the people rather than establishing communication with them.

During the campaign, all party members were ordered to devote two to three months to study and discuss the designated materials, critically analyze their own behavior and attitudes and allow others to criticize them, make public confessions of their failings, and thus rectify their erroneous ideas. The campaign lasted two years and stilled all opposition to Mao. Those who still disagreed with the "Great Helmsman" learned to keep their thoughts to themselves. The guidelines worked out by Zhou En-lai for himself during *zheng feng* are a good example of basic Maoist thought:

1. Study diligently, grasp essentials, concentrate on one subject rather than seeking a superficial knowledge of many.
2. Work hard and have a plan, a focus and a method.
3. Combine study with work. . . .
4. On the basis of principles, resolutely combat all incorrect ideology in others as well as in myself.
5. . . . make the most of my strength and take concrete steps to overcome my weaknesses.
6. Never become alienated from the masses; learn from them and help them. Lead a collective life. . . .
7. Keep fit and lead a reasonably regular life.[15]

In 1942 Mao also addressed himself to the question of art and literature. He attacked writers for having petty bourgeois ideas, for thinking that they knew best what was good for the people, and for wanting independence from party control. Mao declared that literature must serve "workers, peasants, and soldiers"; that writers must study the masses and bring their standards down to the level understandable by the masses; that literature and art are "subordinate to politics, we mean class politics, the politics of the masses"; and that writers must destroy the "creative moods" that are "feudal, bourgeois, petty bourgeois, liberalistic, individualist, nihilist, art-for-art's sake, aristocratic, decadent, or pessimistic."[16] These lectures were added to the *zheng-feng* materials studied by writers and artists.

After two years of the rectification campaign, the CPC Central Committee in 1945 adopted the Resolution on Certain Questions in the History of Our Party, which claimed,

> Ever since its birth in 1921, the Communist Party of China has made the integration of the universal truth of Marxism-Leninism with the concrete practice of the Chinese revolution the guiding principle in all its work, and Comrade Mao Tse-tung's theory and practice of the Chinese revolution represent this integration. . . . In the course of its struggle the Party has produced its own leader, Comrade Mao Tse-tung [who has] creatively applied the scientific theory of Marxism-Leninism, the acme of human wisdom to China. . . .[17]

The resolution then goes on to say that whereas Mao was always correct, the party between 1921 and 1935 thrice suffered serious setbacks because of leftist mistakes made by leaders who had not followed Mao's line (e.g., Wang Ming's left line had resulted in the collapse of the Jiangxi soviet) and that Mao could do nothing about it because his leadership over the party and army was decisively established only in 1935. This reinterpretation of party history became the standard basis for all future history writing until Mao's death. The myth of Mao's infallibility had received party endorsement.

By 1945 Mao, at last in absolute command of the CPC, was ready for the long-awaited showdown with Chiang Kai-shek.

THE FINAL STRUGGLE FOR POWER: 1944–1949

The American Interlude

The Sino-Japanese War had drawn the Americans into the Chinese scene. The large numbers of American military advisors, diplomats, and civilian China experts attached to the U.S. embassy that thronged Chongqing somehow came to believe that they had the power and the wisdom to guide the Chinese revolution and to help in remaking China. Since they were providing aid, it seemed obvious to them that they had the right to intervene in China's internal development. At least they thought so until events proved how limited their understanding was of the Chinese reality. In some ways their failure can be compared to that of the Russians in the 1920s. In 1949, after having been thrown out of China by the Communists, who established the People's Republic in that year, the Americans returned home to debate the issue of which of them had contributed to America's loss of China.

After its entry into World War II, the United States had two basic interests in China: to mobilize the Chinese to help in the war against Japan and to prepare a strong, stable, united, and pro-American China to become the principal stabilizing factor in East Asia after the war. Only such a Chinese state could keep Soviet influence out of the country and become a substitute for Japan in balancing Soviet power in the region.

These two interests began to coalesce in 1944. To mobilize Chinese war potential fully, the Communists had to be included in strategic calculations; to prepare China for its postwar role, the Guomindang government had to be made more liberal and democratic; to avoid a civil war between the Nationalists and the Communists (which would draw Russian support for the Communists and might result in the Soviet domination of China) after the collapse of Japan, Chongqing was to be encouraged to establish a more representative government that would include the Communists; and the Nationalists were not to be given too much aid lest they feel strong enough to start the civil war. But at the same time, aid was not to be too little lest it keep them from economic and political recovery. As one of the American diplomats wrote in 1944, "[We must] use *our tremendous influence* with the Kuomintang [Guomindang] to promote internal unity on a foundation of progressive reform [emphasis added]."[18] There were, of course, differing views on how America was to achieve its policy goals.

The making of U.S. national policy toward China was also affected by the changing personal attitudes of Americans in Chongqing, many of whom were academics (the China experts) and journalists. Their personal sense of democracy, humanity, justice, and efficiency was offended by what they witnessed in Chongqing. They could not tolerate the harsh, dictatorial nature of the government and the corruption, nepotism, incompetence, and apathy that surrounded it. They were more at ease with the left-wing intellectuals in Chongqing and fell in love with the image of the Chinese Communists; with, in the words of John Fairbank, "the sunny vitality and homespun egalitarianism of the CCP [CPC] at Yenan . . . already famous from Ed Snow's *Red Star Over China*. . . . Yenan glowed in the distance."[19]

Although there was a state of undeclared war between the Nationalists and the Communists, the united front was supposedly still intact. In the negotiations carried on between the two sides in May 1944, the position of the Nationalists was that the Communists had broken their original agreement by increasing their army strength and area of jurisdiction beyond what had been authorized; the Communists insisted that the liberated areas were run on Sun Yat-sen's principles and that their armies had been organized for national defense, both legitimate actions; their grievance was that they had received no funds or equipment since 1940.

It is at this stage that the Americans first became interested in trying to break the stalemate. In June 1944 Henry Wallace, U.S. vice-president, visited Chongqing and got Chiang to agree that a small American military observer mission could be posted at Yanan. The observer group was favorably impressed by the idealism and dedication of the Communists (who lacked every modern amenity) and the high morale of their troops. The Communists, realizing that the American mediation could bring them supplies and raise the CPC national profile, were most cooperative and agreed that China needed a coalition government.

In August General Patrick Hurley was appointed personal representative of President Roosevelt in China to smooth the differences between Stilwell and Chiang. By early November Stilwell had been replaced by Wedemeyer and Ambassador Gauss by Hurley. Hurley was now free to devote himself to the task of getting the Nationalists and the Communists to work together. Why were the Americans so ready to include the Chinese Communists in their calculations, when they were so deadly afraid of Russian communism? The answer is that the Americans were convinced that the Chinese Communists were not real Communists but nationalist agrarian reformers. This image was propagated by American journalists who had visited Yanan (witness the *New York Times* report from China: "[The CPC] system now might be described as agrarian or peasant democracy, or as a farm labor party") and was assiduously projected by Mao himself. As he told John Service, an American political officer who was a member of the observer mission,

> Between the people of China and the people of the United States there are strong ties of sympathy, understanding and mutual interest. . . . China's greatest post-war need is economic development. . . . America is not only the most suitable country to assist this economic development of China: she is also the only country fully able to participate. . . .
>
> The Chinese Communist Party . . . is *the* party of the Chinese peasant. . . . The Communist Party will be the means of bringing democracy and sound industrialization to China. . . .
>
> America does not realize her influence in China and her ability to shape events there.[20]

The Russians also aided in establishing this myth. Molotov, the Soviet foreign minister, told Hurley in August 1944 that the Chinese who called themselves Communist had no real relation to communism and that once their economic conditions had improved they would forget this political inclination.[21]

On November 7 General Hurley visited Yanan for three days and worked out a draft Guomindang-Communist agreement with Mao Ze-dong (the Communist Five Point Proposals), which included the clause that the reorganized national coalition government should include the CPC representatives, as should the envisioned United National Military Council. Hurley considered the terms fair to both sides. Chongqing, however, submitted counterproposals that the Communists could not accept, and although Hurley optimistically continued the negotiations right up to the time of Japan's surrender, it was becoming clear that the gap between the two sides was too big to be bridged. As the negotiations proceeded, Hurley increasingly accepted the Guomindang line, which created an anti-American sentiment in the CPC.

When the war suddenly ended with the Japanese surrender, the Nationalists were not in a position to reoccupy immediately all enemy-held territory. The supreme commander of the Allied forces in the Pacific designated the Nationalists as the sole agency for accepting Japanese surrender in all parts of China except Manchuria, where the Russians were given this privilege. After all, the Nationalist government was the internationally recognized legal government of China; even the Russians had signed a Sino-Soviet Treaty of Friendship and Alliance with Chiang on August 14, 1945. So Chongqing ordered the Japanese to surrender only to the Nationalists and not to the Communists, even if this meant that the Japanese had to hold on to their positions and fight off the Communists until the Nationalist forces could reach them. The Communists were ordered to remain in their positions, which of course, they did not; they moved to strengthen their position by seizing as much territory and as many arms from the Japanese as possible.

At the political level negotiations were still being carried on. Indeed, Mao accepted Chiang's invitation for discussions and went to Chongqing in person from August 28 to October 11, 1945. When Mao left Chongqing, Zhou En-lai stayed on to carry on the talks. By November this phase of the negotiations was over: Zhou returned to Yanan, and Hurley resigned his post. The only reason why Chiang had invited Mao and Mao had accepted the invitation was that both sides wanted to impress America with their sincere desire for peace, democracy, and unity. Each side also hoped to win over the neutral Chinese leaders and the third parties in China by this show of reasonableness.

America, however, did not give up the hope of saving China from a civil war. General George Marshall, handpicked by President Truman, replaced Hurley and carried on the good work for another full year. The Americans were now clearly siding with the Nationalists and giving Chiang all the aid they could by flying his troops to North China and by allowing American Marines to disarm and repatriate the Japanese. On the other side, the Russians, who had declared war against Japan on August 8, poured their troops into Manchuria, refused to allow the Nationalists to land at Dalian to take over the northeastern provinces, and covertly helped the Communists to build up their forces and expand into certain areas of Manchuria. However, the Chinese Communists had to depend primarily on their own resources because the Russians when they withdrew from Manchuria took all the industrial and other equipment they could lay their hands on, leaving some limited arms for the Communists. The Soviets, having gotten Chongqing to agree to the concessions that the Allies had promised Moscow in the Yalta conference, finally declared in November 1945 that they would vacate Manchuria by January 3, 1946. Actually the last Soviet troops did not leave until May 3.

Marshall was initially successful in getting the two sides to agree to a ceasefire and allow truce teams to monitor the front lines (January 1946). The truce, however, broke down in Manchuria, where the Communists began to take over areas being vacated by the Soviet troops and which the Nationalist government was determined to occupy. By April the Nationalists completed their takeover of Shenyang (Mukden), the capital of Manchuria, while the Communists had entered Harbin, Siping, and other strategically located towns. In May 1946 the Nationalist troops defeated the Communist army at Siping and took away that town from the CPC. Having suffered heavy losses at Siping, the CPC decided to revert to the policy of strengthening their bases in the countryside and not try to hold towns and cities or maintain an unbroken military front. The Communists renamed their forces the People's Liberation Army (PLA), thus symbolically declaring their independence of the Nationalist government and the end of the united front. In the same month, Marshall persuaded the U.S. government to lay a temporary embargo on all exports of arms and ammunitions to China, hoping that this act would frighten Chiang from proceeding with the civil war. Its futility soon became apparent when Chiang launched a nationwide military campaign to retake towns and cities held by the Communists. In August Mao made his famous statement:

> [T]he atom bomb is a paper tiger. . . . All reactionaries are paper tigers. . . . Chiang Kai-shek and his supporters, the U.S. reactionaries, are paper tigers . . . history will finally prove that our millet plus rifles is more powerful than Chiang Kai-shek's aeroplanes plus tanks . . . the day will come when these reactionaries are defeated and we are victorious.[22]

General Marshall's efforts at getting the Nationalists to make the constitution, which was promulgated in December 1946, more democratic also failed. On January 7, 1947, Marshall left China, attributing his failure to the reactionaries who opposed him in the Guomindang and the "dyed-in-the-wool Communists,"[23] who were ruthlessly trying to gain their objectives.

The Americans had, at last, come to recognize the basic reality of Chinese politics: Chiang Kai-shek could not be bullied or cajoled into giving up his monopoly of power, and Mao Ze-dong could never accept a coalition government in which the CPC did not play a leading role; and the "moderates" and "liberals" who could have helped to democratize Chinese politics lacked "political power to exercise a controlling influence."[24]

During the next two years the United States gradually disengaged from China and cautiously prepared for the Communist takeover. However, because of internal pressures, the government had to continue aiding the Nationalists, even though on a considerably reduced scale. In August 1949 the U.S. government issued a white paper, *United States Relations with China,* strongly critical of the Nationalists, and in his letter Secretary of State Dean Acheson asserted, "Nothing that this country [USA] did or could have done within the reasonable limits of its capabilities could have changed the result [in the Chinese civil war]."[25] Regardless of these actions, the Communists had become alienated and condemned the United States for its imperialistic behavior. The Nationalists, of course, felt that they had been denied support when they most needed it and were also antagonized.

The Civil War

The civil war was launched in earnest by the Nationalists in 1947. Chiang had every reason to be confident that he would win the war. Besides the three-to-one advantage he had in regular troops, he also possessed superior weapons and an air force. But his forces were overextended. Like the Japanese, his troops had occupied the cities in areas otherwise controlled by the Communists; the Nationalists even occupied Yanan, the Communist capital. Major General David Barr, head of a U.S. Army Advisory Group in China, recommended that Chiang withdraw from some of the northern cities and consolidate his position in central China, where he was at his strongest, but Barr's advice went unheeded.

By mid-1947 the Communists began their counteroffensive and isolated the Nationalist-held cities by destroying the railroads and other lines of communications. By summer 1948 the Communists had penetrated central China. In fall 1948, the Communists, who had captured a vast amount of weaponry from the defeated or defecting Nationalist troops and whose forces now outnumbered those of the Nationalists, mounted powerful attacks against the Nationalists in Manchuria, north China, and central China, winning victory after victory.

The new Nationalist constitution was promulgated on January 1, 1948, and in April the new National Assembly elected Chiang Kai-shek president and Li Zong-ren, the one-time Guangxi warlord, vice-president. In midyear the Nationalists appealed to the Allied powers to intercede on their behalf and help in restoring the ceasefire. The powers rejected the appeal. The Communists agreed to reopen peace negotiations on conditions that were totally unacceptable to the Nationalists. Chiang Kai-shek thereupon retired from the presidency on January 21, 1949, hoping that Li could work out a better deal, but the Communists increased their demands, which now amounted to a call for surrender. The Communists used the three-month period of negotiations, when there was a lull in the fighting, to regroup their forces.

The day after the Nationalists, who had shifted their capital to Guangzhou, rejected the CPC demands, the Communists, on the night of April 20–21, moved south across the Yangtze River. By the end of the year China had been "liberated," except for Yunnan, Xinjiang, Tibet (which were absorbed later), and Taiwan.

On October 1, 1949, the People's Republic of China was inaugurated in Beijing with Mao Ze-dong as its head. The Nationalists moved their government from Guangzhou to Chongqing to Chengdu and finally in December to Taipei in Taiwan. Many of the foreign diplomats stayed on in Nanjing; the one surprising exception was the Soviet ambassador, who accompanied the mobile Nationalists headquarters until it moved to Taiwan.

An Assessment of the Communist Success

In the final analysis the Nationalist government was not overthrown by a "spontaneous proletariat uprising" (as orthodox Marxism would have it) or even by a "popular revolution" (as Lenin managed to lead in Russia) but defeated by an organized military government using military tactics and strategy. The success of the Communists was largely due to the failure of the Guomindang leadership, which had fostered a faction-ridden party, wanting in principles; which had perpetuated a corrupt, nepotistic, brutal government that had no support from the peasant masses (who were crushed by taxes and conscription) and had alienated the intelligentsia, the professional classes, the business community, and the bureaucracy; and which had, of all things, even allowed a military system to emerge that depended on incompetent generals and inefficient and demoralized armies that defected by the tens and hundreds of thousands. The result was that many politically important elements of the population had become passive observers—not turning to the Communists but not interested in saving the Guomindang, either.

The CPC had superior leadership, promoting merit and ability and ensuring loyalty from the rank and file. To the areas under its jurisdiction and the population under its control (both comparatively much smaller than those of the Nationalists in 1945) the CPC had brought land reforms, eliminated exploitative landlord and warlord traditions, introduced a just and fair government system, and engendered patriotic and nationalistic enthusiasm. It was this policy, and not any abstract ideology of Marxism-Leninism, that had mobilized the people behind the CPC.

At the establishment of the united front, the CPC had discarded class warfare and accepted milder policies toward landlords and other enemy classes. Even when the united front broke down, these policies were not changed because Mao had realized that they were conducive to a more popular acceptance of the CPC leadership. And they helped in gaining adherents among the intellectuals and third parties in the Guomindang-held areas. Except for a short period in 1947, when a harsh program of class struggle was introduced, mild policies were followed through 1949.

NOTES

1. *Japan Weekly Chronicle*, October 21, 1937, p. 548; cited in Harold S. Quigley, *Far Eastern War: 1937–1941* (Boston: Putnam's, 1942), pp. 59–60.

2. See Roger Pelisser, ed. and trans. Martin Kieffer, *The Awakening of China: 1793–1949* (New York: Putnam's, 1967), pp. 376–77.

3. Barbara Tuchman, *Stilwell and the American Experience in China: 1911–1945* (New York: Macmillan, 1971), p. 377.

4. Ramon H. Myers, *The Chinese Economy, Past and Present* (Belmont, CA: Wadsworth, 1980), p. 185.

5. Ibid.

6. John K. Fairbank, *Chinabound: A Fifty-Year Memoir* (New York: Harper Collins, 1982), p. 262.

7. Chiang Kai-shek, *China's Destiny & Chinese Economic Theory,* with notes and commentary by Philip Jaffe (New York: Roy Publishers, 1947), p. 105.

8. Ibid., pp. 209–10.

9. Ibid., pp. 212–13.

10. Joseph W. Stilwell, *The Stilwell Papers,* arr. and ed. Theodore H. White (New York: William Sloane, 1948), p. 316; cited in Pelisser, *Awakening of China,* pp. 405–6.

11. *Selected Works of Zhou Enlai,* vol. I (Beijing: Foreign Languages Press, 1981), p. 217 [hereafter cited as *Zhou En-lai*].

12. Chang kuo-t'ao, *The Rise of the Chinese Communist Party, 1928–1938* (Lawrence: The University Press of Kansas, 1972), Vol. 2, p. 507.

13. *Selected Works of Mao Tse-Tung,* vol. III (Beijing: Foreign Languages Press, 1967), p. 35 [hereafter cited as *SWM*].

14. *SWM,* vol. III, p. 39.

15. *Zhou En-lai,* p. 144.

16. *SWM,* vol. III, p. 94.

17. *Selected Works of Mao Tse-tung,* abridged by Bruno Shaw (New York: Harper Collins, 1970), pp. 267–68.

18. See Lyman P. Van Slyke, ed., *The Chinese Communist Movement,* A Report of the United States War Department, July 1945 (Stanford, CA: Stanford University Press, 1968), p. 240.

19. Fairbank, *Chinabound,* p. 266.

20. Van Slyke, *Chinese Communist Movement,* pp. 218–19.

21. See Herbert Feis, *The China Tangle* (New York: Atheneum, 1966), p. 180.

22. *SWM,* vol. IV, pp. 100–1.

23. *The China White Paper* (Stanford, CA: Stanford University Press, 1967), vol. II, p. 687.

24. Ibid., p. 688.

25. Ibid., vol. I, p. XVI.

CHAPTER 8

From "Liberation" to "Independence": 1949–1958

When Hurley was trying to get Chiang Kai-shek to form a coalition government in 1945, he proposed as a first step holding a conference that would include representatives of the Guomindang, the CPC, and other parties, as well as nonpartisan leaders. In 1946, after Marshall had managed to get the two sides to declare a ceasefire, a "political consultative conference" was held in Chongqing, with CPC representatives taking part. But by the end of the year the negotiations for a coalition government had collapsed, and the CPC withdrew from the conference. The CPC withdrew because Chiang had unilaterally decided to convene the National Assembly and promulgate a constitution.

The National Assembly did meet, and a constitution was adopted on December 25, 1946. It was a purely Guomindang constitution and ended all hopes for a reconciliation with the CPC. In January 1949, when the Guomindang tried once again to start negotiations with the CPC, Mao demanded that the 1946 constitution be annulled, war criminals be punished (Chiang among them), and a new Political Consultative Conference be formed "without the participation of reactionary elements" (the right-wing Guomindang leaders).

By summer 1949, when the Communists had already occupied Beiping, it was clear that it was only a matter of time before the Guomindang would be ousted and the CPC would take over the government. In preparation for this eventuality, Mao Ze-dong directed that a Political Consultative Conference, representing various friendly parties and personages, be convened by the CPC as the first step in the formation of a coalition government." The CPC thus took over the role of the Guomindang.

In theory, by reforming the Political Consultative Conference—now called the Chinese People's Political Consultative Conference (CPPCC)—Mao not only derived his authority from the Second United Front but also took over the leadership of the "bourgeois-democratic phase of the revolution."

In June 1949 Mao provided the guidelines of the government-to-be in an essay entitled "On the People's Democratic Dictatorship."[1] The article, a mix of orthodox and semi-orthodox beliefs, reflects Mao's view of the Chinese revolution, the current national and international situation, and the direction of future CPC policies. Many elements in the essay were to cause problems later.

The article begins by stating an orthodox Marxian view that the ultimate objective of the revolution, after it had led to the extinction of classes and class struggle, was to reach the stage when the state and the party would wither away. However, Mao argues, the conditions to achieve this end will be provided by "the leadership of the Communist Party and the state power of the people's dictatorship." This truth was above challenge.

Mao then analyzes the modern history of China to show that although Western bourgeois democratic models were tried, they could not succeed in China because the country was "suffering under imperialist oppression." Only with the advent of the Russian Revolution did socialism come to China and the Chinese entered "an entirely new era in their thinking and their life."

Internationally, the "Chinese without exception must lean either to the side of imperialism or to the side of socialism. Sitting on the fence will not do, nor is there a third road." China belonged "to the side of the anti-imperialist front headed by the Soviet Union, and so we can turn only to this side for genuine and friendly help, not on the side of the imperialist front." Evidently, Mao not only had given up his earlier idea of obtaining postwar aid from the United States but also had come to look on the United States as a potential enemy. The division of the world into two clear-cut camps, one headed by the evil American imperialists and the other by the forces of good led by the Soviet Union, did not bode well for China's future adjustment to international affairs.

Internally, the party was to form and lead the united front of workers, peasants, petty bourgeoisie, and national bourgeoisie to establish a "people's democratic dictatorship." Members of this united front were the people, who would enforce their "dictatorship over the running dogs of imperialism—the landlord class and bureaucratic bourgeoisie, as well as the representatives of those classes, the Kuomintang reactionaries and their accomplices. . . . The combination of these two aspects, democracy for the people and dictatorship over the reactionaries, is the people's democratic dictatorship. . . . The state apparatus, including the army, the police and the courts, is the instrument by which one class oppresses another. . . . We definitely do not apply a policy of benevolence to the reactionaries. . . ." Since anyone who was found wanting in socialist virtues could be condemned as a representative of the reactionary classes (as was frequently done later), a "'people' person" could be transformed into a "'nonpeople' person" with the greatest of facility. There being no recourse to law, a victim had the option of accepting the political judgment and the punishment that went with it or committing suicide.

As had all constitutional documents that had preceded it, this document also mentions the people's rights of freedom of speech, assembly, association, and so on. But this was a meaningless concession to Western ideals, which had never been followed in China earlier and were not going to be followed under the Communists.

Under the People's Democratic Dictatorship, declared Mao, the people can "educate and remold themselves on a countrywide scale by democratic methods and, with everyone taking part, shake off the influence of domestic and foreign reactionaries (which is still very strong . . .), rid themselves of bad habits and ideas acquired in the old society, not allow themselves to be led astray by reactionaries, and continue to advance—to advance toward a socialist and communist society." This is a remarkable statement because Mao implies that the party did not represent any particular class or segment of the population, not even the working class, but all the people. Indeed, the enforced shift of the Communists from the cities after 1927 had eliminated their influence over the labor unions and the labor movement. When the cities finally were occupied by the CPC in 1947–1949, it was not through uprisings of the urban workers but through seizure by the People's Liberation Army (PLA). Liu Shao-qi, in a speech to the CPC Central Committee in March 1949, on "Questions Concerning Urban Work," was forthright in stating his suspicions about the reliability of the urban working class:

> We must rely on the workers [for administering the cities and to increase production]. But are they reliable? Marxism holds that the working class is most reliable. Generally speaking, this is correct, but we still have some specific problems. So *we must strive to enable our working class to become completely reliable* [emphasis added]. If we ignore these problems and rely on the workers without doing any work among them, they won't necessarily be reliable.[2]

In his essay Mao also made particular reference to the "education" of the peasantry because, as he put it, "without socialization of agriculture, there [could] be no complete, consolidated socialism." So Mao declared that all classes and all people needed reeducation and that only the party could guide them in this process. However, troubles would arise later, when Mao found that the party itself needed reeducation. Who was to teach the teachers? At that stage many Chinese must have felt that Mao was the sole repository of "the Truth."

INAUGURATION OF THE NEW ERA

On October 1, 1949, Mao Ze-dong proclaimed the establishment of the People's Republic of China (PRC) from Tiananmen (the Gate of Heavenly Peace), the southern entrance to the imperial palace in Beijing (Beiping was now renamed Beijing, "the Northern Capital"). It can be said without exaggeration that the vast majority of the Chinese people, exhausted by 50 years of internal upheavals and wars, welcomed their "liberation" because above all it presaged peace and the reintegration of the nation under a strong central leadership. Few would have disagreed with Mao Ze-dong's proud statement, made in September 1949, "Our work will go down in the history of mankind, demonstrating that the Chinese people, comprising one quarter of humanity, have now stood up. . . . Ours will no longer be a nation subject to insult and humiliation. We have stood up."[3]

In many ways the PRC found itself in an easier situation than the Soviet Union had encountered at its inception: In 1918 the Soviet Union was isolated and alone, whereas the PRC in 1949 had a powerful friend in the Soviets and allies among the Communist states of Eastern Europe. Among the countries of the Third World, most of which were yet under colonial domination, China was looked on with admiration as a symbol of anti-imperialism and anticolonialism; the newly independent countries of Burma and India hastened to recognize the PRC.

But this in no way implies that the PRC was without problems. The sudden collapse of the Nationalists meant that the CPC had to expand its party network to include the vast areas that had fallen under its control. The party membership had to be increased hurriedly to undertake the new tasks; it was worrisome that since most of the new recruits had no experience of the revolution, their ideological commitment could be weak. Also, in the interest of maintaining local administration, many bureaucrats from the old regime were allowed to continue to function as before until they could undergo "thought reform."

The CPC was no longer a party in opposition, functioning with simple administrative structures in the countryside and downgrading the value of the cities. As the party in power, running the most populous state in the world, it had to fashion elaborate political and administrative institutions and learn to deal with the cities (from which it was now going to rule the country) as the centers of industry, commerce, communications, international relations, education, and culture. This task called for skills and techniques that the CPC had had no opportunity to develop.

While consolidating its hold over the country, the CPC also had to rehabilitate the shattered economy, bring inflation under control, and help the recovery of industry and commerce. Here the party was faced with a dilemma: To achieve this goal the CPC had to win over the old-style intellectuals, professionals, managerial class, and industrialists, who otherwise were considered the enemies of socialism and targets for attack. The goals of the revolution could not be achieved and the ideology of the CPC legitimized without introducing socialist reforms; yet these reforms, if they alienated the urban bourgeoisie, would undermine economic recovery and development, which the regime could not allow.

The problems of the CPC were eased partly by its own mild policies represented in the united front approach and partly by the amazing readiness with which the urban bourgeoisie accepted the new regime. This readiness was not due to their love for Marxism-Leninism; rather it reflected a traditional attitude, ironically strengthened by the developments in the twentieth century.

Traditionally, the Chinese have placed a high value on strong, paternalistic leadership that could protect, nurture, and look after the needs of the people and clarify the pattern of hierarchical human relationships that the leaders endorsed. To such a leadership the people readily offered their loyalty and obedience. Moreover, Chinese nationalism (a modern development), having risen as a response to the threat of imperialist aggression, demanded a strong, authoritarian state. This need in turn allowed Chinese politics to turn left and replace democratic models with the Bolshevized single-party authoritarian governments of the Guomindang and the CPC. Most of the intelligentsia and leaders of society supported, rather than condemned, this development.

Another traditional value, the Confucian virtue of harmony, had been attacked since the May Fourth Movement as false and counterproductive, but in fact it was very much a part of the living political culture. It was reflected in the obligation of the leaders to make a public show of consensus and to demand conformity from the citizenry, which the bourgeoisie instinctively accepted.

The urban bourgeoisie had learned to live within the framework of the Guomindang-organized state, using nepotism and the corruption of factional politics as a substitute for more democratic channels to express its sectional or group interests. There was no reason it could not adjust to the new circumstances even better since the CPC was free of corruption and recognized the bourgeoisie's importance to the nation. Had not Mao himself publicly declared,

> The whole Party should try earnestly and painstakingly to make a success of the united front work. We should rally the petty bourgeoisie and the national bourgeoisie under the leadership of the working class. . . it is right and necessary to unite with the national bourgeoisie, the democratic parties, democratic personages and intellectuals. May of them were our enemies before, but now that they have broken with the enemy camp and come over to our side, we should unite with all these people, who can more or less be united with. It is in the interest of the working people to unite with them.[4]

The situation looked good to the bourgeoisie, but only time would tell what working under the working-class hegemony would entail or how the Communists intended to "struggle against them [the bourgeoisie] on the one hand and unite with them on the other."[5] Time, however, was not on their side.

Vast and rapid changes took place within the next decade. By 1959 the so-called enemies of socialism had been eliminated or come under the stern control of the party, the political and social order had been transformed, and the economy had been reorganized. In foreign relations, by 1960 China had declared its independence of Moscow, ending ten years of Soviet domination of the China scene and replacing the fraternal alliance between the two Communist giants with a bitter hostility that was to last for the next three decades.

Naturally, Mao played a key role in these developments, but by 1959 his colleagues in the party had begun to criticize some of his policies for attempting to apply the simplistic Yanan approach to complex national problems. The "two lines" on China's path to modernization that emerged from the inner party conflict have marked all Chinese politics ever since.

Central Government and Regional Administration

The PRC was inaugurated even before all internal fighting had ended. In fact, the PLA fought a major battle in Xigang in October 1950, and Tibet was not absorbed into the PRC until 1951. As the PLA armies advanced and "liberated" the provinces, they established military control commissions to supervise the existing administration of these areas because the party lacked enough civilian personnel to replace the bureaucracy of the old regime. The result was that a civil central government was organized at the capital, but the regional administration was under the control of the military. This situation lasted until 1954, when a constitution was adopted and the government became truly centralized under the CPC.

From 1949 to 1954 the Chinese People's Political Consultative Conference (CPPCC), a multiparty body comprising CPC delegates and several hundred prominent people representing eight minor parties, professional and cultural associations, minorities, and other groups (e.g., the overseas Chinese and the army), acted as a national assembly. The Communists were in a minority, but nobody was under any illusion concerning who ran the show.

In September 1949 the CPPCC passed the Organic Law of the Central People's Government, which set up the new structure of government and the Common Program. Noncommunists were represented in the government, but the key decision-making posts were invariably given to CPC members. The central government oversaw the administration of the entire country.

In the last phase of the civil war the PLA was divided into five field armies and a central military command, which were entrusted with the regional and central administration; the whole country was divided into six administrative regions (Great Areas). Under the Military and Administrative Committees, all of which had considerable autonomy in planning, economic organization, health, and education, the administration of the provinces and the 2,000-odd *xian* (counties) remained basically intact.

The Common Program, as the name suggests, was the CPC's statement on how the various classes in the nation were expected to work together within the framework of the new united front during the "new democracy" period. The document defines in a more systematic and detailed fashion what Mao had already enunciated in his essay "On the People's Democratic Dictatorship" and other writings. The program gave the impression of being liberal in spirit and was designed to appeal to the intellectuals and the industrial and commercial classes. It did not mention class struggle at all and included such patently meaningless clauses as "the right of the people . . . to elect and be elected" (Article 4) and "The people . . . shall have the freedom of thought, speech, publication, assembly, association, correspondence, person, domicile, moving from one place to another, religious belief and the freedom of holding processions and demonstrations" (Article 5).[6]

The Party

The critical element in the new government's drive toward a socialist state was naturally the CPC. The party made the policies that the State Administrative Council (the government) and the mass organizations carried out. The rapid growth of CPC membership in the early years of the PRC reflected the growing needs of the party; it had 1.2 million members in 1945, 3 million in 1948, 4.5 million in 1949 (about 1 percent of the population), 6.6 million in 1953 (over 1 percent), and the figure doubled to 12.7 million in 1957 (over 2 percent), 17 million in 1961, 20 million in 1966, 28 million in 1973, 35 million in 1977, nearly 40 million in 1982, and 46 million in 1987 (a little over 4 percent).

The CPC constitution adopted at the Seventh National Party Congress in 1945, when Mao assumed total control, was still in force in 1949. The central leadership of the CPC was vested in three organizations: the Political Bureau (Politburo), the Secretariat, and the Central Committee. Mao Ze-dong chaired all these bodies. The Central Committee, which had about 40 members, represented the main body of the CPC and its branches in the "liberated areas" and symbolized the authority of the party. It legitimized policies by approving them, but real power lay with the Politburo, which made the policies, and the Central Secretariat, which was responsible for the administration of the party and for ensuring that the Politburo policies were properly followed. Since most of the persons who staffed the Politburo and the Secretariat in 1949 are extremely important in the later history of the PRC, it is worth listing their names:

Politburo
Mao Ze-dong (chair)
Liu Shao-qi
Zhu De
Zhou En-lai
Gao Gang
Chen Yun
Kang Sheng
(Plus four more)

Added Later:
Lin Biao (1950)
Peng Zhen (1950)
Peng De-huai (1953)
Deng Xiao-ping (1954, replaced Gao Gang)

Secretariat
Mao Ze-dong (chair)
Liu Shao-qi
Zhou En-lai

Added Later:
Chen Yun (1954)

In its Eighth National Party Congress, held in 1956, the CPC constitution introduced a Standing Committee of the Politburo. From then on this committee became the most important organ of the party and was authorized to oversee the routine work of the Central Committee. Its membership in 1956 was Mao Ze-dong, Liu Shao-qi, Zhou En-lai, Zhu De, Chen Yun, Lin Biao, and Deng Xiao-ping.

In 1949 the local party organs expanded as the PLA advanced through the country. The most important of these were the six bureaus that provided party leadership over the six military regions; 26 provincial party committees; a certain number of special district committees; and at the very bottom, 2,200 county committees.

The CPC is not a mass organization. Although anyone over 18 can apply, membership is highly selective and is based on recommendations by two party members who certify that the person's past behavior and attitudes have conformed to the revolutionary values of the party. Theoretically, local party members at the county level elect county party congresses, which elect delegates to the provincial party congresses, which in turn elect the delegates to the national party congress. The national party congress elects the Central Committee, which theoretically functions as the highest organ of the party between the national congresses, which are supposed to be convened every five years. The Central Committee of the CPC is supposed to elect the Politburo and the Standing Committee of the Politburo. The Standing Committee of the Politburo exercises the Central Committee's functions and powers.

In practice, the system worked the other way around. Until the early 1980s, the well-recognized, great leaders of the CPC who controlled the Politburo (its composition reflected the rise and fall of factions within the top echelons of the party) nominated the members of the Central Committee, which in turn supervised the selection of delegates to provincial congresses, who helped select the delegates to the county and other local congresses. The elections were pro forma: A single slate of candidates received 100 percent of the votes. The situation has changed only slightly in the post-Mao period.

The formal structures of the party and the authority vested in them have, however, remained fluid; politics in China has depended to a large degree on the amount of power the top personalities have been able to exert to bend the structures to suit their needs.

The relationship between the party and the government was never clearly defined (the first attempt to do so was made only after the death of Mao), but since the leading party officials also occupied leading central and provincial government posts, the party maintained its command over the government through these overlapping appointments. The formal framework of government remained weak, and the practical problems of administration were often unaddressed, although Prime Minister Zhou En-lai was a powerful enough figure to provide some sense of identity and security to the state bureaucracy.

REMOLDING OF THE POPULATION

Two external events involving the two superpowers, each in its own way, helped the CPC to consolidate its hold over the country. One was the signing of a Sino-Soviet Treaty of Friendship, Alliance, and Mutual Assistance on February 14, 1950. The treaty, designed to last 30 years, was personally negotiated by Mao and Stalin and ratified by both sides in April 1950. Directed against the United States and Japan, it linked the defense interests of the two countries; it also provided $60 million in Soviet credits and promised Soviet aid in economic, educational, scientific, technical, and other fields. Although some conditions of the treaty were not entirely satisfactory to China (the Russians were allowed to occupy Port Arthur and Dalian, run the main Manchurian railway under Sino-Soviet joint control until 1952, and set up certain Sino-Soviet joint enterprises in Manchuria and Xinjiang, and Beijing had to recognize the independence of Outer Mongolia), the alliance contributed to a psychological and material sense of security.

The other important event was the Korean War (1950–1953), which broke out in June 1950, two months after the ratification of the Sino-Soviet alliance. The war, started by the North Korean invasion of South Korea, brought the United States back into the East Asian scene; U.S. troops formed the bulk of the United Nations forces that were sent to help South Korea. It is doubtful that the Chinese anticipated their participation in the Korean War, but by November 1950, driven by strategic and political considerations, the Chinese forces, in the guise of Chinese People's Volunteers, were fighting in Korea and succeeded in pushing the United Nations troops out of the North.

America's fear that any expansion of the Communist bloc in East Asia would threaten American strategic interests in that area led Washington to reverse its earlier policy of neutrality in the Chinese civil war. It now declared itself staunchly on the side of the Nationalists by recognizing the Republic of China in Taiwan as the legitimate government of *all* of China. Thus the cold war saved the Nationalists and halted Beijing's drive to unify the country. (The uncompleted "liberation" of Taiwan still remains a sensitive issue that continues to haunt U.S.-China relations even after they were normalized in 1979.) The United States, stunned by developments in Korea, began to look on Beijing as a dangerous enemy; the United States not only refused to recognize China but also got its Western allies, and the United Nations, to join Washington in doing the same and imposing an embargo on the export of strategic materials to China. Beijing was forced to depend even more heavily on the Soviet Union and the Eastern bloc.

Although this unexpected war strained China's economic and military resources, it strengthened Beijing's self-confidence because the Chinese managed to fight the imperialist superpower to a halt and thus win a psychological victory. It also bolstered China's image among the peoples of the Third World, who were strongly anticolonial and anti-imperialist. Most important, the war helped the CPC in its drive to remold the pro-Western and pro-Guomindang (or anti-Communist) elements in the Chinese urban population.

Mass Campaigns

Mao Ze-dong's conviction that the masses, if actuated by "correct thinking," could change history, coupled with his theory of the "mass line," resulted in a peculiarly Chinese use of mass campaigns as an instrument of political communication and the politicization of the people. The mass line theory required the ruling elite to keep in close touch with the masses, to "study the masses" so that they could formulate policies on the basis of the "people's will." Since the "ideas of the masses" supposedly had a "revolutionary content," the policies would naturally push the revolution forward. As Mao defined it, "mass line" meant:

> From the masses—back to the masses! This means: take the ideas of the masses (scattered and unsystematic ideas) and concentrate them (through study turn them into concentrated and systematic ideas), then go to the masses and propagate and explain these ideas until the masses embrace them as their own.[7]

There was little chance that this vague process could be applied to a nation of 500 million. In practice, since the CPC leaders—Mao in particular—always seemed to know what was best for the masses, the CPC policies were taken to reflect the "ideas of the masses," and mass campaigns were used to "propagate and explain" these policies and mobilize the masses to carry them out.

Some mass campaigns were nationwide, such as the Great Leap Forward in 1958, but most were restricted to discrete segments of the population. All mass campaigns needed a real or a symbolic enemy that could provide a negative example and be used as a target for attack. The policy around which a campaign was to be built having been decided, the campaign was initiated by the leadership; the cadres spread the word through party, state, and mass organizations; the media broadcast the issues; and the masses responded by holding rallies and "demanding" that action be taken according to the leaders' ideas. Those who showed lack of enthusiasm were "struggled" against, made to undergo "criticism and self-criticism," and if that did not help, were put in the category of the "enemy."

The Peasantry—Phase One: 1949–1953

The CPC did not need Soviet aid to carry out the land revolution. Their own long experience in organizing the peasantry in the countryside and Mao's guidelines were sufficient. Since 1936 the Communists had been carrying on land reform in areas under their control, although the operation lacked the radical intensity it was to gain after 1949.

Only in 1947 did the CPC adopt the Basic Agrarian Law, which categorically announced that "China's agrarian system is unjust in the extreme. . . . The agrarian system of feudal and semifeudal exploitation is abolished. The agrarian system of 'land to the tillers' is to be realized."[8] The program to uproot landlordism was, however, moderated and was slowed down to help the party gain popular support in establishing the new united front to back Mao's People's Democratic Dictatorship.

The Agrarian Reform Law of 1950, which replaced the 1947 land law, aimed at three things: first, to give all individual, poor peasants a certain amount of land (confiscated from the big landlords, clan lands, and Buddhist/Taoist/Christian temple and church lands) and free them from tenancy and exorbitant rents; second, to avoid chaos and protect production by allowing rich and moderately well-off peasants to keep their surplus land; and third, to politicize the peasantry in the process of land redistribution.

This revolutionary land reform program was completed by the beginning of 1953, except in areas belonging to the minority peoples. A little less than half of all the arable land changed hands, and 300 million peasants became independent holders of small pieces of farmland.

The land settlement, the return of peace to the country, the improvement and repair of waterworks, and the restoration of transportation networks helped the recovery of agricultural production, which now reached or exceeded the highest prewar figures.

On the political and ideological level, the land reform movement was a mass campaign intended to politicize the peasantry by inciting them to organize under the leadership of the party and "struggle" against the landlords, the "class enemy."

In the process of liquidating the class enemy it was hoped that the peasantry would become familiar with the rudiments of socialist ideology, understand the power and authority of the new rulers, destroy traditional social structures, and replace them with more socialistic patterns of relationships.

Guided by outside party activists and agitators, peasant associations, headed by the poorest peasants, were formed in the villages. The rural population was divided into five classes: landlords, rich peasants, middle peasants, tenants, and landless labor. The peasant associations held public accusation meetings in which the local tenant farmers and landless laborers were encouraged to attack the local landlords, who were brought before the audience one by one and made to kneel before their accusers. These public trials, where the peasants poured out their "bitterness," created an atmosphere of mass hysteria and often ended with the peasant mob demanding immediate death of the landlord to "settle old scores." Many landlords were beaten to death or executed on the spot; many others committed suicide to avoid the torture of the trial. The landlord's title deeds were burned and the land redistributed. A reign of terror swept through the country. It is estimated that no fewer than 5 million people died before calm returned. The children of the landlords and rich peasants became political outcasts and until the end of the Maoist era, suffered from the stigma of being "black elements"; the derogatory class designation of "landlord" and "rich peasant" was finally removed in 1979.

The Land Law of 1950 had prohibited the use of force, but the party followed Mao's basic approach to the problem of peasant mobilization, summed up neatly in his dictum of 1927: "To put it bluntly, it is necessary to create terror for a while in every rural area."[9]

The Urban Classes: 1949–1955

Control and Remolding Techniques. Apart from the more formal structures of control (the party, the PLA, and the government), the CPC introduced mass organizations at the local and national levels as subsidiary instruments of control. Every citizen was forced to become a member of one or more of these organizations. The local organization was that of a "small group"; for example, the street committee, the neighborhood committee, the teachers' committee in a school, and the workers' committee in a factory. At the national level there were organizations such as Young Pioneers (children's corps); All-China Students' Federation; and All-China Federations of Trade Unions, of Democratic Women, of Democratic Youth, of Cooperative Workers, and of Literature and Art.

These organizations covered all aspects of an individual's activities: personal, social, and professional. Guided by party members, these organizations looked after local and national peace and security (arbitrating family disputes and hunting out troublemakers, petty criminals, and "counterrevolutionaries"), supervised indoctrination meetings and mass campaigns, recruited activists, and recommended applicants for party membership.

The remolding of the intelligentsia and the urban professional classes was carried out by the reeducation methods first used in the rectification campaign of 1942. These methods, employing techniques of struggle meetings (in which the subjects were criticized and made to recognize their ideological shortcomings) and self-criticism sessions, aimed at "thought reform," often referred to as "brainwashing," which is a translation of a popularly used Chinese term.

The process that the subjects underwent has been likened to a religious conversion. They were first "struggled against"; made to feel guilty; forced to undergo a period of privation, insecurity, and inner tension; and denied the company of friends or family. They were then given time to struggle with themselves, to ruminate over their guilt until they confessed their "crimes." When the deviants were considered to have fully remolded their thinking, they returned to the fold chastened and ready to wholeheartedly support the regime and the new order. Sometimes it was necessary to send the subjects to a village or a factory for several weeks to several months to labor alongside peasants and workers and undergo "reform through labor." It is debatable whether, despite the torture and the torment, there were many whose brains were actually washed clean of their past thought.

As noted earlier, in 1949 the urban professional classes were lulled into a sense of security, and indeed during the first year of the new regime the industrial and commercial groups, the "national bourgeoisie," were treated with care, their authority and properties protected, and they were given help and encouragement to expand their production. As a result, by 1952 rail and road transport networks had been restored, industrial and handicraft production had more than doubled in value, and Chinese exports had begun to expand. Coupled with other state actions, such as price controls and the creation of parity units (based on the price of essential goods) for the payment of wages, national economic recovery was more or less successfully completed by 1952, and the CPC was ready to lead the country's "transition to socialism."

Mass campaigns to reform and cleanse the bureaucracy, the bourgeoisie, and the intelligentsia were now in order. The Korean War had helped to create a climate of state terror, which made the task of the CPC much easier. Even as the administration of the six military regions was being consolidated, those who were considered to oppose the regime had been dubbed counterrevolutionaries, quickly tried by military courts, and executed. This operation was given formal approval and turned into a nationwide campaign, when the Regulations for the Suppression of Counterrevolutionaries were issued in February 1952. The term *counterrevolutionary* covered not only political acts of espionage, revolt, and sabotage but also criminal acts, such as the looting of important public or private properties; disturbing markets or dislocating currencies; and attacking, killing, or injuring public officials or the people.[10] The punishments were harsh: death penalty or life imprisonment. The criminals were tried by mass courts, and over a million were executed. Zhou En-lai was pleased to report to the CPPCC in October 1951 that the government

> . . . stimulated and placed their reliance on the revolutionary initiative of the masses of the people and achieved great nationwide success in the suppression of counterrevolutionaries . . . [who] have been dealt very serious blows with the arrest, execution and imprisonment of large numbers . . . who fall into five categories of bandits, despots, secret agents, members of reactionary parties and organizations and reactionary secret societies.[11]

In fall 1951 the party had begun an in-house "three anti" campaign directed against corruption, waste, and bureaucratism. The campaign had a double goal: It was intended to cleanse the party cadres (whose numbers had increased so rapidly that many careerists had entered the organization) of malpractices, and it put the bourgeoisie on notice that they were the next target because they had corrupted the cadres and encouraged waste and evil bureaucratic practices. Thousands of cadres were purged in the "three anti" campaign.

The "five anti" campaign, launched in January 1952, was a movement against the bourgeoisie to cure it of the evils of bribery, tax evasion, theft of state assets, nonfulfillment of contracts, and theft of state economic secrets. Since the party had no intention of liquidating this vitally important class, as it had the landlords, this was both a mass campaign (in the style of the land reform, with clerks, accountants, and other subordinate staff denouncing the head of their commercial or industrial unit) and a thought reform program that encouraged the erring bourgeoisie to seek rehabilitation by confessing their past sins and condemning their past ideology and attitudes.

All private enterprises were classified according to the gravity of their crimes and dealt with accordingly; the serious law breakers were punished publicly to teach the others a lesson. Since Shanghai was the biggest industrial and commercial center, it naturally held special interest for the party, which found 140,000 of its 164,000 firms guilty of one crime or another. Similar determination was made about the bourgeoisie in other major cities. It is estimated that only about 500 businesspeople were executed, although the numbers of those imprisoned ran to several thousand. When the campaign was wound down in mid-1952, the government itself declared that the cases must be dealt with magnanimously to help the rapid restoration and development of industry and commerce.

The campaign was comparatively short-lived, but it helped to destroy any illusions the capitalists may have had regarding their independence; it softened them for the next phase, which followed in 1954, when the business enterprises were made "public-private," and for the last phase in 1955–1956, when all private enterprises were socialized. The campaign also was successful in enrolling the workers into labor unions and, like their peasant counterparts, making them more politically conscious.

The class that needed thought reform most was the *zhi-shi-fen-zi* ("knowledgeable elements"), comprising virtually everyone who had had any schooling. The term is loosely translated into English as "intellectuals" by the Chinese themselves, although they sometimes refer to "higher intellectuals" as an important subgroup. For our purposes the term *intellectuals* will include only those who belong to the category of teachers, writers, artists, journalists, lawyers, and so on—those who can be considered capable of independent thinking and have the facility to express their thoughts and thereby influence public opinion.

This class has posed a special problem for the CPC, and even today the Communists have not learned how to handle it. The CPC dilemma arises out of the fact that on the one hand the country, if it is to modernize, cannot do without the intellectuals; on the other, it appears almost impossible to remold them to the party's satisfaction.

We observed earlier that most of the intellectuals had been disgusted with the Guomindang Fascist regime and shifted their support to the CPC; many of them were "liberal-leftists," and some had even joined the CPC. The League of Left-Wing Writers, for example, was heavily Communist-influenced. The intellectuals were eager to see China reunified under a strong government, but they also hoped that such a government would ensure their intellectual freedom. Even those who had been in Yanan in 1942 and undergone the rectification campaign were not convinced that the party should prescribe the contents of their artistic and literary expression.

The campaign for remolding the intellectuals was launched in late 1951 by Zhou Enlai. The intellectuals were seen as tainted by their class background (bourgeois or petty bourgeois) and their intoxication with Western ideas and ideologies. Mao was particularly critical of their subjective individualism, their self-conceit, and their knowledge, which according to Mao came from books and was therefore idealistic and impractical. Thousands of intellectuals, forced to undergo thought reform, were duly "struggled against," and they duly made "confessions," which were widely published. Some intellectuals working for the media were demoted or dismissed. Libraries and bookshops were purged of their holdings of imperialist and counterrevolutionary literature.

If it was the intention of the CPC to remold the nation to make it a docile tool in the hands of the party, then it had largely succeeded in its goal by 1953; but if the aim was to prepare the people to become active participants in the political process and to produce from among them the new leadership of the country, it had eminently failed. The peasants, the workers, the intelligentsia, and the national bourgeoisie had all participated in campaigns that made them conscious not of their "rights" but of the capacity of the state to unleash terror. This realization had little immediate relevance to most of the population because all they wanted was a stable government and personal security. It did matter to the intellectuals because they believed that they had a role to play in the modernization of China.

THE TRANSITION TO SOCIALISM: 1953–1957

By the end of 1952, the national economy having made a recovery, the land reform program having basically ended, and the urban classes having been reoriented to the new politics, China was ready to embark on the First Five-Year Plan (First FYP), which was begun in January 1953 (the details were not revealed until 1955). In that year, on October 1, 1953, the fourth anniversary of the founding of the PRC, the party also proclaimed the "general line for the transition to socialism."

The First FYP and the transition to socialism were to go hand in hand. To achieve these goals the country needed to have a far more centralized government authority (which meant it had to end the regional administrative bureaus); collect statistics on natural resources and population; socialize industry, commerce, and agriculture; and win over the intellectuals. These multifarious tasks had to be performed almost simultaneously and required tremendous skill in manipulating the social forces.

The State Planning Committee was created in fall 1952 with Gao Gang, the boss of the northeast region, as the chair, but his demand for a disproportionately high investment in the industrial development of Manchuria led to a leadership crisis. Gao Gang was purged in 1954 for attempting to establish an "independent kingdom" in Manchuria and for conspiring to seize state power. It is possible that one reason for Gao's troubles was his close association with the Russians. But since Rao Shu-shi, who controlled the east China region, was also purged on a similar charge and had no Soviet connection, it is more likely that the two party leaders had to be removed because they were trying to use their influence to strengthen their regional industrial areas at the expense of the rest of the country, thus adding to their personal authority; Mukden in Manchuria and Shanghai in the east were two of the most advanced industrial centers in China. Incidentally, Rao was also a member of the State Planning Committee.

The 1954 Constitution

The Gao-Rao affair may or may not have hurried the decision, but the formal centralization of state authority took place with the adoption of the 1954 constitution, which replaced the temporary state structure established in 1949. The constitution announced in its preamble that the national environment was ready for "planned economic construction and gradual transition to socialism."

The ultimate authority of the state was vested in the National People's Congress (NPC), which headed the pyramidal system of people's congresses: The electorate at the local city or county level "elected" the base-level congress, which "elected" delegates to the provincial congress, which sent delegates to the NPC. During Mao's lifetime the people (men and women over 18 who had not lost their civil rights) voted for a handpicked, single list of candidates.

The 1954 NPC appointed Mao Ze-dong as chairman of the PRC and placed the State Council under the premiership of Zhou Enlai. The NPC was elected for four years and was supposed to meet once a year for about two weeks to endorse policies and legislation. While it was in recess its functions were performed by the Standing Committee of the NPC.

The relationship among the NPC, the government (State Council), and the CPC can be described briefly as follows: The State Council had direct control over the central ministries of the government and the government bureaus at the provincial and county level; just as the NPC was supposed to oversee the functioning of the government at the national level, the provincial and county people's congresses were supposed to oversee the functioning of the government at the provincial and county levels, respectively; the party Central Committee had lines of direct control over the State Council but indirect control over the provincial and county bureaus, exercised through its provincial and county party committees.

The First Five-Year Plan

The First FYP, based on Russian experience and advice, was strongly weighted in favor of the development of heavy industry. The investment distribution reflected this bias: Industry received 58.2 percent; transportation and communications, 19.2 percent; and agriculture, 7.6 percent. The plan could not have been fulfilled without Russian aid, which although limited financially (3 percent of the total plan outlay), was crucial in providing model factories, technical know-how, and technicians. The Soviets supplied 156 industrial units (the core of the industrial construction program), 12,000 engineers and technicians from the Eastern bloc, blueprints and technology for construction projects, and training for 6,000 Chinese students and 7,000 workers. The result was a dramatic growth in industrial output (e.g., steel output rose from 1.4 million tons in 1952 to 5.24 million tons in 1957), but agriculture lagged far behind, with an annual growth rate of about 3 percent, just about keeping pace with the annual population growth of about 2.2 percent.

While this industrial base was being laid, the private sector, as noted earlier, disappeared without much fuss, and all industrial and commercial enterprises still in private hands were nationalized. The capitalists and industrialists were bought out, but the monetary compensation paid to them was deposited in banks, from which they could not withdraw any large sums without permission. Most of these dispossessed capitalists were, however, retained as managers and directors of the companies they once owned.

The Peasantry — Phase Two: 1954–1956

The transition to socialism in agriculture was a more complicated affair. It was apparent from the beginning of the land reform program that many poor peasants who had never owned land before did not have the draft animals and the tools to make a success of their farms. It was also obvious that a whole country divided into such small parcels of land could be conducive neither to agricultural growth nor to agricultural modernization. The party's urging that peasants establish "mutual aid teams" and cooperate with one another at the time of plowing and harvesting was willingly accepted by many. By the end of 1953, 43 percent of the peasants were in mutual aid teams of 4 or 5 families. Some of these basic units had gone a step further and established small "semisocialist" Agricultural Producers' Cooperatives (APCs) of 20 to 30 families, who had pooled their lands and were working on them collectively. The crops were divided among the members of the cooperative on the basis of what they had contributed to the pool in the way of property (land, animals, tools) and in the way of labor and other services.

The campaign to establish lower-level (semisocialist) APCs nationwide was officially launched in December 1953, even before the mutual aid teams had been established throughout the entire country. But the party emphasized that the movement must be voluntary and the pace restrained. This go-slow policy was reflected in the First FYP target, which aimed to place one-third of the peasant households in APCs by 1957. By mid-1955 only 15 percent of the rural population had joined these elementary cooperatives.

Agricultural output was, however, not keeping pace with the demands of industrial production. The question was: Would the speeding up of agricultural cooperativization help solve this problem or aggravate it? Mao was one of the few in favor of rapid collectivization, which according to him would not only increase agricultural production to meet the needs of industrialization but also help in bringing socialism to the countryside. In October 1954 Mao had called for a sixfold increase in the APCs; although the Central Committee had agreed, the results of the drive were mixed. Indeed, in certain areas the APCs were dissolved soon after being formed because of local negative reaction. The party vacillated and reemphasized gradualness.

This situation was intolerable to Mao because land redistribution and the resulting private ownership of land had re-created some evils that had marred life in the countryside before 1949. As Mao put it in his speech to provincial party secretaries and propaganda officials in July 1955,

> What exists in the countryside today is capitalist ownership by the rich peasants and a vast sea of private ownership by the individual peasants. As is clear to everyone, the spontaneous forces of capitalism have been growing steadily in the countryside in recent years, with new rich peasants springing up everywhere and many well-to-do middle peasants striving to become rich peasants. On the other hand, many poor peasants are still living in poverty for lack of sufficient means of production, with some in debt and others selling or renting out their land. . . . There is no solution to this problem except on a new basis . . . the socialist transformation of the whole of agriculture. . . .[12]

According to Mao, what was needed to save the situation was not a go-slow policy but the reverse:

> But some of our comrades are tottering along like a woman with bound feet and constantly complaining, "You are going too fast." Excessive criticism, inappropriate complaints, endless anxiety, and the erection of countless taboos—they believe this is the proper way to guide the socialist mass movement in the rural areas.
>
> No, this is not the right way; it is the wrong way.[13]

The comrades Mao was referring to were the majority of the leaders in the government and the party. Indeed, just a few weeks before Mao's speech, the chair of the State Planning Committee, Li Fu-chun, while reporting on the progress of the First FYP had declared that it would take three 5-year plans, that is, 15 years, "to fulfill this fundamental task of the transition" to socialism. There was, obviously, political opposition to Mao's views. So, Mao, instead of following the proper channel and presenting his ideas to the Central Committee of the party, settled the issue by speaking directly to the provincial cadres, who were the ones actually to perform the task of mobilizing the peasantry. In bypassing the party high command, Mao had put himself above the party; the party was forced to give its formal approval to Mao's policy in October. And once again, as in his 1927 Hunan Report, Mao found the peasants more radical and revolutionary than the party ("the present position is precisely one in which the mass movement is running ahead of the leadership."[14]).

By directing the cadres to start a mass campaign from the bottom (which would exclude the rich peasants from the peasant associations and depend on the support of the poor peasants), Mao had also eschewed the planners and bureaucrats who would have liked to organize a centrally controlled, step-by-step development. Guided by enthusiastic cadres, the movement gathered an extraordinary momentum, and by the end of 1956 all of China's 120 million rural families were distributed in APCs. Mao had been fully vindicated. But his utopian dream did not stop with the establishment of semisocialist APCs. He now looked forward to their conversion to fully socialist or advanced-level cooperatives, comprising 100 to 250 families, which would no longer take into account the peasant's material contribution to the collective. This act would abolish private ownership of land and make all peasants equal. A peasant was to be allowed to retain a small private plot of land (total area of these not to exceed 5 percent of the arable land) for private use and house, but the peasant's income was to be calculated on the socialist principle "to each according to his labor."

Some fully socialist cooperatives had already emerged in 1955. In January 1956 the party announced that the task of shifting to fully socialist cooperatives would be completed by 1958. In fact, over 90 percent of the peasants were in higher cooperatives by early 1957, and the transition to socialism could be declared to have been completed.

The Intellectuals

The transition to agricultural collectivization and the nationalization of industry had been relatively smooth. The problem of winning over the intellectuals proved more bothersome. The early post-1949 campaigns of thought reform had fallen short of their goal to gain the wholehearted acceptance of party policies by the intellectuals.

Matters came to a head when one of the nationally recognized intellectuals, Hu Feng, decided to take a stand against the party and demand that the intelligentsia be given a certain amount of intellectual freedom. Hu Feng, a friend of Lu Xun and a longtime follower of the CPC, was on the editorial staff of the magazine *People's Literature* and a member of the NPC. In 1954 Hu Feng blamed the authorities for the failure of the development of literature and art. He said that the party policies of indoctrination; thought reform; prescriptive writing; and limiting the writers' subject matter, demanding that they seek inspiration from the lives of workers, peasants, and soldiers, were like "five daggers in the backs of the writers" because they were repressive and destructive to the creative soul of the artist.

Hu Feng had given the party an ideal opportunity to attack bourgeois thinking, which the party could now declare existed even among the leftist intellectuals. Quickly the leadership switched to an all-out assault on Hu Feng and made him the target of a nationwide campaign. There was no longer any attempt to get Hu Feng to reform his thinking because it was announced that he was a counterrevolutionary. In mid-1955 Hu was arrested and imprisoned.

The celebrated Hu Feng case and the anti-Hu Feng campaign that was mounted in schools, colleges, universities, and the cultural field cowed the intelligentsia into submission or at least effectively silenced it. The intellectuals could now be given the label *counterrevolutionaries* and punished accordingly; about 80,000 of them were put into that category, and another 300,000 were found politically unreliable and deprived of their civil rights.

By the end of 1955 the party realized that it had gone too far in alienating the members of this important class and was depriving the nation of their contributions. In January 1956 Zhou En-lai, in his "Report on the Question of Intellectuals," admonished the party for its heavy-handed policies:

> It is . . . the opinion of the Party Central Committee that even though the intellectuals were influenced in various ways in the past by the imperialists and the reactionary classes, the overwhelming majority of them also suffered the oppression of the imperialists and the Nationalist Party. Some of them, accordingly, joined the revolution and some others showed sympathy to the revolution. Most of them maintained a neutral and observing attitude toward the revolution. *Only a very small number of them were counterrevolutionaries* [emphasis added]. Facts clearly pointed out to the intellectuals that except for standing together with the working class and the Chinese Communist Party, there was no other way out for them. It is therefore necessary, as it is also possible, to unite [with] the intellectuals. . . .
>
> We must confess that there are many shortcomings in our work . . . [we have failed to place] confidence in intellectuals who deserve it, such as forbidding them to visit factories which they should see and barring them from information which they should possess. . . .
>
> Many intellectuals have the feeling that they spend too much time on non-functional con-

ferences and administrative routines [political study and political conferences].[15]

In 1956 the party relaxed its controls over the intellectuals; indoctrination meetings were reduced, salaries were increased, and greater freedom of expression was allowed. It appears that the party leaders were confident that most older intellectuals had been won over. The future lay with the younger generation, who would, it was hoped, receive the right type of education. During the First FYP the number of primary school students rose from 26 to 64 million and university students from 117,000 to 441,000. But the rub was that the academics still belonged to the pre-1949 class of urban intellectual elites.

YEAR OF REAPPRAISAL: 1956–1957

As the First FYP drew to a close, it became evident that certain tendencies had emerged in China that were not in keeping with Mao Ze-dong's ideas of how the Chinese revolution was to be continued into the future. The basic contradiction was between the Soviet model of a socialist state and Mao's concept of China's path to modernization.

The Soviet model presumed that further socialist transformation of society to true communism would follow the economic modernization of the state, and that artificially created social upheavals to promote social change were counterproductive. If there were to be changes, they would be initiated from above by the party leadership. The Soviets believed in the unchallenged power of the party, stable state structures, centralized planning, bureaucratic controls, elitist technocrats as key elements in running industries and other enterprises, authority vested in the managerial class, hierarchy of ranks, monetary incentives, and accepted differentials in salaries and other benefits. The Soviet model was city-oriented and correlated modernization with urbanization and industrialization.

The CPC, in the absence of any other relevant model, had accepted the Soviet system with certain initial additions, such as the use of mass campaigns as a technique of control. The result was that the party began to lose its pre-1949 revolutionary ardor, and its ideological authority came to be replaced by state policies. The party was fast becoming a bureaucratic organization, and the once-revolutionary party cadres were now civil servants, who evaluated their success not in terms of their capacity to lead and educate the masses but by how fast they could move up the bureaucratic ladder. By 1955 the PLA, too, had been Sovietized and the old ideas of a people's army and guerrilla warfare were being replaced by a greater emphasis on professionalism and hierarchical military structures, with a corresponding deemphasis on political training.

The Soviet model was attractive to all those leaders who saw the need for the modernization of the country through an orderly and methodical process of economic development. These leaders were not against further socialization of society, but they considered increased industrial and agricultural production as a key to future changes in social relations.

On the other hand, Mao, who was by no means against economic modernization, felt that the "economics first" approach spelled the end of the revolution. In contrast, his "politics in command" approach espoused modernization through mass mobilization, which would heighten political consciousness and ensure the continuation of the revolution. As early as 1937 Mao had enunciated his version of the theory of dialectical materialism in an essay entitled "On Contradiction," in which he had said,

> . . . while we recognize that in the general development of history the material determines the mental and social being determines social consciousness, we also—indeed must—recognize the reaction of mental on material things, of social consciousness on social being and of the superstructure on the economic base.[16]

Mao, the populist, the believer in voluntarism, therefore advocated the utilization of the mass line to bring to flower the "boundless creative power" of the masses and raise their social consciousness. Instead of greater centralization of authority, he wanted decentralization of leadership in the area of production, the expansion of the worker and peasant participation in management and decision making, and the replacement of monetary incentives with ideological ones. He also emphasized self-reliance. In keeping with these ideas, Mao in the winter of 1955–1956 proposed a 12-year program for agriculture, which bypassed the party's 5-year-plan approach and called for some rapid socioeconomic changes that would bring "greater, faster, better and more economical results." The party leaders could not reject Mao's proposal, but they managed to shelve it for the next 18 months.

The year 1956 was of historic importance because during it Mao gave the first indication that he was not satisfied with the political line that was evolving at the party center. It was also a year of some confusion because an internal lack of consensus on future national goals and policies was made more complicated by external events.

After the death of Stalin in 1953, the struggle for power in Moscow led the Soviet leaders to adopt a softer line toward China. The unequal aspects of the earlier Sino-Soviet treaties were done away with, and there was even some increase in Soviet aid. In the new, more relaxed political environment of the Eastern bloc, China adopted a flexible approach to the Third World. Sponsored by India to attend the Bandung Conference of Afro-Asian States in 1955, China, represented by Zhou En-lai, emerged from the conference with its reputation vastly enhanced. Indeed, immediately after the conference many developing countries began to view China as a leader and a model to be emulated. China could now look forward to playing a more important part in the East-West confrontation, within and without the Eastern bloc.

But China's troubles with the Soviet Union started soon thereafter with Khrushchev's de-Stalinization speech at the Soviet Twentieth Party Congress in February 1956. Khrushchev's criticism of Stalin for having put himself above the party and developing a "cult of personality" not only made it difficult for the Chinese leaders to explain their earlier glorification of Stalin but also reflected adversely on Mao's leadership style. Moreover, Khrushchev's views on peaceful coexistence with the capitalist nations and détente with the United States implied that China would have to follow suit in the manner of Moscow's East European client states, amending its policies that were built around the idea of the socialist and the imperialist blocs confronting one another in a life-and-death struggle; or China must reject Moscow's stand and break away from the bloc. Mao's sense of independence could never have allowed him to accept the former path.

Mao's reaction to the internal and external situation led him to express his views in three documents, all reiterating his basic, independent position on the nature of the Chinese revolution.

China did not publish Khrushchev's speech, but there was considerable intraparty debate on the issue. Finally, in April the *People's Daily* printed a critique of Khrushchev's speech, the first pronouncement, in an editorial entitled "On the Historical Experience of the Dictatorship of the Proletariat." There is every reason to believe that the editorial was written by Mao himself or at least that he had a major hand in writing it. The document praised Stalin as a "great Marxist-Leninist revolutionary" who had made important contributions to the development of socialism and whose merits were greater than his faults. The article accepted the criticism that Stalin made "some serious mistakes" in his later life, but it put them down to his having divorced himself from the masses. Regardless of how wrong it was of Stalin to misuse "class warfare" to purge his opponents, the article pointed out that "society at all times develops through continual contradictions" and "to deny contradictions is to deny dialectics." The "cult of the individual" was also attacked, but it was emphasized that such a development could take place only when the "mass line" was ignored. The implication was that Mao could never make such a mistake. However, the article added, "it is utterly wrong to deny the role of the individual, the role of forerunners and leaders."[17]

In that same month Mao took up the theme of "contradictions" in a major secret speech, "On the Ten Great Relationships,"[18] which was officially made public only 20 years later. The immediate reason for its secrecy was that Mao had defined a self-reliant Chinese path to modernization, which was critical of the Soviet model.

In this second pronouncement, Mao divided China's problems of modernization and change into ten major contradictions between industry and agriculture, heavy and light industry, coastal and inland industries, economic and defense constructions, state and productive units and individual producers, the center and the regions, Han and other nationalities, party and others, revolution and counterrevolution, and China and other countries. To handle these contradictions properly, Mao proposed a radical change of policy, which would have meant a virtual rejection of the Russian development strategy.

Khrushchev's attack on Stalin had made it possible for the Soviet Communist party to break with its Stalinist past and provide a new legitimacy to the Khrushchev-led party. By the same token the de-Stalinization speech made it possible for Mao to reconsider the "blind faith" with which the CPC had followed the Soviet lead. Mao's speech was thus critical not only of the Soviet model but also of the Soviet socialist system. Directly, it was critical of the CPC leaders who had "blindly" accepted the Soviet path and thereby rejected the Chinese (i.e., the Maoist) approach to socialism and change.

Mao's third pronouncement can be best understood in this context. In a speech delivered to the Supreme State Conference on May 2, 1956, he announced a new policy of "let a hundred flowers blossom, let a hundred schools of thought contend."[19]

The policy promised political and social liberalization. At one level it appeared to be similar to the current post-Stalin liberalization moves in the Soviet Union and Eastern Europe to enlist the intelligentsia in the economic development programs. In fact, the Chinese had contemplated winning over the intellectuals even before Khrushchev's speech, as indicated in Zhou En-lai's January speech. But Mao Ze-dong's motive for encouraging "independent thinking and free discussion" among the intelligentsia was to revive the revolutionary spirit of the party rather than merely to channel their energies into achieving the economic goals of the Second FYP.

Mao accepted Zhou's belief that the majority of the intellectuals had been won over and declared that since the natural sciences had no "class character," the time had come to give freedom to the scientists, who belonged to various schools of thought, to extend and enrich the scientific field. Similarly, the artists and writers should be free to express themselves in differing ways to create a variety of literature and arts, like flowers of different hues. However, since art, literature, philosophy, and history had a "class character," the intellectuals' freedom in these fields was to be contained within the realm of what was acceptable to the "people," and their works must "serve the people."

But what was even more important than this "liberalization" was that the new policy encouraged the intellectuals to criticize the party for the mistakes it had made in dealing with the problems of the intellectuals. Here Mao differed from both Zhou and the European Communists. Mao felt that acceptance of criticism from the outside would mobilize support for the government, help rectify the party's growing elitism and bureaucratism, and thus revive its earlier revolutionary work style. This action of Mao was unprecedented. The intelligentsia, condemned until yesterday for its tainted class background, was being invited to criticize and attack the party!

However, Mao Ze-dong's endeavors failed to move the party to change promptly its current attitude or the twice-bitten intellectuals to respond to his call with eagerness. Although the Hundred Flowers policy was reluctantly endorsed at the Eighth Party Congress in September 1956, many of the top leaders were not enthusiastic at the idea of opening the party to public criticism. These CPC leaders became even more suspicious of the Hundred Flowers campaign when the liberalization that had followed the de-Stalinization speech of Khrushchev in East Europe resulted in a revolt of the intellectuals in Hungary in November. Whatever little blossoming had taken place in the fall of 1956 withered away by the early months of 1957.

In the field of economic development there was a similar dragging of feet by the party center to Mao's ideas. Mao had heated up collectivization without waiting for industrial development to reach a stage at which it could help socialist agriculture to mechanize. Rapid collectivization had brought a large number of problems in its wake. Agricultural production had not increased significantly, and there were not enough trained cadres to run the new collective organizations and maintain complicated accounts of work points earned daily by individual peasants performing widely differing tasks. The peasants, who had been induced to join the cooperatives under false promises of quick gains, had become disillusioned, and there was widespread slaughter of draft animals and hoarding of grain. Half a million peasants migrated to the cities, hoping to escape the hardship in the countryside, but they only added to the strain on urban housing and food supplies. The party cadres, who were responsible for urging the masses to "leap forward" in the winter and spring of 1955–1956, were now attacked for "commandism," "dogmatism," and "blind optimism." This attack naturally resulted in demoralizing the cadres and making them apathetic and cynical.

The standard of living was also a problem in the cities, where an excessive rate of capital construction and indiscriminate growth in the money supply had produced inflationary trends.

The Eighth Party Congress not only ignored Mao's unorthodox economic plan advocated in his Ten Great Relationships but also failed to mention in its new constitution that the party was guided by the Thought of Mao Ze-dong, a clause that had been introduced in the 1945 party constitution. Mao may have agreed to this change as a concession to the anti-Stalinist developments in the Soviet Union, but it could not have pleased him. Mao's hold over the organization was further weakened by the reestablishment of the post of party secretary (abolished in 1937); the post was assigned to Deng Xiaoping. Mao agreed to this change but regretted it later. Liu Shao-qi and Deng Xiao-ping, who gave the principal reports at the congress, stressed that "the question of who will win in the struggle between socialism and capitalism in our country has now been decided,"[20] implying that since socialism had won, it was no longer necessary to carry on a disruptive, Maoist-style class struggle and that national affairs should be controlled from the top through the party.

The targets of the Second FYP (1958–1962) were also announced at the congress. Although some modifications were made to suit the Chinese requirements (the "one-man management system" in industrial units was done away with and replaced with a factory general manager under party leadership, greater investment allocation was made to light industry, and increased autonomy was given to provinces and industrial enterprises), the plan still followed the Soviet model in emphasizing heavy industry, urban industrialization, and urbanization and in putting the leadership in the hands of planners and technocrats.

Despite all his efforts, it appeared that by the end of 1956 Mao was not making much headway in getting the party to accept his ideas and policies. Mao had all along linked social "contradictions" with "class struggle," but now that the transition to socialism had been made and the exploiting classes eliminated, Mao's views on class conflict and class struggle no longer seemed valid. However, the party was mistaken if it thought that Mao had been silenced.

On the Correct Handling of Contradictions Among the People

By the end of 1956 Mao had worked out a new thesis on classes and class conflict in a socialist society. On February 27, 1957, he chose a nonparty forum, the enlarged Supreme State Conference to which many third-party leaders had been invited, to deliver a speech, "On the Correct Handling of Contradictions Among the People," which became the most important part of the Maoist doctrine, influencing one way or another all Chinese politics from 1957 until the death of Mao in 1976. The text of the speech remained secret until June 19, 1957, when it was published with several revisions. It is rumored that many of the CPC members left the hall when Mao made the speech.

By not debating the issues within the Politburo, a majority of whose members may not have supported him, Mao presented the party with a fait accompli.

The contradictions speech[21] stressed that contradictions will continue under socialism, although there was a distinction between the contradictions in the presocialist and postsocialist eras. Those before the transition to socialism were primarily "antagonistic contradictions" (between the people and "our enemies," which could only be resolved through violence and the physical elimination of the enemy); those in the socialist period were primarily "nonantagonistic contradictions" ("among the people" and resolvable through debate and education).

Nonantagonistic contradictions existed everywhere and would continue to do so throughout the socialist period and into the period of communism. They could only be resolved by what Mao was later to call "permanent revolution" because they were a permanent fact of life: "The ceaseless emergence and the ceaseless resolution of contradictions is the dialectical law of the development of things."

In the current situation Mao indicated that there were contradictions between "the government and the masses . . . between those in positions of leadership and the led." He advised the party and the leaders not to be afraid of criticism because "[f]or a party as much as for an individual there is a great need to hear opinions different from its own." These contradictions could be resolved by allowing the Hundred Flowers to bloom, by asking the "democratic (i.e., non-Communist) parties" and intellectuals to "exercise supervision over the Communist Party" under a policy of "mutual supervision."

In working out this thesis, Mao obviously had placed himself above the party. He had not followed the principle of democratic centralism whereby his ideas would have been democratically debated within the party before being accepted as central policies. As Maurice Meisner surmises, Mao's argument freed him "from the Leninist discipline of the Party and enable[d] him to criticize the party from without in his unique role as the representative of the people."[22]

Furthermore, although agreeing that class exploitation had ended, Mao argued that "It will take a considerable time to decide the issue in the ideological struggle between socialism and capitalism in our country," and therefore there was a compelling necessity to wage a continual "ideological struggle." The implications of this new form of class struggle were rather grave. First, anybody holding incorrect ideas could be condemned as an "enemy of the people," posing an "antagonistic contradiction" and therefore worthy of being treated as an element demanding violent elimination. Second, since the party members (party leaders, for that matter) could also be prone to incorrect ideas, the "enemy" may be found to reside within the party itself—which is exactly what happened during the Great Proletarian Cultural Revolution of 1966–1969.

The Hundred Flowers Campaign and Mao's Return to Power

Mao's speech was circulated among party and nonparty leaders, and the intelligentsia was encouraged to join the rectification campaign, which aimed at correcting the three evils of bureaucratism, sectarianism, and subjectivism that marred the party's work style. The intellectuals were still hesitant to "bloom and contend" because they feared that the campaign was a trap. Within a month or two, however, the party managed to overcome their fears, and by mid-May the movement began to unfold in earnest.

Mao could not have imagined the depth of resentment and frustration among the intellectuals that now came pouring out in the form of speeches; letters to the press; and thousands of *da-zi-bao* (posters written in large Chinese characters) posted on the walls of schools, colleges, universities, hospitals, and other public buildings, denouncing the party for usurping state power, for turning itself into a privileged class (ruling by "standing on the back of the masses"), for being undemocratic and violating civil rights written into the constitution, for using the united front as a meaningless facade because third parties were given no political role, for running a one-party government and not allowing free elections, and for committing all kinds of other excesses.

Beijing University students formed the vanguard of the movement. They established a union, held public debates and discussion meetings, and asked many pertinent questions: Why were older faculty members denied the right to teach? Why were academics forced to follow the instructions of ignorant (but arrogant) party cadres? Why were Soviet studies being pushed at the expense of Western science and literature? Why was political reliability more important than ability and talent? Why was Khrushchev's speech not published in China? Why were the people denied knowledge of what was going on in the world? Why was Hu Feng not tried?

The *People's Daily* published a letter allegedly written by a lecturer in Beijing University, which said, "China belongs to the six hundred million people. . . . It does not belong to the Communist party alone. . . . If you carry on satisfactorily, well and good. If not, the masses may knock you down, kill the Communists, overthrow you. This cannot be called unpatriotic as the Communists no longer serve the people."[23]

Similar student and faculty demands were raised in other universities, and there were widespread demonstrations by intellectuals and professionals in many cities.

The party leaders and Mao himself were shocked at the volume and bitterness of the attacks on the party. Within a month of the start of the campaign it was decided to clamp down on the critics. Ironically, the posters put up by the party pledging immunity to those who spoke out boldly had still not been brought down.

Mao's contradictions speech of February was published on June 18, and among the revisions were several criteria that were to be used to distinguish "fragrant flowers" from "poisonous weeds": Words and action should unite, not divide, the people; they should be beneficial, not harmful, to socialist construction; they should consolidate the people's democratic dictatorship and democratic centralism, not undermine them; and they should strengthen the leadership of the Communist party. Free speech that went beyond the parameters of these criteria produced stinking weeds and poisonous fruits, which had to be destroyed quickly before they could harm the people. On June 22 *People's Daily* published an editorial indicating that the party leadership had set a trap for the "bourgeois rightists" to reveal themselves. The rectification campaign was now turned against the rightists.

> "Some ask," said the editorial, "Why does the Party which invites others to rectify its working style, now rectify others? True the Party will continue to ask the broad masses of the people to help its rectification campaign. . . . But can it be said that the reactionary words and deeds of anti-socialist bourgeois rightists should be given protection and must not be criticised? If the revolutionary leaders of all circles do not know how to beware, detect and hit anti-socialist speeches and deeds (whatever sacred name they borrow), such revolutionaries simply have no sense of responsibility towards the people's cause."[24]

By creating an arbitrary distinction between the people and the bourgeois rightists (who did not necessarily have a bourgeois class background) and by dubbing them the "enemy of the people," class struggle had been turned into a supraclass struggle.

Many non-Communist officeholders in the government were made to confess their "crimes" and then dismissed, many other prominent third-party figures were compelled to "repent" publicly, and some "troublemakers" were executed. Entire faculties were closed down so that students and teachers could be struggled against; some of them committed suicide rather than suffer the humiliating punishments imposed on them. The antirightist campaign, which was carried on vigorously for the next two years, was also extended to the party, and thousands of party members were purged and punished. Altogether, several million people were sent to the countryside to "reform their thought through labor."

The surprising result of the 180-degree reversal of the Maoist Hundred Flowers campaign was not, as one would have expected, a weakening of Mao's position but a strengthening of it. Mao skillfully used the antirightist campaign to get rid of his opposition within the party.

THE GREAT LEAP FORWARD: MAO'S INDEPENDENT PATH TO MODERNIZATION

By the end of 1957, Mao was back in full command of the national scene. Some additions to the membership of the Standing Committee of the Politburo had given him the necessary edge over his opposition, but far more important, Mao had regained his authority by advocating his theory of everlasting contradictions and the resulting need for ceaseless rectification of incorrect ideology. The party had been forced to accept Mao's approach to modernization, which linked mass mobilization and mass socialization with economic growth. In October 1957 the Central Committee of the CPC formally approved Mao's radical 12-Year Plan for Agricultural Development, thus settling the debate over economic policy.

During the winter of 1957–1958, millions of peasants were organized to help in construction work, building railroads, canals, river embankments, and dams. Since right enthusiasm and humanpower were now more important than machinery and technicians, Mao even reversed the policies on family planning, declaring that China was short of people! Mao's advice on devolution of authority was also followed, and greater financial autonomy was given to provinces and municipalities, who were also encouraged to practice self-reliance in expanding local light industries.

In January 1958 Mao at a meeting of the Supreme State Conference could announce with arrogant self-confidence, "I stand for the theory of permanent revolution. . . . One revolution must follow another, the revolution must continually advance." It was in the same speech that Mao also announced new economic targets that would be achieved by the whole nation mobilized to take a giant step forward. He said that the national spirit had risen to a level surpassing that of the previous 8 years and that China could now catch up with Britain in about 15 years. "Our nation is like an atom. . . . When this atom's nucleus is smashed the thermal energy released [through the Great Leap Forward] will have really tremendous power. We shall be able to do things which we could not do before."[25] By March Mao felt strong enough to attack Stalin for having declared the Chinese revolution a fake, to reject the Soviet model ("The Soviet Union stresses unity, and doesn't talk about contradictions, especially the contradiction between the leaders and the led"), and to confirm that China would henceforth follow its own path. Mao was critical of party leaders who, when the CPC assumed power, felt diffident to tackle the new tasks of economic, cultural, and educational development on the national scale and so, wholeheartedly and uncritically, accepted the Soviet model:

> In short, the Soviet Union was [considered] tops. . . . The Chinese people had got so used to being slaves. . . . In April 1956 I put forward the "Ten Great Relationships," which made a start in proposing our own line in construction.[26]

In another speech Mao clarified that "it is very necessary to win Soviet aid, but the most important thing is self-reliance."[27]

Like the Soviet Union, the intellectuals could also now be discarded. China could depend on the innate wisdom of the masses and their inherent revolutionary capacity. Mao said that after the shift to the cities, the party had been "terrified" of academics and "felt that we were good for nothing." It was intolerable for a Marxist, who is not afraid of imperialists, to be afraid of bourgeois intellectuals:

> In history it is always those with little learning who overthrow those with much learning. . . . I don't propose to close all the schools. What I mean is that it is not absolutely necessary to attend school.[28]

The second session of the Eighth Party Congress, held in Beijing in May, officially endorsed the Great Leap Forward, which was based on the Maoist principles that had evolved during the Yanan period and on the economic policies enunciated by Mao in the Ten Great Relationships: In addition to self-reliance, a national mass campaign led by Maoist cadres would raise the level of the political consciousness of the masses and channel their enthusiasm and will to ensure spectacular economic results in industrial and agricultural development. The gap between the city and the countryside could be bridged by industrializing the countryside and the interior; the gap between the elite and the masses, by sending the elite to the factories and the villages to work alongside the masses. The people could be made multifunctional by having the peasants set up "backyard furnaces" for making steel and the factory workers plant crops in available land near the factories—the peasants would thus acquire working-class mentality and the workers would help in food production.

Collective effort was to be emphasized, and moral and ideological incentives would replace monetary ones. The advancement of socialism would come through the establishment of communes in the countryside. Mao had once again turned to the peasantry to lead the revolution. Whereas Marxism-Leninism demanded a high degree of industrialization before a society could reach the stage of establishing communism, Mao celebrated China's backwardness even as a means to achieving this end. China, he said, was "poor" and "blank." "That may seem like a bad thing, but it is really a good thing. Poor people want change . . . want revolution. A clean sheet of paper has no blotches, and so the newest and most beautiful words can be written on it."[29]

Mao was in a hurry to cover the blank sheet of paper with everything that was needed for a transfiguration of China, to convert it into an advanced socialist state, with modern industry, modern agriculture, and socialist (modern?) science and culture. The Great Leap Forward immediately and simultaneously was to develop the industrial and agricultural sectors (thereby "walking on two legs"), making steel the "key link," bringing technology to the countryside, and producing a class of "Red" (ideologically pure) and "expert" (technologically advanced) intellectuals and a new selfless, socially dedicated "socialist man."

As the movement unfolded, a spirit of frenzy gripped the nation. The antirightist campaign was still in existence to ensure that those who lagged behind would see the light and find their enthusiasm. Popular enthusiasm for the Great Leap Forward was represented by the voluntary raising of production targets by each locality and collective. Statistics, however, became meaningless and often reflected utopian idealism rather than the real situation.

In April word came that 27 cooperatives in Henan comprising 9,300 households (43,000 persons), presumably as a voluntary act, had formed an enlarged cooperative, liquidating all private plots and private ownership of property. The new organization was big enough to take over control of local farming, industry, commerce, health, and education. Other provinces were encouraged to follow suit. These organizations were soon given the name People's Communes. The communes, with their larger population could use peasant labor more effectively. Men and women were organized in a military fashion into platoons and brigades assigned to special tasks. They marched to work at the call of bugles and labored unbelievably long hours, in the manner of shock troops fighting a battle. Communal kitchens, mess halls, old-people's homes, and nurseries "liberated" the women, who were often forced to live in separate dormitories from the men. In some communes wages were entirely done away with, following the Communist principle that the commune would satisfy the needs of each member; in most others wages were introduced on the socialist principle "to each according to his work"; the peasant thus became a wage earner, a "worker."

In August the party, declaring that the movement represented a popular demand, adopted a resolution making the establishment of communes official national policy. By November 99 percent of the peasantry had been organized into 26,578 communes with an average size of 4,600 households. There was even an attempt to establish urban communes with an emphasis on "street industries" run by women who had been liberated from household work. The urban communes were abandoned a year or so later because they served no useful purpose and because of the complexity of the problems posed by the cities.

In September a new slogan, "everyone a soldier," was introduced, which added another dimension to the communes, turning them into defense units, ready to fight a people's war if the occasion ever arose. It was suggested that a U.S.-backed Nationalist invasion was imminent. In reality, most of the young men and women commune members who joined the People's Militia and received elementary military drill (often with outmoded rifles) contributed to collective discipline rather than to national security.

The local cadres, under pressure to produce results, claimed record outputs far in excess of earlier estimates. The party Central Committee was becoming a victim of its own propaganda. Thus, to take some basic commodities, it was announced that because of the Great Leap Forward, the steel output had more than doubled, from 5.35 million tons in 1957 to 11.08 million tons in 1958; the production of cereals had risen from 196 million tons (including soybeans) in 1957 to 375 million tons. There was therefore no reason not to speed up the process of communization even further.

On the other hand, there were administrators in the government and the party who knew that these figures were exaggerated and who were cognizant of the failures. The haste with which communes were being established was leading to chaos in some places. Soon the whole country was to learn what it had cost the nation to indulge in this wild Maoist experiment. Although the revised estimates of the Great Leap Forward results are in themselves respectable, they bear little relationship to the rigors the country had gone through. Instead of the 70 percent increase in total value of agriculture and industry claimed in 1958, the revised results, issued later, were 39.3 percent for industry and 16.7 percent for agriculture.

The cost was physical and emotional exhaustion everywhere. Resources had been wasted (nearly 3 million tons of the backyard "steel," produced with so much extra toil by 10 million peasants, was unusable); machinery had been overworked and, with no time for maintenance, had begun to break down; there was no synchronization between production and demand, so that many manufactured items lay stored in the open (there was not enough warehouse space), deteriorating in wind and rain; standards had been lost sight of, and many overproduced items could not be used at all; communications had broken down, resulting in acute shortages and surpluses; "deep plowing" (encouraged by the party) had, in some areas, led to soil exhaustion and erosion; many dams burst during the rainy season because nobody had cared to calculate how much water pressure the dam walls could tolerate. All these damaging details were not known immediately and came to be revealed in the years that followed the Great Leap Forward.

The Results of the Great Leap Forward

The Great Leap Forward was a party-run campaign. The party cadres, operating on the mass line principle, had played a key role in activating the masses. In the resulting overdecentralized atmosphere, the government agencies and planning organizations lost their authority to coordinate national economic development. The *xia fang* (down to the countryside) campaigns, which became a part of the new policies, forced many hundreds of thousands of bureaucrats to the villages and weakened bureaucratic economic control organs—this was, of course, apart from the *xia fang* of millions of city youths and urbanites.

At the meeting of the Central Committee of the CPC in December 1958, the party conservatives (sometimes referred to as "pragmatists") got an opportunity to air some of their anxieties and appeal for a period of consolidation. There was no attempt to attack Mao, whose Great Leap Forward policies had been accepted by all the major leaders, but there was a hint of disillusionment in his ultraradical approach. Even Peng Dehuai, the defense minister, who expressed his impressions of a visit to a commune in the following verse, did not take up the issue with the party until mid-1959:

> Millet is scattered all over the ground,
> The leaves of the sweet potatoes are withered.
> The young and the strong have gone to smelt iron,
> To harvest the grain there are children and old women.
> How shall we get through next year?
> I shall agitate and speak out on behalf of the people.[30]

The resolution on "Some Questions Concerning the People's Communes," adopted by the Central Committee in December 1958, set down certain guidelines that reflect the major problems faced by the communes: "It should be publicized among the masses that the means of livelihood owned by members—including housing, clothing, bedding and furniture—and their deposits in banks and credit cooperatives will remain their own property . . . and will always belong to them. . . . Members can retain individual trees around their houses, small farm tools, small instruments, small animals and poultry . . . and [be allowed to] engage in small domestic side-occupations"; work days should be shortened—at least "8 hours for sleep and 4 hours for meals and recreation," must be guaranteed; rest must be ensured to women before and after birth and during menstruation; certain commune members may cook at home (this soon became the general rule); parents may withdraw their children from communal nurseries; wages should be paid in cash for the most part; the production brigade (the equivalent of the old socialist cooperatives) should be made the basic accounting and labor units; the party cadres "dizzy with success" had been guilty of commandism and exaggeration—they should adopt a more "comradely" style of work; the "military work style" should be discarded because it interfered with normal agricultural methods and unified work plans; and the local party branches must ensure orderly operations in the communes by April 1959. In sum, overeager comrades were advised to recognize that "the transition to Communism is a fairly long and complicated process of development," but the communes were still to "go in for industry in a big way.[31]

Mao had agreed to this resolution, seeing in it a temporary phase of consolidation, but he also called for the continuation of the policy of the Three Red Banners, which referred to the Maoist General Line for Building Socialism, The Great Leap Forward, and establishment of the people's communes.

Just at this juncture, in December 1958, Mao announced that he would step down from the post of chair of the People's Republic when his term expired in April 1959. He was succeeded to this post by Liu Shao-qi, who had stood by Mao throughout 1958. There has been considerable debate regarding Mao's retirement. Some scholars feel that he was forced to withdraw under pressure from his critics. There is little evidence to substantiate this view. On the contrary, there is every reason to believe that Mao wanted to be free of the onerous ceremonial duties imposed on him as the formal head of state (e.g., receiving ambassadors) so that he could devote himself to questions dealing with "direction, policy and line of the party and state." What possibly happened was that after the event, many who disagreed with Mao began to take advantage of his retirement and ignore him. Years later, Mao did complain that persons like Deng Xiao-ping stopped consulting him and that others treated him like a "dead ancestor."

Regardless of all the setbacks, 1958 had been a good year, and grain production had touched 250 million tons. Although this was far less than the optimistic claims of 375 million tons, it was sufficient to keep the countryside pacified. Indeed, in many communes, because of a heightened sense of autonomy and communism, there had been excessive sharing out of grain at the expense of the state, which was finding it difficult to reach its procurement targets.

As an overview, 1958 can be considered a year of great success for Mao Ze-dong, who had emerged as the all-powerful reshaper of China's destiny. He had been able to impose his uniquely simplistic and faulty economic vision on an entire nation without anyone daring to challenge or criticize him. The Chinese technocrats and state bureaucracy were paralyzed, as were the Soviet advisers, whose model was being dismantled before their eyes. Mao had liberated China from the Guomindang in 1949; he freed it from the Soviet system in 1958. The year ended without any hint of the opposition Mao was to face during the next few years.

The politics that had given Mao such a free hand to experiment with a nation of 600 million was rooted to an important degree in the Chinese traditional elitist system. Mao had succeeded in establishing himself as a morally superior ruler in the manner of the dynastic emperors and in establishing a consensus based on ideology (even though the ideology was modern and antitraditional). In keeping with traditional political behavior, the people, who did not expect to be told (nor were they) of the secret debates and factional struggles that went on behind the publicly announced consensus, were expected to work (and they did) to uphold the consensus, docilely and with a display of enthusiasm. The state structures, lacking constitutional authority, could not intervene between the leader and the people; indeed, government organizations were expendable. So like the Qin emperor, who in the third century B.C. could order millions of peasants to build the Great Wall, Mao could get 10 million peasants to indulge in the absurd campaign of making steel in backyard furnaces. However, after 1958, as we will witness, Mao's status, unlike that of the traditional emperors, was neither sacrosanct nor above being damaged by intraparty factional struggles.

CHINA'S FOREIGN RELATIONS

Having reexerted China's independence in its internal affairs by replacing the Soviet model for social change and economic modernization, Mao by 1958 also began to guide China's foreign policy toward a more independent stand.

From the late nineteenth century to the establishment of the PRC, most Chinese revolutionaries and leaders had a passionate desire to see China become truly independent and regain the world stature it had traditionally possessed. When at American insistence China was honored as one of the Big

Four during World War II, many Chinese felt that China was gaining no more than its due. However, the action of the Allies was only partially satisfying because China did not have the capacity to play the role of a world power.

The possibility that the Communist government of China could play such a role was nullified even before the PRC was officially inaugurated, when China's economic problems and the international situation led Mao to declare (June 1949) that China would "lean to one side," the side of the Soviet Union. The debate on American recognition of Beijing was over by the time the Korean War broke out. In the early 1950s only about 20 countries recognized the PRC.

Mao was acutely aware of the fact that China could not be truly independent in foreign relations until it had achieved economic self-reliance. He had to depend on the Soviet Union, but he chafed under the conditions imposed by Stalin. This attitude is reflected in an article published by Wu Xiu-quan (a veteran diplomat who had participated in the Sino-Soviet talks between Mao and Stalin preceding the signing of the Sino-Soviet Treaty of Friendship, Alliance, and Mutual Assistance in February 1950) in November 1983:

> Now that the new Chinese government had been established, the Soviet Union ought to hand over unreservedly the right [to run the Manchurian Railway] to China. But [by not doing so] the Soviet Union, in fact, had gained more advantages. . . . The agreement also stipulated that the Soviet Union should hand over without compensation to China a number of factories, mines and machinery they had acquired from Japan in northeast China. However, they took home with them all the machinery and materials that could be dismantled and removed. In the Anshan [industrial complex] only some empty buildings had been handed over "without compensation." Even the pianos and fine furniture . . . had been taken to the Soviet Union.[32]

After Mao had left, Wu stayed on in Moscow to help in negotiating various economic agreements; "It was no smooth sailing when our talks involved the economic interests of the two countries. Differences and disputes soon arose, the comparatively striking one being how to decide on the ratio between the specific value of the Chinese [currency] and the Soviet ruble. . . . The ratio was fixed, in truth, under relatively unequal conditions. . . . [Later other] disagreements arose from time to time."[33]

After China had intervened in the Korean War, the Soviet Union conveniently overlooked the provisions of the Sino-Soviet treaty and, fearing that any escalation of the war might force the Soviet Union to face the Americans, kept its military aid to China limited, even though the Chinese, to their further surprise, had to pay for the armaments. The Soviets then, without prior consultation with Beijing, made a ceasefire proposal in the United Nations in June 1951. The ceasefire negotiations dragged on until 1953, the same year that a negotiated settlement was about to be reached over Vietnam. Whatever the costs of the war, the PRC's participation in the 1954 Geneva Conference on Korea and Indochina put China at the same negotiating table as the United States, Britain, France, and the Soviet Union. America had been forced to recognize China as an enemy of stature, and the post-Stalin Russian leaders could no longer treat China as a minor ally. The unequal aspects of Sino-Soviet treaties were abrogated by Moscow by November, and economic aid was increased. Zhou En-lai's success as a negotiator and his suave, diplomatic behavior won China much respect in the world press.

But the success did not come as an unmixed blessing. The Americans drew up plans to set up a military alliance in the West Pacific—the South East Asia Treaty Organization (SEATO)—which, linked with the Central Treaty Organization and North Atlantic Treaty Organization (NATO), would establish a cordon of military bases around the entire socialist bloc and help "contain" communism. It was, of course, China that was to be contained in the East. Mao, hoping to get the Russians to respond to the challenge, began a bombardment of the offshore

Nationalist-held islands of Quemoy (Jinmen) and Matsu (Mazu) in the Taiwan Straits (September 1954), ostensibly as a first step to the liberation of Taiwan. The Soviets, however, were not at all interested in creating disequilibrium in the straits, which might draw America to the aid of Chiang Kai-shek and force Moscow to intervene. In December the United States signed a mutual defense treaty with Taiwan.

The Soviet Union's response to the crises was to move a resolution in the Security Council of the United Nations (January 1955) calling on the United States to withdraw its forces from Taiwan and urging that all parties in the Taiwan Straits area avoid hostilities. This statement reflected the Soviet Union's national security interest but not that of China. The Chinese looked on hostilities between them and the Nationalists as a legitimate continuation of the Chinese civil war (Taiwan *had* to be liberated), thus a totally internal matter not open to debate in any international forum. If the Americans insisted on starting a war, even an atomic war, China could handle the situation alone. Two days before the Soviet resolution, Mao had said,

> The Chinese people are not to be cowed by U.S. blackmail. . . . We have an expression, millet plus rifles. In the case of the United States it is planes plus the A-bomb. However, if the U.S. . . . is to launch a war of aggression against China, then China with its millet plus rifles is sure to emerge the victor.[34]

Mao's brave words were lost on the Russians and the Americans. In the absence of any solid support from the Soviet Union for China's military action in the Taiwan Straits, Beijing was forced to stop the bombardment, but it cleverly defused the issue by declaring that China's show of will had checked an American threat in the area.

At the Bandung Conference of Afro-Asian states, held in 1955, China could put on a face of moderation and accept the idea of peaceful coexistence between Third World countries and the socialist states. The newly independent Afro-Asian states and those still fighting for independence were, by the nature of their circumstances, anti-imperialist. But when Khrushchev, in 1956, announced his formula of peaceful coexistence and détente with the United States, ostensibly to save the world from nuclear war, China could not accept the Soviet view of coexistence because it was qualitatively different.

In 1956 Mao, who was then establishing his credentials to enforce his policies for China's internal development, also indicated the need to develop the potential for an independent foreign policy. There is a significant passage in his April 1956 speech on "The Ten Great Relationships" that touches on this issue. "In the future," said Mao, "we will not only have more planes and artillery but we will also have atom bombs. If we are not *to be bullied in the present day world,* we cannot do without the bomb [emphasis added]."[35] It is equally significant that China did manage to manufacture its first atom bomb by 1964, even though the Soviet Union had rescinded its offer to provide China with the scientific know-how.

At the end of 1957, when Mao had recouped his power within the CPC and was about to launch the Great Leap Forward, he felt self-confident enough to advise the Soviet Union on how to lead the socialist bloc and deal with the imperialist enemy. Mao went to Moscow in November to attend the fortieth-anniversary celebrations of the October Revolution, the accompanying meeting of Communist parties in power, and the international conference of Communist parties. He made much of the first earth satellite, the Soviet *Sputnik,* which according to him, proved that the socialist camp was ahead of the imperialist camp and that "the East wind prevailed over the West wind." This was the time to increase confrontation with the imperialists and push forward the cause of socialism.

Mao gave his Communist comrades a talk on his favorite subject of contradictions and dialectics, saying that the concepts must be moved "from the small circle of philosophers to the broad masses of the people"; he added that in China even the party branch secretaries "understand dialectics."[36] He also gave a speech (directed primarily to his hosts) on the nature of imperialism. He reiterated what he had said earlier in 1946, that the United States and the atom bomb were "paper tigers." Elsewhere he suggested that even a nuclear war was not to be feared because the worst it could do was to destroy half of humankind; but imperialism would also be liquidated, and there would still be half of humankind left over to make the whole world socialist.[37] Mao hinted that this was no time for the Soviet Union, as the head of the socialist camp, to lose the initiative and compromise with the United States.

Although Mao managed to get Khrushchev's thesis amended to a certain extent, it was clear that the Soviets were not ready to give up their interest in lessening international tensions through a policy of peaceful coexistence with the United States. This policy implied that Moscow was willing to accept the American containment line and therefore the continued existence of two Koreas, two Vietnams, and two Chinas (or one China and one Taiwan). If this implication was correct, it threatened China's goals of liberating Taiwan.

Mao returned home with agreements for large-scale Soviet technical aid, including nuclear know-how, but convinced that China's future policies would have to be more independent of Moscow. After January 1958, when the United States introduced tactical nuclear weapons into South Korea, China asked Russia for equivalent weapons, but Moscow declined unless such hardware could be put under joint command, which proposition Beijing refused. In July Khrushchev was rebuffed again when he suggested the creation of a joint naval command in the west Pacific. Mao could not tolerate the idea of any diminution of Chinese independence and sovereignty.

And in any case this was the wrong time for Moscow to make such proposals because China was in the euphoric throes of its Great Leap Forward. In August Mao, full of confidence in China's capacity to go it alone, ordered the bombing of the offshore islands of Jinmen (Quemoy) and Mazu (Matsu), ostensibly as a first step to the liberation of Taiwan. Yet was it rather a feeler to prove that the Nationalist reactionaries and the U.S. imperialists were paper tigers? Or was it a test to find out whether the Soviet Union would stand by a fraternal power? Whatever the reason, Mao failed on all three counts. In contrast Moscow's policy of détente had worked: The lack of superpower support to their client states stopped the war from escalating. This success encouraged Khrushchev to improve relations with the United States even further, whereas he was alarmed enough by the Chinese adventurous behavior to abrogate the nuclear-sharing agreement in 1959.

For good or bad, Mao, by the end of 1958, had guided China to a stage of internal and external independence it had not had since 1800.

NOTES

1. *Selected Works of Mao Tse-Tung,* vol. IV (Beijing: Foreign Languages Press, 1961), pp. 411–23 [hereafter cited as *SWM*].

2. *Selected Works of Liu Shaoqi* (Beijing: Foreign Languages Press, 1984), p. 419.

3. *SWM,* vol. V (1977), pp. 16–17.

4. Ibid., p. 35.

5. Ibid.

6. Harold C. Hinton, ed., *The People's Republic of China, 1949–1979: A Documentary Survey,* vol. I (1949–1957) (Wilmington, DE: Scholarly Resources, 1980), p. 51.

7. See *Selected Readings from the Works of Mao Tse-tung* (Beijing: Foreign Languages Press, 1967), pp. 234–39.

8. Mark Seldon et., al., ed., *The People's Republic of China: A Documentary History of Revolutionary Change* (New York: Monthly Review Press, 1979), p. 215.

9. *SWM,* vol. I (1967), p. 29.

10. Hinton, *People's Republic,* pp. 74–75.

11. Ibid., p. 82.

12. Ibid., p. 231.

13. Ibid., p. 233.

14. Ibid., p. 224.

15. *Chinese Communist World Outlook,* Department of State Publication 7379, Far Eastern Series 112 (Washington, DC: U.S. Government Printing Office, 1962), pp. 60–61.

16. *SWM,* vol. I, p. 336.

17. Hinton, *People's Republic,* p. 334.

18. For the full text, see ibid., pp. 325–31.

19. For the full text, see *Let a Hundred Flowers Blossom, a Hundred Schools of Thought Contend* (Beijing: Foreign Languages Press, 1958).

20. Liu Shao-chi, *The Political Report of the Central Committee of the Communist Party of China to the Eighth National Congress of the Party* (Beijing: Foreign Language Press, 1956), p. 27.

21. For the full text, see *SWM,* vol. V, pp. 384–421.

22. Maurice Meisner, *Mao's China* (New York: Free Press, 1977), p. 184.

23. Cited in Edward E. Rice, *Mao's Way* (Berkeley: University of California Press, 1972), p. 146.

24. Hinton, *People's Republic,* pp. 552–53.

25. See Stuart Schram, ed., *Chairman Mao Talks to the People* (New York: Pantheon Books, 1974), pp. 92–93.

26. Ibid., pp. 98–101.

27. Ibid., p. 126.

28. Ibid., p. 118–20.

29. "Introducing a Cooperative," *Peking Review,* June 10, 1958, p. 6.

30. Cited in Roderick MacFarquhar, *The Origins of the Cultural Revolution, vol. 2: The Great Leap Forward 1958–1960* (New York: Columbia University Press, 1983), p. 200.

31. For the document, see Hinton, *People's Republic,* vol. II, pp. 720–30.

32. Wu Xiu-quan, "Sino-Soviet Relations in the Early 1950s," *Beijing Review,* November 21, 1983, p. 19.

33. Ibid., pp. 20–21.

34. *SWM,* vol. V, pp. 152–53.

35. Mao Tse-tung, "On the Ten Major Relationships," *Peking Review,* no. 1 (January 1, 1977), 13.

36. *SWM,* vol. V, p. 516.

37. See John Gittings, *The World and China, 1922–1972* (New York: Harper & Collins, 1975), p. 218; and Harrison Salisbury, *War Between Russia and China* (New York: Norton, 1969), p. 118. Khrushchev, in *Khrushchev Remembers* (Boston: Little, Brown, 1974), pp. 254–55, quotes Mao as saying, "We shouldn't be afraid of atomic bombs or missiles. No matter what kind of war breaks out . . . we'll win. As for China . . . we may lose more than three hundred million people. So what? . . . The years will pass and we'll get to work producing more babies than ever before."

CHAPTER 9

From Consensus to Factional Conflict: 1959–1966

During the seven years following the 1958 Great Leap Forward, Chinese politics underwent a radical change. Mao's path to independence had a drastic impact on China's economic modernization program and led to a serious ideological division within the party, with the majority of the party leadership turning against him. Externally, China broke with the Soviet Union and soon found itself isolated from the world community.

Mao lost his grip over the party apparatus, and his economic policies were reversed, but he could not be compelled to retire. Apart from retaining his charismatic national popularity, he managed to maintain control of the armed forces and to continue to direct foreign policy. Using the avenues available to him, he finally fought his way back to power in 1966.

RETREAT FROM MAOISM: 1959–1961

In the early months of 1959, there was little indication of the troubles that lay ahead. At this time Mao was still insistent that the Great Leap be continued, although he recognized that some of the leftist excesses of 1958 needed to be dealt with; he agreed that the "Communist wind" had destabilized the countryside and dislocated supplies to the urban sector. This belief put him on the side of those who, in the interest of economic stability, were advocating a retreat from the commune system.

The immediate problem facing the country was food shortages in the cities. Many, including Zhou En-lai, still believed that the food production had doubled during 1958. Why then the shortages? One reason was that the peasants in the newly formed communes had distributed the grain among themselves and hidden what they could not consume, thus making it exceedingly difficult for the state procurement agencies to make adequate collections. But there were other reasons, too. The excessive use of humanpower in making steel had left few able hands to harvest the grain. In some cases the crops had not been harvested at all and were allowed to rot in the fields. Beyond the waste was of course the fact that the statistics had been incorrect. There had no doubt been a bumper harvest in 1958, but the 1957 output certainly had not been doubled. The droughts and famines in the summer of 1959 exacerbated the situation.

However, Mao was optimistic that with a few adjustments the Three Red Banners could still be kept flying in all their glory. He admitted that he had made a mistake in concentrating on the 10.7 million tons of steel and agreed that central planning and direction could not be bypassed. He even accepted the idea that it would take 15 to 20 years or longer for the entry into communism.

Mao's mild rightist approach may well have led to a compromise solution of economic policies but for three unforeseen developments that forced him to confirm his radical leftist policies.

The Peng De-huai Affair

At the meetings of the Politburo and the Central Committee of the CPC held at Lushan (Jiangxi) in July–August 1959, Marshall Peng De-huai, minister of defense, addressed a "Letter of Opinion"[1] to Mao in which he criticized the policies of the Great Leap Forward and the establishment of the communes as a product of "petit-bourgeois fanaticism." These policies had wasted scarce resources and humanpower and were directly responsible for the economic chaos and disasters that had followed and for the alienation of the party from the masses. The document was circulated to the members of the conference on July 17.

Normally one would not have expected a military figure to become involved in such a political controversy, but it is likely that Peng was worried about the impact of this chaotic situation on the armed forces, who were mostly recruited from the countryside; on the modernization of the PLA, which depended on a planned development of science and technology; and on Sino-Soviet relations. Besides, the establishment of the People's Militia in the communes was anathema to the professionals in the PLA. Peng, who had just returned from a visit to the Soviet Union, was perhaps also aware of Khrushchev's antagonism to China's communes (the Chinese, Khrushchev had said, "do not properly understand what communism is or how it is to be built") and may have feared the Soviet withdrawal of military technological aid. Indeed, in June the Russians unilaterally abrogated their agreement to provide China nuclear technology and a sample atom bomb.

However, Mao, who was the greatest proponent of criticism and self-criticism and had encouraged the whole nation to indulge in it, considered himself above criticism. Like the emperors in imperial China, Mao would periodically make public declarations of self-criticism, but he could not accept criticism, which in his eyes amounted to *lèse-majesté*. He took Peng's criticism as a personal attack. In his speech on July 23 Mao accepted some responsibility for what had gone wrong but counterattacked by declaring that the

> masses still support us. . . . [The Great Leap Forward had been a great school which enabled] a population of several hundreds of millions as well as several million cadres to be educated. . . . [Even illiterates] can learn some political economy. . . . [Petit bourgeois rightists] say "while there is loss, there is also gain." The fact that they put the word "gain" second is the result of careful consideration. . . .
>
> If we do ten things and nine are bad, and they are all published in the press, then we will certainly perish, and will deserve to perish. *In that case, I will go to the countryside to lead the peasants to overthrow the government. If those of you in the Liberation Army won't follow me, then I will go and found a Red Army, and organize another Liberation Army. But I think the Liberation Army will follow me* [emphasis added]. . . .
>
> I am a complete outsider when it comes to economic construction, and I understand nothing about industrial planning.
>
> I have committed two crimes, one of which is the calling for 10,700,000 tons of steel and the mass smelting of steel. If you agreed with this you

should share some of the blame. . . . As for the people's communes, the whole world opposed them; the Soviet Union opposed them. . . . If you talk about haste, Marx also made mistakes. . . .

Comrades, you must all analyse your responsibility. If you have to shit, shit! If you have to fart, fart! You will feel much better for it.[2]

Thus, although accepting some blame for some things that went wrong, Mao, using homely examples and earthy epithets, suggested that others would have to share the blame for the rest. In any case, according to Mao, the gains far outweighed the losses, and so there was no reason to reject his mass-based revolutionary approach. Mao gave his opponents an impossible choice: Accept his leadership and his policies or risk a major confrontation. Even those who may have agreed with Peng found it expedient to keep silent.

By the time the Central Committee meeting ended, Mao had managed to get the party to denounce Peng as the leader of an anti-party clique opposed to the victory of the Three Red Banners, hinting that he was in the pay of the Soviet Union. Peng made a public self-criticism ("I expressed a series of [Right opportunist] absurdities. . . . I attacked the Party's general line . . . and damaged the prestige of the Party Central Committee and Comrade Mao Tse-tung. Now, I have realized that this is a kind of crime"[3]), but he lost his post as defense minister to the Maoist Lin Biao. Because of Peng's popularity and prestige within the army, however, he was allowed to retain his membership in the party and the other positions, which were basically empty titles.

Mao won the battle, but the Lushan developments turned him away from the right-oriented correctional policies he was following before August, back to a more left line. It was, however, a pyrrhic victory, and the pragmatic party leaders in actual control of state affairs continued to carry out policies of retrenchment from the Great Leap Forward, while paying lip service to Mao. These policies led Mao to make an ominous statement in September that hinted that bourgeois elements had infiltrated the party.

The Economic Crisis

The second development that shaped the turn of events was the fact that during the three years 1959–1961, China suffered from severe natural calamities. Widespread floods and droughts caused a drastic reduction in agricultural output and a corresponding decline in light and heavy industry. Crop failures and widespread starvation brought unrest to the countryside. Agricultural output value in 1959 was less than that in 1957 (half the cultivated acreage had been devastated); in 1960 and 1961 it was below that in 1952; in 1962 the recovery began and the output value finally rose above the 1952 figure.[4] It has been calculated that the mortality rate more than doubled between 1957 and 1960 and that about 22 million extra people died during the Great Leap Forward.[5] No doubt the crisis can be attributed to the Great Leap Forward: dislocations caused by the establishment of the communes, labor shortages due to the allocation of labor to rural industries and the drift of peasants to the cities, and the loss of peasant enthusiasm because of the reductions of material incentives. In 1962 Liu Shao-qi suggested that 30 percent of the production difficulties were a result of natural calamities and 70 percent derived from human factors.

Mao's call to the party to oppose "right deviation" after the Lushan conference began to come in direct conflict with those who wished to follow a more pragmatic line that would ensure economic rehabilitation by avoiding the dangers of Maoist-style rapid economic and social development. Liu, the new chair of the PRC, became the main articulator of the new line. The term *leap forward* was not discarded immediately, but it was used as a cover-up for anti-leap-forward policies. Liu began a program implementing the recentralization of industry and the decentralization of the communes under the auspices of the state and party organs. The party apparatus reexerted its hold over the country by establishing six regional bureaus of the Politburo in 1960, and the party Secretariat under Deng Xiao-ping (a strong supporter of Liu's policies) assumed greater importance. In 1962, obviously with Mao in mind, Liu even went so far as to declare that a party member, however capable or important, was no more than "one element in the apparatus"[6] and should lead the party from within and not from without.

By 1962 the people's communes as structured in 1958 had virtually disappeared: The ownership of land, cattle, and agricultural implements was transferred back to the production teams, consisting of 20 to 30 households, and individual peasants were given small private plots as a material incentive; the peasants were allowed to sell the produce of their private plots in free markets that sprang up in rural towns; a system of work points, based on productivity, was used to remunerate the peasants for their work in the collective; the production brigades became responsible for schools and local industries: the People's Communes retained control of only public works and security organs; the size of the communes was reduced and their number increased from 24,000 to 74,000; canteens almost disappeared, as did the nurseries and old-people's homes; enterprises that did not make profits were closed down; and the cases of many rightist deviationists were reconsidered, and they were exonerated. Centrally appointed cadres oversaw the operation of the new policies in the countryside. It looked as if China had gone back to the pre-Great Leap Forward days of the APCs.

Similar policy changes in the industrial sector pushed targets down to realistic levels and brought back a variation of the Soviet-style management system, which emphasized material incentives and profitability and the authority of managers and planners and which recognized the role of market forces. Furthermore, the Soviet withdrawal of their technicians from China in 1960 made it absolutely necessary for the party to turn to the old bourgeois capitalists and businesspeople for their expertise and to the much-maligned intellectuals for help. Not surprisingly, therefore, there was also a return to the pre-Great Leap Forward educational system, emphasizing competition and quality. "Expertise" was given a wide edge over "Redness."

In view of the national economic situation and since the new approach had the backing of the majority of the party leadership, Mao could not deny the need for or the implementation of these policies of "readjustment, consolidation, filling out, and raising standards," but it can be imagined that he was far from happy at the manner in which his revolutionary path was being abandoned. The polarization between the pragmatists or conservatives (condemned by the Maoists as "rightists"), now associated with the name of Liu Shao-qi, and the Maoists could no longer be glossed over.

The Sino-Soviet Split

The third element that affected Chinese internal politics was the emergence of strained relations between China and the Soviet Union, leading to confrontation and an open rift. There had been some strains in the relationship of the two countries from the beginning, but they became critical at the end of the 1950s.

Khrushchev's de-Stalinization policies and his views on peaceful coexistence with capitalist nations, particularly his move toward détente with the United States, were unacceptable to China. Mao had tried and failed to reverse the trend during his visit to the Moscow conference in November 1957, where he debunked the idea that a nuclear war would destroy civilization. Mao's Great Leap Forward policies (which rejected the Soviet model), the establishment of the communes, and the hard line against Taiwan in 1958 widened the gap between the two countries. China's internal and external radical policies came in direct conflict with those of the Soviet Union, which deemphasized revolutionary ideology for greater production at home and coexistence abroad.

Whether Moscow's decision in mid-1959 to rescind its 1957 nuclear agreement was based on the calculation that China was not ready for nuclear technology and that it would become a destabilizing factor or was a reaction to China's refusal to make available naval and other bases, the fact remains that this unilateral act on the part of the Soviet Union was most humiliating to Beijing.

Moscow's view of the Sino-Indian dispute, which suddenly erupted in early 1959, also proved that the Soviets had turned their backs on China. As a consequence of harsh Chinese policies the Tibetans had risen in rebellion, and the Dalai Lama, the religious and secular head of "autonomous" Tibet, was forced to seek asylum in India (April 1959).

When India became independent in 1947, its borders with Tibet were undemarcated, and it inherited the "special position" Britain had occupied in Tibet. However, with the establishment of the PRC in 1949, Prime Minister Nehru, who was exceedingly friendly to new China, not only accepted China's "suzerainty" over Tibet but in a 1954 agreement also gave up all the old privileges, hoping that Beijing would not infringe on Tibetan "autonomy," promised in a Sino-Tibetan agreement of 1951.

With the Dalai Lama's departure, the unsettled boundary between India and China became an explosive issue. China accused India of "abducting" the Dalai Lama and "aiding" the rebels, and also of physical aggression because it was supposedly occupying 50,000 square miles of Chinese territory in the northwest and northeast, which had been "gobbled up" by imperialist Britain.

The Soviet Union disagreed with China that India was a stooge of the imperialists and carrying on the expansive policies of its erstwhile imperialist master and therefore needed to be punished. Russia not only disavowed the Chinese position on India but also sided with India against China. In February 1960 the Soviet Union signed a friendship treaty with India. The deterioration of Sino-Indian political relations led to the flaring up of border disputes between the two countries, which reached a high point of tension in 1962. In that year a border war broke out between India and China; the Soviet Union continued to support India and thereby "proved" its betrayal of fraternal ties with China.

China countered by openly, although in the beginning indirectly, denouncing Soviet foreign policy. A strongly worded polemical article, "Long Live Leninism," definitely approved if not written by Mao himself, was published in the party journal, *Red Flag,* in April 1960. The article argued that peaceful coexistence was meaningless because imperialism could not change its exploitative nature and that as long as there was class exploitation there would be wars. Until the imperialist system was eliminated, wars could not be brought to an end; hence, in the Third World, the parliamentary road to socialism was not preferable to revolution. Ostensibly, the attack was directed against the "revisionist" Yugoslav leader, Tito, who had accepted "bourgeois influence" internally and surrendered to "imperialist pressures" externally, but the real target was the Soviet leaders. Only "modern revisionists," said the article, could recognize the "imperialist chieftain Eisenhower" as the man who established "lasting peace."[7]

Thus Mao, by enunciating a more orthodox viewpoint, challenged the Soviet leadership role as an exponent of correct ideology and confirmed not only Beijing's independence from Moscow but also Beijing's right to lead the world Communist movement. Incidentally, as revealed in December 1984, it was also in 1960 that Beijing decided to develop its own nuclear weapons.[8]

The Soviet Union, irritated by China's internal and external policies, sought to force Beijing to change its stand by summarily withdrawing all the Soviet scientists and technical experts working in China (summer 1960). If the Soviets had thought that the Chinese would knuckle under, they had made a gargantuan error of judgment. Even the pro-Soviet elements in the CPC leadership agreed with Mao that self-reliance was a better alternative to such conditional help.

One wonders whether Mao had not played his cards with this very end in mind. Although economic ties were not immediately broken, the future spelled a worsening of political and therefore all other relations. Chinese students in the Soviet Union were recalled, and Soviet-China trade began to dwindle; it declined from about $2 billion in 1959 to $45 million by the end of the 1960s. Chinese trade with the West increased correspondingly, and China began to look to the Third World as an arena in which to exert its ideological leadership.

By 1962 the Sino-Soviet differences were aired openly, and mutual attacks became more bitter. The Chinese enjoyed Moscow's discomfiture resulting from being forced to withdraw their missiles from Cuba (1962). The Soviet Union was condemned both for "adventurism" and cowardly "capitulationism." That the Soviets, despite this setback, signed the partial nuclear test ban treaty with Britain and the United States in 1963 was a clear sign that Moscow was bent on colluding with the imperialists to keep China from acquiring nuclear weapons. All further negotiations to improve the Sino-Soviet relations came to an end.

These developments liberated Mao from external restraints and gave him a freer hand to deal with internal problems. But by 1962 the internal scene had become far more complex than it was in 1959. Although Mao continued to direct foreign policy and could still influence affairs because of his political stature and although he still maintained a direct hold over the PLA, he no longer controlled the party or state. However, Mao's antirevisionist international stand had a strong bearing on his approach to internal politics.

DRAWING THE BATTLE LINES: 1962–1965

While Mao had been defining the deadly role of revisionism in international communism and reiterating the need to continue class struggle against imperialism, the party leaders handling China's internal affairs were pushing policies that could be criticized for being revisionist (i.e., restoring "capitalism" by extending private plots and making the peasants responsible for profits and losses, allowing private ownership of small enterprises, extending free markets, allowing market forces to link industry and agriculture, and overlooking the existence of classes and the need for class struggle.) The pragmatists' approach is best summed up by Deng Xiao-ping's 1961 remark that it did not matter whether a cat was black or white; it was a good cat as long as it caught mice. To Mao, on the other hand, nothing was more important than the color of the cat. As Mao had put it in 1958, "Those who pay no attention to politics and are busy with their work all day long will become economists who have gone astray and are dangerous."[9]

Looking back in 1981 on the developments in the late 1950s and early 1960s, the post-Mao CPC Central Committee made the following assessment:

> [The shortcoming in the 1958 line] was that it overlooked objective economic laws. . . . "Left" errors, characterized by excessive targets, the issuing of arbitrary directions, boastfulness and the stirring up of a "communist wind," spread unchecked throughout the country. . . . It was due to the fact that Mao Zedong and many leading comrades . . . had become smug about their successes, were impatient for quick results and overestimated the role of man's subjective will and efforts. . . .
>
> In the winter of 1960 . . . [a] number of correct policies and resolute measures [to rectify "left" errors] were worked out and put into effect with Comrades Liu Shaoqi, Zhou Enlai, Chen Yun and Déng Xiaoping in charge. . . . [Around January 1962] most of the "Rightists" had their label removed. Thanks to these economic and political measures, the national economy recovered and developed fairly smoothly between 1962 and 1966.[10]

Although this assessment, coming two decades after the events, has a certain air of clear-cut clarity that may not have been evident at that time, it does indicate the sentiment of the "Liuists," whose policies expressed their disillusionment with the Great Leap Forward.

Removing the rightist label was coupled with the party's liberalization policies, which encouraged the intellectuals, who were primarily the ones being rehabilitated, to help in the economic recovery. The old "Red" versus "expert" controversy was now settled in favor of expertise, and a renewed emphasis was placed on scientific research and uplifting educational standards at the expense of political study and political activity. This policy went totally against Mao's Great Leap Forward call that ideology and politics must remain in command in the realm of education and technology.

In a similar vein, the liberal intellectuals within the party, no doubt supported by the top leaders, went so far as to allow the publication of articles critical of Mao and his policies. In 1961 Wu Han, the deputy mayor of Beijing, a prominent Ming historian, wrote a play entitled *Hai Rui Dismissed from Office,* which attacked a capricious Ming emperor for unjustly dismissing Hai Rui, an incorruptible official who had taken some unpopular actions to help alleviate the suffering of the peasantry. Many who saw the play had no doubts that the emperor, who had lost touch with reality, was Mao and the aggrieved official was Peng De-huai. Among the other important writers who used allegory to criticize Mao was Deng Tuo. Deng, a journalist of long standing, had been editor-in-chief of the *People's Daily* from 1952 to 1959 and was currently a secretary of the Beijing Municipal Party Committee under Mayor Peng Zhen. Deng Tuo published 153 essays in 1961 and 1962 in a series entitled "Evening Talks at Yanshan," and his message was that leaders who lacked practical experience and knowledge should "study more, criticize less, and maintain a humble attitude"; otherwise they would become "arrogant, subjective, dogmatic and arbitrary."[11]

The new policies, based on the principle of democratic centralism, were carried out by a highly centralized party apparatus. Since class struggle had been replaced with planned development, there was no longer any possibility of Maoist-style "spontaneous" mass movements. The result was that the hierarchical party bureaucracy began to exercise greater control and authority; instead of revolutionary cadres inciting popular campaigns, the party members became careerists interested in promotions and special privileges. Since they were now directing the masses to follow the path chalked out by the party center, they became more arrogant and authoritarian.

The situation was obviously unacceptable to Mao and the Maoists. Broadly speaking, there were three interconnected elements that Mao viewed with grave concern: the revisionist economic policies of the party, the decline in socialist cultural values, and the bureaucratization of the party. In 1962 Mao made his first moves to reexert his authority.

Those who had closely followed Mao's public statements since 1959 would not have been surprised at the post-1962 developments. As early as September 1959 Mao had remarked that "bourgeois elements have infiltrated the Communist party." By January 1962, he was warning the party that there was danger that China would follow the revisionist path of Yugoslavia and "become a bourgeois country." Speaking to 7,000 provincial and district party functionaries, Mao declared that policies that overlooked the revolutionary spontaneity of the masses and ignored the mass line principle could not be construed as democratic centralism. He condemned comrades who "suppress the activism of the masses" and "who do not allow people to speak, who think [they] are tigers, and that nobody will dare touch [their] arse."[12]

Mao also raised the ghost of class struggle, saying that people's democratic dictatorship should repress landlords, rich peasants, counterrevolutionary elements, bad elements, and anti-Communist rightists. And he added, very significantly, that "there are some bad people who have infiltrated into our ranks . . . who sit on the heads of the people . . . We must find a way to deal with this type of people, and arrest some and execute a few. . . ."[13]

Mao repeated these sentiments in September 1962 at the Tenth Plenum of the Central Committee of the CPC and inaugurated a mass movement for ideological reeducation. The Socialist Education Movement, as the campaign came to be called, was intended to raise the ideological consciousness of the cadres and the masses and revive their flagging revolutionary spirit. Mao asserted that throughout the historical period of socialism, the bourgeoisie would continue to exist and continue to try to make a comeback. As such it would be a permanent source of revisionism within the party that needed to be struggled against ceaselessly. As an aside he added, "Writing novels is popular these days, isn't it? The use of the novels for anti-Party activity is a great invention."[14]

THE SOCIALIST EDUCATION MOVEMENT

Before we discuss the Socialist Education Movement or the developments that followed, it is necessary to clarify the terms *pragmatist, leftist,* and *ultraleftist,* which will be used hereafter. Those Chinese leaders who believed that economic development should have precedence over further socialization will be referred to as pragmatists. Not all pragmatists agreed wholly with Liu Shao-qi's policies, but by and large they belonged to or leaned toward the Liuist camp. The followers of the moderate Maoist line will be considered leftists; those who supported an extreme Maoist position will be called ultraleftists.

The Socialist Education Movement, which proceeded in several stages, began with a tacit agreement between the pragmatists and the leftists that some of the basic-level cadres needed to undergo ideological rectification (if necessary, punishment and removal) because their bad work style had led to a loss of confidence in the party. The general relaxation of the party's radical policies during the years of recovery, 1959–1961, had indeed resulted in certain "unhealthy tendencies." Acting as bureaucratic chiefs rather than revolutionary leaders, many cadres had become corrupt, misappropriating state funds, falsifying accounts dealing with grain collection and payments to peasants, and taking petty bribes. From Mao's point of view, the source for even greater worry was the emergence of capitalistic and feudalistic tendencies among the peasantry. Many peasants, finding it more profitable to work exclusively on their private plots and sideline occupations, had withdrawn from the collective; some peasants who had become rich through private initiative had started lending money at exorbitant rates; and other peasants had turned away from farming altogether and had become peddlers or moved to the cities to gain contract employment in industry. Feudalistic practices, such as the purchase of brides, witchcraft, and religious festivals, had also made a reappearance in several areas.

Although both sides agreed that some corrective action was called for, trouble between Mao and the pragmatists arose when he tried to use the movement to mobilize the masses to rectify the evil tendencies, whereas the party apparatus tried to control the movement from above. Mao encouraged the establishment of "poor and lower-middle peasants' associations" to oversee cadre reeducation through public criticism, and to identify enemies (former landlords, rich peasants, and bad elements who were supposedly reviving capitalism in the countryside). He wanted the work teams, sent by the party center to investigate local cadres, to collaborate with the masses. In each instance of deviation the Maoists saw the evil role of bourgeois class consciousness and so strove for ideological rectification. Mao's desire was to see that the campaign was firmly based on the slogans "never forget class struggle" and "put politics in command."[15]

But the pragmatists, still worried about production, were more interested in taking action against corrupt cadres rather than in opening a mass campaign against them. Their goal was higher production through discipline and efficiency, not through Maoist-style social upheaval that may or may not raise socialist consciousness. It soon became apparent that there was a wide divergence of viewpoints between the two sides.

As the movement unfolded. Mao felt it necessary to define his goals more clearly. In May 1963 he promulgated a set of guidelines that came to be known as the First Ten Points. Mao stressed the importance for cadres to understand the need for class struggle, which alone could provide correct leadership, and to participate in farm labor to guarantee mass line ties and to keep the peasants from becoming alienated. Mao also recommended that the poor and lower-middle peasant associations be revitalized and mobilized to supervise the work of the basic-level cadres. This would be the proper way to help in the rectification of the cadres and in carrying out the "Four Cleanups" movement; clean up corruption in accounts, grain collection, properties, and work-point distribution.

At the same time Mao called on the youths of China to study Lei Feng. Lei Feng was a PLA soldier who, although he died at a young age, was a model Maoist: Apart from always quoting Mao Ze-dong, he was selfless, anti-individualist, and had dedicated his life to the service of the masses. It was not accidental that the Maoist model was found in the very Maoist PLA and not among the millions in the party or the Communist Youth League.

However, the pragmatists were confident that Mao could not reverse their new policies. In fact, in 1963 Liu Shao-qi, Zhou Enlai, Chen Yi, Peng Zhen, and Deng Xiao-ping all went on state or diplomatic visits abroad, not overly worried about Mao's activities. Indeed, when they felt that Mao's Ten Points were likely to create political confusion, they issued the Second Ten Points in September 1963. The new directive was drafted by Deng Xiao-ping and Peng Zhen.

The Second Ten Points revealed that the party was generally averse to any class-struggle mass movement that would have an unsettling effect on the economy and politics of the country. While paying lip service to Mao, the Second Ten Points restrained the rural masses from any direct political action and played down the evil effect of so-called capitalism, declaring that many of the new marketing and trading practices in the countryside were legitimate. The pragmatists were worried that poor peasants who had improved their economic condition would be reclassified as "upper-middle" and struggled against. In the interest of production, material incentives could not be allowed to be replaced with ideological incentives. This step would run counter to the basic policies that had been introduced to rehabilitate the Chinese economy; in 1962, 30 percent of the grain production came from private plots, although they formed only 5 to 10 percent of the total cultivated area.

The pragmatists also did not see the errant behavior of the cadres as a class product but rather as a deviation that needed disciplining according to the party constitution. The effect of the directive was that work teams sent to the countryside by the party center, instead of inciting and leading peasant struggle meetings, began to work in close collaboration with the local principal cadres to investigate the basic-level cadres. In 1967, when the Maoists had come to power, they condemned the Second Ten Points for "completely [discarding] the line, principle and policies . . . which Chairman Mao had explicitly formulated in the First Ten Points."[16]

Apparently as a countermove the leftists launched a Learn from the PLA campaign (February 1964), which can be considered an attack on the party structure and party work style. The PLA, under Lin Bao, emphasized political indoctrination and unquestioned loyalty to Mao Ze-dong and was supposedly a model of ideological purity, civic virtue, and moral perfection. The officers lived and worked with the common soldiers for a certain period every year (in 1965 they would give up wearing special uniforms or any insignia indicating rank) and delighted in propagating the "living study and living use of Mao Ze-dong Thought." By mid-1964, the General Political Department of the PLA published a small, pocket-sized book with a red jacket entitled *Quotations from Chairman Mao Ze-dong*. After 1966 there was perhaps no one in China, except preschool children, who did not carry the *Little Red Book* on his or her person.

Mao demanded that a political control system, based on and associated with the General Political Department of the PLA, be introduced into regional and provincial organizations, industrial and commercial enterprises, and even the various ministries of the government and the bureaus and departments under them. The party accepted the proposal, but, as it had done with the Socialist Education Movement, it undermined the Maoist thrust by not allowing the new political departments in the higher organs of the government to be staffed by military men and by making the political departments subordinate to the existing structural authority.

The year 1964 was one of confusion. The conflicting approaches to the Socialist Education Movement resulted in neither side gaining ground. Liu could not consolidate the party at the basic level, and Mao could not get the party to reduce the so-called capitalistic tendencies in the countryside or to accept the supervision of revolutionary masses over its ground-level operations. It appears that by mid-1964 Liu Shao-qi, partly because of the findings of his wife, Wang Guang-mei, who had gone incognito to investigate conditions in the countryside, became alarmed at the extent of the corruption among the basic-level cadres. To deal with the situation, and perhaps to appease Mao, Liu issued a new set of directives, Revised Later Ten Points, in September 1964. The directives, which quoted extensively from Mao's writings and were ostensibly intended to implement Mao's policies, in reality continued to blunt the radical thrust of the Maoist movement. Mao later criticized the directive as being left in form but right in essence.

It was also in 1964 that the Maoists realized that they had failed in their attempt to suppress the anti-Maoist intellectuals or to revolutionize the existing world of literature and art, and they began a movement to rectify the situation. The key figure in this movement was Mao's wife, Jiang Qing, who had been a small-time stage and film actress in the 1930s but who thought of herself as a great revolutionary artist. After having succeeded in getting the Hai Rui play withdrawn, she tried in 1963 to get a Beijing opera troupe to drop the performance of a traditional opera and stage in its place an opera she had been working on, *Shajiabang*. Peng Zhen, the mayor of Beijing and the patron of arts and letters, did not take her seriously. The result was that she got Mao to praise her opera and attack the ministry of culture as a protector of bourgeois ideas. Finally, on the urging of Mao Ze-dong, who had criticized the literary workers for being on the brink of revisionism, Liu, Deng Xiaoping, and Peng Zhen agreed (January 1964) to promote socialist art. But once again, apart from empty rhetoric and lip service to Mao, no radical changes were made in altering the tone of the literary and art productions.

As the battle lines became clearer, Mao attacked other aspects of the current policies followed by the pragmatists by launching a whole series of mass campaigns, such as the Five Anti Movement and the Movement to Cultivate Revolutionary Successors. Mao used these movements, which never gained tremendous popular support, to pinpoint areas where the party had failed. For example, he criticized the educational system for producing bourgeois intellectuals rather than "revolutionary successors," those who could carry on the revolutionary ideals after Mao's generation had passed away. He wanted the period of schooling to be reduced and study to be combined with labor. He also felt that there was much greater need for schools to increase the enrollment of children with worker, peasant, and soldier backgrounds. Teachers and students should go to the countryside and live for a certain number of months with the peasants, "to get some experience of class struggle—that's what I call a university. . . . None of the stuff I learned in thirteen years [of my schooling] was any good for making revolution."[17]

Particular mention should be made of the Learn from Dazhai and Learn from Daqing movements. The Maoists upheld Dazhai, a poor commune in Shanxi, as a model for the country to follow because it had prospered by maintaining the collective spirit and emphasizing self-reliance. Chen Yong-gui, the head of the commune, became an overnight hero. (In 1980, four years after Mao's death, the party revealed that Chen was personally corrupt and that he had falsified statistics. The party produced data to show that Dazhai's prosperity had been artificially created by pumping large amounts of state funds into the commune.) Similarly, the workers of the Daqing oil field were eulogized for their herculean efforts to improve oil output without any financial rewards.

It appears that by the end of 1964 Mao had come to the grave conclusion that all his exhortations were in vain and that no mass campaign was likely to succeed as long as the current party leadership was not rectified. On January 14, 1965, he drew up the last of the series of directives for the Socialist Education Movement, The Twenty-three Articles, which stated, among other things,

> In the cities and villages alike, there exists serious, acute class struggle. . . . This class struggle is necessarily reflected within the Party. . . .
>
> The key point of this movement is to *rectify those people in those positions of authority within the Party who take the capitalist road* [emphasis added], and to progressively consolidate and develop the socialist battlefront in the urban and rural areas.
>
> Of those people in positions of authority who take the capitalist road, some are out in the open and some are concealed. Of the people who support them some . . . are at higher levels. . . .
>
> Among those at higher levels there are some people . . . [even in] provincial and Central Committee departments, *who oppose socialism* [emphasis added].[18]

Mao's attempt to radicalize the Socialist Education Movement, however, failed. Indeed, 1965 saw the deradicalization of the movement. In retrospect, it looks as if the pragmatists had decided to take their stand in public. The party, and one can use that term because the majority of the Politburo leaders were against Mao, reemphasized the need for experts and attacked the idea that political reliability and revolutionary consciousness were more important than expertise. In the press and in public forums, people were allowed to decry the waste of time involved in political meetings and compulsory physical labor and to demand more leisure time and improvements in the standard of living. In March, Deng and Liu convened a meeting of the Central Committee Secretariat at which they criticized the 1964 Jiang Qing/Mao campaign against writers and artists as excessive, hampering "prosperity in creation." Deng complained that "right now, some people [do not dare] to write articles. . . . We are forbidden to stage this and that." The decision by the leaders was that in the future any criticism of notable personalities must have the "approval of the Central Committee."[19] Simultaneously, it appears that an attempt was being made to raise the stature of Liu Shao-qi, chairman of the PRC, to that of Mao Ze-dong, chairman of the party. Pictures of Chairman Liu, of the same size as those of Mao, began to appear along with those of Chairman Mao.

The reasons for these developments are not yet wholly clear, but it may be that the commencement of massive bombing of North Vietnam by the United States in February 1965 and the across-the-board failure of China's foreign policy in that year made the pragmatists feel that it was imperative for China to halt all campaigns that could lead to internal turmoil and upheaval. Furthermore, those such as Lo Rui-qing, chief of the general staff, who believed that there was danger of China being drawn into the Vietnam War, argued in favor of a reconciliation with the Soviet Union, as the only country that could guarantee arms aid to China.

The actions of the pragmatists only helped to further confirm Mao's view that the real threat to China came not from without but from within, from the revisionists in the party who were out to destroy China's revolution.

From 1960 to 1965 Mao had carried on a foreign policy that attacked both the imperialists led by the United States and the revisionists led by the Soviet Union. In 1962 he had enunciated the theory of "two intermediary zones"—Asia, Africa, and Latin America as the "first zone" and the more developed countries of Western Europe and Japan as the "second zone." China hoped that the two zones would form a united front to destroy the capitalist-imperialist America and the socialist-imperialist Russia; China, however, concentrated its activities in the first zone (the Third World) to gain client states and foster Chinese-style revolution.

In the beginning the Chinese efforts appeared to meet with success. The world international Communist movement was split between pro-Moscow and pro-Beijing Communist parties, and several Third World countries began to accept Chinese aid and leadership. However, as time passed, it became evident that China's encouragement of socialist revolutions was not welcome to the newly liberated Afro-Asian countries, and so Chinese policies came to be looked on with suspicion. In 1965 Burundi expelled all Chinese diplomats; Dahomey, the Central African Republic, and Ghana broke off relations with China; China could not keep the Soviet Union from participating in the second Afro-Asian Conference scheduled to be held in Algiers; and the Communist party of Indonesia, backed by China, failed in its attempt at a coup. As a generalization it may be said that China now stood isolated from the larger world order.

In this context Lin Biao, speaking for Mao Ze-dong, published an article entitled "Long Live the Victory of the People's War!"[20] (September 1965). The article extolled the self-reliant manner in which the Chinese Communists, relying on the masses and using guerrilla strategy and mobile warfare tactics, working from the countryside and surrounding the cities, had won victory against the Japanese and Guomindang.

The article likened the Third World to the "rural areas of the world," which surrounded North America and Western Europe, "the cities of the world," and suggested that global "people's wars" could liquidate the imperialist enemy. Lo Rui-qing's defensive posture and military professionalism stood in stark contrast to the dynamism of Lin Biao's thesis. According to Lin, if China were attacked, it could defeat the enemy through the well-tried people's war tactics and did not need sophisticated weaponry. Incidentally, the article also implied that other countries could do the same and China did not have to go beyond its borders to help them.

By the end of the year Lo, the organization man, was removed from office for advocating military professionalism, and the path was cleared for the greater participation of Lin Biao and the PLA in national affairs.

However, the open conflict between Mao and his opponents began not over military issues but over cultural ones. Earlier in 1965 Mao did the extraordinary: He appointed Peng Zhen, mayor of Beijing, a member of the Politburo, and a recognized Liuist, to head a five-person "cultural revolution group." Peng was caught in a dilemma. If he rectified the dissident intellectuals, he would be attacking many of his own subordinates and therefore indirectly condemning himself for following incorrect policies. The only way out for Peng was to use tactics of evasion, quite in keeping with the rest of the party leadership, and thwart Mao's effort to revolutionize literature and the arts. In the long run Mao's move proved to be brilliant because Peng became the symbol of the revisionists in the party and an open target for denunciation.

In September 1965, at an enlarged session of the Standing Committee of the Politburo, Mao, irritated no doubt by Peng's foot-dragging, suggested that a campaign to rectify the dissident intellectuals be opened with an attack on Wu Han and his play *Hai Rui Dismissed from Office.* According to Jürgen Domes, for the first time in his career Mao was humiliated by an outright refusal by the party to accept his demand; four persons (including Lin Biao) supported Mao, whereas Liu and Deng had the support of five; Zhou En-lai abstained.[21]

Many scholars feel that at this point Mao

had finally lost control of the party. Whether or not that is true, it can be said with confidence that Mao had indeed lost his personal influence with the majority of the top leaders in the party. Although it may not have been clear at the time, Mao was, however, not wholly without institutional power to affect Chinese politics. In 1965, as the party became less responsive to his directions, Mao deliberately upgraded the role of the PLA in civilian politics. Lin Biao, whose authority had been increased by his appointment as head of all public security forces and the first-ranking vice-premier, had speeded up the radicalization of the PLA by abolishing all military ranks and insignia in May 1965. Later in the year, his authority was enhanced further when Lo Rui-qing was dismissed. Although the PLA had yet to exert its power in the cities, in many rural areas militia and regular PLA cadres had been elected as commune functionaries and had become an active force in the rural political scene by the end of the year. At the same time a Mao-study campaign was launched in the countryside to provide ideological indoctrination to rectify incorrect thinking.

However, since Beijing had become a "watertight kingdom," which, as Mao later put it, "could not be penetrated even by a needle,"[22] Mao retreated to Shanghai to prepare for the onslaught on the party in the form of the Great Proletarian Cultural Revolution.

NOTES

1. For the text in English see *Survey of China Mainland Press,* No. 4032, October 2, 1967.

2. See Stuart Schram, ed., *Chairman Mao Talks to the People* (New York: Pantheon Books, 1974), pp. 131–46.

3. *The Case of P'eng Te-huai* (Hong Kong: URI, 1968), p. 34.

4. See "China's Industry on the Upswing," *Beijing Review,* 27, no. 35 (August 27, 1984), 19.

5. Roderick MacFarquhar, *The Origins of the Cultural Revolution, vol. II: The Great Leap Forward, 1958–1960* (New York: Columbia University Press, 1983), p. 330.

6. Quoted in Jürgen Domes, *The Internal Politics of China, 1949–1972* (London: C. Hurst, 1973), p. 127.

7. See Harold C. Hinton, ed., *The People's Republic of China, 1949–1979: A Documentary Survey,* vol. II (Wilmington, DE: Scholarly Resources, 1980), pp. 839–55.

8. "Developing the First Atom Bomb," *Beijing Review,* 27, no. 50 (December 10, 1984), 31–32.

9. See *Current Background,* no. 892 (October 21, 1969), 6.

10. *Resolution on CPC History (1949–81)* (Beijing: Foreign Languages Press, 1981), pp. 27–30.

11. For these quotations and an extended discussion of the intellectuals' attacks on Mao, see Merle Goldman, *China's Intellectuals: Advice and Dissent* (Cambridge, MA: Harvard University Press, 1981), chap. 2.

12. See Mao Ze-dong's "Talk at an Enlarged Central Work Conference," in Schram, *Chairman Mao Talks,* pp. 159–87, 167.

13. Ibid., p. 184.

14. Ibid., p. 195.

15. For the Maoist position see Hinton, *People's Republic,* vol. II, pp. 952–60.

16. "Struggle Between Two Roads in China's Countryside," *Peking Review,* no. 49 (December 1, 1967).

17. Mao Ze-dong, "Talk on Questions of Philosophy," August 18, 1964, in Schram, *Chairman Mao Talks,* pp. 213–14.

18. See Hinton, *People's Republic,* vol. II, pp. 988–89.

19. Lowell Dittmer, *Liu Shao-ch'i and the Chinese Cultural Revolution* (Berkeley: University of California Press, 1974), p. 61.

20. For the full text see Lin Piao, *Long Live the Victory of the People's War* (Beijing: Foreign Languages Press, 1965).

21. See Domes, *Internal Politics of China,* p. 142.

22. *Survey of China Mainland Press,* no. 4200 (June 18, 1968), 2.

CHAPTER 10

From the Cultural Revolution to Mao's Death: 1966–1976

Shifting the emphasis from socialist education to cultural revolution was not accidental. To Mao Ze-dong, all campaigns of thought reform and socialist education were aimed at changing the ideas, values, and habits of mind that were a part of China's tradition. In other words, Mao wanted to revolutionize inherited culture, replace it with socialist culture, and thus change the nature of the Chinese people.

According to Marx, the superstructure (social consciousness) is a product of the social economic base; and the social system associated with the ownership of the means of production. Socialist social consciousness would therefore rise after the establishment of the public ownership of the means of production and the development of a Communist economic base. This is a rather simplified analysis of the Marxist theory, but it suffices to show that if one were to follow the orthodox Marxist line, China had a long way to go before it manifested any signs of socialist (i.e., Communist) consciousness. Mao, having reached the age of 72 and fearing that he had not many years left, could not wait that long. In any case, he firmly believed that the people, imbued with the correct ideological spirit, acquired an indomitable will and could overcome insurmountable obstacles. These performers of miracles did not need to depend on such materialistic factors as an advanced economic base. In other words, socialist consciousness could be created through a proper dose of indoctrination and could emerge before the objective material stage was reached.

Since Beijing leaders had not responded to Mao's call for a cultural revolution, Mao began his national cleansing operation from the more congenial environment of Shanghai. Although the Great Proletarian Cultural Revolution (as distinguished from the half-hearted cultural revolution conducted by Peng Zhen) officially started in May 1966, its origins can be traced to an article written by a comparatively unknown writer, Yao Wenyuan, and published in a nonparty Shanghai newspaper, *Wen Hui-bao,* on November 10, 1965. The article bitterly criticized *Hai Rui Dismissed from Office* and its author, Wu Han, the deputy mayor of Beijing. Although it was not known immediately that Mao had revised the manuscript several times (as had Jiang Qing and another close friend of Mao's, Zhang Chun-qiao, the head of propaganda in the Shanghai Party Committee), it was obvious that he had approved it for publication. Since Peng Zhen, the party boss in Beijing, had not only been responsible for allowing Wu Han to publish the play but had also, as head of the cultural revolution group, not done anything about it, Yao's article could also be construed as an attack on Peng.

The Central Committee newspaper, *The People's Daily,* produced in Beijing, which had been the forum for so many anti-Mao articles, delayed all action on the article until it was forced to reprint it after *Liberation Army Daily* had published it and thus brought it to national attention. Even when it reproduced the article, the *People's Daily* suggested in its editorials that the matter must be looked on as an academic question. As a result, articles supporting and opposing Wu Han began to appear in the press.

When Peng Zhen realized that this approach would not appease Mao, he finally decided to take a position on the issue and criticized Wu Han's "academic" point of view. Although support for Wu Han suddenly disappeared from the press and Wu Han was forced to make self-criticism, Peng Zhen's cultural revolution group appeared to have succeeded in developing a thesis (the February Outline) that kept the matter from becoming political.

In the meantime the Maoists, Lin Biao and Jiang Qing in particular, working under the aegis of the PLA, produced a document of their own that repudiated the Peng Zhen line and advocated that all academic questions be judged in political terms. The Military Affairs Commission approved the document in March 1966.

Mao also opened another front against the party over the issue of educational reform, reiterating that students should not be spending so much time attending classes and that they

> must go down and engage in industry, agriculture and commerce. . . . Many great inventors, such as Watt and Edison, came from workers' families. . . . Many of the great scholars and scientists did not go through college. Not many of the comrades in our Party's Central Committee are university graduates.[1]

By March 1966 the Red Flag Militant Team had been established by the students in the secondary school attached to Beijing University, which began to pressure the university authorities for reforms.

In late March, Mao, now back in Beijing, unleashed his criticism of Peng Zhen at a meeting of the Politburo. In April, after some foot-dragging, the Beijing Party Committee published a self-criticism in a three-page editorial in the *People's Daily.* All these efforts came to naught, however, because on May 16 the Politburo in an enlarged meeting (enlarged with Mao supporters) revoked the February Outline, dissolved Peng's cultural revolution group, attacked Peng and some of his colleagues for attempting a coup (a totally ridiculous charge), and established the new Cultural Revolution Group made up of recognized Maoists: Chen Bo-da (member of the Standing Committee of the Politburo and formerly Mao's secretary), Kang Sheng (member of the Standing Committee of the Politburo), and Jiang Qing. Peng Zhen disappeared from public view, as did several other party leaders in charge of propaganda and culture. The fact that this purge, and purge it surely was, had been accepted by other pragmatist leaders quietly (there was no public announcement regarding the dismissal of Peng and the others) and without protest meant that the top echelon of the Liuist leadership was trying to save itself by sacrificing their protégés, just as Peng had sacrificed Wu Han. This process, if not halted, could work itself all the way to the top—which is exactly what happened within the next several months.

On May 16, 1966, a circular, said to be drafted by Mao himself, was issued in the name of the Central Committee for circulation among all committees of the party, government, and the PLA organizations, down to the provincial level. The May 16 circular became the programmatic document of the Great Proletarian Cultural Revolution (GPCR). The document attacked Peng's line for "proceeding from a bourgeois stand and the bourgeois world outlook . . . [which] completely transposes the enemy and ourselves, putting the one into the position of the other." It went on to say,

> Our country is now in an upsurge of the Great Proletarian Cultural Revolution which is pounding at all the decadent ideological and cultural positions still held by the bourgeoisie and the remnants of feudalism. . . .
>
> Those representatives of the bourgeoisie who have sneaked into the Party, the government, the army, and the various spheres of culture are *a bunch of counterrevolutionary revisionists*. . . . Some of them we have already seen through, others we have not. Some we still trust and are training as our successors. There are, for example, people of the Khrushchev brand still nestling in our midst. Party committees at all levels must pay full attention to this matter [emphasis added].[2]

The document also made a pointed reference to the academic authorities, who needed to be made a target for attack because they opposed socialism.

The political situation was very anomalous and confusing. Mao was working against the party leadership, yet the new Cultural Revolution Group (CRG) was placed directly under the Standing Committee of the Politburo, which meant under Liu. The CRG, however, took orders from Mao and not the party leaders. Indeed, it was shortly to become responsible for destroying the party structure. Similarly, Mao used the Chinese youths, an outside element, to attack the party; yet the Red Guards, as the Maoist youths soon came to be known, took orders from the CRG.

What was Mao's relationship to the party? It would appear that Mao, whatever his personal feelings about the matter, played God. Since the party, as it existed, was not to his liking, he tried to reshape it by first destroying it, and he destroyed it by using nonparty forces. To that extent he was the leader of all Chinese and not just a party member who could be restrained by the party constitution or party discipline. But since he continued to preserve a linkage with the party and seek party authorization for his actions (e.g., give the CRG a position within the party structure), he can still be considered a party member working from within the party framework, although he purged his opposition from the leading organs of the party in a most unconstitutional manner. The GPCR was a coup from without as well as a coup from within. The rank-and-file party members, who never understood the complexity of Mao's motivations or his style of action, got crushed by the juggernaut that Mao let loose.

It was from the educational institutions that the GPCR was to gain the main body of its fighting force. Large numbers of students were attracted to Mao's call inciting them to rebel against educational authorities. There were many reasons for this attraction. The children from the working and peasant classes in secondary schools were frustrated because they could not compete with the better-prepared children from urban professional families (erstwhile bourgeois families) for the extremely limited seats in institutions of higher learning. Many talented students were disgruntled because children of high party and government officials often managed to get into better schools (which after graduation, meant better jobs) because of their official connections, students in universities were unhappy because they were not allowed to study the subjects of their choice, and there was a general frustration with the rigid party policies and its heavy-handed approach to academic problems. Ironically, the students in the late 1960s were ready to revolt for many of the same reasons that had led the generation of the late 1950s to take up the challenge of the Hundred Flowers campaign, but this time only the leftist students were allowed to participate in the campaign, and Mao was on their side against the party apparatus. The most important reason for participation in the GPCR, however, was the idealism of the young men and women whose imagination was fired by Mao's vision.

In May, as developments in Beijing University showed, the party academic authorities were still not ready to accept a Hundred Flowers-style massive, uncontrolled attack from the students. Indeed, Lu Ping, president of Beijing University, managed to suppress the activities of the volatile Miss Nie, a teacher who had posted a wall newspaper on May 25 that was a passionate call to arms:

> Now is the time for all revolutionary intellectuals to go into battle! Let us unite and hold high the great red banner of Mao Tse-tung's thought . . . resolutely, thoroughly, totally and completely wipe out all monsters and demons and all counterrevolutionary revisionists of the Khruschev type, and carry the socialist revolution through to the end.[3]

Mao, however, endorsed the poster, and under his orders it was broadcast by Beijing Radio (June 1) and published in the *People's Daily* (June 2). Students from various Beijing schools and colleges responded promptly by plunging into revolutionary activity, which at first generally meant holding mass meetings, writing posters attacking those in authority, and categorizing people as friends or enemies according to their class background.

Although various categories were drawn up in different places and at different times, the most popular were the five red categories of good people, who came from the families of workers, poor and lower-middle peasants, Maoist cadres (revolutionary cadres), army men, and martyrs; and the four black categories of bad people, whose family background could be traced to landlords, rich peasants, counterrevolutionaries, and "bad elements." Students compelled the school party committees to hand over confidential records so that the black elements could be located and attacked.

The Liuists, in a manner reminiscent of the Socialist Educational Movement, tried to control the campaign by sending party work teams to the schools and colleges. Mao wanted the order for work teams to be revoked, but the party ignored his request. The work teams often picked the most radical students and attacked them for rightist tendencies and made them "confess" their "crimes." Since the work teams were supposedly also upholding the Thought of Mao Ze-dong, there was confusion concerning who were the legitimate defenders of the truth. Now personal loyalty to Mao became the distinguishing factor. All others, who were acting on orders from the party center, were traitors, "waving the red flag to attack the red flag."

In mid-June middle schools, colleges, and universities were closed for six months, apparently to allow the students and faculty to take part in the GPCR (the schools actually remained closed for the duration of the GPCR, until 1968–1969; the colleges and universities even longer, until the early 1970s). If the Liuists thought that this action would disband the students, they were mistaken. The students simply occupied the schools and made them their headquarters.

During these summer months the cultural revolution also spread to the cities in the provinces, but there the local party committees were in a better position to control the campaign by establishing their own Red Guard groups.

On July 16 Mao did something that no man had done before him or is likely to do after him: He plunged into the Yangtze River and broke all records by swimming 15 kilometers in 65 minutes. There are various theories about the event, ranging from those that declare that it was entirely staged to those that suggest underwater frogmen carried Mao downstream. Anyway, the news story and the photograph of Mao swimming the river proved that Mao was physically in the best of health (there had been rumors that he was ailing) and symbolically that no opposition was too formidable to be overcome. Incidentally, to the ecstatic masses this was another confirmation of Mao's superhuman qualities.

After this feat, Mao came to Beijing ready to attack the party *appartchiks* and turn the GPCR into a genuine Maoist mass movement. Maoist PLA units occupied the offices of the party center and surrounded the residences of the top party leaders, who thus suddenly lost their capacity to counterattack. Mao now came out in public support of the Red Guards and published his own big-character poster, entitled "Bombard the Headquarters."[4] in which he made it clear that his target was Liu and his colleagues, the "leading comrades" who had established a "bourgeois dictatorship" and imposed a "white terror" that "struck down the surging movement of the Great Cultural Revolution of the Proletariat."

To give the movement an air of legitimacy, the Maoists then convened a rump plenum of the Central Committee, which although lacking a quorum, adopted the "Decision Concerning the Great Proletarian Revolution" (August 8) and set the stage for a change in the superstructure by weeding out right deviationists and revisionists in the party, reorganizing education, and establishing new mass organizations such as cultural revolutionary groups and committees. The communique concluded with the admonition:

> In the course of the GPCR it is necessary to hold high the great red banner of the thought of Mao Tse-tung and to place proletarian politics in command. The movement for creatively studying and applying Chairman Mao's works must be launched among the broad masses of workers, peasants and soldiers, cadres and intellectuals. The thought of Mao Tse-tung must be regarded as a compass to the Cultural Revolution.[5]

Ignoring the party constitution that authorized changes only at party congresses, the Maoists purged the Politburo Standing Committee and reorganized it, thereby gaining 8 of the 11 votes. Lin Biao was made the sole vice-chair and Liu was demoted to the eighth position.

Later in the year the second edition of the *Little Red Book* appeared with a foreword by Lin Biao, which indicates to what degree the cult of Mao was being fostered:

> Comrade Mao Tse-tung is the greatest Marxist-Leninist of our time. Comrade Mao Tse-tung has, with genius and in a creative and all-around way, inherited, defended, and developed Marxism-Leninism, advancing it to a completely new stage. . . . Once Mao Tse-tung's thought is mastered by the broad masses, it will become an inexhaustible source of strength and an infinitely powerful spiritual atom bomb.[6]

However, at this stage the PLA itself was wisely kept out of the campaign and allowed to carry out its own low-key cultural revolution.

THE GREAT PROLETARIAN CULTURAL REVOLUTION: 1966–1969

"To Rebel Is Justified"

August 18 marked the beginning of the new order. Over a million young people, wearing armbands with the Chinese characters for Red Guard, rallied in the Tiananmen Square in Beijing and greeted the new leaders, who were all significantly dressed in army uniforms. Mao also wore the Red Guard armband and became their "supreme commander." There were several more such demonstrations, and by the end of the year more than 10 million Red Guards had met the Great Helmsman, as Mao came to be called. The rallies were emotionally charged. Thousands wept hysterically when they saw Mao in person; many who had the unbelievable good fortune of shaking hands with the leader did not wash their hands for days afterward. Hours of singing the hymns "The East is Red" (which likened Mao's appearance in China to the rising of the sun) and "Sailing the Seas Depends on the Helmsman" and of shouting slogans made their voices hoarse, and ceaseless waving of the *Little Red Book* left their arms limp with exhaustion but in no way diminished the euphoria of the youths dedicated to the Maoist cause.

The speeches at these rallies were usually given by Lin Biao, Chen Bo-da, Jiang Qing, and Zhou En-lai. The theme was the reconstruction of China through the complete destruction of old ideologies, old culture, old customs, and old habits (the Four Olds).

The Red Guards, the "revolutionary successors," took their task seriously and began to make revolution the way it made sense to them. Groups of revolutionary rebels, some in their early teens, rampaged in the cities, creating a reign of terror. "Bourgeois" homes were broken into; "black" family members were physically beaten and tortured; and their possessions, such as "old" books and traditional-style paintings and furniture, were thrown into bonfires. Temples, churches, museums, and libraries were ransacked and damaged. Among those beaten to death in Beijing was the great Chinese novelist Lao She.

However, lacking an organizational structure and well-defined guidelines, the Red Guards began to split into factions. Children of high officials tended to be students of the same school and thus have their own organization. Some radical groups denounced class background as "the reactionary theory of lineage" and allowed children from the black category to join them. Red Guards associated with different educational institutions or attached to various departments and bureaus of the government had their own camps. Because of differing loyalties or differing perceptions of how far the radical policies should extend, some Red Guard units considered themselves more elite than others. Then, of course, there were Red Guards who were vying for leadership positions and so decided to take their followers and break away from the main body.

By the end of the year diverse groups of radical workers (who called themselves "revolutionary rebels" and "red rebels"), instigated by the CRG to make revolution in the factories and mines, had joined the Red Guards. Finding the party bureaucracy of the All-China Federation of Trade Unions hesitant in initiating unrest and revolt among the workers, the CRG dissolved that organization and replaced it with the All-China Red Workers General Rebellion Corps.

As the party and government cadres, particularly those in the provinces, managed to resist the Red Guards and stay on in their posts of authority, the goal of the radical Maoists became clearer: The revolutionaries must seize power from the national and provincial power holders, meaning Liu and his supporters in Beijing and party secretaries and the chairs of the regional bureaus. Clearly the old control apparatus was to be destroyed; but what organizational structure was to replace it? The idea that the 1871 Paris commune would provide a model was mooted and obviously accepted by some.

"Destruction Before Construction"

In the winter of 1966–1967, with the logistic aid of the PLA, the Red Guards and revolutionary rebels managed to undermine the existing party and government apparatus in major cities and provincial capitals but failed to unite and establish new political mechanisms. For example, in Shanghai the revolutionaries who had seized power proclaimed the establishment of the Shanghai Commune, but the vast number of radical factions, bickering and clamoring to get their representatives into the ruling committee, proved that they were better at creating chaos than at establishing order.

As the party- and state-controlled structures collapsed and internecine fighting broke out between the less radical and the more radical groups, the Maoists had to call on the regional military forces of the PLA to intervene and "support the broad masses of the Left." The authority of the military was extended over state and party offices, radio stations, transportation, security organs, and industrial and commercial units. Realizing that the country could not do without the help of the experienced cadres and specialists, the CRG now ordered that the country compulsorily follow a new organizational model, the Revolutionary Committee (RC), based on a "triple alliance" among army officers, revolutionary (Maoist) party cadres, and representatives of revolutionary mass organizations. In February the Shanghai commune itself was transformed into an RC. Within the next year or so, the RCs took over the earlier role of the party and state organs and began to administer districts, provinces, cities, factories, mines, schools, and colleges; but in the interim, signs of chaos increased in every province.

The PLA Enters the Scene

As can be imagined, the active introduction of the PLA into the political arena meant an immediate diluting of the power of the masses to make and lead revolution. It also meant that those PLA commanders who were not in favor of continued chaos suppressed the more radical factions (the favored approach was first to dub these factions as counterrevolutionary) in favor of the moderate ones and rehabilitated some of the purged party leaders. Many Red Guard groups that had for one reason or another been left out of the "grand alliances" of rebel groups from which the representatives of the rebel masses were to be drawn for the triple alliances, refused to accept the PLA verdict and responded by attacking the army. Often such armed clashes only helped to strengthen the army's resolve to enforce law and order by arresting recalcitrant Red Guards. For example, by the end of March, 20,000 were in jail in Chengdu alone.

However, just when it appeared that the cultural revolution was possibly drawing to a close, Mao gave it another boost and renewed its momentum. In Beijing the situation had been so far under fairly reasonable control. Some party leaders, like Peng Zhen, did undergo trial by the masses, but both Liu Shao-qi and Deng Xiao-ping, who had been under indirect attack since the fall of 1966, still remained unindicted. In March 1967 Mao decided to get the enlarged Politburo Standing Committee to censure Liu and Deng. Although even then he could muster a majority of only one vote, it was a signal for a massive campaign against Liu, "China's Khrushchev," "the top party person taking the capitalist road."[7]

Liu had made several self-examinations and even a confession, but this in no way saved him from being accused of being an anti-Mao counterrevolutionary and being subjected to Red Guard trials and public humiliation. By the fall, Liu was under detention, and a year later, at the Twelfth Plenary Session of the CPC in October 1968, Liu was officially denounced as a "renegade, traitor and scab hiding in the party, a lackey of imperialism, modern revisionism and the KMT [Guomindang] reactionaries"[8] and was formally expelled from the CPC. Liu died in detention in 1969. Deng, who had abjectly confessed to being a counterrevolutionary, was removed from all posts but allowed to retain his party membership.

Rise of Ultraleftism

The developments in Beijing in March 1967 led to another upsurge of leftism ("ultraleftism," if we have to distinguish it from what was going on earlier), which resulted not only in the establishment of the Beijing Revolutionary Committee (April 1967) but also in new orders to the PLA restraining it from direct involvement in the cultural revolution in the provinces and forbidding it from taking action against mass organizations. The army could no longer declare any local mass organization to be counterrevolutionary without the approval of the CRG.

The ultraleftists now felt arrogantly self-confident enough to start criticizing Prime Minister Zhou En-lai, who had so far, with the cooperation of the PLA, managed to ward off more serious attacks against many of his senior cabinet members. Since the PLA was no longer allowed to intervene, Zhou found it necessary to sacrifice a number of his subordinates. The work of many of the ministries was seriously handicapped, the Foreign Ministry was paralyzed, and by August Red Guards had begun to victimize foreign diplomats and raid the embassies. All Chinese ambassadors, with the exception of the one in Cairo, had been withdrawn, and China's international relations stood at their lowest point.

Under the new guidelines, with the PLA standing by as a neutral observer, the situation in the provinces became progressively worse as armed factions of Red Guards and Red rebels not only fought each other but also continued the "sinister practices of beating, smashing, looting, ransacking, and arresting [people]."[9] Thousands were killed. On June 8 the Central Committee issued new orders forbidding the revolutionary mass organizations from using violence and making arbitrary arrests. The army was once again made responsible for the enforcement of order. However, since the April order forbidding the army to use firearms against mass organizations had not been withdrawn, the army was caught in a dilemma. Some army commanders found a solution in backing amenable revolutionary groups against the more recalcitrant ones. The amenable organizations were, as can be expected, less radical than the others. This approach of the army was naturally unacceptable to the radicals and resulted in a new set of crises. The most notable of these was the Wuhan incident.

The Wuhan Incident

Wuhan, the capital of Hubei, comprises the three cities of Hankou, Hanyang, and Wuchang and straddles the Yangtze at the Beijing-Guangzhou railway bridge. It is one of the more important industrial and political centers of China. General Chen Zai-dao, who had served the Communist cause for 40 years and had been in charge of the Wuhan military region since 1954, had tried to control the course of the cultural revolution as it zigged and zagged through the first half of 1967. The task had not been easy. Not only were the factionalized mass organizations fighting one another, but also the military command itself was split.

Even before the June orders, Chen had been backing a less radical mass organization by the impossible name of Wuhan Area Proletarian Revolutionary Liaison Center of Mao Tse-tung Thought Million Heroic Troops (Million Heroes for short) against a more radical one called Mao Tse-tung Thought Fighting Team's Wuhan Workers General Headquarters (Workers Headquarters). These were large organizations, and their total membership was about a million; the Workers Headquarters included more local students, as well as the Red Guards sent from Beijing to Wuhan. The fighting between the rival organizations had resulted in hundreds of deaths; the closure of factories and mines; and several times, the stoppage of traffic over the Yangtze bridge. By mid-June, the situation in Wuhan was anarchic.

On June 17 and 18 General Chen helped the Million Heroes to surround and attack the Workers Headquarters. Nearly 300 youths were beaten to death and over 1,000 injured. As the days passed, the skirmishes increased, and some 2,000 industrial enterprises had to close down or reduce operations.

The continuing violence alarmed Beijing, and sometime in the first half of July, Zhou En-lai personally went to Wuhan to examine the situation. His findings appear to have been that Chen had erred in supporting the less radical group, the Million Heroes, and that Chen should now shift his backing to the Workers Headquarters and try to help the warring groups establish a grand alliance. Zhou then went back to Beijing, leaving Xie Fu-zhi and Wang Li (two members of the CRG and its troubleshooters, who had arrived in Wuhan on July 14; Xie was also minister of Public Security) to get the various factions to accept Zhou's verdict.

On July 19, after meeting leaders of the different factions, Wang and Xie summoned Chen and various officers of the Wuhan command and ordered them to accept what was essentially Zhou's original assessment. One of the military commanders was so deeply incensed, as were the members of the Million Heroes, that he allowed his troops to join some of the Heroes to kidnap the two emissaries from Beijing and physically rough them up. The following day, July 20, the Million Heroes, no doubt with the help of these mutinous troops, seized the city of Wuhan, occupying such strategic locations as the radio station, the railway yard, the airport, and the approaches to the Yangtze bridge. News of the mutiny reached Beijing, and the Maoists, who had to impress other military commands with the center's capacity to suppress quickly and effectively such acts of open defiance, rushed troops of an airborne division into the city and ordered gunboats of the East China Fleet to steam upriver to Wuhan. The story of Xie's and Wang's release has not been fully told, but it appears that on July 22 some anti-Chen officers helped them reach a safe airport, where Zhou had already arrived. Wang Li, who had been treated more harshly than Xie, became the hero of the left.

Chen was dismissed, the PLA disarmed and dispersed the mutineers, and peace returned to Wuhan, but the center could no longer be sure of the loyalty of the military commanders to the Maoist cause. After the Wuhan incident, there was a nationwide increase in armed clashes between the various groups of the revolutionary masses, as also between the revolutionary groups and the military. A situation close to civil war existed in some areas in Guangzhou and Sichuan.

Jiang Qing and other radical directors of the cultural revolution managed to use the occasion to get several military leaders, who had either opposed their policies or were viewed as personal enemies, dismissed from important posts. Wang Li, who had a particular reason for being bitter against the army, talked about "the two headquarters within the military establishments."[10]

The Wuhan incident also gave the ultraleftists another opportunity to push the cultural revolution further left by calling for the purging of the PLA and the arming of the revolutionary masses. There were accusations of opportunists within the PLA following the capitalist road, and fear was expressed that they might collaborate with the "capitalist-roader-power-holders" in the party. Mao's acceptance of the policy to arm the left changed the nature and the level of conflict qualitatively. The rebels felt justified in raiding arms depots and arsenals and at certain locations came to possess tanks and heavy artillery.

Retreat to Moderation

By late August the conclusion was reached, obviously by Mao himself, that if the PLA structure was allowed to be destroyed, the last viable national institution holding back a total breakdown of law and order would disappear. The party apparatus was in shambles: The Politburo was nonexistent; only 36 of the 93 full members of the Central Committee were still active; only 5 provincial party chairs out of 28 were still in office; and the 6 regional party bureaus were no longer functioning.

On September 5, 1967, an order was issued jointly by the Central Committee of the CPC, the State Council, the Central Military Affairs Committee, and the Central Cultural Revolution Group, which forbade mass organizations from seizing "under any pretext whatever the arms, ammunition, equipment, vehicles, materials and supplies of the PLA . . . [and any such arms and equipment] that have been seized must all be put under seal and stored."[11] The directive also countermanded the April 6 order and authorized the military to use their guns if necessary in dealing with mass organizations. This action was taken on Mao's initiative; Mao, who had just been on a trip of five central and southern provinces, was persuaded that China was in the throes of a "civil war."

The ultraleftist Maoists were now denounced as "left in form but right in essence," and four (out of the current total of ten) leading members of the CRG, including Wang Li, were arrested on the grounds that they were Guomindang agents! Jiang Qing hurriedly changed her stand and attacked the slogan "Seize the handful in the military forces" (which she herself had coined) as reactionary. The moderates at the center, led by Zhou En-lai, took over the direction of the cultural revolution, and the role of Jiang Qing, the leader of the radicals, was temporarily eclipsed. Articles in the press recommended an early establishment of revolutionary committees and reiterated that 95 percent of the cadres were "good or relatively good" and therefore could be rehabilitated. Primary and secondary schools were to be reopened and Red Guards encouraged to leave the streets and go back to their books; the primary and secondary schools were finally restarted in October, but universities and colleges did not reopen until the fall of 1970.

However, the goal of national stability could not be achieved by merely issuing directives. The difficult question facing Mao and the moderate leaders was how to reduce the overwhelming power acquired by the PLA and rehabilitate the party. The army could not be allowed to become a substitute for the party. The anxiety to hurriedly establish provincial revolutionary committees was no doubt to ensure the return of the party into the administrative picture. The process of establishing RCs nevertheless was slow because representatives of provincial party cadres, revolutionary rebels, and military officials had to be carefully approved by the center before a "triple alliance," the basis of an RC, could be worked out. In many cases it was imperative that the feuding leftist factions form a "grand alliance" and then select mutually acceptable representatives. It was not always easy to isolate the ultraleftists from the leftists.

In January–February 1967, when the call was first made, only Heilongjiang, Shandong, Shanghai municipality, and Guizhou had established RCs. They were followed in March–April by Shanxi and Beijing municipality. After six months of almost total inactivity, the majority of the provincial-level RCs were established between November 1967 and May 1968. This, however, still did not mean that law and order had returned to the country.

The Last Swing to the Left and the End of the Great Proletarian Cultural Revolution

The RCs tended to be conservative not only because they brought back to power some of the old party cadres but also because the triple alliances were often still dominated by the PLA. The disciplinary measures taken by the RCs against the ultraleftist students were resented by the radical youths, who felt betrayed; for example, large numbers of students were transferred to the provinces in a new program of *xia-xiang*. After a few months of quiet, complaints against the RCs—that they represented "rightist reversals of verdicts" and were "reactionaries in authority"—were heard again across the country. There were also some in the Beijing leadership who felt the same way, although they would not have gone as far as the Guangzhou Red Guards, who in the summer of 1968 were to call for an overthrow of Mao and Zhou.

The purge of Yang Cheng-wu, the acting chief of general staff and his supporters, the political commissar of the air force and the military commander of the Beijing garrison, in March 1968, allegedly for having conspired in a rightist plot against Zhou En-lai and Jiang Qing, encouraged the leftists to start a new round of antirightist criticism. The reasons for the Yang affair are still murky (after the fall of Lin Biao, he was condemned for having been an ultraleftist working for the scoundrel Lin), but it appears that Yang's dismissal was a victory for the leftist Jiang Qing and her vastly diminished group.

For the next three months, factional fights erupted once again. This was the last bloody gasp of Mao's GPCR. Arms and ammunition were seized by the rebel groups from trains carrying war material to Vietnam; parts of towns and cities harboring the "enemy" came under seige and were fired on with heavy guns; universities and schools became battle grounds; and the outside world saw a glimpse of what was happening within China when over 100 trussed and bound dead bodies, some headless, floated downriver from Guangxi and Guangdong to Hong Kong waters.

Violence also broke out among Beijing students, who had so far maintained relative calm. It appears that this event finally convinced Mao Ze-dong that the radical students could not be trusted with the great task of revolutionizing Chinese culture. He called the leaders of various Beijing student factions to meet with him on July 28, and he told them, with tears in his eyes, "You have let me down, and what is more, you have disappointed the workers, peasants, and soldiers of China."[12] The Great Helmsman thus ended the political role of the Red Guards and called a halt to the GPCR.

With the blessing of Mao and the backing of the PLA, Worker's Thought of Mao Zedong Propaganda Teams were dispatched to universities and schools to bring discipline to the student bodies. Any lingering spirit of extreme radicalism or extreme conservatism was further dispelled when a vast number of students, cadres, and professionals were dispatched to the countryside to be reeducated by the poor peasants. It is estimated that 20 million persons were forced to migrate from the cities between 1968 and 1969.[13]

The leaders still had to depend on the PLA, the only nationwide organization that had any organizational integrity, to complete the task of establishing the RCs in the few provinces that were still without them and at the district, county, and municipal levels. This task was completed by September 1968, and the Central Committee of the CPC met in October to expel Liu Shao-qi, the "renegade, traitor, and scab," from the party.

AN EVALUATION OF THE CULTURAL REVOLUTION

Whichever way one looks at the great upheaval caused by Mao, one finds it a terribly costly failure. At the broadest level Mao wanted to energize the revolutionary masses to take over power or at least to supervise the functioning of the party and state bureaucracies. This did not take place because the Thought of Mao Ze-dong, the ideology underlying the cultural revolution, lent itself to contradictory interpretations and failed to provide a unifying body of ideas. The ruthlessness with which Mao had turned against Liu Shao-qi and other long-standing, loyal party members and condemned them as long-standing traitors had made it impossible for the revolutionary masses to distinguish between friends and enemies. And what is worse, the frenzy and passion with which the cult of Mao was pushed denied the possibility of the revolution's ever being guided by reason and principles.

Despite Mao's insistence to the contrary, it was never clear whether he genuinely believed that the GPCR would inspire a revolution from below. The Shanghai commune, established in January 1967, was a product of spontaneous mass action and therefore truly "revolutionary." However, it was suppressed by the leadership and replaced with an RC, a most arbitrary action initiated from the top, at the insistence of Mao himself. The periodic shifts in policy from right to left confused the revolutionary groups, who in any case proved themselves incapable of unifying and coordinating their activities or of throwing up any great leaders from their midst.

Mao's declaration that "capitalist-roaders" and "counterrevolutionary revisionists" had penetrated the top echelon of the party, government, army, cultural, and academic leadership at the central level and that their agents were holding positions of power at the provincial and district levels had sullied the image and undermined the prestige of the entire party and the government. His unleashing of the masses to overthrow these representatives of the so-called bourgeois class through a *class struggle* not only exaggerated the "crimes" of the offenders but also destroyed the principle of democratic centralism that provided discipline and cohesion to the party. The result was not the remaking and the strengthening of the party but the decimation of its leadership and the weakening of its structure.

Mao's destruction was visible in every sphere of life; his construction of a new order was nowhere to be seen. Mao did emerge as the key power holder, but his power was in effect limited to arbitrating among the radicals who wanted to continue the cultural revolution (the Jiang Qing group); the PLA leaders who had acquired extraordinary authority (the Lin Biao group); and the pragmatists who wanted to rehabilitate the national economy and the party, limit the role of the PLA, and reverse the radical policies of the CRG (the Zhou En-lai group).

Mao had had to accept the entry of the PLA into politics and its dominating role in national and local government. At the Ninth Congress of the CPC held in April 1969, the newly acquired status of the PLA was reflected in the fact that soldiers made up to 40 percent of the Central Committee and it was written into the party constitution that Lin Biao was "Comrade Mao Ze-dong's close comrade-in-arms and *successor*."[14] In 1969 there appeared to be some danger that Mao's long-standing injunction that "the gun will never be allowed to command the Party"[15] was about to be reversed.

Liu Shao-qi was indeed eliminated from the political scene, but most other so-called revisionists were gradually rehabilitated as Mao was driven to compromise with the pragmatists, led by Zhou En-lai, who correctly believed that the country could not do without the experience of the old guard.

As far as the social costs are concerned, the post-Mao leadership has calculated that 100 million persons were adversely affected by the cultural revolution. Since the upheaval was primarily an urban phenomenon, this means that over 50 percent of the city people suffered in one way or another: from loss of life or limb of one or more members of the family, loss of jobs, loss of personal property or physical torture and humiliation. Many writers, teachers, and top-ranking political figures committed suicide. The closing down of universities for four or more years left a gap in the educated class that is currently proving to be a handicap in China's efforts to modernize.

In economic terms, although agricultural production suffered only marginally (the cultural revolution was never really extended to the countryside), there was a drastic decline in industrial production. The combined gross output value of industry and agriculture fell from 600 to 500 (base year 1949 = 100), and there was a similarly significant decline in foreign trade. There was no doubt that China's program for economic modernization had suffered a setback.

The CPC's official reappraisal of the cultural revolution, carried out in 1981 by those who had suffered at the hands of Mao, may be biased but it does appear to be justified. According to the reappraisal, it was Mao's class struggle approach that led to the "confusing of right and wrong" and therefore inevitably to "confusing the people with the enemy." The report goes on to say that the cultural revolution was "divorced both from the party organizations and the masses," that it "paralyzed" party organizations, and that "inner-Party life came to a standstill. . . . Practice has shown that the 'cultural revolution' did not in fact constitute a revolution or social progress in any sense, nor could it possibly have done so. *It was we and not the enemy at all who was [sic] thrown into disorder by the 'cultural revolution'*" [emphasis added].[16]

Gains?

The Maoists tried, after the reopening of the schools, to ensure that Mao's educational policies would become the basis of the reformed educational system. These policies were intended to remove past inequities that favored the children of the urban elite. The most important reforms were that high school graduates were to work in communes and factories before entering institutions of higher learning; age limits and entrance examinations for universities and colleges were eliminated (politically Red students were to be "elected" by their factory or commune units for higher education); tuition fees were reduced and the examination-based grading system was eliminated; the number of school years needed for graduation was reduced; and a teaching system was started that combined theoretical classroom work with practical training in factories and workshops.

As time passed it became obvious that this egalitarian approach to education would not produce the high-quality technicians and scientists the country needed for its modernization program. Even before Mao died, many of the reforms were gradually replaced with the old-style admission and competition processes; after his death they were discarded altogether.

The attempts to reduce the inequities among the working class and the gap between management and labor proved largely abortive. Temporary contract workers continued to provide a high percentage of cheap labor; workers were not allowed to change jobs; a multigrade wage system remained unchanged; and the role of the worker in management was more fictive than real.

Similarly, the transfer of millions of urbanities into the countryside did little to help bridge the gap between the town and countryside, mental and manual labor, or workers and peasants. In fact, since the *xia-xiang* program turned out to be no more than the reduction of the population pressure in the cities, the tendency of the cities was to get rid of their unqualified unemployed. As a result the policy not only failed to raise the technological level of the villagers or increase the socialistic content of the erstwhile city-dwellers' consciousness but was also resented by the villagers, who were forced to accept the financial burden of absorbing so many extra mouths. After Mao's death many of the *xia-xiang* youths returned to the cities to complain about life in the countryside, and the peasants heaved a sigh of relief at the departure of the arrogant outsiders.

It is generally recognized that the GPCR contributed significantly to the change in attitude of the young toward the old. Ever since the New Culture Movement of the 1910s, when Confucianism had first come under open attack, many reformers had criticized the traditional value system for forcing youths to be obsequiously submissive to their elders and had encouraged the young to replace the tendency of unthinking obedience with a greater sense of individualism and independence. The objective of the reformers was to modernize China by strengthening the forces of democracy. This trend was reversed by the authoritarian Guomindang government by policies that attempted to reinforce traditional Confucian values. The GPCR finally fulfilled the goal of the New Culture Movement by effectively destroying the uniquely Confucian attitude of servitude. However, since Mao was not liberating the youths to establish a more democratic system, the results of his action were more negative than positive. Along with the old bond, the youths discarded the traditional attitude of civility and politeness and replaced it with rude and arrogant behavior. Post-Mao China is still trying to deal with this problem: The actions of unruly youngsters are difficult to curb and campaigns aimed at restoring the old courtesies are not bearing much fruit.

One undeniable good that accrued from the GPCR policies was the improvement in the health services in the countryside. Under orders from Mao, hundreds of thousands of paramedics, "barefoot doctors," were trained to serve the basic needs of the peasants. With certain amendments, the resulting nationwide network of primary health-care centers has survived the death of Mao Ze-dong, and these centers, apart from being purely medical facilities, are doing an effective job in providing community-based planned-birth services.

MAO'S LAST YEARS: 1969–1976

Mao, now in failing health, spent his last years trying to bring back unity to the strife-torn country by reconstructing the CPC on Maoist lines. However, he wholly failed in this endeavor and managed to do no more than balance off the various warring opinion groups that had appeared during the period

1958–1966 and further crystallized during the cultural revolution. The only satisfaction he may have gained in his declining years was in the field of foreign relations. As China discarded the self-imposed isolation of the GPCR period, it reemerged into a changed global environment with enhanced status and was finally accepted as a great independent power.

Internal Developments

Two party congresses were held in quick succession during the period 1969–1976: The Ninth Party Congress (PC) met, eight years late, in April 1969, and the Tenth PC in August 1973. The reason for two congresses was that the Ninth PC, although supposedly, in Mao's words, "a Party Congress of unity and victory," could not instantly establish an institutionally strong party. The country still had to depend on the military to enforce public order, to provide the only viable support for new political structures (e.g., the RCs), and function as the link between the leaders and the led. Indeed, it was the military that had to be asked to help rebuild the party itself.

The enhanced political role of the military became evident at the Ninth PC. The new party constitution named Marshal Lin as Mao's heir, stating that,

> Comrade Lin Piao [Biao] has consistently held high the great red banner of Mao Tse-tung [Zedong] thought and has most loyally and resolutely carried out and defended Comrade Mao Tse-tung's proletarian revolutionary line. Comrade Lin Piao is Comrade Mao Tse-tung's close comrade-in-arms and successor.[17]

Forty-five percent of the new Central Committee, whose number had been increased from 190 full and alternate members to 279, was made up of party men with military backgrounds; of the 21-person ruling Politburo, 10 were military commanders (7 of them newly elected), and 1 was Marshall Lin's wife, also newly elected.

Lin Biao's political report to the congress explained that the origins of the cultural revolution lay in the conflict between the "two lines" represented by the "underground bourgeois headquarters" of the "counterrevolutionary" Liu Shao-qi and "his gang" and "the proletarian headquarters headed by Chairman Mao." Lin then analyzed the cultural revolution itself, showing how right and ultraleft deviations had to be crushed, and he emphasized,

> Mao Tse-tung thought is the Marxism-Leninism of the [current] era. . . . Departing from the leadership of Chairman Mao and Mao Tse-tung thought, our Party will suffer setbacks and defeats; following Chairman Mao closely and acting on Mao Tse-tung thought our Party will advance and triumph. . . . Whoever opposes Chairman Mao, whoever opposes Mao Tse-tung thought, at any time or under any circumstances, shall be condemned and punished by the whole Party and the whole nation.[18]

Lin also quoted Mao in his report, saying that, like a human being, the party must "get rid of the stale and take in the fresh, for only thus can it be full of vitality." However, it is significant that despite Mao's stated goal and despite the fact that 60 percent of the members of the old Eighth Central Committee had been dropped, most members of the new Ninth Central Committee were from the generation that had joined the CPC before 1935; revolutionary rebels and the Red Guards had been given only token representation. The average age of the newly elected members of the Central Committee was over 61 years. This figure shows how, in actual practice, the basically conservative PLA, which had been assigned the task of suppressing the Red Guards, had managed to keep new blood out of the restructured party leadership organs.

The composition of the Standing Committee of the Politburo, the apex of all political power, appeared to be balanced in favor of a unified Maoist party. All those who had opposed Mao had been eliminated. Of the Standing Committee's five members, Mao Ze-dong was of course the key figure, Lin Biao represented the ardent Maoist section of the PLA, Chen Bo-da and Kang Sheng were the dogmatists who had guided the GPCR, and Zhou En-lai had managed to survive the cultural revolution by skillfully accommodating his views to those of Mao.

Yet behind the facade of unity, there were strong differences of approach regarding future developments of policy. Among other things, Mao and Zhou wanted to reduce the power of the military and restrengthen the party organization, but whereas Mao wanted to institutionalize the mass line and integrate education with production, Zhou wanted to see the shattered state organs regain their old authority and the country pursue pragmatic educational and economic policies that would modernize China. Lin wanted to consolidate his power, but he was opposed by civilian groups, such as that of Zhou En-lai, and also by the more professional military commanders who wanted the PLA to withdraw from the political arena. And then there were Chen Bo-da and his leftist supporters, who wanted to see the continuation of radical Maoist egalitarian policies to a degree that even Mao was to find objectionable.

This confusing situation was further complicated by disagreement over foreign policy. By the time the GPCR was over, it was becoming clear that the United States, pressured by internal and external factors, was going to pull out of Vietnam and gradually reduce its presence in Asia as a whole. President Nixon's Guam Doctrine (1969) gave an indication of the United States' new policy: Asian security must be primarily the concern of Asians. The prospect of reduced American presence was counterbalanced by a growth of Soviet forces on the Chinese border and the Pacific region.

The Soviet proposal for a collective security system in Asia, first mooted in 1967, appeared (correctly) to China to be a Soviet attempt to take over the earlier American position, which aimed at containing and isolating China. The Soviet Union's invasion of Czechoslovakia in 1968, justified by the theory of limited sovereignty (the Brezhnev Doctrine)—which upheld the principle that Moscow could come to the defense of socialism in any country of the socialist commonwealth where socialism was imperiled—could mean that the Soviet Union had intentions of acting in a similar manner in China. China's strong condemnation of the Soviet act was followed a few months later by a border incident on the Ussuri River (March 1969) when the two sides opened fire on one another.

In April at the Ninth PC, Lin in his political report, referred to earlier, publicly expressed a commitment to continue the old foreign policy line. He attacked both the superpowers for colluding to redivide the world and reiterated the party's goal to confront both U.S. imperialism and Soviet revisionist social-imperialism. Behind the scenes, however, Mao and Zhou decided to make a radical shift in foreign policy by accepting the United States' overtures for a detente. Although the details of inner party debate are still hazy, Lin and his supporters, apparently for ideological reasons, did not favor this policy shift.

Because of differences among the leaders, the work of party reconstruction was delayed and no provincial-level party committees were established during the 18 months after the Ninth PC. The work was speeded up only after the Second Plenum of the new Central Committee, which was held at Lushan from August 23 to September 6, 1970. At Lushan Mao for the first time felt threatened by Lin Biao's ambitions. At the plenum, with the backing of Chen Bo-da and some of his generals, Lin proposed that the post of state chair, which had been done away with after the fall of Liu Shao-qi, be reestablished and that Lin be made chair. To Mao, who had decided to abolish the post and had not included it in the draft state constitution that had been circulated in March, this came as an unpleasant surprise. Lin, obviously afraid of what might happen once the party was fully reconstructed, wanted to ensure his future by becoming head of state. Mao, however, now decided to do away with the heir apparent.

Afraid of a military revolt, Mao made no hasty move but laid out his plan with great care. First he purged Chen Bo-da, declaring that he was an ultraleftist and a political swindler. Then, as chair of the Military Affairs Commission, Mao added his supporters to that body and reduced Lin's influence in it. Last, Mao reorganized the Beijing military region to weaken Lin's military control of the capital.

The process of establishing provincial party committees, taken up in earnest after the Second Plenum, was completed by August 1971. Once again the PLA showed its political clout by placing its senior officers in nearly two-thirds of the key positions of party secretaries. What was even more ominous, many of these persons were also chairs of the local provincial revolutionary committees. Although not all the provincial military leaders were pro-Lin, political power did appear to be shifting into the hands of Lin Biao, who had also filled some of the top military posts with his supporters.

From late 1970 through mid-1971, there was increasing direct and indirect criticism of the PLA for denying the party its proper role and for not paying sufficient attention to democratic centralism and collective leadership. There was, however, still no public sign of any conflict between Mao and his designated successor.

Behind the facade of unity, Mao began to tilt in favor of Zhou En-lai, even allowing the return of "evil" economic practices that encouraged increased production through material incentives and the holding of private plots. Mao also favored deemphasizing his personality cult and criticized Lin for trying to push the idea that Mao was a "genius" and that a "genius" appeared in China only once in a thousand years. In foreign relations, Mao and Zhou used their old friend, the famous American journalist Edgar Snow, to convey China's readiness to open a dialogue with Washington. It appears that Lin objected to this policy. Apart from ideological reasons, détente with the United States meant a containment of Soviet designs through diplomatic means and thereby a lessening of the importance of the PLA. In December 1970 Mao indicated to Snow that President Nixon would be welcome to visit China. Snow, with permission from Beijing, published the interview in *Life* magazine in April 1971. By mid-July Secretary of State Kissinger had made a secret trip to China to arrange for Nixon's visit in February 1972.

The serious struggle over power and policy going on behind the scenes culminated finally in some mysterious events in September 1971, the tremendous significance of which was not immediately obvious. On the night of September 12–13 a Chinese air force plane with nine persons aboard crashed 150 miles inside Outer Mongolia. The following day all airline flights were canceled and the PLA air force grounded. The traditional National Day parade on October 1 was also canceled, but the outside world did not know what to make of these developments. Gradually news began to filter out that the charred bodies found in the plane's wreckage were those of Lin and his close associates, who had plotted a coup against the state and tried to assassinate Mao. The news of Lin Biao's death was officially confirmed, eight months after the event, in July 1972, but an official version of the "coup" was presented only two years later by Zhou En-lai in his report to the Tenth PC in August 1973.

Regardless of the full details, which have yet to be revealed, it appears certain that there was a major crisis in September. It is possible that realizing that he was about to be purged, Lin was planning a takeover of power. If the coup plan that has come to light is authentic, Lin was highly critical of Mao because, according to Lin,

> Today he [Mao] uses this force to attack that force; tomorrow he uses that force to attack this force. Today he uses sweet words and honeyed talk to those whom he entices, and tomorrow he puts them to death for some fabricated crimes. Those who are his greatest friends today will be his prisoners tomorrow.[19]

The Lin affair helped Mao and Zhou to purge a large number of military commanders who had been Lin's supporters; about half the Politburo members appointed at the

Ninth PC disappeared. With the PLA in disgrace, it became possible to reduce the role of the military in politics and to restore the party apparatus to civilian control and to its position of supremacy over all other organizations. In the mid-1960s Mao had called on the party to emulate the PLA; in 1973 the call went out that the PLA should study the fine work style of the party. Coincidentally, no doubt on the grounds that the revitalization of the party needed expertise, Zhou managed to rehabilitate a number of old party leaders who had been removed from office in 1966. One of these was Deng Xiao-ping, who, after being kept under house arrest in Beijing, had been exiled to rural Jiangxi and made to work as a fitter in a tractor factory.[20]

The fall of Lin Biao was no doubt a blow to Mao. Although Zhou and the others around Mao continued carefully to bolster his image as the great leader, thinking Chinese could not avoid wondering whether Mao was a poor judge of character—since both his handpicked successors had to be liquidated as counterrevolutionaries—or that he was indeed, as Lin had evaluated him (and Lin's coup document was circulated throughout the country), a cruel, bloodthirsty Machiavellian dictator. Zhou gained the most from this traumatic affair, perhaps, because Mao had to depend heavily on Zhou's group to help him topple Lin. In any case, Zhou's moderate and pragmatic policies were appreciated by a majority of the contending interest groups. This helped him in steering the country to a middle course between the right and the left—to a position not dissimilar to the one China was following before the GPCR was launched. Zhou's prominence was further enhanced by his skillful handling of foreign affairs; apart from overseeing the PRC's entry into the United Nations (1971), Zhou was universally lauded for the impressive arrangements he made for President Nixon's visit in February 1972.

However, Zhou was not without enemies, and his pragmatism was unacceptable to the left-wing group, which saw it as "reactionary rightism." This group was centered around Madame Mao (Jiang Qing), who along with her leading supporters, Zhang Chun-qiao and Yao Wen-yuan, had been elected to the Politburo at the Ninth PC. Mao, himself, periodically backed this group to balance Zhou's authority and to put a restraint on his policies. The Jiang Qing group favored an increased role for the revolutionary masses, as did Mao, who now called for the triple alliances to combine "the old, the middle-aged and the young." The "young" were to represent the revolutionary masses.

The changed political environment was reflected in the new party constitution adopted at the Tenth PC (August 1973) and in the changed membership of the new Central Committee and the Politburo. The constitution of the Tenth PC dropped all references to Lin Biao and restored collective leadership by appointing five vice-chairs. Zhou En-lai was shown in the number-two position on the Politburo list, but an unknown, Wang Hong-wen, was number three. Wang, 39 years old (there are other conflicting estimates of his age, ranging from 36 to early 40s), recruited into the party after 1949, was a Shanghai cotton mill worker who had risen to local prominence during the cultural revolution. His emergence as an important national leader no doubt symbolized Mao's desire to prove that the GPCR had succeeded in producing youthful "revolutionary successors." Wang also had the backing of Jiang Qing and her other Shanghai-based supporters, Yao Wen-yuan and Zhang Chun-qiao, and was soon to be identified as a member of the Shanghai group (the Gang of Four as it was later disparagingly called). Another relatively unknown figure in the new Politburo who was soon to gain national importance was Hua Guo-feng, the erstwhile chair of the Hunan Provincial Party Committee.

Wang Hong-wen presented the new party constitution at the Congress and was one of the two main speakers, the other being Zhou En-lai, who gave the political report. Both of them stressed repeatedly that the party was in absolute command and that everything must be done to strengthen the centralized leadership of the party. Lin Biao and Chen Bo-da, who had been attacked in 1972 for their ultraleftism, were now condemned for being ultrarightists and expelled from the party (Lin, posthumously). This switch was apparently made at the insistence of the leftists, no doubt with the approval of Mao, who felt that an attack on ultraleftism would help the pragmatists to undo the gains of the GPCR. One can only wonder how the common Chinese reacted to these 180-degree shifts in party policies.

The decline in the influence of the military was further reflected in its reduced representation in the Tenth Central Committee—31 percent as against 44 percent in the Ninth Central Committee—and in the Politburo, down from 55 to 28 percent. In contrast, the representation of the revolutionary masses in the Central Committee went up from 21.5 to 33.5 percent, and in the Politburo from 19 to 38 percent. This was further evidence of Mao's anxiety not to allow the pendulum to swing too far to the right. Incidentally, the party membership now stood at 28 million, a considerable increase over its strength of 17 million in 1961. Millions of professed Maoists had been taken into the party during the GPCR.

The percentage of government and party cadres (Zhou's group) remained unchanged, but Zhou managed to get a large number of rehabilitated cadres back into the higher ranks of the party. Deng Xiao-ping, shown as a member of the Tenth Central Committee, had been appointed vice-premier in April 1973. His name began to appear on the lists of members of the Politburo from January 1974.

The year 1973 saw the first signs of a more open conflict between the pragmatists, headed by Zhou En-lai, and the left-wingers, headed by Jiang Qing—a conflict that was ultimately resolved only after the death of Zhou and Mao. For example, one of the campaigns started in mid-1973 attacked Confucius and his ideology. Some scholars believe that this was an indirect attack on Zhou En-lai by the leftists. By the use of obscure historical references, Confucius was shown to be an apologist for the dying slave society of the Zhou dynasty, a man who tried to perpetuate the old order and stem the revolutionary changes that were advancing China to the feudalist stage. Zhou was the modern Confucius indulging in counterrevolutionary restoration of the rule of bourgeois capitalists. In early 1974 the campaign was enlarged to "criticize Lin, criticize Confucius," supposedly a move by Zhou's group to reorient the thrust of the campaign against the leftists, who were after all, once closely associated with Lin. Whatever the nature of the confusing undercurrents of this period it is now officially recognized that intraparty tensions did exist and that Mao had personally approved the launching of the campaign.[21] The campaign wound down by the end of 1974, having achieved no noteworthy results.

Beyond the field of ideology the conflict between the leftists and the pragmatists, or the moderates, affected policies concerning higher education and economic development. Some of the issues that China had faced during the Great Leap Forward and the GPCR reappeared; for example, should professionalism, planning, and technology be emphasized over the willpower of the masses and their enthusiasm?

The celebrated case of the rusticated youth, Zhang Tie-sheng, is a good example of this controversy. At the end of the GPCR it was decided that college enrollments would no longer be based on entrance examinations, which favored the children of the city elite, but on proper class background and political behavior, strengthened by two years' stint in a factory or countryside. In 1973 an admissions examination was reimposed because the colleges and universities complained that the egalitarian system had resulted in the influx of academically poor students who were not ready for a college education. Zhang, who had all the requisite political qualifications, applied for the admissions test but, finding it difficult to answer the questions asked, wrote instead an essay on the un-Maoist nature of the test and how it reflected the return of bourgeois practices. The leftists took up Zhang's case and made him out to be a hero but, in the long run, failed to change the direction of the educational system.

Although Zhou sometimes had to make some compromises, he usually managed to carry out his policies. Under his guidance, both industrial and agricultural output, which had declined during 1966–1968, continued to increase. However, since the gains were offset by the growth in population the government, from 1973, began to put a stronger emphasis on family planning and birth control. The campaign encouraged late marriages, longer spacing between children, and fewer births.

Struggle for Succession

The Tenth PC was to be the last congress led by the veteran leaders Mao Ze-dong and Zhou En-lai. Even in 1973 it was obvious that Mao (79) and Zhou (75) had only a few years left. Both of them were suffering from serious debilitating illnesses and were getting physically incapacitated; Mao, who remained mostly in seclusion, was a victim of Parkinson's disease, and Zhou was dying of cancer. Although this information was kept "secret," foreign visitors noticed that Mao was feeble and found it hard to concentrate on any one subject for too long. Zhou was hospitalized in 1974 and, except for a few occasions, did not leave his hospital room until his death in January 1976.

As was to be expected, factions contesting for power began to ready themselves for the inevitable succession struggle. The most important factions were:

1. Jiang Qing's left-wing Maoist group. The group wanted to protect the gains made during the GPCR. It controlled the propaganda apparatus (radio, television, party papers) and had some support from a section of the military.
2. Zhou En-lai's group, moderates who wanted to undo the radical policies of the GPCR. Its important members were Deng Xiao-ping and Li Xian-nian, who took over more and more of the prime minister's responsibilities. It had the backing of the organizational, bureaucratic apparatus; the economic apparatus; and the scientific establishment; it also had connections with certain sectors of the military establishment.
3. Hua Guo-feng's group. Hua, who had followed Maoist policies in Hunan when he was chair of the Hunan Party Committee, appears to have had the backing of Mao. This newly emerging faction had a close association with the security apparatus and the Beijing military command.

These groups also tried to build up provincial-level support through appointments of loyal followers. From 1973 to 1976 the most serious contenders for power were the Jiang and Zhou groups, and while their struggle intensified, Hua Guo-feng and his people remained neutral.

The year 1975 was good for the moderates. The Fourth National People's Congress (NPC) was convened in January, and although the new state constitution, which replaced the 1954 constitution, and the reports presented at the congress must have had Mao's approval, Mao did not attend the session. In his absence Zhou was by far the most important national leader at the congress, although the leftists were given significant visible representation. Thus although Zhou, who had been premier from the inception of the PRC, delivered the report on the work of the government during the 12 years that had passed since the last NPC, Zhang Chun-qiao introduced the revised constitution. Both stressed the need for "revolutionary unity" based on a "revolutionary united front which include[d] the patriotic democratic parties, and patriotic personages in all walks of life."[22]

This balancing of interests of various groups was also evident in the appointment of state ministers and other high officials. It appeared as if Zhou was preparing China for collective leadership. Hua Guo-feng was appointed minister of public security; the Jiang Qing group was represented by offices given to Zhang Chun-qiao and Yu Hui-yong (the composer of Jiang Qing's revolutionary operas). Yu was made minister of culture; Zhang was appointed second-ranking vice-premier and director general of the PLA Political Department.

But behind the facade of collective leadership, Zhou, by strengthening his own group, tried to ensure that his policies would be continued after his death. And obviously Deng was being groomed to take over as prime minister. Deng, who had been appointed to the Standing Committee of the Politburo and a vice-chair of the party just before the meeting of the Fourth NPC, was made first vice-premier, vice-chair of the Military Affairs Commission, and chief-of-staff of the PLA. Deng was thus given leading positions in the party, the state, and the PLA—the three institutions of national power. It is also significant that although Zhang Chun-qiao's posts paralleled those of Deng, they were a step lower and that Jiang Qing, Yao Wen-yuan, and Wang Hong-wen were given no bureaucratic positions at all.

In the absence of a well-defined legal system, the new constitution was as meaningless as any that had been promulgated since the 1911 revolution. For example, what is one to make of Article 28: "Citizens enjoy freedom of speech, correspondence, the press, assembly, association, procession, demonstration [etc.]"?[23]

Basically, the 1975 constitution reflected the changes that had transformed Chinese polity since the promulgation of the 1954 constitution. Thus the description of the PRC was changed from "people's democratic state" to "a socialist state of the dictatorship of the proletariat." The leadership of the CPC was emphasized: "The Communist Party of China is the core of the leadership of the whole people." The party chair was given supreme command over the armed forces. The post of state chair (equivalent to state president—Liu Shao-qi's last post) was abolished. Marxism-Leninism-Mao Ze-dong Thought, "the theoretical basis guiding the thinking of our nation," was prescribed study for state employees. The institution of the communes, which had come into existence only after 1954, was constitutionally confirmed, as was the new leadership principle of "three-in-one": the combination of the old, the middle-aged, and the young.

On Mao's insistence the workers'right to strike was added to the fundamental rights, although many wondered why the ruling class would strike against itself—could it mean that Mao was protecting the working class from the reactionary rightists if they usurped state authority! The power and function of the judiciary was reduced, implying that the power of the security organs and police was enhanced. No doubt to restrain the activities of the intellectuals and the movements of the youth who had been sent to the countryside, two freedoms in the 1954 constitution were deleted: "the freedom of citizens to engage in scientific research, literary and artistic creation, and other cultural pursuits" and the "freedom of residence and freedom to change their residence."

The constitution conceded that "people's commune members may farm small plots for their personal needs, engage in limited household side-line production, and in pastoral areas keep a small number of livestock for their personal use."[24]

In his report on the work of the government, Zhou went to excessive lengths to praise Mao and his Thought, but it was clear to all who understood Zhou that the heart of his message was that China must turn to the task of economic development:

> The first stage is to build an independent and relatively comprehensive industrial and economic system . . . before 1980; the second stage is to accomplish the comprehensive modernization of *agriculture, industry, national defense and science and technology* [emphasis added] [the basis for post-Mao China's drive for the four modernizations] before the end of the century so that our national economy will be advancing in the front ranks of the world.[25]

Zhou had modified his stand on self-reliance by quoting Mao to the effect that "subsidiary" external assistance was acceptable. To modernize its economy, China began to import considerable amounts of technology from the West and Japan. It was estimated that

China's trade deficit for the year 1975 was as high as $3 billion.

As Zhou's health failed, Deng took on more and more of the work load. The leftists were not happy with the pragmatic policies and began to voice fears that the system was generating new bourgeois elements and that the GPCR verdicts were being reversed. They also made some indirect attacks on Zhou's foreign policy line and started a campaign against the evil of "empiricism" and against "empiricists." By the end of 1975 Mao, who had earlier suppressed the anti-Lin, anti-Confucius campaign because the left had gone too far in its criticism of the moderates, began to side with the left to restrain the moderates. The New Year's message, published as a joint editorial by the leading party and army organs, introduced a new comment by Mao: "Stability and unity do not mean writing off the class struggle; class struggle is the key link and everything else hinges on it."[26] According to the post-Mao assessment of this period, "Comrade Mao could not bear to accept the systematic corrections of the errors of the 'cultural revolution' by Comrade Deng Xiaoping and triggered the movement to 'criticize Deng and counter the Right deviationist trend to reverse correct verdicts,' once again plunging the nation into turmoil."[27]

Even though the turmoil of the cultural revolution was not repeated, Mao's actions after the death of Zhou did plunge the nation into another period of renewed power struggle and political uncertainty.

Zhou died on January 8, 1976, at the age of 78 and was cremated according to his wishes. His death, although expected, nevertheless stunned the nation, and there was a spontaneous outpouring of genuine grief. Deng Xiao-ping, the first vice-premier, delivered the funeral eulogy, but to the surprise of most Chinese, Mao neither attended the memorial ceremony nor paid any public tribute to his late comrade; was he really that upset with Zhou's pragmatic policies?

It was expected that Deng would automatically succeed Zhou. However, on February 7, it was officially announced that Hua Guofeng had been appointed acting premier. There is no doubt that Mao was personally responsible for this appointment, which must have pleased the Shanghai group even though they could not get one of their own into this key position.

Deng disappeared from the public scene and was soon under attack in the press, without being named, as "the unrepentant capitalist-roader in power in the Party." It was also recalled that during the GPCR, he had once said that "it did not matter whether the cat is white or black; if it catches mice it is a good cat," which went to prove that he had little regard for ideology. Leaflets, posters, and articles in the party organs warned of leaders "influenced by bourgeois ideology," who had "not accepted the Party's education and remolding."[28] In one of his comments, Mao endorsed the campaign and identified Deng as the target: "This person does not grasp class struggle; he has never referred to this key link. [He still continues] his theme of 'white cat, black cat,' making no distinction between imperialism and capitalism."[29]

Zhou also came in for criticism for his "revisionist" four modernizations program. This action of the Maoists enraged many, who showed their love and support for Zhou and resentment of the new policies by using the occasion of Qing Ming (a traditional spring festival when Chinese honor their dead elders by sweeping their graves and putting flowers on them) to pay homage to Zhou. In 14 major provinces and in the metropolitan cities of Nanjing and Beijing, citizens gathered at the local martyrs' memorials and placed wreaths there in the memory of Zhou; posters were also put up eulogizing him.

From March 30 to April 4, thousands flocked to the Heroes' Monument in Tiananmen (the Gate of Heavenly Peace) Square in Beijing. As the wreaths, many bearing Zhou's portrait, and posters began to pile up, rising ultimately to a height of 50 feet, the Maoist party leaders issued orders to all units to suppress the movement on the grounds that the Qing Ming festival represented an outmoded feudal custom that recognized ghosts. In fact these leaders were rightly afraid that the demonstrations were becoming more and more an overt expression of support for Zhou (and therefore of Deng) and an attack on the leftists, if not on Mao himself. Beijing citizens refused to obey the restrictive orders and continued to come in droves to the Square of Heavenly Peace.

It is possible that Mao was not informed of these developments and that the order to the Beijing municipality to remove the wreaths (morning of April 5) and to the security forces to stop further demonstrations was taken by someone else. However, it appears definite that Mao was told that the clashes between the infuriated citizens and the government forces that followed these orders and that led to the death of hundreds and the arrest of thousands were the result of a conspiracy by Deng. On April 6, an editorial in the *People's Daily* warned that "the counter-attack on the Right deviationist attempt is bound to meet with rabid resistance and trouble-making from class enemies . . . particularly the bourgeois in the Party."[30] On April 7 the Central Committee, "on the proposal of our great leader Chairman Mao,"[31] appointed Hua prime minister and first vice-chair of the CPC. Deng, although allowed to keep his party membership, was dismissed from all posts inside and outside the party. Thus Hua, Mao's protégé, emerged as the victor in the power struggle; Zhou's plans appeared to come to naught; and the Shanghai group still held on tenuously to a position at the top. That Hua had been chosen by Mao as his successor became fully apparent when it came to light that, on April 30, Mao had given Hua a handwritten note saying, "With you in charge, I am at ease."[32] Deng moved to Guangzhou to reside under the protection of his supporter, General Xu Shi-yu, the commander of the southern military region.

But political decisions in Beijing brought only an uneasy peace to the country. Even as Mao lay dying, the Gang of Four began to snipe at Hua; officials in the provinces waiting for the final solution began to slow down the antirightist campaign; respect for authority declined, and social undiscipline increased. And as if to confirm the correctness of the traditional superstition that large-scale natural disasters presaged the end of a dynasty, summer crops were affected by bad weather and, at the end of July, an earthquake measuring 8.2 on the Richter scale leveled the mining town of Tangshan (near Tianjin) and killed or injured hundreds of thousands.

On September 9 Mao Ze-dong died. Many grieved his death, but it was noted by several reliable witnesses that there was no outpouring of sorrow on the scale that had marked Zhou's death.

Mao's death brought to an end an era in the modern history of China.

Conclusion

Under Mao China finally regained its independence, and the nation was more fully integrated, although some problems remained with the absorption of the national minorities. Mao's approach to foreign relations showed his will to get China recognized as a great power, and he succeeded in seeing the world give China this recognition before he died.

But however great a revolutionary, Mao failed to bring true liberation and democracy to the people. He and the people were both caught in a dilemma created by the coexistence of traditional habits of mind and the demands of a modern state. Mao's difficulty lay in his lack of understanding that whereas one man could be extremely important in leading a political revolution, no one man could ever radically transform the nature of humankind and reshape the character of an entire society. Mao's absolute faith in his own ideology, his incapacity to accept criticism from his peers (he did not believe he had any peers) or to work as a member of a team, his ruthless suppression of those who disagreed with him, and his scorn for the intelligentsia meant that his so-called respect for the "wisdom of the masses" was an empty gesture—he knew that all that the masses could do was to worship him as a hero.

In 1956 Edgar Snow had asked Mao to comment on the Soviet criticism that Mao was building up a cult of personality. Mao replied that there was good reason for fostering a cult of personality, adding that "probably Mr. Khrushchev fell because he had no cult of personality at all."[33] In a later interview in 1970, Mao reiterated that there was a cult of personality but added that it may have been overdone. "It was hard," he said, "for people to overcome the habits of 3,000 years of emperor-worshiping tradition."[34] But had Mao tried to destroy these habits? Yes and no. He wanted the people to discard the traditional vices of fatalism and passivism, of blindly following authority, and of emphasizing harmony over struggle (i.e., conflict). Yet he promoted their passive, unquestioning acceptance of *his* authority so that they could *struggle* unthinkingly against his enemies. Was not Mao, himself, a traditional-style totalitarian ruler, who in an authoritarian fashion propagated a single ideology that, ironically, was supposed to "educate" the people to become "democratic"?

His biggest failure lay in strengthening the traditional ideal that made personalities more important than laws and institutions. The individual rights enshrined in the constitution were not worth the paper they were written on. By the time he died, he had weakened all three national institutions—the party, the government, and the army.

EXTERNAL AFFAIRS

Mao Ze-dong's internal policies failed to establish the social-political infrastructure that would have helped realize his vision of national reconstruction; however, the framework for foreign relations established by Mao before 1969 was successful in helping China emerge as a global actor in the 1970s.

Mao shared the overriding desire of all twentieth-century Chinese reformers and revolutionaries to restore China's independence and greatness—in other words, the desire to eradicate the hold of the foreign imperialists over the country and the memory of how they had humiliated China. Mao wanted to see China recognized as a global power and its voice heeded by the world. He therefore found all ties that made China dependent on a foreign power truly abhorrent. In April 1949, even before the PRC was established, future CPC foreign policy was outlined in the following terms:

> We must not seek foreign aid without being self-reliant. If foreign aid holds benefits for China, of course we want it; but we cannot be dependent on it. *We should not be dependent even on the Soviet Union and the New Democracies* [emphasis added].[35]

It is in this context that China's break with the Soviet Union, followed by a period of hostility to both the superpowers and Mao's policies of economic autarchy and nuclear independence, can be best understood.

As early as 1956, in a speech ("Ten Major Relationships") made public only 20 years later, Mao said, "In the future . . . we will also have atom bombs. *If we are not to be bullied in the present world we cannot do without atom bombs*" (emphasis added).[36] In 1959, on the eve of the Sino-Soviet split, when the Soviet Union decided to withhold atomic bomb technology from China, Beijing decided to go it alone. In 1964 China exploded its first nuclear device; in 1967, at the height of the GPCR, China detonated its first hydrogen bomb. Mao, elated at the speed with which China had acquired its nuclear arsenal, commented,

> "Modern weapons, guided missiles and atomic bombs were made very quickly [in China], and we produced a hydrogen bomb in only 2 years and 8 months. Our development has been faster than that of America, Britain and France. We are now in the 4th place in the world." And he went on to add, "China should not only be the political center of the world revolution, it must also become the military and technical center of the world revolution."[37]

At this time, when China appeared to have voluntarily withdrawn from the larger world order, the militancy of Mao Ze-dong's thought was reflected in optimistic pronouncements about world revolutionary movements. In April 1968, commenting on the assassination of Martin Luther King, Jr., Mao said,

> It has touched off . . . a storm which has swept well over 100 cities in the United States such as has never taken place before in the history of the country. It shows that an extremely powerful revolutionary force is latent in the more than 20 million black Americans.
>
> . . . The Afro-American struggle is not only a struggle waged by the exploited and oppressed black people for freedom and emancipation, it is also a new clarion call to all the exploited and oppressed people of the United States to fight against the barbarous rule of the monopoly capitalist class. . . . I hereby express resolute support for the just struggle of the black people in the United States.[38]

Mao was soon to change this stand because, in the final analysis, what Mao wanted was not a world revolution but a recognition of China's world stature and security for China. Mention has already been made of the Sino-Soviet border trouble in 1969 and the subsequent détente between China and the United States. It needs to be added, however, that this development should not be taken to mean that Mao had capitulated to Soviet pressure. As far as Sino-Soviet relations are concerned, after both sides had made irreconcilable statements of their stand on the border issue, border negotiations were opened on October 20, 1969, which vastly reduced, if not eliminated, the possibility of war between the two Communist states. Beijing felt so confident of this relationship that by 1973 it had developed a new foreign policy strategy, which emphasized that the Soviet Union was only "making a feint in the East while attacking the West."[39] Although there has been limited progress in the border talks, Sino-Soviet relations have gradually improved after Mao's death.

China and the United States

The reorientation of China's foreign relations should be viewed in the context of the radically altered dimension of international politics. Mao, who had in the 1950s tilted toward the Soviet Union because the United States represented the greatest threat to China and who had equated the Soviet Union with the United States in the 1960s, shifted toward the United States against the growing threat of the Soviet Union in the 1970s. But he did this largely on his own terms—the major policy change was made by the United States. As revealed by Nixon in 1972, Washington itself was eager to reestablish contact with China even before the Sino-Soviet flare-up:

> Within 2 weeks of my inauguration [January 1969] . . . I ordered that efforts be undertaken to communicate our new attitude through private channels, and to seek contact with the People's Republic of China. . . . [The USA] began to implement a phased sequence of *unilateral measures* [emphasis added] [e.g., relaxing trade and travel restrictions] to indicate the direction in which the Administration was prepared to move.[40]

The United States, conscious of growing Soviet interest in Asia and the limited capability of Japan to fill the vacuum created by the anticipated U.S. withdrawal, sought to increase China's participation in world affairs so that a new balance of power could be created to replace the earlier East-West confrontation—a balance of power that would align the United States, China, and Japan against the Soviet Union. Mao had succeeded in getting China recognized as a significant world power: The Soviets were afraid of it; the United States had come wooing it. This would not have happened if China had not shown its "will" to challenge both the superpowers and if it had not developed an independent nuclear arsenal.

Nixon's visit to China in February 1972 symbolized the success of Mao's foreign policy. After all, the head of the most powerful capitalist country in the world was coming to Beijing without China having made any explicit or implicit concessions. In the famous Shanghai Communiqué, issued at the end of the visit, both sides agreed to begin a process of "normalizing relations," which meant eventual diplomatic recognition. The United States accepted China's five principles of "peaceful coexistence" and agreed to oppose "hegemony" (a clause directed against the Soviet Union and its allies) and attempts by "major countries [meaning the Soviet Union] to divide up the world into spheres of interest." The critical question of Taiwan was glossed over by keeping references to it deliberately ambiguous. The United States acknowledged that "all Chinese on either side of the Taiwan Strait maintain there is but one China and that Taiwan is a part of China" and "affirmed" its intention to withdraw, in due course, its military from Taiwan. Whereas Beijing reaffirmed its right to consider "the liberation of Taiwan [as] China's internal affair," the United States expressed its interest in seeing the affair settled peacefully.[41]

The new ties between China and the United States developed rapidly, and within a year the two countries established diplomatic liaison offices in Beijing, and Washington, which for all practical purposes functioned as full-fledged embassies. The position of the PRC (Taiwan) embassy in Washington became increasingly anomalous, although the strong Taiwan lobby kept the U.S.-Taiwan relations from deteriorating too quickly. Large numbers of Americans now had an opportunity to visit China, a country that had been closed to them for nearly a quarter century, but Beijing gave most of the visas to Americans who were "friendly" to the PRC.

There was an initial spurt in the growth of American trade in China, but by 1975 the Americans realized that their euphoria was misplaced; China's internal economic and political considerations posed a serious handicap to any sudden opening up of the vast market envisaged by optimistic businesspeople. The total Sino-American trade in 1974 was only $1 billion and not quite that high in 1975. The conflict between the leftists and the Zhouists, Zhou's failing health, Mao's tilt toward the leftists and antagonism to Deng, and the U.S. efforts to promote détente with the Soviet Union after the Helsinki accords (1975) all meant a certain cooling of relations. Under these conditions, President Ford's visit (December 1975), although cordial enough, was a nonevent: No joint communiqués were issued, and no obvious results ensued.

In 1976 all attention was focused on internal intraelite conflict, and foreign affairs assumed a secondary importance. After the death of Zhou En-lai, the radicals, aiming to undermine the moderate group and strengthen their position vis-à-vis Hua, made vicious attacks on Deng for being a "capitalist roader," who was

> *importing foreign techniques and equipment . . . copying foreign designs and technological processes and patterning our equipment on foreign models . . . [asking] for foreign loans by selling out China's natural resources and sovereignty* [emphasis added].[42]

Such attacks continued even after Deng had been dismissed from all his posts. Mao was almost on his deathbed. Nobody could be sure what direction internal politics was about to take and how that would affect foreign relations.

China and the Rest of the World

The change in the U.S. attitude toward China helped the PRC to replace Taiwan in the United Nation's Security Council and its General Assembly in 1971. A number of countries that had withheld recognition of Beijing because of pressure from the United States now hastened to establish diplomatic relations with Beijing. To offset the Soviet Union's growing menace, it was important for China to receive recognition from as many nations as possible. It was therefore with some degree of satisfaction that Zhou En-lai could report to the Fourth NPC (January 1975) that "the number of countries having diplomatic relations with us has increased by nearly 100 [over double the number in 1968], and more than 150 countries and regions have economic and trade relations and cultural exchanges with us. . . . We have friends all over the world."[43]

However, China's new world status was not cost free. China's rapprochement with America came as a shock to China's allies and brought fears to some of its neighbors. China had to reassure North Korea, the Democratic Republic of Vietnam (DRV), and Laos that détente with the United States would not lead to the sacrifice of old friends. Relationships could, however, never be the same again, particularly with the DRV, which was still fighting a war with the United States and so was naturally more suspicious of the détente. And there were reasons for being suspicious. As late as 1971 China had condemned U.S. proposals for a ceasefire in Vietnam, but shortly thereafter China was eager for a negotiated peace. In the eyes of China a quick U.S. collapse in South Vietnam could only benefit the Soviet Union. Prince Sihanouk, the head of the Cambodian government-in-exile, who had been told by Zhou in 1971 that "China did not break her word,"[44] summed up the changed situation rather well in 1973: "China," he said, "is playing a power game with the US now and so cannot help as much as she would like."[45] China managed to maintain good relations with North Korea and Laos, but Vietnam continued on a more independent tack, playing off the Soviet Union and China to its advantage.

The rest of the Third World countries were also concerned about changes in Chinese foreign policy. They had been exhorted for so many years to look on the United States as their main enemy—was China now going to join forces with that enemy? Would China, allied to America, itself become a threat to Third World nations, particularly the ones in Asia? China tried to calm their fears by enunciating, in 1974, Mao's new theory of three worlds: the superpowers (the United States and the Soviet Union) constituted the First World; the developed countries (East and West Europe and Japan), the Second World; and the developing countries, the Third World. The First World powers had reduced the Second World countries to a position of dependency and were contending to enslave and control the Third World countries. China insisted that it belonged to the Third World, and it recommended that the Second and the Third Worlds join hands to fight the First World.

In fact, China appeared to have lost much of its earlier interest in most of the Third World, particularly in South America and Africa. It gave up its frenzied revolutionary rhetoric and shifted its activities from the field to the United Nations, where it could present itself as a protector of the Third World and its voice. It did not give up its verbal assaults on the superpowers, calling them biggest international oppressors and exploiters, although in practice China supported the United States in many of its moves against the Soviet Union.

Japan was the greatest benefactor from the changes in Asian international politics. After being "shocked" that America could open relations with China without first informing Japan, Tokyo quickly seized the new opportunity and by the end of 1972 had established full diplomatic relations with Beijing and opened the PRC to Japanese trade. Representatives from some of Japan's largest firms and banks were soon establishing bridgeheads in Beijing and Japan shortly became China's biggest international trading partner. However, the two sides failed to sign a peace treaty because Japan resisted China's pressure to include an "antihegemony" (i.e., anti-Soviet) clause in the treaty. The hurdle was finally overcome in 1978.

Relations between China and India worsened before they improved. As a response to the Sino-American rapprochement, India signed a treaty of friendship with the Soviet Union in August 1971. This act no doubt helped to keep China from giving active support to its ally, Pakistan, in the Indo-Pakistan war, which led to the dismemberment of Pakistan and the establishment of Bangladesh (December 1971). As a consequence Indo-Chinese relations were strained even further. However, in 1975 the pro-Indian Bangladesh government was overthrown by a military junta that wanted to reduce India's influence in Dacca. Beijing hastened to recognize the new government, but it also accepted the reality that India had emerged as the major power in South Asia, far more powerful than any of its neighbors. It was in the interest of China to recognize the new balance of power in the region and try to keep India from drawing too close to the Soviet Union. The exchange of ambassadors in 1976 (withdrawn 15 years earlier) was a tentative move in the direction of greater mutual accommodation.

As can be expected, changes in China's foreign relations added new issues to China's internal debate. The pragmatists were eager to open China to foreign investment and technology; as Deng said in his address to the United Nations in 1974, "Self-reliance in no way means 'self-seclusion' and rejection of foreign aid."[46] The leftists, however, still favored self-reliance. The pragmatists, fearing that American withdrawal from Southeast Asia (the United States was finally driven out of South Vietnam in 1975) would weaken Japan and invite Soviet penetration of the area, wanted to encourage the United States to continue its presence in East Asia and also wanted Japan to strengthen its armed forces; this course went against everything the leftists had held dear in foreign policy. The Zhouists also wanted to reassure the Association of Southeast Asian Nations (ASEAN) that Beijing would not encourage Communist insurrectionary groups in the area; the leftists found this policy anathema because by giving up ties with local Communist parties, the CPC was discarding its ideological commitment to international Communist revolution. Prime Minister Lee Kuan Yew, during his visit to Beijing in May 1976, touched upon this part of the Chinese dilemma when he said, "Premier Hua says that, being a Socialist country, China supports the revolutionary struggles of all countries. But Premier Hua also states that China does not interfere in the internal matters of other countries and that how Singapore Government deals with its Communists is a matter for the Singapore Government to decide. Based on non-interference, I believe that we can develop our relations."[47] As 1976 ended, it was still uncertain as to how China would resolve these contradictions.

NOTES

1. See Stuart Schram, ed., *Chairman Mao Talks to the People* (New York: Pantheon Books, 1974), p. 237.

2. See Harold C. Hinton, ed., *The People's Republic of China, 1949–1979: A Documentary Survey,* vol. III (Wilmington, DE: Scholarly Resources, 1980), pp. 1508–11.

3. New China News Agency, June 1, 1967, quoted in Stanley Karnow, *Mao and China* (New York: Viking Press, 1973), p. 174.

4. For the text of the poster, see Hinton, *People's Republic,* vol. III, p. 1553.

5. Ibid., p. 1568.

6. Ibid., p. 1460.

7. Jürgen Domes, *The Internal Politics of China, 1949–1972* (London: C. Hurst, 1973), p. 182.

8. Hinton, *People's Republic,* vol. IV, p. 2194.

9. See Edward E. Rice, *Mao's Way* (Berkeley: University of California Press, 1972), p. 393.

10. Ibid., p. 403.

11. See Hinton, *People's Republic,* vol. IV (1980), p. 1923.

12. See *Far Eastern Economic Review,* 35 (August 1968), 377–78.

13. See Karnow, *Mao and China,* p. 446.

14. Hinton, *People's Republic,* vol. IV, p. 2239.

15. *Selected Works of Mao Tse-tung* (Beijing: Foreign Languages Press, 1967), vol. II, p. 224.

16. *Resolution on CPC History (1949–81)* (Beijing: Foreign Languages Press, 1981), pp. 32–36. The resolution was adopted by the Sixth Plenary Sessions of the Eleventh Central Committee of the CPC on June 27, 1981.

17. For the English text of the constitution, see *Peking Review,* no. 18 (April 30, 1969), 36–39.

18. For the English text of the report, see *New China News Agency,* April 27, 1969.

19. See "Outline of 'Project 571,'" in *Chinese Law and Government,* Autumn-Winter 1972–73, p. 54.

20. For an interesting account of Deng's years in disgrace, see Mao Mao, "My Father Deng Xiaoping's Years in Jiangxi," in *China Reconstructs,* April 1985, pp. 28–30.

21. See *Resolution on CPC History,* p. 39, where it says, "Jiang Qing and others directed the spearhead at Comrade Zhou Enlai."

22. For English translations of Zhou's and Zhang's speeches, see *Peking Review,* no. 4 (January 24, 1975), 6–25.

23. For the text of the new constitution and a side-by-side comparison between it and the 1954 constitution, which it replaced, see *China Quarterly* no. 62 (June 1975), 386–406.

24. Ibid., p. 390.

25. *Peking Review,* no. 4 (January 24, 1975), 23.

26. For the full text see *Peking Review,* no. 1 (January 2, 1976), 8–10.

27. *Resolution on CPC History,* pp. 39–40.

28. For the various criticisms leveled against Deng, see Roger Garside, *Coming Alive: China After Mao* (New York: McGraw-Hill, 1981), pp. 7–24.

29. *Peking Review,* no. 14 (April 2, 1976), 4.

30. Quoted in "Quarterly Chronicle and Documentation," *China Quarterly,* no. 67 (September 1976), 662.

31. Hinton, *People's Republic,* vol. V, p. 2558.

32. Ibid., p. 2602.

33. Edgar Snow, *The Long Revolution* (New York: Random House, 1971), p. 70.

34. Ibid., p. 169.

35. *Selected Works of Zhou Enlai,* vol. I (Beijing: Foreign Languages Press, 1981), p. 360.

36. Mao Tse-tung, "On the Ten Major Relationships," *Peking Review,* January 1, 1977, p. 13.

37. Kwan Ha Yim, ed., *China and the U.S.: 1964–1972* (New York: Facts on File Publication, 1975), p. 161.

38. Quoted in Yuan-li Wu, *As Peking Sees Us* (Palo Alto, CA: Hoover, 1969), p. 74.

39. Zhou En-lai, "Report to the 10th National Congress of the Communist Party of China," *Peking Review,* nos. 35 and 36, September 7, 1973, p. 22.

40. Yim, *China and the U.S.,* pp. 215–16.

41. For a text of the communiqué, see Hinton, *People's Republic,* vol. V, pp. 2362–63.

42. "Comments on Teng Hsiao-p'ing's Economic Ideas of the Comprador Bourgeoisie," *Peking Review,* no. 35 (August 27, 1976).

43. Chou En-lai, "Report on the Work of the Government," *Peking Review,* no. 4 (January 24, 1975).

44. "Quarterly Chronicle and Documentation," *The China Quarterly,* no. 48 (October–December 1971), 804.

45. Ibid., no. 57 (January–March 1974), 214.

46. See Special Supplement in *Peking Review,* no. 15, April 12, 1974, p. iv.

47. *Far Eastern Economic Review* (Hong Kong), June 4, 1976.

CHAPTER 11

China After Mao: "A New Revolution"

In 1976 few could have foreseen the rapidity with which Deng Xiao-ping and the pragmatist faction would rise to power, discard Maoist ideology, and reverse Maoist policies. Fewer, if any, could have predicted that in their haste to follow an economic-oriented path to modernization, the pragmatists would not only throw the country wide open to Western (the term includes Japan) investment capital, Western technology and know-how, and Western business collaboration but also introduce several key capitalist development techniques. Finally, none could have envisaged the possibility of a handful of Beijing students starting a "democracy movement" (in 1989) that would snowball into a major confrontation between them and the government and force Deng to use guns to crack down on the dissidents. The decade that had started with such promise ended in bloodshed, confusion, and the loss of national direction.

However it is to Deng's credit that in the first few years following Mao's death he managed to manipulate Chinese politics so skillfully that his return to power was carried out in a relatively smooth fashion, without creating any acute succession crisis that could have thrown the country into a period of political chaos.

POLITICAL SUCCESSION: FROM HUA TO DENG

Mao's dismissal of Deng Xiao-ping (the "unrepentant capitalist-roader"), his appointment of Hua Guo-feng as premier, and his note to Hua stating that "with you in charge, I am at ease" were all actions no doubt intended to ensure a smooth transfer of power after his death. But the very reason that made Hua an attractive candidate also reflected the weakness of the choice. Mao had chosen a centrist, a person who was not committed to the extreme left or right but one who was supposed to be able to project Maoist ideology and work with all sides. Hua, a latecomer to national politics, had had no time to build central and provincial power bases of his own, and his support from existing institutional and party factions was tentative and weak.

In the months preceding Mao's death, with Deng out of the way, members of the Jiang Qing group tried to bind Hua to their radical policies by heightening their attacks on the "capitalist roaders." And as soon as Mao died, Jiang Qing's group put forward a candidate of its own for the post of chair of the party. But the country as a whole and most of the leaders in the party, the military, and the state bureaucracy were tired of radical left policies, and there appeared to be limited support for Mao's widow and her friends. There was, however, serious danger that the Jiang Qing group could create—and some troubling signs that it was attempting to create—a political crisis.

On October 6, 1976, Hua, with the support of the military-bureaucratic complex and senior party cadres in the Politburo, took preemptive action by arresting all members of the Jiang Qing group, hereafter referred to by the Chinese press by the pejorative term the *Gang of Four.* An important role was played in this operation by Politburo member Wang Dong-xing, one-time bodyguard of Mao Ze-dong and currently in charge of the military unit 8341, which protected the lives of the leaders in Beijing. The government also took swift action to disarm the pro-left militia in Shanghai and destroy the power of the pro-Jiang Qing leaders in the other provinces. The Gang of Four was accused of having conspired to take over party and state power by a coup. The people welcomed the news of their fall.

Thus, within a month of Mao's death, the ultraleft had been eliminated from the national power struggle, and Hua hastened to legitimize his position by establishing links with Mao's personal and ideological legacy. On October 8, six days before the purge of the Gang of Four became public knowledge, it was announced that Mao's body would be placed in a crystal sarcophagus in a memorial hall to be built in Tiananmen Square, enshrining forever Mao's physical body, and that Hua would edit the fifth volume of Mao's collected works, enshrining forever Mao's ideology. Hua's authority was further enhanced when the Politburo decided to make him chair of the party and of the Military Affairs Commission. On the face of it, these developments made Hua the most powerful leader China had known since the establishment of the PRC; he now combined in his person the erstwhile power and authority of Chairman Mao and Premier Zhou En-lai. And both the major opposing factions—the ultraleftists and the ultrapragmatists—were out of grace. Hua also tried to win over the middle-of-the-road pragmatists by becoming an outspoken patron of the Four Modernizations program, which had been first proposed by Zhou En-lai in his speech to the Fourth NPC in 1975.

But behind this facade of strength Hua remained a vulnerable figure. He had been elevated to this high status by those who wanted the country to return to a state of normalcy. As long as the succession was in dispute, local leaders were hesitant to carry out orders. There was a breakdown of discipline, resulting in the reemergence of factional fighting in the provinces, widespread disruption of production, and even cases of deliberate sabotage. With the installation of Hua as party chair and premier, full attention could be paid to the problem of internal law and order. The price Hua had to pay for his promotion could not have been entirely to his liking; his pragmatist backers forced him to rehabilitate Deng Xiao-ping.

In anticipation of the conflict that was bound to arise when Deng returned to the political arena, Hua tried to entrench himself by emphasizing his loyalty to Maoist values and Maoist work style. He even tried to foster a cult of personality and had huge portraits of himself, in which he had altered his hair style to look very much like Mao's, hung next to those of the Great Helmsman. Ultimately, all this activity proved to be counterproductive because Hua, who had been a member of the Politburo for only 3 years compared with Deng's 21, was a political novice in comparison to his opponent. Moreover, he misread the spirit of the times; many people who had been hurt so deeply by the GPCR not only had no desire to see a return of Maoism but also wanted the leaders to go beyond the arrest of the Gang of Four and critically examine the party's role in that campaign.

In July 1977, at a plenary meeting of the Central Committee of the CPC, Deng was restored to all the positions he had occupied before his dismissal: vice-chair of the party and membership in the party Central Committee, the Politburo, and the Standing Committee of the Politburo; he was also appointed vice-premier, vice-chair of the Military Affairs Commission, and chief of the general staff. It is significant that Deng's return was not accompanied by even a pro forma confession of any wrongdoing. Hua had resisted Deng's rehabilitation because it meant that if Deng was without guilt, then those who had participated in his ouster, including Hua, were the guilty ones. It also meant that similar amnesty would have to be extended to other Mao-dismissed political figures. Before the situation could deteriorate further, Hua had his position legitimized at the national party and people's congresses, which were held in quick succession in 1977–1978.

The Eleventh Party Congress, convened in August 1977, confirmed the new leadership group (led by Hua as chair of the party) and officially declared that the GPCR had come to an end. However, from Hua's point of view, the composition of the new Central Committee and the Politburo reflected an ominous shift in the balance of power. Seasoned veterans, who had been pushed aside by Mao during the GPCR, made a stunning comeback. The average age of 146 of the 201 members of the Eleventh Central Committee was over 60 years; 84 percent of the members had joined the CPC before 1949, and 38 percent had been purged during the GPCR and rehabilitated since 1972. Representation of ultraleft mass organizations was reduced from 18 percent, as it had been in the Tenth Central Committee, to 12 percent. Yet it is noteworthy that Hua in his seven-hour inaugural address still praised Mao as a genius without flaws (the "greatest Marxist of our time") and made no reference to the Tiananmen Square incident.

Like the Central Committee, the new Politburo (23 full members and 3 alternates) also saw the return of many veterans. The following five figures who were elected to the Standing Committee of the Politburo represented the new leadership core:

- Hua Guo-Feng (56), chair of the party and a middle-of-the-road Maoist.
- Marshal Ye Jian-ying (80), vice-chair of the party and representative of the central military machine.
- Deng Xiao-ping (73), vice-chair of the party and representative of the hard-line pragmatists who were purged during the GPCR.
- Li Xian-nian (72), vice-chair of the party and representative of the civilian bureaucratic complex that had survived the GPCR.
- Wang Dong-xing (61), vice-chair of the party. One-time body guard of Mao Ze-dong, Wang had risen to become vice-minister of public security and was made a full member of the Politburo in 1973. At the Eleventh PC, Wang was also made secretary-general of the party.

The congress adopted a new party constitution, which stressed discipline, stability, and unity, and dropped all references to the Red Guards as a party institution.

It was obvious that although Deng had been rehabilitated, he still lacked majority support within the Politburo and therefore was not yet in a position to challenge Hua's authority.

As far as Hua and his backers were concerned they were in a superior position but, at the same time, caught in a situation with a built-in contradiction: They were ideologically committed to upholding Maoism, while being forced to attack the members of the Gang of Four, who had been the most ardent proponents of Maoism. Hua tried to make out that the Gang of Four was in reality anti-Mao and ultrarightists and, at the Eleventh PC, officially denounced Zhang Chun-qiao as a "Guomindang agent," Jiang Qing as "a renegade," Yao Wen-yuan as "an alien class element," and Wang Hong-wen as "a new bourgeois element; all old and new counter-revolutionaries who [had] sneaked into our Party." And as a good Maoist, he also made the following declaration, which must have made large numbers of Chinese feel very uneasy:

> *Stability and unity do not mean writing off class struggle.* The victorious conclusion of the first Great Proletarian Cultural Revolution certainly does not mean the end of class struggle. . . . Throughout the historical period of socialism the struggle between the two classes, the proletariat and the bourgeoisie, and between the two roads, socialism and capitalism, continues to exist. . . . Political revolutions in the nature of the Cultural Revolution will take place many times in the future [emphasis in original].[1]

Within a few months of the Eleventh PC, the Fifth National People's Congress was convened from February 26 to March 5, 1978. Hua, as premier, presented the report on the work of the government and laid down the goal of making China a "modern, socialist great power" by the year 2000. In the first phase of his grandiose plan, from 1978 to 1985, Hua called for an annual gross national product (GNP) growth rate of at least 8 percent. However, the targets were to be achieved by policies reminiscent of Mao's 1958 Great Leap Forward.

In contrast, the 1975 state constitution was revised again, and the new document reflected the desire of its framers, many of whom were pragmatists, to strengthen law and order and limit Maoism by making the authority of the judiciary and other institutions more explicit and by reinstituting the procuracy (the equivalent of an attorney-general's office). Marshall Ye, in his report on the revision of the constitution, called for "unity and iron discipline" and, ironically, also quoted Mao to emphasize the need for socialist justice:

> Within the ranks of the people, it is criminal to suppress freedom, to suppress the people's criticism of the shortcomings and mistakes of the Party and the government or to suppress free discussion in academic circles.[2]

The new constitution gave the citizens "the right to lodge complaints with organs of State at any level against any person working in an organ of State, enterprise or institution for transgression of law or neglect of duty."[3] Incidentally, among the citizens' fundamental rights, the clause granting freedom to engage in scientific and literary pursuits, which had been deleted in the 1975 constitution, was also reintroduced.

Pragmatists, particularly Deng's supporters—who had hoped that the NPC would, in keeping with pre-1976 practice, separate the office of the chair of the party from that of premier and appoint Deng to the latter post—were disappointed. The opposition not only managed to confirm Hua in his post of premier but also kept Deng from becoming head of state (a new post that substituted for the earlier chair of the People's Republic of China); Ye Jian-ying was made head of state.

Obviously, the struggle for power was far from over. A still-insecure Hua now tried to legitimize his position further by promoting the "two whatever's" policy—the party must uphold whatever policy decisions Mao had made (e.g., appoint Hua as premier) and adhere to whatever instructions Mao had given (e.g., class struggle must never be abandoned)—because an infallible Mao provided the best defense for Hua's position. Deng countered this policy by separating Mao the man from Mao the revolutionary thinker. By tacitly rejecting Mao's post-1956 policies as dogmatic and unworthy of Maoism, and using Mao's early writings, Deng established a new "Maoist" guideline: "Seek truth from facts." Had not Mao, himself, repeatedly said that Marxism-Leninism must not be viewed as a dogma, but as a guide to action? This conflict between Hua and Deng was waged on a theoretical plane through published articles with oblique historical allegories. This method ensured that the intellectuals understood what was going on, whereas the masses remained ignorant and popular opinion was not inflamed.

At a more practical level, the pragmatists, exploiting their official positions and influence, encouraged changes that reversed Maoist policy patterns; Deng as first vice-premier in charge of the Four Modernizations, naturally played a crucial role in furthering these designs. Apart from Deng's supporters at the center, the pragmatists by 1978 had been able to replace leaders of 26 of 29 province-level governments with their own men. The result was that material incentives and wage differentials were restored to boost industrial production; foreign trade and import of technology made a mockery of "self-reliance"; emphasis on private plots, side-line production, and free markets brought profit-oriented economy to the countryside; and entrance examinations to colleges and universities were reintroduced and professional standards and expertise made respectable again. Jiang Qing's revolutionary operas and ballets were no longer performed, and what was once dubbed decadent literature was available once more. The veteran theorist Hu Qiaomu went so far as to suggest that "methods of economic management in capitalist countries contain factors worth our study" and conclude his thesis with the call, "The proletariat can and must learn from the bourgeoisie."[4] As a logical conclusion of this line of thinking the decision was reached to send thousands of students to the West to study advanced scientific techniques.

The pragmatists also encouraged youths to embarrass Hua by airing their views through a poster campaign. The posters, critical of the Maoists, were pasted on the so-called Democracy Wall (a short stretch of wall about a mile west of Tiananmen Square) and strongly endorsed Deng's liberalizing policies. The writers asked for a reversal of the official verdict on the April 1976 Tiananmen Square incident, for an enquiry into the injustices perpetuated during the GPCR, and for a rehabilitation of leaders such as Peng De-huai. They demanded "socialist democracy," which would free them from enslavement to feudal despotism. They also asked for greater personal freedom and legal protection for this freedom. The protesters rapidly enlarged their activities and began to publish a number of unauthorized journals. Deng's use of this Democracy and Human Rights Movement to advance his cause was not dissimilar from Mao's periodic use of the masses.

The confrontation between Hua and Deng that had been taking shape for a year, ended with the Third Plenum of the Eleventh Central Committee (December 1978), where Deng finally emerged as the clear victor. The meeting[5] vindicated Deng's 1975 policies and canceled the documents issued in the anti-Deng campaign of 1976; it confirmed that the Tiananmen events of April 5, 1976, "were entirely revolutionary actions"; it rejected the "two-whatever's" policy and accepted the slogan "seek truth from facts" as the guiding principle; it discarded the slogan "take class struggle as the key link" and replaced it with policies that emphasized planned economic development; and except for Liu Shao-qi, it rehabilitated most of the living and dead leaders purged since 1958, such as Peng Zhen (living) and Marshall Peng De-huai (posthumously), and declared that socialist democracy and the socialist legal system would be strengthened so that such injustices could not take place in the future.

The Politburo was increased to include, among others, such pragmatists as the economic specialist Chen Yun; Zhou En-lai's wife, Mme. Deng Ying-chao; and Hu Yaobang, a long-time younger associate of Deng Xiao-ping, who had been active in the Communist Youth League and was soon to become one of the most important members of the new leadership group. The strategy used by the antileft group was to allow Hua supporters to retain their Politburo positions but to reduce their voting strength by adding increasing numbers of Dengists. By the end of 1979, the membership of the Politburo had been increased to 28 and Deng could count on 13 or 14 votes, against 7 for Hua.

Despite all his efforts and all his high posts, Hua had lost the succession struggle; it was only a matter of time before he would be removed from his leading positions in the party and the state. The "reversal of verdicts" by the Third Plenum of the Eleventh Central

Committee, however, went far beyond marking the end of the Hua regime by implying that Mao, too, was not without fault and shortcomings; the path was now opened for a reappraisal of Mao Ze-dong.

As was to be expected, there was a considerable backlash from the left, and fears were expressed that socialism was being discarded. Deng's liberalization approach had caused many human rights protesters even to question the merit of socialism and to attack the party itself for having allowed itself to be misused by the leftists. This reaction could only embarrass Deng, who in any case no longer needed a popular poster campaign to support his struggle for power. The result was that the government began to curb the movement and arrested many of the political activists.

The most notorious arrest was that of the 28-year-old Wei Jing-sheng who had become an outstanding spokesperson of the Democracy movement. Wei, like many other young intellectuals, had written graphically about the widespread grinding poverty in the countryside that he had witnessed during the cultural revolution and about the backwardness of the country (thus directly or indirectly criticizing the party under Mao), but it was his poster on "The Fifth Modernization—Democracy" that brought him into prominence. In this piece Wei questioned the motives of the pragmatists and warned that the Four Modernizations program, unless accompanied by democracy, would not liberate the people from exploitation by the party and a state of thralldom. In a later poster entitled "Do We Want Democracy or New Dictatorship," Wei went so far as to attack Deng for turning into a dictator. Wei was arrested in March 1979 and indicted as a counterrevolutionary who had supplied state secrets to a foreign journalist (a wholly phony charge).

In the same month, Deng warned the seekers of "ultra-democracy" that their antinational activities would not go unpunished, and to score the need for the people to uphold the party's leadership, he announced the Four Cardinal Principles that were to be dutifully upheld by all Chinese: unquestioning loyalty to the socialist road, the dictatorship of the proletariat, the leadership of the CPC, and Marxism-Leninism-Mao Zedong Thought. The Four Cardinal Principles were written into the party and state constitutions in 1982.

The Democracy and Human Rights Movement was now brought to an end on the grounds that the party and government would themselves take over the responsibility of extending socialist democracy and socialist legality.

And indeed Peng Zhen, who had spent years in jail during the GPCR, was put in charge of the legal affairs commission to draw up a comprehensive legal system. The new laws, which came into effect on January 1, 1980, indicated the desire of the leaders to reduce the power of the public security authorities and increase that of the police and the judiciary. For example, under the new laws, criminals were entitled to legal council and had a right to appeal their sentence. Frame-ups and torture were explicitly forbidden. Law codes were also drawn up to reassure the increasing number of foreign traders and investors that their contracts, monies, and goods were fully protected.

Laws were also passed to reestablish local people's congresses at the county level and above and to replace revolutionary committees with people's governments. Elections, theoretically, were made more democratic by allowing more than one person to be nominated.

As early as 1978, Deng, who was acutely conscious of the need to gain the willing cooperation of the intellectuals for China's modernization program, had announced that "brain workers" were also proletarian workers and had gotten the rightist designation removed from intellectuals, many of whom had been under a shadow since 1957. In 1979 thousands of intellectuals (professors, scientists, writers, and artists), who had been exiled to the countryside as rightists and revisionists during the GPCR, were finally rehabilitated and restored to positions of honor. Also in 1979 the stigma of "black elements" (children of landlords, rich peasants, and counterrevolutionaries) was removed from all those who had been so categorized during the cultural revolution. In a correlated action the government urgently began to upgrade and expand the damaged educational system; in a population of nearly a billion, there were only 16,000 persons with postgraduate degrees and 1.55 million college graduates.

Recognizing the necessity to rebuild the faith of the masses in the party, the pragmatists encouraged the people to air their complaints. According to Beijing figures, the party, the government, and the courts reviewed nearly 4 million cases of persons who had been persecuted during the GPCR and redressed most of them.

So despite the banning of the Democracy Wall and the persecution of a few protesters, the social and cultural atmosphere improved dramatically. Foreign movies, books, plays, and music added to the richness of cultural life. Consumer goods began to increase in quantity and improve in quality. After the official recognition of the PRC by the United States in January 1979, the number of American tourists increased by the tens of thousands. Tourism as a whole was growing by leaps and bounds, resulting in vast building projects and improvement of transportation. English became the most popular foreign language. There was a new liveliness in the once-drab cities of China.

By 1980 it was readily accepted, both inside and outside China, that Deng, even though he was neither chair of the party nor premier in the State Council, was the new leader of the country. However, Deng still had a long way to go before he could acquire anywhere near full control of China's affairs. Even Mao, whose charisma was far greater than that of Deng, had failed to achieve that elusive pinnacle of power.

THE 1980s: DENG LAUNCHES HIS REVOLUTION

After a short foray into active international politics that produced debatable results, Deng from 1980 on turned his full attention to internal affairs. He was convinced that without economic modernization, China could not play a significant role in international affairs.

If Deng's plans for China's modernization were to succeed, he had to ensure that there would be no succession problem after his death. Having gained a majority in the Politburo, Deng by mid-1980 also managed to strengthen his forces in the State Council. One of the additions to the list of vice-premiers was a loyal Dengist, Zhao Zi-yang. As first secretary of the Sichuan Provincial Party Committee, Zhao had applied Deng's rural policies in his province in 1979 and proved their amazing effectiveness. He had veered away from the Hua-supported Dazhai large-collective model and allowed small groups of four or five peasant families to contract for land and keep all their production beyond a fixed amount guaranteed for state procurement. Although the amount of land so distributed amounted to only 12 percent of the total land under cultivation, the results were staggering. The incentive for private gain led to the doubling or even tripling of earlier production figures. By the end of 1980 the Maoist Dazhai model was denounced, and its much-touted success was revealed to be a result of secret investment of state funds and not self-reliance.

A much more self-confident Deng now moved to the next phase of his strategy, which involved removing Hua and other veteran leaders who could thwart Deng's actions, getting his own men into key positions, and making the party and state organs supportive of his policies. Deng began to promote the idea that the functions of party and state must be separated (one person should not hold posts in both systems), the bureaucratic organizations must be made more efficient by eliminating excess personnel, tenure must not be lifelong (aged leaders should retire), leaders must possess professional knowledge and skills, and the party must be cleansed of unqualified members (the target was mainly the leftists who had been recruited during the GPCR). By the fall of

1980 most of Deng's suggestions had been accepted by the Politburo, and since then Deng, not always successfully, has been trying to get the party and the state to implement them.

The Dismissal of Hua Guo-feng

In the Fifth NPC convened in September 1980, Hua, whose support in the party Politburo had been further eroded earlier in the year with the dismissal from that body of Wang Dong-xing and three others, reduced the numbers of his multisystem appointments by resigning from the premiership. Zhao Zi-yang (born 1918) took over as premier. But if Hua believed that he could thus appease Deng and retain the chair of the party and that of the Military Affairs Commission, he was mistaken. Before the year was out, Hua was bitterly attacked in a Politburo meeting for not having fully recognized his past mistakes. He was forced to make self-criticism. Hua confessed that he had followed leftist style in leadership and economic work, upheld the "two whatever's" policy, and not been enthusiastic in rehabilitating purged leaders or in reversing the verdict on the Tiananmen Square incident. He also requested to be relieved of all his leadership posts. Although the formal transfer of power did not take place until June 1981, Hua for all practical purposes was immediately replaced as chair of the party by Deng's protégé Hu Yao-bang and as chair of the Military Affairs Commission by Deng himself. At the Twelfth Party Congress (September 1982) the posts of party chair and vice-chair were abolished and replaced with that of secretary-general; Hu became the first secretary-general of the CPC.

The Great Trial

Hua's departure from the political scene was followed by the dramatic public trial of the Gang of Four and the Lin Biao Clique, which lasted from November 1980 to January 1981. Apart from the Gang of Four there were six other defendants—five generals associated with Lin and Mao's secretary, Chen Bo-da. The accused were indicted for four major crimes: (1) framing and persecuting party and state leaders (e.g., Liu Shao-qi, Deng Xiao-ping, and Peng De-huai) and plotting to overthrow the political power of the dictatorship of the proletariat (e.g., by falsely accusing 88 of the 193 members of the Eighth Central Committee and even Zhou En-lai of antiparty activities); (2) persecuting and suppressing large numbers of cadres and ordinary people (number persecuted 729,511; number persecuted to death 34,800); (3) plotting to assassinate Mao and engineer a coup d'état; and (4) plotting an armed rebellion in Shanghai. Lin Biao and his generals were primarily responsible for the third; the other indictments were basically against the Gang of Four. All the defendants except Jiang Qing confessed to their crimes. Jiang Qing not only refused to acknowledge any guilt but also accused the prosecutors for being anti-Mao counterrevolutionaries. The final sentence was "death with two years reprieve and permanent deprivation of political rights" for Jiang Qing and Zhang Chun-qiao; the others were sentenced to various prison terms. The death sentences were never executed, and the period of reprieve has been quietly extended indefinitely.

Although the Great Trial was no doubt intended to show the Chinese and the outside world that the new Chinese legal system had been brought into operation, it was clearly a political, rather than a legal, trial. The Gang of Four had worked within the given system to take over power; they could not be made solely responsible for the harshness and cruelty engendered by the GPCR. To have passed the death sentence on Jiang and Zhang but not on the generals connected with the Lin Biao coup hardly made any legal sense. Similarly, the tendency to attack the Gang of Four for all the ills that China had suffered since 1966 was stretching the imagination beyond acceptable limits. Obviously the time had come to reevaluate Mao's role in post-1956 Chinese politics.

The Resolution on Party History: June 1981

At the Sixth Plenum of the Eleventh Central Committee held at the end of June, Hua Guo-feng was officially relieved from his posts as chair of the party and of the Military Affairs Commission, which were taken over by Hu Yao-bang and Deng Xiao-ping, respectively.

An even more significant action of the plenum was the adoption of the Resolution on Certain Questions in the History of Our Party since the Founding of the PRC. The resolution, although insisting that the CPC must be guided "for a long time to come" by Mao Ze-dong Thought, openly and severely criticized post-1956 Mao for becoming "arrogant," for erring in criticizing Peng Dehuai, for overlooking objective economic laws during the Great Leap Forward, for overturning the correct policies of Liu Shaoqi and Deng Xiao-ping in the 1960s, and for ignoring both Marxism-Leninism and "Chinese reality" when he plunged "the nation into turmoil" by initiating the GPCR. An evaluation was also made of the "leftist errors" of the Gang of Four and Hua Guofeng.[6]

Thus the resolution, while evaluating Mao's role in the historical context, also spelled out the place Maoism was to hold in the future. Mao Ze-dong Thought would always be considered a "valuable spiritual asset of our Party," but it was to be limited to providing the guidelines encompassed by the three points: seek truth from facts, do not ignore the mass line, and do not give up independence and self-reliance. As Hu said in his speech on July 1, 1981, presenting the resolution

> Mao Zedong Thought, coming into being and developing in the course of the Chinese Revolution, is the crystallization of the collective wisdom of our Party . . . [it] will remain the guiding ideology of our Party.
>
> However, Comrade [note that the appellation chairman has been dropped] Mao Zedong had his shortcomings and mistakes just like many other outstanding figures in the forefront of the march of history. Chiefly in his later years, having been admired and loved for so long by the Party and people, he became overconfident and more and more divorced from reality and the masses and, in particular, from the Party's collective leadership, and often rejected and even suppressed correct opinions that differed from his.[7]

Liu Shao-qi's posthumous rehabilitation was symbolic of the new ideology. The country could now put Mao behind and move on to establishing collective leadership and more institutionalized rule. There was a certain amount of regrouping of factions; although Deng was still not in absolute control, he did have a working alliance with other groups that allowed him to pursue his major goals. Deng wanted to streamline the government and make the bureaucracy and economic units more efficient and modern. The obstacles he faced were too many aged leaders with fixed ideas, too many inefficient and underemployed cadres, too many persons with multiple offices in the party and the state organs, too many factions, too many leftists still in the party, and increasing corruption.[8]

In 1982 several actions were initiated to reform the situation. In the State Council (the cabinet) the number of vice-premiers was reduced from 13 to 2, and the number of state ministries and commissions was reduced from 98 to 52 and finally to 43. To cushion the impact of this drastic action, many of the aging veterans who lost their posts were made "advisers" so that they could retain their salaries and other privileges. Similar actions were taken in the party. The Central Advisory Commission (CAC), with Deng as chair, was established, to which the aged senior veterans could withdraw and give way to more youthful leaders.

At the Twelfth Party Congress, held in September 1982, only 48.5 percent of the members of the old Central Committee were reappointed to the new Central Committee; the others were shifted to the CAC, demoted, or retired. The post of party chair was abolished (to avoid future one-man dictatorship) and replaced with that of a secretary-general. The General Secretariat of the party was made the leading body of the CPC. The Standing Committee of the Politburo was now staffed by Hu Yao-bang, Ye Jian-ying (83 years old but refusing to shift to the CAC), Deng Xiao-ping, Zhao Zi-yang, Li Xian-nian, and Chen Yun. With the obvious purpose of weeding out diehard Maoists and other undesirables, Hu proposed that beginning in 1983 and proceeding in three stages over three years, the party would be rectified. In the last stage all members of the party would be called on to reregister (no doubt, to allow the leaders to reject the unwanted).

A revised state constitution (the fourth) was approved in December 1982. It further strengthened institutional revival by restoring the posts of president and vice-president of the PRC, by establishing a State Central Military Commission, and by transferring administrative power from the communes to local government bodies. The constitution also abolished life tenure in leading posts and declared that state leaders could not serve more than two consecutive terms in office. But the fact that Deng (79 years old in 1983) continued to retain his chair of the Military Commission and his seat in the Politburo Standing Committee meant that he was not yet confident that his protégés, Hu Yaobang and Zhao Zi-yang, were well enough entrenched in their posts and also that it was as yet difficult to get the old guard, such as Ye Jian-ying, Li Xian-nian, and Chen Yun, to comply with the new orders.

In 1983 the publication of *Selected Works of Deng Xiaoping,* which contained Deng's key policy speeches from 1975 to 1980, evidenced further consolidation of Deng's power and of his policies that encouraged economic growth and political reform.

The New Economic Policies

From the time Deng returned to power he made China's economic modernization his single most important concern. Every policy framed or approved by Deng, whether it revamped the educational system, streamlined the party, reduced the size of the military, forced couples to have only one child, or experimented with capitalist-style market mechanisms, was directly aimed at carrying out Deng's "second revolution." In more concrete terms his goal was to quadruple China's GNP from $250 billion in 1980 to $1 trillion by the year 2000.

To achieve this historic goal China began to make far-reaching and determined efforts to seek foreign loans, acquire foreign technology and machinery, and invite foreign investors to participate in Chinese economic enterprises. China also sent thousands of students to the advanced countries of the West, primarily America, to gain scientific, technological, and managerial skills. Between 1978 and 1989 the number of Chinese students who had or were studying abroad had exceeded 90,000—80,000 of them in the United States.[9]

From 1980 on, the reform leaders repudiated elements of both the Maoist model, which emphasized collectivism and egalitarianism, and the Soviet model, which considered centralized state planning and state administration of the economy as basic to the socialist economic infrastructure. The record of economic achievement in the Maoist era had by no means been unimpressive (the average annual growth rate between 1952 and 1980 was 8.2 percent[10]), but it had been marred by periodic ideological campaigns that had resulted in social upheaval and economic regression. Thus, for example, famine and hunger had reemerged during the Great Leap Forward and the Cultural Revolution. Maoist strategy had supported the growth of industry, particularly heavy industry, at the expense of agriculture, and the policy of holding procurement prices of agricultural products artificially low had kept the standard of living of the masses from improving. In economic terms accumulation had been emphasized over consumption.

The new approach of the reformers discarded Mao's overriding commitment to ideology and aimed at reducing party and state controls over planning, production, and pricing of commodities (except commodities of national interest such as steel and energy) and allowing market forces to have freer play. Unfortunately, the new policies, although still at an experimental stage, created contradictions that exploded in the Tiananmen Square incident and brought to focus the dilemmas currently facing the leadership.

One of Deng's biggest predicaments was a consequence of the fact that he, like Mao before him, had to work with various factions within the party. Deng was, without doubt, the Supreme Leader, but the only way he could keep his program from collapsing was by skillfully balancing factional interests. There were several factions to contend with, and since they often shifted their alliances, the story of factional infighting, which in any case was hidden from public view, is not easy to comprehend. At the broadest level the factions were divided into two groups: the conservatives and the reformers. However, the conservatives ranged from diehard Maoists to those who approved the reforms as long as they did not go too far in reducing the authority of the party or the state. Similarly, the reformers ranged from radicals who were prepared to dismantle the old party and state structures, and virtually Westernize China in order to modernize it, to moderates who wanted to proceed slowly to ensure that economic liberalization policies did not destabilize the country.

Rural Reforms. Of all the reforms, the ones affecting the countryside, where nearly 80 percent of the Chinese still live, have so far been the most successful. The reformers moved quickly to decentralize state authority in management and to privatize production. By 1982, the communes had been quietly disbanded and replaced by the Household Responsibility System (HRS). In this system agriculture was decollectivized and land was divided into parcels that were leased to individual peasant households, who were entitled to produce whatever they wished as long as they met their contractual obligation to the state. The peasants, free to sell their surplus in the open markets, now had an incentive to maximize their gains by increasing production. As a further encouragement the government increased procurement prices of agricultural commodities, paid higher than contracted prices for purchases in excess of the contracted amount, and allowed pricing of these commodities to be even higher in the open markets where the peasants sold their surplus. When the peasants, afraid that the policy would soon be reversed, began to overexploit the land, the government lengthened the lease period up to 15 years to encourage them to put some of their profits back into land improvement. The state also allowed the peasants who could afford to do so to hire labor and to buy and own trucks and other farm machinery.

The reformers then went a step further and invited the peasants to "contract out" forests, ponds, and nonagricultural land and get into very profitable specialized activities such as growing fruit and raising fish, chicken, ducks and pigs. Under this new liberalized environment the peasants did not need much goading to start other side-line businesses dealing with handicraft products, repair services, and local transportation.

These policies resulted in rapid and visible changes in the countryside. The average gross annual agricultural output value grew at the rate of 6.2 percent between 1979 and 1988, from 170 billion yuan to 587 billion yuan in money terms, and average per capita rural income tripled during this period.[11] In the beginning the leaders, enthused by the success of the profit motive, lauded the prosperity of the "specialized" households that had attained an annual income of 10,000 yuan (about $5,000 at the current exchange rate) and held them up as models for others to emulate; later when disparities in income began to cause social problems, the leaders had to play down this kind of success. Although many of the rural areas have not done so well as others and many of the peasants have not done so well as the 10,000-yuaners, the general living standard of most peasants has risen considerably. As a result, although comparatively few peasants own impressive private houses, cars, trucks, and tractors, as the very rich ones do, large numbers have brought themselves luxury articles such as cassette recorders, television sets, and even refrigerators.

This development, in turn, led to a growth of rural towns, which brought light and service industries to the countryside and absorbed surplus rural labor, thus solving, to a considerable degree, the problem of rural migration to the cities and the consequent growth of urban slums and unemployment. It is estimated that by 1988, 20 percent of the rural labor force was involved with nonagricultural economic enterprises in the villages and rural towns.[12]

Although the success of the agricultural reforms is undeniable, the reforms did also, to a degree, engender some social and political problems that contributed to the 1989 crisis. The party's decision in 1985 to phase out mandatory quotas in agriculture and to decontrol prices of agricultural commodities, other than grain and cotton, had particularly serious side effects. The decision was based on two assumptions: (1) that the removal of quotas would relieve the government from subsidizing agriculture (the state was paying higher procurement prices than it was charging urban consumers for the same commodities) and (2) that the high growth level of agricultural produce would keep the free market from pushing prices too high. The assumptions proved to be incorrect. Released from the burden of supplying the state, the peasants naturally shifted to growing more profitable cash crops; the percentage of land used for cash crops rose from 9.6 percent in 1978 to 14.8 percent in 1988.[13] As a consequence there was shortfall not only in the grain supply but also in the supply of such commodities as pork and poultry, since pigs and chicken are fed on grain, and a steep rise in prices. The cost-of-living index for staff and workers was 172 percent higher in 1988 than it was in 1980. This rise hurt the fixed-wage earners, whose anger, as can be expected, was turned not against the peasants but against the reformers.

The change in the pattern of agricultural development also raised fears that China would not be able to feed its growing population unless the trend was reversed. Some effort was made to persuade the peasants to grow more grain, but the country failed to reach the declared targets. Grain production in 1988 fell to 394 million tons from the high of 407 million tons in 1984, and China had to increase its importation of cereals from 6 million tons to 15.3 million tons in 1988.[14]

What was perhaps even more important, the reform policies, by diminishing the role of state-organized collectives, undermined the authority, status, and local leadership role of the party cadres. This development, plus the new social environment that had replaced Maoist ideology of selflessness and altruism with materialism and personal profit, convinced many cadres that the time had come for them to enter the growing business world and "make money." These cadres left their jobs to become commercial agents, in which capacity they could exploit their old official connections to procure scarce commodities, such as fertilizers, and sell them at exorbitant prices to the needy peasants. Some of the more acquisitive cadres literally became black-marketeers and racketeers. The phenomenon of rural cadres abandoning their jobs to join the ranks of rural entrepreneurs caused the party to lose its prestige and respectability and led to a further erosion of the party's local authority.

It is obvious that the impressive growth in agriculture, based as it is on small, private plots, is bound to reach a plateau, and when it does the leaders will be faced with another dilemma. In the interest of continuing growth they will then have to decide whether to take the land back from the peasants so that it can be consolidated into sizable farms, where more efficient large tractors and more modern machinery can be used, or to make the ownership of land a truly private affair and allow the affluent peasants to increase their holdings by buying out the poorer peasants. The latter action, if followed, would spell the end of socialism.

As it is, by reducing its investment in the countryside, the state is already depending heavily on the richer segment of the rural population, and thereby accepting the widening gap between the richer and the poorer regions and between the richer and the poorer elements in the rural society. It has been estimated that there were 79.2 million people living in poverty in rural China in 1985, and that figure rose to 101.3 million in 1988.[15] The poorer peasants are also finding it difficult to pay for educational and health services, the financial burden for which has been shifted by the government to the peasantry.

The reform programs have also had a negative impact on the one-child-per-family policy. During the initial phase, when harsh punitive action was taken against couples who had more than one child, the policy did change the demographic pattern in the countryside. Later, when the policy was toned down and the government tried to achieve the same results through a system of rewards (job security, job promotion, better housing, and subsidized schooling and health care) and punishments (demotions, fines, reduced food rations, etc.), the measures began to fail. The system was more applicable to the cities than to the countryside, where the HRS had made the peasants relatively autonomous. Apart from the pressure of traditional values, many peasants felt the need to increase the family labor potential by having more male offspring. The richer peasants, of course, were happy to pay the fines imposed by the government for having a second or a third child. In several cases the poorer peasants' response to the population control policy was to resort to female infanticide to keep their options open for having a male child.

As indicated, the one-child policy has been more successful in the cities than in the villages because administrative pressures can be applied more directly on urban couples, who depend so heavily on the government for jobs, housing, and other facilities. However, 80 percent of the population still lives in the countryside, where population control problems continue to exist. It is worth noting that regardless of all the difficulties, there has been an overall drop in the population growth rate, from 2.6 percent in 1970 to 1.4 percent in 1988, even though the government will find it almost impossible to achieve the declared target of zero growth by the year 2000.

Urban Reforms. Compared with the success in the countryside, reforms in the urban industrial and commercial sectors have been slow to take hold. As a first step, the reformers tried to eliminate the extreme socialistic equalitarian thinking that characterized the inherited industrial system, popularly expressed in the phrases "everybody eats out of one big pot" and "the iron rice bowl." Under the old system, since the state guaranteed financial support to an economic unit (EU) regardless of the quality of its produce or the fact that it was running at a loss, the workers and management did not feel any sense of responsibility because they were all assured a part of the "big pot"; and since the workers could neither be fired for poor work nor their salaries reduced for low performance, their "rice bowls" (their jobs) were said to be as secure as if made of "iron." In contrast, an EU that showed profits or a worker who was more productive than the others received no material rewards.

The initial reforms gave the EUs some autonomy in the arena of decision making, allowing them to retain a part of their profits to refurbish their plants and to provide material incentives to workers by awarding bonuses for outstanding work. However, since old habits were difficult to break and since the issue of central control versus EU autonomy had not been fully resolved, the results of the reforms were very mixed.

In 1984, strengthened by the success of the rural reforms, the leaders turned their full attention to urban reforms and declared their intention to make the EUs truly independent economic entities, which would have the authority to plan and market their products and the right to retain all profits that accrued after they paid their taxes and, of course, to suffer the consequences of any losses. To achieve this end, the reformers decided (1) to strengthen the EU directors' role and make them fully responsible for the running of the enterprise (including the right to hire and fire); (2) change the rigid wage system to reflect the diversity of needs and individual performance; (3) substitute banks for government agencies as a source of financial loans; and (4) push China toward a more open market by freeing prices from central control, a process that had been started gingerly in 1980 but was now going to be accelerated.

The reforms also introduced new regulations for the ownership of small enterprises. Private individuals or collectives, not old-style state-run collectives but collectives formed by private citizens and by economic units, were allowed to take over state-owned enterprises on contract and even encouraged to set up their own businesses on a contractual basis. As a generalization, the privately owned businesses, limited to retail shops, repair workshops, and restaurants, were much smaller in size than the collectively owned urban enterprises such as hotels and trading companies. But both, run independently and without state interference, were extremely lucrative and rapidly grew in numbers. The flourishing collective and individual small-scale businesses, which soon came to absorb millions of urban unemployed, made a tremendous contribution in stimulating the economic environment and providing much-needed services.

The leaders also reaffirmed their commitment to the Open Door. Five Special Economic Zones (SEZs), restricted areas where special facilities and attractive financial considerations were given to foreign capitalists to establish their firms, were created along the coast in Guangdong and Fujian provinces. The firms were supposed to export their products and bring advanced technology to China. By 1990 the SEZs had attracted over $4 billion and set up 5,700 projects; their exports during the last decade accounted for a tenth of China's total exports and earned China $3.85 billion in foreign exchange. Foreign capitalists were also invited to set up joint ventures and to provide capital investment for upgrading the 400,000 aging economic units built in the 1950s.

There was some inner-party criticism against this policy because it appeared to undermine national autonomy and open the country to "bourgeois corrosion," but Deng managed to win the debate and confirm that being open to the world would remain a "fundamental policy for China."[16] By the end of 1988 China had signed agreements for 16,325 projects involving $79.2 billion in foreign investment, of which $47.7 billion had already been utilized. Separate agreements were concluded for 10,732 Sino-foreign joint projects, 7,573 Sino-foreign co-operative enterprises, and 1,090 enterprises run exclusively with foreign capital.[17]

The Tortuous Path of Reforms

In the five years from 1984, when urban reforms were accelerated, to the crisis in 1988–1989, China achieved impressive overall results. Chinese official figures, which have proven to be fairly accurate,[18] indicate that between 1985 and 1988 the national GNP increased from 856,800 million yuan to 1,401,500 million yuan, the total output value of agriculture from 361,900 million yuan to 586,500 million yuan, and that of industry from 971,600 to 1,822,400 million yuan (the figures are based on the prices for the year cited).

Why, then, the crisis in 1989? Troubles arose because the radical reformers, led by party general secretary Hu Yao-bang and premier Zhao Zi-yang, moved too fast in reducing the supervisory role of the state over planning and production and in lifting price controls without making adequate changes in the economic-political infrastructure. Thus economic structural imbalances developed that had a devastating impact on the economy as a whole and on the wage earner in particular.

Released from central controls, the EUs in the national and provincial sectors and the individual and cooperative enterprises blindly expanded investment in construction. The random but rapid growth in capital investment led to shortages in construction materials and energy; for example, raw materials provided by agriculture (growth rate: 3.9 percent) could not keep up with industrial demand (growth rate: 17.8 percent). The proportion of state revenue to national income dropped from 37.2 percent in 1978 to 26.2 percent in 1985 and to 21.3 percent in 1988, while the ratio of unbudgeted investment to budgeted investment rose from 31 percent to 81 percent and then to 92.4 percent during the same years. Excessive capital investment and large subsidies resulted in huge financial deficits (98.7 billion yuan between 1984 and 1988).[19]

Salaries were increased, but because of the low investment in consumer goods the gap between supply and demand rose from 4.6 percent in 1983 to 16.2 percent in 1988. Consumers had the money but there was little they could buy with it. At the same time unfair differences in salaries and incomes began to exist. Generally speaking, employees of state-owned enterprises were paid less than their counterparts in collectively owned enterprises, who in turn earned less than those in private businesses or in Sino-foreign joint ventures; and the income of the intelligentsia ("mental workers" such as teachers) fell far behind that of physical laborers.[20] Though this development was bad enough, it became even more intolerable for the wage earners, whose surplus purchasing power was further reduced by inflation, to see profiteers and corrupt businesspeople flitting around in imported cars and entertaining one another lavishly in expensive restaurants.

As early as 1985, the highly respected economist Chen Yun, a moderate reformer, cautioned the radical reformers that without proper macroeconomic controls, experiments with microeconomy (e.g., price decontrols) would result in chaos and that the naked pursuit of wealth would have severely negative side effects. Chen was proven correct when by the end of the year newspaper reports shocked the reading public with stories of unbelievable corruption in high places. News of the biggest scandal came from Hainan Island, where state and party officials connived with 872 companies and 88 government departments to improperly, indeed illegally, use their foreign exchange allocation to import, tax free, nearly 3 million color television sets, 252,000 videocassette recorders, 122,000 motor cycles, and 89,000 motor vehicles (more cars than were imported in the entire year by the rest of the country) and resell these items "all over the country at double or triple the prices." Several persons made more than a million yuan in corrupt money.[21] This scandal, involving a sum of $1.25 billion, was only the largest of innumerable similar affairs. Also in 1985 prices of several food items were allowed to float, resulting in price increases of up to 50 percent. That these developments resulted in popular dissatisfaction was revealed by some small-scale riots and student demonstrations.

The leadership tried to assuage popular feelings by cracking down on corruption and economic crimes and, in 1986, launched a drive to "rectify the party's work style." The need to reform the political structure was now more openly recognized, and Deng agreed with the radical reformers that the time had come for party functions to be separated from those of the state and for the party to leave issues "that fall within the scope of the law to the state and the government." Deng was cognizant of the fact that the country had "no tradition of observing and enforcing laws" and that devolution of power was not easy because of ingrained attitudes; according to Deng, state institutions "simply [took] back the powers that had been delegated to the lower levels." However, Deng wanted a sincere start to be made in working out plans for political reform.[22]

The opening provided by Deng was used by Hu Yao-bang and Zhao Zi-yang to go much further in the direction of intellectual liberalization than the limits Deng may have had in mind. Hu Yao-bang initiated a full-fledged debate on the essence of Chinese socialism, going so far as to declare that "Marxism is [almost] obsolete" and that "No advanced philosophical thought should become dogma. It should instead be a spiritual force that incites people to ceaselessly search and create. It should develop in step with the development of actual situations."[23] In a symposium held at Beijing in late 1986, scholars and intellectuals aired their views on political structural reform. They all agreed that China faced a problem in the over-centralization of power and that apart from separating the functions of the party and the government, efforts should be made to increase public participation in politics by reforming the legislative system and strengthening its supervisory role over the government. The main criticism was directed against the party for usurping the functions of the state.[24]

The relatively free academic environment produced a plethora of daring and unorthodox ideas. At the heart of the new political thinking was the realization that China needed to consider afresh the theoretical basis for its development. Some went so far as to suggest that China should go in for "wholesale Westernization" because Western science and technology and Western market techniques could not be understood or fully utilized without a proper comprehension of Western political thought and culture and the fostering of individual, civil, and human rights. Only true democratic pluralism could usher in an era of genuine modernization.

One of the most articulate exponents of this line of thought was Professor Fang Lizhi, vice-chancellor of the University of Science and Technology (UST) in Hefei. An internationally recognized astrophysicist, Fang traveled from university to university giving highly provocative speeches. He soon became the idol of the university students, and we can get some idea of his thinking from the speech he gave at Tong Ji University in Shanghai in November 1986:

> As for myself, I think that complete Westernization is the only way to modernize (enthusiastic applause). I believe in thorough, comprehensive liberalization because Chinese culture is primitive, not just backward in any particular aspect. . . . [T]he call for complete Westernization is nothing new . . . the roots of our backwardness lie in our history. We have changed a lot over the past century, yet we are still far behind the rest of the world [because] these decades of socialist experimentation since Liberation have been—well, a failure! (long applause) This is not just my opinion. It is clear to all eyes. . . . [I]t is important to note that . . . the critical component of the democratic agenda is human rights, a touchy issue in our country. Human rights are fundamental privileges . . . but we Chinese consider these rights to be dangerous.[25]

In early December 1986, 10,000 students of UST, who had been told repeatedly by Fang that "democracy must be won, not handed down from above," marched to the party's headquarters in Hefei (capital of Anhui province) to demonstrate against the local elections for the National People's Congress, which had just been held, and to demand that the electoral system be reformed. The agitation spread to 150 universities and colleges in other parts of China, including Beijing, taking the party by surprise. It appears that the cause of the unrest lay more in the poor educational system and the crisis created by urban reforms (inflation, corruption, etc.) than in any deep-seated desire for democracy, a concept not fully understood by the students; the students had every reason to be upset with the poor food and the poor classroom equipment provided by the universities and the manner in which the government arbitrarily appointed graduating students to unsuitable jobs in undesirable locations. However, slogans such as "Marxism, Leninism, Thought of Mao Ze-dong, Go to Hell" gave the conservatives a handle to attack the reformers, who themselves were shaken by these developments.

Student demonstrations petered out by February 1987, but apart from giving an indication that all was not going well with the reforms, they helped widen the rifts between the party factions. Deng moved in quickly and stabilized the situation by punishing the radical reformers and reconfirming his commitment to party dictatorship. He was particularly incensed by Fang's activities and ordered that he "be expelled, not just persuaded to quit" the party. Deng also warned the party and the people that "bourgeois liberalization would plunge the country into turmoil once more."[26]

Deng Xiao-ping was caught in a dilemma. He had no wish to see his economic reform program fail, nor did he want the party to lose its leadership role. He placated the conservatives by removing Hu Yao-bang, his hand-picked successor, from the post of party general secretary (January, 1987) and by expelling Fang Li-zhi and some other prominent right-wing figures such as Liu Bin-yan, the nationally recognized journalist, from the party. On the other hand, Deng replaced Hu with Zhao Zi-yang, who was as committed to the reform programs as Hu Yao-bang. Deng's action, however, did not resolve the contradiction inherent in the situation: Economic reforms demanded a lessening of, and not an increase in, the party's role. Taking advantage of this contradiction, the leftists used their temporary gains to reassert some of Maoist-style central controls. They even went so far as to revive Mao's Learn from Lei Feng campaign, which decried material incentives and exalted the Maoist ideology of self-sacrifice in the service of the collective (see Chapter 9).

Obviously, the crisis of winter 1986 had reopened the all-important issue of succession and placed Deng's reform programs in jeopardy. Inner-party conflict, and the resulting policy shifts, had confused the masses and the officials; in some rural areas cadres had begun to attack private entrepreneurs and the household responsibility system for being capitalistic.

By the end of 1987, Deng managed to contain the leftist trend and restrengthen the hands of the reformers by removing some of the key senior conservatives from positions of power. Under the guise of "rejuvenating the party," Deng pressured the veteran leaders to retire voluntarily and make place for younger colleagues. He, himself, led the way by stepping down from all the posts he held, retaining only the chair of the Military Affairs Commission. As a consequence, ten leaders, including four important conservatives, resigned from the Politburo. Though Deng thus managed to work out a rough parity between the left and the right in the Standing Committee of the Politburo, with the balance tilting in favor of the reformers, he had to pay a price: He had to elevate Li Peng, a moderate reformer, to the post of premier (November 1987), a position that until then was concurrently held by the party general secretary, Zhao Zi-yang.

When the personnel changes were officially announced at the Thirteenth Congress of the Communist Party of China (convened from October 25 to November 1, 1987) it appeared that the reformers had gained a victory. In his address to the Congress, Zhao provided a fresh theoretical basis for capitalist-style reforms. China, said Zhao, was "now in the primary stage of socialism" and embarked on a process of industrial modernization, which took place under "capitalist conditions" in other countries. Therefore, China had to "keep reforming" and pursue the Open-Door policy, develop a market economy, let private and public ownership play a dominant role, and "encourage some people to become rich first." Although economic development was to be made the "central task" and the country had to persevere in carrying out reform policies, it all had to be done "while adhering to the four cardinal principles." In this way China could establish a true modern, socialist society and not a capitalist one, even though the path followed involved capitalistic elements. Zhao then presented a farfetched economic plan that envisaged the separation of coastal areas from the hinterland so that the coastal belt could be modernized first by being opened to foreign investment and foreign management of Chinese enterprises. Modernization would later trickle westward to lesser and lesser developed areas.

Zhao also spoke of plans for structural reforms in the political realm, but here he went no further than to reiterate what had been said many times earlier, that there was a need to separate the party from the state, to delegate greater authority to the lower levels of government and to the economic enterprises, to make the functioning of bureaucracy more efficient and corruption free, and to strengthen the legalist system. The only reference to the need for a more democratic system was, strangely enough, enfolded in the statement that the party must carry on the fine Maoist tradition of "from the masses to the masses" and let the people "know about important events and [let them] discuss important issues."[27]

Before Deng's grand vision of a New Economic Order could be realized, developments in 1988 intervened to postpone the introduction of the new reform programs. A year later, in 1989, the vision was totally shattered.

Though political troubles in 1987 had kept China's economic reform programs in abeyance, the problems of an overheated economy and inflation had not been resolved. The double-digit rise in food prices in the cities (46.4 percent for grain products!) meant a continuing alienation of the urban population. The situation became worse in 1988, proving that, rhetoric apart, the leaders had failed in their attempts to control the money supply and the high rate of capital construction, which were feeding the inflationary spiral. Similarly, despite all talk of harsh action against corruption and profiteering, the government could do little to stop party, government, and public organizations from joining the ranks of private profiteers by establishing business companies that were often economically nonproductive but excellent sources for making money. After the 1989 crisis, the government itself reported that in 1988 the number of such companies jumped to 400,000, and according to the government report,

> Private businesses, collective enterprises and state-owned factories were not the only units involved in the *nationwide craze for business.* Party and government organizations, public organizations and even the army, public security and judicial departments eagerly entered the distribution field of materials. Abusing their power and taking advantage of incomplete reform measures, many companies engaged in *illegal management activities reaping huge profits by buying and reselling critically short raw materials and common, everyday commodities in high demand.* Their activities . . . disturbed the nation's economic order, drove up the price index and the rate of inflation, and disrupted the normal reform process. [emphasis added].[28]

Involved in this scandalous development were 47,956 cadres of the party and government, and the companies run by them made millions of yuan through corruption, bribery, and "1.3 million cases of illegal dealing."

An August 5, 1988, editorial in the *Worker's Daily* expressed what must have been the popular sentiment of the day:

> It is incomprehensible that profiteering by officials continues despite the Party Central Committee's repeated injunctions. Why do bureaucrat profiteers flourish? . . . The reason is that dishonest officials are backing them. . . . People always associate the phenomenon of bureaucratic profiteering with influence. . . . Relying on their parents' prestige, the children of high-ranking officials also can get items for their companies. No one dares to displease them. . . .
>
> Enterprises must be separated from the government. At the same time economic order must be based on the rule of law rather than the "rule of man."[29]

Also in August, the consumer price index soared by nearly 20 percent, and rumors that price controls were going to be removed on September 1 led to panic buying, hoarding, and massive corruption; similarly, rumors of currency devaluation resulted in runs on the banks.

In the face of mounting public opposition the reformers had to give in to the moderates and introduce a policy of retrenchment. It was announced that in the coming year, 1989, price reforms would be limited and that the prices of 72 major commodities would continue to be controlled.

THE TIANANMEN INCIDENT AND AFTER

The year China was to celebrate the fortieth anniversary of the founding of the People's Republic, 1989, should have been a year of great festivity. But there was little to celebrate. The inordinate escalation of corruption and inflation and the growing disparities in personal income had cast a deep shadow over the entire reform program, and the people had begun to grumble and lose faith in their leaders. There were even some who looked back wistfully at the Maoist era and said that they would much rather "have the stable prices of Mao than the high prices of Deng."[30]

It was under these circumstances that the students, once again, began to demonstrate against the government. As early as mid-1988, students at Beijing University had put up posters criticizing Zhao Zi-yang, Li Peng, and Deng Xiao-ping for the troubles facing Chinese society. Instead of enquiring into the causes for student demands for democracy and liberalization, the leaders clamped down on them, warning them that "rightist troublemakers" would be severely dealt with. Hints were also dropped that foreigners and the Voice of America were encouraging dissidence.

The "foreign hand" theory got some credibility when President George Bush, during his visit to China in February 1989, included Professor Fang Li-zhi among the list of invitees to his state dinner. Fang had just a month earlier angered Deng Xiao-ping by writing a letter to him (later endorsed by several other liberal intellectuals) asking for the release of Wei Jing-sheng and other political prisoners. Deng had taken no action on Fang's letter, and Chinese leaders, particularly the conservatives, were upset at the provocative action of the American president. They resolved the issue by using the police to keep Fang from attending the dinner.

The liberal intellectuals, no doubt, were upset by this action of the government, but it was the university and college students who, six weeks later, displayed their outrage by massive pro-democracy demonstrations. reasons for student unrest were basically the same as those that had led to campus trouble in 1986. After the lapse of two years, the students were still living in cramped quarters (often six to a room), eating indifferent food in cafeterias that did not even have enough seating capacity (many just filled their rice bowls and ate their meals walking back to their dormitories), and studying in poorly lit classrooms and ill-equipped laboratories. And their disgruntled, low-paid teachers could hardly be expected to inspire them with a sense of unthinking loyalty to the state. Indeed, the students, although apathetic on the surface, had many unspoken grievances against the political system.

The death on April 15 of Hu Yao-bang, the patron of liberal intellectuals, came as a shock to the students of Beijing and reawakened their instinct for activism. Overnight Beijing University became the center of the new agitation. From the few hundred students who gathered at Tiananmen Square on April 16 to pay homage to Hu, by laying wreaths and flowers at the foot of the Monument of the People's Heroes, the numbers of mourners grew to several thousands within days. Technically the students had breached the law against demonstrations,* but initially the police had not taken notice, perhaps, because "mourning" was not "demonstrating." However, when the students went beyond mourning to demand that the leaders rehabilitate Hu's name, end corruption in the party, publish details of personal assets of high officials and their family members, put price controls on consumer goods, lift restrictions on the press, and increase funds for higher education, the marches did turn into demonstrations; by then, however, Beijing authorities were helpless in the face of the growing numbers of students involved. On April 22, the day of Hu's funeral,

*The law was passed in 1986 following student turbulence that year, and it forbade all gatherings of people for purposes of demonstration except when official permission had been sought beforehand and the names of the organizers registered with the police.

tens of thousands gathered at Tiananmen Square.

The continuation of the demonstrations after Hu's funeral made them truly illegal. If the party had not been split between the soft-liners, led by Zhao Zi-yang, and the hard-liners, led by Deng Xiao-ping, Li Peng, and other senior conservatives, it is quite possible that the student problem could have been concluded to everyone's satisfaction. Official declarations that those who defied the ban on public protests would be "severely dealt with" came to mean nothing because the leaders were divided on how to deal with the students, and without any clear-cut directives the local authorities took no action at all.

In the absence of any concrete action by the leaders the students became more belligerent and escalated the confrontation by making harsh, and often crude, personal attacks on Deng and the other leaders and by ridiculing the party. Demonstrations, sometimes violent, also spread to many other cities of China. Deng Xiao-ping made his position bluntly clear on April 26: In the absence of Zhao Zi-yang, who had gone to North Korea on a state visit, the *People's Daily* published an editorial that characterized the student movement as an organized conspiracy whose aim was to "poison people's minds, create national turmoil and sabotage the nation's political stability [by] *negating the leadership of the party and the socialist system*" (emphasis added).[31]

Clearly, the Politburo was still not unified on the issue, and the editorial was not followed by any directive to the Beijing authorities on how to proceed against the students. The students, however, responded to the editorial by a massive demonstration; it is estimated that over 100,000 of them, cheered by thousands of bystanders, demonstrated on April 27.

Zhao returned from Korea on April 30 and was apparently caught in a dilemma. He could not ignore Deng's analysis of the current situation, but his own views were at total variance with those of the hard-liners. On May 4, when 150,000 students, journalists, and workers paraded in Tiananmen Square to celebrate the seventieth anniversary of the 1919 May Fourth Movement for science and democracy (see Chapter 5), Zhao, in a speech to the delegates of the Asian Development Bank, publicly contradicted Deng's policy line. He said that the students were "by no means opposed to our fundamental system. Rather they are asking us to correct mistakes in our work,"[32] which presumably was also the policy of the leaders. The split in the party leadership had come out in the open, but the two voices only confused the people and confounded the issues. Newspapers suddenly became more generous in their coverage of the demonstrations, and on May 9, 1,000 journalists from official news organizations, misreading the political signs, sent a petition to the government asking that press censorship be lifted.

There is no doubt that at this stage Mikhail Gorbachev's scheduled state visit, starting May 15, affected all parties concerned in the brewing political crisis. Deng Xiao-ping, anxious to make the first Sino-Soviet summit in 30 years a memorable one, softened the government stand and proposed that students hold "dialogues" with officials at various levels. On May 12 a government spokesperson met with the students and requested them not to demonstrate during the summit meetings; it was necessary for students to keep out of Tiananmen Square, where the Soviet president was to be welcomed, and off adjacent roads that converged on the square. The students, however, took the occasion of Gorbachev's visit as an opportunity to embarrass the government further. On May 13, they occupied a section of the square, set up tents, and started a seven-day hunger strike by 1,000 students (later reaching the figure of 3,000), supported by 15,000 of their colleagues. On May 14, the Beijing Students' Dialogue Delegation did meet with some high officials from the party Central Committee and the State Council, but the meeting was aborted for various reasons, basically because the government was not sincere in its efforts and the student leaders themselves were split over the issue.

The consequence of the hunger strike was a personal humiliation for Deng because his moment of glory was lost: Gorbachev had to be welcomed at the airport instead of at Tiananmen Square; he had to cancel his wreath-laying ceremony at the Heroes' Monument; he had to be brought to the Great Hall of the People (that flanks the square) for an official function through a rear door; and his visit to the Forbidden City (situated at one end of the square) also had to be canceled. On the seventeenth, the day Gorbachev left China, 1 million citizens of Beijing gathered at the square to show their support for the innocent, courageous, youthful hunger strikers.

Foreign journalists and television reporters, who had come to report on the summit meetings, were more enraptured by the student "democracy movement" than the summit. They stayed on to cover what many considered to be the most exciting development in post-Mao China. The students, eager to be seen and heard across the globe, helped the reporters in many ways: They gave interviews freely; they went out of their way to facilitate the work of the journalists; and they began to write their placards in English, some of which were obviously meant to cater to foreign sentiment ("Give Me Liberty or Give Me Death"; "I Have a Dream"; "Hello, Mr. Democracy") and some to show their bravado ("Deng Xiaoping Has an Addled Brain"; "Down With Deng Xiaoping"; "Hang Li Peng"). When the official media blacked out news of Tiananmen Square, the students became avid listeners of the Voice of America, thus confirming the "foreign hand" thesis.

From Deng's point of view, the situation had become intolerable, and within two days of Gorbachev's departure he lined up the conservatives behind him to reassert party authority by putting Beijing under martial law. Though party factionalism may not have wholly disappeared, this decision meant that Zhao's faction had lost out. The intensity of the party infighting can be gauged from Zhao's remark to Gorbachev that the CPC Central Committee (obviously in a secret meeting) had made a decision in 1987 that all important national issues had to be approved by Deng; the implication was that Deng was an emperorlike autocrat and responsible for perpetuating undemocratic practices. Zhao was later condemned for having revealed a "state secret" to the Soviet leader.

Zhao's last public act was a visit to the hunger-striking students on May 19, the day before martial law was declared. He told the students, with tears in his eyes, that he was sorry that he had "come too late." However, he added that the students should give up the hunger strike and that the problems they had raised would eventually be resolved.

The students, who had learned of Deng's secret decision to impose martial law, possibly from Zhao's associates, forestalled the entry of the troops by setting up barricades. The citizens of Beijing, outraged and alarmed by the government's action, came out in large numbers to support and help the students. Faced by such massive popular defiance, the leaders were caught in a dilemma. They had hoped that the declaration of martial law, coinciding with an unannounced entry of troops into Beijing, would make the students disperse, but that had not happened. Deng's only alternative now was to order the army to force its way into Beijing, but he could not get the Politburo to agree with him.

The failure of the leaders to agree on the next step created the impression that martial law had failed; and in the absence of any clear-cut policy the local authorities turned a blind eye to an increasingly liberal Beijing press, which joined the students in demanding the lifting of martial law. Censorship was finally imposed on May 24, the day after Deng managed to get the Politburo to dismiss Zhao Zi-yang as party general secretary and replace him with hard-liner Jiang Ze-min, currently secretary of the Shanghai party committee. With the head of the opposition out of the way, the hard-liners took steps to regain control of the party propaganda machine and the mass media.

However, it is significant that the final decision to use troops and tanks to suppress the democracy movement was taken by Deng (85 years old), with the backing of veteran leaders President Yang Shang-kun (82), Chen Yun (85), Li Xian-nian (80), Peng Zhen (87), Vice-President Wang Zhen (81), and Deng Ying-chao (85), none of whom was a member of the Standing Committee of the Politburo, or except for Yang, even an ordinary member of the Politburo. In fact many of these party stalwarts had been retired from active party work between 1985 and 1987. The resurrection of this veteran group meant that Deng had not been able to get the kind of support he wanted from the fractured party.

On the evening of June 3, after making repeated announcements over the television, the radio, and the local loudspeaker systems that the citizens must keep off the streets and allow the PLA troops to carry out their martial law tasks, the government ordered fully armed troops, backed by tanks and armored vehicles, to move into the city from various directions. The troops had to battle their way through barricades and crowds of angry citizens who fought back with Molotov cocktails, metal clubs, and rocks. Many soldiers were beaten to death; others were forced to remain within burning trucks or were doused with gasoline and incinerated. The soldiers responded with live ammunition. The bloodbath ended on the morning of June 4 when the tanks rolled over the tent city in Tiananmen Square and demolished the 27-foot-high plaster statue of the "Goddess of Democracy," modeled after the Statue of Liberty, which had been raised by the students on May 30. As to how many were killed in the square itself, accounts differ widely: According to the government no persons died there because the military allowed the students to withdraw before the tanks were sent in; according to some of the student leaders there were certainly some deaths, though the figure may not have been too high.

At 7:30 A.M., June 4, the government announced that the "rebellion" had been put down.

RETURN TO NORMALCY

During the next four days, while mopping-up operations continued in the city, no senior leader made a public or television appearance to allay rumors that the party was paralyzed by a power struggle and that the generals were readying for a civil war. Some embassies began to evacuate their nonessential personnel and advise their nationals to leave the country. A shocked world condemned the Chinese government for the use of lethal force against an unarmed citizenry, and many Western powers and Japan suspended high-level government contacts and imposed economic sanctions.

Rumors were finally laid to rest when, after two weeks of total silence, Li Peng made a television appearance on June 8 to praise the troops and call on the student leaders of the "rebellion" to surrender to "face punishment." On the following day, June 9, Deng, who also had been absent from the public scene for several weeks, addressed the Central Military Commission and provided an explanation of the "storm," which he said, "was bound to happen sooner or later" because of the "international and domestic climate." Deng said that the country had withstood the storm because "*we have a large number of veterans who have experienced many storms and have a thorough understanding of things* [emphasis added]." Deng cautioned his audience that they "should never forget how cruel our enemies are," and he praised the army for having made great sacrifices to save the "state and the party" from being overthrown and "*a bourgeois republic entirely dependent on the West* [emphasis added]" from being established. He added that "after serious work we can win the support of the great majority of comrades within the Party." Obviously, then, the majority had not favored his action. Deng reemphasized the need for the party and the people to adhere to the

Four Cardinal Principles and eradicate ideas of bourgeois liberalization through political education. He also reiterated the need for China to continue on its path of economic reforms and Open-Door policies.[33]

By the end of the month, the Central Committee of the CPC and the Standing Committee of the National People's Congress met to endorse Deng's June 9 speech and formally dismiss Zhao Zi-yang from his various party and state posts.

At the NPC Standing Committee meeting the mayor of Beijing provided an authorized version of the Tiananmen incident. He revealed that Zhao's liberal-minded supporters had promoted the "democracy virus" and the idea that Deng should be replaced by Zhao; he said that one of them had gone so far as to refer to Deng as "the super old man." The mayor explained in detail how the students had been incited to rebellion by intellectuals such as Fang Li-zhi, and he countered the rumors "spread by the Voice of America" about "thousands of people massacred" in the "Tiananmen Square bloodbath" with the following figures: "Several dozen" troops and security police and 200 civilians, including 36 students, had been killed; over 6,000 soldiers and security police and over 3,000 civilians had been wounded; and 1,280 military and other vehicles had been destroyed.[34]

With the propaganda machine totally under party control and the security force back under party discipline, it was not long before the Chinese people were deluged with stories that offered convincing proof that only a small group of antiparty elements, backed by foreigners, had misled the students and created the crisis; that the massacre was a myth; and that the common citizens had helped the glorious army to put down the thugs and counterrevolutionaries.

Thousands of "evil-doers" were promptly imprisoned and a few hastily executed to set an example to the good citizens. Arrest warrants were also issued for 21 student leaders (some escaped to the West and some went underground) and for the arrest of Fang Lizhi and his wife, professor Li Shu-xian, both of whom had taken refuge in the American embassy.

Those who know China were not surprised by the swiftness with which life in Beijing and other cities returned to normal. As in previous occasions, the Chinese people, who are well known for their capacity to hide their real feelings, responded to aggressive authority by returning docilely to their everyday activities as if nothing extraordinary had taken place.

The leaders, not oblivious to the immediate causes that lay behind the student trouble and popular unrest, confirmed their decision to continue the policy of price controls for the next two years and tackle the problem of corruption with greater severity. More significantly, the decision was taken to slow down the entire reform program and pursue a long-term policy of economic retrenchment. Almost two years later, at the time of this writing (fall 1990), the government has not yet succeeded in its endeavors to halt capital construction projects and reexert central controls over township and collective or private enterprises. Although the desired balance in the nation's capital construction has not been reached, what little has been done has resulted in further unemployment.[35]

The perception that the evil of "bourgeois liberalization" had spread because the hold of ideology had weakened persuaded the leaders to revive various Maoist practices. The party was admonished to cultivate "democratic centralism" and follow Mao's mass line in its dealings with the populace. Not surprisingly the leaders felt that the PLA could play an important role in this arena. There was a spate of stories in the press of how soldiers and military officers lived modestly and how they diligently served the people in construction and other work without ever demanding any special treatment. To inculcate ideological discipline among university students, the party ordered that starting in fall 1989, all freshmen entering Beijing University (the university that had given the most trouble) had first to take ten months of military training. The very Maoist Learn From Lei Feng campaign was also revived. However, it is becoming increasingly apparent that the party and the people are finding it almost impossible to combine ideological values that demand simple living and self-sacrifice for the common good with economic modernization based, as it is, on private entrepreneurship and the profit motive.

CHINA'S FOREIGN RELATIONS: 1976–1990

Before Mao died, he had the satisfaction of seeing China recognized as a global power whose friendship was actively sought by the United States. However, after the 1972 Nixon visit and the joint Shanghai Communiqué, moves toward a full normalization of relations were stalled because of U.S. incapacity to reorganize its relations with Taiwan to the satisfaction of Beijing. Anyway, because of the struggle for succession that preceded and followed Mao's death, foreign relations remained virtually dormant until Deng's return to power.

At the beginning, regardless of his other differences with Mao's ideology, Deng, who had enunciated Mao's three world theory at the United Nations in 1974, accepted Mao's anti-Soviet stand as the key element in the formulation of foreign policy. In 1978 the international political climate was generally favorable to China, and while there was a spate of goodwill visits to Beijing, top Chinese leaders, too, led delegations to countries in Europe, Africa, South Asia, and Southeast Asia. There was a marked increase in China's cultural exchanges with other countries and in its foreign trade and commerce.

The high points of the year were the signing of the Treaty of Peace and Friendship with Japan (in which Japan agreed to introduce an "antihegemony" clause aimed at the Soviet Union) in August and the declaration by the United States in mid-December that Sino-American relations would be fully normalized on January 1, 1979. In return for acknowledging China's claim to Taiwan, the United States was allowed to maintain "unofficial relations with the people of Taiwan."

Apart from the Soviet Union, which posed no immediate threat but was considered the main enemy of China, the only real trouble spot in China's foreign relations was Vietnam. Hemmed in between a pro-United States China and a pro-China Cambodia (under the ruthless, Maoist government of Pol Pot), Vietnam drew closer to the Soviet Union. Hanoi began to put pressure on the overseas Chinese population, most of whom had been involved in capitalist-style trade in preliberation South Vietnam and whose loyalty to Vietnam was doubted, to leave the country. The Sino-Vietnamese friction reached acute proportions when, soon after the Washington declaration regarding diplomatic recognition of Beijing, Vietnam invaded Cambodia on December 25, 1978, and on January 10, 1979, set up a government in Phnom Penh headed by Heng Samrin.

In February 1979, after the exchange of ambassadors, Deng went to America on a state visit. Although his official position in China was vice-premier, the Americans recognized him as the true leader of post-Mao China and gave him a welcome worthy of a head of a major state allied to the United States. Deng rose to the occasion, taking banquets and press conferences in his stride, kissing little children, putting on a ten-gallon hat in Texas, and achieving the distinction of becoming a darling of the American television public. The euphoria created an impression that China and the United States had developed extremely close ties.

Deng, convinced that China had indeed become, as National Security Adviser Zbigniew Brzezinski put it, "a central facet of U.S. global policy,"[36] talked in America about the need to "teach Vietnam a lesson." The absence of any clearly stated objection from the U.S. State Department no doubt strengthened this conviction and gave Deng the impression that he had gained clearance from Washington to mount a military operation against Vietnam. The Chinese invasion of North Vietnam, on grounds of "self-defense," began on February 17, 1979. It involved about 80,000 Chinese troops and lasted 28 days. The operation was a failure from every point of view. It embarrassed America because the United States did not want to be forced into a confrontation with the Soviet Union; it failed to have any impact on Vietnamese forces in Cambodia, none of which were withdrawn; the Soviet Union did not get involved; and when, after considerable destruction of Vietnamese property, the Chinese troops returned home, it had become humiliatingly clear that the Chinese army had lost its fighting prestige and that China had failed to lessen Vietnam's hegemony over Laos and Cambodia. As some cynics put it, "Vietnam had taught China a lesson." In the larger context it became questionable whether China, which could not control its own backyard, could help in the global balance of power.

Rhetoric apart, Chinese leaders soon realized that the United States, Western Europe, Japan, and the Third World were not about to satisfy Chinese world political strategies by establishing a united front against the Soviet Union. China had tried, rather naively, to play the "U.S. card" against the Soviet Union and failed. There was much greater danger that sooner or later, the United States may play the "China card" to the disadvantage of China. Beijing also realized that before China could be an active participant in global politics, it needed to modernize its armed forces. Beijing, however, also wisely concluded that economic modernization must precede military modernization. In the 1980s Chinese policies, although allowing for limited purchases of arms, concentrated on economic exchanges and international trade. The new awareness has also led to a more sober reappraisal of foreign policy goals, a withdrawal from the close strategic collaboration with the United States, and a more equidistant relationship with the two superpowers. In any case, the breathtaking events of 1989–1990, which saw the collapse of communism in Eastern Europe and the radical reorientation of Soviet foreign policy and which brought to a conclusion the cold war era of ideological confrontation, not only reduced China's value as a "card" in the Soviet-American strategic game but also ended China's fears of an expansive Soviet Union. China, if anything, is now worried about how the movement toward political openness in the U.S.S.R. will affect Beijing's current drive to preserve the authoritarian role of the CPC.

China's post-Vietnam foreign policy is constructed on the premise that China needs a period of prolonged peace to build its economy while maintaining flexibility and independence in foreign affairs. China is no longer a champion of world revolution, and its active interest in the Third World is limited to Indochina, where it would like to see a neutral, if not a pro-Beijing, regime replace Heng Samrin. With the lessening of Soviet interest in Vietnam and Vietnam's withdrawal from Cambodia, Beijing is now ready to improve relations with Hanoi and has accepted the idea that a political solution of the Cambodian problem, under the auspices of the United Nations, is both feasible and desirable. This change of stand has eased China's relations with Malaysia, Singapore, and Indonesia, states that have large overseas Chinese populations and were suspicious that China wanted to dominate the region. The new political environment has resulted in the restoration of diplomatic relations between China and Indonesia in August 1990 (ending a 23-year rift between the two countries) and the establishment of diplomatic relations between China and Singapore in October 1990.

Elsewhere in Asia, there are signs of a Sino-Indian rapprochement, although China remains a close ally of Pakistan and India recognizes the Heng Samrin government in Cambodia. Though there have been some irritants, China's relations with Japan are close and fairly cordial, and Japan has emerged as China's biggest trading partner.

The greatest triumph for China's foreign policymakers during this period was the successful conclusion of the Sino-British negotiations on the future of Hong Kong. After two years of secret discussions, a joint declaration signed in Beijing in December 1984 by Prime Ministers Margaret Thatcher and Zhao Zi-yang announced that Hong Kong shall be restored to the PRC on July 1, 1997, but it shall become a special administrative region (SAR) with a high degree of autonomy and shall be allowed, for a period of 50 years, to maintain its nonsocialist political, ideological, and economic system. Although Hong Kong residents have expressed dissatisfaction with the manner in which their future is being worked out, Beijing expects the policy of "one country, two systems" to function satisfactorily and even help in the reunification of Taiwan with the motherland. Beijing's hope is that Taiwan, in due course, would come to realize the benefits of reuniting with the motherland as another SAR—a notion that, it may be added, the affluent and more democratic Taiwan finds wholly repugnant.

China and the United States

From 1980 to 1989, China's primary foreign policy concerns continued to be its relations with the superpowers. Those with the United States swung from hot to cold to warm. The focal point of contention was Taiwan. Beijing expected that the establishment of Sino-U.S. diplomatic relations would end Washington's diplomatic relations with Taiwan, terminate the defense treaty between the United States and Taiwan, and lead to a withdrawal from Taiwan of U.S. military personnel. In the eyes of Beijing the Taiwan Relations Act adopted by the U.S. Congress in April 1979, which established the American Institute in Taiwan as an unofficial body to maintain mutual relations between Washington and Taipei, contravened the principles underlying normalization. The United States also continued to export arms to Taiwan or allowed Taiwan to manufacture arms under coproduction arrangements. Beijing was appeased to a degree with an assurance given in 1982 that the United States would gradually reduce arms sales, "leading over time to a final solution,"[37] but in the words of Beijing, "these actions continue to cast a shadow over Sino-American relations."[38] During the U.S. presidential elections in 1984, both the Republican and the Democratic party platforms included clauses supporting the Taiwan Relations Act, which led the Chinese to demand that the Taiwan statements be removed from the platforms and to advise the Republican and Democratic parties to "refrain from intervening in China's internal affairs."

Relations were also strained because of other reasons. China was angered at the imposition of quotas on textile imports by the United States and its reluctance to allow the export of certain high-technology items. There was a brief escalation of friction in 1983, when the United States granted political asylum to the Chinese tennis star Hu Na and Beijing canceled cultural and sports exchanges for that year. On the other side, there was irritation in American academic circles that the American scholars in China, who were outnumbered 20 to 1 by the Chinese scholars in the United States, were not being given proper research facilities by their host country. China's image in America has also suffered from press reports and publications critical of life in China. The U.S. public was particularly shocked by revelations of how the regime was ruthlessly enforcing the "one child per family" policy through coerced abortions (as late as in the sixth month of pregnancy) and forced sterilization and how this policy had resulted in widespread female infanticide. As a consequence, the U.S. Congress condemned China for violation of human rights and the U.S. government stopped funding population-control agencies, such as the United Nations, operating in China.

Efforts were made by both sides to accommodate one another, although the general impression was that the United States had given in more than the Chinese. A two-year low in Sino-U.S. relations ended in fall 1983 when U.S. Defense Secretary Caspar Weinberger visited Beijing and approved China's purchase of high-technology items that could be put to dual (civil and military) use.

In 1984 a high-ranking Chinese military delegation visited America and managed to purchase 70 percent of the items on its shopping list. By 1986 the United States had publicly announced that it was helping to modernize the Chinese navy and planning to sell $550 million worth of aviation electronics to China.

To strengthen this thaw in relations, Premier Zhao Zi-yang and President Reagan exchanged state visits in 1984. Although this summitry was richer in symbolic value than in substance, an agreement enabling China to buy civilian nuclear power reactors was initialed during Reagan's trip. To the chagrin of the Chinese, on his return home Reagan did not submit the agreement for congressional approval because it was feared that in the absence of any detailed and well-defined Chinese assurances that the U.S. nuclear material would not be used for military purposes by China or a pro-Chinese third country, Congress would reject the agreement. The question was taken up again in 1985, when President Li Xian-nian, the nominal head of China, paid a state visit to Washington. The agreement was finally signed, and the U.S. Congress approved the sale, but in 1986 the Chinese decided to put the deal on hold because of foreign exchange considerations. Incidentally, just prior to leaving Beijing, Li vehemently attacked the U.S. stand on Chinese population-control policies as interference in China's internal affairs. There were some other low-level irritants in U.S.-China relations in 1987–1988 arising out of China's alleged sale of missiles to the Middle East, but they were smoothed over by Chinese assurances after the Iran-Iraq ceasefire.

Despite all these problems, the trend toward greater economic intercourse between the two countries continued to strengthen until the Tiananmen incident, when many aid-giving countries, the United States included, condemned the massacre of unarmed citizens and suspended further aid and high-level government contacts. Washington also halted military sales to China and made it easier for Chinese students in America to extend their visas. China protested these actions as interference in China's internal affairs and was particularly disturbed by the diplomatic protection granted to the "criminals" Fang Li-zhi and his wife, who had taken refuge in the American embassy.

However, behind the facade that there would be no "business as usual," President Bush sent two high-level secret missions to China, headed by acting secretary Eagleburger and national security affairs assistant to the president, General Scowcroft; the first trip was made in July 1989 (a month after the Tiananmen incident) and the second in December 1989. When forced to explain the reason for the secrecy, the White House asserted that China's tradition and unique circumstances made it a special case that needed patient handling and that quiet diplomacy could persuade the Chinese leaders to liberalize their policies in the interest of better relations with the United States. The lifting of martial law in January 1990, accompanied by the release of 573 detainees, was seen by Washington as a sign that Beijing was moving in the right direction. The Chinese, hurt by the economic sanctions, were also anxious to present a milder image. They finally removed the most visible impediment in Sino-U.S. relations in June 1990 by allowing Fang Li-zhi and his wife to emigrate to Britain. Washington hailed the action as a "farsighted" humanitarian action that "will improve the atmosphere for progress in bilateral relations."[39]

By the end of 1990, the United States had confirmed China's "most favored nation" status and reduced the sanctions against commercial transactions. Following the U.S. example Japan, too, resumed its multibillion-dollar aid program to China. At the time of this writing, the rest of the world also appears to have forgotten the Tiananmen incident and is fast resuming its old ties with Beijing. However, events in Europe have reduced China's strategic importance, and in any case, China has lost much of its pre-1989 attractiveness.

China and the Soviet Union

For three years after the death of Mao Zedong, the relationship between China and the Soviet Union continued to be marked by the bitter rhetoric that gave the impression that the two Communist giants were out to destroy each other. However, in 1979, soon after the Sino-U.S. normalization and the Vietnam border war, Beijing, although informing Moscow that it would not renew the 1950 30-year Treaty of Peace and Friendship, initiated talks with Moscow to improve bilateral relations. The talks were quite steadily carried on even though they were periodically suspended by Beijing to express condemnation of some particular Soviet foreign policy action. Thus, for example, the Soviet invasion of Afghanistan in December 1979 brought a long break in the meetings.

Beijing's de-Maoization policies and its acceptance of certain capitalistic economic practices resulted in a reappraisal of the Soviet Union's role in the 1960 break between the two countries; it was tacitly accepted that Mao's leftist policies were to blame for much that went wrong, and Beijing stopped using the pejorative term *revisionist* when referring to the Soviet Union—after all, China was becoming as "revisionist" as the U.S.S.R.

The Chinese leaders, having decided that a Sino-American alliance was not possible on their terms and that on American terms might prove too costly and counterproductive, turned to an independent foreign policy. It was sufficiently evident to China that it could buy the science and technology it needed without tying itself to any one superpower and that the Soviet Union did not pose any immediate threat. Furthermore, the increase of tensions between the United States and the Soviet Union during President Reagan's first term meant that China was coming to occupy an advantageous position between the superpowers; it could strengthen its operational flexibility by establishing more equidistant relations with both of them.

Beijing appears to have then decided to allay Soviet fears of a Sino-U.S. strategic alliance by using the Sino-Soviet talks to hint that improvements in relations were possible and in the offing. On the surface, the Chinese continued to maintain a rigid stand: Relations could not be normalized until the Soviets eliminated the threat to China's security by (1) reducing their armed forces on the Sino-Soviet border and in Outer Mongolia, (2) discontinuing their support of Vietnam, and (3) withdrawing from Afghanistan. In practice, the Chinese showed a remarkable forbearance and gradually recognized the fact that it was possible to ease tensions without giving up their "righteous" stand.

In 1980, in response to the Soviet invasion of Afghanistan, China, which had already suspended the Sino-Soviet talks, joined the U.S. bloc in boycotting the Olympic Games, which were being held in Russia. In June 1981 Moscow signed a treaty with Afghanistan, which among other things, settled the borders between the two countries and legalized the Soviet occupation of a piece of territory in the Pamirs claimed by the Chinese. The treaty was loudly protested by Beijing, but in the same year China allowed a team of Chinese gymnasts to participate in a gymnastic competition in Moscow. This move can be compared to the "Ping-Pong" diplomacy that had preceded the Sino-U.S. détente. As may be recalled, a U.S. table tennis team competing in Japan in 1971 was invited by the Chinese team to visit China; the Chinese also allowed Western journalists to enter China to cover the event.

The thaw in the relations quickened in 1982 with the reopening of the suspended talks and the signing of a Sino-Soviet trade agreement; it envisaged a 45 percent increase in trade, which had hit the low point of $300 million, and allowed for a resumption of border trade. The Soviets, in turn, agreed to reduce Soviet border troops as long as China did the same and also to withdraw their forces from Mongolia. Cultural and other bilateral exchanges increased in number while the war of words continued unabated. The most important development in 1983 was the visit to Beijing in September of the Soviet Deputy Foreign Minister M. S.

Kapitsa, the first high-ranking Soviet official to come to China in over 20 years. In the following month and also for the first time in nearly 20 years, the first group of Russian tourists arrived in China. In February 1984 President Li Xian-nian sent a condolence message to the Soviet Union on the death of President Andropov, and a Chinese delegation headed by Vice-Premier Wan Li attended the funeral. During his stay in Moscow, Wan Li invited China's "old friend" First Deputy Premier Ivan Arkhipov, who had been the economic advisor in China in the 1950s, to visit China. Sino-Soviet trade in 1984 showed a 60 percent increase over 1983, and during Arkhipov's visit (December–January) further agreements on economic, scientific, and technical cooperation were signed and a joint committee to promote such cooperation was established. In July 1985 Chinese Deputy Premier Yao Yi-lin paid a return visit to Moscow and signed another accord with Arkhipov, under which the volume of trade was expected to double to $3.5 billion by 1990. The Soviet Union was to supply machinery, transport equipment and chemicals, and assist in building seven new plants and in modernizing 17 others in the field of energy, metals, and machinery manufacturing, coal, chemicals, and transportation. In return China agreed to provide agricultural and industrial raw materials and consumer goods.

China's new approach to the Soviet Union

China Today

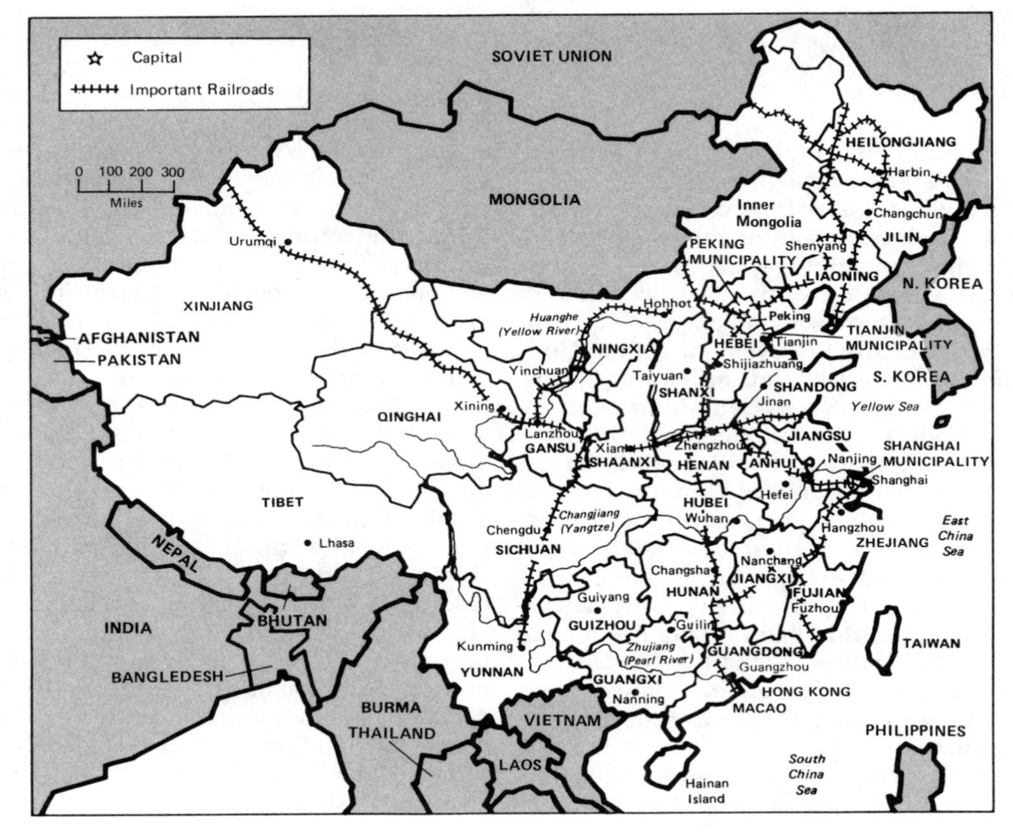

could be explained in the context of China's new foreign policy orientation enunciated by President Zhao Zi-yang in May 1984:

> We [Chinese] take a principled stand in handling our relations with the United States and the Soviet Union. *We will not refrain from improving relations with them because we oppose their hegemonism, nor will we give up our antihegemonist stand because we want to improve relations with them* [emphasis added]. This is not only in the interests of the people in the three nations, but also benefits world peace.[40]

To this statement, one may add what a Chinese foreign policy analyst had to say about the superpowers:

> At one time the Soviets thought China could develop its economy and contend with the U.S. only with Soviet support. Later the U.S. thought China would be willing to make political concessions in order to import advanced technology for its modernization drive. Both countries were wrong. China cannot be bullied. . . . China will never attach itself to any big power or power blocs or submit to their pressures.[41]

Trade and bilateral exchanges between China and the Soviet Union continued to increase over the next four years, paving the way for the historic summit meeting between Gorbachev and Deng Xiao-ping in May 1989, which ended a three decades' rift and normalized Sino-Soviet relations. Much of the credit for this achievement goes to Gorbachev, who from the time he became general secretary of the Soviet Communist party in 1985, made the improvement of relations with China a matter of high priority. From China's publicly expressed point of view, the breakthrough came because Moscow had eliminated the "three obstacles" (support for Hanoi, troops on the Sino-Soviet border, and the invasion of Afghanistan). Gorbachev's tacit acceptance of China's claim of being a regional power no doubt also helped.

Gorbachev, who had already gained international recognition for his liberalizing policies, landed in Beijing in the middle of the Tiananmen crisis, but he was careful not to take sides in the CPC inner-party conflict or, later, to criticize the Tiananmen massacre. The Chinese leaders, too, have maintained a posture of studied silence over developments in Eastern Europe and the Soviet Union, though it is well known that they are not overly pleased with them.

Economic relations between the two countries have not been affected by their internal politics or the Tiananmen incident. The envisaged trade target of $3.5 billion for 1990 was reached in 1989, and trade in 1990 was expected to increase by 36 percent over the previous year. However, since this figure still accounts for only 3.5 percent of China's total trade volume, both sides are optimistic that there is vast potential for future growth.[42]

CONCLUSION: CHINA IN SEARCH OF A MODERN POLITICAL ORDER

From the time in the late nineteenth century when China accepted the idea that change and modernization were necessary, it also discovered that the hold of traditional culture was so strong that such change could not be introduced through a program of reforms. It took a revolution to discard the imperial political system, but this revolution found the country unprepared for a constitutional, democratic, republican order and ended in the birth of warlordism. A second revolution, combining elements of tradition and modernity, established a single-party (Guomindang) government, which theoretically aimed at leading the country to independence and constitutional democracy but in reality managed to do little more than impose a harsh military dictatorship over a fractured and bankrupt nation. Finally, nearly 40 years after the first revolution, a third revolution, lead by a Marxist revolutionary party (CPC), brought national reintegration and independence to China. Thus, the foremost demands of the national will (fostered by modern nationalism through the first five decades of the twentieth century) for national unity and for the recovery of national rights usurped by the imperialist powers were fulfilled.

In 1949 China regained its pride and the independence it had sought to shape its own polity. Thus it could, at last, establish a political order that would help modernize the country. Although the country was not without elements of modern industry, commerce, communications, and education, these sectors were still extremely weak, and China was still a backward, largely illiterate, primarily agricultural, premodern society.

From 1949, and particularly from 1956, until Mao Ze-dong's death in 1976, it can be said as a generalization that Mao's need to use charismatic leadership to fulfill what had increasingly become a highly personal vision of China's future clashed with the needs of a modernizing state: a stable political system with rational, efficient institutions based on permanent organizational principles. When, after the Great Leap Forward, Mao felt that power was slipping from his control, he used the cult of personality to regain mass support and launch the antiestablishment GPCR. The resulting attacks on the party-state apparatus not only weakened national institutions, which could have provided the framework for growth and modernization, but also ironically led to the colossal failure of the GPCR because no policies can succeed without supporting organizational mechanisms.

For China the tragedy was not that Mao failed to create the new "socialist man" but that Mao, in trying to achieve his noble vision, had to belittle the role of modern knowledge and expertise in economic modernization; keep China from benefiting from international economic, scientific, and technological exchanges; and, perhaps even more important, make constitutions and legal codes irrelevant by subordinating them to personal whim.

After Mao's death, it was only with the emergence of Deng Xiao-ping as China's key leader in 1978 that the Maoist era was brought to its ignoble end. Under the pragmatists, China has opened itself to the outside world and appears to be fast becoming a part of the global economic order and an active participant in international society. China's long-delayed economic modernization is under way, and there is optimism that by the year 2000 China will have increased its per capita GNP to $800.

However, the rapidity of political-social change in China during the last few years and the speed of economic growth do not necessarily mean that Chinese leaders have finally succeeded in putting China securely on the path to modernization. In fact, the leadership is faced with many problems, some of which have already proved to be destabilizing.

There are problems connected with the new economic reforms. First, the new policies have yet to establish the balance among socialist public ownership, the nonsocialist economic sector (enterprises with foreign investment), and private enterprise; between centralized control and the decision-making independence of the economic enterprises; between centralized planning and decentralization of authority; between unified state-fixed wages and prices and the role of free market forces; and between the ideal of socialist egalitarianism and the freedom for enterprises and private persons to accumulate profits.

Second, the increase in agricultural production may have been dramatic, but being based on small farms and labor-intensive methods, may already have reached its limit. The very success of the household contract system puts obstacles in the way of further progress, which demands the large-scale use of fertilizers and mechanization. Even if farm-labor productivity is increased by the use of capital-intensive methods, it will mean a further increase in rural unemployment or underemployment. It is yet to be seen whether rural industries and rural towns, which are expected to do so, will absorb excess labor released from the countryside.

Third, there is the problem of urban unemployment. According to Chinese calculations in 1979, it was estimated "that there will be 37 million urban people waiting for employment [Chinese way of saying unemployed] between 1980 and 1985 (excluding people whose jobs will be assigned by the state invariably according to state policy)."[43]

Deng's decision (June 1985) to reduce the size of the 4-million-strong PLA to 3 million also increased unemployment, although the impact was softened to a degree because many of the demobilized soldiers were retired on military pension. Peking has tried various tactics to increase employment but so far has had limited success. The post-Tiananmen economic retrenchment policies have only worsened the situation. In the meantime, urban unemployment is leading to an increase in such crimes as thefts, bank robberies and black marketeering and in the rise of gangs, mostly involving youths who have lost faith in socialism and generally feel that they have been denied the material wealth that everybody around them is grabbing with unconcealed gusto.

For Deng Xiao-ping, 87 years old in 1991, a far bigger problem is the transition of power after his death. He is naturally anxious that his "second revolution" not die with him. Until the tragic events of June 1989 reversed the course, Deng had taken several steps that appeared to establish the concept of collective leadership and to institutionalize the policy-making process.

To ensure that power would not become overcentralized, Deng abolished the prestigious chair of the CPC and made the Secretariat the top body of the party; the secretary-general, the head of the Secretariat, became one of the most important persons in the party, but he did not have the power once enjoyed by Mao. The once all-powerful Politburo also lost some of its top-level decision-making powers to the party Secretariat and was further weakened by the replacement in 1985 of nearly half of the senior Politburo members, including Ye Jian-ying, by younger, more reform-minded party members. In a similar action 64 of the 340 members of the party Central Committee were replaced by younger (average age: 50), better-educated (76 percent with college degrees) leaders.

The leadership of the party was also separated from that of the Military Affairs Commission. Earlier, the party chairperson was also the head of the Military Affairs Commission, but since 1981, when Deng took over the post, the two offices were separated. The party control over the military was reduced further when the 1982 state constitution established the Central Military Commission, a new organ with strong statutory powers. Deng was made chair of the Central Military Commission. Thus the executive control over the party, the army, and the state was divided among three leaders, and the daily functioning of the government supposedly came to rest with the State Council.

Deng also did away with overlapping offices that undermined the functional division of the party, the state, and the judiciary. At the grass-roots level, the communes, which had merged the party and government bureaucracies, were dissolved and village and township governments reestablished. The hierarchical party committees and bureaucracies that paralleled the structure of the government organizations were supposed to make sure that party policies were being carried out, but they were no longer supposed to get directly involved with the functioning of the state. However, old habits lived on, and changes on paper could not be realized in practice.

Ultimately, it was Deng himself who sabotaged what little had been done to give political authority and policy formulation a legal-rational base. Deng's approach to the institutionalization of politics was flawed by a serious contradiction: He wanted to introduce collective leadership without giving up his own power. In 1987, when Hu Yao-bang was dismissed, Deng, though not permitted to do so under the rules of the party constitution, called an enlarged meeting of the Politburo, packed it with cronies, and forced Hu to resign. In 1989 the situation was even worse. Deng decided to use the military on June 4 by going outside the party center and mustering the support of the "large group of veterans who [had] experienced many storms and [had] a thorough understanding of things"[44] but who had no official standing. In the face of this wholly unconstitutional action, the point that Zhao Zi-yang's departure from power was "legalized" after the event is a detail of little consequence. In November 1989, Deng relinquished the last of his formal posts, the chair of the Central Military Commission, and handed it over to his third hand-picked successor, Jiang Zemin. But no one in China had any doubts that it was Deng who continued to make the final decisions.

This style of personalized authority has kept China from developing mechanisms for a smooth transition of power and weakened national institutions, which are needed to provide the framework for growth and modernization. And the traditional cultural propensity to locate power in a single strong leader is far from dead.

After the Tiananmen crisis the hardliners have tried to win back the hearts and minds of a disillusioned populace by reemphasizing Maoist ideology and reintroducing Maoist-style ideological mass campaigns, but the clock cannot be turned back. Furthermore, the fractured and factionalized party, which itself is corrupted and lacks unity and discipline, can hardly be expected to set an example to the people. Repeated declarations that the party is guided by Marxism-Leninism-Mao Ze-dong Thought means little in the context of Deng's new economic policies, which have downgraded Maoist ideology and have accepted, indeed encouraged, the emergence of capitalist practices and profit-oriented market mentality, which in turn have led to rampant individualism and the naked pursuit of private wealth. Indeed, there has been a phenomenal spread of corrupt practices such as bribery, misuse of state funds, and nepotism among party and state cadres at various levels. In one of the most notorious cases of corruption revealed by the Chinese press in 1985, an ex-cadre "netted an illegal gain of Rmb 12.6 million [$5 million] by selling nonexistent color TV sets" to officials in his native village. An official commentary said, "This case shows that some of our cadres . . . are obsessed by a lust for wealth and attempt to grab huge gains, only to be taken in by others."[45]

From 1987 to 1989, 100,000 party members were found to have violated discipline; in 1988 alone action was taken against 21,100, of whom 3,700 were "leading cadres." After June 1989, the government issued 20 administrative laws and regulations to combat corrupt practices and launched a nationwide campaign against graft and corruption but failed to halt the evil. A declaration of amnesty for those who voluntary surrendered themselves to the authorities between August 15 and October 31, 1989, resulted in 18,030 "criminals" turning themselves in and handing over 102,000,000 yuan ($25.5 million) worth of "illicit money and spoils."[46] The government has continued to publicize the cases of erring cadres and the severe punishments meted out to them, but so far this practice has failed to make the party or society more disciplined or socialistic. During the first six months of 1990, 17,757 government officials were punished for corruption, a 75 percent increase over 1989.[47]

By 1983, there was a growing debate about whether the opening to the West had brought spiritual pollution in its wake. A campaign against "spiritual pollution" was mounted, but since nobody was sure what the phrase meant, anything that had a foreign flavor was attacked, from the content of paintings and short stories to hair styles, clothes, music, makeup, and dancing. Once again, the Chinese intellectuals and youths felt intimidated, and the campaign was halted by Deng himself because it dampened enthusiasm for change and threatened the future of liberal economic policies.

It did not take long for spiritual pollution to become dovetailed into the more serious "bourgeois liberalization" movement, which exploded in the student crisis of 1987 and was closely related to the 1989 Tiananmen incident. Deng then reversed his stand and jettisoned both his chosen successors, Hu Yao-bang in 1987 and Zhao Zi-yang in 1989. By removing these leaders and punishing the so-called dissident intellectuals, Deng gained temporary respite; but he should be aware that guns and brutality cannot still the demands for greater freedom for all time to come or close the widening gap between hollow ideological pronouncements and Chinese social reality.

Ultimately it is not punishment of intellectuals and stray cadres or political campaigns that will regulate official and private behavior but the revitalization of the legal system. The regime has promulgated a code of criminal law (first promised in 1950) and codes of criminal and civil procedure, increased the number of law colleges, and is encouraging more students to graduate in law. But it will take many years before the legal system can be properly entrenched. At the moment the country lacks lawyers and judges and, more important, a psychological attitude among the people that would make them accept a rule of law as a substitute for a rule by personalities. As party Secretary General Jiang Ze-min confessed in late 1989, "the building of democracy and a legal system still remains an extremely arduous task."[48]

Thus we see that although China has made considerable progress in improving its economy by liberalizing it, the country has a long way to go before it can truly modernize the economy. Indeed, economic liberalization demands that the political system also be liberalized, and if this is not done, further efforts at modernizing the economic infrastructure are likely to fail.

The time has come for the leaders of China to realize that they must make a conscious attempt to loosen the grip of the traditional political culture that permits the emergence of an emperorlike supreme leader (Yuan Shi-kai, Sun Yat-sen, Chiang Kai-shek, Mao Ze-dong, and Deng Xiao-ping) who believes that he alone has the wisdom to guide the nation and the moral duty to do so. As long as this psychological environment is not changed, the supreme leader, once in power, will demand that society submit to his will and that he be universally honored, if not worshipped.

Since this leader, in reality, does not possess absolute power, he has to work through factional alignments that are destructive to the smooth working of government and a smooth transition of power. However, the leader cannot tolerate any public expression of opinions critical of his policies. Because such criticism comes largely from modernizing intellectuals, who have the intellectual courage to break the hold of the past and seek innovative ideas from the outside world, it is not surprising that it is they who have suffered most grievously at the hands of these leaders.

When Deng Xiao-ping returned to power, he appeared to have understood the need to broaden its base and draw the much maligned and harassed intellectual community into the decision-making process. But events have proved that even he could not accept the call for a political change that would have reduced the authoritarian role of the party and opened politics to popular participation. Deng's suppression of the intellectuals and the students, followed by quick action on price controls and corruption, have brought him some respite, but these moves have in no way solved the basic contradictions created by the reform policies. His quick fixes cannot stem the waning public confidence in the party and the state or undo the damage inflicted on the reform process and the reputation of the reformers or win back the allegiance of the intellectuals to a defunct political system.

China is caught in many crosscurrents as it moves into the last decade of the twentieth century, and at this stage it is difficult to foresee the possibility of any kind of collective leadership emerging after Deng Xiao-ping's death or of the realization of Deng's vision of socialist modernization. For a considerable time to come, China is likely to continue on the zigzag course of advances and retreats that it has followed ever since the People's Republic was established.

NOTES

1. *The Eleventh National Congress of the Communist Party of China (Documents)* (Beijing: Foreign Languages Press, 1977), p. 52.

2. *Documents of the First Session of the Fifth National People's Congress of the People's Republic of China* (Beijing: Foreign Languages Press, 1978), p. 210.

3. For the English version, see "The Constitution of the People's Republic of China," *Peking Review,* no. 11 (March 17, 1978), 5–14.

4. Quoted in *Asia 1979 Yearbook* (Hong Kong: Far Eastern Economic Review), p. 172.

5. For the communiqué released at the end of the meeting, see Harold C. Hinton, *The People's Republic of China, 1949–1979: A Documentary Survey,* vol. V (Wilmington, DE: Scholarly Resources, 1980), pp. 2722–27.

6. For a complete official English text of the resolution, see *Resolution on CPC History (1949–81)* (Beijing: Foreign Languages Press, 1981).

7. Ibid., pp. 94–95.

8. For details, see William deB. Mills "Leadership Change in China's Provinces," *Problems of Communism,* May–June 1985, pp. 24–40. Mills gives an excellent analysis of the problems faced by the Dengists in trying to achieve their goal.

9. See Leo A. Orleans, "Chinese in America: The Numbers Game," *China Exchange News,* 17, no. 3 (September 1989), 9–10. It is reasonable to presume that at least 10,000 other students went to countries in Western Europe and to Japan.

10. "Guidelines Old and New," in *Economic Readjustment and Reform* (Beijing: Beijing Review Press, 1982), p. 12.

11. See *Changes and Development in China (1949–1989)* (Beijing: Beijing Review Press, n.d.), pp. 17, 80, 118. The absolute value in yuan has been rounded to the nearest billion.

12. "Economic Growth Between 1983–1987," *Beijing Review,* 31, no. 23 (June 6–12, 1988), 28.

13. *Changes and Development in China,* p. 115. The percentages have been calculated from the figures in the chart.

14. Ibid., pp. 120, 184.

15. *World Development Report 1990* (New York: Oxford University Press, for the World Bank, 1990), p. 43.

16. "Open Policy Essential to Socialism," *Beijing Review,* 28, no. 13 (April 1, 1985), 15.

17. *Beijing Review,* 32, no. 45 (November 6–12, 1989).

18. See ibid. no. 40 [there were two issues with the same date—no. 39 and no. 40] (October 2–8, 1989), 29.

19. See "Economic Structural Imbalance: Its Causes and Correctives," *Beijing Review,* 32, no. 36 (September 4–10, 1989), 22–28.

20. See Liu Guoguang, "Changes in Ownership Forms," *Beijing Review,* 29, no. 19 (May 12, 1986); and *Changes and Development in China,* p. 65.

21. *Beijing Review,* 28, no. 32 (August 12, 1985).

22. Deng Xiaoping, *Fundamental Issues in Present Day China* (Beijing: Foreign Languages Press, 1987), pp. 145–48.

23. Quoted in Willy Wo-Lap Lam, *The Era of Zhao Ziyang* (Hong Kong: A.B. Books & Stationary, 1989), p. 69.

24. See "Symposium on Theory of Political Structures," *Beijing Review,* 29, no. 46 (November 1986), 14–15.

25. *China Spring,* 1, no. 2 (March–April 1987), 12–18.

26. Deng Xiaoping, *Fundamental Issues in Present Day China,* pp. 162, 165.

27. For the text of Zhao Zi-yang's report to the Thirteenth NC of the party, see *Beijing Review,* 30, no. 45 (November 9–15, 1987).

28. Ibid., 32, no. 46 (November 13–19, 1989), 18.

29. Ibid. 31, no. 41 (October 10–16, 1988), 39.

30. Wo-Lap Lam, *Era of Zhao Ziyang,* p. 252.

31. Fred C. Shapiro, "Letter From Beijing," *The New Yorker,* June 5, 1989, p. 76.

32. "Documents," *Beijing Review,* 32, no. 9 (July 17–23, 1989), viii.

33. For the full text, see ibid., 32, no. 28 (July 10–16, 1989), 18–21.

34. Ibid., 32, no. 29 (July 17–23, 1989), i–xx.

35. Ibid., 33, no. 20 (May 14–20, 1990), 23.

36. Zbigniew Brzezinski, *Power and Principle* (New York: Farrar Strauss Giroux, 1983), Annex 1, p. 1.

37. *Department of State Bulletin,* 82, no. 2067 (October 1982), 20.

38. Zheng Wei-zhi, "Independence Is the Basic Canon: An Analysis of the Principles of China's Foreign Policy," *Beijing Review,* no. 1 (January 7, 1985), 18.

39. *The Times* (London), June 26, 1990, p. 10.

40. Zheng Wei-zhi, "Independence Is the Basic Canon," p. 19.

41. Ibid., p. 18.

42. Gu Guanfu and Chun-tu Hsueh, "Sino-Soviet Ties Grow Steadily," *Beijing Review,* 33, no. 36 (September 3–9, 1990), 12.

43. See Feng Lanrui and Zhao Lukuan, "Urban Employment and Wages," in Yu Guangyuan, ed., *China's Socialist Modernization* (Beijing: Foreign Languages Press, 1985), 579.

44. *Beijing Review,* 32, no. 28 (July 10–16, 1989), p. 18.

45. Quoted in "Corruption: The Dark Side of the Liberalism Coin," *Far Eastern Economic Review,* March 21, 1985, p. 68.

46. *Beijing Review,* 32, no. 52 (December 25–31, 1989), 23–29.

47. Ibid., 33, no. 35 (August 27–September 2, 1990), 10.

48. Ibid., 32, no. 41 (October 9–15, 1989), 19.

Suggestions for Further Reading

GENERAL AND REFERENCE WORKS

BAI SHOUYI, ED. *An Outline History of China.* Beijing: Foreign Languages Press, 1982.

BIANCO, LUCIEN. *Origins of the Chinese Revolution, 1915–1949,* trans. Muriel Bell. Palo Alto, CA: Stanford University Press, 1971.

BOORMAN, HOWARD L., AND RICHARD C. HOWARD. *Bibliographical Dictionary of Republican China,* 4 vols. New York: Columbia University Press, 1967–1971.

BRANDT, CONRAD, BENJAMIN I. SCHWARTZ, AND JOHN K. FAIRBANK. *A Documentary History of Chinese Communism.* Cambridge, MA: Harvard University Press, 1959.

CLUBB, O. E. *20th Century China.* New York: Columbia University Press, 1964.

CRESSY, GEORGE B. *Land of the 500 Million.* New York: McGraw-Hill, 1955.

CROWLEY, JAMES B., ED. *Modern East Asia: Essays in Interpretation.* San Diego: Harcourt Brace Jovanovich, 1970.

DE BARY, WILIAM THEODORE, ET AL., COMP. *Sources of Chinese Tradition.* New York: Columbia University Press, 1960.

FAIRBANK, JOHN K., ED. *The Cambridge History of China, vol. 10: Late Ch'ing. 1800–1911, Part 1.* Cambridge, Eng.: Cambridge University Press, 1978.

———, ED. *The Cambridge History of China. vol. 12: Republican China 1912–1949, Part 1.* Cambridge, Eng.: Cambridge University Press, 1983 (reprinted 1987).

———, AND ALBERT FEUERWERKER, EDS. *The Cambridge History of China, vol. 13: Republican China 1912–1949, Part 2.* Cambridge, Eng.: Cambridge University Press, 1986.

FAIRBANK, JOHN K., EDWIN O. REISCHAUER, AND ALBERT CRAIG. *East Asia: The Modern Transformation.* Boston: Houghton Mifflin, 1965.

FAIRBANK, JOHN K., AND K. C. LIU, EDS. *The Cambridge History of China, vol. 11: Late Ch'ing 1800–1911, Part 2.* Cambridge, Eng.: Cambridge University Press, 1978.

HINTON, HAROLD C., ED. *The People's Republic of China, 1949–1979: A Documentary Survey,* 5 vols. Wilmington, DE: Scholarly Resources, 1980.

HO, KAN-CHIH. *A History of Modern Chinese Revolution.* Beijing: Foreign Languages Press, 1959.

HSIEH, CHIAO-MIN. *Atlas of China.* New York: McGraw-Hill, 1973.

HSU, IMMANUEL C. Y. *The Rise of Modern China, 4th ed.* Oxford, Eng.: Oxford University Press, 1990.

HSÜEH, CHÜN-TU, ED. *Revolutionary Leaders of Modern China.* Oxford, Eng.: Oxford University Press, 1971.

HU SHENG. *Imperialism and Chinese Politics,* Beijing: Foreign Languages Press, 1955.

KLEIN, DONALD W., AND ANNE B. CLARKE. *Biographic Dictionary of Chinese Communism, 1921–1965*, 2 vols. Cambridge, MA; Harvard University Press, 1971.

KUO, WARREN. *Analytical History of the Chinese Communist Party*, 4 vols. Taipei: Institute of International Relations, 1968–1971.

LANGER, W. L. *The Diplomacy of Imperialism*, 2 vols., 2nd ed. New York: Knopf, 1950.

MACFARQUHAR, RODERICK, AND JOHN K. FAIRBANK, EDS. *The Cambridge History of China, vol. 14: The People's Republic, Part 1: The Emergence of Revolutionary China, 1949–1965*. Cambridge, Eng.: Cambridge University Press, 1987.

SHABAD, THEODORE. *China's Changing Map: National and Regional Development, 1949–71*. New York: Praeger, 1972.

SPENCE, JONATHAN D. *The Search for Modern China*. New York: Norton, 1990.

TENG SSU-YU, JOHN KING FAIRBANK, WITH E-TU ZEN SUN CHAOYING FANG AND OTHERS. *China's Response to the West*. Cambridge, MA: Harvard University Press, 1954.

TOWNSEND, JAMES R., AND BRANTLY WOMACK. *Politics in China*. Boston: Little, Brown, 1986.

VOHRA, RANBIR, ED. *The Chinese Revolution*. Boston: Houghton Mifflin, 1974.

NINETEENTH-CENTURY CHINA AND THE BACKGROUND TO THE 1911 REVOLUTION

AYERS, WILLIAM. *Chang Chih-tung and Educational Reform in China*. Cambridge, MA: Harvard University Press, 1971.

BLAND, J. O. P., AND E. BACKHOUSE. *China Under the Empress Dowager: Being the History of the Life and Times of Tzu Hsi*. London: William Heinemann, 1910.

CAMERON, M. E. *The Reform Movement in China, 1898–1912*. Palo Alto, CA: Stanford University Press, 1931 (reprinted by Octagon, 1963).

CHANG HAO. *Liang Ch'i-ch'ao and Intellectual Transition in China, 1890–1907*. Cambridge, MA: Harvard University Press, 1971.

CHANG HSIN-PAO. *Commissioner Lin and the Opium War*. Cambridge, MA: Harvard University Press, 1964.

DRAKE, FRED W. *China Charts the World: Hsü Chi-yü and His Geography of 1848*. Cambridge, MA: Harvard University Press, 1975.

ESHERICK, JOSEPH. *Reform and Revolution in China: The 1911 Revolution in Hunan and Hubei*. Berkeley: University of California Press, 1976.

FAIRBANK, JOHN K., ED. *The Chinese World Order: Traditional China's Foreign Relations*. Cambridge, MA: Harvard University Press, 1968.

FEUERWERKER, ALBERT. *China's Early Industrialization: Sheng Hsuan-huai (1844–1916) and Mandarin Enterprise*. Cambridge, MA: Harvard University Press, 1958.

———. *The Chinese Economy, ca. 1870–1911*. Michigan Papers in Chinese Studies, no. 5. Ann Arbor: University of Michigan, Center for Chinese Studies, 1969.

FORSYTHE, SIDNEY A. *An American Missionary Community in China, 1895–1905*. Cambridge, MA: Harvard University Press, 1971.

GASSTER, MICHAEL. *Chinese Intellectuals and the Revolution of 1911: The Birth of Modern Chinese Radicalism*. Seattle: University of Washington Press, 1969.

GREENBERG, MICHAEL. *British Trade and the Opening of China, 1800–1842*. Cambridge, Eng.: Cambridge University Press, 1951.

HAO, Y. P. *The Comprador in 19th Century China*. Cambridge, MA: Harvard University Press, 1970.

History of Modern China series. Beijing: Foreign Languages Press, 1976:
The Opium War
The Taiping Revolution
The Reform Movement of 1898
The Yi Ho Tuan Movement of 1900
The Revolution of 1911

HO PING-TI. *Studies on the Population of China, 1368–1953*. Cambridge, MA: Harvard University Press, 1959.

HOU CHI-MING. *Foreign Investment and Economic Development in China, 1840–1937*. Cambridge, MA: Harvard University Press, 1965.

HSIAO, K. C. *A Modern China and the New World: K'ang Yu-Wei Reformer and Utopian, 1858–1927*. Seattle: University of Washington Press, 1975.

HSU, IMMANUAL C. Y. *China's Entrance Into the Family of Nations: The Diplomatic Phase, 1858–1880*. Cambridge, MA: Harvard University Press, 1960.

JEN YU-WEN. *The Taiping Revolutionary Movement*. New Haven, CT: Yale University Press, 1973.

LEVENSON, J. R. *Liang Ch'i-ch'ao and the Mind of Modern China*. Cambridge, MA: Harvard University Press, 1965.

LEWIS, CHARLTON M. *Prologue to the Chinese Revolution: Transformation of Ideas & Institutions in Hunan Province, 1881–1907*. Cambridge, MA: Harvard University Press, 1976.

LO JUNG-PANG. *K'ang Yu-wei: A Biography and a Symposium*. Tucson: University of Arizona Press, 1967.

PERKINS, DWIGHT H., WITH THE ASSISTANCE OF YEH-CHIEN WANG, KUO-YING WANG HSIAO, AND YUNG-MING SU *Agricultural Development in China 1368–1968*. Chicago: Aldine, 1969.

PORTER, JONATHAN. *Tseng Kuo-fan's Private Bureaucracy*. Berkeley: University of California Press, 1972.

POWELL, RALPH. *The Rise of Chinese Military Power, 1895–1912*. Princeton, NJ: Princeton University Press, 1955.

PRICE, DON K. *Russia and the Roots of Chinese Revolution.* Cambridge, MA: Harvard University Press, 1974.

PURCELL, VICTOR. *The Boxer Uprising: A Background Study.* Cambridge, Eng.: Cambridge University Press, 1963.

RHOADES, EDWARD. *Chinese Republican Revolution: The Case of Kwangtung, 1895–1913.* Cambridge, MA: Harvard University Press, 1975.

SCALAPINO, ROBERT A., AND HAROLD SCHIFFRIN. "Early Socialist Currents in the Chinese Revolutionary Movement." *The Journal of Asian Studies,* XVIII (1959).

SCHIFFRIN, HAROLD Z. *Sun Yat-sen and the Origins of the Chinese Revolution.* Berkeley: University of California Press, 1968.

SCHRECKER, JOHN E. *Imperialism and Chinese Nationalism: Germany in Shantung.* Cambridge, MA: Harvard University Press, 1971.

SCHWARTZ, BENJAMIN I. *In Search of Wealth and Power: Yen Fu and the West.* Cambridge, MA: Harvard University Press, 1964.

SHARMAN, LYON. *Sun Yat-sen, His Life and Its Meaning: A Critical Biography.* Palo Alto, CA: Stanford University Press, 1968.

TAN, CHESTER C. *The Boxer Catastrophe.* New York: Columbia University Press, 1955.

WAKEMAN, FREDERIC. *Strangers at the Gate: Social Disorder in South China, 1839–1861.* Berkeley: University of California Press, 1966.

WANG, Y. C. *Chinese Intellectuals and the West, 1872–1949.* Durham: University of North Carolina Press, 1966.

WEHRLE, EDMUND S. *Britain, China and Antimissionary Riots 1891–1900.* Minneapolis: University of Minnesota Press, 1966.

WILBUR, C. MARTIN. *Sun Yat-sen: Frustrated Patriot.* New York: Columbia University Press, 1976.

———, ED. *China in Revolution: The First Phase, 1900–1913.* New Haven, CT: Yale University Press, 1968.

WRIGHT, MARY C. *The Last Stand of Chinese Conservatism: The T'ung-chih Restoration, 1862–1874.* Palo Alto, CA: Stanford University Press, 1957.

YOUNG, ERNEST. *The Presidency of Yuan Shih-k'ai: Liberalism and Dictatorship in Early Republican China.* Ann Arbor: University of Michigan Press, 1977.

REVOLUTION IN THOUGHT AND CULTURE

ALITTO, GUY S. *The Last Confucian: Liang Shu-ming and the Chinese Dilemma of Modernity.* Berkeley: University of California Press, 1978.

CHOW TSE-TSUNG. *The May Fourth Movement: Intellectual Revolution in the Modern China.* Cambridge, MA: Harvard University Press, 1960.

DE FRANCIS, JOHN. *Nationalism and Language Reform in China.* Princeton, NJ: Princeton University Press, 1950.

GRIEDER, JEROME. *Hu Shih and the Chinese Renaissance: Liberalism in the Chinese Revolution, 1917–1934.* Cambridge, MA: Harvard University Press, 1970.

HSIA, C. T. *A History of Modern Chinese Fiction, 1917–1957.* New Haven, CT: Yale University Press, 1961.

HU SHIH. *The Chinese Renaissance,* 2nd ed. New York: Paragon, 1964.

ISRAEL, JOHN. *Student Nationalism in China: 1927–1937.* Palo Alto, CA: Stanford University Press, 1966.

LANG, OLGA. *Pa Chin and His Writings: Chinese Youth Between the Two Revolutions.* Cambridge, MA: Harvard University Press, 1967.

LEE, LEO OU-FAN. *The Romantic Generation of Chinese Writers.* Cambridge, MA: Harvard University Press, 1973.

LEVENSON, JOSEPH R. *Confucian China and Its Modern Fate,* vols. I, II, and III. Berkeley: University of California Press, 1958, 1964, 1965.

LIN YU-SHENG. *The Crisis of Chinese Consciousness: Radical Anti-traditionalism in the May Fourth Era.* Madison: University of Wisconsin Press, 1978.

LYELL, WILLIAM A. *Lu Hsun's Vision of Reality.* Berkeley: University of California Press, 1976.

SCHWARTZ, BENJAMIN I., ED. *Reflections on the May Fourth Movement: A Symposium.* Cambridge, MA: Harvard University Press, 1972.

TAN, CHESTER C. *Chinese Political Thought in the Twentieth Century.* New York: Anchor Books, 1971.

VOHRA, RANBIR. *Lao She and the Chinese Revolution.* Cambridge, MA: Harvard University Press, 1974.

WANG, Y. C. *Chinese Intellectuals and the West, 1872–1949.* Durham: University of North Carolina Press, 1966.

CHINESE SOCIETY TO 1949

BUCK, JOHN L. *Land Utilization in China.* New York: Paragon, 1964.

FEI HSIAO-T'UNG. *China's Gentry.* Chicago: University of Chicago Press, 1953.

———. *Peasant Life in China: A Field Study of Country Life in the Yangtze Valley.* New York: Dutton, 1939.

FREEDMAN, MAURICE. *Family and Kinship in Chinese Society.* Palo Alto, CA: Stanford University Press, 1970.

———. *The Religion of the Chinese People.* New York: Harper Collins, 1975.

FRIED, MORTON. *The Fabric of Chinese Society.* New York: Praeger, 1953.

HSU, FRANCIS L. K. *Under the Ancestors' Shadow: Chinese Culture and Personality.* New York: Columbia University Press, 1948.

LANG, OLGA. *Chinese Family and Society.* New Haven, CT: Yale University Press, 1946.

LEVY, MARION. *The Chinese Family Revolution.* Cambridge, MA: Harvard University Press, 1949.

MYERS, RAMON. *The Chinese Peasant Economy.* Cambridge, MA: Harvard University Press, 1970.

PECK, GRAHAM. *Two Kinds of Time.* Boston: Houghton Mifflin, 1950.

SKINNER, G. W. "Marketing and Social Structure in Rural China." *Journal of Asian Studies,* 24, nos. 1, 2, and 3 (November 1964, February and May 1965).

TAWNEY, R. H. *Land and Labor in China.* San Diego: Harcourt Brace Jovanovich, 1932.

WEBER, MAX. *The Religion of China.* New York: Free Press, 1951.

YANG, C. K. *Religion in Chinese Society: A Study of Contemporary Social Functions of Religion and Some of Their Historical Factors.* Berkeley: University of California Press, 1961.

THE NATIONALIST REVOLUTION

BELDEN, JACK. *China Shakes the World.* New York: Harper Collins, 1949.

CHANG KIA-NGAU. *The Inflationary Spiral: The Experience in China, 1939–1950.* New York: Wiley, 1958.

CH'I, H. S. *Warlord Politics in China 1916–28.* Palo Alto, CA: Stanford University Press, 1975.

CHIANG CHUNG-CHENG (CHIANG KAI-SHEK). *Soviet Russia in China: A Summing-up at Seventy.* New York: Farrar Straus Giroux, 1957.

CHIANG KAI-SHEK. *China's Destiny.* New York: Macmillan, 1947.

CH'IEN TUAN-SHENG. *The Government and Politics of China, 1912–1949.* Cambridge, MA: Harvard University Press, 1950.

CHOU SHUN-HSIN. *The Chinese Inflation, 1937–1949.* New York: Columbia University Press, 1963.

EASTMAN, LLOYD. *The Abortive Revolution: China Under Nationalist Rule, 1927–1937.* Cambridge, MA: Harvard University Press, 1974.

EUDIN, XENIA, J., AND ROBERT C. NORTH. *Soviet Russia and the East, 1920–1927: A Documentary Survey.* Palo Alto, CA: Stanford University Press, 1957.

GILLIN, D. G. *Warlord: Yen Hsi-shan in Shansi Province, 1911–1949.* Princeton, NJ: Princeton University Press, 1967.

IRIYE, AKIRA. *After Imperialism: The Search for a New Order in the Far East, 1921–1931.* Cambridge, MA: Harvard University Press, 1965.

ISRAEL, JOHN. *Student Nationalism in China, 1927–1937.* Palo Alto, CA: Stanford University Press, 1966.

LEONG, S. T. *Sino-Soviet Diplomatic Relations 1917–26.* Honolulu: University of Hawaii Press, 1976.

LIU, F. F. *A Military History of Modern China, 1924–1949.* Princeton, NJ: Princeton University Press, 1956.

NATHAN, A. *Peking Politics, 1918–1923.* Berkeley: University of California Press, 1976.

PEPPER, SUZANNE. *Civil War in China: The Political Struggle, 1945–1949.* Berkeley: University of California Press, 1978.

PYE, LUCIAN W. *The Spirit of Chinese Politics: A Psycho-Cultural Study of the Authority Crisis in Political Development.* Cambridge, MA: MIT Press, 1968.

SHAO CHUANG-LENG AND NORMAN D. PALMER. *Sun Yat-sen and Communism.* New York: Praeger, 1960.

SHERIDAN, J. E. *Chinese Warlord: The Career of Feng Yü-hsiang.* Palo Alto, CA: Stanford University Press, 1966.

TIAN HUNG-MAO. *Government and Politics in Kuomintang China, 1927–1937.* Palo Alto, CA: Stanford University Press, 1972.

TING, LEE-HSIA HSU. *Government Control of the Press in Modern China, 1900–1948.* Cambridge, MA: Harvard University Press, 1975.

TSOU, TANG. *America's Failure in China, 1941–1950.* Chicago: University of Chicago Press, 1963.

WILBER, C. MARTIN. *The Nationalist Revolution in China, 1923–1928,* Cambridge, Eng.: Cambridge University Press, 1983.

YOUNG, ARTHUR N. *China's Nation-Building Effort, 1927–1937: The Financial and Economic Record.* Palo Alto, CA: Hoover Institution Press, 1971.

———, *China's Wartime Finance and Inflation, 1937–1945.* Cambridge, MA: Harvard University Press, 1965.

YU, GEORGE G. T. *Party Politics in Republican China: The K.M.T., 1912–1924.* Berkeley: University of California Press, 1966.

CHINESE COMMUNIST MOVEMENT: 1921–1949

BRANDT, CONRAD, *Stalin's Failure in China, 1924–1927.* Cambridge, MA: Harvard University Press, 1958.

CHANG KUO-T'AO. *The Rise of the Chinese Communist Party, 1921–1927. Volume One of the Autobiography of Chang Kuo-t'ao.* Lawrence: University of Kansas Press, 1971.

———, *The Rise of the Communist Party, 1928–1938. Volume Two of the Autobiography of Chang Kuo-t'ao.* Lawrence: University of Kansas Press, 1972.

CHASSIN, LIONEL M. *The Communist Conquest of China: A History of the Civil War, 1945–1949.* Cambridge, MA: Harvard University Press, 1965.

CH'EN, JEROME. *Mao and the Chinese Revolution.* Oxford, Eng.: Oxford University Press, 1967.

CHESNEAUX, JEAN. *The Chinese Labor Movement, 1919–1927,* trans. H. M. Wright. Palo Alto, CA: Stanford University Press, 1968.

The Chinese Communist Movement (A Report of the U.S. War Department). Washington, D.C., 1945. Reissued with an introduction by Lyman P. Van Slyke. Palo Alto, CA: Stanford University Press, 1967.

COMPTON, BOYD. *Party Reform Documents, 1942–44.* Seattle: University of Washington Press, 1952.

HINTON, WILLIAM. *Fanshen: A Documentary of Revolution in a Chinese Village.* New York: Monthly Review Press, 1966.

HSIUNG, JAMES CHIEH. *Ideology and Practice: The Evolution of Chinese Communism.* New York: Praeger, 1970.

HUANG, PHILIP C. C., ET AL. *Chinese Communists and Rural Society, 1927–1934.* Berkeley: University of California Press, 1978.

ISAACS, HAROLD. *The Tragedy of the Chinese Revolution.* Palo Alto, CA: Stanford University Press, 1951.

JOHNSON, CHALMERS A. *Peasant Nationalism and Communist Power: The Emergence of Revolutionary China, 1937–1945.* Palo Alto, CA: Stanford University Press, 1962.

KATAOKA, TETSUYA. *Resistance and Revolution in China: The Communists and the Second United Front.* Berkeley: University of California Press, 1974.

KIM, ILPYONG, J. *The Politics of Chinese Communism: Kiangsi under the Soviets.* Berkeley: University of California Press, 1973.

LEE FEIGON. *Chen Duxiu.* Princeton, NJ: Princeton University Press, 1983.

MEISNER, MAURICE. *Li Ta-chao and the Origins of Chinese Marxism.* Cambridge, MA: Harvard University Press, 1967.

RUE, JOHN E. *Mao Tse-tung in Opposition, 1927–1935.* Palo Alto, CA: Stanford University Press, 1966.

SCHWARTZ, BENJAMIN I. *Chinese Communism and the Rise of Mao.* Cambridge, MA: Harvard University Press, 1951.

SELDON, MARK. *The Yenan Way in Revolutionary China.* Cambridge, MA: Harvard University Press, 1971.

SNOW, EDGAR. *Red Star Over China.* New York: Random House, 1938.

SWARUP, SHANTI. *A Study of the Chinese Communist Movement 1927–1934.* Oxford, Eng.: Clarendon Press, 1966.

THORNTON, RICHARD C. *The Comintern and the Chinese Communists 1928–1931.* Seattle: University of Washington Press, 1969.

WILSON, DICK. *The Long March, 1935: The Epic of Chinese Communism's Survival.* New York: Penguin Books, 1982.

THE PEOPLE'S REPUBLIC

Note: The following periodicals provide a valuable source of materials on contemporary China: *China Quarterly, Asian Survey, Far Eastern Economic Review, Modern China, Issues and Studies, Journal of Asian Studies, Pacific Affairs, Chinese Law and Government, Chinese Studies in History and Philosophy,* and *Beijing Review.*

BAO RUO-WANG (JEAN PASQUALINI) AND RUDOLPH CHELMINSKI. *Prisoner of Mao.* New York: Penguin Books, 1976.

BARNETT, A. DOAK. *Cadres, Bureaucracy and Political Power in China.* New York: Columbia University Press, 1967.

———. *China After Mao.* Princeton, NJ: Princeton University Press, 1967.

———. *China and the Major Powers in East Asia.* Washington, DC: Brookings Institution, 1977.

———. *China on the Eve of Communist Takeover.* New York: Praeger, 1963.

———. *Communist China: The Early Years, 1949–55.* New York: Praeger, 1964.

———. *The Making of Foreign Policy in China: Structure and Process.* Boulder, CO: Westview Press, 1985.

BARNETT, A. DOAK, AND RALPH N. CLOUGH, EDS. *Modernizing China: Post-Mao Reform and Development.* Boulder, CO: Westview Press, 1986.

BAUM, RICHARD, ED. *China's Four Modernizations: The New Technological Revolution.* Boulder, CO: Westview Press, 1980.

———. *Prelude to Revolution: Mao, the Party and the Peasant Question, 1962–1966.* New York: Columbia University Press, 1975.

BAUM, RICHARD, AND FREDERICK C. TEIWES. *Ssu-Ch'ing: The Socialist Education Movement of 1962–66.* Berkeley: University of California Press, 1968.

BENNET, GORDON. *Yundong: Mass Campaigns in Chinese Communist Leadership.* Berkeley: University of California Press, 1976.

BERNSTEIN, THOMAS P. *Up to the Mountain and to the Villages: The Transfer of Youth from Urban to Rural China.* New Haven, CT: Yale University Press, 1977.

BURNS, JOHN P., AND STANLEY ROSEN, ED. *Policy Conflicts in Post-Mao China: A Documentary Survey, with Analysis.* Armonk, NY: M. E. Sharpe, 1986.

BURTON, CHARLES. *Political and Social Change in China since 1978.* New York: Greenwood Press, 1990.

The Case of P'eng Teh-huai, 1959–1968. Hong Kong: Union Research Institute, 1968.

CHANG, PARRIS. *Radicals and Radical Ideology in China's Cultural Revolution.* New York: Research Institute on Communist Affairs, Columbia University, 1973.

CH'EN, THEODORE, H. E. *Thought Reform of the Chinese Intellectuals.* Hong Kong: Hong Kong University Press, 1960.

CHEN JO-HSI. *The Execution of Mayor Yin.* Bloomington: Indiana University Press, 1978.

COHEN, JEROME ALAN. *Contemporary Chinese Law: Research Problems and Perspectives.* Cambridge, MA: Harvard University Press, 1970.

———. *The Criminal Process in the People's Republic of China, 1949–1963: An Introduction.* Cambridge, MA: Harvard University Press, 1968.

Collected Works of Liu Shao-ch'i, 3 vols. Hong Kong: Union Research Institute, 1968–1969.

CROIZIER,RALPH C. *China's Cultural Legacy and Communism.* New York: Praeger, 1970.

DAVIN, DELIA. *Woman-Work: Women and the Party in Revolutionary China.* Oxford, Eng.: Oxford University Press, 1976.

DENG XIAOPING. *Selected Works of Deng Xiaoping (1975–1982).* Beijing: Foreign Languages press, 1984.

———. *Speeches and Writings.* New York: Pergamon Press, 1984.

DITTMER, LOWELL. *Liu Shao-ch'i and the Chinese Cultural Revolution: The Politics of Mass Criticism.* Berkeley: University of California Press, 1974.

DOMES, JÜRGEN. *China after the Cultural Revolution.* Berkeley: University of California Press, 1977.

———. *The Government and Politics of the PRC: A Time of Transition.* Boulder, CO: Westview Press, 1985.

———. *The Internal Politics of China, 1949–1972.* London: C. Hurst, 1973.

DREYER, JUNE TEUFEL, ED. *Chinese Defense and Foreign Policy.* New York: Paragon, 1989.

ECKSTEIN, ALEXANDER. *China's Economic Development: The Interplay of Scarcity and Ideology.* Ann Arbor: University of Michigan Press, 1976.

FRASER, STEWART E., ED. *Education and Communism in China.* Hong Kong: International Studies Group, 1969.

FROLIC, B. MICHAEL. *Mao's People.* Cambridge, MA: Harvard University Press, 1980.

GARSIDE, ROGER. *Coming Alive: China After Mao.* New York: McGraw-Hill, 1981.

GITTINGS, JOHN. *The Role of the Chinese Army.* Oxford, Eng.: Oxford University Press, 1967.

———. *The World and China, 1922–1972.* New York: Harper Collins, 1974.

GOLDMAN, MERLE. *China's Intellectuals: Advise and Dissent.* Cambridge, MA: Harvard University Press, 1981.

HAMRIN, CAROL LEE. *China and the Challenge of the Future: Changing Political Patterns.* Boulder, CO: Westview Press, 1990.

HAN, MINZHU, ED. *Cries for Democracy: Writings and Speeches from the 1989 Chinese Democracy Movement.* Princeton, NJ: Princeton University Press, 1990.

HARDING, HARRY. *China's Second Revolution: Reform After Mao.* Washington, DC: Brookings Institution, 1987.

———. *Organizing China: The Problem of Bureaucracy, 1949–1976.* Palo Alto, CA: Stanford University Press, 1981.

HOUN, FRANKLIN. *To Change a Nation: Propaganda and Indoctrination in Communist China.* New York: Free Press, 1961.

HSU, KAI-YU. *Chou En-lai: China's Gray Eminence.* Garden City, NY: Doubleday, 1968.

JOHNSON, CHALMERS, ED. *Ideology and Politics in Contemporary China.* Seattle: University of Washington Press, 1973.

KIM, SAMUEL S., ED. *China and the World: Chinese Foreign Policy in the Post-Mao Era.* Boulder, CO: Westview Press, 1984.

LAM, WILLY WO-LAP. *The Era of Zhao Ziyang: Power Struggle in China, 1986–1988.* Hong Kong: A.B. Books & Stationary, 1989.

LEE, HONG YUNG. *The Politics of the Chinese Cultural Revolution.* Berkeley: University of California Press, 1978.

LEWIS, JOHN W. *Leadership in Communist China.* Ithaca, NY: Cornell University Press, 1963.

———, ED. *Party Leadership and Revolutionary Power in China.* Cambridge, Eng.: Cambridge University Press, 1970.

LIFTON, ROBERT JAY. *Revolutionary Immortality.* New York: Random House, 1968.

LINDBECK, JOHN, ED. *China: Management of a Revolutionary Society.* Seattle: University of Washington Press, 1971.

LIPPIT, VICTOR D. *The Economic Development of China.* Armonk, NY: M. E. Sharpe, 1987.

LIU, ALAN P. L. *Political Culture & Group Conflict in Communist China.* Santa Barbara, CA: Clio, 1976.

LIU, BINYAN.*China's Crisis, China's Hope,* trans. Howard Goldblatt. Cambridge, MA: Harvard University Press, 1990.

———. *People or Monsters? and other Stories and Reportage from China after Mao,* ed. Perry Link. Bloomington: Indiana University Press, 1983.

LIU BINYAN ET AL. *"Tell The World": What Happened in China and Why,* trans. Henry L. Epstein. New York: Pantheon Books, 1989.

MACFARQUHAR, RODERICK. *The Origins of the Cultural Revolution, vol. 1: Contradictions among the People; vol. 2: The Great Leap Forward, 1958–1960.* New York: Columbia University Press, 1974, 1983.

NELSON, HARVEY W. *The Chinese Military System.* Boulder, CO: Westview Press, 1977.

OKSENBERG, MICHEL, ED. *China's Developmental Experience.* New York: Praeger, 1973.

PYE, LUCIAN. *The Dynamics of Chinese Politics.* Cambridge, MA: Oelgeschlager, Gunn & Hain, 1981.

———. *The Mandarin and the Cadre: China's Political Culture.* Ann Arbor: Center for Chinese Studies. University of Michigan, 1988.

RICE, EDWARD. *Mao's Way.* Berkeley: University of California Press, 1972.

RISKIN, CARL. *China's Political Economy: The Quest for Development Since 1949.* Oxford, Eng.: Oxford University Press, 1988.

SCALAPINO, ROBERT A., ED. *Elites in the People's Republic of China.* Seattle: University of Washington Press, 1972.

SCHRAM, STEWART R., ED. *Authority, Participation and Cultural Change in China.* Cambridge, Eng.: Cambridge University Press, 1973.

———, ED. *Chairman Mao Talks to the People: Talks and Letters, 1956–1971.* New York: Pantheon Books, 1974.

SCHURMAN, FRANZ. *Ideology and Organization in Communist China.* Berkeley: University of California Press, 1966.

SCHWARTZ, BENJAMIN. *Communism and China: Ideology in Flux.* Cambridge, MA: Harvard University Press, 1968.

Selected Works of Mao Tse-tung, 5 vols. Beijing: Foreign Languages Press, vols. I, II, III (1967), IV (1961), V (1977).

Selected Works of Zhou Enlai, vol. I. Beijing: Foreign Languages Press, 1981.

SHAW YU-MING. *Power and Policy in the PRC.* Boulder, CO: Westview Press, 1985.

SHERIDAN, MARY, AND JANET W. SALAFF, ED. *Lives: Chinese Working Women.* Bloomington: Indiana University Press, 1984.

SIDEL, RUTH. *Women and Child Care in China.* New York: Hill & Want, 1972.

SOLOMON, RICHARD H. *Mao's Revolution and the Chinese Political Culture.* Berkeley: University of California Press, 1971.

STARR, JOHN BRYAN. *Continuing the Revolution: The Political Thought of Mao.* Princeton, NJ: Princeton University Press, 1979.

———. *Ideology and Culture: An Introduction to the Dialectic of Contemporary Chinese Politics.* New York: Harper Collins, 1973.

TEIWES, FREDERICK C. *Leadership, Legitimacy, and Conflict in China: From a Charismatic Mao to the Politics of Succession.* New York: Macmillan, 1984.

TOWNSEND, JAMES. *Political Participation in Communist China.* Berkeley: University of California Press, 1967.

VOHRA, RANBIR. *China: The Search for Social Justice and Democracy.* New York: Penguin USA, 1991.

WHITSON, WILLIAM W. *The Chinese High Command: A History of Communist Military Politics, 1927–1972.* New York: Praeger, 1972.

WHYTE, MARTIN KING, AND WILLIAM L. PARISH. *Urban Life in Contemporary China.* Chicago: University of Chicago Press, 1984.

WOLF, MARGERY, AND ROXANE WITKE, EDS. *Women in Chinese Society.* Palo Alto, CA: Stanford University Press, 1974.

YANG, ZHONGMEI. *Hu Yaobang: A Chinese Biography.* Armonk, NY: M. E. Sharpe, 1988.

YU GUANGYUAN. *China's Socialist Modernization.* Beijing: Foreign Languages Press, 1984.

ZAGORIA, DONALD S. *The Sino-Soviet Conflict, 1956–61.* Princeton, NJ: Princeton University Press, 1962.

Index

D

E

F

G